£6.59

W9-BBH-401

Popular Disturbances in England
1700–1870

Themes in British Social History

edited by Dr J. Stevenson

* already published

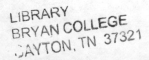
LIBRARY
BRYAN COLLEGE
DAYTON, TN 37321

Popular Disturbances in England
1700-1870

John Stevenson

Longman
London and New York

To Jack

Longman Group Limited London

Associated companies, branches and representatives
throughout the world

Published in the United States of America
by Longman Inc., New York

©John Stevenson 1979

All rights reserved. No part of this publication may be
reproduced, stored in a retrieval system, or transmitted
in any form or by any means, electronic, mechanical,
photocopying, recording, or otherwise, without the
prior permission of the Copyright owner.

First published 1979

British Library Cataloguing in Publication Data

Stevenson, John
    Popular disturbances in England, 1700–1870
    – (Themes in British social history)
    1. Great Britain – Politics and government – 18th century   2. Great Britain – Politics
    and government – 19th century   3. Collective behavior
    I. Title   II. Series
    322.4'4'0942   DA486   78–40986

    ISBN 0-582-48325-5
    ISBN 0-582-48326-3   Pbk

Printed in Great Britain by Richard Clay (The Chaucer Press) Ltd, Bungay, Suffolk

Contents

Preface

The aim of this study is to examine popular disturbances in England from the beginning of the eighteenth century to the latter part of the nineteenth. As indicated in the first chapter, this is a topic which has generated increasing interest amongst historians and students, but it has not yet been made the subject of a connected survey. In attempting to review the origins, impact and nature of such events over nearly two centuries, I am conscious primarily of my debt to other scholars. A work of this kind could only be embarked upon with the aid of the distinguished corpus of studies which have emerged in this field in recent years. At times indeed, the emergence of fresh theses, articles, and full-length studies has presented a considerable problem of assimilation. The extent of my debt to the work of colleagues should be evident from the references and bibliography at the end of this book.

The introductory chapter has been used to establish some of the main features of this study. As explained in that section, the principal focus of interest is popular disturbances, what some historians would term collective violence. It is not a study of all popular movements or even of all 'crowds'. My main concern can perhaps best be summed up in the question 'Why do people rebel?' What are the conditions and contexts in which collective violence occurs and what is its relationship to wider social, economic, and political processes.

By confining this survey to England, I recognise that some of the advantages of a comparative study have been lost, but considerations of length and the difficulties of making effective cross-cultural comparisons within one volume have restricted the area that could be covered. Other scholars have already tackled some aspects of these comparisons, and it was my main intention to provide a survey over a relatively long period, even if this meant circumscribing the geographical area being examined. Fortunately, neither Scotland nor Wales lack their own historians of popular movements who will no doubt fill these gaps in due course. Although Ireland was part of the United Kingdom for much of this period and remains one of the most under-researched fields for movements of this kind, I have had to exclude it from this study because of the special problems it raises. To avoid confusion, however, I ought to make it clear here that I have included some reference to events in Scotland, Wales, and Ireland where they are relevant to an understanding of what was happening in England. Where the geographical limits of this study appear particularly arbitrary, as for example in discussions of such groups as the United Irishmen or the Chartist movements in Wales or Scotland, I have indicated in the references where further information can be found.

I would like to express my particular thanks to Dr R. M. Hartwell and Miss B. Kemp for their encouragement of my own interests in this field. I also owe a considerable debt to many colleagues in Oxford and Sheffield for their advice and interest. I have been greatly assisted by the kindness of the staffs of several libraries and record offices, including the Bodleian Library, the British Library, the Devon County Record Office, the London Corporation Record Office and Guildhall Library, Nuffield College Library, the Prior's Kitchen Library, Durham, the Public Record Office, Sheffield City Library, and the University libraries of both Manchester and Sheffield. The typing of the manuscript was carried out by Mrs Shingler and the secretaries of the History Department at Sheffield. I am extremely grateful to them for coping with it so efficiently. The book is dedicated to my wife.

J. Stevenson
Sheffield
1978

Acknowledgements

Cover illustrations: Mary Evans Picture Library.

1 Introduction

There is a story, possibly apocryphal, that a prospective research student who confessed to wanting to work in the field of popular disturbancies was asked by a famous constitutional historian 'Why are you interested in these bandits?' It is a question unlikely to be framed in quite the same way today perhaps not even asked at all. Few areas of social history have attracted more attention in recent years than the study of popular movements. It may be an exaggeration to suggest that interest in 'the deserter, the mutineer, the primitive rebel, the rural bandit, the market rioter, the urban criminal, the pickpocket, and the village prophet' dominates every Senior Common Room and Examination Hall, but one knows what Richard Cobb meant when he spoke of the almost 'alarming respectability' which the subject has attained.[1]

Historians of modern Britain have always had some interest in questions of popular protest and public order if only for their bearing on the topic of the *revolution manquée*, why and how Britain in the eighteenth and nineteenth centuries escaped a revolutionary upheaval similar to those experienced on the continent. Riots, rebellions and industrial conflict have frequently been viewed - explicitly or implicitly - as a barometer of social and political stability. British historians have tended to regard periods of concentrated and violent protest as potentially revolutionary: R. J. White, for example regarded the period following the Napoleonic Wars as the time when the country came closest to revolution; other favoured candidates have been the Reform crisis of 1830-2 and the peak years of Chartist agitation.[2] There has also been a strong tradition of social and labour history which traced the sometimes violent responses to industrial and agricultural change. The Hammonds provided the first substantial accounts of the Luddite outbreaks and the disturbances in the agricultural counties in 1830-2 in their studies of the rise of industry and the impact of agricultural change.[3]

To some extent, however, the study of popular disturbances remained somewhat incidental to the main concerns of historians. The presence of 'riots' or other kinds of violence has more often been treated as the inevitable outcome of distress and the absence of an efficient police force than as a subject worthy of study in its own right.[4] Popular disturbances have generally been seen as indicating moments of particular crisis and as evidence of a 'primitive' stage of social and political development which preceded the acquisition of political rights, the growth of organised trade unionism, and the gradual amelioration of social conditions. Thus R. F. Wearmouth, the historian of Methodism, produced what is still one of the most useful chronicles of riots and disturbances in eighteenth-century England to provide evidence of the brutal character of eighteenth-century society before its subsequent improvement under the influence of Methodism.[5] This is not to belittle earlier generations of historians, simply to recognise that their interests often led them to treat popular movements of various kinds as a peripheral phenomenon, more to be regretted than examined for their own sake.

In common with many other aspects of social history, the study of popular movements, riots, and crowds received considerable impetus from the work of the *Annales* school and their concern with 'total' or at least 'broader' history. Some interest in crowd psychology had been shown by writers such as Gustave Le Bon at the turn of the century, but it was George Lefebvre's study of 'Foules revolutionnaires', published in 1934, which provided the first serious attempt to examine the role of crowds and mobs in the social and political context of the French Revolution.[6] After the Second World War a number of historians began to give more serious attention to popular movements, including the nature and role of the 'mob' or 'crowd'. Among the pioneering works in this field were E. J. Hobsbawm's *Primitive Rebels* and G. Rudé's *The Crowd in the French Revolution* and *Wilkes and Liberty*. These works, together with a number of articles, opened many new lines of enquiry.[7]

The work of Rudé brought the 'mob' within the orbit of national political events. The crowds involved in the French Revolution were shown to be something more than spasmodic and irrational phenomena and the London mob of the eighteenth century was put within the context of the 'political nation without-doors', which could on occasions act with other elements as an opposition to the Government of the day. Of the agitations surrounding John Wilkes and Lord George Gordon, Rudé wrote: 'Anomic and associational movements, social protest and political demands, well-organised and clear-sighted interest groups and "direct-action" crowds, leaders and followers came together in a chorus of united opposition.'[8] But as well as illustrating the role of popular disturbances in some of the major political upheavals of the eighteenth century, the work of Rudé and others provided a greater understanding of the composition, nature and ideology of the eighteenth-century mob. It was shown, for example, that the stereotypes commonly applied both by contemporaries and some later historians were highly misleading. Analysis of the participants in some larger disturbances in eighteenth-century London and Revolutionary Paris suggested that the majority were neither criminals nor unemployed, but often a fairly typical cross-section of the working population; moreover, when examined closely, many were revealed as disciplined and highly ritualised forms of protest, in which the populace acted in accordance with a coherent set of beliefs and values. Hobsbawm showed how protest movements in pre-industrial Italy operated within a framework of traditional concepts about the 'just King'. Studies of food riots in both England and France suggested that these too were frequently selective, disciplined and ritualised protests directed at obtaining 'fair' or 'just' prices. Similarly Hobsbawm's study of the Luddites placed them within the context of a traditional process of 'collective bargaining by riot' which provided a means by which early trade groups could negotiate with their employers.[9]

Popular disturbances also provide an opportunity to investigate the ideas and beliefs of otherwise largely inarticulate sections of the population. The London mob, for example, showed a recurrent emphasis upon its 'rights' and 'liberties', intermingled with 'No Popery' and popular chauvinism.[10] Taking some of these points further, E. P. Thompson has argued in a series of articles and full-length studies that the activities of English crowds in the eighteenth century indicate an 'extraordinary deep-rooted pattern of behaviour and belief' – a 'moral economy' – which legitimised popular action against those who transgressed customary practice. For Thompson the actions of the crowd reveal some of the underlying assumptions of what he terms the 'plebeian culture', assumptions which often ran contrary to those of the authorities in a period of economic change. As a corollary of this, he stressed the need to see these actions from the point of view of the participants and to de-code the ceremony and symbolism which many of them displayed, rather than to see them solely through the eyes of the authorities.[11]

As a result, historians have increasingly been making sense of what have often been regarded as aimless incidents. A useful example is the furore which surrounded the introduction of the Gregorian calendar into Great Britain in September 1752 as a result of an Act passed in the previous year. It is still possible to find accounts of this episode which attribute it to the ignorance and folly of the eighteenth-century populace, with such references as the 'howls of the uninformed mob to "give us back our eleven days"'.[12] In fact, the removal of eleven days from the calendar in September 1752 (the 3rd to 13th) to bring the country into line with the continent excited popular concern not because people thought they were 'losing' days, but because the alteration created considerable difficulties over such matters, as debts, contracts or other formal agreements which either fell due during the 'lost' days or spanned the changeover. A symptom of the confusion and difficulties caused was revealed when the newspapers had to provide complex tables showing how to calculate wages, taking the change into account, and to explain laboriously the legal position in relation to services fixed by the calendar. That the date on which the year began was changed from 25 March to 1 January also served to upset the timing of many annual payments, as well as complicating hirings, rents and apprenticeships. Protest about the 'lost' days was not simply a display of irrational ignorance, but one based on concern about interference and complication of many important transactions.[13] As such it throws some light on contemporary society and can be rendered at least comprehensible by a closer examination of the impact of a particular piece of legislation.

There are obviously dangers here, principally that of investing incidents with too much significance. The sources at our disposal are often inadequate for a completely satisfactory appraisal of the motives and rationale of those who participated in popular disturbances and one of the subtler forms of condescension in historical writing is to see all violence as 'protest' and all the participants in riots as sobersided and self-conscious proletarians. A degree of tact and sensitivity is required in dealing with episodes for which the source materials are often limited. The issue is complicated by the sociological perspectives which argue that no social action is meaningless. Even the most casual-looking and seemingly unrestrained brawl might be regarded as having some 'meaning' to those involved and subject to certain normative constraints. Recent work on such subjects as football crowds is an example of an attempt to understand the motives of those concerned in events which are sometimes labelled as 'senseless'.[14] Although studies of this kind arouse controversy, either from those who believe them too naive in their application of anthropological theory or from those who believe that to understand motivation is in some way to condone the events themselves, they nonetheless provide an important parallel to some of the work being done by historians on hitherto obscure or little explored areas of the past.[15]

As well as providing historians with a kind of 'window' on the attitudes and assumptions of otherwise inaccessible sections of the population, there has been a tendency in recent work to widen the scope of enquiry from a concentration on popular disturbances per se to an examination of social relationships at large. One strand of research has been concerned with the relationship between 'order' and 'disorder' and the process by which these terms are defined; another has been an exploration of what some sociologists call the 'negotiation of order', the processes by which events are defined as 'disorderly' or 'disturbances' and the way these definitions could alter according to circumstance.[16] The concept of 'social control' and the more informal processes by which frequent outbreaks of collective violence are discouraged and contained have also attracted discussion.[17]

Studies such as Dr Bailey's investigation of the differential patterns of law enforcement in relation to popular disturbances in late Victorian England, Dr Storch's examinations of the use of the professional police as an agency of regulating popular recreations, and Dr Hay's account of the role of the law in eighteenth-century England illustrate a more sophisticated approach to the question of 'order' than one confined solely to the mechanics and technicalities of policing.[18] Within limits, 'order' – and by implication 'disorder' – are being recognised as elastic terms which vary according to changing social and political attitudes. Historians have increasingly asked what were the pressures and circumstances within society which led to changes in the definition and regulation of conduct. If, however, there is a relative quality in the attitude of the authorities to certain forms of activity, such as strikes, mass petitioning of parliament, and aspects of popular recreation, it is important that the processes which are believed to be at work should be made explicit. One danger of the approach which sees the definition of what is 'orderly' or 'disorderly' as 'socially constructed' is that it can too easily degenerate into a kind of conspiracy theory in which *the* authorities, *the* press, *the* police are seen in a solely manipulative role. These collectives are in their own way just as crude as *the* 'mob'. While it may be true that on occasions the law has been manipulated to serve sectional interests and that the definition of 'order' can shift to accommodate the purposes of ruling groups, it is important that this does not coarsen our understanding of the complexities and subtleties which govern attitudes and responses to events.

Disturbances, riots, crowds, and mobs

In the context of discussions of public order, the world 'disturbance' is normally defined as any interruption of tranquillity by tumult or uproar. Needless to say, such a definition begs many questions and it is important to examine the kinds of definition available for the study of popular disturbances. There are four types of definition available, those provided in law, those derived from the social sciences, those used by contemporaries in the period being studied, and those applied by other historians in their attempt to delimit a discrete area of enquiry.

The law dealing with public order in England covers a wide range of offences. Some breaches of public order have in the past been considered as treason by an extension of the Statute of Edward III which covers levying war on the King. The great majority of such crimes, however, are covered by the common law offences of riot, rout, unlawful assembly and affray. The essential features of these offences was recognised as early as the sixteenth century when Chief Justice Hale provided distinguishing criteria for the different offences which were followed, with minor modifications, by later legal writers, including Blackstone. The basic offence is unlawful assembly, defined as any gathering of three or more persons, on public or private property, with common intent to commit either a lawful or unlawful act in such a way as to give any person of reasonable courage and firmness fear of a breach of the peace. 'Rout', a virtually obsolete offence even by the eighteenth century, is defined in similar terms but involves some 'moving towards' an execution of the common purpose. Riot is by far the most common of these offences in law. The modern legal definition is

> a tumultuous disturbance of the peace by three persons or more, who assemble together of their own authority, with an intent

mutually to assist one another against anyone who shall oppose them in the execution of an enterprise of a private nature, and afterwards actually execute the enterprise, in a violent and turbulent manner, to the terror of the people, whether the act intended were lawful or unlawful.

The common features of these offences are numbers (three or more), mutual intent, and violence. The distinction between these offences and an affray was regarded from at least the sixteenth century as lying in the 'accidental' nature of the quarrel or fight.[19]

The definition of some riots as felonies or as treason rested upon interpretations of these essential ingredients. Some riots had been classed as felonies from the reign of Edward IV and Acts of Mary I and Elizabeth I also particularised as felonies those riots which offered violence to the Privy Council or tried to change the laws of the Kingdom. In the period from the death of Elizabeth to the accession of George I these Acts were allowed to lapse. The famous Riot Act of 1715 (1 Geo. I, st. 2 c. 5), enacted in response to a wave of riots following the Hanoverian succession, aimed to provide a more serious offence than misdemeanour, but which fell short of treason; it was also designed to expedite the suppression of disturbances because by making certain riots felonies it indemnified the civil and military authorities from prosecution for any injuries caused in dealing with them. The statute made it a felony for twelve or more persons riotously to assemble and not to disperse an hour after the reading of a proclamation commanding them to do so; to oppose the making of the proclamation and not to disperse within an hour after the making of the proclamation had been opposed; and unlawfully to assemble to the disturbance of the public peace and when so assembled unlawfully and with force to demolish or pull down any church, chapel, any building for religious worship, certified or registered, or any dwelling-house, barn, stable, or outhouse. (For the background of the Riot Act see p. 22 below.)

The Riot Act illustrated the way in which the legal status of disturbances could be altered to meet particular circumstances. The Act itself had far-reaching implications in that it effectively made unlawful assembly a felony: a felonious offence was committed by simply remaining assembled after the reading of the Proclamation, even though no specific acts of violence followed. A similar example of the changed status of offences came with the 'Black Act' of 1723 which made capital a number of offences of trespass, killing game, going in disguise, arson, and breaking down fences, some of which would previously have been regarded as only riotous misdemeanours.[20]

Definitions of riots as treasonable rested on the Statute of Treasons of 1351, by which serious riots could be considered as levying war on the King. This interpretation had been used both in Messanger's Case (1668) and in Dammaree's Case (1710). In the case of Lord George Gordon in 1780, Lord Mansfield declared that an attempt to force repeal of a law by intimidation and violence was a levying of war against the King and therefore high treason. This view was restated in 1795 in one of the 'Two Acts', in which any attempt to

> levy war against his Majesty, his Heir and successors within this realm, in order, by force or constraint, to compel him or them to change his or their Measures or Counsels, or in order to put any force or constraint upon, or to intimidate, or overawe, both houses, or either House of Parliament . . . shall be deemed, declared, and adjudged to be a Traitor and Traitors . . .[21]

The definition of a treasonable riot in the eighteenth and nineteenth centuries rested on a distinction between a public and general design which challenged royal authority and a private design. Essentially, the distinction rested on the intentions of the participants in a disturbance, for in the words of one commentator: 'The intent, not the act, constitutes the treason; the open act being only evidence of and auxiliary to the design, and it is by no means essential that the means used should be efficient enough in their nature and tendency to produce in physical execution the end intended.'[22] Hence Dammaree was convicted of treason following the Sacheverell riots because it was held that behind the riots lay a plan to destroy all meeting houses which, as an object of 'a general nature', was constructive treason.

Thus the law of riotous offences involves three essential elements in the form of violence displayed in such a manner as to alarm at least one person of reasonable firmness and courage, intent or joint design to help one another in the inception and execution of the common purpose, and numbers of three or more for a riotous offence to take place. In determining the gravity of the offence, the law required an increase in numbers from three or more to twelve or more to come under the provisions of the Riot Act of 1715. The same Act took an important departure from previous legal sanctions by in regarding the act of remaining assembled as a felony. Lastly, the law was much concerned with the intention of participants in determining the gravity of offences. The distinction between an affray and a riot rested on whether there was evidence of mutual intent, while the objective of the participants played a crucial role in determining whether treasonable actions had taken place.

In the social sciences, the study of disturbances, riots, and collective violence falls within the field of collective behaviour, and there is a substantial literature dealing with various aspects of riots and allied phenomenon. *The Encyclopedia of the Social Sciences* defines a 'riot' as 'an outbreak of temporary but violent mass disorder'.[23] In its essentials this is little different from the legal definition of riotous offences. Riots are considered as a qualitatively different category of events than individual violence, characterised by their mass character. This reflects a long tradition of study in the social sciences of crowd behaviour. Early writers, such as Gustave Le Bon, were concerned with the nature of crowd psychology and its effects on human behaviour.[24] Collective mentalities included not just crowds, but also audiences, publics, and even whole nations. This theme of inquiry was developed further by men such as R. E. Park and members of the Chicago school of sociologists who extended the study of collective behaviour into a major branch of sociological enquiry.[25] One of the most influential and comprehensive attempts to fit collective behaviour, including riots, into an overall scheme has been made by N. Smelser. He defines collective behaviour as 'mobilisation on the basis of a belief which re-defines social action' and includes riots with panics and crazes in the subcategory which he terms the 'hostile outburst'. Smelser excludes from this field all 'institutionalised' actions, such as patriotic demonstrations, ritual rebellions, and ceremonial behaviour; while admitting that these might provide the setting for riots and disturbances, he claims that they are qualitatively different from 'true' episodes of collective behaviour.[26] From many points of view this appears a rigid and possibly irrelevant distinction, separating episodes which appear to have much in common, and bringing together others which do not. The point has already been made that there are many aspects of popular disturbances which can be described as at least partly institutionalised. The work of Hobsbawm, Rudé, Thompson and others has shown the semi-organised and ceremonial nature of many disturbances in the eighteenth and early nineteenth centuries.

The social sciences can, however, help to clarify some of the categories into which we might group episodes of collective violence. English law, for example, places a great deal of emphasis on the question of mutual intent or 'joint design' in its definition of riot. The various studies of crowd behaviour that have been undertaken by sociologists and crowd psychologists suggest that the legal definition is inadequate. Participants in modern riots have frequently been shown to have had no intention of taking part in a riot when they assembled, and sometimes of having no intention to assemble at all. Thus R. Turner in the *Handbook of Modern Sociology* uses the phrase 'not volitional but impulsive' to describe riot behaviour.[27] The point has been stressed in Turner and Killian's study of collective behaviour when they claim that 'people may come to a crowd, even to the most violent mob, with quite different initial motives and interests'; they illustrate their case with examples of people who claim to have been 'swept up' in riots without any prior intent.[28] Arguing on the basis of his studies of eighteenth-century 'mobs', Rudé has also made the point that 'we must allow considerable importance to spontaneity in the origin, development, and climax of popular disturbances'.[29] The emphasis on intent as a defining characteristic of riots in the legal sense is also undermined by the existence in modern case studies of a wide variety of forms of crowd behaviour in riots, so that it becomes extremely difficult to talk of participants having a common purpose. Turner and Killian list five different kinds of participation in a riot and Smelser quotes from the Chicago Commission on Race Relations, *The Negro in Chicago*, to show that crowds engaged in race riots displayed different types of behaviour. Recent studies of riots in American cities during the late 1960s have confirmed the complexity of behaviour and motivation which can lie behind involvement in disturbances.[30]

As well as questioning the adequacy of some of the legal definitions, the social sciences also provide an important distinction between collective violence and criminal activity. Criminal gangs which use violence to steal or for some other purpose might appear at first sight to share many features with the legal definition of riot, in terms of numbers, violence, and mutual intent. In fact, the social sciences generally make a distinction between criminal gangs and rioting crowds on the grounds of organisation. The organisation of crowds is seen as both rudimentary and temporary, whereas crime, at least organised crime, shows a greater degree of permanence and sophistication. Clearly there can be some overlap between popular disturbances and crime, and such incidents ought to be included in any comprehensive study, but there remains a distinction between a professional criminal gang and a shortlived disturbance.[31]

As in law, violence might appear the most obvious defining character of collective behaviour which disturbs the public peace. But 'violence' is not as clearcut a concept as it would seem at first sight. While the commonsense definition of 'physical damage to persons or property' can be invoked on many occasions, there are and were many episodes where the violence is more implicit than explicit. A parade of large numbers through the streets could by their bearing and demeanour appear threatening and exert force even though no overt violence occurred. Large crowds around the hustings at election times, mass pickets, and even some mass meetings might be said to border on explicit violence even though none in fact occurs. However the law provides an interesting consideration here through the concept of 'public terror'. The definition of riot, rout, and unlawful assembly as common law offences rests on someone of 'reasonable courage and firmness' being frightened by what was going on about them. Although this concept also begs many questions in that what is construed as 'reasonable' might alter according to changing cultural values and political situations, it nonetheless provides a case for the inclusion of events which exist on the borderline between intimidatory force and explicit violence.[32]

How did Englishmen of the eighteenth and nineteenth century speak of popular disturbances? In legal circles, the main lines of definition of riotous offences already existed by the eighteenth century. The main differences were that Blackstone was definite that an unlawful assembly only existed where people assembled 'to do an unlawful act', leaving their legal status somewhat ambiguous. By the early nineteenth century, however, the law of riotous offences was in almost every respect similar to that of modern authorities.[33] Outside legal circles the words 'riot' and 'affray' were in common use in eighteenth-century newspapers and periodicals to denote a disturbance, but with little regard to the precise legal meaning. The words 'riot', 'riotous', and 'riotously' were, for example, frequently applied to behaviour which was merely extravagant or noisy. A newspaper in 1810 reported as a 'riot' an incident in the

Strand in London where a number of people had assembled and let off some fireworks during a patriotic demonstration.[34] Individuals indulging in noisy or outrageous behaviour were commonly accused in the press of creating a 'riot', a usage which was nonsensical in strict legal terms: what were in law affrays were often termed 'riots', although the press sometimes used the word 'affray' to describe fights and brawls. In the eighteenth century it was still possible to find the word 'insurrection' being used to describe a disturbance over a non-political subject; other common terms were 'tumult', 'outrage', and 'disorder'.

The word most frequently used to describe popular disturbances was not a description of events but of the people involved. The term 'mob' appears to have come into common use in the late seventeenth century to describe an assembly of the populace. A contraction of the Latin term *mobile vulgus*, meaning the excitable crowd, it was used in two distinct senses during the eighteenth century: one was that of the hired gang which acted on behalf of external interests, usually in elections, fights with political opponents, and occasionally against dissident minorities, such as Catholics or dissenters; the other was to describe the common people, the multitude, or the lower orders generally. Its implication was usually of the 'rabble', the lowest sections of society, driven by criminal dispositions and immorality to participate in disturbances.

Historians of popular movements have been reluctant to accept these categories and usages uncritically. Rudé preferred to talk in terms of crowds rather than mobs, defining his area of study as the 'aggressive' crowd which became involved in riots, strikes, rebellions, insurrections and revolutions. He excluded passive crowds such as audiences, casual sightseers, revivalist, ceremonial, or 'expressive' crowds, such as those who came together for carnivals and student rags. As 'mob' contained the implication either of hired thugs or of a criminally-inclined group of slum-dwellers, Rudé argued that on the basis of his findings about crowd composition and behaviour in disturbances in both England and France, the term 'crowd' or even 'revolutionary crowd' was more appropriate than 'mob'.[35] Thompson has gone a stage further in the search for a 'value-free' terminology, questioning whether 'riot' is adequate to express the more sophisticated expressions of popular action. 'Riot', he considers, implies a spasmodic view of what were highly complex forms of popular action, more likely to be viewed by their participants as acts of 'popular justice' than mere breaches of public order. The implication being that 'riot', like 'mob', is a term imposed from 'above' which does little to reveal the motivation and attitudes of the people involved.[36]

Unfortunately, the term 'crowd' is not without its own pitfalls and dangers. As an organising concept derived from the social sciences it has a tendency to imply a greater unity and homogeneity of feeling and action than is necessarily warranted. Although the use of 'crowd' may impart rather more dignity to the proceedings of many protestors in the eighteenth and nineteenth centuries, it is likely to fit some situations better than others. The variations in behaviour and levels of participation found in modern studies of disturbances should warn against too lazy a use of the 'crowd' label. Phrases such as the 'language of the crowd' or 'the politics of the crowd' are extremely treacherous once it is recognised that people in crowds often behave in different ways and that to typify the actions and attitudes of the whole from those of a minority or section may well be to misrepresent the actions of many of those present. It takes very little effort of historical imagination to see that in any so-called mob or crowd it is unlikely that everyone was doing the same thing at once: only one or two people could carry a banner or flag, seize and open grain sacks, or break down the doors of a building. Violent acts are often only committed by some members of crowds; some may take a lead in shouting slogans or addressing the authorities, others tag along on the fringes of a parade or stationary crowd, only half-involved with the events concerned. Such considerations need not destroy the concept of the crowd as an organising concept for the study of popular movements, but it is important that it is used carefully, otherwise it presents too simplistic a view of what were often very complex events. It has been argued too that if the 'crowd' is a valid basis on which to examine popular movements it would be as well to extend the range of crowds studied from those merely engaged in protest to those who assemble for ceremonial, celebratory, recreational or religious purposes. Only by doing so, could the place of crowd activities in communal life be fully established.[37]

The study of popular disturbances is narrower than the broadest definitions of crowd studies. Its defining characteristics are numbers and violence. Numbers differentiate collective violence from individual or criminal assault: in common with the legal definition of riotous offences, three or more people have been taken as constituting a disturbance, although in practice the numbers involved were usually larger. Violence is regarded as physical damage to persons or property, but some allowance has been made to include incidents which bordered upon explicit violence. By using the term 'popular disturbance' an attempt has been made to embrace a broader field than that covered by the legal term 'riot', such as some brawls and affrays; where 'riot' is used, it is in the dictionary sense of 'a violent disturbance of the peace' and no more. Similarly, 'mob' has been used in the loose sense of a crowd, primarily to provide some variation in terminology with no implications about the nature of the people in the assembly.

Sources and methods

The principal sources available to historians of popular distur-bances are the various classes of government records, memoirs, diaries and other similar classes of material, judicial records and criminal statistics, and the press. These sources present their different problems, some of which are discussed in specific instances in the text. In general terms, government records provide information only on the more serious disturbances, but during a period of particular excitement, there has been a tendency for the amount of material and the range of information to increase considerably. The Home Office is the principal organ of government responsible for law and order (before 1782 the Secretaries of State for North and South) and it is in Home Office correspondence that most of the information about the state of the country can be found. Public order is not the only function of the Secretary of State or Home Secretary and with the correspondence about public order are filed petitions for clemency, material relating to the transportation of criminals, and papers dealing with the militia, yeomanry and volunteers. In practice, the Home Office has had very limited executive authority over the conduct of public order in the country at large and its main function has been to act as a channel through which local authorities could request troops or inform the government of a situation which worried them. The files also contain unsolicited information, threatening and anonymous letters, and general requests for assistance from magistrates, Lords Lieutenant and army commanders. After the French Revolution the number of files increased and separate files were opened to deal with 'disturbances'. The various Home Office files, together with some material in the Treasury Solicitor's files, the Privy Council papers, and the War Office papers provide the main government sources. Although the government records provide one of the richest caches of material available for the study of popular disturbances, they have some important limitations. By dealing primarily with the larger events or those with political significance, they often exclude many that were less spectacular or mundane; for the study of a large wave of disturbances or of, say Luddism, they are invaluable, but it is rare to find evidence of more minor and individual episodes in the government records. Unless a magistrate or some other person was particularly concerned to inform the Home Secretary, perhaps to request military assistance, many disturbances simply went unnoticed by the government. The problem is less severe in the nineteenth century than in the eighteenth, but even as late as the mid-Victorian period many minor episodes of disorder fell outside the attention of government.[38]

Such government sources as exist must also be treated with a degree of caution. A food riot in a provincial town, even in a 'bad' year such as 1795, may be recorded by only a single letter from a magistrate or some local official. Inevitably the majority of letters written by those in authority reflect their attitudes and prejudices. Although in some of the larger events, the sheer quantity of evidence allows a more critical treatment of the information, it has to be recognised that knowledge of important events sometimes rests on only one or two letters or documents. Sufficient attention has been given to the question of 'tainted' evidence, the role of spies and informers, by other historians not to have to reiterate it fully here. The crucial considerations, however, can be stated as those of reliability and consistency of treatment. Historians have traditionally

regarded the principal problem as that of the alarmism and exaggeration
of informers who are paid according to the value of the information they
provide. Richard Cobb has observed of Revolutionary France:

> Of all these contemporary historians of popular movements, the
> informer is undoubtedly the least reliable. He has to convey the
> inestimable and unique value of his information, for, to be
> successful, he needs to prove that he has access to secrets that
> would otherwise be unknown to the authorities, and, in order to
> make money, he needs to provide a great deal of information,
> whatever its worth, information generally being paid for by
> bulk ... it follows too that an informer will often construct an
> elaborate 'plot' where there is an open and probably harmless
> association, that he will make machiavellian conspirators of
> simple and angry men, and that he will scent daggers – or
> pretend to scent daggers – where there are kitchen knives and
> spoons.[39]

Such observations, perhaps bolstered by the practice of Joseph Fouché,
Napoleon's chief of police, of tipping all informers' reports in the
wastepaper bin, has led to a concurrence of opinion that the evidence of
paid spies and informers is almost worthless: certainly it must be treated
with caution. The problem for the historian, like that of the recipients, is
not shortage of information, but distinguishing good intelligence from
bad. Informers were no more a monolithic category than anyone else: the
crucial distinction lay between the 'casual' informant, usually dis-
regarded unless there was corroborative evidence from other sources, and
the semi-professional agent who was paid a regular stipend and put in
more or less regular reports. These men were far less likely to indulge in
idle alarmism, nor were their masters likely to pay them for very long
should they do so. Men such as Sir Robert Walpole, Henry Dundas, and
Lord Sidmouth did not rely on any casual informant that happened their
way to provide them with vital and often politically valuable
information. As recent work has shown, the intelligence services of both
early and late Hanoverian England were conducted with a good deal
more professionalism than has usually been imputed to them.[40] This is not
to suggest that informers' reports can be accepted uncritically, but that
they must be evaluated on their merits. The quality and reliability of
informers varied considerably, some being more prone to alarmism than
others.

Memoirs, diaries and private papers present similar problems of
accuracy and bias. In many cases the only accounts of disturbances that
we possess come from the educated upper classes. Although many were
clearly well-informed and sensitive to the situations around them, they
often reflect characteristic prejudices which limit their value in providing
evidence of the feelings of the people actually involved. As a result they
are frequently more useful as evidence of attitudes among the governing
classes than of the events themselves. A particular difficulty lies in the

paucity of first-hand accounts by the participants in disturbances, especially in the eighteenth and early nineteenth centuries. Such accounts become more common in the nineteenth century, in the autobiographies and memoirs of people who had been involved in early radical and reform movements. These again present difficulties, many falling into a *genre* of writing by 'improved' working men, who sometimes exaggerated their own roles and wrote with a conscious desire to stress the 'improvement' thesis. Many were written long after the events they describe and for obvious reasons have to be treated with caution.[41]

English judicial and criminal records for this period are not as revealing about offenders as those of other countries, notably France, where more bureaucratic systems of administration prevailed. Notwithstanding, historians have made increasing use of the various provincial and metropolitan court records to discover both the incidence of disturbances and the nature of those tried in connection with them. Rudé, in particular, has made extensive use of such records to examine crowd composition. This method provides an alternative to reliance on eye-witness reports and newspaper accounts, many of which are often rather vague, with phrases such as 'a mixed multitude', or use stereotyped terms such as 'mob' or 'rabble'. As a technique this can be criticised on the grounds that its tendency to atomise the 'crowd' destroys its collective identity in a breakdown of occupations, but there is little alternative if we want an accurate picture of those committed for trial or convicted for taking part in disturbances. The central problem here is whether those arrested and committed are indeed representative of the participants in a particular episode. The authorities often intervened at a late stage in a disturbance and the composition of the crowd might have changed, particularly if crowds had been assembled for several hours. It is possible, for example, that those who remained assembled even when they had been told to disperse or the Riot Act had been read might be unrepresentative of those who assembled in the first place. There was also a tendency to seize those who were 'most forward'. Certain groups, such as women, who were often declared by eye-witnesses to be prominent, were not always as frequently represented in the numbers of those committed for trial.[42] These difficulties are compounded when dealing with smaller incidents where only a few people were arrested. The number seized varied considerably from disturbance to disturbance according to purely fortuitous factors, such as the attitude and strength of the police or other authorities. Similarly, we can never be sure that those committed for trial are representative of those arrested, still less of those who took part in a disturbance. Thus whereas this technique offers a valuable tool for the analysis of larger disturbances, it is important to bear in mind some of its limitations, especially when applied to smaller incidents.

Judicial records and criminal statistics present problems familiar to historians of crime in general, notably of the relationship between recorded crime and 'actual' crime. The problem of the 'dark number' of unrecorded offences poses very considerable problems for the historian of popular disturbances as it does for other categories of crime.[43] The issue is complicated still further when one turns to the increasing amount of criminal statistics which become available during the nineteenth century. Some of these issues are dealt with at a later point in the text, suffice it here to say that it is not only the relationship of 'known' crime to 'actual' crime which presents difficulties, but also that the relationship between these two elements cannot be considered as constant. Changes in legal processes, in police strength, and in policy can alter the balance between the two. Criminal statistics have therefore to be used judiciously and somewhat tentatively in analysing patterns and levels of disturbances.

The press, including periodicals such as the *Annual Register* and the *Gentleman's Magazine*, are a staple source for popular disturbances in both eighteenth- and nineteenth-century England. The press, like crime, always appears to be 'rising', but it is undoubtedly the case that the number and scope of newspaper sources was increasing in this period. Inevitably there were variations in coverage over so long a period. In the early eighteenth century, for example, probably only in the capital did the press provide a variety of sources for examining disturbances. In the course of the century the rise of the provincial press and an increasing number of metropolitan papers make them more valuable.[44] Not all areas were equally well served, the remoter country areas and some of the early industrial towns were not covered to the same degree as the capital and well-established commercial centres and county towns. Reporting of local news was often exiguous and erratic, and coverage of disturbances sometimes exceedingly so. When dealing with political events, it is obviously necessary to consider the bias and prejudices displayed by individual papers. The variety of press sources available in the nineteenth century often illustrate the nuances of meaning and selectivity which can easily distort the view of a particular event, especially when dealing with politically sensitive issues. By the nineteenth century too, we have to consider to what extent the press reflected the attitudes of certain sections of society. As an important component in shaping opinion over such issues as parliamentary reform and Chartism, it is crucial to be aware of the role of the press as a purveyor of values and assumptions about English society.

A survey of sources for examining popular disturbances in modern English history brings us to one of the major methodological questions. There has been considerable effort by some historians to quantify popular disturbances in precise terms. Charles Tilly, for example, has used the concept of 'man-hours spent rioting' to bring some objectivity to discussions of the 'level' of popular protest in France and other European countries during the nineteenth century.[45] This raises several problems, notably that by reducing events to statistics, the human and subjective dimension can be lost; a statistically 'large' disturbance can be of considerably less importance than a 'smaller' one in historical terms. A broken window on the King's coach in October 1795 provoked far greater comment than the killing of at least a score of colliers in a militia riot at

Hexham in 1761. Although it is important to be as precise as possible in terms of numbers, the sources impose limitations upon the accuracy of quantification, particularly in the eighteenth century. There is also the difficulty of defining precisely what category of events are being quantified. Even if this is done, it is usually necessary to qualify purely quantitative analyses with more subjective ones, such as the mood and appearance of the people involved, as well as the normal questions of the causes, objects and effects of the incident concerned. This is not to dismiss the quantitative school, but simply to recognise its limitations. A degree of quantitative data is valuable to put the reactions of contemporaries in perspective and to temper the tendency of inflation in terminology which has led one historian to resort to the term 'hyper-crisis'[46] to express his view of a particularly disturbed period. What follows cannot be described as a quantitative study in the fullest sense of the term, but it does make use of such statistical material as appears relevant, whether derived from my own researches or that of other scholars.

2 The age of riots

Riot and disorder form part of the stock image of eighteenth-century society, an age which succeeding generations were often to characterise as peculiarly brutal and violent. In recent years historians have gone a long way towards qualifying this image, if not by claiming that popular disturbances did not occur, at least by examining their nature more closely and trying to understand better the context in which they occurred. While we can agree with E. P. Thompson that there is little to mourn in the end of 'Gin Lane, Tyburn Fair, orgiastic drunkenness, animal sexuality, and mortal combat for prize money', we can also accept the need to put the 'age of riot' in perspective by looking at the principal occasions and nature of popular disturbances in eighteenth-century England.

The 'rage of party'

A writer in 1740 dated the use of the term 'the mob' to the gatherings of the Green Ribbon Club and the Exclusion Crisis, when 'the Rabble first changed their title, and were called *the mob*.'[1] The Exclusion Crisis certainly witnessed many examples of mobs in action, and the release of the Seven Bishops on bail in 1688 was celebrated by crowds in Sunderland and Lichfield who believed them to have been acquitted. Similarly, although the 'Glorious Revolution' has usually been considered as a peculiarly peaceful transfer of power, at least in England, there were widespread popular disturbances in the winter of 1688-9. There were attacks on Catholic premises in London in September and October 1688 and disturbances occurred in York, Newcastle, Norwich, Cambridge, Bristol and Oxford during the autumn. On 27 November it was reported that thirty of the King's troops had been killed in a clash with the populace at Uxbridge. In the main the targets were Catholic mass houses and the property of Catholics. With the flight of James from the capital on 10 December, there was a widespread assault on Catholic property in London, including the Spanish, Venetian and Florentine embassies. In the country there were more attacks on Catholic chapels and property at York, Bristol, Gloucester, Worcester, Shrewsbury, Staffordshire, Wolverhampton, Birmingham, Cambridge, Bury St Edmunds, Hull and Newcastle. The counties of Northamptonshire, Cambridgeshire, Norfolk and Suffolk were the chief centres of the riots, although they were reported as far apart as the south coast, the Welsh Marches and the North-East.[2]

With the immediate transition over, disturbances continued to occur which displayed a mixture of political and religious rivalry. The most usual occasions for these disturbances were royal anniversaries and the celebrations of them by rival factions (see Table 2.1).

Table 2.1   Political anniversaries and festivals in eighteenth-century England

8 March	Accession of Queen Anne
23 April	Coronation of Queen Anne
25 May	Landing of Charles II at Dover
28 May	Birthday of George I
29 May	Entry of Charles II into London
10 June	Birthday of James III
7 September	Birthday of Queen Elizabeth I
20 October	Coronation of George I
30 October	Birthday of George Prince of Wales
4 November	Birthday of William III
5 November	Guy Fawkes' day. Landing of William III at Torbay
17 November	Accession of Queen Elizabeth I

For example, at Stamford popular rejoicing to celebrate the coronation of William and Mary was suppressed by a pro-Jacobite mayor, who called on the local militia to douse 'the presbyterian rogues' with the town fire engine. In London on the anniversary of the Prince of Wales's birth on 10 June 1695, Anthony Wood recorded:

> Yesterday being the birth of the sham prince of Wales, a great number of Jacobites assembled in a tavern in Drewry lane [sic] and made great revelling with musick, drinking the late king's health, and at night came into the street and stopt the coaches for them to give money for a bonfire. Upon which the mob assembled, beat away the Jacobites, broke open the taverne dore, filled themselves with wine, carried away all the plate, and broke all the glass in the house.[3]

Parliamentary elections were another major source of political disturbances in this period. It has sometimes been suggested that the eighteenth century saw the beginning of election disturbances in Britain, but the researches of Professor Hirst have shown that the tradition of election disorder stretches as far back as the late Middle Ages. The statute of 1430 which fixed various aspects of election procedure and limited the county franchise to the forty-shilling freeholder did so allegedly because of the 'homicides, riots and battles' which they were said to occasion. There is also evidence of disturbances at elections in the course of the fifteenth and sixteenth centuries, but municipal contests appear to have caused more disturbances than parliamentary ones, except when elections were influenced by some other issue, such as enclosure.[4]

Although election procedure became increasingly formalised in the course of the seventeenth century, the pre-conditions for tumultuous elections remained in the centralisation of polling, extensive and customary treating of electors, and the prolongation of divisions over days or even weeks. The carnival atmosphere of a contested election to which people might flock from miles around to share the excitement of the hustings has often been commented on. But it was the increasing bitterness of party strife after 1689 which underlay the frequency of election riots. Not only did the Triennial Act of 1694 make elections more frequent, but they also took place in a political climate which was almost unique for the intensity of party conflict. Professor Holmes has written:

> The occurrence of no fewer than ten General Elections in the space of twenty years between 1695 and 1715 was something quite without precedent in English history, and as things turned out it had no parallel in the 250 years that have followed. The result was that throughout these two decades the political temperature at the grass roots of politics, in the constituencies (counties where the party balance was fairly even, cities and boroughs with large, volatile electorates, and many smaller incorporated boroughs where control of the council or even of the mayor was a crucial factor in commanding parliamentary seats) the temperature was feverishly high for much of the time.[5]

Moreover, compared with the mid-eighteenth century, the elections of the early decades were marked by a relatively large number of contests. In 1702, eighteen counties in England went to the polls, twenty-six in 1705, and twenty-three in 1710. Similarly over half the English boroughs went to the poll in 1710, and again in 1722. One obvious pre-condition for election violence was a contest, particularly where an 'independent' interest might seek to unseat an established family or interest, leading to a process of 'bidding up' both in electoral bribery and in violence at the polls. The frequency of contest brought party and electoral organisation to new levels. The hiring of mobs to intimidate opponents became a common practice and violence was facilitated by the tendency of government to withdraw any troops from places where they were quartered during an election. An increasing electorate during the late seventeenth and early eighteenth centuries also contributed to the vigour of political life, both at Westminster and at the polls.[6]

Beloff has recorded that notable election riots occurred in 1695, when disturbances took place at Oxford, Exeter, Westminster and elsewhere. In 1698 there were more disturbances in Westminster, establishing that populous constituency as one of the most turbulent in the country, a place it was to hold at various points during the next hundred years. The election of 1705 was also notorious for the electoral violence to which it gave rise, with the worst disturbances at Coventry, where 600 or 700 men defied the orders of the mayor to keep out of the town. Overpowering the civil authorities at dead of night, they took possession of the town hall and held on to it throughout the election; with the focal point of the election in their control they were able to attack the supporters of their opponents. The election was subsequently declared void, but when assizes were held there in the following year, the rival candidates appeared with their supporters to assist them. Chester, Honiton, and Salisbury were also disturbed.[7]

The 1710 election has been called 'the most riotous election campaign of the period'. It followed the raising of political and religious passions by Dr Sacheverell's preaching in the autumn of 1709 and his prosecution by the Whig administration for his High Church views. During the spring and autumn of 1710 political and religious rivalries flowed into each other. (The disturbances in London in 1710 are described in more detail later, see p. 53–7.) The promulgation of the sentence against Sacheverell led to widespread demonstrations in his support; its lightness was seen as a vindication as his views and clergy with High Church inclinations were reported to be preaching violent sermons against the Whigs. Disturbances broke out at Oxford, Exeter, Hereford, Barnstaple, Gainsborough, Frome, Cirencester, Sherborne, Walsall, West Bromwich, and across the border into Wales. There was also an identifiable anti-Sacheverell disturbance at Ely. The places disturbed were a mixture of cathedral cities, where a degree of High Church and High Tory sentiment could have been expected, and also the cloth towns of the West Country. During Sacheverell's summer progress, his presence led to renewed violence at Ely and Bridgnorth. The autumn election was fought amid intense party feeling, the many contests allowing scope for electoral rowdiness and intimidation. The county contests at York, Canterbury, Norwich, Nottingham and Northampton all provoked violence. In the boroughs, there were disturbances at Taunton, Liverpool, Chester, Northwich, Marlow, Whitchurch, Coventry, Chippenham and Newark, and in London itself.[8]

The Proclamation of George I in August 1714 provoked little discontent in England. The King's arrival in September and preparations for the coronation led to a few brawls in London, but the coronation provoked only one serious disturbance, at Bristol, where a small mob attacked a shop alleged to contain an effigy of Dr Sacheverell. Other houses were attacked, mainly belonging to town officials, and a Quaker who attempted to pacify the crowd was trampled to death.[9] It was only in the spring of 1715 that disturbances between Jacobite and Hanoverian factions became more numerous. Street demonstrations and attacks on Presbyterian meeting houses in London in April and May were paralleled in the North-West and the Midlands. As in the capital, the targets were recently constructed dissenting chapels; at least thirty Nonconformist place of worship were attacked during June, July, and August 1715. At Manchester, trouble had broken out in May, when on the fifth, some townsmen proclaimed the Pretender as King. Hanoverian celebrations on the 28 May were also broken up by Jacobite mobs. On the following day, a mob under a Jacobite blacksmith, Tom Sydall, attacked the Cross Street Presbyterian chapel, in 1694 the first dissenting chapel to be built in Manchester, and the most opulent and dominating symbol of dissent in the community. The mob smashed the doors and windows, wrecked the pulpit and pews, and made a bonfire of the wreckage. An award of £1,500 was later granted by parliament to repair the damage. Other meeting houses were attacked in Lancashire, including some at Wigan and Pilkington, to cries of 'Down with the Rump' and 'Church and King'. On 10 June, the Pretender's birthday, there were disturbances in South Lancashire. At Warrington, crowds were summoned by the pealing of the bells of the parish church and a mob went through the streets crying 'The Church in Danger!', 'Down with the Dissenters!' and 'God save King James the Third!'[10]

Disturbances also spread to the Midlands. Meeting houses were gutted at Wolverhampton, Worcester, Birmingham, Stourbridge, Shrewsbury, Newcastle-under-Lyme, Walsall, Whitchurch, Burton-on-Trent, Lichfield, Dudley, Leek, Stafford and Uttoxeter. At Shrewsbury a 'proclamation' was issued which ran:

> We gentlemen of the loyal mob do issue this proclamation to all Dissenters of what kind soever, whether Independents, Baptists, or Quakers. If you, or any of you, do encourage or suffer any of that damnable faction called Presbyterians to assemble themselves in any of your conventicles at the time of Divine worship, you may expect to meet with the same that they have been treated with. Given under our hands and seals on the eleventh day of July, 1715. God save the King!

In Staffordshire it was said that 'scarcely a Whig or Dissenter could escape insult or more serious injury'. Several days of rioting occurred in Oxford, partly as a result of the incautious behaviour of the Whig Constitution Club. Meeting for a dinner on the evening of 28 May, they ordered a bonfire prepared outside their hotel, upon which to burn an effigy of the late Queen Anne and as a result some leading Tories urged a crowd to demolish the bonfire, which was speedily accomplished. The pro-Tory mob then went on the rampage, gutting the Presbyterian meeting house, burning its pulpit 'in a public place' near Carfax, and locking the chapel clerk into the stocks when he tried to interfere. Gangs paraded the streets throughout the evening, loosing off firearms into the air; some of the rioters were shot at from the windows of Oriel College, one of the centres of the Whigs, but their marksmanship was poor. The following day, the city was a blaze of lights, 'as hath not been known since the Restoration' wrote a contemporary. People were reported running through the streets, crying for 'King James the Third'. The 'True King! No Usurper!' and drinking toasts to a new restoration. During the evening the Quaker and Baptist meeting houses were attacked and badly damaged, while a mob swarming around the gates of Oriel was again fired on and a man wounded.[11] Colourful as the events in Oxford were, the most serious casualties were at West Bromwich where the soldiers caught up with a crowd demolishing the meeting house and fired on them: reports of the dead varied between two and twenty.[12]

The geography of these disturbances clearly reflected the distribution of strong Tory sentiment. Oxford was disturbed again a year later when a recruiting party visited the town and was prevented from reading the recruiting proclamation by cries of 'Down with the Rump'; the recruiting officer was covered in filth and mud and noisy illuminations once again enforced. Shropshire, Lancashire, parts of the West Midlands, and the Marches were to retain strong Tory and Jacobite feeling well into the eighteenth century. Moreover, the Midlands and Lancashire were also areas with a strong dissenting tradition, where the newly opened chapels clearly marked them out as an increasingly self-confident and permanent part of the community. The clash of these two forces in the heated atmosphere of the Hanoverian succession accounts for the concentration of the rioting in these areas. Significantly, it was to be Birmingham and Manchester, three generations later, who saw the most serious disturbances in England in the aftermath of the French Revolution. Once again, the dissenters were to bear the brunt of attack.

A direct result of these disturbances was the Riot Act (1 Geo. I, st. 2, c. 5). Coming into force on 1 August 1715, its preamble stated:

> Whereas of late many rebellious riots and tumults have been in divers parts of this kingdom, to the disturbance of the publick peace, and the endangering of his Majesty's person and government, and the same are yet continued and fomented by persons disaffected to his Majesty, presuming so to do, for that the punishments provided by the laws now in being are not adequate to such heinous offences; and by such rioters his Majesty and his administration have been most maliciously and falsely traduced, with an intent to raise divisions, and to alienate the affections of the people from his Majesty.

The intention was to strengthen and clarify the law relating to riots. Under its provisions a crowd of twelve or more which 'unlawfully, riotously, and tumultuously' remained assembled for an hour after the reading of a set proclamation was guilty of a felony and therefore liable to capital punishment. Although much confusion was caused about the precise way in which the Act was to be used, this strengthening of the law illustrated the seriousness with which the Government saw the situation.

It did not, however, end unrest. The autumn of 1715 was marked by disturbances in London and faction fights continued into 1716. Nor was the country entirely pacific. Strong Jacobite sentiments in many parts of the North and West of England, as well as in some cathedral and university cities, contributed to a tense atmosphere. A good illustration of this occurred in Derby where there was a disturbance in All Saints' Church when the cleric conducting the service prayed publicly for King James, but after a few moments hesitation, quickly corrected himself with

'I mean King George'. The slip, if slip it was, caused an uproar in the congregation and the offending clergyman was driven from the church with drawn swords by soldiers from the congregation. That the incident was more of a political demonstration than an accident was indicated when other clergy in Derby showed strong pro-Jacobite sympathies. The Rev. Harris of St Peter's was repeatedly called to order by the magistrates for irregularities and the Rev. Cantril was said to drink the Pretender's health on his knees. There were also disturbances at Cambridge in May 1716 and further riots in Oxford in October. Oxford had been garrisoned with troops since the Jacobite rebellion of the previous year and the officers were entertained by the Whig Constitution Club to celebrate the Prince of Wales's birthday on 30 October. During the course of the evening the windows of houses which failed to illuminate were smashed and the Mayor of Oxford roughly handled, the Major of the garrison being accused of ordering his men to the work with words 'Come in, Boys, and drink, and then go out and at it again'. The behaviour of the soldiers was made a source of political capital when the Tories led by the Vice-Chancellor complained to the Privy Council. Such charges were rebutted by the Whigs who seized on Paris reports of the disturbances as evidence that 'our British Jacobites' were trying to encourage the Pretender.[13]

The intensity of party feeling magnified almost any incident out of all proportion and there were quite deliberate attempts by a Whig administration to 'license' favourable demonstrations of support: through the control of the army and its garrisons in notable centres of Jacobite activity the Whigs had considerable scope to play the game according to their own rules. Thus when in January 1717 George I returned from Hanover, anti-Jacobite demonstrations were staged in London and effigies of the Pretender, the Pope, the Duke of Ormonde, a Jesuit, and a cardinal were carried in mock procession through the streets and burned at Charing Cross. Similar preparations for processions and bonfires were made at Oxford and when the heads of the colleges objected because of the threat of disorder, the garrison commander pleaded insufficient force to prevent the Whigs celebrating 'in such manner as they lik'd best'. When the heads appealed to the Secretary of War, he prohibited the procession only on condition that they 'set all their Bells a-ringing' on the 'first notice of his Majesty's happy arrival'. Having exacted their agreement, the procession was banned and a more restrained celebration held with bonfires and fireworks, effigies of the Pope, the Pretender and Ormonde being exhibited for money rather than carried through the streets. Small flurries of pro-Jacobite sentiment continued to erupt on appropriate festivals or at elections in strong Tory areas. At a Lichfield election in 1718 the Whig candidate's supporters were 'kept out the Hall and barbarously beaten and abused, and their lives endangered by a very great mob' with the Pretender's white emblem stuck in their hats. At Leicester in July 1722 it was reported that a group of seven or eight people proclaimed James III at the Market Cross, though the suggestion was that this was simply the outcome of prolonged entertainment during the evening.[14]

The age of oligarchy

But with the growing security of the Hanoverian succession and the increasingly oligarchic tendency of electoral control, the occasions of open political violence became more limited. After the Septennial Act of 1716 elections were less frequent and there were also fewer contests than in the heyday of the 'rage of party'. A vigorous anti-Jacobite policy made displays of even Tory sentiment dangerous at a time when Walpole was only too ready to use any real or imagined threat to the regime as a means to rally the 'independents' and divide the Tories. Election disturbances were less frequent during the 1720s, but Chester in 1732 provided an interesting illustration of a mayoral election causing disturbances in a confused interplay of local issues and national politics. The local Whigs were trying to wrest control of the city from the Tory Grosvenor family who dominated its representation (the family held a seat there without a break from 1715 to 1874). The Whigs were headed by Thomas Brereton, a Chester alderman, and Richard Manley, the author of a scheme for reviving the declining trade of the city by widening the River Dee. The scheme proved popular and the cry of 'for Mr Manley and Navigation' became the slogan of the Whig candidate for the mayoralty. The Grosvenors were blamed when the Bill was lost in April 1732 and during subsequent disturbances were reported to be 'daily insulted'. The city was said to be 'hardly ever free' from riots in the run-up to the mayoral election in October. Walpole arranged through his son-in-law Lord Malpas, the son of the Lord Lieutenant, for a 'swarm of excise, salt and customs house officers' and 'common soldiers' to be brought in to vote for Manley when he stood for Mayor. On 10 October a Whig mob demolished the city hall on hearing that the Tories were intending to create 300 more freemen voters, but the Tories now rallied their forces. Watkin Williams-Wynn, MP for Denbighshire and a leading ally of the Grosvenors, raised the Welsh tenantry of the Tory gentry and issued orders for them to go to Chester 'to beat the Whiggish rascals'. There arrived in the city '8 or 9 hundred Welshmen . . . armed with clubs, staffs and other dangerous and offensive weapons', headed by Wynn's liveried servants armed with pistols. It was reported that the Welshmen 'knocked down every man that declared a Manley, or for King George'. The Tory candidate got home, though not without extensive treating to accompany the intimidation.[15]

The apparent weakening of Walpole's position after the Excise Crisis led to a more heated election contest in 1734. Both Walpole and his opponents mobilised more actively than for many years, with more secret service money being spent than in any other year between 1728 and 1760.[16] The resulting election campaign was violent as well as expensive, the usual result of a seriously contested election in the eighteenth century. There were disturbances at the county elections in Yorkshire, Suffolk and Norfolk, and a particularly fierce clash at Great Yarmouth. There the appearance of the Tory candidates led to a rampage by their supporters through the town, followed by further riots when the Whig candidates appeared with their supporters. But the most serious disturbances were seen on the Welsh Marches, reaching as far north as Chester and as far south as Gloucestershire. Opposition to turnpikes may have played a part in the disturbances in the southern areas, as this had been the cause of rioting as recently as 1731.[17] In the northern Marches the riots were more directly political. At Newcastle-under-Lyme colliers assembled and threatened to 'wash their hands' in the 'Heart's Blood' of one of the candidates, and in nearby Bridgnorth, the troops had to be called in to restore order. Both of these were fairly populous boroughs by contemporary standards, Newcastle having about 500 voters, while Bridgnorth was one of the widest franchises in England, polling over a 1,000 votes in the elections of 1727, 1734, and 1741.[18]

The Jacobite Rebellion of 1745–6 provided the next major occasion for political disturbances outside the capital. In the aftermath of the rising two Manchester Jacobites, Adjutant Sydall, the man who had led the attack on the Cross Street chapel thirty years earlier, and Lieutenant Deacon, were executed in London and their heads sent to Manchester and exhibited at the Exchange. To the fury of local Whigs, Jacobite sympathisers insisted on paying the gruesome relics every respect, never passing without stopping and raising their hats. In this climate it was hardly surprising that a reaction should take place. On a day of public thanksgiving for the suppression of the rebellion in October 1746, a bitter sermon against the 'traitors' encouraged a Whig mob to attack the houses of Deacon's father and of Sydall's widow; the latter was forced to contribute to the illumination by putting candles in her windows.[19] Elsewhere, Catholics became a convenient scapegoat for loyalist sympathisers. In Sunderland a 'popish Chapple' was pulled down by a band of sailors and apprentices. There were also two separate incidents in spring 1746 at Liverpool, where on 30 April a mob of ship carpenters, sailors, and others attacked and set fire to a Roman Catholic chapel, completely destroying it and four adjacent houses. Towards the end of May the disturbances recurred when a mob attacked a house containing a private Catholic chapel. Although the mayor read the Riot Act, he and his constables were driven off by the mob, who fired the house and chapel.[20]

There were fewer overt Jacobite demonstrations after 1745. But that the 'good old cause' could still provide some focus for protest was shown in the continuing undercurrent of incidents in areas with known Jacobite leanings. At Oxford on 23 February 1748 (the birthday of the Pretender's youngest son) some undergraduates created a small disturbance. One declared 'I am the man that dare say God bless King James the Third and tell you my name is Dawes of St Mary Hall. I am a man of independent fortune and therefore am afraid of *no one* or *no man*.' Another was even more explicit: 'God Damn King George and all his assistants. God Bless King James the Third of England, Prince Charles and Prince Henry, Duke of York.' The Government was sufficiently alarmed by what was little more than a drunken prank to bring the offenders to London and charge them with uttering treason. The year before a contest for the county seats in Staffordshire – the first for a hundred years – saw a trial of strength between Whig and Tory interests. After the election result had been contested by the Whigs, the Tories under Sir Watkin Williams Wynn assembled in September to raise money to fight the petition. It was reported that 'one hundred and fifty of the Burton mob, most of them in plaid waistcoats, plaid ribbon round their hats and some white cockades' entered the town and were joined by a crowd from Birmingham. A soldier who cried out 'God Bless His Majesty King George and damn the Plaids' was assaulted, but the crowds largely confined themselves to drinking the Pretender's health and singing Jacobite songs. The North-East also harboured some Jacobite feeling. In April 1750 during a strike of the Tyneside keelmen, a number of people in keelmen's clothing gathered at Elswick Fields, near Newcastle, where one of them made the following pronouncement:

> *I proclaim* Prince CHARLES *King* of England France *and* Ireland *Defender of the Faith, and let every one of my way of thinking say Amen.*

At least four persons were reported to have contributed an 'Amen'.[21] But the most remarkable incident took place in the West Midlands, so frequently one of the most turbulent areas of Tory support, and once again on the anniversary of Charles II's restoration, 29 May. A Captain of Dragoons reported:

> ... about twelve o'clock at noon, a crowd of people assembled, to the number of near three hundred, in a riotous and tumultuous manner upon a certain place or street in the said town of Walsall, called The Hill, and then and there had a image or figure dressed up in the likeness of a man, his head was a barber's block, with an old wig upon it, and there was fixed to the hinder part of it a horse tail which reached down all along the back; that he had upon his hands white gloves and upon his legs white stockings; that his clothing appeared to be chiefly rags, or anything else that could make it look mean and disgracefull [*sic*]; that about the neck was a thick rope twisted round three or four times, and upon the breast was a paper or label, with these words wrote upon it: 'This is King Geo: the Second', and a little lower down, upon the belly, was another paper or label expressing these words: 'Evil to him that evil thinks, it is this that makes the nation stink'; in one hand was an orange, and in the other a bunch of turnips; they raised and fixed a gibbett in the street called The Hill, and upon this gibbett they hung by the neck the aforesaid figure or image, with a pair of horns set upon the head; and after many revileings [*sic*], attended with frequent shoutings and huzzaings,

and uttering many scandalous and treasonable expressions, they next had the impudence and insolence most audaciously to fire shots at the body as it hung upon the gibbett, and with much mirth and joy, many times shouting and clapping their hands; and this they continued doing till two o'clock next morning and after that they burned the body.[22]

The years which followed were relatively undisturbed. The gradual closing up of political representation offered fewer opportunities for displays of election disorder. In particular, the counties with their wide electorates, were less frequently contested. Between 1741 and 1768, 18 of the 40 English counties were uncontested, and 4 others only once. Whereas 65 per cent of counties had gone to the poll in 1705, only 7.5 per cent did so in 1747.[23] In the general election of 1754, there were only 56 constituencies that went to the poll in England, 5 counties and 51 boroughs. The most bitter contests occurred at Appleby and in Oxfordshire, but whereas the former had virtually no electors and the dispute was between Whig magnates for control of a pocket borough, the latter was fought out between Whig and Tory candidates in a county with an electorate of some 4,000. With a great deal of money being spent in an area with strong High Church and Jacobite associations, it was almost inevitable that some disorder would result. The Tories were alleged to have guarded the approaches to the hustings in Broad Street with men twenty deep, although the Whigs were allowed through Exeter College and cast their votes, much to the annoyance of the Vice-Chancellor. In the most serious incident of the election a Whig cavalcade was pelted as it passed over Magdalen Bridge and an attempt made to heave some of the gentlemen into the river. One retaliated and shot a chimney-sweep who was in the crowd.[24] At Leicester, another populous constituency gave rise to disorder: the local Whigs sought to capitalise on discontent with the Corporation's plan to enclose the southfield. A Whig mob marched to the fields and pulled down the fences erected by the Corporation in accordance with an advertisement they had placed in the newspapers some time before; both sides recruited freemen for the contest, while the Tories were alleged to have imported 'three hundred colliers . . . armed with bludgeons in which iron spikes had been inserted'. With or without this assistance, the Whig challenge was beaten off and the Tory candidates got home.[25]

Elections continued to occasion sporadic violence throughout the eighteenth century. Two men were killed at a by-election in Taunton in December 1754, and in 1756 soldiers had to be called in to keep the peace between cloth-workers and wealthier citizens over the choice of candidate. At Pontefract in 1768, a burgage borough which had been skilfully and tactfully managed by its two patrons, an East India nabob, John Walsh, bought up one of the patron's interests and determined to end the treating of electors and to bring in dummy voters. The burgage holders and the rest of the population, deprived of their customary privileges, reacted by bringing in rival candidates. During the election, the crowd surrounded the polling booth, kept out certain voters, and forced the election of the less guilty of the two patrons and one of their own candidates. This disturbance illustrated one theme of eighteenth-century election riots, the belief in customary treating by the candidate, an infringement of which could easily lead to trouble. Thus at Northampton in 1774, when after a particularly ruinous contest in 1768 the candidates refused to treat the electors, a crowd broke the windows of the inn where the candidates had put up. Similarly at York, in the same year, one of the sitting members caused a disturbance because he objected to treating the voters.[26]

Although the furore surrounding the Wilkes affair was primarily a metropolitan phenomenon, recent work has shown that there was wide provincial interest in Wilkes's campaign, and very widespread demonstrations of support, some of which led to minor disturbances, such as window-smashing, the burning of effigies, and rowdy illuminations.[27] For example on the day following Wilkes's first return for Middlesex in March 1768, there were noisy rejoicings in his old seat at Aylesbury; a local attorney recorded: 'Here were great rejoicing last night – Bonfires, Illuminations & every thing of the Sort. The Bells began ringing at 12 yesterday & are ringing now. Windows all broke that did not illuminate on account of Mr Wilkes being elected for Middlesex.'[28] Similarly his release from King's Bench Prison in April 1770 triggered off popular demonstrations in many parts of the country with the usual round of illuminations, bonfires, and some sporadic rowdiness and window-smashing. But the violence never reached the same proportions as had accompanied earlier celebrations for popular heroes such as Dr Sacheverell.

Similarly, the Gordon Riots provoked little response in the country at large. Demonstrations of anti-Government and anti-Catholic feeling were largely confined to petitions and meetings. The growth of more organised opinion in the provinces, seen in the county movement of the 1770s and 1780s, eschewed popular violence. Outside London, England was virtually free from popular political disturbances in the middle and late eighteenth century. Elections remained an important exception. In 1784 there were serious riots at Westminster, Liverpool, Buckingham, Coventry and Leicester, and again in 1790 there were riots at Carlisle, Leicester, Nottingham, Beverley and York.[29] Election riots continued into the 1790s amid the larger issues created by the French Revolution and the war with France. Norwich, the scene of riots during a by-election in 1786, was again disturbed ten years later, when in a campaign enlivened by the presence of the radical orator John Thelwall and considerable anti-war feeling there was much disorder and violence at the poll. On the final day of voting the *Norfolk Chronicle* recorded that for three hours gangs of desperadoes attacked anyone who had the courage to show the colours of the sitting member, William Windham, while Thelwall complained that he was attacked and twice knocked down.[30]

Religious riots

As suggested above, religious disputes were a characteristic feature of the early part of the century, involving attacks on the dissenters, and Roman Catholics. Many were bound up with the rivalry between Whig and Tory and between Hanoverian and Jacobite. Attacks upon dissenting meeting houses and Roman Catholic chapels were likely to occur at times of political controversy, and these two minorities were often the scapegoats for political factions. With the growing stability of politics after 1716, attacks on Catholics or Dissenters tended only to reappear at times of political tension. Thus attacks on Catholic chapels took place in the aftermath of the Jacobite rising of 1745 and during the campaign of the Protestant Association in 1778–80. Even in the latter period, the most serious rioting outside London occurred in Scotland, with only an isolated attack on a Catholic chapel in Bath as a demonstration of violent anti-Catholicism in England.[31] The dissenters too, were only objects of attack in the harsher political climate after 1789 when their identification with radical opinion led them once again to become the targets of 'loyalist' abuse.

Generally speaking, religious violence in the eighteenth century seemed to fluctuate far more with the political climate than anything else. Thus in some freemen boroughs, an added bitterness could be added to electioneering where urban politics were divided along religious lines. John Brooke has suggested a number of boroughs, such as Exeter, Leicester, Liverpool and Norwich, where Anglican control of the Corporation was contested by an independent party based on a nucleus of dissenters; at Nottingham it was the dissenters who controlled the corporation and this may well have contributed to the frequent rowdiness of its elections.[32] Nonetheless, the overall impression for eighteenth-century England is that both Catholics and dissenters, although objects of suspicion and even attack at times of political excitement, were generally tolerated within their communities and that communal violence on specifically religious issues was rare. Whether its absence was due primarily to the growing stability of the regime in the years after 1716 and, at least until the last decades of the century, an easing in political tension, or to a growing tolerance and sophistication within English society is a difficult question to answer. The argument for greater tolerance seems belied by the Gordon Riots and the antagonism shown to the dissenters in the early 1790s, in the wake of the French Revolution. In the years that preceded these events, however, it would not have been difficult to sustain the view that disturbances occasioned by religious belief were a thing of the past. The reasons behind the re-emergence of rioting on ostensibly religious grounds after 1789 must be examined in due course (see pp. 137–42 below).

Quakers and Methodists

Two groups stand out from the general pattern of religious disturbances: Quakers and Methodists. The Society of Friends were an interesting example of a group who were not only tainted with the mark of dissent, but also earned considerable hostility because of their involvement in commerce and industry, particularly the grain trade. As late as 1823, that bundle of prejudices, William Cobbett could rail against the Quakers' involvement in the wholesale trade for farm produce: 'Thus the *Quaker* gets rich, and the poor devil of a farmer is squeezed into a gaol. The *Quakers* carry on the far greater part of this work. They are, as to the products of the earth, what the *Jews* are as to gold and silver.'[33] This involvement led to their being blamed for high prices in times of scarcity. As we shall see later, the central government and provincial authorities were often guilty of passing the blame for shortages onto a convenient scapegoat, namely the middlemen in the grain trade: as a result there were attacks on Quakers in both 1766 and 1800.[34] Apart from these incidents the Quakers were generally tolerated outside periods of severe shortage.

The Methodists became a frequent target for attack in the middle years of the eighteenth century. The *Journals* of John Wesley contain many examples of anti-Methodist disturbances, particularly in the early years of the movement. The Methodists suffered a variety of assaults, some of which involved no more than rude horseplay, but others caused serious injury and even death. Dr Walsh's researches into the character of these disturbances have suggested a number of significant features. Much violence took the form of what he characterises as 'psychological humiliation', the sort of ill-treatment usually meted out to offenders against moral standards or who in any way earned the displeasure of the local community. Methodists were subjected to attacks on their property, personal assault, including sexual abuse in the case of women, and ritual chastisement. The houses of local Methodists were frequently attacked and where a chapel or meeting house was constructed, they usually became the primary target as being a tangible expression of the new movement, and symbols of permanency. In many instances the violence was directed at the itinerant preacher, an obvious target who often daringly courted a 'confrontation' with attackers.[35]

It would be wrong, however, to regard the reception given to Methodism as typically violent. Although the early struggles play an important part in traditional histories of Methodism, as they tend to in the history of most movements (a parallel case is trade unionism), there is plenty of evidence from the *Journals* and elsewhere to show that in many places the Methodists were welcomed with a range of reactions from open friendliness to complete apathy. 'Mobbings' happened often enough to give them a place in almost every local history of the movement, but open hostility was by no means automatic. Wesley's more peaceful reception in some of the mining districts of Cornwall and the dock area of Newcastle bear this out,[36] but elsewhere, his presence, or that of other Methodist itinerants, stirred up the antagonism of the established clergy. When Wesley made his second visit to Wednesbury in April 1743 and attended the local parish church, he claimed he had never heard 'so wicked a sermon' inveighing against the Methodists. Two days later a drunken clergyman attempted to ride down Wesley's listeners. On his third visit, almost a month later, there were nine days of rioting in which the houses and persons of local Methodists were attacked with the encouragement of the local curate and magistrate. Three weeks later a crowd assembled in Wednesbury churchyard, apparently under the direction of the churchwardens, and went on to attack eighty houses belonging to Methodists. Wesley himself was roughly handled there in October; the mobs who attacked him on this occasion believed themselves to be acting within the law, for on 12 October the justices had issued an order to apprehend and bring before them 'several disorderly persons styling themselves Methodist preachers who go about raising routs and riots'. The rioters who buffeted Wesley through the streets of Wednesbury on 20 October insisted that he go with them to find a magistrate, and it was only when they were unable to find one that they consented to release him.[37]

Similarly, on Charles Wesley's visit to Cornwall in July 1743 the vicar of Illogan hired his churchwarden and a mob to chase him from the district, an event celebrated at an alehouse in Pool and recorded in the parochial accounts as nine shillings expended at 'Anne Gartrell's on driving out the Methodist'. When John Wesley arrived in Cornwall a month later, he only encountered violent resistance in the parish of St Ives, where the vicar and curate, Hoblyn and Symonds, were openly hostile. The chapel built by the local Methodists was destroyed during the subsequent winter, an act in which the churchmen were strongly suspected of being involved. On John Wesley's next visit to St Ives in April 1744 he recorded that the 'persecution here was owing, in great measure, to the indefatigable labours of Mr Hoblyn and Mr Symonds'. On 11 April, the church in St Ives was full when Hoblyn preached on the text 'If they have called the Master of the house Beelzebub, how much more then of his household?' Wesley recorded that 'Mr Hoblyn fulfilled them by vehemently declaiming against *the new sect*, as enemies of the Church, Jacobites, Papists and what not!' The result was almost inevitable: the houses of several Methodists were attacked on the following day. The antagonism was probably intensified by Wesley's intention of making St Ives the headquarters for the evangelisation of West Cornwall. In spite of manifestly poor relations with the established Church, Wesley persisted in his plan, even though for some time afterwards Sunday evenings were often the occasion for an attack upon Methodist property 'from some of the devil's drunken champions, who swarm here on a holy-day, so called'.[38]

As well as the opposition of resident clergy, Methodism also inherited the fear of sectaries and levelling from the seventeenth century and a continuing 'Church and King' tradition which manifested itself in periods of political tension. Hence the meeting house at St Ives was burned down by a mob celebrating a naval victory over the Spaniards. The attacks on Methodists in cathedral towns such as Exeter in 1745 and Norwich in 1751–2 at least partly derived from this tradition. Moreover the coincidence of the early years of the movement with the threat of invasion and the Jacobite rebellion only served to heighten the sense of unease. As the sermon quoted above shows, Methodists were frequently branded as political subversives and accused of being crypto-papists and Jacobites. These charges were at their height in the years 1744–6; the incidents at St Ives, for example, took place at a time when there were real fears of a French descent upon Cornwall. The atmosphere of these years was shown in the wild rumours which circulated about the political activities of Wesley, who was variously alleged to have visited the Pretender in France and brought him to England, and was at one point believed to have been committed to the Tower for treason.[39]

Methodism also provoked more basic fears in many communities. Initially, at least, the preacher was seen as an intruder, a stranger, and a disruptive force. The 'enthusiasm' of early converts was regarded with considerable suspicion and conjured up some of the stereotypes often attached to strange new movements. Hence early Methodists were accused of kidnapping children, encouraging sexual licence, disrupting family ties, and practising sorcery. Not all these charges were fanciful: conversion could divide families and its attraction of the young, especially young women, could arouse strong and violent passions, and the riots at Wednesbury were reported to have been partly caused by a man's wife going missing for several days and then being found in the company of a Methodist preacher.[40] Early Methodists were often warned against 'marrying with the world'; an instruction which could easily lead to bitter conflicts within relatively closed and isolated communities. Converts often formed a community within a community, marking themselves out from non-Methodists by their conspicuous piety and ascetic practices. Wesley's strictures on certain forms of behaviour could also create tensions within a community; his attack on smuggling, and perhaps more important upon the trade in smuggled goods, aroused great hostility in the Cornish fishing villages where it struck at a virtual pillar of the local economy.[41]

The antagonism to Methodism was most prevalent during its initial impact on an area, when still an unknown quantity and rumours about behaviour were most likely to be given credence. In general terms the opposition to the Methodists began to slacken from the middle of the century but it could still flare up when they evangelised new areas; for example disturbances recurred in Cornwall towards the end of the century when the Methodists moved into the eastern part of the county. Most of these were on a small scale, with the most serious incident at Wadebridge where some gunpowder was placed under the doorstep of the Methodist meeting-house. Preachers were attacked at Quethiok, St Germans, and Mevagissy.[42]

As in many other areas, the disturbances here were only an aspect of the hostility shown towards the Methodists. Persecution also included humiliating practical jokes, social ostracism, and economic sanctions. At St Mellion a goat was pushed into the congregation and at St Germans a reputedly fierce mastiff was set loose in the chapel. Social displeasure and economic pressure could prove more decisive and longer lasting than occasional violence. At St Breock the rector effectively destroyed the local Methodist community by persuading shopkeepers not to sell to them. Methodists could also be impressed in the armed forces under the laws permitting magistrates to draft the idle and disorderly; manipulation of the laws of settlement, the withholding of charity, and sackings also played a part beside more violent opposition.[43]

The pace of persecution did slacken during the late eighteenth century, as familiarity with the Methodists stilled the worst fears and they achieved either a stable relationship with local communities or cultural hegemony over them. The relatively stable political atmosphere from the 1740s until the French Revolution permitted the Methodists to consolidate their position in a climate less hostile to the new movement. Wesley himself took every opportunity of stressing loyalty to King and constitution. As well as fulsome protestations of loyalty during the 1740s, his ultra-loyalism expressed itself as a firm conservatism in the years up to 1789. His basic position that 'the powers that be are ordained of God' was reiterated on several occasions. When French invasion threatened in 1756, Wesley offered to raise two hundred men for the Crown. In 1768 he reproved anyone for speaking ill of either the King or his Ministers and suggested that methodist preachers refute any slanders on the monarch. In 1775 he committed himself to extinguishing the 'flame of malice and rage against the King, and almost all who are in authority under him', and when the threat of invasion recurred he again offered to raise 'some men'.[44]

The tight control which Wesley exercised enabled him to enforce this policy at the grass roots of the movement. For example, in 1789 the superintendent preacher at St Austell received a letter from Wesley instructing him to advise all Methodists who had votes to cast them in the coming election for Francis Gregor of Trewarthenick, who was described as 'a lover of King George and the present administration'.[45] The outbreak of the French Revolution only strengthened Wesley's conservatism, and he was reported in May 1790 to declare 'That if the best of Kings – the most virtuous of Queens – and the most perfect Constitution, could make any nation happy, the people of this country had every reason to think themselves so'.[46] This loyalist stance was maintained after Wesley's death and undoubtedly helped the Methodists to escape a renewed bout of persecution. Though they came under suspicion, the Methodists made repeated and public professions of loyalty, particularly at the height of the reaction against Jacobinism in 1792–3. In August 1792 a conference of Methodist preachers in London answered the question 'What directions shall be given concerning our conduct to the civil government?' with:

1. None of us shall, either in writing or conversation, speak slightly or irreverently of the government under which he lives.
2. We are to observe that the Oracle of God Command us to be subjects to the higher powers; and that honour to the King is there connected with the fear of God.[47]

Subsequent conferences during the 1790s reiterated these sentiments and enforced the expulsion of members who displayed radical tendencies. Compared with other dissenters, who were to bear the brunt of Church and King attacks in the early 1790s, the Methodists escaped largely unscathed.[48]

3 Manifold disorders

Politics and religion by no means exhaust the range of issues on which popular disturbances occurred in eighteenth-century England. Indeed, the frequency of riots and disorders on a wide variety of other occasions has done much to produce the impression of a period in which this was the most characteristic response to impositions of any kind. In fact, as the following sections show, popular disturbances were usually directed against some innovatory or unusual practice. It would be wrong to assume that every enclosure, every press gang, or every turnpike excited violent opposition. Disturbances were the exception rather than the rule and the reasons why they occurred in one place rather than another and on some occasions rather than others have to be considered.

Recruiting riots

The only branch of the armed forces raised on a systematic basis in eighteenth-century England was the militia.[1] Until 1757 it remained a decayed and little-used force, but an Act of that year, passed under the pressure of the Seven Years' War, remodelled its organisation and recruiting procedures. A force of 60,000 men was envisaged, the bulk of whom were to be obtained by county quotas. Each county was to take a census of able-bodied men between eighteen and fifty years of age (later reduced to forty-five) and select a proportion of them from each parish by drawing lots. The procedure was for the chief constable of each hundred to produce a list of all the men within his jurisdiction who were fit to serve. This he obtained from the parish constables, who were instructed to place a copy of the list of those going into the ballot on the door of the parish church on the Sunday before the return was made so that men who believed they should be exempt could make a challenge and claim their exemption. When the returns from parishes and hundreds were collected, a meeting of magistrates apportioned the quota between each parish and took a ballot to decide who would serve.

Militia service was for three years, when the procedure was repeated to refill the ranks. The Act permitted the men chosen to provide a substitute or pay a fine of £10; if they paid a fine, they were automatically appointed to serve again in three years time. Service involved training each Sunday between February and October in the locality and a few days drill at Whitweek; under normal conditions discipline was imposed by the civil authorities by fines or imprisonment. If embodied to deal with a local or national emergency, the militia received army pay and was subject to military law. Officers were selected according to graded property qualifications. The major burden of the new militia fell upon the poor. The gentry bore no charge for the militia, as its expenses were paid out of general taxation, but many poorer men viewed the militia as a burdensome inconvenience and a form of taxation. One result was that the bulk of the men were poor manual workers who could not afford to find a substitute or pay the fine. Very quickly the Militia Act gave rise to a trade in substitutes which drew on the same sources as the regular army, including the 'crimp' houses of the capital, centres of trade, and the poorer regions of the country. Some parishes attempted a system of offering bounties in order to fill their quota with volunteers, thus relieving the district of the whole business; others employed insurance agents to obtain the men required.[2]

The attempt to put the Act into operation in the summer of 1757 met with widespread opposition, partly inspired by the sheer novelty of the legislation. There were widespread misunderstandings about the operation of the Act and its intention especially fears of arbitrary power and of being sent abroad but in fact it used the normal machinery of local government and specifically excluded service overseas. Widespread concern was felt that men would be forced to join the militia wholesale and the procedure of listing the inhabitants and posting names on the church door undoubtedly aroused a myriad apprehensions among a largely illiterate population, possibly reawakening long buried fears of poll-tax and parliamentary commissioners. In the more rural areas the first levy with its fairly complicated procedure and only half-understood provisions, created an atmosphere of near panic. A major grievance came from a sense of inequality, that the poor were being made to serve, while the rich could simply pay the fine or find a substitute. But opposition was not confined to the poor: many farmers and yeomen reacted strongly to the Act in a mood which was strikingly similar to the strong resentments shown towards the nobility during the county movement of the 1770s and 1780s. Western comments that the resentments of poor and middle-class opponent to the Act led to it being 'viewed as an upper class plot and reminded middle and lower class alike of other grievances against their rulers' and describes a threatening letter sent to two Lincolnshire justices as 'virtually a middle-class political manifesto', threatening to destroy gentlemen's houses if the lists were drawn up and suggesting that if the gentry wanted militiamen they should hire them 'by the assistance of your long green purses'. If militia service left families destitute the letter asked, 'which of you buntin-ars' coated fellows will maintain his family?'[3]

It was hardly surprising that such opposition would manifest itself in some violence, but even the Government was startled by the scale of disturbances which occurred. The Act came into force in June 1757 and the riots mainly took place in August and September when the local authorities began to put into operation the machinery for raising the 32,000 men envisaged. The riots were often sparked off by the act of making the lists in individual parishes and the most usual form they took was of preventing the returns being made. Meetings of magistrates to execute the ballot were often disrupted, and attacks were also made on the property of magistrates and county officials. The most disturbed part of the country was the East Riding of Yorkshire: at Birdsall 'a very numerous body of farmers and country people, out of 40 townships in the weapon of Buckrose, armed with scythes and Clubs, rose on account of the Militia Act'. While confessing their willingness to serve their King and Country, they declared that they would not 'submit to the Act as it stood'.[4] On 12 September a mob assembled near Beverley and made the chief constable give up the lists being prepared for the lieutenancy meeting the following week; invading the town, they threatened to burn it down, demolished one house and were only bought off when given some money. The houses of the gentry were visited, threats issued to them and their property if they operated the Act, and on several occasions contributions demanded and the occasional house pillaged. A short-term success was obtained when the lord lieutenant issued a proclamation on the 15th, ordering no lists to be returned pending instructions from the King.[5]

Similar events took place in the North Riding. A mob from the Wapentake of Bulmer prevented magistrates from their own district from attending the meeting at York, and proceeding to York themselves destroyed the inn where the meeting was to have taken place and seized such lists as they could find. They were only pacified when the lord lieutenant and the Mayor of York told them that a meeting at Thirsk would be abandoned and further meetings would not be held. Less serious disturbances also occurred at Doncaster and Sheffield. Lincolnshire was much disturbed, with a general rising in the area around Lincoln forcing the abandonment of the lieutenancy meeting on 6 September. Contributions were levied on the local gentry by the mob and there were reports of 'great outrages' at Boston. The disturbances also spread into the Midlands and South. At Mansfield in Nottinghamshire the magistrates were assaulted when trying to administer the Act and fifty lists were seized around Nottingham when a mob armed with clubs entered the meeting place and rough-handled Sir George Savile and Lord Robert Sutton. Lists were destroyed in East Bedfordshire and Hertfordshire, while disturbances occurred in Cambridgeshire, Norfolk, Huntingdonshire and Middlesex. A few disturbances also broke out in Gloucester and Kent.[6]

Although many counties submitted to the Act peacefully, two years after its operation only half the number of troops required had been selected. In some districts the local gentry refused to implement the Act in the face of widespread hostility, while in others, as in Yorkshire, its political opponents sought to take advantage of the riots in order to frustrate its operation. Eventually a determined effort by the administration, making support for the militia almost a test of loyalty to the Government, coupled with a convenient invasion scare in 1759, helped to establish the militia. It did not, however, mean an end to disturbances. There were renewed riots in Huntingdonshire in 1759 and 1761, but the most serious took place in the North-East. In Durham a mob 'armed with clubs' marched to Gateshead and told the magistrates that 'they who have lands should hire men to maintain them' and extracted a promise that 'the Gentlemen in the County would find men to fill up the vacancies'. In Northumberland the issue was settled less amicably. After compelling magistrates at Morpeth to stop their attempt to implement the act, 5,000 marched to Hexham where they were met by the Yorkshire Militia, who fired on the mob, killing and wounding more than a hundred: this was the most serious disturbance caused by the Militia Act, with over twenty people killed. Sporadic opposition continued, with riots in Buckinghamshire in 1769, Sussex in 1778, and much of eastern England in 1796.[7]

Even when embodied, the militia proved extremely troublesome. Desertion was rife whenever a regiment was put on active service and most were under strength in normal times. Most serious was the shortage of capable officers, as a result of which many regiments lapsed into a permanent state of ill-discipline. As well as participating in food riots on a number of occasions, there were riots at Plymouth in 1759 among the Devon militia because one of the sergeants had been imprisoned for illegally selling ale. Using their muskets and swords, the sergeant's fellows attempted to break into the prison, firing on the guard. They were beaten off with some casualties. Significantly, the colonel, the Duke of Bedford, was an absentee politician.[8] Plymouth was the scene of more riots among the militia in 1780 when there was a violent affray between the Somerset and Brecon militiamen, in which one man was killed. A 'mutiny' took place in the Derbyshire militia in 1778 and among the Duke of Atholl's Highlanders at Portsmouth in January 1783.[9]

Service in the regular army was regarded with particular hostility, not only on constitutional grounds, but also because of the army's bad reputation for indiscipline and lawlessness. Acts such as those of 1703 and 1779 drafted paupers, debtors, criminals and the unemployed into the armed forces, inevitably lowering its reputation and leading to the situation in which the army has been described as 'a midden fit only for outcasts'.[10] Conditions of service were poor, with low pay and harsh discipline but recruiting for the regular army never provoked hostility on the same scale as the militia or as persistent as the navy, mainly because it was carried out on a less regular basis. Unlike the navy, the army had no clear legal right to take men by force, even in wartime; the recruiting parties of the army had none of the powers of seizure enjoyed by the press-gangs; army recruits had to be persuaded to volunteer and accept the 'King's Shilling', after which they were legally bound to enlist. Cajolery, threats, bribery, and any amount of skulduggery were employed to fill the ranks, and recruiting parties were not particularly scrupulous about the law if the need for recruits was pressing. For example in 1702, it was reported that the army had employed a naval press-gang to kidnap men for Marlborough's army in Flanders; the men were overpowered, blindfolded, and placed on the transports.[11]

During Anne's reign a number of recruiting Acts were passed which made it legal to conscript the able-bodied unemployed for the army. The result was a series of disturbances in which the local magistrates sometimes showed themselves sympathetic to the populace. There were disturbances at Coleshill (Warwickshire) in June 1704; at Exminster (Devon) in the same year; at Romsey (Hampshire) and Newbury (Berkshire) in 1706; and Leigh (Gloucestershire) in 1707. These were fairly minor affairs in which members of the local population attempted to rescue men taken for the army. Frequently the local authorities took the part of the population, obstructing the operation of the Acts and even sometimes joining in the riots themselves. Recruiting parties aroused popular reaction even after the War of Spanish Succession. In Oxford, in August 1715, a recruiting party which attempted to read a proclamation of recruiting for the King aroused the hostility of the populace and was pelted by the mob to the accompaniment of pro-Jacobite cries.[12]

The navy was legally entitled to man its ships by the use of press-gangs. Although their actions have passed into the realms of folklore, the press-gangs operated under certain restrictions: press warrants specified that only men who 'used the sea' were to be taken and legal problems could arise if these restrictions were transgressed, and bound apprentices, certain trades, members of the militia and volunteers were all at least in theory exempt. These rules were often abused if a shortage of men became critical, especially in the later stages of a war when a particularly 'hot press' was in operation. During the eighteenth century the impress system developed into a regular operation. Rendezvous houses were opened in the major ports when hostilities started, acting both as centres for volunteers and lock-ups for pressed men. They operated openly, usually in a tavern, with a flag and posters offering inducements to volunteers, but also acted as headquarters for the press-gangs. From the middle of the century, 'regulating captains' were appointed to examine volunteers and pressed men. Civil authorities were also empowered to press men, usually with instructions to take them to the nearest 'rendezvous'. By the time of the American War, the impress service had premises in over forty ports in England and Wales, manned by over a thousand officers.[13]

Not surprisingly affrays with press-gangs were of frequent occurrence in many coastal areas, particularly in ports such as London, Bristol and Liverpool. Crews on inward or outward-bound fleets were often pressed and some of these encounters led to miniature battles, with boarding parties, firearms, and even cannon being used. Thus in 1759 the

Liverpool whaler, *Golden Lion* beat off a boarding party from the *Vengeance* man of war and fought her way out of harbour under fire.[14] When an East India convoy arrived at the Downs in 1740, Admiral Wager wrote:

> We had three men-of-war there, they sent all their boats, but they fired on them from the ships and wounded several men. One was drowned; in the evening the East India men got into their boats with arms and went ashore, but were attacked by our boats who took some, but most of them escaped; so that we got, in the whole, but 156 men when we should have 500; they passed the Nore and would not bring to there, though several shots were fired at them.

The American War led to more conflicts. At Liverpool it was said that during 1776 'attempts at impressment gave rise to desperate battles, in which many lives were lost'. In November of that year, a seaman forcing his way into a house to impress another was shot dead, and in May 1778 the mayor complained of groups of armed seamen going through the town in 'a riotous and unlawful manner', rescuing impressed seamen.[15]

Although there was often a degree of exaggeration about the brutality of the press-gangs by pamphleteers and moralists alike, they were involved in innumerable vicious conflicts throughout the century. In June and July 1790 there were widespread clashes as ships were manned in preparation for war with Spain; in London a group of journeymen coachmakers attacked a press-gang which had taken one of their fellows and beat up the gang. The lieutenant defended himself so vigorously that his sword was broken to the hilt, but he 'had his face so cut, that scarce a human vestige could be traced'.[16] Nor did resistance cease when men had been taken. Often the pressed men were placed on a tender and some desperate attempts were made to escape. A group of pressed men overpowered the guard on the *Tasker* tender in 1755 and beached the ship and so made their escape. Less lucky were the men on the *Melville Castle*, anchored in the Thames in 1792. Although they wounded an officer, marines were called in and firing on the 'mutineers' killed two of them.[17] The Napoleonic Wars simply saw a heightening of the scale of the violence as the navy became more and more ruthless in their search for men. Even the introduction of quotas to supply men from the maritime districts did not dispense with the use of the press-gangs.

Enclosures and turnpikes

The impact of the enclosure movement of the eighteenth century has been a lively source of controversy for decades. The Hammonds argued that the poor were 'bitterly hostile' and that this 'appears not only from the petitions presented to parliament, but from the echoes that have reached us of actual violence'.[18] Other historians have taken a different view. W. E. Tate wrote:

> Some well-known and very scholarly books of the left suggest that the change it [enclosure] involved was forced upon the countryside in the teeth of a bitterly resentful peasantry. It was quite usual, it is implied, for the opposition to exhaust all legal methods of protest. Then in despair at the extent to which the dice were loaded by the landed class in its possession of pulpit, courts and parliament, the peasantry might well rise in revolt. Its ringleaders would then find in death or transportation a somewhat harsh punishment to be imposed merely because they had resisted by the only means in their power their own expropriation and that of their class. I suggest that, in general, this picture is overdrawn and that a remarkable feature of the eighteenth century enclosure movement is the care with which it was carried out and the relatively small volume of organised protest which it aroused.

Drawing his evidence from the Commons' *Journals*, Tate argued that 'such opposition as there was must have been either marvelously small or remarkably unvocal'.[19]

Tate was primarily concerned with 'organised protest' in the form of counter-petitions and obstructions to parliamentary enclosure, but other writers have confirmed the view that the level of protest to enclosure was small given the scale of the movement in the years up to 1800. With innumerable private agreements to enclose and over 2,000 parliamentary Enclosure Acts between 1750 and 1800 alone, the incidence of disorder was relatively small. Even if local research unearths the same number of disturbances again as we know at present, we will still be forced to conclude that in the eighteenth century, at least, enclosures did not normally encounter violent resistance. Many reasons have been suggested for this. Gilbert Slater in his extensive survey concluded that 'it may be regarded as axiomatic that in a corn growing country, enclosure which does not diminish tillage, does not provoke riot and insurrection'.[20]

Much eighteenth-century enclosure was for intensive arable husbandry and has, in large part at least, been absolved from the charge of depopulation which attended many earlier enclosures where the intention was to convert from arable to pasture; it is perhaps unfortunate that Goldsmith's *The Deserted Village* has become the favourite epitaph for a movement which commonly did not depopulate. Enclosure was not necessarily the economic disaster envisaged by the Hammonds, who believed they saw in it a movement parallel to the factory system in industry, pauperising and proletarianising the agricultural labourer. Historians have been increasingly aware that enclosure was not the sole, nor even the main, cause of the rural poverty and misery so eloquently described by Cobbett and others. Population growth, rural unemployment and the operation of the poor laws rather than enclosure were the major causes. Moreover the process was not such as to encourage popular resistance; much enclosure was by communal agreement and even in the case of parliamentary enclosure was rarely carried out without some measure of negotiation, facilitated by the protracted nature of the procedure for obtaining the Act, surveying and apportioning the land. The distribution of land was carried out equitably in the main; Chambers and Mingay have written that 'it almost always worked fairly as between the various classes of proprietors'.[21] Even where non-proprietors had a grievance, the piecemeal nature of enclosure was not such as to generate nationwide or even countywide discontent, similar to that aroused by the Militia Act of 1757 or the agrarian 'Captain Swing' disturbances of the 1830s. Where hostility was felt, it seems in the main to have taken the form of passive grumbling, sometimes expressed in threatening letters, or in individual acts of sabotage rather than large-scale disorder.[22]

That enclosure was not normally met by widespread opposition is confirmed from Beloff's study of the period 1660–1715, where he concluded that it played 'little part in the history of disorder in this period'. He indicated instances of anti-enclosure riots at Coventry in 1689 and in Northamptonshire in 1710, but argued that the main opposition to enclosure came when the making of parks or the enclosure of wastes threatened local poaching. This confirms Slater's major qualification to his axiom of little resistance when he argued that anti-enclosure riots 'may occur on the enclosure of waste, where the enclosed wastes gives a livelihood to a considerable specialised population'. He cited the example of the fens which were considered by Beloff to be the major area of enclosure disturbances up to 1714. There was a history of resistance to fen drainage schemes which deprived the local population of game and some grazing. In Lincolnshire in June 1697 fences and dams were fired at Epworth and in 1699 it was reported that 1,000 men destroyed the drainage works in Deeping Fen, as well as houses, mills and barns. Small-scale disturbances continued throughout the first decade of the eighteenth century, by which time the major drainage work had been completed; even so, occasional disturbances continued to occur during the eighteenth century. In November 1757 in the West Fen near Boston, 200 people assembled and with 'drum beating and colours flying' cut down some new dams. Twelve years later, there were renewed disturbances.[23]

Another 'special case' was the Royal Forest of Dean. The 'free miners' of the Forest frequently found themselves in contention with the attempts by the Crown or its lessees to enclose and replant parts of the forest. Enclosure deprived the miners of access to pasture and fuel which they considered their customary rights and they frequently rioted to protect them. Disturbances were recorded in 1612, 1629–32, 1640, 1659, 1670, 1688 and 1696. Most of these involved breaking down fences and hedges, burning new saplings, preventing the felling of mature wood, and rescuing animals from the pounds set up by the forest authorities. For example, in 1707 twenty oak saplings were stripped of bark and in 1735 several pounds were broken down and forest lodges destroyed. These disturbances bear a remarkable similarity to the events described by E. P. Thompson in the vicinity of Windsor Forest, which led to the 'Black Act' of 1723, covering a wide range of offences including poaching, destroying trees, animal-maiming, various forms of aggravated trespass and assault.[24]

Thus where violent opposition to enclosure was expressed it was often over the loss of rights to common and wastes. While the legal owners of common rights were usually compensated by an allotment of land for the enclosure of common land, many marginal groups, such as squatters, lost their access to pasture, firewood and game which provided a significant portion of their livelihood. The extent to which the enclosure commissioners were prepared to recognise customary rights of common varied considerably and there was undoubtedly some truth in the allegation, even if exaggerated, that the loss of common rights removed one support for the poorest sections of rural society. Thus at Shaw Hill in Wiltshire in June 1758 'a large mob of weavers, labourers, and other disorderly persons' assembled and cut down 'the banks and fences of the gardens and orchards in that neighbourhood, under pretence that they were purloined from the common'. At North Leigh Heath, near Witney (Oxon), in 1761 a mob armed with 'bludgeons and pitchforks' attempted to destroy the fences put up by a recent enclosure. On two separate days they attacked the soldiers guarding the heath, but were repelled. Enclosure of a common sometimes united the opposition of the several parishes who shared the rights to it; for example the enclosure of Haute Huntre Fen in Lincolnshire was opposed by the people of eleven parishes who broke down the fences; in a similar incident the enclosure of waste ground at Redditch (Worcestershire) in 1791 also led to disturbances.[25] At Sheffield in 1791 there were riots because of the enclosure of the commons at Stannington and Hallam; the rioters fired several ricks of hay and a number of houses, including that of the vicar of Sheffield, before being dispersed by troops. This was one of the few instances where enclosure rioters showed any inclination to voice wider protests, for there were reports of cries of 'No King', 'No Taxes', and 'No Corn Bill'.[26] A more typical concern affected one of the last disturbances of the eighteenth century aroused by enclosures at Wilbarston in Northampton in 1799, when 300 people were dispersed by the Yeomanry after avowing 'their determination to resist the fencing out of a piece of land allotted to them in lieu of the common right'.[27] Once again, it was a flagrant abuse rather than the issue of enclosure itself which triggered off violent demonstrations.

Opposition to turnpikes was remarkably similar, with relatively few disturbances in proportion to the scale of the activity. Turnpikes were not an unmixed blessing, for toll charges could prove inconvenient and burdensome. Some feared that turnpike development would drain the district of produce to more distant markets, others that they would simply put an extra charge on produce brought into the area. These feelings contributed to a spate of disturbances in the Bristol area in the middle decades of the century; there were riots at Bristol in 1727, Gloucester in 1731 and 1734, Ledbury in 1734, Gloucestershire and Herefordshire in 1735 and 1736. At Bristol in July and August 1749 farmers and labourers destroyed toll-gates on roads leading to the city, and on the Somerset side of the city, another mob destroyed turnpikes on the Ashton road. In Gloucester more turnpikes were destroyed, so that by early August 'almost all the turnpikes and turnpike houses about the city' had been destroyed. Four years later in Yorkshire there was a report that 'Rioters have destroy'd all the Turnpikes about Leeds and threatened more mischief'. Another group was active in Wakefield, while at Beeston a group of rioters were arrested in the attempt to destroy a turnpike; an attempt at rescue by a mob was resisted by the military, who killed ten and wounded another twenty-four.[28]

But these reactions to turnpikes were strikingly localised. If we examine the rate and geographical distribution of turnpike Acts, it is clear that the instances of disturbances coincided neither with the peak period of enactment (the 1760s) nor with the distribution of Acts through the country as a whole (see Table 3.1.[29])

Table 3.1   Turnpike Acts, 1663–1839

Distribution by periods

1663–1719	37
1720–9	46
1730–9	24
1740–50	39
1751–60	184
1761–72	205
1773–91	65
1792–1815	173

Distribution by area

Home counties	73
Southern counties	134
East Anglia	61
Western counties	102
Far West	68
Northants., Cambs., Hunts., and Bedfordshire	45
South Midlands	58
North Midlands	84
East Midlands	75
Yorkshire and Lancashire	148
Far North	64

Hence the disturbances against turnpikes in the Bristol area appear to stand out as being largely determined by local considerations. Some years ago, D. G. Isaac suggested an important clue to the disturbances in the area when he recorded that it was the Kingswood colliers who provided the main opposition to turnpikes in 1727 and 1748. Their concern was that a toll should not be imposed upon the provisions necessary to supply a growing manufacturing area. This reaction from an especially turbulent group of workmen, accustomed to defending their food supply by riots and demonstrations where necessary, suggests one reason why this locality should have been more disturbed than others by the advent of turnpikes.[30]

Smugglers, wreckers and poachers

Smuggling was a way of life in many parts of eighteenth-century England. Heavy excise duties promoted a lucrative trade in coastal districts which embraced not only the poor, but also artisans, shopkeepers, merchants, and gentry. The Government maintained a revenue service to check smuggling, with the result that there were innumerable small-scale disturbances: the situation on the Sussex coast in the 1740s was described by one writer as 'a guerrilla war between the smugglers of Sussex and Kent and the officers of the government'. A well-organised trade in wool, tea, brandy, and other valuable commodities became so prevalent in the 1740s that a determined effort was made by the Government to suppress it. The result was an increased level of violence along the coast in which the smugglers were frequently the aggressors, attacking revenue officers, rescuing contraband goods, and even on one occasion laying siege to the town of Goudhurst. These conflicts took a toll of lives: a Customs officer was killed in 1740; three dragoons killed in 1743; and two smugglers killed at Goudhurst in 1747.[31]

Although the Government proved ready to send in troops whenever necessary, imposed exemplary punishments and levied communal fines in an attempt to stop smuggling, the trade was both too profitable and too much part of the local economy to be easily suppressed. The defiance of local people to the revenue officers was supported by a widespread belief in the rectitude of the actions: smuggling was 'no crime'. What distinguished them from many other disturbances was their violence, particularly the access to and use of firearms. Where enclosure protestors were more commonly equipped with the ubiquitous bludgeons and agricultural implements, the smugglers were often armed with 'blunder-busses, carbines, and other offensive weapons'. Some smuggling vessels were veritable small arsenals, one carrying fifteen men, 'eight swivel guns, and two carriage guns, and two chests of small arms'. The semi-professionalism of the smuggling gangs of Sussex and Kent seem to have marked them out from the community as a whole, although there was much sympathy with them and many who profited from their trade.[32] Smuggling was as prevalent in Cornwall, But here seems to have been more casually organised. Even so frequent clashes between smugglers and excise officials were reported throughout the eighteeth century, some of which led to serious casualties.[33]

Cornwall was more associated with wrecking. For Victorian moralists and novelists, wrecking meant luring ships on to the coast and plundering their cargoes. Although this may have happened in a number of cases, 'wrecking' more often involved looting the cargoes and materials of wrecked ships. This practice was common on many parts of the English coast until the early nineteenth century. Primarily associated with Cornwall, the Wirral peninsula, and the Norfolk and Channel coasts, as well as the coasts of Wales and Ireland, were also frequently scenes of looting and pillage. Although technically illegal while any creature remained alive from the vessel, the right to the 'harvest of the sea' was clearly considered by many local inhabitants as 'fair game' even if it meant resisting the local authorities to get it. For example during the American War a Liverpool privateer, the *Mersey*, brought a French prize into the river, but ran her aground near New Ferry, on the Wirral. While lighters were taking off the rich cargo of sugar and coffee the local inhabitants assembled, equipped themselves with firearms and, in a battle in which one man was killed, captured the cargo. On the Wirral, so-called fishermen were said to make a living out of wrecking, the village of Hoylake being especially associated with the activity. Generally speaking, however, wrecking appears to have been an *ad hoc* business to which the inhabitants of particularly dangerous sections of coast could become accustomed, so much so that some developed in the opposite direction and became salvagers. Interference frequently led to violence; several people were killed at Dartmouth in 1721 when soldiers fought off a crowd attempting to plunder an East Indiaman, and three more were killed at a similar incident near Bridgend in 1782. Serious affrays were less common than in the case of smuggling, mainly because the Government was rarely in a position to intervene effectively to prevent plunder and took less direct action to prevent it. Although the plunder of wrecks and occasional clashes with the authorities continued into the nineteenth century, it began to die out with more effective policing, improved navigational aids, and the growing disapproval of evangelicals and Methodists.[34]

Poaching too provided an almost continual undercurrent of violence in many rural areas. The epidemic of disturbances in the vicinity of Windsor Forest in the 1720s between 'Windsor Blacks' and gamekeepers came, according to E. P. Thompson, from 'the attempted reactivation of a relaxed forest authority'. Widespread resentment among the local inhabitants, but especially in the case of deer-poachers, led to a more organised resistance in which armed bands encountered the gamekeepers in an attempt to defend their customary rights. Keepers were attacked and intimidated, seized property and game rescued, and deer driven off. The disturbances reached out to Enfield Chase and Richmond Park. Thompson writes that 'by 1721 the Chase was in uproar and skirmishes between keepers and deer-stealers frequent'. When Richmond Park came into control of the Walpole family in 1725, their 'improvements' led to a spate of disorders over deer-stealing, rights to firewood, and access.[35]

As in the case of the Sussex smugglers in the 1740s, or the opposition to the enclosure of the Fens, much of the disorder arose out of what appeared to the people involved to be interference with their customary rights. An equally detailed study of Cannock Chase by Dr Hay has also turned up many instances of disorder. In the middle years of the eighteenth century 'poachers from the villages near the Park and the Chase waged a small war on the keepers and the game'; affrays on the Chase, acts of revenge, and a stream of fines and sentences marked a growing hostility in the area; and a bitter conflict arose over the refusal of the Earl of Uxbridge to control the extensive rabbit warrens which the local inhabitants believed were destroying the grazing. Lurking at the back of their minds was also the fear of enclosure which might deprive them of their grazing rights altogether. Convinced that the rabbit warrens were an infringement of customary rights to the Chase, the local people went to law, but faced with interminable delays and mounting costs took direct action in 1751 by beginning to dig up burrows and kill the rabbits. Although the rioters were dispersed and the leaders arrested, the attack on the warrens began again in mid-winter 1753-4: on 28 December 1753 the warrens were attacked with considerable ceremony and in two weeks most of the rabbits were killed. Hay suggests that the actions of the local inhabitants had been encouraged by similar incidents at Charnwood Forest in Leicestershire where, starting in 1748, the warrens had been destroyed in the face of troops, constables and gamekeepers, and a favourable settlement reached which established rights to the common. The rioters of Cannock Chase were less lucky, for though several thousand rabbits were killed, a warrener's lodge damaged, and several keepers attacked or intimidated, many of the participants were ejected from their cottages and others were pursued through the courts.[36]

Popular disturbances and the local community

Many disturbances arose entirely from local issues. There were riots in Lincoln in 1726 because reconstruction work on the cathedral towers excited a popular fear that the spires were to be demolished altogether; crowds broke into the cathedral close, the Riot Act was read, and the crowds only with great difficulty persuaded to disperse. The ex-mayor was widely suspected of having stirred up the furore, but it seems to have been a genuine protest by the local inhabitants against a threat to a familiar landmark. Not untypically, the issue had arisen out of a misunderstanding about the nature of the repair work, and the discontent subsided when the full story was explained.[37] Local administration also provoked disturbances in Suffolk in 1765 when there was violent resistance to the erection of some new workhouses.[38] An attempt in 1788 to put an end to the Stamford bull-running, widely regarded by the local authorities as a source of disorder and crime, also provoked disturbances.[39] In 1786 a Maldon miller recorded in his diary that an attempt to resite the village pump at Dunmow had ended in uproar for 'the gentlemen of the Mob Class were determined it should not be moved and at the alteration a great mob got together and a great riot ensued'.[40] A rather similar incident occurred in Banbury in February 1826 when the Corporation planted some trees as a piece of municipal improvement. After one of the new trees was persistently broken, the man whose house it stood outside was hauled up before the Quarter Sessions but, as no one had seen him do it, got off; on his discharge he was chaired through the streets by a large crowd, the trees were torn down and their protective casings burnt in a bonfire. The reading of the Riot Act by the mayor had no effect, for backed up by only four constables he was completely helpless. A local spectator recorded that the matter was allowed to drop, 'but there were no more trees planted. The people thought by planting trees they were wasting the town's money.'[41]

In many rural areas, the 'skimmington', 'skimmity' or 'stang' ride provide a tumultuous form of public disapproval in which the victim, usually a notorious offender against conventional morality, was paraded in effigy, often to the accompaniment of cacophonous 'rough music' produced on an assortment of instruments and household implements.[42] The 'skimmington' was most likely to be found in communities where at least some of the inhabitants had a clear sense of 'proper' behaviour and where a public display of disapproval could be regarded as sufficient both to punish the victim and to assert community standards. It could also, no doubt, be a good bit of fun for the participants, if not for the victims, many accounts giving an impression of something between an elaborate 'lark' and a more serious attempt to express disapproval. A. J. Peacock quotes an example of a 'skimmington' from the village of Yaxley in Huntingdonshire in January 1824, in which the actions of the village pindar (pound-keeper) in fining a woman the considerable sum of two shillings for allowing her geese to stray provoked a 'skimmington' against the pindar's father, who was notorious for having at the age of sixty fathered an illegitimate child which had to be supported by the parish. When asked to pay the fine the woman rounded on the pindar, saying that 'he might put sixpense to and buy a frock coat for his father's bastard'. The next night a crowd assembled outside the father's door with an effigy of a man on a pole which they repeatedly threw to the ground whilst others cried out in mock concern not to hurt the 'old fellow', as he would be unable to get another child. The following night crowds paraded outside the house carrying the effigy of a child.[43]

As a rowdy rather than particularly violent form of expressing disapproval which derived most of its force in closely knit societies, the 'skimmington' lasted in some rural areas until the early twentieth century. In Herefordshire in the 1860s and 1870s it was reported to be tolerated by the police provided that the performance occurred on not more than three successive nights, the participants kept on the move, and the name of the offender and the offence was not openly shouted out; other variants on this practice have been noted which allowed the 'skimmington' to survive into the era of borough and rural police forces, although it came under increasing attack.[44] Its origins are more obscure. That some means of expressing community hostility existed in the early modern period is entirely likely, but it may well have become more common after the ecclesiastical courts fell into disuse in the late seventeenth century so that no official sanctions were available against those who transgressed conventional moral standards. The 'skimmington' was the most highly ritualised expression of 'community justice' and elements of it can be found in attacks on strike-breakers, informers, or members of press-gangs. It was a short step from the 'skimmington' to stripping blacklegs naked and running through the town, putting a lieutenant of a press-gang under the nearest pump, or making excise officers run a gauntlet from one end of the town to another. Although they usually stopped short of causing death, the 'justice' meted out was sometimes harsher. Informants under the Gin Act were killed in London during the 1730s and the semi-professional 'Hawkhurst' gang of smugglers were involved in a notorious murder of an informer and an excise officer on the Sussex–Hampshire border in February 1748.[45]

Another and often more violent aspect of 'community justice' occurred in attacks on those suspected of witchcraft. Although the last recorded witch trial in an English civil court took place in 1717 at Leicester and the Witchcraft Act of 1736 prohibited accusations of witchcraft and sorcery as such, popular belief in witchcraft lasted much longer. At its mildest hostility to suspected witches could take the form of a 'whispering campaign' and general hostility, sometimes leading to the accused being forcibly driven from the area. Sometimes suspected witches were subjected to the 'swimming test', the rationale of which was that water, being the instrument of baptism, would reject those who had renounced it. Cast into water, a witch would float, whereas an innocent person would sink.[46] Instances of the swimming test being applied have been noted on several occasions in the first half of the eighteenth century; one of the most notorious occurred in 1751 at Tring, where an elderly couple were accused of having bewitched cattle which were dying in the neighbourhood. According to one report, 'one of their enemies paid the criers of the towns and villages about to give notice that on Monday next a man and woman were to be publicly ducked at Tring, in this county, for their crimes'. A crowd duly assembled and, when the couple took refuge in the workhouse, attacked it and broke down several walls to get at them. Seeking refuge next in the church vestry, the couple were seized and carried two miles to Marlston Mere. Here, it became clear that the object was not a 'ducking' but a 'swimming test' for the couple were tied in a sheet and thrown in the water, treatment from which they both subsequently died.[47]

Nor were such examples of 'community justice' restricted to country areas. Late Hanoverian London offers several examples of people being maltreated for particular actions. In July 1790 an elderly pickpocket was seized by a crowd in the Strand, dragged to the Thames and thrown in the water. On struggling out and begging for mercy, 'a fellow not deeming the punishment he had received sufficient, gave him a blow which drove him a second time into the river'. The pickpocket failed to emerge a second time.[48] As late as the Regency period, it is possible to find similar incidents, with attacks on individuals for 'offences' as diverse as indecent exposure or looking like Oliver the spy.[49] In 1799 a prostitute, Jane Gibbs, aroused considerable hostility when she was accused of murdering a client: crowds gathered around Bow Street when she was examined and tried to assault her when she was acquitted for lack of evidence. Over the next few weeks she was attacked on sight when she appeared in the streets of the capital, once being stripped of her clothes by a crowd in Bedford Square.[50] Another aspect of popular hostility to particular crimes was shown in 1810 when a group of suspected homosexuals, the 'Vere Street gang', were taken to Bow Street. Those who were released were set upon and knocked about, while the coach conveying others to prison was attacked and the occupants forced to take refuge in an inn. Over the next months there was a spate of attacks on homosexuals and people suspected of being members of the 'Vere Street gang'.[51]

The pillory provides an interesting example of an institution where formal judicial proceedings and popular feelings overlapped, the severity of the punishment being largely determined by the attitude of the populace towards the offence and the offender. It was in a sense, an instance of 'licensed' community justice, which could backfire if the authorities misjudged the temper of the spectators. There were, for example, cases of noted Jacobites in Lancashire being pelted with flowers, the symbol of the Pretender; in the 1790s there were occasions when radicals imprisoned in the pillory were not only pelted with the customary refuse, but also released by a sympathetic crowd (see pp. 165, 330 n. 55). On other occasions, crowds around the pillory chose to give the offenders a particularly severe time; In 1756 a group of men who had faked a highway robbery in order to obtain the large rewards being offered at the time were sentenced to the pillory and given a pelting so severe that one of them died and the others were severely injured.[52] Similarly, it was reported in 1810 that members of the 'Vere Street gang' were 'heartily pelted' when they appeared in the pillory in 1810. Place recorded that pelting with refuse was reserved in his day for those convicted of 'unnatural crimes'.[53] Attempts by the authorities in Regency London to punish those convicted of seditious words or libel by the pillory ended in humiliation in May 1812 when Daniel Eaton was simply applauded by the bystanders as he stood in the pillory for publishing part of Paine's *Age of Reason*. Recognition that the punishment offered by the pillory was 'apportioned solely by the caprice of the multitude' played an important part in its virtual abolition in 1816.[54]

Wakes, fairs, faction fights and saturnalia

Eighteenth-century England had a rich calendar of annual wakes, fairs, trade holidays, and popular festivals. From the perspective of the Victorian era, these events contributed to the 'disorderly' and riotous character of eighteenth and early nineteenth century life. A long campaign to regulate or abolish these activities accompanied their erosion under the impact of changing attitudes and conditions. The Victorian perception of popular celebrations as 'disorderly' was far from unfounded, but it was one which needs to be qualified. Although much of the fighting, quarrelling, and general rowdiness which accompanied many of these events can only be described as casual and accidental, there was also a sense in which they were an almost routine expression of conflicts between different groups or localities. Faction fighting has been called the principal pastime of young adults (usually males) in the early modern period and popular holidays provided one of the main occasions for it.[55] Faction fights between different parts of a town, between different villages and towns, between the men from rival counties, and between different occupational groups, provided not only an outlet for high spirits but also expressed an intense localism. The Victorian historian William Borlase recorded that such activities were common in eighteenth-century Cornwall. He noted one instance when 'the men of Redruth' swore to take the life of the first living thing they found in the neighbouring village of Gwennap. This happened to be a dog. Dyeing a handkerchief in its blood they used this as a form of standard in a pitched battle with their neighbours in which they were ultimately routed and one of their number killed. At the May Day wakes in Shropshire, it was customary for the Wrekin colliers to fight the local farm labourers for possession of the summit. It was said that the men of the market town of Wellington only joined in if the fight appeared evenly balanced. Fights between the colliers and Severn bargemen took place regularly on market days in Ironbridge until the early nineteenth century.[56]

Many wakes and fairs were built around a 'sporting' contest which expressed these rivalries in a semi-institutionalised form. Annual football matches between villages and townships were often little more than an excuse for a battle between the young men and adults of the area. Although the contest might be seriously pursued and its outcome regarded as a matter of great concern, there was usually a good deal of fighting during and after the event. By the early eighteenth century the Shrovetide football match at Derby was one of the most celebrated of these contests, 'played' between the parishes of All Saint's and St Peter's. The ball was thrown into the Market Place from the Town Hall and the result of the ensuing brawl-cum-football match announced by ringing the parish bells. At Chester-le-Street (Durham) the game was played between 'Up-streeters' and 'Down-streeters', each side endeavouring to keep the ball at their own end of town; at Dorking (Surrey) the contest was between the east and west ends of the town; at Alnick (Northumberland) between the parishes of St Michael's and St Paul's. Other sports served the competitive instincts of rival communities. By the late seventeenth century the bull-running at Tutbury on the border between Derbyshire and Staffordshire was effectively a trial of strength between the men from each county, each side trying to drive the animal into their own territory. At Ludlow there was a grand tug of war between the members of different wards on Shrove Tuesday which usually ended with fighting and quarrelling. At Scarborough, Shrovetide was celebrated by an indiscriminate contest on the beach between men, women and children armed with sticks and coloured balls bought from hawkers. At Witney, all pretence of a game was set aside with a regular fight between the 'up-town' and 'down-town' boys on 5 November.[57]

4 Eighteenth-century London

London, with an estimated population of over half a million people in 1700, was by far the largest urban community in England. As a stronghold of dissent and a major commercial city, the capital had played an important role in the constitutional and religious struggles of the seventeenth century in which the people of London earned a formidable reputation for intervening on major issues. Their actions were usually intricately bound up with opposition from within the City administration to the government or its policies. At several points in the late seventeenth and eighteenth centuries the City of London, or sections of it, were in opposition to the administration of the day, as during the Exclusion crisis when City politicians and the London 'mob' were recruited to the aid of Shaftesbury's 'country party'. Opposition could emanate from the City's concern for its commercial interests or from divisions within the merchant community, with the 'middling sort' opposing administrations with which the richer citizens were allied. Still more important was the use to which oppositions within parliament could put the organised 'support without doors' which the City could provide. As Dame Lucy Sutherland has written:

> City leaders were expert, from long experience of organising commercial agitation affecting both London and the 'outports', in the art of bringing pressure to bear on authority from without. Petitions, instructions, from the Common Council to the City representatives, pamphlets and press campaigns were rapidly planned there, while whenever political excitement ran high the London crowd could be relied on to emerge and give the added support of their clamour to the Opposition cause.[1]

The Sacheverell riots and popular Toryism in London

The most serious disturbances to take place in London during the early decades of the eighteenth century were in support of the

London in the reign of George I

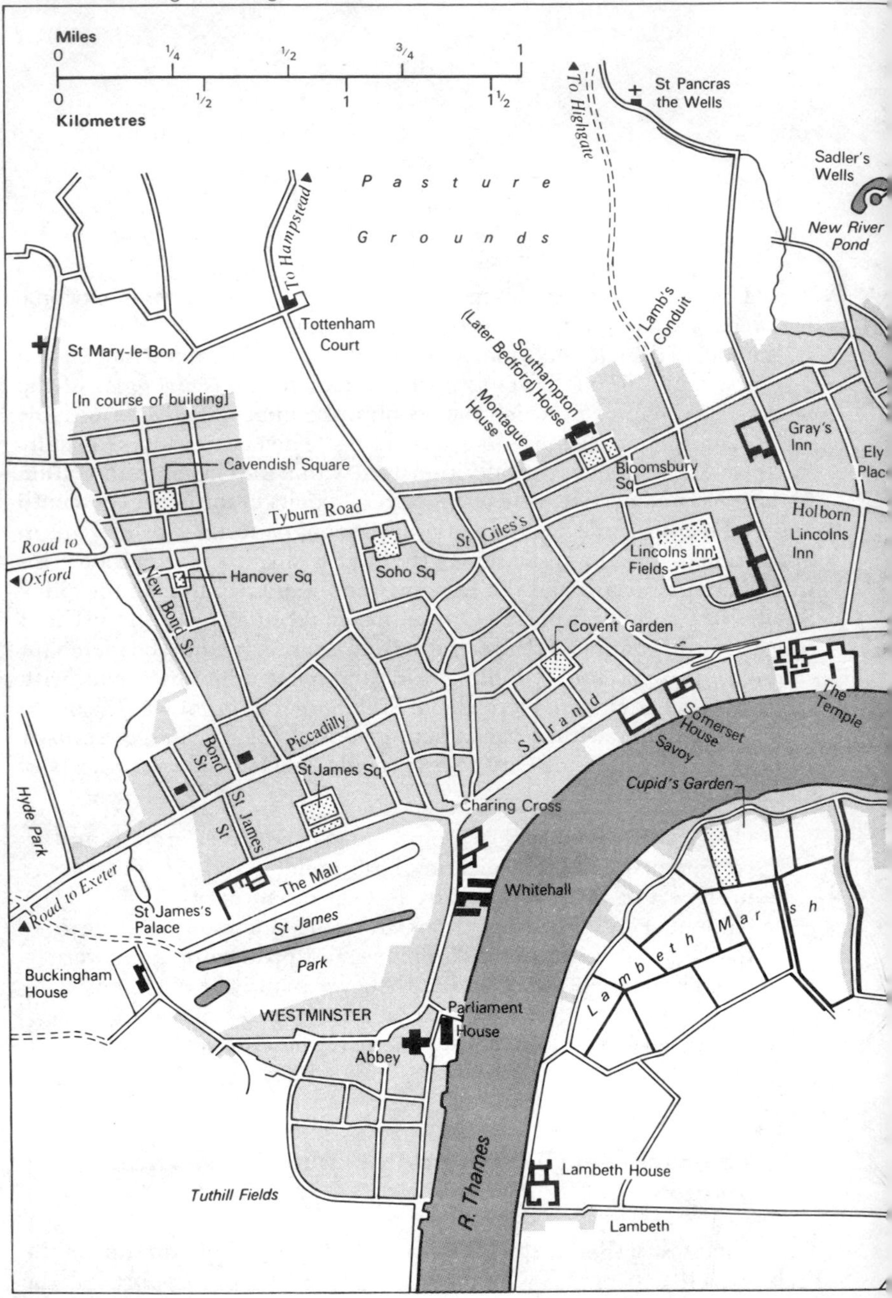

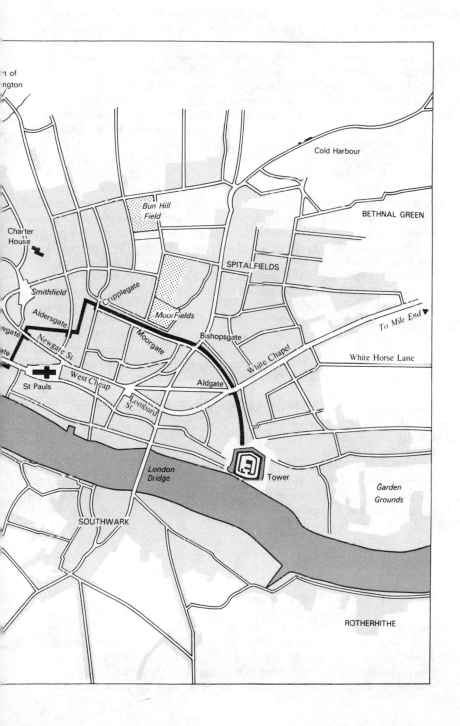

Court of
Islington

Cold Harbour

Bun Hill
Field

BETHNAL GREEN

Charter
House

SPITALFIELDS

Smithfield

Cripplegate

Aldersgate

MoorFields

To Mile End ▶

Newgate St

Moorgate

Bishopsgate

White Horse Lane

White Chapel

Newgate

gate

West Cheap

Aldgate

St Pauls

Lombard
St.

London
Bridge

Tower

Garden
Grounds

SOUTHWARK

ROTHERHITHE

controversial High Church Tory, Dr Sacheverell. On the night of 1-2 March 1710 occurred the first and one of the most significant of eighteenth-century London's disturbances. Within a few hours, several of the largest dissenting chapels in the capital were attacked, sacked and partly demolished by crowds shouting 'High Church and Sacheverell'. The background to this slogan lay in the progress of the War of Spanish Succession and the increasing hostility felt towards both Whigs and dissenters by the City of London and sections of the population. By 1709-10 war-weariness had begun to affect many of the smaller merchants and artisans in the capital, heightened by a year of high prices in 1709, and the continuation of the war was widely blamed on Whig financiers who supported the Godolphin-Marlborough administration. The dissenters were identified with the Whig ministry as its financial supporters while as a community their growing assurance was given tangible expression by the completion of a number of large chapels. Thus when on 5 November 1709, the anniversary of the landing of William III at Torbay, Dr Sacheverell preached a sermon at St Paul's on the text 'In perils among false brethren' advocating the doctrine of non-resistance, condemning toleration, and attacking the dissenters, he became a symbol of discontent with the Whig administration. The printed version of the sermon achieved a wide circulation and forced the Whigs to act against this dissident voice. On 13 December a complaint was made to the House of Commons and, after some debate, the sermon in question, and one preached at Derby, were denounced as 'malicious, scandalous and seditious libels highly reflecting her majesty and her government, the late happy revolution, and the Protestant succession as by law established'. Sacheverell and his publisher, Henry Clements, were summoned to attend at the Bar of the House of Commons on the next day.

In fact there was considerable delay before Sacheverell could be brought to account and in the interim his trial was moved from the Commons to Westminster Hall, where it opened on 27 February and continued for three weeks. It was the linking of wartime discontent, native dissent and the prosecution of Dr Sacheverell which provided the occasion for the crowd's actions during the trial. From the outset, Sacheverell was treated on the streets as a popular champion, greeted with cries of 'Sacheverell and the Church for ever'. He attended Westminster Hall with an impressive retinue of clergy and undoubtedly performed his part in the spectacle with considerable aplomb. Investigations of the economic background to the disturbances which broke out in the first week of his trial reveal that social conditions were unexceptional for the time of the year and that the fervour of the demonstrations in support of Sacheverell and the Church of England cannot be directly related to price movements.[2]

Although the Sacheverell riots appeared to some contemporaries as a senseless outrage committed by impassioned and irrational mobs, more careful analysis of the disturbances has suggested they they conformed in many respects to the characteristics found in later episodes. The rioters acted with considerable discrimination and discipline in their attacks, at least in the initial phase of the disturbances. They went to considerable pains to avoid destroying property other than the chapels and ornaments and furnishings from the buildings were often carried a considerable distance in order to burn them in safety in an open space or a broader street. No reports of damage to private dwellings or of indiscriminate looting were made during the disturbances, although the crowds had ample opportunity. The only incident which seemed to suggest escalation into a more general movement was when a crowd reported to be on its way to attack the Bank of England in Grocers' Hall was dispersed by the military at Blackfriars. Even here, however, the crowd would have been assaulting the symbol of the Whig financiers so widely blamed for perpetuating the war. Professor Holmes's account of the riots which he describes as the 'second worst' of the century, makes the telling point that destruction of such large and well-built structures as the chapels could not be carried out as an act of casual vandalism. Instead demolition took place in a well-disciplined and coordinated manner, carried on with the air of a drilled operation; the rioters came to the scene with the necessary tools to carry out the complicated process of removing the furnishings and razing the chapels to the ground without killing themselves or endangering neighbouring property. Analysis of the crowd has also proved interesting, for it has been argued that these rioters must have been some of the most 'respectable' of the eighteenth century; the great majority were fully employed and several were self-employed tradesmen or professional men.[3]

The role of the City was also significant. Pro-Tory sentiment showed itself in the election of City MPs in 1708 and 1710, and strong Tory support within the City, especially within Common Council, may well have encouraged the rioters to take the law into their own hands. The newly elected Lord Mayor, The High Tory Sir Samuel Garrard, had been present at Sacheverell's sermon and congratulated him on it, suggesting that it should be printed. Although the more Whiggish Court of Aldermen declined to print it, because of its controversial nature, Sacheverell printed the sermon at his own expense and dedicated it to the Lord Mayor. Thus the London 'mob' could be in no doubt that at least some sections of the City authorities were sympathetic with Sacheverell and might not act too savagely against their demonstrations. So it turned out. The rioters were able to carry out several hours of destruction with very little interference, and although direct 'collusion' is impossible to prove, the suspicion remains that the City authorities turned a blind eye. In the aftermath, when Sacheverell's sermons were ordered to be burnt at the Royal Exchange, the Lord Mayor ostentatiously absented himself. The verdict against Sacheverell was greeted in London with bonfires and illuminations in his support, so much so that Queen Anne complained publicly to the Court of Aldermen. Only then were the riots investigated, the ring-leaders rounded up and bound over to the sessions.[4]

The accession of George I gave rise to a period of 'High Church' rioting and further attacks on the dissenters. The proclamation of George I during the early days of August 1714 provoked nothing more serious than a few brawls between rival factions, which recurred upon George's arrival in the country in September. The first serious disturbances occurred in spring 1715. On 23 April, the anniversary of Queen Anne's Coronation, there were noisy demonstrations in the capital, and houses were forced to illuminate at the behest of crowds who roamed the streets, crying 'God Bless the Queen' and 'High Church for ever'. Disturbances were widely expected at the end of May when the coincidence of two royal anniversaries promised rival demonstrations. George I's birthday occurred on the 28th, the day before the anniversary of the restoration of Charles II. The magistrates were prepared for a degree of disorder, but could not prevent bonfires and illuminations in the City nor mobs parading the streets to cries of 'High Church and Ormonde'. At Highgate a mob entered a Presbyterian meeting house, carried off the window casements, and damaged the pews; at Aldersgate Church, the bell ropes were cut to prevent peals of celebration for the King and when the constables attempted to interfere they were resisted and several were wounded. The riots continued on the 29th. A party of Life Guards were insulted and forced to join in the cries of 'High Church'; a print of King William III was publicly burnt at Smithfield, and the mob carried all before them until the constables of Cheapside ward dispersed them.[5]

During the countrywide wave of disturbances which led to the passing of the Riot Act in August 1715 the capital was relatively quiet. There were, however, a number of affrays between rival factions in and about the alehouses in the Strand and Fleet Street and a number of celebrations of the Pretender's birthday in Clerkenwell and Whitechapel. A meeting house at Blackfriars was attacked by over 400 assailants on 9–10 June, some of them disguised as women, while Lord Oxford was conducted to the Tower by a 'great Mobb' crying for 'High Church and down with the wiggs'. Political anniversaries continued to cause a series of faction fights and demonstrations during the autumn and winter of 1715–16. To rally loyalist sentiment, the Government organised elaborate Hanoverian celebrations, fiercely prosecuted any symptoms of discontent, and encouraged Loyalists in their attacks on Tory and Jacobite sympathisers. A pope-burning ceremony was organised on 5 November 1715, in which effigies of the Pope, the Pretender and Tory rebels were drawn through the streets with halters about their necks, hung on a 'high gallows', and eventually burned. Other demonstrations displayed a rich theatre of political symbolism, not just in effigies, ribbons and cockades, but also in more elaborate pageants including re-enactments of the 'warming-pan' scene, floats depicting the Pope flanked by the Devil and the Pretender, and cavalcades bedecked in loyal emblems. Loyalist societies, based on a number of taverns in central London, many sited conveniently for forays upon opponents, engaged in a series of brawls with Tory demonstrators, known as 'Jacks'. One of the most serious of these

'Mug-house' fights happened on 16 November when 500 'Jacks' attacked the head-quarters of the Duke of Newcastle's loyalist society at the Roebuck taven in Cheapside: met by musket fire, two men were killed and several wounded. Renewed clashes occurred during the spring of 1716 and concern that the spirit of opposition was far from dead led the Government to garrison the capital with troops. In demonstration on the Pretender's birthday and through late June and July a number of people were killed or seriously injured. After an attack on Read's tavern, off Fleet Street, five rioters were hanged on the site under the provisions of the Riot Act – the first executions under the Act in the capital.

In his important study of these disturbances, Dr Rogers has shown that the majority of those brought to trial were petty tradesmen, craftsmen, and casual labourers with a smaller number of professional people and gentlemen. He notes that many of the anti-Hanoverian demonstrations originated in the out-parishes where the crowds were drawn together, not as hired gangs, but with 'rough music' and disguises to emphasise the ceremonial and legitimate character of their enterprise. While undoubtedly some of the participants, especially those on the loyalist side, were hired mobs in the traditional sense, many of the pro-Tory demonstrators showed a more spontaneous desire to express hostility to Whigs, Hanoverians and dissenters. Encouraged by Tory clergy in sermons, broadsheets and pamphlets, some sections of the London population renewed the antagonisms to the Whigs and dissenters which they had shown in the war years. A hard winter in 1715-16, demobilisation, and troubled trading conditions added to dislike of the old 'war party'. Spectres of a return to military rule and authoritarian government, partly encouraged by the introduction of the Riot Act, also played a part in branding the Whigs as a threat to traditional 'liberties'. Such Jacobite feeling as emerged in these demonstrations was often only part of a more complex opposition to the new regime.[6]

The Age of Walpole

The gradual consolidation of the Hanoverian succession was marked by recurrent disputes between the government and the City of London. Running like a thread through their relations was the government's determination to assert its control over a potentially dangerous source of opposition, particularly in the more popular branches of the City's government, Common Council and Common Hall, who sought to maintain independence. Arguments about the conduct of municipal elections and the passage of troops through the City were followed by a bitter dispute about Walpole's City Election Act of 1725. As well as restricting the City franchise only to those who paid all municipal charges and taxes, thus disqualifying an estimated 3,000 voters, the Act also imposed an 'aldermanic veto' on all acts of Common Council. This was seen as an attempt to restrict the Common Council's power of independent action and place it firmly in the hands of the pro-ministerial 'monied interests' who sat in the Court of Aldermen.[7]

Although the Act passed, in spite of petitions and protests, it left Walpole with many opponents. The introduction of his proposals for the Excise scheme offered his enemies their opportunity. Many of the merchants and tradesmen of the City were violently opposed to the scheme and saw it as a possible means of destroying Walpole's position. The Excise Bill was introduced on 14 March 1733, creating scenes in London which contemporaries regarded as reminiscent of the trial of Dr Sacheverell. Pamphlets, handbills and broadsides poured out; parades of artisans bearing wooden clogs on long poles were accompanied by cries of 'No slavery – no excise – no wooden shoes'. Thus Walpole's financial reforms aroused popular indignation and the Excise was linked with foreign despotism, popery and slavery. Two City members, Sir John Barnard and Micaiah Perry, led the campaign against the Excise in parliament and their speeches were accompanied by noisy demonstrations outside the House. A petition from the City of London was presented on 10 April and rejected by only seventeen votes. On 11 April when Walpole attempted to postpone the Bill until 12 June, the crowd outside became so tumultuous that the magistrates had to read the Riot Act. Even so Walpole was mobbed as he left, being forced to flee his pursuers by running from one coffee house to another. Several of his close friends who had tried to make him take a more discreet exit were themselves recipients of blows and abuse.[8]

On the news that the Bill had been abandoned effigies of Walpole and Queen Caroline were burnt in Fleet Street, Smithfield and Bishopsgate Street. In one incident, Walpoles's effigy was burnt in the company of a notorious murderess, Sarah Malcolm. Coaches were stopped and forced to declare for 'No excise', bonfires lit, and mobs of apprentices enforced an illumination. So memorable a victory for the populace was one which it was hoped would be celebrated for years to come and a subscription for the purpose was opened. The more sober City politicians, however, already feeling the strengthening of Walpole's position after the dropping of the Excise, issued orders for anyone who lit bonfires or caused a disturbance to be arrested. For his pains, the Lord Mayor, Sir William Billers, had his windows smashed and was pelted by the crowd when he appeared in public. Notwithstanding, the Court of Aldermen rallied around this stand upon order and with the end of united City opposition the disturbances over the excise came to an end.[9]

In 1736 there were renewed agitations against Walpole's administration. A Gin Act was passed which attempted to prevent the retailing of gin by imposing a prohibitive duty and a retailer's licence of £50. On the day the Act was to take effect retailers draped their signs with black and organised mock lyings in state and funeral processions for 'Madame Geneva' or 'Mother Gin'. In fact, no riots occurred until the following year when there were a series of attacks on informers who, attracted by the prospect of a £5 reward, were responsible for bringing several retailers to court; the chief magistrate responsible for convicting six retailers had his house threatened. On 28 July an informer was stoned to death by a crowd in New Palace Yard and two more were killed in the course of the next month. A series of further attacks on informers, two more of whom were killed and several injured, virtually rendered the Gin' Act ineffective, in spite of attempts on the part of the Government to protect informants.[10]

The summer months of 1736 were also affected by anti-Irish disturbances. The laying-off of English workmen and the employment of Irishmen in the building and weaving trades sparked off a two-day riot in East End parishes. The cry of 'Down with the Irish' was raised on 26 July by a large crowd assembled in Shoreditch; on the next day a crowd of 2,000 assembled and attacked public houses owned or frequented by Irishmen. When the Riot Act was read and the soldiers called the crowd broke up, but reassembled on Wednesday evening, 28 July, and only dispersed when the Tower Hamlets Militia were called out against them. Melting away through the alleys and courts of the East End, they escaped the soldiers and attacked Irish houses in Whitechapel. Other attacks took place in Southwark, Lambeth, and Tyburn, but were put down by fresh parties of Guards. Although the Government believed that Jacobite agents, as well as some of its opponents, were behind the disturbances, there was little evidence that this was so. The Gin Act, and others such as the Smuggling Act, were acting to arouse grievances for which the Irish proved a convenient scapegoat.[11]

During the first half of the eighteenth century, subtle changes were affecting the course of popular movements in the capital. Nicholas Rogers has detected a decline in Tory–Jacobite demonstrations from the 1720s as well as a slackening of intensity in religious disputes. In its place developed a more 'patriotic libertarian ideology . . . a more forthright vindication of the Englishman's "birthright"; a more adamantly anti-absolutist posture'.[12] During the struggle which eventually led to Walpole's resignation in February 1742, there were many displays of bellicose patriotism in the City: the capture of Porto Bello by Admiral Vernon in November 1739 was greeted with widespread popular rejoicing and Vernon's birthday was marked by illuminations and demonstrations for several years.[13] The 1745 rebellion also released a flood of popular loyalism, assiduously cultivated by the Whigs. Anti-Catholic prejudice was involved in a stream of prints, broadsheets, and ballads. Towards the end of 1745, with the Pretender's forces carrying all before them in Scotland and northern England, loyalist demonstrations gathered in intensity. The King's birthday was celebrated on 30 October with illuminations and bonfires, while the anniversary of the Gunpowder Plot was celebrated by burning effigies of the Pope and the Pretender. On 12 November the declaration of the Pretender was burnt at the Royal Exchange and his effigy carried through the streets on a gibbet, 'attended by six butchers with their Mock Musick'. Otherwise, a few brawls in

London alehouses marked the only evidence of popular commotion during the rebellion. London Jacobitism was by the 1740s a minority movement and loyalism genuinely popular with wide sections of the labouring population; Rogers has written that 'In the popular mind, the Jacobite cause symbolised the return of absolutism and the denial of national identity'. The heady concoction of popular chauvinism, anti-popery, and libertarianism had developed in the City mobs by the 1740s.[14]

'Independent' Westminster

During that decade, however, Westminster also became a focus of popular agitation. By the middle years of the eighteenth century Westminster elections had become noted for their turbulence. Because the borough lacked the municipal machinery and corporate status of the City, its opposition tended to be expressed at elections. Its wide burgess franchise, estimated at 9,000 in 1761, made it the largest parliamentary borough in the country, and like the City, Westminster contained a high proportion of craftsmen, tradesmen, professional men, and a relatively high proportion of courtiers and noblemen.[15] The proximity of the Court and the Houses of Parliament also gave the Westminster elections a potential for embarrassing government which was utilised by opposition elements. Meetings, parades, and demonstrations provided a means of displaying opposition 'without doors' and goes a long way to explain the elaborate pageantry of these contests. Equally tempting was the possibility of defeating court nominees at the polls, on the very doorstep of parliament. Some cooperation with City politicians was possible in mid-century because significant numbers of liverymen and aldermen had taken to living in the fashionable districts and were therefore capable of bringing their influence to bear both in City politics and Westminster elections.[16]

It was at the peak of discontent with Walpole's policies that the 'patriot' opposition chose to contest the Westminster election of 1741. The 'Independent and Worthy Electors of the Ancient City of Westminster' supported Charles Edwin and Admiral Vernon, the hero of Porto Bello, against the Court candidates Sir Charles Wager and Lord Sundon. The patriot opposition organised a mob at the hustings in Covent Garden to intimidate court voters. On the afternoon of the opening of the poll, the mob forced the candidates, the High Bailiff of Westminster, and the elected officials to take refuge in St Paul's Covent Garden to escape a barrage of 'Dirt, Stones, Sticks, Dead Cats and Dogs'. The violence continued until the sixth day when Lord Sundon called on the Horse Guards to protect him and persuaded the High Bailiff to shut the poll and declare the Court candidates elected. Even then he was forced to escape the hustings like a fugitive, pursued by a mob which pelted his coach with dirt and stones, injuring both himself and his footman. Sundon's retreat from the husting had to be protected by the Guards who with loaded muskets prevented the mob from following him to his home and carrying out their threat to demolish his house. But his understandable decision to call out the troops gave the opposition their opening. Within a month the Grand Jury of Middlesex placed a writ at King's Bench against the partiality of the High Bailiff and the use of military power to terminate the election. As a result Wager and Sundon were unseated and the anti-Court candidates installed.[17]

In the election of 1747 the Independents were defeated in a wave of anti-Jacobite reaction, and Admiral Sir Peter Warren and Lord Trentham returned. Trentham's appointment to a Lordship of the Admiralty forced him to resign his seat and seek re-election in 1749; the Independents put up Sir George Vandeput to oppose. The election took place against a background of violence in the capital which owed little to the election, but which spilled over on to the hustings. On a Saturday evening in early July three sailors who visited a brothel in the Strand were robbed; returning to Wapping they collected some colleagues and returned to wreck the house, burning its contents in the street. The crowd continued to grow and threatened another brothel before being broken up by troops in the early hours of the morning. That evening a crowd reassembled and attacked the house of the local beadle who had called out the troops, rescuing two men arrested the previous night; two other brothels were wrecked before a magistrate and some soldiers arrived. The ringleaders of the crowd were arrested and taken to Bow Street. Crowds now assembled in the street crying 'To the rescue', and when the men were committed to Newgate an escort of Guards had to be used to beat off attempts to rescue the men. Although there were rumours of 4,000 sailors assembling at Tower Hill in readiness to march on the Strand – rumours taken seriously enough to cause near panic among shopkeepers and householders who moved their belongings out of the area – the precautions taken by the magistrates John Fielding and Saunders Welch in posting troops and constables in the area prevented further disturbances.[18]

Two of the rioters were tried under the Riot Act at the Old Bailey, convicted, and sentenced to death. The result was an outcry; the Riot Act had been little used in the capital since its inception in 1715 and there had been repeated demands for its repeal.[19] The jury which convicted the men sent a petition for reprieve to the King and another came from 900 inhabitants of the Strand. As a result, one of the men was reprieved but the other, Bosavern Penlez, was hanged. A riot was only just avoided at his execution by the action of the magistrate in dismissing the soldiers sent to guard the gallows, an action described as an example of the 'Old British spirit' which proved 'that His Majesty's Reign was that of the Laws and not of the sword'.[20] Fielding, was accused of taking protection money from the brothel keepers and the Duke of Newcastle was pilloried as callous, cruel and oppressive. The Riot Act was widely condemned as an 'oppressive innovation' and 'dangerous to the liberty of the subject'. Penlez himself was elevated into the status of a public martyr who had died in defence of English liberty. Fielding was forced to publish a rebuttal of these charges in *A True State of the Case of Bosavern Penlez*, in which he argued that Penlez was not only a rioter but also a thief and that the Riot Act, far from being oppressive, guaranteed individual liberty. Notwithstanding, great political capital was made of Penlez's death during the Westminster election. His effigy was paraded in a coffin and, at appropriate moments, an actor dressed in a shroud would 'resurrect' and harangue the crowd on the threat to English 'liberties'.[21]

This Westminster election was also enlivened by the opposition aroused by a group of French actors who visited the Little Theatre, Haymarket. Popular chauvinism led the crowd to pelt the players and generate an atmosphere of intense hostility to foreigners. Squibs and broadsides accused the English aristocracy of adopting foreign manners and developing French subservience. The Court party was forced to produce several printed replies, and when the poll was finally declared for the Court candidate in May 1750 there were widespread disturbances in which Court sympathisers were insulted and Trentham's house threatened.[22]

'Wilkes and Liberty!'

During the 1750s William Pitt became something of a champion with the small tradesmen and craftsmen of the capital, but there were few examples of popular demonstrations in his favour until 1761, when following Pitt's resignation the Earl of Bute, the King's chief minister, was pelted and hooted by the crowd when he visited the Guildhall for Lord Mayor's Day.[23] The capital's support for Pitt and its opposition to Bute was to provide the background to the elevation of Wilkes into a popular champion.

The Wilkes affair brought together a number of strands. The current of persistent opposition to the Court which had been suspended for the duration of Pitt's period of office was abruptly terminated with his resignation. Opposition to George III and his favourite, Bute, provided the political background to the support given to Wilkes. But the City was also developing a distinctive political character of its own; Rudé has suggested development in three significant directions in the latter part of the eighteenth century: firstly, the City developed a more independent line of its own, no longer merely mirroring opposition within parliament; secondly, City radicals began to formulate a programme of parliamentary reform, including the demand for shorter parliaments, reform of the 'Rotten' boroughs, and a widening of the franchise; thirdly, the appeal was extended to those who did not possess the vote, the nation 'without doors'. Moreover, the development of a vocal independence in Westminster and the growth of urban development in Middlesex, extended the influence of City politics beyond the confines of the City proper and involved the electors of Westminster and Middlesex.[24] The growth or 'revival' of metropolitan radicalism in the 1760s was one of the most significant aspects of the period. Wilkes and his City ally William Beckford, became the political mouthpieces for this 'radicalism'.[25]

Another strand in the affair was the growth of industrial disputes in the capital. The 1760s have been called 'the most remarkable decade of industrial disputes of the whole century' for the London trades.[26] 'Combinations' existed in a number of trades, and the demonstrations, strikes and riots of workmen formed a recurrent theme throughout the decade, running parallel to the campaigns of Wilkes. They drew on the strong traditions of collective action among the London trades which had made them among the best organised in the country. During these disturbances complaints about high prices were mingled with demands for higher wages and the use of trade union tactics of a strikingly modern character were mingled with traditional attempts to force government intervention to protect craft privileges.[27] Some of the groups involved, especially the silkweavers, coalheavers and seamen used violence to back their demands; others, including the hatters, tailors, shoemakers, watermen and coopers remained within the law while pressing their claims. The impact of the Wilkes controversy was to be greatly increased by unrest in several trades.[28]

In 1763, the thirty-six-year-old John Wilkes, MP for Aylesbury, supported Pitt, Beckford and the City 'Patriots' against George III. The famous issue No. 45 of Wilkes's *North Briton* attacked the peace preliminaries of 1763 and denounced the King's Speech in terms which led to his being arrested on a general warrant and committed to the Tower on a charge of libel. A week later he was released by Chief Justice Pratt who declared the warrant a breach of parliamentary privilege. At the hearing in Westminster Hall on 6 May Wilkes made the first claims that his cause was of more than personal significance, identifying his cause with 'that of all the middling and inferior set of people'. On his release he was escorted to his house by a large crowd who cried 'Wilkes and Liberty!' and 'Whigs for ever'. His successful claim for damages for unlawful arrest and confiscation of his private papers led to popular rejoicing and bonfires in the streets of the capital.

In order to keep in the limelight, Wilkes had printed an obscene parody of Pope's *Essay on Man*, called an *Essay on Women*, which was bound and sold with copies of No. 45 of the *North Briton*. Summoned to appear before the Commons on a charge of blasphemy, Wilkes escaped to France. But when the common hangman was ordered to ceremonially burn No. 45 at the Royal Exchange, the supporters of Wilkes turned out in force. More than 500 gathered and pelted the sheriffs who came to conduct the proceedings; one of their coaches had its windows smashed and the tumult prevented the burning from taking place. The mob then took No. 45 in triumph to Temple Bar, where they lit a large bonfire and burnt a large boot (a pun on Lord Bute) to shouts of 'Wilkes and Liberty!'[29]

Wilkes was to remain out of the country until 1768, but in the interim the hand of 'Wilkes and Liberty' was suspected in many disputes with which he had nothing at all to do. In 1763 the silk-weavers in East London drew up a scale of wages and when it was rejected left their workshops, broke their tools and destroyed materials. According to a contemporary report the silk-weavers 'masked and disguised in Sailors Habits and otherwise, and armed with Cutlasses and other Dangerous Weapons' attacked journeymen who refused to join them and paraded the streets with the effigy of an unpopular master in a cart, 'with a halter about his neck, an executioner on one side, and a coffin on the other'. The effigy was hung and burnt before the weavers dispersed. A detachment of Guards had to be placed in Spitalfields to overawe the weavers. In May 1765 there was renewed violence when a Bill to prohibit imported silks was supported by demonstrations of the Spitalfields weavers. Eight thousand marched on parliament from the East End and mobbed the entrances to the Houses of Parliament. Members were jostled and roughly treated as they arrived and the Duke of Bedford, suspected of being against the Bill, had his coach wrecked; he was pursued to his house and the crowd was only with difficulty persuaded from demolishing it. A few evenings later his house was attacked again and the mob only beaten off when the Riot Act was read and soldiers unleashed. This display of collective pressure was symptomatic of the organisation and strength of some of the London trades and eventually the Act to prohibit foreign silk goods was passed. Although a few commentators claimed that the weavers had been organised by Wilkes, in fact these demonstrations were entirely free from his influence. They did, however, provide the background to the trade disputes with which Wilkes became involved on his return to England in 1768 and illustrated the potential which could be tapped by a skilful popular demagogue.[30]

Wilkes returned to England on 6 February 1768, at a time of considerable social and industrial unrest. Poor harvests had caused food rioting in the country at large during the preceding two years. London had escaped the provincial rioting but suffered from relatively high prices for bread in both 1767 and 1768; bread reached over eight pence for the quartern loaf in 1767 and remained at very high levels through the winter and spring of 1767-68.[31] Moreover, many London trades were suffering from depression. Normally the variety of the capital's crafts provided some cushion against depression in any particular field of activity, and while skilled clockmakers could hardly turn to, say, coalheaving, selective unemployment meant that people possessing a settlement would be able to obtain parochial relief without much difficulty. More serious were the problems of the large East End parishes, where the concentration of numerous bodies of particular trades, such as silk-weaving, created difficulties. Because the parochial system of relief was self-financing from poor rates, depression in a trade which was the livelihood of a large proportion of the inhabitants, including small masters and employers, could prove disastrous.

By the winter of 1767-8, severe weather also meant that the poor had to spend more on fuel, while the freezing over the Thames brought unemployment to the numerous workmen employed on the wharves, barges, and lighters which normally made the port of London a hive of activity. In addition, there is some evidence that numbers of the provincial poor moved into London during the preceding years, swelling the ranks of the unskilled and semi-skilled workers in the poorer parishes to the east and south of the capital. Shelton writes that: 'this influx of labour as a result of provincial distress in 1768-9 aggravated a crisis already developing from a combination of post-war adjustment, trade realignment and an increasingly frequent *laissez-faire* policies of the government.'[32]

Wilkes's return had witnessed a few outbursts of popular enthusiasm. When he stood for the City of London in the elections of 1768 he was greeted by enthusiastic cries of 'Wilkes and Liberty', but was unable to win a seat. A fortnight later, Wilkes was elected for Middlesex amidst tumultuous scenes. Spitalfields weavers assembled in Piccadilly and gave out blue favours and papers inscribed with 'Wilkes and Liberty'; opponents to Wilkes were pelted or roughly handled and when news of his victory broke, the crowds turned upon any house which refused to illuminate in celebration. 'No. 45' was chalked on walls and doors, the Austrian ambassador dragged from his coach, and the windows of the Mansion House smashed. Mobs crisscrossed London from east to west, smashing windows in the fashionable districts and enforcing a general illumination. The tumult was generally goodnatured, although the bill for damage to the Mansion House alone was over £200.[33]

Sporadic disturbances in support of Wilkes continued into April. When he was brought up before the Court of King's Bench on 20 April there were crowds to greet him, who on his release enforced a general illumination of Ratcliffe Highway. A week later, when he was escorted to prison in Southwark, the coach in which he was travelling was 'hijacked' by the crowd, the horses taken from the shafts, the coach turned around and dragged by the crowd back to the City and on to Spitalfields. There Wilkes appeared at the window of the Three Tuns tavern to the acclaim of his followers, before surrendering himself to the authorities.[34] On the following day, crowds mobbed the King's Bench prison and had to be driven away by soldiers. On 10 May, the opening of Parliament, when Wilkes should have been released to take his seat in the Commons large crowds assembled. As the crowd became more daring, the ranks of the soldiers guarding the prison were broken and a poster stuck on the prison wall. A magistrate, called Ponton, ordered a constable to remove it; at this the crowd started throwing stones, hitting magistrates and soldiers and a group of soldiers took off in pursuit of some of the stone throwers, chasing one into a cowshed where they bayoneted and shot a publican's son, William Allen, whom they mistook for their quarry. By this time the temper of the troops was well and truly roused. After the Riot Act had been read twice in an attempt to disperse the crowd outside the prison, the troops opened fire and killed five or six people, wounding a score of others. The 'Massacre of St George's Fields', as it was quickly dubbed, resulted in further disturbances. The houses of the magistrates concerned in the incident, Ponton and Gillam, were attacked. In the City, the Lord Mayor was pelted with stones and the windows of the Mansion House were smashed again; further demonstrations also took place outside parliament, but without serious damage or casualties.[35]

At this stage industrial disputes in London began to create a series of disturbances which ran parallel to and sometimes flowed into the Wilkes affair. The year 1768 witnessed a wave of strikes and demonstrations among many London trades, including the coalheavers, silk-weavers, watermen, sailors, hatters, sawyers, tailors, and coopers. The coal-heavers dispute had been running since the end of 1767; they were a body of about 700 men employed in unloading coal on to the wharves of the port of London. A fairly homogeneous group, mainly Irish, they earned high but irregular wages. Their greatest weakness was that the work was at best only semi-skilled, and coal-heavers were always threatened by the recruitment of new labour. Middlemen, known as undertakers, who were often publicans dominated the workmen, making deductions from wages, charging for the use of shovels, and paying wages in drink. A later writer, Patrick Colquhoun, described the coal-heavers, as 'a very depraved but useful and frequently ill-used class of men'.[36] Their attempts to establish their trade as a Fellowship had failed in the past, as had their attempts to check the abuses of the undertakers, but in 1758 they obtained an Act which placed the coal-heavers under the direction of an Alderman for Billingsgate, William Beckford, who was to compile a register and act as the middleman between coal-heavers and ships' masters. The Alderman was supposed to collect wages, taking a deduction to cover operating expenses and a scheme to provide a sickness, burial and dependants' benefits. However, no wage-fixing machinery was created, nor was the scheme compulsory; as a result many of the coal undertakers and ships' masters carried on the normal trade. By 1767 the official scheme had gradually fallen into disrepute through the embezzlement of its funds. Instead many of the coal-heavers signed up with the rival scheme of a 'trading justice' from Tower Hamlets, Ralph Hodgson, which licensed workers, established wage rates, and provided for a benefit fund. The coal-heavers also organised into a society, which held regular meetings and rapidly developed a strong trade-union style organisation.[37]

This development of a stronger organisation was timely. The coal-heavers were under renewed pressure from the recruitment of cheap labour, using the 'coal-whipping' technique to unload the colliers, a system of baskets and pulleys which required both less physical effort and less skill. By 1768 wage levels were being pushed down by an influx of unskilled labour and the coal-heavers were conscious of a significant drop in their status. Encouraged by news of a coal dispute in the North-East, they demanded higher wages, and when this request was refused they struck, bringing the coal trade to a standstill. At this point Beckford, who was opposed to the strike, re-opened his register and offered higher wages, attempting to break the position of the coal-heavers. Beckford's agents advertised for men to register in April 1768 and offered an attractive wage to would-be strike-breakers. Two ex-undertakers and victuallers, John Green of the Round About Tavern, Shadwell, and Thomas Metcalf of the Salutation Inn, Wapping, were the principal agents of the scheme.[38]

The coal-heavers reacted violently. Salutation Inn was attacked in February 1768, the bar was wrecked and Metcalf threatened. In March and April further attacks were made upon undertakers who attempted to recruit men and anyone who signed on with them. On 21 April, a gang of coal-heavers armed with bludgeons attacked Green's tavern, arriving at about eight o'clock in the evening with cries of 'Wilkes and Liberty'. Mistaking the cause of the tumult several neighbours put candles in their windows, but Green, with the assistance of his sister and a sailor, defended his tavern with musket fire and killed several of the mob. All night the attack continued, several coal-heavers were killed and not once did the magistrates, troops or constables interfere. The coal-heavers brought up muskets themselves and virtually riddled the tavern with shot. Running out of bullets, they were reported to have broken pewter pots and fired the pieces. Breaking into the door, they were beaten out again by the sailor. During the night, Green made a somewhat ungallant escape over the rooftops, no doubt believing that as he was the principal object of the assault his sister would be left unmolested. He was mistaken. The coal-heavers returned to the assault with cries of 'Green, you bouger, why don't you fire?', swearing they would 'have his heart and liver, and cut him to pieces and hang him on his sign'. Finding their prey gone, they dragged his sister from the house and murdered her in the street. Seven coal-heavers were eventually hanged for the murder and three others transported. Green and the sailor were also arrested for murder by Hodgson, though later acquitted.[39]

The coal-heavers, undaunted by these measures, tried to bring pressure to bear on parliament. On 11 May, the day after the 'massacre' in St George's Fields, a mob of coal-heavers marched on the House of Commons, but John Fielding hurried from Bow Street to head them off. Addressing the mob, he persuaded them to surrender their flags and drums and to send a deputation to meet him in Bow Street. Although negotiations were opened, the masters refused to allow a rise in wages and continued to engage sailors to break the strike. Inevitably further violence was the result. The Wharves from Limehouse to Westminster were brought to a standstill, barges were prevented from unloading, and coal-carts unharnessed. Men who attempted to work were made to ride a wooden rail and beaten with lengths of rope and sticks. Sailors were frequently attacked during May and June and in one battle in which sailors from the *Thames and Mary* sallied on to the shore, coal-heavers armed with cutlasses and bludgeons murdered a young sailor. Affrays continued as the coal-heavers maintained pickets on the wharves, and even exchanged shots with ships in the river. Eventually in June soldiers were stationed in the riverside districts and the ringleaders of the strike arrested. The assailants of the murdered sailor were brought to trial and hanged. Unable to enforce the stoppage, the coal-heavers were forced to return to work at the old rates of pay.[40]

The coal-heavers strike was only the bloodiest of several bitter disputes which were conducted during 1768–9. With a tradition of 'collective bargaining by riot' stretching as far back as the seventeenth century, the Spitalfields silk-weavers were also engaged in a protracted dispute. Overseas competition, the use of 'engine looms' and cheap apprentice labour were constant sources of dispute between weavers and masters and between different groups of workmen.[41] In October 1763, a group of several hundred journeymen had smashed the looms of other workmen, wounded several of them and burned a master in effigy.[42] In 1765 the weavers lobbied parliament and in November 1767 were reported to be determined to destroy engine looms which they believed were ruining the trade. Well-organised groups of weavers, probably operating by agreement through their illicit societies which met in public houses in Spitalfields, Bethnal Green, and Stepney, attacked looms in Stepney.[43] Attempts by the masters to reduce wages by fourpence per yard in January 1768 provoked violent opposition. The weavers armed themselves with cutlasses, pistols, and bludgeons and destroyed looms and silk in the workshops. On 20 August, they were reported to have 'rose in a body', broke into a workshop in Pratt's Alley, cut to pieces some silk in looms and shot a young silkworker; the garrison of the Tower was called out, but was resisted by the weavers, leaving several dead and wounded.[44]

An attempt at a negotiated settlement in autumn 1768 failed, as a result of which the weavers formed themselves into committees for the various branches of the trade. Calling themselves the Bold Defence they levied strike contributions on willing and unwilling alike. Refusal to pay, resulted in written threats or nocturnal visitation by armed weavers. By spring 1769 the affair was reaching a crescendo; in March the throwsters held 'tumultuous assemblies' and intimidated the masters. During the spring and summer well-organised weavers terrorised the eastern parishes. Gravener Henson described how the weavers

> could be drawn out of the various purlieus of Bethnal-green [sic] and Spitalfields, in less than an hour. The waving of silk handkerchiefs, the turning out of their pigeons, with a cry or watch-word, set them instantly in motion, generally armed, in which the bullock hunters acted as their advanced guard, than which a more active, agile, desperate, and determined number of young men never existed.[45]

In one incident. 1,500 weavers 'cut' seventy-six looms in reprisal for a master's failure to contribute to the weavers' subscription fund.

By the autumn, the Government had decided that events had gone far enough and authorised the use of troops to put down the weavers' organisations. In late September magistrates and military raided the Dolphin tavern in New Cock Lane, one of the weavers' usual rendezvous. A vicious battle developed in which both sides used firearms and three people were killed, a soldier and two 'cutters'; one of the leaders of the strike was sentenced to death.[46] The Spitalfields area was garrisoned with troops, supported by funds collected by the master weavers. In a move which foreshadowed the suppression of radical societies in the 1790s, publicans who allowed the weavers to hold meetings on their premises were threatened with loss of their licence. With the execution of two more of the weavers in December 1769, the violent phase of the weavers' strike was virtually ended. In 1773 the Spitalfields Act (13 Geo. III, c. 68) restored the magistrates' control of wages for the industry, and a permanent body of masters and men was set up which could present the case of the weavers to the magistrates. As a return to the more paternalistic system of wage regulation, it flew in the face of the general drift of policy in this area during the late eighteenth and early nineteenth centuries. Whatever its consequences for the future of the silk industry in London, and in spite of the wrath of a later generation of *laissez-faire* theorists who saw it as a retrogressive step, the Act was successful in its short-term aim, that of securing peace in the silk-weaving districts. Although often the object of concern by the authorities in subsequent years, they rarely again participated in large-scale popular disturbances.[47]

The coal-heavers' and silk-weavers' disputes were only the most violent of several which took place in the capital in 1768-9. The seamen too were involved in a protracted dispute. They had been in difficulties since the end of the Seven Years' War in 1763 when rapid demobilisation brought unemployment and pressure on wage rates. Economic fluctuations prevented the trade from declining steadily and the seamen were faced with severe difficulties at a time when prices were high, and as the largest port in the kingdom, London was the home port of many of those who were unemployed. Abuse of apprenticeship regulations by the ships' masters and various attempts to reduce wages, including non-payment for time spent in foreign ports, led to an appeal to the authorities for the application of the Elizabethan Statute of Apprentices. The authorities had been forced to deal with disturbances among the sailors as early as 1763, but it was only with the development of a strike in the ports of the North-East that the seamen of London reacted. In May 1768 a party of them boarded ships at Deptford, unreefed the sails, and vowed no ships should sail till the merchants had consented to raise their wages. The London seamen demanded a wage of 35s. a month and by 9 May had immobilised every ship on the Thames; their representatives visited each ship, investigated the monthly wage rates and conditions of service, and disabled the ship if they were below 40s.[48]

A meeting of between 5,000 and 6,000 sailors assembled in Stepney Fields to discuss the next step and a group from St George's Fields marched 'with colours flying, drums beating and fifes playing', to St

James's Palace, where they handed in a petition. On 10 May a large group descended on parliament with another petition, before peacefully dispersing. Representatives from the sailors met with the owners to present their demands, but no general agreement was forthcoming, though some individual shipowners and companies, such as the Hudson's Bay Company, did agree to increase wages. Generally only those shipowners most vulnerable to an interruption of work came to a settlement. By July most of the seamen were back at work, although there were reports of isolated strikes in August. In comparison with the coal-heavers' and silk-weavers' disputes, there was very little violence, except when sailors were attacked by coal-heavers for unloading coal ships. The absence of violence was certainly aided by the abstention of the shipowners from any attempt at strike-breaking. Because no disturbances of serious consequence had occurred, the authorities were prepared to allow the strike to take its own course without sending in the troops.[49]

These large-scale demonstrations occurred contemporaneously with a series of disputes among other trades, notably, the watermen, hatters, tailors, shoemakers, and coopers. Two thousand watermen demonstrated at the Royal Exchange and Mansion House in May, complaining about high prices and the competition of private craft in the trade. After an interview with the Lord Mayor, the watermen were persuaded to draw up a petition, which he offered to present to parliament for them. His action sent the watermen away in a peaceful frame of mind. On the same day as the watermen's demonstration, the hatters struck work for higher wages. Their disputes lasted some weeks and mobs of hatters went about the capital enforcing the stoppage. Assemblies to present petitions from various trades and occasional damage to machinery and equipment occurred, but the majority of these disputes proceeded without violence.[50]

These years saw the largest wave of industrial disturbances in London before the 1790s. Occurring at the same time as the Wilkes disturbances, the two movements have often been considered together. In fact, although there was some individual support for Wilkes among trade groups such as the coal-heavers and silk-weavers, the industrial disputes and the violence which arose from them were almost completely divorced from the political movement headed by Wilkes. Wilkes undoubtedly became a kind of symbol – one historian has recently cast him in the role of a 'Lord of misrule' – but there was little political influence in the disturbances. The various disputes ran parallel with the Wilkite movement, occasionally overlapping with it, but not principally inspired by it. Wilkes for his part was content to allow striking workmen to adopt him as a champion, provided they did not compromise his position. Each dispute derived its impetus from the conditions of the trade, but above all from the movements in the price of bread. May 1768, when many of the protests about wages began, was also the peak in wheat and bread prices. It is almost certain that strikes, demonstrations, and petitions from the London trades would have been taking place, whether Wilkes had appeared or not.[51]

What of Wilkes? After the 'massacre' of St George's Fields, there was a lull in activity other than the trade demonstrations and disturbances. But Wilkes's birthday on 28 October 1768 provided the opportunity for his supporters to come out on the streets again. 'A great number of disorderly persons' went through the principal streets breaking the windows of those who refused to illuminate in honour of their champion. The Middlesex election on 8 December caused by the death of Wilkes's fellow-member, George Cooke, led to disturbances, but they were primarily the work of the Court candidates, Sir William Beauchamp Proctor, who employed a body of men armed with bludgeons and with 'Liberty and Proctor' on their hats to drive voters from the hustings. In spite of these tactics the Wilkite candidate, Serjeant Glynn, was elected and pro-Wilkes crowds enforced an illumination in the centre of London. Wilkes's expulsion from the Commons on 3 February 1769 provoked a riot in Drury Lane which was only put down when the troops were called.[52]

There followed the famous series of elections in which Wilkes was returned as member for Middlesex, but was each time disqualified from sitting or had his election annulled. During this time Wilkes was consolidating his City position by becoming an Alderman for the Ward of Farringdon Without, while his supporters became more organised with the formation of the Society of Supporters of the Bill of Rights. The amount of disorder occasioned by these events was minimal, but on 22 March 1769 an attempt by 'loyal' merchants to present a petition to the King at St James's Palace was interrupted by a Wilkite mob. The merchants were pelted and insulted as they passed through the City of London. At one point the passage of the merchants' cavalcade was interrupted by a hearse decorated with prints and pictures, representing the death of Allen in St George's Fields and the death of another rioter at Brentford. Drawn by one black and one white horse, with a coachman in black, the hearse paraded outside the royal palaces. Only a dozen of the 'loyal' merchants arrived at St James's in their mud-bespattered coaches. Although a number of rioters were taken by the troops, and five later indicted, they were all discharged by the Westminster Grand Jury, much to the chagrin of George III.[53]

Wilkes's fourth election to Westminster on 13 April 1769 was the occasion for a parade through London to the King's Bench Prison with banners and music, and several thousand supporters in attendance but these demonstrations were peaceful, even when his election was declared null and void on the following day. There was no renewal of violence until the 'Printers' Case' of 1771, in which the City championed the cause of printing details of parliamentary debates in the metropolitan newspapers. Taking a stand on the City's liberties, the Lord Mayor, Brass Crosby, backed by Wilkes and other aldermen, defied and frustrated attempts to arrest the printers. When Crosby was summoned to parliament on 19 March a vast crowd accompanied him, and on his return from the House his carriage was dragged by the mob through the streets. His subsequent attendances were also supported by large crowds who mobbed the entrances to parliament. Court supporters were attacked and Lord North's coach broken to pieces. Eventually the crowds were persuaded to disperse and Crosby was committed to the Tower for a breach of privilege.[54]

This action gave rise to further popular demonstrations. Effigies representing the Princess Dowager, Lord Bute, the Speaker, and the two Foxes were 'beheaded' by a chimney-sweep and burnt on Tower Hill. There followed the 'execution' of other opponents of the City. When the City men were released from prison on the prorogation of parliament, tumultuous popular demonstrations followed. A ritual illumination of the City had its inevitable result when the windows of the Speaker of the Commons were smashed. A year later, when Wilkes was passed over for Lord Mayor in defiance of precedent, his supporters demonstrated against the successful candidate. Three thousand sailors mobbed the entrances to Guildhall and pulled down the temporary staging erected in the yard, spectators were forced to drink to Wilkes's health, bonfires were lit, and the crowd was only dispersed in the early hours of the morning by the Honourable Artillery Company. The last episodes of the Wilkes affair took place in 1773, when his election as Lord Mayor was greeted with popular rejoicing, his coach was pulled in triumph, and his opponents' windows were broken. In December he regained his seat in parliament. Following his period as Lord Mayor, Wilkes dropped out of radical politics, taking a City sinecure in 1779.

The support which Wilkes achieved among a broad spectrum of opinion within the metropolis seemed a culmination of extra-parliamentary agitation, propaganda, and organisation. They did not spring 'new born' from the reign of George III, but built on traditions established before 1760 and apparent in the 'Patriot' opposition to Walpole. The excise crisis and the Westminster contests in the 1740s were clear forerunners to the campaigns of Wilkes, but propaganda, demonstration and riot, had never before been so sustained. Extra-parliamentary agitation reached new levels of sophistication and a wider audience. The role of the crowd in these events was complex. Rudé's exhaustive study of the composition of the Wilkite mobs has shown that they were drawn from the typical occupations and trades of the capital, including large numbers of wage-earners and self-employed artisans. He concludes that these were not 'criminal' mobs, for there is 'no evidence of the "hiring" of bands of demonstrators; and loot played no part in the disturbances'.[55]

By identifying himself so closely with the cause of English 'liberties', Wilkes was able to evoke once more the complex medley of atavistic passions which had led City mobs to support Sacheverell, oppose the Excise, and resist Jewish naturalisation. His conscious attempt to present himself as no better than his supporters both enhanced his following and stimulated their political activities. A master of a propaganda, Wilkes bombarded the populace with pamphlets, handbills, ballads and cartoons; cheap chapbooks also made his writings available to a wider audience than ever before, not only in the capital but in many towns and cities in the country at large. In return he became the centre of the elaborate ritual and pageantry of the London crowd. He was accorded a symbolic status, awarded presents, celebrated on artifacts, drawn through the streets on his public appearances, and treated almost as a monarch and ruler. Illuminations, the wearing of badges and cockades, plays on the number '45' all played their part in what Brewer has called the 'deliberate theatricality' of much of the crowd's behaviour. Wilkes was only too ready to respond. Colourful, gregarious, and with his ready wit, he could act the role of a kind of 'lord of misrule'. Certainly contemporaries recognised that power of personality in winning the plaudits of the populace, so that Burke could shrewdly remark that 'the crowd always want to draw themselves from abstract principles to personal attachments'.[56]

Taking their lead from the 'middling sort' represented among City merchants and Middlesex freeholders, some of the better educated artisans and workmen saw Wilkes as the symbol of opposition to an unpopular monarch and the 'corruption' with which he and his ministers were tainted. Above all, however, the lower classes of the capital were motivated by social and economic grievances which also triggered off the series of wage disputes in the capital. Demonstrators outside the House of Lords on 10 May 1768 chanted not only 'Wilkes and Liberty' but also 'It is as well to be hanged as starved'. Although by no means all the pro-Wilkes demonstrations coincided with high prices, the strikes and demonstrations by coal-heavers, silk-weavers and tailors, among others, which added so much to the atmosphere of 'misrule' in the years 1767-9 were principally a response to economic fluctuations. Although individual artisans no doubt supported Wilkes for other reasons, the actions of the trade groups had a more direct relation to trading conditions and price movements.[57]

The significance of the support gained by Wilkes has been examined by several historians. However traditional the alliance between the 'middling sort' and the 'mob', the scale and persistence of the agitation marked a significant development in eighteenth-century politics. Rudé, in particular, has argued that in the 'groping, tentative, and immature displays' of the Wilkite crowds can perhaps be seen the first stirrings of the 'mass Radical movement'; only later, he argues, would the concept of 'liberty' be presented in more tangible form as demands for annual parliaments, the rights of electors, or the extension of the franchise. Similarly, E. P. Thompson has argued that the supporters of Wilkes were 'a transitional mob, on its way to becoming a self-conscious Radical crowd' and 'a half-way house in the emergence of popular political consciousness'. On the one hand 'the leaven of Dissent and of political education was at work', but on the other 'the London crowd of the 1760s and 1770s had scarcely begun to develop its own organisation or leaders'.[58] As Brewer has observed, Wilkes himself was largely unconcerned with political education or long-term organisation, he focused the disparate grievances of his supporters but did little to create a permanent base for political radicalism among the wage-earners and artisans of the capital.[59] Such links as exist between the Wilkite crowds and the political societies of the 1790s, notably the London Corresponding Society, are tenuous to say the least. As Thompson has argued, the crowds whose slogan was 'Liberty', 'were highly volatile and might equally well swing round to attack "alien" elements or smash the windows of citizens who failed to illuminate them on "patriotic" occasions'.[60]

The Gordon Riots

The most serious riots of the eighteenth century displayed to the full these contradictions. The Gordon Riots of 1780 stand out as the largest civil commotion in England since the Monmouth Rebellion. No civil disorder since, in England, has led to greater bloodshed or more widespread destruction of property; more people were killed or executed than during the Luddite outbreaks, the Reform struggle, or the various Chartist episodes. A Catholic Relief Act passed in 1778 met with little resistance either in the House of Commons or in the country at large, but when the repeal of the corresponding penal laws in Scotland was proposed, violent opposition was encountered. In 1779 a Protestant Association was formed and there was rioting in Edinburgh, Glasgow and other small towns in Scotland although no loss of life was reported. In the face of this antagonism the Scottish provisions were abandoned, which led the Protestant Association to attempt the repeal of the measures south of the Border. In February 1779 a Protestant Association was founded in London to campaign for repeal of Catholic Relief. Lord George Gordon, who had been active in the Scottish movement became president of the English Association in November and began to collect signatures for a petition to parliament. Gordon was a somewhat eccentric young man of twenty-eight at the time of his becoming leader of the Protestant Association. Although a member of parliament for a Wiltshire pocket-borough since the age of twenty-three, he still had a political career to make, and had already shown himself willing and able to manipulate popular feeling to his own advantage. Gordon, like Wilkes, sought to channel popular sentiment for his own purposes and the theme of 'No-Popery' played into his hands: he was able to put himself at the head of an undoubtedly popular agitation and threaten the direst consequences if he was not taken seriously. Thus on 25 November he told the House of Commons: 'The indulgences given to Papists have alarmed the whole country, and they are determined, with the utmost resolution, to guard against a people that are become such favourites in the eyes of the Ministry. I do not deliver my own sentiments only; government will find 120,000 men at my back who will avow and support them!'[61]

But Gordon was no mere demagogue. He set out to obtain support for a petitioning campaign against Catholic relief. In mid-January 1780, advertisements were placed in the *Public Advertiser* calling on the clergy, churchwardens and dissenting congregations of the metropolitan parishes to recommend the petition. Handbills announcing the opening of the petition to the populace were posted throughout the capital and were sufficiently influential to obtain several thousand signatures. Moreover, like Wilkes, Gordon could count on the support of the City of London. Discussion of the question of Catholic relief was deferred by Common Council in March 1780, but on the 31 May a motion was passed which declared that the passing of any Acts of parliament in favour of Papists, or repealing any Act against Popery, was repugnant to the true interests of the country. The City of London MPs were directed to support any moves against the Catholic Relief Act of 1778.[62]

With the petition prepared, the question was how to present it. On 29 May a meeting of 2,000 members of the Protestant Association at Coachmakers' Hall heard Gordon declare that unless 20,000 attended him he would not present the petition. He argued that the only way to stop the spread of Popery 'was by going in a firm, manly and resolute manner to the House, and there shew [*sic*] their representatives that they were determined'. For his own part he pledged that

> he would run all hazards with the people, and if the people were too lukewarm to run all hazards with him they might get another President, for he would tell them candidly that he was not a lukewarm man himself, and that if they meant to spend their time in mock debate and idle opposition they might get another leader.[63]

However ominous these remarks appeared after the rioting of the following week, Gordon was doing little more than ensuring that his followers turned out to show their active support. Mass lobbies of parliament and demonstrations of support timed to coincide with petitioning were nothing new and had been used during the excise crisis and during the Wilkite agitation.

Gordon urged the whole of the Protestant Association to assemble in St George's Fields on 2 June to accompany him to the House of Commons and present the petition. For good order, he moved that they should arrange themselves in four divisions and that each member of the association should wear a blue cockade. Arrangements for the four divisions were posted in the *Public Advertiser* on 31 May, 1 June, and 2 June. The magistrates of London, Westminster and Southwark were requested to attend so 'that their presence may overawe and control any riotous or evil-minded persons who may wish to disturb the legal and peaceable deportment of His Majesty's Protestant subjects'. Gordon was ostensibly pursuing a legitimate, if dangerous, policy of attempting to orchestrate extra-parliamentary pressure in support of his cause; that he expected the outcome to be severe rioting is extremely doubtful. What is more likely is that he expected his followers to fulfil the role of 'opposition without doors', enabling him to rally sympathetic MPs, including those of the City of London, win the support of the independents and panic the King and administration into repealing the Catholic Relief Act. Just as Walpole had been forced to relinquish the excise project, so Gordon could legitimately hope to produce an equally effective swell of opinion against the Act of 1778.

On Friday 2 June an estimated 60,000 supporters of the Protestant Association assembled in St George's Fields. The weather was sultry and oppressive, violent thunderstorms having taken place on the last two or three days. The crowd was later described as being composed of 'the better sort of tradesmen; they were all well-dressed decent sort of people'. While awaiting the arrival of Gordon, they paraded with flags, chanted hymns and psalms, and arranged themselves into the prearranged four divisions for the march to Parliament. The initial proceedings went peacefully; the crowd listened to a harangue from Lord George Gordon and, after parading three or four times around the Fields, marched out six to nine abreast, singing hymns and heralded by blue banners. Using separate bridges, the sections of the Association moved to Palace Yard; the section crossing by Westminster Bridge preceded by a man carrying on his shoulder the great parchment roll containing upwards of 100,000 signatures, inscribed on different skins tacked together the night before by a tailor. The section which passed over London Bridge had the longest route, a three-mile journey through the City; its leader was one of Gordon's chief links in the City of London, Alderman Bull, MP for the City. This detachment interrogated passers-by who were not wearing blue cockades and was later claimed to have been swollen by hangers-on recruited from the City and Spitalfields.[64]

Between half-past two and three o'clock in the afternoon, the crowd reassembled in Palace Yard. Some crowded into Westminster Hall and seeing Dunning, the seconder of the Bill for Catholic Relief, addressing the Court of King's Bench, they interrupted his speech. They then blocked up the avenues to the Lords, from which they were rebuffed by the door-keepers. By now the crowd was boisterously unruly: members attending the Lords or the Commons were forced to join in cries of 'No Popery'; known supporters had their coaches drawn to the doors of the House, while opponents were pelted with mud, insulted and maltreated, usually to tumultuous cries of 'No Popery'. The proposer of the Catholic Relief Bill, George Savile, had his coach demolished, and the Archbishop of York was covered in mud; the Bishop of Lincoln had the wheels taken off his coach and was half throttled; Lord Bathurst, Lord President of the Council, lost his wig; Lord Mansfield, the Chief Justice, had his coach windows smashed. A rush was made at Lord North and before he was rescued he lost his hat to a man who opened the carriage door. Inside the Lords could be heard the sounds of the crowd thundering on the doors, while battered, shaken, and dishevelled peers arrived in dribs and drabs to report on the state of the crowd; Lord Ashburnham, for example, was dragged into the House over the heads of the crowd. At half-past eight the

Lords adjourned and Lord Stormont, the Minister of State for the South, called for military assistance to free the Commons.

In the lower House Gordon informed members that he had a petition with 120,000 signatures and moved for it to be brought up, seconded by Alderman Bull. In the ensuing debate, Gordon frequently left the chamber and addressed the crowds from the gallery stairs, giving them news of the progress of events and also the names of those opposing the petition. Eventually, however, he reported that the debate was adjourned until Tuesday, but that he expected the repeal of the Act and therefore urged the crowd to depart; he was also reported to have warned them 'to beware of evil-minded persons, who would mix amongst them to incite them to mischief, the blame of which would be imputed to them'. Many members were increasingly irritated at the proceedings; Colonel Holroyd was reported to have warned Gordon: 'My Lord George, do you intend to bring your rascally adherents into the House of Commons? If you do, the first man of them that enters, I will plunge my sword, not into his, but into your body.' Henry Herbert followed Gordon about the House, claiming that at the first entry of the mob he would kill him instantly. Some of the more respectable members of the crowd had already left, when the intervention of the Guards allowed the members of the Commons to disperse at about eleven in the evening.

A section of the crowd, however, moved off to attack Catholic property. The chapel attached to the Sardinian embassy in Duke Street, Lincoln's Inn Fields, and that attached to the Bavarian embassy in Warwick Street, St James's were attacked. The former was burned to the ground and the other ransacked and its contents burned in the street. Attempts by groups of rioters to attack the Portuguese chapel and the Moorfields district, with its large Irish Catholic population, were prevented by the troops and several rioters arrested. Gordon, meanwhile, had left the Commons in the company of Alderman Bull and retired for the evening, taking no part in the night's proceedings. Saturday was relatively quiet; although crowds gathered outside a Catholic chapel in Little Moorfields, no disturbance took place. On the following day, Sunday 4 June, the crowd assembled at nine in the morning and broke the windows of the chapel; in the evening the building was pillaged and the contents burned in the street.

The conduct of the Lord Mayor at this point was open to serious question. It was widely alleged that he had allowed the mob to go about its business unimpeded, even at one point encouraging them. The Mayor, on the other hand, later explained that he had found his constables unwilling to attack the mob, and that although he had called up military assistance from the Tower, the commander offered him only seventy-three men and even these were sent in small detachments. Lord Stormont eventually accepted this explanation and issued fresh orders to the commander at the Tower. Nonetheless the suspicion remained that the City authorities were holding back from intervening in a cause with which they sympathised. One marshalman openly refused to obey a summons to deal with the rioters, declaring that he would not go to protect 'any such Popish rascals'.[65]

On Monday 5 June a crowd paraded in front of Gordon's house in Welbeck Street bearing a pulpit and other trophies taken from the various chapels, before burning them in the nearby fields. In the evening parties of rioters moved into the eastern parishes, heading for the Catholic districts in Wapping and Spitalfields. A Catholic chapel in Nightingale Street was set on fire and the priests' house ransacked. Troops were reported to have been present with a justice of the peace, but to have done nothing to intervene. Houses and a school were attacked in Moorfields and another school demolished in Hoxton. The mob also turned its attention to the justices involved in arresting men for the attacks on the Sardinian chapel. The houses of Mr Rainsforth in Clare Street and of Mr Maberly, in Little Queen Street were attacked and demolished; at midnight a mob attacked George Savile's house in Leicester Square, damaging the windows, railings, and some of the furniture before the Guards intervened. Burke's house too was threatened and he began to sort out his most valuable papers in order to effect an escape, but a party of troops arrived and prevented any attack.

When parliament met on Tuesday 6 June large crowds, festooned with blue cockades, assembled outside. Burke, whose property had escaped the night before, was accosted even before he reached the House, being asked to promise to vote against Catholic relief. So pressing did the crowd become that he was forced to draw his sword to protect himself. At twenty to one in the morning, Lord Stormont had requested extra troops from the Commander-in-Chief, Lord Amherst, and these had begun to operate in the metropolis. In the City too, the Lord Mayor was requested by the Court of Aldermen to take effective measures against further rioting.[66] In spite of these precautions, a party of 500 congregated outside Lambeth Palace and made repeated attempts to enter the gates; when prevented from doing so they milled about and forced the inhabitants to call on the soldiers for assistance. At noon, several groups of rioters assembled at a shop in Moorfields and destroyed the contents. Outside the Houses of Parliament, Foot and Horse Guards provided avenues for members to attend unmolested, although the crowd continued to parade about with flags, music, and assorted weaponry. A detachment of the crowd tried to break through the troops to the Queen's House but were prevented. Meanwhile the Commons had again adjourned debate on Catholic relief and concentrated on a series of resolutions to deal with the rioters of the previous days.

About five o'clock Justice Hyde read the Riot Act and ordered the Horse Guards to disperse the crowds outside parliament. One of the crowd hoisted a red and black flag and shouted 'To Hyde's house a-hoy', and the crowd surged off to St Martin's Street where Hyde's house was located and turned its furniture into the street where it was devoured by half a dozen bonfires. Some troops under an Ensign attempted to stop them, but the jeers of the crowd proved too much and the soldiers retreated without interfering. The crowd kept a bonfire blazing in Leicester Fields until two in the morning, forcing the inhabitants to illuminate their windows. By then, however, the majority of the rioters had moved to Newgate where the rioters from 2 June were lodged. On the way a group destroyed the Bow Street police office of Sir John Fielding, using sticks, iron bars and choppers to force an entrance. The crowd that arrived at Newgate was also well supplied with crowbars, chisels, and ladders. The keeper's house was set on fire, the prison gates broken open, and the ten-year-old building set on fire when the prisoners had been released. A party of a hundred constables who attempted to interfere were encircled by the crowd, beaten up, disarmed, and their staves used as extra firebrands. Gordon made an appearance in his coach, being dragged by a large crowd of 500; passing Newgate as the riots were in full spate, he called on the mob to stop, but to no avail and that evening, he lodged at Bull's house, unable to control his followers.

The same evening the crowd attacked Clerkenwell, Bridewell and the New Prison, releasing the captives. Lord Mansfield's house was another target and its contents were destroyed, even though the soldiers opened fire killing several of the mob; an attack on Lord North's house by a mob brandishing torches and bundles of faggots was frustrated at one o'clock on the morning of Wednesday 7 June by the intervention of a detachment of the Light Horse. Other houses of Catholics in Bunhill Row and Golden Lane were also destroyed and the Ship Alehouse in Gate Street and a Catholic school in Little Russell Street were also attacked. The same evening the King urged Lord North to deal vigorously with the riots and to use 'exemplary punishment' on the rioters. Responding to widespread criticism at the inactivity of the City authorities, the Lord Mayor wrote to the Secretary of State requesting additional military aid and was assured that this would be made available, at the same time, he was urged to take steps to protect the Bank of England, widely rumoured as the next target of the mob.

This day, 'Black Wednesday', marked the culmination of the riots. In many parts of the metropolis, houses, shops, alehouses, and other premises belonging to Roman Catholics came under attack. The City was galvanised into action: the Court of Common Council was summoned; the sheriffs raised the *posse comitatus*; the services of a Military Association were accepted; officers of the City Militia offered their assistance and were put under the command of the sheriffs. During the afternoon two assaults were made on the Bank of England, but the rioters were repulsed. King's Bench and the Fleet Prisons were set alight, and at one point thirty-six fires were raging in the City. In Broad Street, the Honourable Artillery Company and the London Military Association fired on the mob, killing several.[67] In the East End the major targets were public houses in Golden Lane and Whitechapel; one of the most spectacular incidents came at the premises of Thomas Langdale, a wealthy Catholic distiller, containing an estimated 120,000 gallons of gin. Throughout the day Langdale had been pressing money and drink on the crowds in order to buy time, but as dusk fell his house and premises were fired, igniting the great vats storing liquor. Over twenty houses were destroyed in the blaze which was described as throwing into the air 'a pinnacle of flame resembling a volcano'. A number of rioters were killed when they attempted to loot the burning buildings and men, women, and children were observed drinking the burning alcohol as it ran down the gutters or collected in pools on the street.

While these events provided a lurid climax, the authorities were busy mobilising troops with which to suppress the disturbances. The number of troops on the march towards the capital grew steadily during the week, and there were several thousand in and around the capital by Black Wednesday. Regiments of every description were hurried into the metropolis, the Northumberland Militia making a forced march of twenty-five miles in order to arrive in time to take part in the defence of the Bank of England. Because of an acute shortage of barrack accommodation the troops were bivouacked in the parks, turning Hyde Park into an armed camp. The ground was cleared for the freer use of the troops against the rioters when on Wednesday morning the Privy Council had wrung from the Attorney-General the crucial opinion that the troops could fire on rioters without the Riot Act having been read. 'Then so let it be done,' was the King's pithy comment. A Proclamation was prepared, issued in Thursday's newspapers, 'exhorting all our loving subjects to preserve the peace', and warning that 'it is necessary, from the circumstances before-mentioned, to employ the military force . . . for the immediate suppression of such rebellious and traitorous attempts'.

In the City, however, Common Council was debating the question of an appeal to Parliament to repeal Savile's Act. A resolution was passed, even as the riots worsened, that the repeal of the Act would be 'the most probable means of immediately quieting the minds of the people'.[68] Thus, much to the anger of the administration, the City appeared to be stirring the discontent to new heights by taking the part of the Protestant Association and the mob. Indeed, when a messenger arrived to inform Common Council that military law had been established by the King's Proclamation, Wilkes showed a flash of his old radicalism by demanding that the messenger be committed, but nobody seconded him. Several members of Common Council who had taken a relatively tolerant attitude towards the mob as a means of forcing the hands of the administration, now realised that the situation was getting out of hand; an informant wrote to Lord Stormont that 'Mr Alderman Wilkes, however moderate before, upon my appearance with Mr Thorp, began to grow active and take up the lesson of loyalty. . . . There are, I am persuaded, many of those who were active in spiriting up the mob to commit devastation that have now changed sides.'

Judging from the actions of Wilkes and other city politicians, this appears remarkably accurate, for shortly after the Common Council meeting at six in the evening the bulk of the members, including Wilkes, reported to the Guildhall to take their orders for the defence of the City.

During the later afternoon and early evening, rioters had fired the New Gaol on the Surrey side of the river. The toll-keepers' houses on Blackfriars Bridge were the next target; they were soon reduced to ashes and the toll money carried off, but not before many of the rioters had been killed. Mobs coming into the City were broken up by the London Military Association, but reassembled and attacked the Bank at about eleven o'clock, led by brewer's drayman riding a horse stolen from Newgate Prison. Several volleys of musket fire were required before the attack was beaten off. Wilkes himself shouldered a musket and entered in his diary:

> Fired 6 or 7 times on the rioters at the end of the Bank towards Austin Friars, and towards the middle of the Bank. Killed two rioters directly opposite to the great gate of the Bank; several others in Pig Street and Cheapside.[69]

The fighting raged on into the night. Another assault on the Bank between three and four o'clock in the morning by a mob armed with muskets was dispersed by the Horse and Foot Guards in the neighbouring streets.

On Thursday morning, parliament met briefly and then adjourned until the 19th. Rioting continued in Southwark, Bermondsey, and the City. But the riots were dying down, with an estimated 10,000 troops now in the capital as well as several militia regiments and groups of armed volunteers. The troops went about removing blue flags and cockades and Wilkes himself helped to round up rioters and place them in gaol. On Friday morning, 9 June, the Lords of the Council issued a warrant for the arrest of Gordon, who was taken from his house in Welbeck Street and lodged in the Tower.

Even as the riots were being concluded, the City broke into an acrimonious dispute with the administration about the arms of the London Association. The Government chose to decide that the London Association was unauthorised to carry arms and ordered that they should give them up. The Association protested, claiming that the Bill of Rights permitted every Protestant subject to bear arms, and demanded a copy of the order. When this was produced the Court of Aldermen appealed to Lord Bathurst, the president of the Council, who eventually conceded that the arms could be retained provided the association did not muster as an armed body without the King's commission.[70]

The cost of the riots was considerable: 210 people were killed outright and 75 died subsequently in hospital. The legal toll was smaller: of 450 arrested, 62 were sentenced to death, of whom 25 were eventually hanged and 12 others imprisoned. Subsequently individuals received compensation to the value of over £70,000, and damage to public buildings was estimated at over £30,000. Both in terms of the human cost and the physical damage, the riots were easily the most serious of the eighteenth century. But in spite of their extraordinary effect, they bore many of the characteristics of other disturbances in eighteenth-century

London. Rudé has shown that those rioters for which we have information represented a fairly typical cross-section of the working population and 'do not appear, in the main, to have belonged to the very poorest sections of the working population'. The initial objects of attack were Roman Catholics, drawing upon the tradition of xenophobia and 'gut patriotism' observed on many occasions in the past. But in the course of the disturbances, the attacks tended to be made upon wealthy rather than poor Catholics; they had not so much the character of a 'pogrom' aimed indiscriminately at Roman Catholics of every class, as an assault on symbols of authority, the prisons, the Bank, toll-gates, and the houses of wealthy supporters of the Catholic Relief Act.[71] The riots grew out of a not unfamiliar situation, a mass lobby of parliament in which the 'pressure from outdoors' was brought to bear on the deliberations within, but which then increasingly got out of hand. The ritual humiliation of the wealthy, intimidation, and a certain degree of 'levelling' rhetoric marked the first phase of the disturbances. But even when violence broke out, the rioters were remarkably discriminating. Particular objects of attack were sought out and, as in the Sacheverell riots, the mob went on to assault bigger targets, such as Newgate, with the necessary equipment, including crowbars, ladders, and axes. Catholic premises were sought out and dealt with even in the later stages of the disturbances when the mobs appeared to many observers to have passed out of all normal restraints. Thus the rioters ignored the districts in their possession in central London to go out to Kenwood to attack Mansfield's country residence, having already sacked his town house, and to Islington to wreck the country residence of Justice Hyde.

Rudé has shown clearly that the crowds were not solely concerned with indiscriminate plunder and looting, although these undoubtedly took place at several points in the proceedings. In fact, sections of the crowds seem to have conducted themselves in different ways. Some of the crowd which turned up in Palace Yard in the early stages of the disturbances had already set to pickpocketing and thieving, but even contemporaries were prepared to acknowledge that the rioters often acted with considerable discipline. Thus Horace Walpole recorded:

> One strange circumstance in the late delirium was the mixture of rage and consideration. In most of the fires the mob threw the furniture into the street, did not burn it *in* the houses; nay, made several small bonfires lest a large one should spread to buildings. They would not suffer [fire] engines to play on the devoted edifices; yet, the moment the objects were consumed, played the engines on contiguous houses on each side.[72]

At the attack on Langdale's distillers, often treated as the most desperate of the whole episode, the rioters showed sufficient restraint to allow the fire engines to play when it was realised that the flames were spreading out of control. So disciplined seemed some of their actions that it was widely believed that a 'hidden hand' directed them. They appeared to know where to proceed next, to obey 'captains', and to act in accordance with some preconceived design. Lord Mansfield spoke of 'a systematic plan to usurp the government of the country' and others sought potential conspirators in the ranks of the opposition, the Protestant Association, dissenters, the French, the Americans, or even the Papists themselves. None of these charges can be sustained; probably the crowds took their discipline from the tradition of semi-ritualised pageants and parades which played so prominent a part in London life in the eighteenth century. Some degree of collusion with City authorities and members of the Protestant Association is entirely possible, but the captains obeyed by the mob appear to have been leaders thrown up spontaneously in a way similar to many earlier occasions. No firm evidence of foreign or domestic conspiracy was ever revealed and the two handbills that appeared during the disturbances, *True Protestants No Turncoats* and *England in Blood,* though directed against Popery were not in themselves proof of a conspiracy to foment riots, but only of attempts to whip up support for the Protestant Association.

There is no evidence that food prices played a significant part in the disturbances of 1780. The year witnessed virtually no food riots in the country at large and was a moderate one for prices; the average price of wheaten bread in London was lower than many previous years and several of those which followed (Table 4.1).

Table 4.1

Average price of bread in London (old pence per 4 lb)

1777	6.6	1780	5.7
1778	6.5	1781	7.0
1779	5.5	1782	7.0

Even though the month of June was traditionally one of high prices and frequently disturbed by food riots in the country at large, the assize price for bread in London remained constant from January to June 1780 at 1s. 11d. for the peck loaf. Thus whatever discontents were realised in the Gordon Riots, they appear to have owed little to short-term movements of the price of food.[73]

Why did the Gordon Riots prove so extensive? Traditionally they have been regarded as evidence of the strength of anti-Catholic feeling in eighteenth-century England; an attitude which had its origins in the conflicts of the previous century and was to reappear on several occasions in the nineteenth, notably in the anti-Catholic disturbances of mid-Victorian Lancashire (see pp. 279–82) Eighteenth-century London had also seen evidence of anti-Irish rioting, in the 'Mother Gin' disturbances of the 1730s and the almost perennial brawls between English and Irish communities in the slum districts of the capital. As observed earlier, the strain of 'No-Popery' played an important part in the xenophobic and patriotic attitude characteristic of many eighteenth-century disturbances. However, Rudé has done much to show that the disturbances quickly tapped other sentiments, especially the social antagonisms which manifested themselves in the attacks and humiliations inflicted on the wealthy, the members of the House of Lords, prominent Ministers, and the symbols of authority. But the intensity of the riots owed more to fortuitous factors than to either the strength of anti-Catholic feeling or of social conflict. Lord George Gordon and his supporters in the City had appeared to license the mob to attack Catholic property, from which a more general outbreak of violence resulted. In addition, a number of purely technical features of the apparatus of public order allowed the riots to get out of control. They could probably have affected any disturbance earlier or later, but it happened to be the campaign of the Protestant Association which provided their occasion.

However unbalanced Gordon was later to become, the initial plan to orchestrate pressure 'without doors' was no more than had been exercised by earlier claimants to public attention. The attacks on members approaching parliament were very similar to the uproar that had occurred during the Excise Crisis and during the Wilkes affair; the initial assaults on Catholic property were not dissimilar to those made over half a century before against dissenters during the Sacheverell riots. For a day or two at least, until parliament eventually postponed its sitting for a fortnight, Gordon could believe that by keeping up the popular clamour, he might force the Ministry to concede to the demands of the Protestant Association. On a number of occasions he appeared on the streets during the disturbances and attempted to stop the rioters from endangering the cause by indiscriminate violence. Outside Newgate on Tuesday evening, Gordon was reported to have urged the rioters to go home with the words, 'While you behave in this unpeaceful way nothing in your petition can be complied with; the House will never consent to it'. On the morning of Wednesday, 7 June, he sought an audience with the King 'because it would be of effectual service in suppressing the riots', but the King refused to see him. Later in the day, Gordon was called to a house in Colman Street by Alderman Pugh which was being threatened by rioters and the officer in charge of soldiers drawn up there allowed him to address the crowd who had already begun the demolition. Gordon urged them to disperse and signed a document testifying that the proprietor of the house was 'a staunch and worthy friend of the cause'. He also appeared outside the Bank of England that evening and urged the populace to stop their attack, offering to stand by with one of the army officers in an attempt to end the disturbances, but the officer refused to believe him. At his trial for high treason in February 1781 Gordon's defence hinged upon his intentions during the initial lobby of parliament. In his charge to the jury, Lord Mansfield put the issue in a nutshell when he said 'If there was no intent of intimidation, either in the mob or prisoner, then he is to be acquitted. If you find he has any hand in inciting the people to commit those acts of violence, and that he intended it, you will find him guilty.' Among the evidence which helped the jury to bring in a verdict of 'Not Guilty' was Gordon's demeanour when told that disorderly elements were assembling in Palace Yard: he was reported to have decided at that point to advise most of the crowd not to attend Parliament.[74]

Equally, the Protestant Association distanced itself from the riotous consequences of the campaign. After the riots had been suppressed, the Protestant Association made its position clear in an advertisement placed in newspapers on 12 June:

> The Protestant Association think it their duty, as loyal subjects and members of Civil Society, in the most public manner to disavow any connection with those lawless rioters who have, for several days past, under pretence of opposing Popery, and promoting the success of the Protestant Petition, committed the most flagrant and dreadful depredations in and about the Metropolis. They cannot but feel the deepest concern for the distress that has been brought on many individuals by such unprecedented and illegal proceedings, and hereby publicly declare their utmost abhorrence of such atrocious conduct.[75]

Gordon's true intentions will probably never be known with complete certainty. Perhaps the nearest he came to explaining himself was in the comment which he made to his followers as they crowded the lobbies: 'The King is a gracious monarch, and when he hears that the people are gathering ten miles round he will send private orders to his Ministers to repeal the Popery Act'. His later actions in attempting to subdue the riots when they got out of hand were entirely consistent with this attempt to orchestrate extra-parliamentary pressure; unfortunately he had by that time little authority with the majority of the rioters, many of whom had nothing to do with the Protestant Association. Wittingly or not, Gordon provided the occasion for an outbreak of violence and destruction in the capital unprecedented between the Great Fire and the Blitz. Like Wilkes, Gordon appeared to legitimise popular demonstrations and to provide an opportunity for some sport with the rich and powerful. Romilly took a not unshrewd view of events when he wrote: 'The monstrous excesses appear to have been the accidental effects of the ungovernable fury and licentiousness of a mob, who gathered courage from their numbers, and, having ventured on one daring act, found their only safety in universal havoc and devastation.'[76]

Not only Gordon, but also the City politicians should be regarded as playing an important part in encouraging the development of the riots out of an ostensibly peaceful demonstration. The City politicians were culpable on at least two different, but related, counts. Several were undoubtedly sympathetic to the cause of the Protestant Association and were prepared to add an air of legitimacy to the actions of the rioters. In his exhaustive study of the riots, de Castro put his view of their behaviour trenchantly: 'When the rabble perceived that the City magistrates were fully prepared to give the petitioning enthusiasts all the rope they required, their self-appointed leaders seized the opportunity and snatched the rope.'

Aldermen Pugh, Sawbridge and Bull played a prominent part in the Protestant Association. Gordon lodged with Alderman Bull during part of the disturbances and was at one point using his coach to convey himself about the capital. The action of Common Council in passing a resolution against Catholic relief while the disturbances were at their height was widely regarded as an encouragement to the rioters; moreover, when the riots were over and Parliament re-assembled on the 19th, the City insisted on presenting its petition. Alderman Bull, seconding, left no doubt as to his sympathies:

> Although through the baneful influence of the Crown, the
> former petitions have been spurned at and trampled upon, I yet
> hope the House will comply and without delay, lest the
> multitude lately at your doors should suspect that under the
> specious mask of moderation and tenderness for the Papists we
> have a design to sacrifice the security of the Protestant religion
> to the shrine of Popery'.

The scarcely veiled threat, was symptomatic of the attitude of Gordon's supporters in the City.[77]

More seriously, it was many of the same men, as magistrates, who had been in charge of the civil power at the initial stage of the disturbances and had appeared to encourage the rioters by their tolerant attitude, an attitude which seemed to derive from sympathy with the rioters' cause. The constables from Bull's ward were actually seen wearing the blue cockades of the Protestant Association and the Lord Mayor was reported to have unburdened himself of the comment on Sunday, 4 June, that 'the mob had got hold of some people and some furniture they did not like and were burning them, and where was the harm in that'. Whatever difficulties the City magistracy claimed to be operating under as the riots worsened – and they highlighted the inadequacy of military support and the threat to their own property – there remained the clear suspicion that they refused to act with the necessary determination to prevent the riots gaining a hold.[78]

In addition, the riots were assisted by the widespread confusion about the law of riot. Not only were several magistrates sympathetic with the rioters, but even those who were not feared that any severe action taken might rebound upon them. Thus the magistrates frequently stood by watching the disturbances without taking effective action. As a later writer commented:

> What appeared most to excite the public indignation was the
> criminal supineness of the Magistracy of London during these
> horrible commotions, apparently threatening to lay the
> Metropolis of the Empire level with the ground, and which
> actually presented in many parts the image of a city stormed
> and sacked . . . it most assuredly was not forgotten that Mr

Gillan, an excellent Magistrate of the County of Surrey, was tried in the Old Bailey for his life, in consequence of the order given by him at the riots in St George's Fields, A.D. 1768, for the military to fire after long and patiently enduring the severest provocations from the rioters, and twice reading the riot act.[79]

It was widely believed by both magistrates and officers that troops could not be used until the Riot Act had been read, and even then a chain of prosecutions for murder against justices and soldiers had taught both to act warily. Soldiers, in particular, were extremely reluctant to interfere without the authority of a magistrate and before the reading of the Riot Act. Another confusion arose from the belief that an hour had to be allowed after the reading of the Act before action could be taken. As a result a kind of paralysis affected the soldiers and magistrates in the early days of the riots as their uncertainty permitted the situation to escalate. It was not until the Attorney-General and, later, Lord Mansfield made a clear declaration of the law that the rioters were dealt with firmly. Even so, confusion about the law of riot remained through the period and was to recur as a source of dispute in the nineteenth century.[80]

The political significance of the Gordon Riots is undeniable. Throughout the eighteenth century, but especially from the 1760s, various forms of extra-parliamentary pressure had been developing. At the time of the Gordon Riots Lord North's administration was also being faced by the demands of the Yorkshire Association and the Irish movement. Both these movements, in common with the Protestant Association, tended to resort to a degree of sabre-rattling in an attempt to obtain their ends. Hence Herbert Butterfield regarded the latter years of the eighteenth century as a period in which these various movements had not yet achieved 'recognised channels' to translate their activities into effective political pressure. As a result, they tended to rely upon 'forms of menace' and 'unspecified threats' which might easily produce an 'accident'. The Protestant Association's campaign occurred at a time

> when the paralysis that afflicted the arms of government, the bitterness of the conflict amongst the governing classes, the continued disparagement of the houses of commons, and the special problems of the capital cities were weakening the brakes of the whole vehicle, making traditional inhibitions less effective, and robbing authority of its former majesty.

Thus the 'accident which many people feared in this period ... did actually occur when the Gordon Riots reduced London to terror'.[81]

The immediate impact of the disturbances was to strengthen the administration of Lord North. Although criticised at first for their tardiness in suppressing the disturbances, the restoration of order 'vindicated the authority of government and raised the prestige of the King'. One effect was to overshadow the campaign being waged by the Yorkshire Association for parliamentary reform. By 1780 the petitions against Catholic relief completely outnumbered those in favour of economical or parliamentary reform. The Gordon Riots were gathering momentum even as the Duke of Richmond introduced a Bill providing for annual parliaments and universal suffrage over the age of eighteen; the riots undoubtedly contributed to the hostile reception given to the proposal and the Lords' refusal to allow him leave to introduce the Bill. The disturbances served to reinforce the antagonism felt by moderates towards petitioning, associations, and the whole process of extra-parliamentary agitation, seeming to fulfil the fears of Speaker Norton who confessed that 'he totally disapproved of the committees and associations. If they were not illegal, they were, in his opinion, extremely improper, and might terminate in consequences which every good man, upon cool reflection, would wish to avoid.'[82] As well as discrediting the reform movement and its methods the disturbances divided the opposition, helping to destroy the uneasy coalition of forces under Shelburne and Rockingham.[83]

The Gordon Riots had longer-term importance. For politicians in the City of London the spectre of mob violence was one which would make them more hesistant about the mobilisation of popular clamour in the future, though it was not to exclude it altogether. Dr Sutherland quotes Joseph Brasbridge, who commented: 'From that moment . . . I shut my ears against the voice of popular clamour.'[84] The riots certainly severed many of the links between City radicalism and the mob. The deliberate incitement of a mob was something which after 1780 would only be embarked on by the most desperate or the most foolish. For the country at large, the Gordon Riots formed part of the consciousness which people carried into the revolutionary era. As I. R. Christie has remarked: 'For a moment the governing class found itself faced with the nightmare of mob rule, and even between bitter political opponents there was a reknitting of the ranks in defence of the established order. The riots were a warning that there were limits beyond which public campaigns for discrediting the government could not be carried without serious risk.'[85] Peter Brown has written that the riots helped to frustrate the campaign for parliamentary reform by destroying support for even moderate reform, and prepared the ground for the reaction which greeted the French Revolution.[86] Many of the worst fears of conservatives and the propertied were realised in these disorders and these fears were to be emphasised in the years which saw the toppling of the French monarchy and the threat of invasion.

5 Food riots in England

The most persistent and widespread disturbances in eighteenth-century England were those associated with food. Food riots covered a wide range of activities, such as stopping the movement of grain, the seizure and resale of grain, flour and bread at 'fair' prices, attacks on mills and warehouses, the spoiling of foodstuffs, and various degrees of tumultuous assembly to force dealers or local authorities to reduce prices. Disturbances of this kind can be found in many parts of Europe between the sixteenth and twentieth centuries, often sharing common features, such as the ritual of price-fixing, the use of ceremonial elements, a relatively high degree of discipline among the participants, and concentration on those specifically concerned with the trade in foodstuffs and the setting of prices usually occurring in years of high prices.[1] The fluctuation of prices of wheat and bread are shown in Table 5.1.

The origin of food riots in England is shrouded in obscurity and there is, at present, no conclusive evidence of such disturbances before the 1520s. This may reflect more on the inadequacy of the available sources and the absence of detailed research than on lack of a medieval tradition of food rioting in England. Nonetheless, we know that periods of scarcity and high prices led to food disturbances in 1527, 1551, 1587, 1595-6, 1622-3, 1630-1, and 1647-8. Although a recent study has concluded that years of dearth in early modern England 'were not marked by widespread rioting', the authors have identified forty incidents from central government records between 1585 and 1660. A study of Kent between 1558 and 1640 has also provided evidence of food rioting during the early modern period, especially in the years 1594-7 and 1630-1. It was not until the end of the seventeenth century that food riots became more common, with disturbances in 1662-3, 1674, 1681, and 1693; in the last of these there were food riots at Worcester, Shrewsbury, Lyme, Wearmouth, Oxford, Northampton, Chipping Norton and Banbury. But it was during the eighteenth century that food disturbances became most common, occurring with increasing frequency as the century wore on and only dying out in the Victorian period. A number of nationwide waves of food rioting have been identified after 1700, such as those of 1709-10, 1727-9, 1739-40, 1756-7, 1766-8, 1772-3, 1783, 1795-6, 1799-1801, 1810-13, 1816-18.[2]

Table 5.1 *Prices of wheat per bushel at Windsor and of the quartern loaf in London*

	Wheat		Bread		Wheat		Bread		Wheat		Bread
	s.	d.	d.		s.	d.	d.		s.	d.	d.
1700	4	9		1734	5	3		1768	6	11¾	6½
1701	4	2		1735	5	9	5½	1769	5	6¾	6
1702	3	7		1736	5	3	5¼	1770	6	10½	6½
1703	5	3		1737	4	7½	5¼	1771	7	3	7¾
1704	4	4		1738	4	8	5	1772	8	6	8
1705	3	6		1739	4	11	6	1773	8	3	7½
1706	3	3		1740	7	10½	7¼	1774	8	0	8
1707	3	10		1741	4	6	5½	1775	6	1½	6½
1708	6	6		1742	3	9	4¼	1776	6	0	6½
1709	11	6		1743	2	11	4½	1777	7	3	7¼
1710	8	0		1744	3	1	4¼	1778	5	4½	6
1711	7	3		1745	3	8	4¾	1779	5	0	5¾
1712	4	9		1746	4	6	5½	1780	6	9	7¼
1713	8	0		1747	4	1	5	1781	6	9	7
1714	4	10		1748	4	9	6	1782	8	1½	8¼
1715	6	3		1749	4	9	5¼	1783	7	0	7¼
1716	6	0		1750	4	3	5¼	1784	7	1½	7½
1717	5	9		1751	5	6	6	1785	6	6	6¼
1718	4	6		1752	5	3	5½	1786	6	0	6½
1719	4	8		1753	5	6	6½	1787	7	0	6½
1720	4	9		1754	4	0	5	1788	6	9	6¾
1721	4	4¼		1755	4	6	5	1789	8	0	7¼
1722	4	6		1756	6	9	7½	1790	7	6¾	7½
1723	4	6		1757	6	6	7¼	1791	6	3	6½
1724	4	9		1758	5	6	6	1792	7	6	7¼
1725	6	10½		1759	4	8	5	1793	6	4	7½
1726	5	0		1760	4	9	5½	1794	7	0	7½
1727	5	10½		1761	3	9¾	4½	1795	11	6	12¼
1728	6	8		1762	4	9	5½	1796	8	0¾	8½
1729	5	6		1763	5	6	6	1797	6	9	9½
1730	4	6		1764	6	3	6½	1798	6	9	8
1731	4	0		1765	6	6	7	1799	11	7	13
1732	3	3		1766	6	6	8	1800	16	0	17½
1733	3	6		1767	8	3	8¼	1801	10	0	10

Source: J. Marshall, *Digest of All the Accounts* (Statistical display of finances, &c.), pp. 88–9. Prices of wheat at Michaelmas, of bread at beginning of each mayoralty on 9 November.

The preconditions for the frequent appearance of food rioting in this period were the dependence of the majority of the population on a limited range of staple foods, of which the most important was bread. Eighteenth-century budgets make it clear that bread formed the single most important item of diet and consequently of expenditure for the working population. At the end of the eighteenth century, Sir Frederick Eden estimated from a survey of workhouse dietaries and family budgets that an average of between a pound and a pound and a half of bread was consumed per day. Although skilled workers were able to afford a wider range of foodstuffs, including meat and dairy products, bread still took up a considerable proportion of the weekly budget; Rudé has calculated that London artisans spent about a quarter of their income on bread alone and that the average weekly consumption of London labourers was about eight pounds of bread per week; nor did the situation alter very much in the early nineteenth century, Cobbett claiming that a family of five, including one baby, would require five pounds of bread per day.[3] The bread consumed was largely wheaten bread by the mid-eighteenth century. In 1765 Charles Smith estimated that out of a population of six million people in England and Wales, 3,750,000 ate wheaten bread, 880,000 ate rye (or the rye-wheat mixture 'maslin'), 739,000 ate barley, and 633,000 oats.[4] Oats, barley and rye remained important in the poorer areas of the West and North until the early nineteenth century, but were increasingly overtaken by the more expensive wheaten bread in larger towns and cities. Potatoes were cultivated as a cheap food for the poor from early in the eighteenth century, but were not regarded as providing a complete alternative to the staple bread grains except in periods of extreme scarcity.[5]

By the eighteenth century England possessed a highly developed trade in foodstuffs, of which the grain trade was easily the most important. In normal years the total grain consumption of the country was estimated at about one quarter per person per year. Until the 1750s, England was a net exporter of grain, but from mid-century domestic production had to be supplemented by a growing quantity of imports as population growth began to outstrip supply, especially in years of harvest failure. Between 1775 and 1786 the annual average quantity of wheat imported was 180,000 quarters, representing about 2½ per cent of total requirements; during the next decade, the figure rose to 325,000 quarters, and reached 700,000 quarters in the decade 1799-1810. Apart from population growth, which made an insufficient harvest more likely, an increasing urban population was more and more dependent on a market economy to supply them with food. During the course of the eighteenth century the chain between consumer and food producer became steadily longer and more specialised. As early as the Tudor period, London's large urban population was stimulating a highly developed trade in foodstuffs in the home counties; by the eighteenth century, the capital's supply network for grain embraced much of southern England and reached even farther afield for more specialised produce. Existing manufacturing populations, such as the Cornish tinners and the cloth-workers of East Anglia and the West Country, were, like the growing commercial cities and towns, already dependent on a relatively complex network to provide them with basic foodstuffs. With the growth of commerce and industry, especially in the latter half of the eighteenth century and the early nineteenth, larger sections of the population became totally dependent on an efficient marketing system.[6]

Relatively few people in the eighteenth century actually produced grain for their own consumption, most were dependent on buying grain, flour, or meal from dealers. Grain might be taken to a professional miller or to a manorial mill, or flour bought direct from the miller who purchased the grain himself. One of the principal features of the commercialisation of the food trade in eighteenth-century England was the rise of the professional miller to a position of dominance. The transition from home baking to the purchase of ready-baked bread was also taking place in these years, although the development varied considerably from one part of the country to another. Professional bakers were already well-established in London at the beginning of the eighteenth century, but did not penetrate many rural areas and some of the new manufacturing centres until the early years of the nineteenth century.[7]

The location of food disturbances

Two features stand out in the incidence of food rioting in England, the influence of the communications network and the distribution of the manufacturing population. A very substantial portion of all disturbances took place at ports, market towns, or transhipment points. This factor seems to have operated whether disturbances occurred in relatively prosperous or marginal areas; indeed, one of the heaviest concentrations of disturbances took place in East Anglia, where grain was frequently being moved by cart or coastal vessel to the capital. In times of high prices the sight of grain being moved out of an area or shipped from small ports could easily excite popular indignation. As early as 1565 the town of Cambridge protested to the Privy Council about grain being moved to London, and again in 1581 there were complaints against the effects of water transport moving grain from country areas.[8] These complaints multiplied with the development of the transport network in the seventeenth and eighteenth centuries.

Water transport played the most important part in moving grain about the country, as the principal means of moving a bulky commodity at reasonable cost. But ease of transport was a mixed blessing in times of scarcity for it meant that grain could be taken out of an area as easily as it could be brought in. Improved water and road communications were bringing more of the inland counties into the larger markets of London and the export trade, and many local authorities were aware that this might deprive them of their natural reservoir of supplies in times of scarcity. This explains the hostility of some corporations towards canal and river improvements in the late seventeenth and eighteenth centuries; Nottingham Corporation, for example, opposed the Trent Navigation Bill which would have eased access to the town for bulky products because it feared that it would destroy the town's monopoly over local foodstuffs. The same concern was shown about the turnpike network. In 1769 Arthur Young commented that 'all the sensible people attributed the dearness of their country to the turnpike roads; and reason speaks the truth of their opinion . . . make but a turnpike road through their county and all the cheapness vanishes at once'![9] In the shortage of 1795-6, canals were blamed by one correspondent to the Home Office for opening up the inland areas to the national market, so that 'the whole Kingdom is become for the purpose of exportation, a seaport'. this view seems to have been taken by the Government itself during this scarcity, for it decided to send relief supplies of grain to the coastal districts in an attempt to keep grain in the inland counties.[10]

Thus the incidence of disorder bore a close relationship to the transport network. In 1766 the first incidents occurred in proximity to the western grain port of Lyme, where it was reported that the mob blamed exports for the high prices. Berkshire, another scene of disturbances, saw a great deal of grain passing through it. W. J. Shelton has written that: 'Always in times of crisis Berkshire felt the draining power of London. The upper Thames valley provided a readily accessible route to the leading grain exporting port in the country.'[11] The actions of rioters in the Midlands speak for themselves. After the disturbances in Birmingham, a 'well-armed' gang made its way along the route to the inland port of Stratford-upon-Avon, stopping all the grain wagons on the way and selling their contents.[12] Disorders were closely linked to the communications network in the shortages of 1795-6 and 1800-1. The most striking pattern overall is that of 1795-6, when at least fifty food disturbances took place at communication centres, either coastal ports, canal or river ports, or towns within easy carting distance of major population centres. In 1795 many of the disturbances took place at small ports such as Seaford, Chichester, Wells, Boston, and Wisbech. Others took place inland at canal or river termini, such as Bedford, Ipswich, Winchester, and Lewes,[13] and also at small market towns from which grain was normally carted to London, such as Hitchin, Halstead, Potters Bar, and Buntingford. In the Midlands a similar pattern emerged, for there were disturbances in the towns from which grain was being sent to Birmingham; at Tewkesbury a mob of women unloaded barges bound there, and in Burford carts bound for the same destination were forcibly unloaded. In the North the catchment area for south Lancashire was much disturbed, with riots in many of the small ports and market towns of North Wales, such as Abergele, Conway, Mold, and Denbigh. Most of these were explicit against the activities of dealers from Lancashire. In Carlisle there were disturbances against the export of grain by Liverpool dealers.[14]

Similarly in the shortage of 1800-1 a number of disturbances occurred at transhipment points, such as the disturbance at Midhurst at the end of the navigable section of the River Arun, and at ports such as Southampton, Plymouth, and Bristol. Through the subsequent shortages of 1810-13 and 1816-18 the communications factor continued to play a part. In 1816 serious disturbances took place around Ely, in an area which was one of the richest grain-producing areas in the country, but where grain was being taken out of the area in the pre-harvest months.[15]

Therefore in seeking a pattern for this period, one of the most important factors is the transport network and the relationship of local markets to those of London and the growing manufacturing towns. Although, as we shall see, there were many other factors which could influence the incidence of food riots, one of particular relevance was the impact of communications. This is particularly important in the case of East Anglia; the area least likely to suffer an absolute shortage of grain. It almost certainly enjoyed a surplus to its own requirement throughout the eighteenth century – nonetheless, as the main source of supply for the capital, it was frequently the most disturbed area of the country. The market towns of Essex, Suffolk, Norfolk, Cambridgeshire, and Huntingdonshire figure prominently in the various waves of food rioting after 1700.

Equally important was the presence of a large non-agricultural population, dependent on local market towns for supply and vulnerable to rapid fluctuations in prices. For much of the eighteenth century colliers were the most important such group. The Kingswood colliers, one of the most persistent groups of food rioters, took part in at least eight separate incidents, including almost every major wave of food riots. The Black Country colliers took a prominent part in frequent disturbances in the Midlands, while the miners of the Forest of Dean were active in 1756, 1795 and 1800. In the North-East it was pitmen and keelmen who attacked the Guildhall of Newcastle in 1740. In the riots of 1757 colliers from Ashton came into Manchester and attacked a mealhouse and some mills before being beaten off by troops, while the colliers from St Helen's marched into Prescot market to force reductions in prices. Their influence was still being felt in the early nineteenth century, with disturbances among the colliers in Radstock in 1817 and at Whitehaven in 1818.[16]

The Cornish tinners were another prominent group during the period, participating in every wave of disturbances. Riots broke out in Cornwall, in 1709, 1727-9, 1748, 1757, 1766, 1773, 1795-6, 1810-13, 1831 and 1847. Typically they involved the local miners coming into the market towns and small ports to obtain grain. A typical incident occurred in 1748 in Penryn, where

> the tinners, suspecting that some merchants had laid up vast quantities of corn for exportation, assembled in great numbers, men, women and children, and broke open one of the cellars and took thence 600 bushels of wheat. They then started to rob the country people carrying their corn to market, and afterwards returning to Penryn in great numbers, armed with clubs and bludgeons, threatened further mischief, till the soldiers sent for from Falmouth to quell the tumult fired upon them, by which two were killed and many wounded.[17]

Little had changed by the end of the century; for example, on 30 March 1796 five hundred tinners assembled in Penryn to force a reduction in the price of provisions, and the tinners continued to participate in food riots up to the middle of the nineteenth century.[18]

Cloth-workers formed another group with a long tradition of defending their interests by crowd activity. The textile centres of Yorkshire, the Midlands, and West Country were often vulnerable to sudden changes in prices. The weavers of the West Country and East Anglia were heavily involved in the food riots of 1766. Similarly in 1795, in South Devon, Honiton, Topsham, Ashburton, Totnes, Okehampton, and Chudleigh were amongst the first to react against high prices. Frome, a mining and weaving town in Somerset, was frequently disturbed in the period. It experienced food riots in 1757, 1766, 1795, 1810, and 1816. Bradford and Trowbridge in Wiltshire were also frequently disturbed. In the Midlands, Nottingham had about half a dozen food riots during the period, disturbances which can be clearly distinguished from wage disputes or machine-breaking. Similar conditions affected places such as Kidderminster, with riots in 1756, 1757, 1766(2), and 1800. The presence of groups of cloth-workers often marked a town out for disturbances when others remained tranquil. In 1800 the Witney weavers led disturbances in the town, whilst at Banbury in the same year stocking-weavers from the neighbouring village of Middleton Cheney were blamed for disturbances which lasted for several days.[19]

Groups of itinerant workmen were frequently blamed for disorder. The canal boatmen earned an unenviable reputation for participation in disorder of many kinds, and though they may simply have been a useful scapegoat for the local magistrates they were certainly involved in riots at Great Marlow in 1757 and at Banbury in 1800. In East Anglia in 1795 many of the food riots were not the work of the local population but of the canal 'bankers' who were engaged in building and repairing the dykes and canals of the Fens; they were said to have been responsible for the disturbances at Ely, Boston, and Wisbech. The riots in the Thames valley in 1766 were said to have been started by gangs of workmen engaged in building turnpikes, and at Stony Stratford in 1800 the 'navigators' building the Grand Junction Canal rioted over the price of bread and meat. These disturbances illustrated the precarious situation of groups of workmen in semi-rural conditions, where provisioning was often difficult, and completely dependent on the vagaries of the local market.[20]

Soldiers played a large part in the riots of 1795-6. Barracked and encamped all along the east and south coast to meet the threat of invasion, they seriously affected the local corn trade as well as the price of other provision. From Weymouth in 1795 a correspondent wrote that the area was accustomed to importing grain from the Isle of Wight, but that the soldiers encamped there had used up the surplus, and at King's Lynn on the east coast the local authorities complained that 700 soldiers and their families were exhausting the town of supplies.[21] The most spectacular evidence of the effect of the soldiers on local price levels was in South Devon in spring 1795, when the outward bound fleet was held up offshore for a number of weeks with around 25,000 men on board. A local correspondent pointed out that this was a number equal to the resident population of the towns and villages of that area.[22] The result was a rapid increase in the price of grain and other provisions; by 14 March the average price for a quarter of wheat in Devon was five shillings above the national average. Between 11 and 18 April the average price soared to seventy shillings, eight shillings above the national average. The result was a wave of rioting in the towns of South Devon and the Tamar valley, in which it was reported that the soldiers had taken an active part. The militia in particular were proved extremely riot-prone; newly raised, poorly disciplined, and often with their officers billeted far from the rank and file, they instigated a whole series of riots along the south and east coast in April 1795. Because their food allowance was fixed at fivepence a day they were vulnerable to the high level of prices which their presence aggravated.

The interplay of the communications network and the presence of a large non-agricultural population is reflected in the experience of the South-West, especially Cornwall, an area of marginal subsistence which maintained a precarious equilibrium between supply and demand. Although the fertile lands along the north coast, around Newquay, Padstow, and Camelford, and those near the Tamar, produced a surplus of wheat and barley, the mining districts of Poudre, Kerrier, Penwith, and Pydre produced virtually nothing for themselves. Thus a mid-eighteenth-century writer commented that 'in a plentiful year we may spare a little quantity for exportation, in a moderate year have enough for ourselves, in a year of scarcity not near a competency'.[23] The poverty of internal transport and the unproductive nature of agriculture in the mining districts made these workmen vulnerable to shortage; frequently their food supply seems to have broken down so that they were forced to march on the local market towns and ports in order to find grain. The poverty of inland communications, however, contrasted with the position of the small ports which dotted the coast, so that at the same time as it might be difficult to obtain food inland, grain might be being exported from coastal areas.[24] In periods of scarcity dealers from London often scoured the Cornish ports and give substance to the worst fears of the tinners, clay-workers, and clothiers of the inland districts. This complex of factors helped to make Cornwall one of the chief centres of food rioting in the country.

As well as places which were prone to disturbances, there were others which had fewer. The North-East, although not entirely undisturbed, appears to have had relatively few riots compared with areas such as Cornwall and East Anglia. Here the communications network seems to have helped food supply because the industrial towns were close to the coast and were often ports. For much of the eighteenth century, the northern counties of England as a whole were less disturbed than the south; in the great wave of food riots which spread through the country in 1766, for example, they had relatively few. A greater readiness to use other food grains, such as oats, barley and rye, as well the more extensive use of potatoes may have contributed to this relative tranquillity. Shelton has shown that magistrates in the North-East insisted on grain being put on sale in the open market to counter allegations of profiteering and withholding from market. The North too, was not always affected by the same weather as the South, nor was oats, its normal bread grain, so readily upset by heavier than average rainfall. In 1766 the North enjoyed the best harvest for corn for several years, whilst the southern counties were suffering from one of the worst. Less grain was moved from the North and this also reduced one of the major precipitants of disorder. It was only as the northern towns began to industrialise that they posed a greater problem of food supply.[25] Significantly, food disturbances did occur in the larger towns, such as Newcastle, Manchester, and Sheffield, and by 1783 there were disturbances in some of the smaller industrial communities such as Halifax, Huddersfield, and Rochdale.

Another area where food disturbances were surprisingly infrequent was the capital. The largest city in Europe by 1750, it was already ten times as large as the next largest in the British Isles. It posed acutely the problem of feeding a vast urban community at prices which would not excite popular commotion. Yet, as we have seen, it was largely dependent on the existing marketing arrangements for its food supply and the smooth functioning of the normal trade in foodstuffs. Moreover it had large bodies of workmen who had a strong tradition of collective action on religious or political issues. London would have seemed to present a potential danger-spot for popular food rioting, but in fact the most striking feature of these waves of food riots is their relative absence there. London shared in the major periods of high prices, 1740, 1756-8, 1766-8, 1772-3, 1794-5, 1800-1, 1810-13 and 1816-18, but witnessed only minor incidents of food rioting. George Rudé has commented that 'there was not in London – as there was in English rural districts, and for that matter, in Paris both before and during the Revolution – a close general concordance between high food prices and popular disturbances', and has suggested that because London was separated from the countryside by the semi-urban county of Middlesex, this might have absorbed the impact of food riots in neighbouring counties and prevented them from spreading into the capital. In addition, in contrast to Paris, the suburban area of Middlesex could prevent the inrush of people from country areas to the markets in the capital in search of grain.[26]

Probably most important, however, was a favourable position in the national food trade. London's basic advantage was its well-developed supply system and its dominant position as a market for much of southern England. As a result it could be supplied provided its normal channels of trade were left open. As early as the sixteenth century the central Government had made it a policy to provide for the London market by adopting a tolerant attitude to middlemen in the corn trade and taking any measures within its power to maintain the normal flow of grain to the capital.[27] Thus the Government's policy of refusing to interfere with

London's supply arrangements, and preserving the normal circulation of grain, effectively discriminated in favour of the capital, which was able to continue to draw on its traditional areas of supply and expand its catchment area without interference. London's magistrates devoted considerable attention to prices by watching the principal markets and fixing the Assize of Bread; if the situation demanded it, exemplary punishments of traders for one or other of the monopolistic offences or for failing to observe the Assize were usually sufficient to assure the populace that the authorities were vigilant and that the most excessive forms of profiteering would be dealt with. The Assize allowed the magistrates to mitigate the most severe fluctuations of the price of bread, at least in the short term, and maintain the psychological initiative in a period of scarcity. Extensive relief operations in the poorer areas of the capital were also taken, to provide cheap substitute foods such as soup or non-wheaten bread, which helped to overcome immediate hardship.[28]

There were, however, indications that the incidence of food rioting was shifting. In the seventeenth century food riots were most common in East Anglia, the Thames Valley, and the cloth towns of the West Country. This pattern remained well into the eighteenth century for relatively few disturbances took place in the North until the end of the century. By the Napoleonic Wars the manufacturing areas of the North and Midlands were more frequently disturbed, a pattern confirmed in the post-war disturbances of 1816–18.[29]

The food disturbances of the Regency period were the last really widespread waves to occur in England. Thereafter food riots became confined to two principal areas: the remoter marginal areas of the British Isles, including the South-West and some of the poorer urban slums. There were food riots in Cornwall in 1830–1, in 1847 (as well as in the Scottish Highlands), and in Devon in 1867.[30] In urban areas, there were attacks on food shops in Manchester in 1826 and in other parts of Lancashire in 1829. Provision shops were looted in the potteries in 1842, and in Liverpool in February 1855. Unemployment and distress also led to similar events in East London in 1855, the winter of 1860–1, and again in 1867.[31]

The participants

Food disturbances in eighteenth- and early nineteenth-century England were usually composed of a cross-section of the local inhabitants. As most took place in market towns or manufacturing centres, they tended to reflect urban populations rather than rural. In comparison with France, one of the most striking features was the relatively small part played by agricultural workers, although they did sometimes become involved after other groups.[32] Living on the land they had far less reason to fear absolute scarcity than their urban compatriots. There is evidence that in times of scarcity farmers withheld corn from market, whether to use as seed, for fear of disorder, or simply to profit from the rise in price, but it meant that country areas were rarely short of grain. Agricultural workers therefore had easier access to grain in times of shortage; there were several reports from harassed urban magistrates in 1795–6 that farmers were selling off what little grain was available for sale at artificially low prices to their labourers.[33] Even before the introduction of the Speenhamland system in 1795, the practice of subsidising or supplementing wages was quite common in the southern counties. With the spread of the practice of fixing poor relief in relation to the current price of bread or wheat, agricultural workers were effectively cushioned from fluctuations in food prices.

The major exception to the pattern in which farm-workers played little part in food rioting is the outbreak of disturbances in East Anglia in the spring of 1816, where agricultural labourers played the predominant part in the disturbances centred upon Ely, Littleport, and Downham. In this area, however, agricultural change had created a large population of wage-labourers, living in populous 'open' parishes.[34] In East Anglia the position of agricultural labourers most closely resembled that of those engaged in manufacturing, and it was significant that in 1816 they combined demands for a reduction in food prices with one for higher wages. Significantly, in the great wave of disturbances which spread over southern England in 1830–2, there were few instances of food rioting outside the South-West.[35]

Women played a prominent part in English food riots during this period. It was women who had to go to market and were faced with the stark imperatives of feeding their family and satisfying all the complex demands of preference and status that went into the family budget. At Olwen Hufton has written of eighteenth-century France: 'The woman had both to procure food and to cook it; all her husband had to do was eat what she prepared and judge whether he was hungry or not. What she got was often the result of hours of waiting.'[36] It is hardly surprising then that market riots were so often the province of women, it was they who felt most acutely the frustrations and anxieties of fluctuations in prices. Instances abound of the involvement of women in food riots: on 12 September 1800 the *Leicester Journal* could remark as a commonplace truth that 'all public disturbances generally commence with the clamour of women and the folly of boys'. At Dover in 1740 a crowd of women 'rose in a tumultuous manner, cut the sacks, and took away the grain that some farmers were bringing to the Ports for shipping'; they also 'pelted the teams and their drivers with stones for three miles out of town'. At Taunton in 1753 women demolished a weir providing power to a mill and when its repair was announced by the local bellman, some hundreds of weavers and woolcombers', with 'the women going on in front', entered the town to 'the beating of a frying pan' and vowed they would drown anyone who attempted to repair the mill. In September 1800 again, the Major of Blandford Forum wrote to the Home Office, complaining that his house was surrounded by women demanding food at fair prices.[37]

Women sometimes acted at one remove, returning from market to bring news to their husbands and menfolk about the state of prices. Mixed mobs of men and women were common too. During the London food riots of 1800, the crowd which went about the capital attacking the shops of dealers was described thus: 'the van was clean, decent-looking young fellows, mainly journeymen tradesmen. The centre was draymen, dustmen, and many women. The rear was composed of boys and girls'.[38] Women were often seen urging men on to violence, as at the Snow Hill riots in Birmingham in 1795. Women too, seemed to have had some immunity and believed that they would not be arrested as readily as men; this perhaps explains the appearance at riots of men dressed as women. At Stockport in 1812, mobs who attacked food shops and threatened power looms were headed by two men dressed as women and hailed as 'General Ludd's wives'.[39]

Descriptions of mobs also suggest that it was the 'poor' who were the most frequently involved. Although it is important to recognise that contemporary descriptions were usually composed by the middle and upper classes, they often distinguished between 'respectable' or 'decent-looking' elements and 'the poor', whilst those at Newbury were blamed on 'a great number of poor people'.[40] In 1773 'the poor of Bedfordshire' were blamed for the series of disturbances in the Midlands, and at Chesterfield in 1800 we hear of two hundred 'of the dirtiest men'. In London, in November 1816, a crowd which plundered shops in Westminster was said to be composed of 'boys and poor-looking men'.[41] Whatever the prejudices of those reporting riots and mob activity, there is sufficient evidence to suggest that these comments were significant. It may well have been those people who were close to the margin of destitution who reacted most violently when prices rose. The distinction between poverty and destitution was felt most acutely by those poised on its margin and threatened by dependence upon the poor law or charity.[42]

Types of food riot

In many ways food disturbances conformed to the classic pattern of eighteenth-century riots as described by Rudé, Thompson, and others. The transportation or storage of food in times of scarcity was often prevented by the populace, and the food resold at 'fair' prices. On other occasions the disturbances could take the form of assemblies in the marketplace to compel the dealers to reduce their prices to a just level; sometimes the intimidation was directed at the local authorities to compel them to intervene in the marketing of provisions.[43] Stopping the movement of grain and preventing its export was particularly common. Sea-going vessels, barges, and carts were frequently stopped and unloaded, sometimes having the contents sold at a 'fair' price or simply spoiled. This type of disturbance could be found in all the major waves of rioting and illustrated the hostility created by the movement of grain in times of scarcity. Fear of exports was particularly prevalent in the transhipment points and ports. In 1740 several hundred people in Colchester prevented grain from being taken out of the town in wagons; and in 1751 the miners from the Forest of Dean stopped barges on the Wye which they believed were going to France. In the following year, the Kingswood colliers rifled a ship bound for Dublin that was lying in Bristol harbour.[44] These disturbances also occurred in many places in 1766 and 1772. Nor did they lessen with the later waves of food rioting. High prices seems to have produced a further wave of attempts to stop the movement of grain in 1795-6 and 1800. So serious did the situation become in 1795 that the government passed an act to prevent the stopping of grain by making the whole hundred liable to fine and imprisonment.[45] This did not, however, have much effect upon the succeeding periods of disturbances. In 1800 there were frequent reports of attempts to prevent the movement of food. A group of incidents occurred in Yorkshire where barges were stopped on the Aire and Calder from taking grain to Leeds and Bradford.[46] Similarly in 1812, carts passing through Manchester had their contents seized and re-sold, while in 1816 a cargo of potatoes was prevented from leaving Bideford harbour by a body of men armed with bludgeons and other weapons.[47]

On other occasions the dealers had their goods seized in the market place and forcibly re-sold. For example along the south and east coast in 1795 the soldiers usually went straight to market where they enforced a fair price for provisions. In the same year a mob at Aylesbury, largely composed of women, seized the wheat in market and sold it at their own price.[48] In 1800 dealers were commonly intimidated to reduce prices; at Oxford, for example, a large crowd assembled and compelled the food dealers to reduce their prices; those who refused to comply had their stalls or carts overturned.[49] At Manchester in 1812 it was reported that a 'sort of maximum' price for potatoes had been forced on the dealers by women at the market.[50] At Oldham and Sheffield shop-keepers were presented with price lists and threatened with attack if they refused to comply. At Macclesfield a mob entered the town and interrogated the dealers, who giving unsatisfactory answers had their goods spoiled.[51]

Mills were the tangible symbol of the middlemen and were extremely vulnerable to attack by outraged crowds. Mills and millers were often unpopular and when the Albion Steam flour mills burned down in London in 1791 the crowd was reported to have danced and rejoiced in the streets.[52] Attacks on mills were common in most outbreaks of food rioting, especially in those of 1765-6. From Devon, it was reported in 1766 that several thousand people rose and attacked mills at Ottery, Tipton, Sidbury, Cullopton, Bradnick, Tiverton, Silferton, and Exeter itself. At Norwich, a mob destroyed a mill, threw the flour into the river, and destroyed or carried off the accounts, furniture, plate and money belonging to the proprietors.[53] So serious did these attacks become that in

1769 the Riot Act was extended to make attacks upon mills a felony, and therefore a capital offence (9 Geo. III, stat. 2 c. 5). But this did little to alter the pattern of mob activities in later food riots. In June 1795 a band of Dudley colliers attacked a mill and were only driven off after a party of dragoons opened fire, killing one person and wounding two others, and in October 1816, colliers from Walsall marched a mile out of the town to destroy some new mills which had been set up. They were gutted and their contents carried away.[54]

The property of dealers and millers was also considered 'fair game' by rioting crowds. In September 1800 a mob at Banbury set fire to an inn belonging to a local farmer and corn-dealer. In London in September 1800, a series of attacks took place upon the shops of bakers, food wholesalers, and the houses of men prosecuted for monopolistic offences. The spoiling of food, rather than its resale or theft, was often the means of showing the anger, or even contempt of the populace for the activities of the middlemen. Corn and flour was scattered over the floor of marketplaces or tipped into rivers, growing corn trodden into the fields, cheeses rolled through the gutters, and vegetables thrown from their carts. The destruction of sacks, breaking of mill machinery, and dams or weirs all played a part in punishing the dealers.[55]

Accounts of the large waves of food rioting give an overwhelming impression of movement. The sense of riots occurring in one town after another partly accounts for this, but there was the unmistakable, and to the Government alarming, prospect of bodies of people moving about the country and out of the control of the local authorities. Food-rioting often triggered off conflicts between town and country, and market towns were threatened with invasion by workmen from neighbouring mines, quarries, and factories. The tinners regularly invaded the small ports and market towns of the South-West, and Bristol was often invaded by the Kingswood colliers who intimidated dealers and local magistrates. Actual instances of invasion soon became compounded by alarmist rumours. Parson Woodforde's fears in the autumn of 1792 that the 'county mobs' were mobilising was only one example of this.[56] In 1795 the Mayor of Gloucester reported to the Home Office that the town was being threatened by the Forest of Dean colliers, a not altogether unnatural fear given their reputation for disorder and participation in earlier forays to obtain provisions. It was reported in 1800 that the town of Banbury expected the colliers from Warwickshire to descend on them in the search for grain.[57] In the Lancashire and Cheshire disturbances of 1812, such fears were realised: mobs assembled in the fields outside Macclesfield before entering the town to interrogate the dealers about the price of provisions, while in East Anglia in 1816 rioters proceeded from the rural villages into the market towns of Ely and Downham.[58]

Elsewhere the movement was reversed, with mobs going out from the towns to secure grain in the countryside. During the disturbances of 1766 mobs from the weaving towns of Gloucestershire visited villages and farms around Gloucester, Stroud and Cirencester requesting that corn be brought at fair prices to the market. In the Thames valley, a crowd calling themselves 'the Regulators', went round the farms demanding food from the farmers.[59] At Oxford in September 1800 it was reported that every day a body of 50-200 people assembled in the midst of the town, went out to neighbouring farms and villages and demanded that farmers bring their wheat to market on the following Saturday, but they were said to march back in good order and disperse at the command of a leader.[60] Similarly, the Cornish tinners in 1812 scoured the countryside with empty sacks which they hoped to fill with grain. Seventy years earlier, they had been doing exactly the same, filling their sacks from farm stocks, malt houses, and cellars, then offering the full sacks for sale at one shilling a sack to anyone who wanted it. On one occasion, the tinners were reported to be visiting farms with a noose in one hand and an agreement to bring corn to market at reduced prices in the other. If the farmers showed any hesitation in signing, they had the rope fastened around their necks until they were 'terrified into compliance'.[61] Sometimes groups of workmen levied contributions of money and drink from neighbouring villages and farms; in 1756, for example, the village of Bitton, near Bristol, was reported to have had to pay 'danegeld' to the Kingswood colliers, while farmers were obliged to provide money and drink in lieu of grain.[62]

The great majority of these disturbances exhibited strong ceremonial and ritual elements. Mobs were frequently headed by someone blowing a horn, beating a drum, or carrying a flag or other emblem. In 1800 there was a report of carts on their way to Newcastle-under-Lyme being stopped at Lane End by a mob wearing blue ribbons and headed by a woman ringing a bell. The East Anglian crowds in 1816 marched on the local market towns bearing a banner inscribed 'Bread or Blood', headed by 'fife and drum'.[63] Loaves draped in black crêpe or smeared with blood often provided the emblem under which crowds gathered and marched on the marketplace or on food shops.[64] The loaf draped in crêpe made its appearance even in London, accompanying the demonstrations of 1795 and a march through the West End in November 1816 when some food shops were attacked. In using these ceremonial devices, the people concerned were often showing their sense of the legitimacy of their actions, endowing them with a ritualism which put them within the context of a form of 'popular justice'.[65]

Although there were instances of pilfering and violence, the most remarkable feature of these food disturbances was the element of discipline and restraint. The resale of food was often followed by a return of the money (and even the sacks) to the dealers from whom it had been taken.[66] Even the destruction of food was often carried out with an orderly deliberation far removed from the frenzied looting that was feared by the authorities (see pp. 312–14). The general run of disturbances were directed at property rather than persons. Threats were certainly made, especially to unpopular dealers or to dealers as a group, but they were rarely carried out: English crowds appear to have killed no one deliberately in the various food disturbances which occurred from the beginning of the eighteenth century to the beginning of the nineteenth, although several rioters were killed by authorities, and some were executed.[67] Even in Cornwall, where the tinners were regarded as almost beyond the pale of civilisation, the most serious casualties inflicted by the miners were a few broken bones and cracked heads, Hamilton Jenkin writes: 'No doubt the appearance of the tinners was wild, ragged and unkempt, but, taken as a whole, their behaviour on these occasions was remarkably ordered and peaceable.'[68]

Where food rioting survived as a traditional form of protest, as in Cornwall, it retained ceremonial elements. Price-fixing occurred in the Cornish disturbances of 1847, both for grain and butter; at Callington the miners who had seized stored grain sold it at 'their own price' and gave the money to the dealers.[69] Elsewhere however, and even in some Cornish disturbances, the plunder and looting of shops became the more common practice, with few, if any, ritualistic elements (see p. 293). The traditional food riot with its relatively disciplined and restrained character had virtually disappeared, to be replaced by other forms of protest and bargaining.

The causes of food riots: prices and disturbances

The relationship between price movements and the outbreak of food disturbances is complex. Although disturbances tended to occur in periods of high average prices for grain and other foodstuffs, food rioting was more likely to occur at some times of the year rather than others and not always at the period of maximum prices. Within periods of shortage, riots tended to occur most frequently in two periods, in the months before the harvest and in those immediately after. The late spring and early summer months were usually the time when grain was in shortest supply because the previous year's stocks were almost used up. Prices therefore tended to be higher, and also more volatile, in April, May, June and July. The post-harvest months may seem more difficult to explain, but there was usually a period when the harvest had just been gathered in when it was not yet available for market. Assessments of its quality were usually difficult until it had been threshed, with the result that many areas would still be existing on the last of the stored grain. Anticipation and speculation would be at their highest in September, leading often to complaints about the holding back of grain by farmers and malpractice by dealers. Thus the pre-harvest months were the ones when real discontent about prices was most likely to surface, while the post-harvest months were a classic period for rumour and resentment.[70]

Often, then, disturbances did not occur when prices were highest. If we take two of the biggest waves of rioting, those of 1766 and 1795–6, the most important factor appears to have been not the absolute level of prices but the *rate* and *direction* of price movements. In 1766 the yearly averages conceal the speed with which prices increased on local markets in the summer and autumn. Rudé has shown that prices for wheat rose in Gloucester from around 6s. per bushel in June to almost 8s. in September. He has argued that it was the sharpness of this rise rather than the peak price reached in the winter of 1766–7, which provoked the first large outbreak of disturbances in the first days of August. A short lull followed during which prices fell back in the dry August weather. Then in September prices began to rise sharply again with the relaxation of a government embargo on grain exports, and rioting broke out early and continued throughout the month. At Exeter mobs objected to prices of 9s. 6d. per bushel for wheat.[71]

In the war-time crisis of 1795–6, the bulk of disturbances occurred in the former year, although the average price of grain was highest in the latter. The largest numbers of disturbances also took place in months with relatively low prices, such as April and July, when prices were considerably lower than they were to be in other months. July 1795 was the month when prices increased most rapidly in the country as a whole and the most unsettling from the point of view of the consumer. The disturbances carried on through the harvest months before petering out in late autumn and winter. In the period of highest prices, January–April 1796, there were some disturbances, but fewer than the previous July when prices were several shillings lower. Similarly in 1800–1 the majority of food riots occurred not in the months of highest prices, but when the rate of increase in prices was most rapid. The pre-harvest months of 1800 and the early months of 1801 were relatively undisturbed, although prices were very high. In fact two-thirds of all food disturbances occurred in September 1800, the month with the second lowest average price for wheat that year, but when prices had begun to rise sharply after a fall with the harvest. In spring 1812 there were a number of riots in the north against a rapid rise in the price of potatoes and meal.[72] In East Anglia in 1816 the price of grain leapt by almost sixteen shillings per quarter in the month of the disturbances, one of the most rapid rises in the whole period.[73]

To say that price movement had an important influence on the outbreak of disturbances is not to accept uncritically what has been called the 'spasmodic' approach to disturbances. The reactions of crowds were not solely dictated by price movements and at most they were only one component which could help to accumulate resentment and ultimately perhaps lead to a disturbance. Some food disturbances occurred when prices were virtually normal and seem to have been caused entirely by rumours of the expectation of a rise in prices.[74] The complex psychology of the populace is well illustrated by the report from a correspondent to the Home Office in mid-September 1800 who explained that in the East Midlands the poor had been patient in the hope of relief from the harvest: 'A hope that two or three weeks since appeared to be realised, the price of wheat having fallen to nine shillings and some I believe to eight shillings, but upon the first shower of rain . . . the farmers made it a pretence to increase the price even to its former amount.' He claimed that this disappointment had been the direct cause of the riot in Nuneaton.[75]

The role of the middlemen

As well as reacting to the movement of prices, the populace also had to feel that direct action could be effective in some way, either in reducing prices by a forced sale or by forcing the local authorities to intervene. The source of the discontents had to be felt as within the immediate scope of direct action and this often involved finding scapegoats. The obvious targets were the middlemen who were accused, sometimes with justice, of exploiting the condition of the people; in many areas, corn dealers were resented as interlopers both by local magistrates and by the country people. Corn merchants complained in 1756 and 1766 that they were not being given the full protection of the laws but were made the scapegoat for them. W. J. Shelton has argued that a 'crucial feature of the hunger riots of 1766 was the initial encouragement given to mobs by the ruling orders in the countryside', and that the failure of local magistrates to act quickly to snuff out the riots was tantamount to sanctioning them. Moreover, the magistrates not only held their hand but 'abetted other members of the landed and industrial interests in their encouragement of the people to regulate markets and reduce the prices of provisions by force'. This diverted the rioters away from attacks on the landed interest; only when the disturbances appeared to be getting out of hand did the authorities step in to quell them.[76]

Many of the actions of local and national government in time of scarcity served to focus discontent on the grain dealers. The common reaction of many urban magistrates was to set an Assize, hoping to placate the populace by preventing profiteering. Unfortunately, it often had the opposite effect, convincing the populace that what they had suspected was correct, that the food-dealers were to blame for the situation. Wittingly or unwittingly, the habit of proclaiming the statutes against monopolistic offences in times of shortage also served to 'legitimise' action by the populace against the middlemen.[77]

Riots and near-riots

Sharp increases of price did tend to arouse greater hostility than the maintenance of high prices at stable levels. Moreover, the failure of prices to move in anticipated directions could be important. Many riots in September 1766 seem to have been partly caused by disappointment that prices had not fallen with the harvest. Thus expectation and anticipation played an important part in mobilising discontent. Rumours, newspapers and letters provided a means by which hostility could be passed from one market to another. Thus in 1766 it was rumoured that the Quakers were hoarding grain in Uxbridge and stories of hoarding or conspicuous consumption became current,[78] and at Nottingham in autumn 1800 a handbill alleged that the proprietors of the Arnold Mill had vast stocks of grain whilst the poor starved outside. Thus reactions to real or anticipated price movements, as well as resentment against the dealers, especially when condoned by the local magistracy, played an important part in most disturbances.

Certain places were 'riot-prone', as we have seen, because of local conditions. Transhipment points, market towns, and ports were commonly affected, whilst the presence of a large non-agricultural population was also important. But a great deal depended upon individual circumstances and the particular turn of events. Time and again the phrase 'symptoms of disturbance' suggests a point at which disturbances failed to break out although there was reason to believe that they would. Many places experienced the 'knife-edge' situation where crowds assembled, hissed or hooted the dealers, threatened them with dire punishment if they did not comply with their wishes, or sought the intervention of the magistrate to act against the dealers or even preside over their activities in conducting a resale of produce. For example, in August 1766 when miners entered Truro, the farmers insisted upon the prevailing prices for wheat and barley, but the magistrates intervened and the grain was sold to them at reduced prices.[79] At Banbury in 1800 the stocking-weavers from neighbouring Middleton Cheney came into town and demanded a meeting with the farmers: to reinforce their point they attacked some butter-makers and bakers. The mayor then spoke to them and issued handbills calling a meeting to which the weavers were invited. While the meeting was taking place, however, the crowd which was still assembled in the marketplace proceeded to duck some dealers and start the resale of food. As a result the mayor broke off negotiations, calling on the local armed association to stand to; by seven in the evening they were under arms, but were unable to prevent the crowd attacking the house of a local innkeeper. At this juncture, the weavers, having conducted their resale, offered to withdraw if the soldiers were called off: this was done, and the disturbance came to an end by mutual agreement.[80]

Generally, magistrates sought to placate rioters if they could. One way short of price-fixing was to open a subscription for the poor or to provide grain at reduced prices. In 1756 the Liverpool Corporation borrowed £2,000 to buy corn which they rationed and sold to the poor at cost price. At Nottingham in 1800, the Corporation purchased 130 quarters of wheat for the use of the poor which they sold at below the market price, and in the manufacturers Davison and Hawksley bought grain and ground it free in order to sell it below cost. In Norwich the mayor and Corporation were active in both 1795-6 and 1800-1, raising subscriptions for the poor and attempting to head off discontent: in 1795 they called together the millers and made them agree not to send any wheat or flour out of the country; when discontent against the middlemen was at its height in 1800 the mayor, Robert Harvey, prevented retail dealers from buying in the market before midday and a handbill was put out saying that the magistrates would exert every legal expedient to reduce the price of bread.[81]

Such negotiations could, however, go badly wrong, as shown by the ferocity with which the Tyneside colliers and pitmen sacked the Guildhall at Newcastle in 1740 after the dealers had promised to reduce prices but failed to do so, and a gentleman had killed one of the aggrieved crowd.[82] The refusal of local authorities to comply with the crowd's demands could easily precipitate a disturbance. In November 1757, colliers from Ashton-under-Lyne marched into Manchester and ordered the High Sheriff to fix a maximum price for oatmeal, potatoes, and flour 'for twelve months to come', and his refusal to obey led to a pitched battle with troops, known as the 'Shudehill fight'.[83] Time and again it was the product of these 'negotiations' between assembled crowds, magistrates, and dealers which determined whether or not a disturbance took place. An obdurate dealer, an insensitive magistrate, or an ill-judged move by any party could make all the difference to the outcome of these confrontations.

The role of agitation in these disturbances is hard to evaluate. Many disturbances were accompanied by 'levelling' threats and ill-feeling against the rich which seem to have been part of the repertoire of eighteenth-century crowds. The period after 1789 deserves separate consideration elsewhere, for the cries of popular radicalism and the changed circumstances of the Revolutionary period added a new dimension to food disturbances and their implications. The occasional appeal to the Pretender, Cromwell, or British heroes seems to form part of a rhetoric which did not need to be present in order to bring about disturbances: such organisation as riots had owed far more to the similarity of regional circumstances and spontaneous reactions to movements in the price of grain. In that sense, it is misleading to speak of riots spreading, disturbances were clustered because they were part of a regional reaction to price movements, and riots appeared to flow along the lines of communication because these governed the movement of prices. We need rarely look further for an explanation of the outbreak of groups of disturbances; only occasionally does it appear that some other factor was at work, as in 1757 when rioting colliers at Prescot were said to have been led by a stocking-loom maker who had been present at the riots in Nottingham.[84]

Famine or scarcity?

In the absence of a definitive study of English demography in the eighteenth century, the evidence for subsistence crises in eighteenth-century England is somewhat conflicting. It is not at present clear that a 'famine' in the strict sense of the term can be found anywhere in England after 1700, or indeed after 1630.[85] R. S. Schofield's study of fifty-four parishes between 1537 and 1809 is one of the most complete that we have available. Taking any doubling of the mortality rate as designating a mortality 'crisis', he has found that the number of parishes experiencing a 'crisis' was usually under eight per decade after 1710 and very few coincided with periods of high prices; only four parishes experienced a 'crisis' in 1740-1, only one in 1795, and none in the years 1800-1.[86] A number of studies have investigated smaller areas or particular crises. An examination of Midland parishes by Dr Gooder has suggested that in this area at least the high prices of the years 1727-30 did see 'a positive correlation between burials, harvest years and grain prices'. However another study of mid-Wharfedale in Yorkshire has found 'complete freedom from the heavy mortality' which affected other areas in the 1720s and 1740s. A recent attempt to discover the demographic effects of the high prices of 1766-7 suggests that only a small increase in mortality and a similarly small decrease in conceptions can be detected. A major difficulty here is that such demographic movements need not be directly related to the price of food, as the conditions which could bring about a poor harvest and high prices, such as a severe winter or a wet, humid summer, were often also favourable to epidemic disease. Simply to establish that an increase in mortality occurred in a year of high prices does not prove the presence of a subsistence 'crisis'. The issue is further complicated by the difficulty in assessing the contribution of malnutrition to epidemic disease.[87]

The problem can be exemplified by examining the demographic impact of scarcity during the Napoleonic period. A recent study of the Yorkshire experience between 1793 and 1802 illustrates some of the difficulties. Burials increased in some parishes by up to 69 per cent in 1795-6 and in 1800-1 there was a widespread increase in mortality of between 16 and 41 per cent. In both periods there is evidence of outbreaks of epidemic disease and it remains difficult to establish the precise contribution of high prices to these mortality increases.[88] Moreover, mortality totals for the whole country show a significant increase in burials in 1795, 1800, and 1816, but nothing approaching the definitions of 'famine' applied by some demographers who require a much larger increase in mortality to establish a clear 'subsistence crisis'.[89]

Nevertheless, there is ample evidence from contemporary sources that periods of high prices produced distress. Poor relief may have allowed a minimum subsistence and avoided mass starvation, but there were always numbers of people who had lost their entitlement to relief by moving, immigrants (such as the Irish) who fell outside the system, as well as an increasing number of manufacturing workers who would overwhelm any system of relief that was operating.[90] As food disturbances became more common in the Northern and Midland manufacturing areas, they tended to be concerned with the basic commodities of subsistence: grain, meal and potatoes. In much of Southern England, however, a striking feature of food disturbances is that they were often concerned with foods which were not essential, such as meat and butter; although hardly luxuries, they illustrated that these were not always riots of desperation by starving men and women, but displayed a wider 'consumer consciousness' and resistance to high prices over a range of commodities. They were price riots, rather than reactions to famine, more plausibly placed within the context of scarcity, high prices, and resentment than of major demographic crises. Commodities included meat (Redruth, St Austell: 1766; Wisbech, Coventry, Portsea: 1795; Oxford, Nuneaton: 1800; Brandon: 1816); cheese (Exeter, Coventry, Oxford: 1766; Seaford: 1795; Nuneaton; London 1800); butter (Stourbridge, Kidderminster: 1767; Bury St Edmunds: 1772; Liverpool: 1793; Wells, Aylesbury, Deddington: 1795; Oxford, Banbury: 1800; Carlisle: 1812; Callington: 1847): Other price riots involved green vegetables, bacon, malt and household commodities such as candles and soap. These were usually treated in much the same way as grain or bread, with attempts to 'fix' the price and spoiling the goods if this was not complied with.

The decline of food rioting

The survival of food rioting into the nineteenth century should not obscure the most important feature of the period after 1800, namely the decline of food disturbances. Food riots were declining in numbers after the Napoleonic Wars, but they were being replaced by other forms of protest more suited to an industrial environment. Even in the shortages of the Napoleonic Wars, and as far back as the 1760s, there was some overlap between strikes and food riots: by the Luddite period food rioting and frame-breaking went on side by side in Lancashire and Cheshire, sometimes flowing into each other; during the East Anglian disturbances in 1816 demands for lower prices were combined with those for higher wages and in many Midlands towns 'collective bargaining by riot' overlapped with food riots as workers moved about the area enforcing a stoppage of work and demanding cheap provisions. During the 1820s, boycotts were sometimes directed against shopkeepers who were alleged to be offending against 'just prices' in what were known as 'food strikes'. The traditional forms of food disturbance gradually gave way to other forms of protest, with trade union activity and strikes becoming the most common means of defending living standards.

6 Labour disputes before the Combination Laws

Labour disputes formed one of the most frequent causes of popular disturbances in eighteenth- and early nineteenth-century England. The graphic phrase 'collective bargaining by riot' has been used to describe the conduct of many early trade disputes and a degree of violence was often associated with bargaining between masters and men and between different groups of workmen. In the years before the growth of strong and legal trade unions, workmen frequently resorted to violence as a means of bringing pressure to bear on employers or local authorities. This could range from tumultuous assemblies, parades, and lobbying of employers and local authorities to the destruction of tools, material, and machinery and the intimidation of strike-breakers or blacklegs. Violence for early trade unions formed not only a mode of bargaining to be used in place of or in conjunction with more peaceful negotiations, but also a crucial means of enforcing a degree of solidarity on fellow workmen.[1]

The cloth-workers

The cloth industry had a history of disturbances stretching back into the seventeenth century, long before its extensive mechanisation and the introduction of the factory system into woollen manufacture. The industry in the eighteenth century was still largely organised on a domestic basis in which the clothiers organised the distribution of raw materials, the finishing of cloth and its eventual sale. Although combinations of cloth-workers against their employers were prohibited by an act of Edward VI, the weavers had begun to develop something more than ephemeral organisations by the beginning of the eighteenth century. In 1717 a widespread combination of woollen-workers in Devon and Somerset was involved in a dispute which led to a series of disturbances in Exeter and Taunton, where the weavers were reported to have pulled down the houses of clothiers and defied the magistrates, but carried royal effigies to show their loyalty. Although a Proclamation was issued in 1718 against 'lawless clubs and societies', the weavers' organisations continued in existence. In 1720 there were serious riots at Tiverton against imported Irish worsted. The wool-combers were the main instigators, seizing and burning combed Irish wool.[2]

The combers have been called 'the "aristocracy" of the worsted workers'. Highly skilled and well organised, they fought a protracted campaign to preserve their craft status in which they employed a wide variety of tactics including violence. At Crediton in 1725 several hundred weavers attacked looms and set fire to the wreckage, and when the Town Clerk tried to read the Riot Act the 'rioters pulled off his hat and wig and put dirt upon his head'. They were reported to have been led by a 'captain' carrying a flag made of serge cut from one of the looms. The reaction of the masters was to obtain an Act against combinations in both the weaving and woolcombing branches of the industry. Neither had much effect, and in November 1726 there was extensive rioting in Wiltshire and East Somerset, in which bands of weavers marched about the woollen towns enforcing a stoppage. The weavers were reported entering the houses of masters and strike-breakers 'spoiling of wool, and cutting and destroying the pieces in the looms and the utensils of the trade'.[3] The claims of the weavers that they were being underpaid did elicit some sympathy from the local gentry and even some clothiers with the result that an Act was passed which abolished truck payments and permitted magistrates to fix wages. At Trowbridge, the magistrate made a table of the grievances and brought them to the clothiers, obtaining a pledge that they would not increase the workload of the men. Although these agreements soon fell into abeyance, they illustrated that in the short term at least 'collective bargaining by riot' could obtain results.[4]

A seemingly unrelated incident took place in 1729 when a body of weavers at Bristol attacked the house of an employer 'while the corporation were at church'. More serious was the extensive rioting which affected the West Country in 1738–40. There were riots at Tiverton over the resale of cloth, while at Melksham in Wiltshire the workmen cut the chains on looms of an employer 'on account of his lowering of the prices', and groups of weavers and shearmen toured the area demanding higher prices for their work. Gravener Henson later wrote that 'a system of riot, respecting wages, was continually in motion, and a cordon of troops was necessarily formed to cut off the communication of the rioters with other counties'.[5] The weavers' complaints were articulated in an 'Essay on Riots', published in the *Gloucester Journal*, in which the clothiers were blamed for their unfair practices. Even so, several of the rioters were hanged and there were fears of renewed disturbances at Trowbridge and Bradford in 1741 because the clothiers refused to improve wages. The weavers' conduct had generally been well ordered, and violence came only as a last resort. One historian of the West Country cloth industry has argued that 'The most noticeable point about the whole series of disturbances is, on the one hand, the anxiety of the weavers to act in a legal manner to get what they believed to be their legal rights and, on the other, the clothiers disregard of any legal obligations.'[6]

A similar attitude prevailed in the next serious round of disturbances in 1755-6. Disturbances had occurred in 1750 between woolcombers and weavers over the use of Irish wool, but the more serious issue of wage regulation was raised in 1755. The Gloucestershire weavers complained that legislation of 1726 and 1728 to regulate their wages had been ignored by the clothiers and that in the absence of summary provisions in the Act, enabling the weavers to bring the clothiers speedily to justice, they could only use the more expensive procedures of law. An application to parliament was preceded by an appeal to a magistrate and the preparation of a table of wage rates. The weavers' leaders held a week of meetings with their fellows in order to instruct them in the course they were taking before applying to parliament for a new Act. Parliament complied with the men's request, empowering the justices to fix wages. When the men applied to the justices at the October Quarter Sessions at Gloucester to take action under the new Act, the masters countered with their own petition. In the face of the inaction of the justices, the weavers resorted to violence and it was reported that the men 'appeared in a very tumultuous manner ... committed great Outrages'; confronted with disorder, the justices broke the stalemate by fixing a scale of wages relatively favourable to the men. Even so many masters refused to comply and to prevent further disorder troops were brought into the area; within a year the masters had obtained an Act which repealed the wage regulation of the previous legislation. Thus both peaceful and violent tactics had availed the men nothing, even though they represented some of the best organised workers in the country.[7]

The disturbances in the cloth industry during the first half of the eighteenth century were the result of disputes either over the level of wages or over practices which effectively reduced earnings by causing underemployment. Hence there was considerable concern shown among cloth-workers, as among many other craft industries, about the dilution of the trade by abuse of apprenticeship laws. Increasingly, however, the quickening pace of economic activity and of technical innovation presented workmen with the threat of machinery. In the West Country objections to the use of machinery culminated in the widespread disturbances aroused by the use of gig-mills in 1802-3 (discussed in more detail later) but some isolated disturbances broke out in the South-West over the use of machinery in different branches of the industry before the end of the century. An experimental spinning machine was broken at Shepton Mallet in July 1776 by mobs from Frome and Warminster and another machine was broken at Frome in June 1781. These violent reactions appear to have contributed to the slow and uneven progress of machinery into the preliminary processes of the West Country woollen industry. The introduction of the flying shuttle met with a mixed reception, being used peacefully in Gloucester from the middle of the eighteenth century but provoking disturbances elsewhere, as at Trowbridge in Wiltshire in 1792; this issue also contributed to disturbances at Frome in 1801 and at Chippenham in 1801-3.[8] As in many other areas of technical innovation, whether violence occurred depended on a complex of factors, especially the speed of introduction, the strength of the local workmen, and the state of the trade. Reorganisation of manufacture could also lead to violence where the men feared that their livelihoods were in danger: there were riots at Trowbridge and Bradford (Wilts) in 1787 over the grouping of looms in shops and the use of untrained apprentices, and the same issue led to riots in Gloucestershire in June 1792.[9]

The weavers of East Anglia figure less prominently in the disturbances of the eighteenth century. There had been disturbances at Colchester in 1675 because of abuse of the apprenticeship regulations, and there was widespread fear of disturbances in 1696 because of unemployment.[10] During the course of the eighteenth century the East Anglian industry reached the zenith of its prosperity. Norwich was the centre of the worsted industry by the middle of the century, but gradually began to decline through competition from Yorkshire and the effects of the American War. Although East Anglia never recovered her position in the trade, the process of decline was a slow one, Norwich alone employing 10,000 looms as late as 1818. In spite of the severe competition from Yorkshire which might have provoked manufacturers to introduce machinery in an attempt to survive, the East Anglian industry remained fairly peaceful. In part, this was because the East Anglian manufacturers recognised that Norfolk possessed none of the natural advantages to permit the efficient use of machinery. Also, they were faced with a potentially hostile population which would have reacted with violence to any attempt to introduce machinery.[11] The ability of the East Anglian workers to resist innovation was therefore never put to the test as much as elsewhere because manufacturers regarded the potential advantages as too small to be worth the opposition they would encounter. Indeed throughout the eighteenth century the Norwich weavers 'were remarkably successful' in keeping up wage rates in the face of the gradual decline of the trade. Thus in 1719 there was rioting in Norwich and Colchester against weavers working on East Indian fabrics, mainly calicoes, at the same time as agitation in London and Canterbury. Similarly, the woolcombers of East Anglia struck in 1752 to prevent the employment of a workman called Trye of whom they disapproved, leaving their work until he was discharged and sending agents to other districts to prevent the enlistment of strike-breakers. Three hundred retired from the city of Norwich to set up booths on a neighbouring heath where they were supported from funds collected from other workers. The man was eventually expelled from the trade and work resumed. Organisation was the secret of this success. The weavers of the Norwich industry pursued a general policy of refusing reductions of prices even when work was slack, preferring unemployment to reduced rates. They were strong enough to force up their wage rates during the Napoleonic Wars even while the trade was in evident decline, and as late as 1822, they resisted a wage reduction by resort to violence, beating up an unpopular master: the manufacturers capitulated, restoring the old prices.[12]

Although normally considered freer from craft restrictions than the traditional areas of woollen manufacture, the Yorkshire industry did not escape labour troubles. A strike was recorded in Leeds as early as 1706, when a small group of weavers threatened to strike if not paid 1½d. per hour instead of the existing 1d; in 1743 a group of cloth workers assembled in Leeds, terrorising other workers who were accepting less than 12d. a day. As elsewhere, the worsted weavers were the most turbulent group, frequently taking part in 'riot and outrage'. In 1770 to demonstrate against the prices being offered for their work, a group of thirty-two stuff-weavers gathered in Leeds and returned unwoven worsted yarn to the clothiers and two years later a group of worsted workers attacked a master with 'force and arms'. In the summer of 1775 Keighley was the scene of a serious dispute in which between 800 and 900 weavers 'paraded the town several days, and would suffer none to work at the usual prices'; workmen who refused to join the strike had their work destroyed. The carpet-weavers of Leeds 'turned out' in 1787 in pursuit of a wage advance, and several disturbances were reported during the dispute; it was hardly surprising that in the face of these persistent activities, the Corporation of the Borough of Leeds appointed a committee to consult with the Recorder 'as to the necessary and proper measures to be adopted for the amending and explaining the Acts of Parliament for punishing Servants and Workmen for breach of their contracts and for preventing combinations of workmen'.[13]

Other branches of the textile industry were being increasingly affected by technological change. In 1768–9 there were riots in Blackburn when the spinners attacked the house of James Hargreaves, the inventor, and destroyed his spinning-machines. A more serious and systematic campaign opened in October 1779 against the machines for carding and roving invented by Arkwright. The American war had brought depression to the textile trade of Lancashire and many workmen blamed the introduction of spinning machines and those for carding and roving for their lack of employment. Richard Arkwright was one of the men who had set up in the Lancashire area. His new carding machine had been patented in 1775 and in 1776 he built a factory at Birkacre, near Chorley. The disturbances were sparked off at the end of September by the offer of work on a large spinning machine at reduced rates. As a result crowds, estimated at up to eight thousand strong, consisting not only of weavers and spinners, but also of colliers, nailmakers, joiners, and general labourers, made attacks upon machinery at Aspull, Westleigh, Worsley Golborne, Blackburn, Little Bolton, Pemberton, Wensleyford and Balderstone. On 4 October the Birkacre factory was attacked when 'a most riotous and outrageous Mob assembled in the Neighbourhood, armed in a warlike Manner, and after breaking down the Doors of the Buildings, they entered the Rooms, destroyed most of the Machinery, and afterwards set fire to and consumed the whole Buildings, and every Thing therein contained'. The damage was estimated by the proprietors at

£4,400, the cost of the entire undertaking. During the attack two people were killed and eight wounded.[14]

The assaults were directed almost exclusively at larger workshops and factories. Domestic machines were left untouched as were spinning jennies of under twenty spindles, which the mobs regarded as 'fair' machines. Some sympathy with the complaints of the workmen was evident from the magistracy, for there was widespread antagonism to Arkwright as a newcomer to the district and one who threatened the livelihood of hand-workers. Thus the magistrates at Wigan responded to the disturbances by suspending the use of machines for carding, roving, or spinning until parliament had deliberated on the subject. But when the cotton-spinners petitioned parliament in 1780, a committee appointed to investigate reported in favour of the use of machines. These riots, in which almost a hundred machines were broken, have been described by the Hammonds as the last attempt by the cotton spinners to resist the use of machinery for spinning; they were the last largely because the vast expansion of the industry absorbed any labour displaced by technical innovation.[15]

The hundred or so frames broken, the two deaths, and a few minor convictions, stand in marked contrast to the disturbances aroused by the use of power looms in the weaving branch of the industry. A foretaste of the Luddite outbreaks in Lancashire and Cheshire after 1810 came with an attack in March 1792 on the factory of Messrs Grimshaw in Manchester, the first to use Cartwright's power loom. The factory was burnt down by handloom weavers, only two years after it had started operations, and its destruction was said to have inhibited the development of powerloom weaving for several years in the area. Even so, the amount of violent opposition to machinery was trivial compared with the scale of the transformation taking place in the industry. Technical innovation could, and usually did, take place without open discontent.[16]

The framework knitters

The framework knitters of the Midlands were also faced with technical change. The industry was of relatively recent growth in the area, the number of frames rising rapidly in the course of the eighteenth century reaching 17,350 by 1782, as against only 5,500 for the whole English provinces in 1727. Primarily supplying stockings and other knitted goods, the industry became specialised according to the type of plain or fancy goods produced, and the type of yarn used: Nottingham became the centre for 'fancy' cotton stockings, while the surrounding villages made the plain; Derby produced silk stockings, and Leicester mainly woollen. Although yarn production operated on a highly capitalised basis with increasing cross-fertilisation of capital, entrepreneurship, and innovation from the textile industries of Lancashire and Yorkshire, the knitters were still organised on a domestic basis, either owning their own frames or renting them from an employer. Their condition varied considerably with the prosperity of particular branches of the trade, but one example of resistance to machinery occurred in Leicester in 1788 when a mob destroyed machinery which applied Arkwright's cotton-spinning machinery to the spinning of woollen yarn for stockings.[17]

The main source of discontent was wage levels. In 1778–9, the framework knitters attempted to obtain a minimum wage. Petitions to Parliament were organised and preparations for a Bill 'to regulate the Art and Mystery of Frame-Work knitting' prepared. After prolonged resistance by a group of employers, the Bill was finally defeated at the Committee stage. News of the loss of the Bill reached Nottingham on Saturday 10 June 1779. In the evening crowds assembled, drawn not only from the town itself but also from the neighbouring villages. The windows on the Market Place were broken and then an attack made on the houses of the principal hosiers. Although the Mayor swore in 300 special constables and read the Riot Act, the crowds continued to destroy the frames and property of the hosiers. Three hundred frames were broken at the mill of Arkwright and Need, the latter being one of the principal opponents of the Bill. The crowd then set out for Need's house at Arnold, where they broke open his coach-house, destroyed his coach and harness, and tipped the wheels and ironwork into the Trent. After a pause on Sunday, the riots broke out again on Monday when a group of country weavers carried a frame to the Malt Cross in the Market Place and demolished it, the Riot Act was again read and troops brought in to patrol the streets. By this time negotiations were taking place between the town authorities, the hosiers, and the workmen. The streets were cleared by a promise that a meeting would be held to deal with the men's grievances and, although further violence did break out, the hosiers were prevailed upon to offer to 'remove every oppression', providing the violence ended, and 'to bring all the manufacturers up to a fair price, not the highest rate, but the best generally given'. This resolution brought the dispute and the violence to an end. Only one man was tried for the riots and he was acquitted. The riots had, in fact, proved successful from the workmen's point of view. A table of prices was eventually agreed and largely observed during the next twenty years. At other centres of industry, no riots were needed, for example, at Derby, where the dispute was settled amicably.[18]

In July 1783, however, there was renewed discontent in Nottingham. During a period of slack trade, a Mr Fellows, one of the leading hosiers of the town and also mayor, reduced wages and threatened that if the men did not comply 'their Frames should stand still'. It was reported that the angry stockingers

> assembled in a large body, made an Effigy by Way of Ridicule

against the first Magistrate, and placed it on the Back of an Ass,
carrying it through the Principal Streets of the Town; at length
they came to the Mayor's House, where they tied it to the
Knocker of his Door and scourged it for a considerable Time.
Then they broke his windows and did some other damage.

The family reacted by 'firing upon the Rioters very smartly', wounding
several, but the attack was only beaten off when some troops arrived. The
houses of other prominent hosiers were then attacked and a full regiment
had to be brought into the town to keep order.[19] Seven years later, there
was a three-day riot in Nottingham because the framework knitters
would not accept the prices offered by the hosiers. The men paraded the
streets and went on to carry out an almost routine attack on the houses of
prominent hosiers. The soldiers were called in to suppress the
disturbances and wounded several when they opened fire.[20]

The major disturbances amongst the metropolitan textile industries
are dealt with elsewhere, as they intertwine with the Wilkes affair, but in
the first part of the eighteenth century, the London framework knitters
were one of the most important branches of the industry. In 1727 there
were 2,500 frames in London, after which the number began to fall as a
result of competition from the provinces. In spite of regulations to the
contrary, excessive numbers of apprentices were taken on and in 1710 the
weavers attacked the offending masters, breaking over a hundred frames.
None of the rioters were arrested and the men's action seems to have
proved effective in the short-term, for the masters agreed to abide by the
existing apprenticeship regulations.[21]

The Spitalfields weavers had a history of violence in defence of their
livelihood, with riots against Dutch looms in 1675-6 and the French
weavers working them. Similarly when a Bill enjoining the wearing of
woollens was before parliament in 1689, a mob of weavers reported to be
20,000 strong bore down on the Commons in support of their spokesmen
who were opposing the measure. The use of East India goods, such as
calicoes, provoked considerable hostility from the silk-workers who feared
widespread unemployment. A Bill was introduced into parliament on 21
January 1697 to limit the import of East India silks and the weavers with
their families filled the lobbies of the House of Commons and were only
prevented from entering the Commons by locking the doors. Eventually
the City members managed to pacify the weavers and they left the
Commons. In the evening, however, the weavers attacked East India
House, breaking its windows before being dispersed. The following
March when the Lords hesitated over the Bill, there was further violence,
the house of an importer of East India goods being attacked. Two weavers
were killed before they dispersed. Further riots took place two days later
upon the loss of the Bill.[22]

The threat which calicoes posed was recognised in an Act of 1700
which forbad the import of printed calico into the country. Notwithstanding, plain calico could still be imported and a growing threat to the

English silk and woollen weavers came from domestic calico production. Calico presses were set up in London and it was the capital's silk-weavers who took a lead in opposing them. Their tactics were novel: in June 1719 women wearing calicoes were attacked in the streets and handbills posted which asked 'Must the poor weavers starve?' The majority of these disturbances occurred in the Spitalfields area, but one group moved out to Lewisham to destroy some calico presses; they were overtaken by a party of troops and one of the weavers killed. Although soldiers were sent into Spitalfields and a strong reinforcement put in the Tower, the attacks on women continued during the summer. In response to a petition from the Weaver's Company a Bill to prohibit the use of calicoes was passed through the Commons early in 1720, but was held up in the Lords. The result was further rioting in May, with attacks on women and on a French calico printer in Spitalfields. With the passing of the Act, the disturbances came to an end. The silk-weavers were not to be engaged in serious disturbances again until the middle of the century when their trade disputes became bound up with that of John Wilkes. [23]

The keelmen

The keelmen of the Tyne and Wear are an interesting example of a group who frequently used 'collective bargaining by riot' to some effect. The keelmen were responsible for transporting coal in small boats, keels, from the stocks and staithes on the banks of the Tyne and Wear to the collierships waiting at the mouth of the river, and were employed on a yearly basis by 'fitters', members of the Hostman's company of Newcastle who held a monopoly on this traffic until the end of the eighteenth century. The history of the trade in the seventeenth century is obscure, though the keelmen are reported to have 'mutinied' in 1654 and 1671 'for the increase of wages'. During the next century they became notorious for their strikes and the strength of their organisation, which has led to them being considered 'among the first trades to be organised in a primitive form of trade union'. [24] In 1710 they struck for higher wages and 'threatened to pull down Houses and commit other great disorders unless their grievances be redressed'. The civil authorities and the local militia were unable to deal with the strike and the regular troops were called in to force the men back to work. Although the keelmen had threatened violence, they had also petitioned the Queen to amend their conditions. Similarly, two years later they again petitioned for a charter of incorporation, sending one to the Queen, several to the Commons, and at least one to the Lords. Over 900 keelmen signed one petition and over 1,000 another; the expenses of the petitioning were met from a charity which they had set up as early as 1699 to support their poor and aged. [25]

The attempt at incorporation failed and in May 1719 the Tyne keelmen entered into a combination with the men of the Wear for an increase in wages. The magistrates certainly feared it; one wrote: 'Though I cannot yet call it a Rebellion yet as so great a Number as eight hundred men upon the Were [sic], and two Thousand upon the Tine [sic] are above the reach of the Civil power, it is uncertain how long Such a Body made desperate by their Obstinacy and Poverty may contain themselves within any legal Bounds.' In fact, there was relatively little violence and the men confined themselves to enforcing the stoppage. When negotiations with the Newcastle authorities and the fitters failed to produce a settlement, the men assembled and affirmed their refusal to work until their demands were met. The authorities reacted by ordering a naval captain sent to the port to impress any keelmen who refused to work; the justices also commited the 'abusive and most active' to prison. The men then negotiated for their release which on a return to work was granted.[26]

A strike in 1738 was enforced by the keelmen threatening any man who attempted to go to work. The strikers were defeated by some of the skippers being persuaded to pass the boats of the 'Mutineers' and, unable to enforce the strike, the men drifted back to work. In 1744 a strike was occasioned by the practice of overloading the keels, at no extra recompense to the men. The strike became so bitter that the Riot Act had to be read and troops stationed in the Sandgate district of Newcastle. The dispute was settled by the drawing up of a 'Contract' detailing the wages and terms of the keelmen, this brought no lasting peace. Over-production by the colliery owners led them to offer free coal to the ship-owners which they were tempted to carry as an extra perquisite.[27] On 19 March 1750 some skippers and keelmen stopped work and brought work to a standstill on Newcastle quay; the next day, bodies of keelmen went to Shields, boarded keels, broke open cabins, destroyed tackle, and created a general stoppage. Once the strike was effective the men presented their grievances to the Newcastle magistrates, especially the issue of overloading the keels. After a second and more detailed table of grievances, the negotiations broke down, even after the men were offered solemn assurances that the 'Contract' of 1744 would be adhered to. Demands now included a wage rise and the issue had reached a stalemate. After six weeks, the magistrates and fitters prosecuted sixteen keel skippers who were committed to the House of Correction, a list of 800 keelmen on strike was issued by the fitters and anyone who employed them was threatened with prosecution, while strike-breaking labour was recruited from the many unemployed sailors and carriers along the river. At this, on 4 May, 1,000 keelmen assembled in Sandgate, manned the keels and placed them in mid-river to intercept any loaded vessels; several such vessels were stopped, their tackle smashed, and the crews beaten up. These actions were rendered futile, however, by the intervention of troops who dispersed the strikers and protected the strike-breakers. As a result the strike collapsed.[28]

A further strike took place in 1768 on the overloading issue and a stoppage was temporarily enforced, but was ended after the men sought legal advice on the issue of the measure of coal they had to carry and decided to appeal to parliament; the dispute continued to erupt with stoppages in July 1771, although no serious violence was reported. Again in 1785 the Sunderland keelmen were reported to be 'demanding exhorbitant wages, threatening and doing much mischief'. The soldiers were called in and the strikers dispersed.[29] The keelmen continued to be a turbulent and tenacious group. Although increasingly threatened by technical innovation, in particular 'the spout', a device for unloading coal from the staithes direct on to the colliers, the keelmen continued to defend their position: indeed the strike in 1771 was partly aimed against the use of the 'spout' and set the pattern for a series of strikes through the Revolutionary and Napoleonic period to maintain their position. As late as 1787 the keelmen obtained an Act of Parliament restricting the loads keels could carry. The continued expansion of the coal trade and the inability of colliers to load further upstream than Newcastle because of its low-arched bridge gave the keelmen the opportunity to maintain one of the most protracted battles of all early trade groups.[30]

Seamen's strikes

During the course of the eighteenth century sailors became prominent in strikes and the disturbances associated with them; the middle years of the century, in particular, led to a number of disputes. The Seven Years' War brought a great expansion of labour, but this prosperity was threatened with the end of the war and the release of large numbers of seamen from the naval service; higher prices in the 1760s also added to the discontents. Still on the crest of expansion in December 1762 the Liverpool seamen struck to establish a minimum wage of forty shillings a month. After some disturbance three of them were arrested, but on their way to Lancaster Gaol they were released by a sympathetic crowd at Ormskirk.[31] As economic recession began to bite after 1763 the seamen attempted to keep up living standards by enforcing the Elizabethan apprenticeship laws which were being widely abused. In April 1768 there were demonstrations for higher wages in the ports of the North-East. The seamen of the Tyne and Wear used tactics which have been described as representing 'an interesting transitional stage between the provincial poor's usual stress upon lowering prices by attacking the middlemen and farmers, and the metropolitan poor's stress on forcing employers to grant increased wages'. Ships were prevented from leaving port, attacks made on property, and magistrates were petitioned for increased wages; in addition the strikers attacked bakers and butchers in an attempt to force down the price of food.[32] In the short term these actions were successful and promises of higher wages were made, though it is not known how far they were honoured. This strike movement spread to London where it became part of the wide-ranging series of industrial disputes which ran parallel to the Wilkes affair (see Chapter 4).

That depressed conditions would not permit seamen's wage rates to remain at wartime levels was confirmed in a violent dispute which broke out at Liverpool in August 1775, when an attempt was made to lower the wages of the seamen in a slaveship, the *Derby* of Captain Yates. The cut came at a time of severe crisis amongst the Liverpool seafaring trades. The outbreak of the American War and resulting trade embargoes coincided with the end of the whaling season, producing considerable unemployment among the 6,000 or so sailors who worked from the port by the 1770s. The strike broke out at seven in the evening of Saturday, 25 August, when the sailors on the *Derby* cut away their rigging to immobilise the ship and went on to do the same to other ships on the river. A crowd on the waterfront paraded behind a red flag and made a 'proclamation' for an increase in wages. The sailors developed an efficient, yet simple organisation for the strike, pickets were set on the docks, and groups of sailors, usually armed with bludgeons, boarded vessels and took off or assaulted anyone whom they found working. While this was occurring, the strikers were also negotiating with the merchants at the Exchange. They had already achieved one success in intimidating the authorities, for when some of the sailors were arrested, 2,000 of their fellows assembled and attacked the gaol; the prisoners were given up without a struggle and the triumphant seamen paraded the streets. The situation turned uglier on the Tuesday. The sailors came in a body to the Exchange to carry out negotiations but were fired on and between two and seven killed; the next day 1,000 sailors rallied on shore, decked in red ribbons and bringing two cannon off a whaler on the river, and with these and other arms taken from gunsmiths' shops they made a violent attack on the Exchange, again hoisting a red flag and systematically bombarding the building; they also attacked the houses of those believed responsible for the deaths of the fellows on Tuesday. Several houses of prominent citizens who had played a part in the defence of the Exchange were attacked, although the sailors were reported to have behaved well to everyone else. On Thursday the appeals of the mayor for troops were answered and the sailors were dispersed, forty or fifty of them being taken prisoner.[33]

The colliers

Coal-miners formed an expanding industrial group in the eighteenth century. But although they intervened in local markets to protect their food supply in times of high prices, there were relatively few examples of industrial disputes before the end of the eighteenth century. An exception was the North-East coalfield where the industry had developed to a greater degree than elsewhere through the east coast trade to London. Here the colliers appear to have been much more conscious of their bargaining power in a highly capitalised trade and were also faced by an increasingly competitive group of coal-owners. As early as 1740 the colliers were able to obtain a wage rise by wrecking and burning pit-head machinery in response to high prices.[34]

These events were only a prologue to one of the most remarkable industrial disputes of the whole century. In August 1765 the miners of the North-East struck against an attempt by the coal-owners to tighten their control over the colliers by extending the customary yearly bond into virtual life-service through an agreement among the owners not to hire each others' men. Paradoxically, the situation had partly arisen from a relative scarcity of labour in the booming coal industry, causing the coal-owners to complain that they were being forced to pay heavy fees to induce men to sign on for their yearly contract. The men resisted the proposed agreement by striking work on 25 August, and when an attempt was made to start up some pits on 13 September in defiance of the strike, a body of colliers came and broke up the machinery. The owners were intimidated by the solidarity of the strikers which effectively prevented them employing the legal sanctions available to them. A letter to the Earl of Northumberland explained that legal proceedings might seem appropriate

> Where two or three or a dozen men desert their service, and [the law] has been many times properly executed with good Effect, but where there is a general Combination of all the Pitmen to the Number of 4000, how can this measure take Effect? in the first place it is difficult to be executed as to seizing the men, and even if they should not make a formidable Resistance which scarce can be presumed, a few only can be taken, for which upon the Face of the thing it is obvious that the whole persons guilty can not be secured, so the punishment of probably twenty or forty by a month's confinement in a House of Correction, does not carry with it the least Appearance of Terror so as to induce the remaining Part of so large a Number to submit, and these men that should be so confined would be treated as Martyrs for the good Cause, and be supported and carressed, and at the end of the time brought home in Triumph, so no good effect would arise.[35]

The coal-owners therefore attempted a lockout. An advertisement was placed in the Newcastle papers which requested 'all Persons not to retain or employ any of the said Pitmen till they have performed their bound Services to their present Masters, as they have not till then a Right to serve any other'. The colliers responded with their own paper, emphasising the legality of their proceedings, and also complaining that the masters proposals were designed 'to reduce the industrious Poor . . . to the greatest Misery: as all the Necessaries of Life are at such exhorbitant Prices'. As a result of the agreement of the masters, the men asserted that they would be 'obliged to serve in the same Colliery for Life, which they conjecture will take away the antient Character of this Kingdom as being a free Nation'. A return to work finally took place on 4 October after the masters abandoned their attempt to bind the men beyond the yearly contract.[36] Again in March 1789 there were renewed disturbances amongst the Tyneside colliers during a strike which was marked by quite exceptional violence. The details of the dispute are unknown, but several pits along the Tyne were affected and the men were reported to have destroyed several pumping engines, smashed other machinery, thrown lighted lamps down the pits and set one of them on fire.[37]

The shipbuilding trades

The various skilled trades involved in the shipbuilding industry provide an excellent example of effective industrial action in the absence of permanent trade union organisation. Situated in an expanding industry, although one subject to severe fluctuations, the shipwrights, caulkers, ropemakers, ships carpenters and other skilled crafts had a tradition of strike activity stretching back to the end of the seventeenth century. The most important centres of the industry were the Royal dockyards at Deptford and Woolwich on the Thames, Chatham and Sheerness on the Medway, Portsmouth and Plymouth on the south coast and the private yards on the Thames. Although shipbuilding was beginning to expand on the Mersey, the Tyne, Wear, Humber and Severn, it was the southern yards which supplied most of the naval and merchant shipping of the eighteenth and early nineteenth centuries.

War tended to lead to strikes in the industry as demands for ships increased and the bargaining power of the shipyard workers grew, and the Anglo-Spanish war of 1739 led to a wave of strikes among the various trades in the Royal yards. The men's demands were for changes in conditions of work and pay which were clearly regarded as innovatory by the authorities but cast as restoration of 'lost privileges'. The strikes, on the whole, were conducted peacefully, most being over within a few days as the authorities capitulated to the men's demands. Only at Woolwich were troops sent to overawe the strikers and the strike broken. By the end of 1739 there had been nine strikes or petitions from different trades and yards in less than six months, so that it was little wonder that Commissioner Mathews felt that 'insolence was then in fashion'. Further strikes took place as the war progressed. At Portsmouth in December 1742 the Riot Act had to be read as striking shipwrights assembled and refused to allow men who were still working out of the yard; the besieged strike-breakers had to be supplied by sea, and it was not until troops were called up that the strike was broken. In August 1744 the smiths at Deptford and Woolwich struck and went 'down to Chatham in a Riotous manner, to prevail upon the Smiths there to do the same'; they also forced men in forges at Greenwich to stop contract work; eventually, some of the men were impressed and troops brought in. In May 1745 a long strike of ship's caulkers at Chatham, Woolwich and Plymouth was broken when the men tried to resist the imposition of extra work without compensation.

These strikes of the 1740s did not on the whole occur over delays in paying wages, a common cause in the past. Usually the men were effectively striking for extra pay or opportunities to increase earnings, but couched their demands in terms of 'lost privileges', and the Navy Board pursued a policy of appeasement, particularly towards the shipwrights, the best organised and most essential of the trades. During a war the main concern was to avoid disruption of supply, a situation seized upon by the men to further their position. At the outbreak of the American War there was a strike in the Portsmouth dockyard when the Admiralty tried to introduce a piecework system in place of a day-rate. As well as stating their case in the *Hampshire Chronicle*, the men made contact with other Royal Yards and tried to petition the Crown. After a three-month stoppage, marked by virtually no disorder, the strike collapsed as fresh workers were brought in from Deptford and the Admiralty delayed the introduction of the new system to entice the men back to work.

Thus by the 1780s the shipyard trades had a long tradition of collective bargaining which included joint activity with other yards, public petitions and appeals, and strikes; compared with some other groups their strikes were generally less likely to cause disturbances, partly because there was no obvious 'breaking' to be done and because the authorities were frequently ready to compromise with well-timed strikes in wartime. During the revolutionary and Napoleonic Wars, the shipyard workers again became one of the most 'strike-prone' groups in the country. A detailed study of the Portsmouth dockyard has shown a stream of petitions and minor disputes there and in other yards, culminating in an extensive strike in spring 1801 during a critical moment in the war, when the fleet was being prepared for the expedition to Denmark.[38]

The 1790s

Strikes and combinations became increasingly common during the 1790s. Although the Friendly Societies Act of 1793 provided an important opportunity for workmen to combine legally and a 'cover' for trade union activity, there was evidence of 'a very general spirit of combination amongst all sorts of labourers and artisans' before then. Liverpool, which had witnessed strikes amongst several skilled groups in the latter part of the eighteenth century, was the scene of an extensive strike movement in August and September 1791 by seamen, ship repairers, and carpenters. Although public notices were put up against riotous assemblies and troops brought into the city, the strike appears to have occasioned no disturbances.

The year 1792 saw a veritable explosion of strike activity both in the capital and in the country: in April the ships' carpenters at Liverpool threatened to pull down houses if the slave trade were abolished and their wages were not raised; in the autumn, along the East Coast, at places as far apart as Yarmouth and Tyneside, sailors assembled and demanded higher wages. At North Shields the strikers were reported to be forcing the recalcitrant to join them and to be organising their strike with care, boats being sent to each ship in the harbour, and watches 'under chiefs' keeping guard on both sides of the estuary. A correspondent to the Home Office described how 'the mob at this moment are driving some seamen or officers that have discovered a reluctance to comply with their mode of proceedings naked through the town before them'. Several ship-owners gave the increase for as the above writer commented: 'The fear from the mob, the temptation of a fair wind, the great demand for coals for London, and no support in view were the causes, and are still the causes why the owners of the load ships complied and still comply with their unreasonable demands.' After protracted negotiations in which Rowland Burdon the Tory MP for Durham played an important part, the strike was concluded in November.[39]

Elsewhere in 1792, the colliers were especially active. There were demands for higher wages from colliers at Bristol, Sheffield, Somerset, and Newcastle. At Wigan, the miners struck and collected 'in a riotous manner' to obtain a wage advance, giving the magistrates until the next afternoon 'to consider of it and if their demand is not complied with they threaten to destroy the works by pulling up the engines, throwing down the wheels, and filling up the pits'. Eventually the miners were dispersed by troops. The same year also saw agitation for higher wages amongst the Banbury shag-makers, who complained of illegal apprentices being taken; the Dudley nailmakers; and several of the smaller trades in the North-East.[40]

Activity continued through the winter of 1792–3, causing considerable alarm to the Government at the time of the most intense phase of the reaction to events in France. Although a dispute with the Northumberland miners was settled in February 1793, the Wear keelmen struck in the same month, attacking any delinquents until the arrival of Dragoons from Newcastle effectively broke the strike. February also saw a strike amongst the Durham colliers. Sporadic disputes, some of them accompanied by violence, occurred throughout the 1790s. There were two strikes among the Manchester spinners in 1795 and also amongst the Chatham shipwrights. In 1796 the Tyne seamen struck again but were defeated by the impresss officers taking the ringleaders. On the eve of the Combination Laws there were disputes amongst the Pennine lead miners, the Tyne sailors and an extensive movement among the Lancashire weavers for an increase in wages. None of these appear to have led to disturbances.[41]

The trades in the capital were also active during the later years of the century. After the extensive combinations of the 1760s several groups retained their organisation, though much of it was forced to be clandestine because of Acts prohibiting combinations in their specific trade. Thus Francis Place recalled that he joined the Breeches Makers

Benefit Society in 1790, which though a benefit club, 'was intended for the purpose of supporting the members in a strike for wages'.[42] Place records an unsuccessful strike in the spring of 1793, but also one in 1795 which raised wages from twenty-two shillings per week to twenty-five shillings.[43] Combinations were reported in other skilled trades before 1789, including the wheelwrights (1782), bookbinders (1786), and feltmakers or hatters (1786).[44] The last group could claim a continuous existence as far back as the reign of Charles II and can be regarded as almost a model of the well-organised London trades, obtaining effective protection under the apprenticeship laws; in 1775 they were strong enough to gain a wage rise and also ensure the exclusive employment of 'clubmen'.[45]

The majority of the combinations in London during the 1790s involved the skilled crafts and there were reports of combinations or strikes in the following trades: shoemakers (1791, 1792); curriers (1792); leather-breeches makers (1793, 1795); journeymen bakers (1793, 1799); ropemakers (1793, 1796); hatters (1794); coal-heavers (1795); paper-makers (1795); printers (1795); shipwrights (1797); sugar-coopers (1798). Most of these disputes were conducted peacefully, suggesting a tolerance of combination among the craftsmen of the metropolis by employers which was to survive the Combination Laws.[46] Some, however, witnessed intimidation and violence. When warrants were issued against 170 journeymen shoemakers who struck in February 1793, a thousand shoemakers demonstrated on the streets outside the Litchfield Street Rotation Office when the first cases were heard.[47]

The role of violence

The role of violence in eighteenth-century labour disputes requires some analysis. In the first instance, machine wrecking, the destruction of raw or finished goods, and attacks upon private property constituted a form of bringing pressure to bear. This form of action has been called 'a traditional and established part of industrial conflict in the period of the domestic and manufacturing system, and the early stages of factory and mine'.[48] For agricultural workers, these actions could take the form of sporadic rick-burnings, cattle-maiming, and the spoiling of crops. The destruction of part of an employer's property was an obvious extension of a stoppage of work itself, threatening his livelihood. In the textile industry, for example, frames were often owned by the masters and 'put out' at a rent to the workmen, and their destruction or threatened destruction marked a serious loss of capital. As industry and machinery developed on a larger scale, the vulnerability of employers increased; the greater the amount of capital sunk into a factory or new machinery, the greater the manufacturers' risk from a stoppage of work and damage to his investment. On more than one occasion entrepreneurs were driven from an area by the destruction of their property.[49] This, however, was rarely the primary object of those engaged in labour disturbances, more often than not, the aim was to ensure a successful platform for negotiation and settlement; indeed, the violence often occurred in the initial phase when the strike was commenced. This could be an almost spontaneous cessation of work, as in the Liverpool sailors' strike of 1775, in which the first action was to disable the ships in the river. Similarly, news of a strike could often only be carried by the strikers touring the neighbouring workplaces and producing a general stoppage; sporadic violence could then occur as the workmen sought to enforce the strike.

Although groups such as the keelmen and the Norwich weavers proved themselves capable of maintaining a prolonged strike with an effective fund, the ability to enforce the stoppage was shown time and time again to be vital to a successful outcome. Hobsbawm has argued that the destruction of tools was one way of ensuring that a return to work could not take place in the short term.[50] The attack on pits which began to operate midway through the colliers' strike of 1765 illustrates the way in which violence was used to ensure the maintenance of solidarity during a dispute; and among the keelmen, the first reaction was to prevent keels working, and if necessary prevent strike-breaking by violence. In many of these disputes, the intervention of the military proved decisive, by preventing the strikers from enforcing the stoppage. This was the crucial difference between the eighteenth century and the era of more permanent and open trade unionism: unless a body of workmen could enforce a stoppage, they were almost certainly doomed to failure. It is significant that even the woolcombers, the virtual aristocracy of the woollen trades, were alleged to have imposed regulations in their trade to the effect that

> no man should comb wool under 2s. per dozen; that no master should employ any comber that was not of their club; if he did they agreed one and all not to work for him; and if he had employed twenty they all of them turned out, and oftentimes were not satisfied with that, but would abuse the honest man that would labour, and in a riotous manner beat him, break his comb-pots, and destroy his working tools.[51]

Thus even the most well-organised groups had sometimes to enforce working conditions by intimidation. Violence in labour disputes has often been seen as a symptom of the 'primitive' stage of trade unionism and a function of the characteristic weakness of early trade groups in the face of their employers. In fact, the most noticeable feature of disturbances arising from eighteenth-century labour disputes is that they were commonest among the best organised groups. The woollen workers, like the metropolitan craftsmen, derived their bargaining strength from their position in a tightly organised and relatively prosperous industry. The keelmen and miners of the North-East were also in an expanding industry, albeit subject to fluctuations, which made them some of the most prosperous workmen in the country. As with the origins of trade unionism, it is not to the most depressed sectors and lowest paid group, such as the agricultural labourers, to whom we should look for labour troubles in the eighteenth century, but to the groups who were the effective 'aristocracy' of the working population.

It would also be unwise to place too much emphasis on violence in the course of eighteenth-century labour relations: disturbances were often only the tip of an iceberg of peaceful negotiation and orderly adjustments. Whether a strike occurred, and whether violence broke out, depended on a set of relatively fortuitous factors, which included the twists and turns of negotiations, the actions of the local authorities, and the degree of organisation among the strikers themselves. Conditions varied considerably between the more spontaneous reactions of the Liverpool sailors in 1775 and the more considered actions of the West Country weavers in their series of disputes with the master clothiers. The latter group only resorted to violence as part of a sophisticated campaign to preserve their living standards and prevent erosion of their craft status. The weavers in 1738-40, like the keelmen and the North-East colliers in 1765, were perfectly capable of conducting negotiations with their employers and with local justices, preparing petitions, or obtaining the help to do so from sympathetic gentry or townsmen. In short, these were not 'primitive' rebellions marked by indiscriminate violence and looting, as has sometimes been inferred, but considered, rational actions in pursuit of definite objectives. Hence labour disputes and the violence which often accompanied them were not blind or spasmodic movements, any more than those of food rioters or other protesters.

One aspect of these early disputes is the emphasis placed on legality, seen in the petitions to parliament, the appeals to local magistrates, and the general discrimination of the violence that occurred. That many of these trade groups were defending customary practices, such as apprenticeship regulations, existing work practices, and traditional rates of pay, only emphasises the point: the overwhelming character of eighteenth-century labour disputes was defensive in the face of changed circumstances or new technology. The long process had already begun in which craft and unskilled workers alike were adjusting to the increasingly rapid organisational and technological changes of the industrial revolution. In many cases the process was extremely gradual, not least because of the resistance put up by groups such as the Norwich weavers or the Tyneside keelmen. It meant that such violence as occurred was directed usually at specific targets, innovating employers, 'unfair' competitors such as immigrant labour, and new machines. As earlier writers have shown, however, even in resistance to machinery, the reaction was less hostility to machines as such, but opposition to those machines which seemed most directly to threaten living standards.[52] In the riots of 1779 care was taken to single out the large spinning machines which appeared a gross threat to the Lancashire workmen. The keelmen objected to the persistent problem of overloading, with a good deal of justice on their side.

Nor should we assume that the workmen who took part in these disputes were necessarily faced with the monolithic opposition of the upper classes. In many cases, magistrates were empowered under earlier legislation to regulate wages and arbitrate between workmen and employers, and while local justices had a legitimate concern to preserve public order, they also had a fear of aggravating the situation. Often a genuine desire to find a settlement from within the local community helps to explain the reluctance of magistrates to call on outside help, hence it was usually only when affairs had clearly got out of hand that the troops were called in.[53] Disputes therefore frequently took on the character of three-sided negotiations between magistrates, employers and workmen, in which the justices sometimes took the side of the men against the employers. During the seamen's strike on Tyneside in 1792 the magistrates pressed for a settlement but were faced with an obstinate group of shipowners who refused to comply with the demands of the men and the magistrates; significantly when troops and naval personnel were brought into the conflict, some of the officers acted as a fourth partner in the negotiations, attempting to bring about a settlement.[54] Workmen could often call on a greater degree of sympathy from magistrates and local gentry than has sometimes been allowed by historians determined to see in these conflicts a class dimension which serves only to obscure the complexity of the relationships involved.

Two other aspects of early industrial disputes reinforce this view. On a number of occasions, strikers were able to obtain a reasonably favourable press; the *Essay on Riots* printed in the *Gloucester Journal* in 1738, extracts of which were later published in the *Gentleman's Magazine*, blamed the disturbances in the West Country cloth industry upon the employers.[55] The Hammonds remarked upon the favourable reaction to the colliers in the London press during the strike of 1765;[56] and the sailors in 1793 received a fairly even-handed treatment among the press of the Newcastle area.[57] Though some reports of combinations in the 1790s breathe a violent spirit of anti-Jacobinism, others remained sane and balanced, and did not preclude reasonably humane treatment. The behaviour of the authorities towards strikers was not always as draconian as has sometimes been depicted; following the amicable settlement of a coal-heavers' dispute in 1795, the *General Evening Post* commented, 'Thus has the timely interference of his lordship the Lord Mayor of London pacified a class of about a thousand industrious men, whose hardships certainly demand serious attention.'[58] Even when relatively serious disturbances had taken place the reaction of the authorities was commonly quite lenient by contemporary standards; thus of the forty or fifty sailors arrested following the violent strike at Liverpool in 1775, true bills were found against only eight, who were discharged on entering the navy. Yet more striking was the reaction to the machine breaking in Lancashire in the autumn of 1779: for the destruction of Arkwright's factory, three people were sentenced, one for two years, one for twelve months, and one for four months, and after the riots in Nottingham earlier in the year because of the failure of the framework knitters Bill the only rioter sent to the Assizes was acquitted.[59]

In seeking any overall pattern for the labour disturbances of the eighteenth century, we come up against the familiar problem of disputes which left no permanent record or have yet to be discovered. The work of a group of historians in the North-East has done much to uncover a more intense degree of industrial conflict than might have been expected; similarly my own researches on London have revealed a large number of trade disputes, some of which occasioned violence. Undoubtedly further work, particularly on local newspaper and court records, will add to the picture, nevertheless some tentative conclusions can be put forward. Many disputes were solely dictated by the fortunes of their particular trade and bore only an indirect relationship to the movement of the economy as a whole. Thus the various disputes in the cloth industry in the 1720s and 1730s reflected the problems created by fluctuations in the trade and some of the consequences of gradual changes in production and organisation. It is likely, however, that the disputes in 1738-41 in the West Country derived some impetus from a situation in which high prices coincided with trade depression, for as one reporter commented of the weavers in 1740, 'Trade and they have *shook Hands* and *took leave* of each other.'[60] Over-production and cost-cutting contributed to the strikes of the Tyneside keelmen in 1744 and 1768; wartime depression also exacerbated the conflicts at Liverpool in 1775 and in the Lancashire cotton industry in 1779. The cross-currents of food prices, trade depression, and wage regulation could combine to produce a dispute on almost any occasion in the eighteenth century.

This being said, there were some periods of greater activity than others. Several historians have recognised the importance of the 1760s as a decade of relatively intense industrial conflict. This is not to say that the claims of other periods should be ignored: the period from the mid-1730s through to the 1740s was also marked by several disputes, especially in London and the North-East, but the 1760s have with some justice been described as one of the most remarkable decades for industrial disturbances in the whole century.[61] The scale, and above all, the range of disputes of that decade marks them out from any comparable earlier period. Trade depression and wartime dislocations undoubtedly played their part in these disputes, but the most important factor was the movement in prices which began to be evident during the decade; as well as being a period of a severe short-term harvest failure with extensive food rioting in 1766, it also saw the beginning of a long-term upswing in prices which was to culminate during the Napoleonic Wars. The year of the protracted colliers' dispute in the North-East, 1765, was chosen by Thomas Tooke as marking the beginning of a new era of rising prices for the century as a whole.[62] This long-term turnround in price conditions was exacerbated by a short-term crisis to provoke extensive combinations, strikes, and industrial disturbances. It is significant that the Webbs also dated the first modern use of the term 'strike' from the year 1768, when it was used in reference to a hatters' dispute in the capital.[63]

Disputes became increasingly common during the latter part of the eighteenth century, and the decade preceding the Combination Laws of 1799 and 1800 saw a renewed peak of activity. Undoubtedly there are some special factors which must be borne in mind here; we probably know more about disputes in these years because of the concern about popular movements and organisation among the lower classes engendered by the fear of popular radicalism in the aftermath of the French Revolution. Nonetheless, the number of combinations and strikes seems to have gone beyond anything experienced before. Wartime conditions and high prices again played an important part. The year 1789 witnessed trade depression and high prices; the winter of 1792–3 was also one of shortage and growing trade depression; the war years after 1793 saw violent fluctuations in prices and trading conditions, providing the background to the disputes of 1795–6 and 1799–1800. Moreover, these short-term crises coincided with a long-term movement in prices which aroused growing concern about 'distress' in the manufacturing districts.[64]

One of the most remarkable features of the years immediately preceding the introduction of the Combination Laws was the number, and one might add, the success, of groups of workmen in obtaining their ends through combination.[65] As the Webbs pointed out many years ago, the object of new penal legislation was to combat 'the marked increase of Trade Unionism among workers of various kinds'.[66] Attempts to check the growth of combination had already led to the passing of forty laws in particular trades by 1799 and the immediate occasion of the general Combination Act of 1799 was a complaint about a strike of London millwrights. The first reaction was the preparation of a Bill against combinations in the engineering trade, which was dropped in the House of Lords in favour of a more comprehensive measure; this law was designed to check what Professor Aspinall described as 'a *growing* and illegal practice'.[67] Combinations in many trades were already illegal under particular Acts, while the law of conspiracy, Acts against workmen breaking their yearly bond, and specific legislation against wrecking and damage could all be used. The expense of proceedings, concern for exacerbating a difficult situation, and sheer fear of reprisal were all factors which had previously led magistrates to operate the available legal sanctions only intermittently. The aim of the Combination Laws was to rationalise and expedite proceedings but, as we shall see later, they did not prevent these earlier obstacles from limiting their impact, particularly against the better organised skilled trades. What is important about the immediate background to the Combination Laws is that they attacked a 'growing' practice; they were as much a reaction to the growing and proved strength of combinations in the 1790s as a mere extension of what Place chose to call 'Pitt's reign of terror'.[68]

Thus even by the beginning of the eighteenth century some groups of workmen were already accustomed to industrial action to preserve or improve their living standards. Many of them engaged in both industrial action and food rioting, as in the case of the West Country cloth-workers and the Tyneside keelmen. But there was an increasing tendency for these groups to rely on various forms of industrial action to protect living standards and resist encroachments upon their status; that these actions sometimes took the form of violence and intimidation should not obscure the sophistication of the organisation of groups such as the metropolitan craftsmen, the cloth-workers, and the trades of the North-East. Some of the actions of the seamen and colliers were in a clearly transitional phase, combining strikes for higher wages and demands for the reduction of prices. By the end of the century groups such as colliers had begun to use strikes to raise wages. Among the unskilled groups these activities often still only arose out of ephemeral organisations, and coal miners, amongst others, also continued to play a large part in food riots during the Napoleonic period.

Thus an important transformation was beginning to take place by the latter part of the century. Even outside the factory districts skilled, and some unskilled, workers were beginning to use industrial action as a substitute for food rioting. Sometimes the two forms merged, as on Tyneside in the 1760s, while during the shortages of 1795-6 and 1800-1 there was an overlap of strikes and food riots. Thus in 1795 when the Chatham shipwrights struck work on some naval vessels, they assembled that evening in the market to reduce the price of provisions. In September 1800, the cloth-workers of Wooton-under-Edge were reported to have struck work to reduce the price of bread. By the end of the Napoleonic Wars, strikes and frame-breaking went on side by side with traditional food riots and in 1829 we hear of 'food strikes' amongst the weavers of Bolton, Wigan, and Preston.[69] The direction of change was clear even before the Combination Laws. Strikes and trade union organisation sometimes, but by no means always, accompanied by violence, were becoming the most popular form of protest over wages and living conditions

7 The age of revolution

The French Revolution brought new issues into British politics, while at the same time exacerbating existing conflicts. Most obviously, the traditions of eighteenth-century mob activity were given a new dimension by the rise of popular radicalism and the threat of a revolutionary ideology being imported from France. Moreover, beyond the direct impact of events in France there were also the changes being wrought by industrialisation and urbanisation. Threats of political disaffection and revolutionary activity were not occurring in a static society, but one which was experiencing the major dislocations of early industrialisation. Some years ago, the Hammonds contrasted sharply the more tolerant atmosphere of the eighteenth century with the situation after 1789:

> The poorer classes no longer seemed a passive power: they were dreaded as a Leviathan that was fast learning his strength. Regarded before as naturally contented, they were now regarded as naturally discontented. The art of politics was not the art of keeping the attachment of people who cherished their customs, religion, and the general setting of their lives, by moderation, foresight, and forbearance: it was the art of preserving discipline amongst a vast population destitute of the traditions and restraints of a settled and conservative society, dissatisfied with its inevitable lot and ready for disorder and blind violence. For two revolutions had come together. The French Revolution had transformed the minds of the ruling classes, and the Industrial Revolution had convulsed the world of the working classes.[1]

While undoubtedly overdrawn by the Hammonds in this passage, few historians would doubt that the years after the French Revolution presented many problems different in type to those which existed in the eighteenth century as a whole.

Church and King riots

Initially the most significant effect of the French Revolution was the renewed stimulus given to 'Church and King' disturbances. Although part of the reaction to events in France and their impact on English politics, the background to the disturbances lay in the political tensions which had developed in the years leading up to 1789. During the 1780s the formation of Revolution Clubs to celebrate the 'Glorious Revolution' of 1688 provided a focus for political rivalries and social divisions in several towns and cities. Patronised by Whigs and dissenters, it was the latter group who provided the most important ingredient in the tensions which were to erupt after 1789. The campaigns of dissenters for the repeal of the Test and Corporation Acts, which still technically excluded them from civil offices, parliament, and municipal politics, had been rejected by a dominant Tory and Anglican majority in the House of Commons. Increasingly for the dissenters, religious and political liberty were linked. Already involved in organisations such as the London Revolution Society and similar provincial societies before 1789, they welcomed the French Revolution because it championed religious toleration and political reform. It was at a general meeting of the London Revolution Society in November 1789 that Dr Price, the leading Unitarian Minister in the capital, preached on the text 'The love of our country', which he proposed could best be pursued by obtaining repeal of the Test Acts and reform of parliament. It was this sermon which provoked Edmund Burke's *Reflections on the Revolution in France* and launched the debate on the French Revolution in England.[2]

Even before this debate opened, the campaigns of the dissenters against their legal disabilities had contributed to a revival of political activity in several towns and cities. At Leicester, for example, a Revolution Club had been founded as early as 1782. Its annual dinners caused little comment until 1788 when it carried a resolution 'that this town is improperly represented in Parliament'. Within a year, the Church and King party had founded a Constitutional Society in self-conscious rivalry. In Manchester one of the leaders of the reformers in the early 1790s, Thomas Walker, dated the growth of 'virulent party feeling' to 1789 and the campaign of that year against the Test Act. A 'Church and King' club was founded in 1791 whose members wore uniform and on their buttons bore the emblem of the 'Old Church'; their toast was 'Church and King and down with the Rump'. These developments laid the seed of future conflict, for even before the French Revolution had a major influence on English politics, traditional rivalries had already been exacerbated. The dinners organised in July 1791 to celebrate the fall of the Bastille which provoked the first and most serious bout of Church and King riots; preparations for dinners went on in many towns and in several there were threats of violent opposition, and although the Manchester dinner passed off peacefully, there had been handbills put about which threatened to demolish the house at which it was taking place on the grounds that 'the brains of every man who dined there would be much improved by being mingled with brick and mortar'.[3]

The most serious disturbances took place in Birmingham in 1791. The centre of a powerful dissenting community, including the notable scientist and theologian, Joseph Priestley, it was also host to a distinguished circle of scholars, literary men, and scientists, not all of whom were dissenters, who met in the Lunar Society. As well as being prominent employers, the dissenters had already come to the fore in local politics over the campaign to repeal the Test and Corporation Acts, in which Priestley played a major part. Relations between dissenters and Anglicans were already soured by this and the enthusiasm shown by Priestley and others for the French Revolution only added to the spirit of acrimony, to such an extent that riots were widely expected during the winter of 1790-1. By June 1791 Priestley was engaged in organising a Warwickshire Constitutional Society, pledged to universal suffrage and shorter parliaments. Meanwhile events in France seemed to confirm the worst fears of loyalists: the King's flight to Varennes on the night of 20 June and his subsequent recapture and closer confinement signalled the beginning of a more radical phase of the Revolution. The Civil Constitution of the Clergy encouraged in many Anglicans the fear of similar moves in England should French ideas spread, yet this was precisely what they appeared to be doing as English reform societies corresponded with the French *clubs* and a two-way traffic of curious observers and messages passed between the two countries.

When a dinner was advertised for 14 July at a Birmingham hotel, inviting 'any Friend of Freedom' to celebrate the fall of the Bastille, a confrontation of 'loyalists' and dissenters became likely. Although the dinner was entirely for the 'respectable', at five shillings a head, 'loyalist' anger was aroused by the publication of a revolutionary handbill urging the deposition of the King and declaring that the 'peace of slavery is worse than the war of freedom'. While the promoters of the dinner denounced the document, rumours of disturbances on the 14th began to circulate and slogans were chalked on the walls calling for 'destruction to the Presbyterians'. The diners took every precaution short of abandoning the event to avoid trouble; the dinner was held in the afternoon and Priestley himself did not attend. Nonetheless, as the eighty diners left the hotel in the early evening, 'some hundreds' pelted them with mud and stones before entering the hotel and breaking its windows, then moving on to burn Priestley's chapel, the New Meeting House, and wreck the furniture of the Unitarian Old Meeting which was carried out and publicly burnt in the street. The crowd then marched out to Priestley's house at Sparkbrook. Although he escaped before they arrived the house was sacked and burnt, destroying his laboratory, library, and manuscripts. Induced to leave the ruins on the next morning by the Earl of Aylesford, who led them back to Birmingham, the crowds found themselves unopposed and began to attack the houses of prominent dissenters; the town prison and debtors' gaol was also attacked and the prisoners released. Although checked in the centre of Birmingham by a hastily assembled group of special constables armed with mop-sticks, parties of rioters moved out to fresh targets in the suburbs. The house of a prominent Unitarian manufacturer, John Rylands, was sacked at Easy Hill and, in a bitter battle, the constables sent to stop them were defeated and disarmed, losing one killed and several wounded. The rioters were now able to range far and wide round Birmingham, attacking the houses of dissenters and levying contributions of food, money and drink from the neighbourhood. Groups of colliers from neighbouring towns also joined in, a party from Wednesbury marching into Birmingham, where they did some looting before returning 'laden with spoils'. The last major incident occurred on Sunday 17 July, when a band of thirty men attacked Egbaston Hall, the home of an Anglican member of the Lunar Society, Dr William Withering. But Withering had hired some boxers and recruited some local workmen to defend him and their joint efforts repulsed the attack; in the evening the first soldiers arrived from Nottingham – two troops of dragoons.

As a result of the riots about twenty buildings were seriously damaged or destroyed, including three Unitarian meeting houses and one Baptist meeting place. It was the dissenters, especially the Unitarians, who bore the brunt of the riots. As R. B. Rose has commented, attacks also extended to people associated with the progressive Lunar Society, and the opportunity was taken to attack the prisons, the homes of local justices, and the shop and premises of the local historian William Hutton, who had earned unpopularity as Commisioner for debts. Some rioters displayed confusion about which minority they were to attack, for cries of 'No Popery' were raised more than once. In many respects, however, the disturbances conformed to earlier Church and King disturbances: property rather than individuals were the targets and although some looting took place the crowds also showed a degree of restraint. For example Rose records the 'curious discipline' shown by the rioters in leading to safety the elderly Anglican Dowager Carhampton, with her possessions, before burning down Mosely Hall.[4]

Although the riots were eventually suppressed, two of the rioters executed, and compensation of £23,615 paid out to the victims, the Birmingham dissenters had suffered severely. Many of them, including Priestley, leaving the town altogether. Although stories of a government plot to chastise the dissenters can be dismissed, the local magistracy was more culpable; in spite of rumours of trouble before the dinner, the magistrates allowed themselves to get drunk and virtually gave the mobs free reign to attack the dissenters. It was only on the Saturday when events seemed to be getting out of hand that they took any action, by which time they were unable to cope with the situation; after initial success in the centre of Birmingham, the special constables were defeated and disarmed. Appeals from the magistrates to end the riots were ignored and they were left powerless to deal with the bands of rioters moving about the suburbs and neighbouring contryside. The crucial time had been on the evening of the dinner, when the magistrates made no effort to stop the crowd gathering outside the hotel, virtually indicating to the population that the dissenters were fair game. Even after the riots, the magistrates were slow to prosecute those arrested and gave the impression that their sympathies still lay with the 'loyalists'.

Although the Priestley riots stand out as the most celebrated of the Church and King disturbances of the early 1790s, the real *annus terribilis* for reformers and French sympathisers was 1792. The radicalisation of the Revolution in France and the growth of popular radical societies in England created an atmosphere of reaction in which reformers of all shades of opinion were subjected to persecution and assault. As in Birmingham, this was most evident in places where the fears aroused by the French Revolution aggravated existing rivalries in local politics. Nottingham was noted for its 'violent party spirit' and turbulent elections before 1789, but it was not until spring 1792 that the revolution began to influence local politics with attacks on the mill of Benjamin and Charles Morley and the home of Alderman William Smith, all three Unitarian dissenters.[5] In Manchester, the formation of the Church and King club had been followed by the formation of a Manchester Constitutional Society which, by sending addresses and deputies to Paris, quickly established itself as one of the most prominent provincial reforming societies, declaring itself in favour of the 'free suffrage of the people at large', but carefully dissociating itself from any charge of sedition. But on 4 June, the King's birthday, the Church and King club met to organise an address to the King, welcoming the Government's proclamation against seditious writings, issued on 21 May. Crowds gathered in St Ann's Square to see some loyalist illuminations, then marched on the Cross Street chapel, crying 'Church and King', 'Down with the Rump' and tried to force an entry. Failing to do so, they made a similar attempt on the Unitarian Mosley Street chapel before dispersing.[6]

Similar incidents occurred during the autumn and winter of 1792. The suspension of the French King in August, the September massacres in the Paris prisons, and the Jacobin declaration of Fraternity on 19 November created a situation of acute alarm. The formation of associations to preserve 'Liberty and Property' marked the organisation of loyalist opinion in the capital and the provinces to counteract the threat perceived from domestic radicalism. The circulation of cheap editions of the second part of Paine's *Rights of Man* and a number of strikes and riots in the provinces added to an atmosphere of near panic, in which all reformers were labelled 'Jacobins' and became objects of suspicion, persecution and outright attack. At least in part genuinely alarmed, the Government responded by issuing fresh proclamations against seditious writing, mobilising the militia, and fortifying the Tower. The most serious provincial disturbances were in Manchester again, where the loyalists held a meeting on 11 December. Rumours had already circulated that a riot would take place that evening. A large procession wended its way through the streets with music and placards; congregating in the marketplace, they smashed the windows of the *Morning Herald*'s premises – the principal organ of the reformers. Unopposed by the local magistracy the crowds then went on to attack the house of Thomas Walker, the leader of the Manchester Constitutional Society. Walker however, had assembled some friends with firearms who defended the house against successive attacks. Although the occupants only set off some charges of gunpowder to frighten the crowd, they were later tried at the Lancaster Assizes on a charge of conspiracy to overthrow the Government, but eventually acquitted.[7]

The most common butt of loyalist demonstration in 1792 was Thomas Paine: his books were burnt in June at Exeter and in November almost as many effigies of Paine were burnt as of Guy Fawkes. During the winter such burnings continued in many provincial centres and country districts. On New Year's day in Coventry it was reported:

> The effigy of Tom Paine, with the *rights of Man* fastened upon his breast, was placed in a cart (with a chimney-sweeper as his companion) and drawn through all the principal streets . . . he was taken to the Cross Cheaping, where a gibbet had been previously erected for his reception; where, after hanging the usual time, a fire was lighted under the gallows, which consumed him instantly to ashes, amidst the acclamations of a loyal multitude of surrounding spectators, who all joined heartily in the chorus of *God save the King*.[8]

Such activities were only part of a widespread persecution of those suspected of 'Jacobin' principles in which booksellers and printers were prosecuted, meeting places denied to reformers, and a boisterous loyalism encouraged by public declarations of support for King and Constitution.

The declaration of war with France on 1 February 1793 brought added passion to local rivalries. In Nottingham the houses of people thought sympathetic to the French Revolution were attacked in August. A committee formed by supporters of the war hired navvies engaged in cutting the Trent Canal to intimidate opponents by ducking or manhandling them, treatment from which one man died. The tenements and mill workshops of one of the prominent dissenters who opposed the war, Robert Denison, were burned down while the magistrates stood by. The Mayor, a noted Tory, actually encouraged the mob to break into the homes of people suspected of harbouring arms: this was the ostensible motive for the attack on Denison's property, though the charge was entirely false.[9]

The most serious Church and King disturbances were over by 1794, except in London. Victories in the war provided opportunities of loyalist celebration, but there were no disturbances comparable to the events in Birmingham in 1791. They illustrated that in most provincial towns, the reformers, whether moderate or radical, were faced with a hostile establishment which was prepared to 'license' popular action against them in much the same way as Roman Catholics, Methodists, or other minorities had been persecuted in the past in times of political unrest. The loyalist mobs were occasionally hired, as in the case of the Nottingham navvies, or at least well supplied with free beer, but often the local authorities had little more to do than make it clear that they would permit some disorder to occur. The Manchester deputy-constable in December 1792 was reported to have told someone who asked him to disperse the rioters, 'They are loyal subjects; let them alone; let them frighten them a bit; it is good to frighten these people.'[10] By this time the disturbances were only part of the campaign being waged against popular radicalism on several fronts. Although there is some evidence to suggest that the Priestley riots were carried out by quite small groups of men, with a hard core of perhaps thirty or so, it is important not to fall into the trap of regarding all radical crowds as 'spontaneous' and all 'loyalist' mobs as hired. In many areas popular Toryism provided at least as spontaneous an appeal as popular radicalism. Perhaps most strikingly, both Birmingham and Manchester had been the most disturbed towns during the struggles between Dissent and Anglicanism in the early eighteenth century. It cannot be without significance that the towns which experienced the most serious manifestations of 'Church and King' rioting had a history of uncomfortable relations between this economically powerful minority and an Anglican establishment. Equally there were other towns, for example Coventry, Leicester, and Portsmouth, where such divisions also existed, but did not produce serious disorder.

Popular radicalism and popular disorder

The fear which these Church and King riots revealed were largely misplaced. The middle-class dissenters and aristocratic Whigs who supported the rash of reform societies which sprang up in the early 1790s operated within a tradition of constitutional action which derived primarily from the county movement of the 1780s. Although contract theories of government could be used to justify rebellion should oppression prove unbearable, the tone of most provincial and metropolitan societies was moderate and non-violent. The ideology of the English reformers was derived more from Saxon 'democracy', Magna Carta, and the constitutional struggles of the seventeenth century than from direct borrowing from France. Indeed sympathy with France had derived primarily from the view that they were acting within a tradition already established in England. Even those societies with a strong artisan element often breathed the same spirit; their aims were correspondence and discussion with the object of promoting political education among the working classes. In doing so, the majority subscribed to an impeccably constitutionalist position. Even in an artisan stronghold such as Sheffield the Society for Constitutional Information, founded late in 1791, organised itself into Saxon *tythings* and urged each member to declare himself 'an enemy to all conspiracies, tumults and riotous proceedings' and oppose 'any attempt that tends to overturn or in any wise injure or disturb the Peace of the People or the laws of the Realm'.[11]

Nonetheless there was widespread alarm on the part of the governing classes that rising prices and radical agitation would lead to a serious situation. The atmosphere in the autumn of 1792 is well captured in the diary of Parson Woodforde, recording how the situation appeared to a country cleric dependent on papers brought from Norwich and the gossip of friends. On 12 October he entered in his diary: 'Mr Jeans informed us that there would be a great mob collected at St Faith's Fair on Wednesday next, on account of the dearness of Wheat and other provisions, but I believe rather from the late long propensity of the discontented to a general disturbance, so prevalent at present in France. The Norwich Mob to meet the Country Mob on the above day at St Faith's.' Further entries in November and December breathe the same spirit of alarm that disturbances would break out because of the price of provisions and the machinations of the 'disaffected'. On 28 November he recorded that there was 'Much talking about mobs rising in many parts of the Kingdom especially in Norfolk and in Norwich'.[12] In fact no 'meeting of Mobs' occurred in Norwich, nor any serious disturbances in the city. But the occasional food riot such as that at Yarmouth in October 1792 and the disturbances associated with the sailors' strikes on the East Coast were sufficient to create alarm out of all proportion to the actual number and seriousness of the incidents concerned.

Concern focused on the fear of disaffection, especially that disturbances were being fomented by radical agitators and above all by the circulation of cheap editions of the second part of Paine's *Rights of Man*, published in May. Although these fears were much exaggerated, there were enough incidents to fuel the anxieties of the Government and the propertied classes. There were undoubtedly occasions when disaffection seemed to have taken root. At an enclosure riot in Sheffield in July 1791 there were cries of 'No King', 'No taxes', and 'No Corn Bill'. Whatever the resolutions of the Sheffield Society for Constitutional Information, it was also true that printed bills bearing the word 'No King' appeared on the walls and that in November 1792, 5,000 people paraded through the streets to celebrate the French victory at Valmy, bearing effigies of Edmund Burke and Henry Dundas, the Home Secretary.[13]

In the main, however, the radical societies avoided open challenges to the authorities. In the grain shortage of 1795-6, there were many who feared that an opportunity would be given to the disaffected to mobilise the populace. A correspondent to the Home Office in August 1795 warned that 'a want of food must and will keep the popular mind in such a state of irritability as to be easily worked upon by mischevous men', and another warned that 'the democrats are taking every pains to persuade them the people that this scarcity is occasioned by the bad management of ministers'.[14]

In fact the majority of the food disturbances in 1795-6 owed nothing to radical agitation. There were, however, one or two exceptions; the disturbances in London in July and October, discussed elsewhere, were part of a more broadly-based, if somewhat inchoate, anti-war spirit in which the denunciation of the war by the radical societies, the City of London, and the Foxites undoubtedly added a political element to discontent about the price of food (see p. 170).

Sheffield too witnessed a series of disturbances, in some of which at least, a case can be made for radical involvement. It was one community in which the case for arming by the radicals can be authenticated and in which a more militant temper had appeared during the years 1794-5. Following some market disturbances in June 1795, there was a threat of mutiny among some of the soldiers garrisoning the town because of grievances over pay. A handbill was circulated, the first verse of which ran:

> Treason! Treason! Treason!
>   Against the People!
> The People's Humbug'd! A plot is discovered!
> Pitt and the Committee for Bread are combined
> Together to starve the Poor into the Army and Navy!
> And to starve your Widows and Orphans!
> God help ye Labourers of the Nation!
> You are held in requisition to fight in a bad cause;
> A cause that is blasted by Heaven, and damned by all
> good men!

When the soldiers mustered on 4 August a crowd gathered and urged them 'to push matters on'. Ordered by the officer to march, the men refused and a troop of volunteers had to be called up to control the situation; when the crowd began to stone the soldiers, the Riot Act was read, and the volunteers eventually opened fire, killing at least two people. Even before the Riot Act had been read, the volunteers' commanding officer, Colonel Althorpe, had gone into the crowd with a drawn sabre to arrest someone, and in doing so wounded several people.[15]

With the disturbances in London, this was the clearest instance of an attempt to capitalise upon disorder during the summer of 1795. The majority of food disturbances occurred without the obvious involvement of radicals and were a spontaneous reaction to high prices and fear of food shortages. It is possible that the disturbances in Sheffield might have taken place without the circulation of the handbill, alleging a *pacte de famine* by the Government to force men to join the army. Service in the army was rarely popular and it was likely that crowds in a town like Sheffield would have been sympathetic to the troops' protest. Nevertheless, the situation did contain a potent fusion of the food and anti-war issue. Only a week after the disturbances a meeting was held organised by the Sheffield Society for Constitutional Information which condemned the war, deplored food shortages, and demanded annual parliaments and universal suffrage. Elsewhere anti-war feeling and the opposition to the Two Acts provoked considerable political activity in the form of petitions and meetings, but on the whole, this was organised by respectable Whigs such as Christopher Wyvill and Charles Grey. Wyvill called a meeting of freeholders at York to condemn Pitt's repressive legislation and demand reform as a means of ending the war. But Wyvill was outflanked by the mobilisation of the Ministry's supporters who at a more numerously attended meeting pledged their support to the government.[16]

Although several petitions for an end to the war were presented during 1795–6, the failure of the reformers to carry a majority at the York meeting illustrated that there were still many who supported both the war and the ministry. Loyalist petitions flowed in after the attack on the King's Coach and the number of petitioners in favour of the Two Acts was said to outnumber those against by four to one. In a famous passage, Francis Place commented on the popular support for repression: 'Infamous as these laws were, they were popular measures. The people – ay, the mass of the shopkeepers and working people – may be said to have approved them without understanding them. Such was their terror of the French regicides and democrats, such was the fear that "the throne and the altar" would be destroyed.'[17] Nor did the opposition to the Government carry sufficient weight to overcome popular 'loyalism' and Tory support in the country at large. Only two counties, Derby and Northumberland, petitioned against the Two Acts. In Liverpool addresses for reform drawn up by a society of friends of peace at the end of 1794 were torn up by a mob which invaded the town hall and called for a new 'loyal' address which was 'tumultuously voted' and received 12,000 signatures. In Norwich, in spite of two petitions for peace in 1795, one signed by 5,500 people, a crowd of 3,000 assembled to celebrate the Queen's birthday in May, while a popular small-scale military review was held to celebrate the King's birthday in June. In Manchester, the war had been positively welcomed, Archibald Prentice writing that 'the war spirit was kindled and it flamed up as fiercely as king, or aristocracy, or church could desire. The war was decidedly popular; if it had not been declared, the people would have used compulsion to have it declared'. Even after bankruptcies and depression in 1793 and food riots in 1795, Prentice recorded that although there was discontent 'it scarcely found audible utterance. . . . Glory and want went hand in hand; splendid reviews and meal mobs were contemporaneous.'[18]

But the burdens of the war were real enough. The continual demand for men led to a quota system for seamen being imposed by two Acts in March 1795. The first imposed quotas on each county, the magistrates being responsible for assembling a specified number of men within three weeks; any parish failing to produce its quota could be fined. The second Act ordered specified ports to produce a set quota of men, until which time a total embargo was placed on shipping leaving the port. Municipal authorities usually offered bounties to raise the men required: Liverpool was asked to provide 1,711, and bounties of £31 5s. were offered to able seamen, £23 10s. for ordinary seamen, and £17 10s. for 'landsmen'; the mayor and corporation processed through the dock area and streets with drums beating and colours flying to fill the quota, which they accomplished. The London quota of 5,704 men was filled with 1,371 seamen (equal to 2,742 landsmen), 2,522 landsmen, and 440 pressed men at an average bounty of 25 guineas.[19]

Whilst these demands for the navy were met without serious disorder, the army and militia remained acutely short of men. Recruitment into the various volunteer corps and armed associations – in themselves a not inconsiderable focus for loyalist activity – carried exemption from militia service. The Government was forced to introduce a supplementary Militia Act to raise 63,878 men from the counties. The result was a renewal of rioting against the balloting provisions – almost a carbon copy of the events of 1757 – which occurred mainly in October and November 1796 when the lists were prepared. The most widespread disturbances were again in north Lincolnshire. Deputies were prevented from attending the meetings scheduled to compile the lists and at Caistor a crowd of 500 broke up the meeting and seized the lists; at Alford, crowds demanded money from every propertied person in the area; and further south, crowds at Norwich broke up a general meeting on 15 November and disturbances spread to Cambridgeshire, Northamptonshire, and Buckinghamshire. Meetings were disrupted and lists destroyed in places as far apart as Ulverstone in Lancashire, Oswestry in Shropshire, and Penrith in Cumberland. Although the riots occurred on a smaller scale than in 1757, they revealed similar anxieties. They were preceded by rumours that the men balloted would be sent to the East Indies and that buying a substitute would be exorbitantly expensive. Although there was an occasional sign of anti-war feeling, as at Norwich, where the crowds who paraded the streets burned effigies of Pitt and Windham, the sentiments of the rioters were more typically represented by the cry at Caistor of 'God save the King, but no militia'. The concentration of disturbances in north Lincolnshire may have been caused by a failure of the Lord Lieutenant, the fifth duke of Ancaster, to call a county meeting to explain the situation; they were soon put down by sending troops and yeomanry to the affected areas. Even more important, an effort was made to explain that militia service was only for home duty, not overseas. Explanatory notices in newspapers, manifestos by lord lieutenants, and an appeal to patriotic sentiment also helped to quieten ill-feeling. Radical involvement had been minimal, the only incident to cause alarm being a pike found on the road between Spilsby and Louth in Lincolnshire.[20]

Hardly had the militia riots died down than the country was plunged into the naval mutinies of spring and early summer 1797. Incidents of indiscipline sufficient to be called 'mutinies' were not uncommon in the British armed forces of the late eighteenth century. The incident at Sheffield in 1795 illustrated that pay was one common source of grievance, particularly among militia regiments. John Prebble's work on Scottish regiments raised for British service has shown that 'mutinies' were frequent, occurring most often when troops were about to be embarked for duty overseas.[21] A savage illustration of such an incident was given in August 1795 when a newly raised Irish regiment at Exeter refused to accept amalgamation with another line regiment. The men had been raised from the tenants of Viscount Cunningham, who commanded the regiment, and quite what their objection was is not clear. Called into a circle and the articles of war read to them, the men still refused to obey orders, one of them interrupting the ceremony by damning the articles and all who belonged to them. When shots were fired at officers some men were taken prisoner, but the regiment fixed bayonets and tried to release them from Exeter Castle. Frustrated in this effort by the officers closing the gates, the men remained assembled and when addressed by a colonel and ordered to dismiss they refused. Finally squadrons of dragoons were brought up. The men were given a time limit to 'recover their senses', but when they still refused to obey orders the dragoons were ordered into the midst of the Irishmen, cutting down all who showed any opposition and driving the rest into their quarters; it was later reported that 'some had their noses cut off, others their arms; in short a great many had been disabled'.[22] The militia too proved extremely troublesome, participating in the provision riots of 1795 and on more than one occasion refusing to obey orders because of disputes about their complex position regarding pay and allowances.[23]

Nor was the navy as immune from unrest as has sometimes been alleged. A study of the major naval base of Portsmouth between 1780 and 1800 records ten incidents to which the term 'mutiny' or 'mutinous' can be applied. In the largest of these in April 1783, men from three ships paraded on the shore with a boy dressed up to represent an unpopular midshipman whom they compelled to clean the shoes of anyone they met. In front of the group marched a petty-officer 'greedily gnawing a bone with little or no meat on it'. A body of seamen marched to London to present a petition to the King about arrears of pay and harsh discipline. While the Admiralty dragged its feet, the men of one ship threatened to pull down the house of the navy prize-agent. Another ship refused to sail when ordered to do so, the men demanding their pay and immediate release at Portsmouth; they were eventually forced to give in when other ships were brought up and the guns of Southsea battery trained on them, the Admiral threatening to sink them if they did not submit; three of the crew were later hung for mutiny. Such agitations about pay and grievances were not infrequent. Their usual character was a refusal of ships to sail, sometimes backed by a petition or other statement of grievances. In a sense, they were similar to strikes among merchant seamen, but threatened with much more harshness because of naval discipline.[24]

Wartime inflation had greatly eroded the value of seamen's wages by 1797, rates still being what they had been in Charles II's reign. Although in theory naval discipline was less harsh than in the army, it varied considerably from ship to ship, and was often still brutal in the extreme. Traditional grievances about lack of shore leave (virtually non-existent for fear of desertion), the inequitable distribution of prize money, and the embezzlement and quality of provisions on board ship continued to fester. The situation was undoubtedly exacerbated by the rapid expansion of the navy, bringing into its ranks merchant seamen, some at least of whom must have heard about, if not being involved in, strikes and action for higher wages in the course of the 1790s. It also brought in large numbers of Irishmen, some of whom may have been involved in the United Irishmen. The expanded navy also included some better-educated 'quota' men, such as Richard Parker, the leader of the Nore Mutiny, who were both less prepared to accept poor conditions and more able to formulate and organise opposition.

The naval mutinies of April–June 1797 took on the character of a protracted strike until grievances were met. Demands for higher pay had been aired in March, but ignored; on 15 April the Spithead fleet refused to sail when ordered to do so. On the next day the men formed a committee, which met on the flag-ship *Queen Charlotte*; some unpopular officers were sent ashore, and a petition of grievances drawn up. A few officers were roughly handled and some men killed in a fight on the *London*, but the mutineers retained strict discipline on the whole, even flogging one man who became drunk. After attempts to persuade the men to return to duty failed, the Government was forced to capitulate to the demands. But delays in implementing them led the men to continue to refuse to weigh anchor. Eventually Lord Howe was despatched to Spithead to convince the men of the Government's good faith. After visiting each ship, on 14 May Howe was carried ashore in triumph by the sailors and chaired to Government House and three days later the fleet put to sea.

On 10 May the first signs of mutiny appeared in the Nore fleet, off Sheerness. Two days later, the crew of HMS *Sandwich*, led by Richard Parker, persuaded eleven other ships to mutiny and send delegates to Portsmouth to coordinate action with the Channel Fleet. Ignoring a Royal Proclamation of the 23rd offering improved conditions and a pardon, the mutineers blockaded the Thames and were joined by thirteen more ships from the fleets of Duncan and Onslow. Gradually running short of supplies, however, the men's morale flagged and most of the ships surrendered, the *Sandwich* renouncing Parker's authority and coming into Sheerness harbour on 15 June. A fortnight later Parker was hanged and twenty-two other mutineers executed.[25]

The mutinies were primarily apolitical. Only at the Nore did the rhetoric of popular radicalism appear with references to 'the Age of Reason' and the 'Floating Republic', and even there the sailors fired salutes on 29 May to honour the restoration of Charles II, and on 4 June for the King's birthday. Although Parker and some of his closer associates may have seen further than a simple revolt over pay and conditions, the conduct of both fleets during the mutinies owed little to radical agitation. An investigation conducted by two London stipendiary magistrates at the behest of the Home Office into the involvement of London

Corresponding Society members with the mutiny at Sheerness concluded that although several people of 'mischievous dispositions' had fraternised with the delegates on shore and encouraged the mutineers with 'inflammatory language', they had not 'in the smallest degree been able to influence the proceedings of the mutineers'. Firm evidence of a connection between United Irishmen and the mutinous fleets was equally lacking. Although it is possible to accept E. P. Thompson's observation that a widespread mutiny in the fleet could have provided an opportunity for an alliance between 'bread and butter' grievances and 'the aspirations articulated by the politically conscious minority', there is very little evidence that the seamen were prepared to allow themselves to be so used. Indeed the men at Spithead went so far as to warn the Nore fleet not to be misled by 'French principles and their agents, under whatsoever mask'. While individual radicals, including a 'shadowy gentleman in black' may have made contact with Parker and the mutineers at the Nore, the mutiny exposed the conflict between the more constitutionally minded radicals, like Francis Place, and those who were beginning to be involved in the conspiratorial activity of the United societies. The limited objectives of the sailors and the still dominant constitutionalism of the LCS deprived the mutinies of any 'revolutionary' significance except within the widest use of that term.[26]

The Government was also dealing with a tremor of mutiny in the army at the same time. A week after the Spithead mutiny had broken out soldiers were given a pay rise which had been urged by commanding officers for several years. Fear that the naval revolt might spread led to part of the London garrison being paraded on 15 May and assured that their conditions would be made better 'in consequence of their uniform good conduct'. The Order confirming the rise was somewhat delayed and in the interim the Government was alarmed by a number of handbills distributed among the troops in London, Reading and Maidstone. A handbill found on 21 May in Maidstone urged the troops to throw off the 'tyranny' of discipline and agitate for better pay and conditions; the troops in London, they were assured, were with them: 'The regiments which send you this are willing to do their part. They will show their countrymen they can be soldiers without being slaves. . . . Be sober, be ready.' On the 26th came news of a disturbance among the privates in the Royal Artillery regiment at Woolwich. Pitt was awakened with the news and hurried to confer with the Duke of York, Marquis Cornwallis, and the Secretary for War and the Colonies. Cornwallis and the regiment's commander, Earl Harrington, were speedily despatched to Woolwich with troops. Although the men were assembled and told to state their grievances, eleven ringleaders were arrested. On the following day the Ordnance Board confirmed that the pay of the artillery was being raised in line with the rest of the army. The soldiers were reminded of their previous good order and 'that it was not in the power of the most artful traitor to seduce the soldiers of the Regiment'. The Coldstream Guards were also paraded on 27 May and told by the Duke of York that 'His

Royal Highness rests assured that these new instances of the liberality of Parliament and his Majesty's paternal care will rivet the affection for their King and Country'. With this the incident ended, but the precaution was taken of hurriedly passing an Act making inciting mutiny among the troops a capital offence.[27]

The impact of popular radicalism in the late 1790s is difficult to gauge accurately. Some more cautious and moderate men were driven out of political activity by government repression and disillusion with the progress of events in France. Of those who remained, some maintained a constitutional stance, while others were increasingly drawn into the shadowy conspiracies of the United Irishmen. Some oscillated between the two approaches. The suppression by name of the principal radical societies in 1799 left in existence groups who continued to agitate against the war and its consequences. There was some agitation during the food riots of 1799–1801, though the degree varied from area to area. It is also important not to confuse agitation with actual involvement or sole responsibility for the disturbances; many took place without any radical involvement whatsoever, marking a traditional response to a period of high prices and widespread distress. But in some areas there was a more complex picture: in Lancashire, bodies of United Irishmen remained active and many magistrates were convinced that the radicals were using the shortage to foment disorder. The pass-word of the United Irishmen at Bolton was said to be 'a Big Loaf'; at Wigan handbills were put about which declared 'When we erect the Tree of Liberty then you the magistrates like others will wish you had acted otherwise . . .'. Posters declaring for 'No K—g!' appeared in Manchester and the spring of 1801 saw several night-time meetings, after one of which a poster nailed to a tree demanded 'an equal representation of all the people of England by Universal Suffrage; A reduction of the National Debt; a lowering of Provisions of all sorts'.[28]

In West Yorkshire too, there was considerable political activity during the scarcity. Christopher Wyvill attempted to revive the spirit of the Yorkshire Association on the basis of a peace campaign, with the hope of leading on to a change of ministers and parliamentary reform. By 1800 the war had begun to affect the fortunes of the manufacturers, and petitions for peace were presented from Leeds, Wakefield and Bradford, but this movement was largely divorced from the food rioting which occurred and many of the disturbances during the first half of 1800 in Yorkshire owed little or nothing to political agitation. A more militant temper existed in Sheffield where the local volunteer infantry showed considerable reluctance to put down food riots and those that did turn out were stoned by the populace. During the autumn and winter of 1800–1 there were reports of nocturnal meetings and magistrates passed on to the Lord Lieutenant, Earl Fitzwilliam, reports of arming, secret committees, and contacts with groups across the Pennines in Yorkshire. Although Fitzwilliam played down these reports, there was undoubtedly some attempt by a determined group of radicals in the area to broaden the attack upon the Government, using the issues of distress and the war. Meetings continued to be held in the spring and summer of 1801 and there was talk of a 'general rise' to take place at the end of July. Agents sent from Lancashire at the behest of the Bolton magistrate, Colonel Ralph Fletcher, claimed to have been told of a 'revolutionary plan' by the United Englishmen to take place at a time thought proper by leaders in London.[29]

The easing of food shortages from the summer of 1801, government vigilance, and the possibilities of peace with France led to a reduction in both agitation and food riots. While there is little doubt that in areas like Lancashire and Yorkshire, there had been attempts to mobilise the populace by determined groups of radicals, the extent to which these can be described as creating a 'mass movement' remains open to question. Nor can 'aggressive self-confidence' and 'political awareness' among the populace at large be deduced from the presence of inflammatory handbills and reports of nocturnal meetings.[30] The former could and often did emanate from small groups whose activities were not necessarily an accurate reflection of the state of mind of the population as a whole; the latter were exaggerated and some at least were concerned with trade union activity rather than specifically political issues.

Similar problems have been raised by discussion of the so-called 'Black Lamp (or Lump)' conspiracy in Yorkshire during 1802. Reports of plans for a general rising in November came in from informers and magistrates in Yorkshire; nocturnal meetings and 'business' committees were said to be active laying plans for an insurrection which would have coincided with Despard's coup in London. Although much of the evidence for this conspiracy rests on informers' reports, in late November 1802, after Despard had been arrested, two Sheffield men, William Lee and William Ronksley, were brought to trial for administering secret oaths. It was alleged that they had manufactured and buried pikes in preparation for an attack on the local barracks, organised a secret association of a thousand members, and drilled during the night. They were said to have been ready to act 'when the late disturbances happened at Woolwich', but, being disappointed in the result, postponed their action. Lee on the other hand said he had given up 'all political matters' when 'provisions became cheaper' and Ronksley that when the 'arms had been buried he hoped they would remain so forever'. Even if the details of the conspiracy were exaggerated by the Government's agents, the trial provided some evidence of West Riding activity in these years. Lee and Ronksley were sentenced to seven years' transportation.[31]

Industrial disputes under the Combination Laws

In spite of their repressive reputation, there is a wealth of evidence that trade union activity continued under the Combination Laws, and with it the traditional tactics of 'collective bargaining by riot'.[32] The Webbs claimed that the London craft trades were never more completely organised than between 1800 and 1820 and, although there were a number of prosecutions against combinations of workmen under the Combination Laws or earlier legislation, magistrates were often prepared to tolerate strikes providing there was no serious disorder.[33] In 1802, in one of the most violent disputes in the capital, the Thames shipwrights conducted a prolonged strike in which they used intimidation to prevent strike-breakers from being brought in from the Royal Yards. Although this strike was eventually broken by the use of troops and the Riot Act, highly skilled or strategically well-placed groups both in the capital and in the country were able to organise strikes through the agency of Friendly Societies, clandestine meetings, and *ad hoc* combination. The various groups involved in the shipbuilding trades carried out a coordinated strike in the dockyards of the Thames and South Coast in 1801-2.[34] The Tyneside keelmen fought a successful strike in 1809 to increase piecework rates: during a three-week stoppage, they prevented all movement on to the river until the magistrates compelled the coal-owners to come to terms.[35]

In the South-West woollen industry a tradition of 'collective bargaining by riot' continued to be used to coerce employers. In 1802-3, two movements flowed into each other, resistance to gig-mills and to masters setting up shops with untrained men against the ordinances of the Statute of Apprentices. As already shown, machinery had been making sporadic inroads into the area during the late eighteenth century, sometimes resisted and at other times not. Another complicating factor in 1802 was the return of discharged soldiers and sailors during the Peace of Amiens. The Wiltshire machine-breaking of these years has been described as 'less a sign of strength than despair', as the Wiltshire shearmen or 'croppers' were increasingly faced with competition with Yorkshire. While the Yorkshire 'croppers' were able to control the introduction of machinery through the strength of their organisation, the Wiltshire men were forced to negotiate from an unfavourable position and with the added disadvantage of the presence of the Combination Laws. In the face of these difficulties machine-breaking was part of a determined campaign to enforce Tudor statutes against gig-mills, the grouping of looms in large shops, and the use of unapprenticed labour. Subscriptions were raised to fight test cases and employ counsel to resist the masters' attempt to secure the repeal of all protective legislation in the woollen industry. In Bradford and Warminster, the shearmen refused to finish cloth produced on gig-mills, destroying property and even firing into the houses of unpopular masters or their workmen. On 21 July mills at Littleton and Steeple Ashton were fired and threatening letters sent out to masters.

The campaign by the croppers was conducted by a committee of thirteen based on Trowbridge and the threats and violence provided evidence of the determination of the workmen to obtain a settlement with the masters, whether in terms of a phased introduction of the machinery, with safeguards for unemployed workmen, or the full enforcement of the protective legislation. Cooperating with the Yorkshire croppers, who conducted successful strikes at Leeds and Huddersfield against un-apprenticed labour and gig-mills, the shearmen of the South-West were described as being 'not an assembly of a common mob but a body of armed, regulated, and systematical people' and the coordination of activity between Yorkshire and the South-West by delegates and letters aroused the suspicions of the Government who feared the presence of an organisation 'at once so efficient and so dangerous both from the amount of its force, and from the facility and secrecy with which . . . that force can be called into action . . .'. In the end the croppers' campaign failed. Annual Suspending Acts allowed manufacturers to introduce the gig-mills until a general repeal of paternalistic regulation of the woollen trade was passed in 1809.[36]

The struggle of these workmen to regulate their industry illustrated many traditional features, as well as some which were to influence Luddism. The workmen had carried out their campaign using petitions, appeals to the magistracy, test cases, threatening letters, and occasional violence. In fact, the last component was of relatively little significance in the campaign, being over by the end of 1802; one man was executed for it after trial at the Salisbury Assizes in March 1803. The Combination Laws had been used to convict large numbers of shearmen summarily to short terms of imprisonment, a London magistrate sent to the area to supervise the operation commenting: "Two or more Justices meet daily at one or other of the Manufacturing Towns and as the Combination Act affords a very convenient pretext for summoning and examining upon Oath any suspected persons I have continually some before them. It answers the double purpose of keeping the Magistrates at their Post and of alarming the disaffected.' The law against administering illegal oaths, passed in the aftermath of the naval mutinies, was also used in an attempt to break up the shearmen's committee, but the five men arrested were acquitted [37] The remarkable feature in the face of these measures was the persistence of the men's agitation through constitutional channels, putting a Bill to Parliament in 1805 backed by petitions and even signed by many small masters. When this failed, attempts to reach a compromise settlement continued. With the passing of the 1809 Act, the shearmen were defeated and could legitimately claim that parliament had sacrificed their interests to those of the masters.

Gig-mills and other disputed practices now made more rapid advances in the South-West. Significantly, however, these developments were slower in Yorkshire where the strength of the shearmen's organisation had earned them the title of the 'Tyrants of the Country' from Earl Fitzwilliam. Although ultimately forced to accept gig-mills, the Yorkshire workers had shown a striking ability to organise themselves in spite of the harassment of the Combination Laws and other legislation. As Earl Fitzwilliam recorded: 'The advantage these people derive from their system of combination becomes an example to every other branch of trade and manufacture, and the pains they take to disseminate their system among other trades, gives just cause for apprehension that the trouble they take in this cause, will not be without its consequences.'[38]

Wartime fluctuations and the impact of technological change also affected the textile districts of Lancashire. The major focus of activity was in the weaving branch of the trade where handloom weavers, still outnumbering factory operatives by two to one in 1816, were being undermined by the introduction of the power loom and by the flooding of the labour market with immigrant labour. The weavers petitioned parliament for a Minimum Wage Bill in 1799 and 1800, and again in 1807, when they secured 130,000 signatures from Lancashire, Cheshire, and Yorkshire. The news of the rejection of their Bill in May 1808 led to serious rioting. The Manchester weavers assembled near St George's Church on 24 May and sent delegates to the principal manufacturers and town officials to demand redress of grievances. A distribution of bread, ale, and butter milk did not prevent 10,000 or 15,000 assembling on the next day. Taking fright the magistrates read the Riot Act and the crowd was dispersed by soldiers, killing one man and wounding several. The weavers started a strike, which gradually spread through the cotton district, demanding an increase of wages by a third. The strike was enforced by the men removing the shuttles of all workmen, threatening those who refused to give them up. When the Rochdale magistrates deposited two bags of shuttles in the House of Correction, the weavers broke in and burned the place down. Near Manchester a manufacturer who paid particularly low wages was forced from his bed and made to sign a minimum wage agreement kneeling in the street. Small-scale disturbances took place in Blackburn, Wigan, and Preston when weavers assembled, and some food riots occurred at Clitheroe and Burnley. By June over 60,000 looms were idle and the employers were forced to come to an agreement during July. Some of the Manchester weavers remained unsatisfied, however, and tried to enforce the stoppage by attacking weavers who went to work, destroying finished work with vitriol and burning effigies of the masters. On the whole, however, the strike had been conducted with relatively little violence and the legal retribution was small, one man receiving two years' imprisonment for the firing of the Rochdale House of Correction and several others receiving light sentences for extorting money and breaking machines.[39]

Although this successful strike did little to halt the long decline of the handloom weavers, it illustrated the familiar range of tactics available to skilled workers. The spinners too conducted strikes in 1799, 1800, 1802, and 1803, and in 1810 they were only defeated after a four-month stoppage supported by subscriptions totalling £17,000 drawn from several parts of the North. Some mills were attacked in Manchester, but there was little other disturbance. The weavers' and the spinners' actions illustrated the growing organisation of old and new branches of the textile industry. The cotton-spinners had begun to organise effectively from the

1790s and although in common with other unions they were forced to operate in semi-legality, they provided the springboard for industrial action by cotton-workers in the post-war period, notably in the 1818 spinners' strike. The development of Luddism should not obscure the most obvious feature of these years, of which Luddism was a part, the continuing ability of workmen to organise themselves and to deploy a range of tactics, including intimidation or machine breaking, to negotiate with their employers.

The Luddites

In 1811 outbreaks of machine-breaking, particularly in the stocking-frame industry, began to be associated with letters and proclamations bearing the 'signature' of 'Ned Ludd', 'King Ludd', or 'General Ludd'. These documents threatened to wreck stocking frames or other machinery and also occasionally the life of employers, magistrates, and even the Prime Minister, Spencer Perceval. Some letters bore the address 'Shirewood Camp', 'Shirewood' or 'Sherwood' forest. The term 'Luddism' has therefore become applied to the widespread machine-breaking and other disturbances chiefly associated with the years 1811–12, although incidents continued sporadically afterwards. Three main trades and geographical areas were affected: the framework knitting trade in Nottinghamshire, Leicestershire and Derbyshire; the woollen industry in Yorkshire; and the cotton industry in Lancashire and Cheshire. In the framework knitting trade it was chiefly the frames used for the production of hosiery and lace which were attacked; in the Yorkshire woollen industry the shearing-gigs which replaced the hand-shearing of woollen cloth; and in the cotton industry the power looms which were displacing hand-loom weavers.

At one time seen as a blind and spasmodic attempt to halt industrialisation, more sophisticated analyses of Luddism have placed it within the context of earlier episodes of 'collective bargaining by riot' and the industrial conditions of each area. In a more controversial interpretation, E. P. Thompson has stressed the political significance of Luddism, arguing that it represented 'a quasi-insurrectionary movement which continually trembled on the edge of ulterior revolutionary objectives'. Luddism he argues, should be seen as 'arising at the crisis-point in the abrogation of paternalistic legislation, and in the imposition of the political economy of *laissez faire* upon, and against the will and conscience of, the working people'. Other historians of Luddism have argued that it was primarily an industrial movement. A recent work has put the counter-argument trenchantly: 'Luddism was industrial in its origins and industrial too in its aims. . . . It remained devoid of any tendencies to develop into a political revolutionary movement, and even on the industrial front it was not demanding a new structure but seeking rather to salvage what it could from the wreckage of the old paternalist, protective legislation.'[40]

Amidst these conflicting interpretations it is important to gauge the extent of the movement known as Luddism – difficult in itself because of its wide geographical spread and the habit of some contemporaries of lumping together machine-breaking, food-rioting, and political agitation under the same label. The main wave of Luddite activity occurred in Nottingham, Leicester and Derby during 1811–12, subsequently spreading to the Yorkshire croppers and the Lancashire weavers. Smaller waves occurred in mid-1814 and again in the summer and autumn of 1816. Each trade was affected by general causes of distress which resulted in unemployment, short-time working, wage cuts, and price rises, but they were also influenced by highly complex particular circumstances which influenced the character of the disturbances in each area.

The framework-knitting trade of the East Midlands had been hard hit by the closure of the American market to British goods under the American Non-Intercourse Act of February 1811, reducing British exports to North America from £11m in 1810 to £2m in 1811. Unemployment and wage cuts followed, while harvest failures pushed the price of wheat as high as 160s. per quarter in August 1812. These industrial and harvest difficulties brought to a head the festering grievances. There had been a history of disputes about frame rents, the price paid for finished goods, payment in truck, and the production of cheap 'cut up' stockings by unskilled labour. None of these grievances was new in 1811, many had existed for a generation or more, and attempts by the hosiers and stockingers to eliminate them and achieve better regulation of the trade had continued throughout the Napoleonic Wars with increasing hostility shown to the 'cut-ups'. In 1811 efforts to regulate the trade had failed, and in the midst of growing distress the stockingers turned to more direct methods of bringing pressure to bear on the hosiers.

The immediate cause of the outbreak of Luddism in Nottingham was a wage dispute in March 1811. Following the failure of the framework-knitters' leader, Gravener Henson, to obtain the intervention of the Nottingham justices against some hosiers who had reduced the prices paid for finished work, a large group of stockingers gathered in Nottingham marketplace on 11 March, 'clamouring for work and a more liberal price'. That evening sixty frames of the underpaying hosiers were broken at Arnold. Although more frames were broken during the spring and early summer, it was not until November that serious alarm developed as the machine-breaking attacks spread into Derbyshire and Leicestershire. Even so, most reports emphasised the selectivity of the machine-breakers, who concentrated on the frames of masters who either underpaid or made 'cut-ups', and the discipline of the bands, meeting secretly and moving from village to village, often armed with muskets, hammers, and clubs. During the most active phase of the attacks between March 1811 and February 1812 it has been calculated that 1,000 frames were destroyed, in about a hundred different attacks. The passing of an

Act making frame-breaking a capital offence in February 1812 and the drafting of 2,000 troops to Nottingham – the largest force ever sent to quell a local disturbance – brought the major phase of Midlands Luddism to an end. It was replaced by the formation of a 'United Committee of Framework-Knitters' to promote a Bill in parliament to regulate the trade. When the bill was rejected in the Lords and the framework-knitters prosecuted under the Combination Laws in July 1814, frame-breaking was resumed, continuing intermittently until 1816.

By January 1812 machine-breaking had spread to Yorkshire. The highly skilled croppers who had earlier resisted the introduction of gig-mills now attacked the shearing-frame which threatened to destroy their livelihood. Resisted by legal means before 1812, the croppers turned to machine-breaking in the midst of unemployment and high prices. A mill at Leeds containing gig-mills was fired on 19 January and a series of attacks by small groups of armed men with blackened faces took place around Huddersfield. Threats were issued to anyone using shearing-frames and the Yorkshire Luddites began to organise attacks on larger factories. On 11 April 1812 150 armed croppers met to attack the mill of William Cartwright of Rawfolds. Some new frames for his mill had already been broken when a convoy of wagons carrying them had been ambushed by a band of Luddites on Hightown Moor and the frames broken with hammers. Five soldiers and four employees were garrisoned at the mill and the attackers failed to break in, two of them being killed by shots from the defenders. In spite of this reverse, events took a more violent turn. On 18 April there was an attempted assassination of William Cartwright and nine days later William Horsfall was assassinated.

April 1812 has been called by Thompson the 'crisis' of Yorkshire Luddism in which machine-breaking became the focus for a 'diffused (and confused) insurrectionary tension'.[41] Whatever the accuracy of this description the disturbances were certainly spreading beyond the textile districts. There were food riots at Rotherham and Barnsley, while at Sheffield a market disturbance on 14 April turned into an attack upon the militia depot in which 198 muskets were broken and 78 others stolen. Whether this was an insurrectionary attempt is not clear; the Home Office investigator concluded that 'this affair was without plan or system, and I should suppose totally unconnected with the proceedings at Leeds, Huddersfield, etc . . .'. We now know that one of the principals in the attack was John Blackwell, a journeyman tailor of Sheffield, who was later to be involved in what look like insurrectionary attempts in 1816 and 1820. How widespread the support for Blackwell's initiative at Sheffield was is difficult to determine, a section of the crowd urging the young men who made the assault to destroy the arms rather than carry them away.[42]

In the textile districts raids for arms, bullets, and money marked the last phase of Yorkshire Luddism, but the precise motivation for the acquisition of arms is uncertain, at a time when the machine-breakers may have felt they needed arms with which to carry out raids against increasingly well-defended targets or to leave people unprotected against future attacks. Thus on 25 July 1812 Earl Fitzwilliam could report to Lord Sidmouth that while well planned and perfectly executed arms raids had taken place, 'it goes no further than in the execution of robbery . . . the reports of nocturnal training and drilling, when one comes to close quarters on the subject, and to enquire for evidence of fact, dwindles down to nothing; they are the offspring of fear, quite imaginary, and mere invention'.[43] By summer, even these raids petered out to be overshadowed by food riots at Knottingley, Leeds and Sheffield. The Leeds disturbances were led by a woman calling herself 'Lady Ludd', but the connection between these disturbances and the machine-breaking went no further. After a couple more breaking incidents in September Yorkshire Luddism came to an end. At the York Assizes in January 1813, sixty-four people were tried, seventeen of whom were hanged; three for Horsfall's murder, five for the attack on Rawfolds mill, and nine for stealing arms and money.

Lancashire and Cheshire were the scene of a particularly confused mixture of machine-breaking, food-rioting, and political agitation. Rumours of delegates from Nottinghamshire making contact with the Lancashire weavers began to circulate in the winter of 1811–12 and in February anonymous letters began to threaten attacks on power looms. On 20 March an unsuccessful attempt was made to burn down the Stockport warehouse of William Radcliffe, the inventor of an improved power loom. At Bolton there were reports of large numbers of weavers being 'twisted in' (sworn into) secret committees in more than a dozen towns and villages about Manchester and Stockport. Although several threatening letters were circulated, the next disturbance occurred on a political occasion. A meeting called by the Manchester Tories to congratulate the Prince Regent for retaining the existing ministers had to be cancelled when placards threatened to oppose it, nevertheless crowds attended a meeting in St Anne's Square where they passed resolutions deploring the continuation of the Perceval administration. A group entered the Exchange and began to wreck the interior before they were dispersed by soldiers. Although not a very serious incident, it was significant that some of the crowd later went on to attack a factory believed to contain power looms.

During the next weeks food riots spread to several of the Lancashire and Cheshire towns, several of which also involved attacks on factories. Following a market-place disturbance at Macclesfield on 15 April, a crowd threatened a factory on the outskirts of the town. Not only weavers, but also colliers, carters, and spinners were involved in the disturbances. The day before at Stockport, crowds led by two men dressed as women who described themselves as 'General Ludd's wives' had milled about the streets, threatening to wreak vengeance on the owners of steam looms; attacking the house and premises of Joseph Goodair, they broke up looms and destroyed finished work. During the following days and nights parties of workpeople moved into the surrounding countryside collecting subscriptions. Following a food riot in Oldham on 19 April, an armed crowd marched on Middleton and attacked the steam loom factory of Mr Burton, but were beaten off by a heavy guard which killed five attackers and wounded eighteen others. On the next day, the crowd was reinforced by colliers from Holmwood, some of them armed with 'muskets with fixed bayonets, and others with colliers' picks' and marched to Middleton headed by 'a *Man of Straw* . . . representing the *renowned* General Ludd whose standard-bearer waved a sort of red flag'. In spite of several losses to the musketry of the soldiers, the attack was pressed home and the mill destroyed.

Apart from an attack on a mill at Westhoughton which had been rumoured for several weeks, the machine-breaking phase of Luddism was now over. At this point accounts diverge, for where some historians have seen the end of Lancashire Luddism in the Westhoughton attack, Thompson has argued that machine-breaking gave way to 'more serious insurrectionary preparations' with reports of oath-taking, arming, and drilling during May and June. There was undoubtedly talk of a 'general rising' to occur on 1 May, but nothing in fact occurred other than isolated raids for arms and money which continued into the summer. More seriously, it has been argued that the evidence for this phase was much exaggerated in informers' reports, especially those of the informer called 'B', or Bent, who operated from Manchester.[44]

The full story of Luddism will perhaps never be known. Almost every category of evidence that we possess about it can be questioned in some way and historians have been left weighing the balance between inadequate sources. Luddism was both geographically widespread and diverse in character; it also developed as it went along. The Midlands Luddites appear to have operated most closely within the traditions of collective bargaining by riot, using machine-breaking as a supplement to more orthodox forms of negotiation. The role of the trade union leader, Gravener Henson, remains obscure, for while he officially condemned machine-breaking, suspicion remains that he oscillated between illegal and legal activity. Certainly frame-breaking in the East Midlands seemed to vary in intensity in direct proportion to the progress of more peaceful agitation being conducted by the framework knitters.[45]

The situation in Yorkshire was more complex. The croppers had a tradition of both legal and illegal activity to protect their interests. The repeal of protective legislation in 1809 left them with few legal remedies and the Luddite attacks were an obvious means of putting pressure on the employers during a period of severe distress. But there also existed at least some groups whose aims went further in places such as Sheffield, Barnsley, Halifax and Leeds. It is less clear how far this support extended or what its relationship to the croppers' movement was. In Lancashire there was undoubtedly some conspiratorial activity, but it is difficult to assess its true dimensions. Lancashire Luddism came nearest to being a spontaneous protest movement, the overlap with food rioting being highly significant. Although we know that secret committees containing representatives of various trades did meet to discuss a 'general turn-out' and machine-breaking to put pressure on the employers, F. O. Darvall believed them to be only very indirectly involved in the attacks on the power looms.[46]

Whether the Luddites posed a 'revolutionary' threat has exercised the mind and imagination of more than one historian. It is important here to distinguish between what might be described as a 'revolutionary crisis' and 'revolutionary' objectives among the Luddites themselves. Wartime distress and dislike of the Government were widespread in 1811–12. Middle-class agitation against the war and the Orders in Council were accompanied by what almost all observers of the industrial districts recognised as severe distress among the working population. The temper of parts of the country at least was shown when the news of Spencer Perceval's assassination by John Bellingham on 11 May was greeted in Nottingham and Leicester by bonfires and tumultuous celebrations. Archibald Prentice learned the news at Newcastle-under-Lyme when he encountered a man 'running down the street, leaping into the air, waving his hat around his head, and shouting with frantic joy, "Percival [sic] is shot, hurrah! Percival is shot, hurrah!"'.[47] In this atmosphere of middle-class disenchantment and lower-class distress, it was hardly surprising that some historians have opted for 1812 as the most likely year for a revolutionary outbreak to occur.[48] Disappointment that the Prince Regent had not changed the administration when he assumed full powers in spring 1812 also added to popular discontent as was shown in the Manchester Exchange riots. Some Luddite letters at least talked of unseating by force 'that damned set of rogues, Perceval and Co.' and of 'shaking off the Yoke of the Rottenest, wickedest and most Tyrannical Government that ever existed'. But middle-class opinion was frightened off by the Luddite outbreaks and appeased by the repeal of the orders in council. Moderate reformers like Wyvill were terrified by the prospect of revolution and temporarily gave up all hope of harnessing the 'least informed and worst disposed men in the Country, already prone to insurrection' to any reform programme. Major Cartwright, who began his first missionary tours of the manufacturing districts in the summer of 1812, hoped to turn popular discontents away from disturbances and 'into a legal channel favourable to Parliamentary reform'. With middle-class opinion alienated and some of the most prominent national leaders of popular radicalism unprepared openly to espouse Luddism, there was little chance of it developing beyond its base in the disturbed counties.[49]

Moreover in assessing the threat of revolution, it is important to recognise that some of the most reassuring reports came from the agents of the Government itself. In his reports from the 'Northern District', General Maitland, the effective supreme commander of the military forces sent to deal with the Luddites, played down the threat of revolution, claiming in the critical late spring of 1812 that he believed the Lancashire magistrates 'had rather over-thought the whole situation' and that such revolutionary agitation as existed was confined to a small minority. Earl Fitzwilliam in Yorkshire also maintained a distinctly unruffled profile, condemning the 'lawlessness' of the Yorkshire Luddites but dismissing any revolutionary intent as exaggerated. Although individual magistrates in the affected areas voiced alarm akin to panic on occasion and the local press in the disturbed districts often reflected acute anxiety, the impact of the disturbances on opinion both in the local communities and in the Home Office can be exaggerated. Incidents were sporadic and dispersed. Parliament was slow to respond to the situation and did not seem particularly alarmed when it did. Darvall concluded from his study of the Home Office papers that the 'astonishing thing about all the early Regency disturbances was not that they should have provoked anxiety on the part of the authorities and terror on the part of some manufacturers and members of the public but that this anxiety and terror should have been so restrained'. The source of this equanimity, according to Darvall, was an assurance on the part of the authorities that it was within their power 'to restore and maintain order, once their arrangements had been completed'.[50] That these arrangements included the garrisoning of the affected counties with 12,000 troops, the employment of spies and informers, and initiating the prosecution of offenders, should not obscure the absence of panic and alarmism within the Government itself.

In the absence of a paralysing 'crisis of the ruling order', even those radicals who maintained a desire to take advantage of the movement were rendered impotent. The case for a 'revolutionary' temper among the Luddites themselves is based on more fragmentary evidence. Although Thompson has stressed his view that an extensive system of delegates and secret committees lay behind the outbreaks and that the urbanity of Maitland's and Fitzwilliam's opinions illustrate only their inability to penetrate the 'opaqueness' of working-class culture, it remains the case that no 'general rising' beyond the immediate industrial objectives of the Luddites took place. The nearest occasions we have are the Sheffield incident in April 1812 and some of the arms raids that occurred in Yorkshire about the same time, but it is not clear whether these arms were intended to be used for machine-breaking attacks or a wider purpose. Moreover, the case for genuine 'insurrectionary' activity also depends on accepting that there was an element of truth in the assertions of informers that there was a well-organised conspiracy afoot, at least in Lancashire and Yorkshire, and on the evidence of papers found near Wakefield after a Luddite attack which contained an 'oath' and 'constitution', similar to those found in the 'Despard conspiracy' of 1802.

Historians have disagreed about the status of this evidence, but there is agreement that Luddism was more than a blind and spasmodic movement, especially in the Midlands and Yorkshire. Although condemned as 'banditti' by some sections of the press and authorities, a criminal element only became involved in the later stages. It appears that the Luddite gangs represented a cross-section of the local population, heavily dominated by the particular trade involved, but with participants drawn from other workmen in the locality. Organisation sprang from within the community, throwing up its own leaders, and usually meeting at a well-known local rendezvous to carry out the attacks. Accordingly the Luddites killed in both the Midlands and Yorkshire were treated as local heroes with large crowds attending their funerals. Indeed in both areas there was also considerable support for the stockingers and croppers by the smaller manufacturers, who equally resented the sharp practice and innovative techniques of some of their colleagues.[51]

A sense of grievance and injustice pervades the majority of letters and addresses issued by the machine-breakers; the phrase 'Army of Redressers' illustrates that they saw themselves as dispensing justice when the authorities had failed them. Talk of Ned Ludd's 'court', and of fines or retribution to be levied on offending hosiers, were intermingled with assertions of past 'rights' and ancient 'liberties'. These backward-looking sentiments have been a commonplace of many early popular movements and would not have been out of place among Tudor rebels or the peasants of 1381.[52] What was new about Luddism was its scale: it indicated long-existing patterns of response to change carried to a new level. The outbreaks were only part of a protracted response to rapidly changing circumstances, in which a wide range of tactics were employed according to the circumstances of the groups concerned. It was significant that by the end of 1812 the Scottish weavers were conducting one of the most impressive strikes in early trade union history, in which 40,000 looms remained idle for six weeks over an area stretching from Carlisle to Aberdeen.[53] It was a pattern that was to be repeated in many instances during the late eighteenth century and early nineteenth, a gradual transition from collective bargaining by riot to more peaceful strike activity. Even so, the traditions of 'King Ludd' were to reappear in Lancashire in 1826 and, more extensively, in the person of 'Captain Swing' in the agricultural disturbances of 1830–2.

8 London in the age of revolution

By the end of the eighteenth century London had become a huge metropolis of over three-quarters of a million people; half as big again as Paris, it dwarfed in size and importance every other town and city in the British Isles. And it posed commensurate problems: if there was a problem of 'public order' in the growing towns and cities of the industrial revolution because of population growth and urbanisation, the capital shared them to the full. Most of the population growth of the capital was concentrated in the out-parishes of Middlesex and Surrey, beyond the jurisdiction of the traditional municipal administrations of the City of London and Westminster, thus the capital was faced with an acute version of the problem which harassed the manufacturing areas – the growth of virtually unregulated urban populations. Moreover as we have seen, the London mob had a tradition of intervention on a wide range of issues. The Wilkes agitation and the Gordon Riots seemed evidence of the ability of the populace to break free from traditional restraints almost at will and overwhelm, at least for a time, the normal peacekeeping forces of the capital. The events in Paris in 1789 served only to confirm the dangers of urban insurrection in a large capital city.

Moreover following the outbreak of the French Revolution, London was faced not only with the consequences of urban growth, but also with the impact of popular radicalism. The threat of simultaneous insurrection in the capital, the manufacturing districts, and Ireland in support of a French invasion was one to haunt the worst nightmares of government. Even after the defeat of Napoleon radical activity formed one of the principal preoccupations of the authorities and was to remain so for much of the first half of the nineteenth century. Lord Liverpool's comment to Chateaubriand as he stared gloomily through his windows at the urban sprawl of Regency London, that 'one insurrection in London and all is lost', serves as a pithy reminder that popular disturbances in the capital remained the first concern of any government in late eighteenth-century and early nineteenth-century England.[1]

The Westminster elections

The years which preceded the French Revolution witnessed a series of tumultuous election contests at Westminster. The seat of Charles James Fox from 1780, Westminster played a prominent part in supporting the petitioning movement of the 1770s and 1780s; moreover its large number of voters and scope for political propaganda had often given its elections a rowdy character. Once again in the 1780s, Westminster became a cockpit of political activity in which the struggle between Pitt and Fox spilled over into election riots.[2] The tone of these contests was illustrated in February 1784 when Pitt attended Grocer's Hall to receive the freedom of the City and the gift of a gold box. On his return from the banquet his carriage was drawn by a cheering mob towards his brother's house in Berkeley Square, but as it passed Brooks's, the chief social centre of the Foxites, a rush was made by a crowd armed with sticks and the broken poles of sedan chairs, while missiles were showered from the upper windows on to the cavalcade. The doors of Pitt's carriage were stove in and Lord Chatham had to ward off the blows aimed at his brother. Cries of 'Fox and popular government' were heard on the one hand and 'Pitt and the constitution' on the other. As the tussle swayed to and fro, the windows of Brooks's were smashed by Pitt's supporters, but Pitt himself was forced to retreat to White's to escape the mêlée. Although Fox was widely condemned for organising the attack and the chairmen and servants of his club appeared the most prominent of Pitt's attackers, he was not at the club that evening: he had an alibi – that he was in bed, and a witness – Mrs Armistead.[3]

Trivial as the incident was, it foreshadowed the rowdiness of the coming Westminster election, regarded by many contemporaries as notorious even by eighteenth-century standards. It showed the highly personalised world of metropolitan politics where the appearance of prominent figures in the streets frequently invited voluble abuse and even physical confrontation. For Pitt this was only the first of many occasions when he was to be confronted by a hostile crowd and subjected to personal assault. The more immediate consequence was to raise the temperature of the election. In the provinces, Fox – the 'black animal' – was reviled by supporters of Pitt, but in Westminster he could still count on a considerable personal following. The intervention of the Duchess of Devonshire, decked out in his colours of buff and blue – the colours of George Washington's regiment – was only the most famous incident of a six-week poll in which Fox and his opponents used almost every trick in the formidable armoury of eighteenth-century electioneering. Plentiful liquor and a series of large dinners helped to persuade Fox's supporters to brave the hired mobs which surrounded the hustings. A mammoth procession greeted the result in which Fox took second place in the poll.[4] If anything, the 1788 election was even more violent. The Government employed gangs of sailors, while the opposition paid Irish chairmen five shillings a day. Operating in mobs of 200 or more, the hired bruisers clashed with the Westminster constables on more than one occasion, leading to several deaths. Both sides tried to use their men to prevent opposing voters from reaching the poll, while the hustings themselves were guarded by young men who interrogated voters in violent terms.[5]

The impact of the French Revolution

These election contests marked the most serious disturbances in the capital during the 1780s. Nor did the French Revolution produce an immediate impact. In comparison with Birmingham, Manchester, and Norwich, the capital was relatively undisturbed in the early 1790s. Celebrations to commemorate the fall of the Bastille in July 1791, which provoked the riots in Birmingham, passed off quietly in London. A dinner was held at the Crown and Anchor Tavern, attended by over a thousand guests, including a representative from Nantes. Fox, Sheridan, and the Whig peers declined invitations, but the dinner itself was conducted, according to one report 'in a manner as peaceable as solemn'. The diners even toasted Burke 'in gratitude for his having provoked the great discussion which occupies every thinking person'. In order to 'rob the ill-disposed of every pretext', the dinner broke up at nine o'clock. But two hours later there was some minor disturbances when, according to Horace Walpole, 'some glaziers and tallow chandlers broke a few windows in the Strand and Cheapside, to force people to put out lights, but all was immediately suppressed by the magistrates'. The smallness of this incident proved encouraging to supporters of the administration.[6]

Even during the autumn and winter of 1792-3 when anti-Jacobin feeling was at its height, the capital remained virtually untouched by political disturbances. The orgy of Paine-burnings and Church and King disturbances which occurred in the provinces was largely absent. In fact, the first clear manifestation of popular feeling came when John Frost, an active radical and LCS delegate to the Jacobin Convention, was convicted in June 1793 of sedition and sentenced to stand in the pillory at Charing Cross: the appointed time was advertised by handbills and a large crowd assembled. Instead of pelting Frost with the customary refuse, the crowd demolished the pillory and released him. The occasion was intended as much as a demonstration of support and disapproval of the sentence than a simple escape, for Frost was escorted on the arm of Horne Tooke back to prison. His release from prison several months later led to another display of popular support when his carriage was dragged through the streets by a rejoicing crowd.[7]

From 1794, however, several currents influenced popular disturbances in the capital. The reforming societies began to stage a series of mass meetings which continued into 1795 and became the vehicles for expressing the demand for radical parliamentary reform and growing opposition to the war. Although remarkably peaceful, the series of mass meetings in the capital during 1794–5 contributed to the alarm of the government. This reached a peak in the spring of 1794 when Thomas Hardy, the founder of the London Corresponding Society, was arrested with eleven other prominent reformers and charged with High Treason. The committal of these men and the subsequent trial in autumn 1794 provided the occasion for displays of both 'loyalist' opinion and support for the reformers' cause. The most celebrated of the 'loyalist' demonstrations came while Hardy and his fellows were languishing in the Tower awaiting their trial. Starved of military success, news of the successful naval battle of 'the Glorious First of June', sparked off three nights of patriotic demonstrations in the capital on 11, 12 and 13 June. On the night of the 11th Hardy's house was attacked by a mob which broke the windows and tried to break into his shop. In terror, Hardy's pregnant wife made an escape, an event which was widely believed to have contributed to her death some weeks later.[8]

The anti-crimp-house riots

By 1794 a more powerful current of opinion was beginning to flow in the radicals' favour. As so many times in the eighteenth century, a war embarked on with high hopes had met with early defeats and frustrations. War involved inevitable difficulties; disruption of trade; higher taxation, and the burden of recruitment. It was the last of these which provoked the greatest hostility in 1794, and it was to provide a recurrent theme of discontent throughout the decade. The war against revolutionary France put an unprecedented strain on the recruiting system and it was upon the capital that the greatest burden of recruiting fell. As the largest concentration of population in the country it provided unparalleled opportunities for naval press-gangs and army recruiting parties. In addition, there were a number of 'rendezvous houses' where volunteers could sign on and where pressed men could be secured before being put on board ship. There were also a number of 'crimp' houses; crimps were agents who traded in recruits when men were in great demand either for the armed forces or to man merchant vessels which were on the point of sailing and were desperate for crewmen. The crimps made their money out of the bounty offered to recruits in wartime or the advance wages of the sailor. Men who were short of money would surrender themselves into the hands of the crimps in order to pay off their creditors; sailors would often be induced by crimps operating from an alehouse to run up expenses on credit, which they would be forced to redeem with the bounty from enlistment or the advance wages for a voyage; others were simply decoyed by prostitutes and kidnapped, eventually finding themselves in the army, militia, or navy.

The early years of the war witnessed a rapid expansion of manpower in the armed forces. The navy alone was increased from 16,613 in 1792 to

87,331 in 1794. In the spring of 1794 Francis Place recorded that a further 85,000 men were voted for the navy, 40,000 for the army and 100,000 for the militia. As a result there was an acute shortage of recruits and the bounties offered to induce men to enlist in the army rose as high as £30. This was a situation in which the crimps flourished, for as the *New Annual Register* noted: 'One of the great evils of war is the encouragement given to deceit, fraud and cruelty in procuring recruits for the service. . . . The recruiting houses of London, kept by crimps and kidnappers, were the general scenes of enormities committed in this atrocious and inhuman traffic.' The radical societies, led by the LCS, also condemned the activities of the 'crimps' as a symptom of a war which they opposed: 'For fresh supplies of blood, the liberties of our country are invaded! the seamen is forcibly torn from his family! the peasant kidnapped from the plough! and the starving labourer is compelled to sell his life and his liberty for bread.'

A number of rumours about men being kidnapped passed into circulation in the summer of 1794, undoubtedly expressing a growing concern about the expansion of the armed forces and the consequent threat of being pressed or abducted by crimps. Another source of discontent in the capital by summer 1794 were the arrangements for selecting the City of London Militia. The City was in the process of balloting for its newly organised militia in the summer of 1794. The procedure meant that the individuals selected would either have to serve in person or bear the full cost of finding a substitute at a time when they were particularly expensive. This caused much popular unrest as it was widely felt that a more equitable and less onerous system, at least for the individuals concerned, would have been to levy a general rate on the City wards and purchase the appropriate number of substitutes. Although there was widespread opposition to the Militia Bill in Common Hall and some Whigs, notably Sheridan, had opposed its passage through the Commons in July 1794, the Act with its balloting provisions was put into operation. The process of balloting went ahead in the City wards with the lists due to arrive at the Guildhall by the 18 August, the last day on which appeals against the ballot would be heard.

On Friday 15 August the body of a young man, George Howe, was found outside a notorious crimp house in Johnson's Court, Charing Cross; according to some reports his hands were tied and it was widely assumed he had jumped or fallen from an attic window. A large crowd assembled and threatened to pull down the house and had to be dispersed by the Horse Guards. Over the weekend there were renewed disturbances around Charing Cross and recruiting houses in Petty France and Charing Cross were also attacked.

On Monday the 18th a crowd of several thousand thronged the Guildhall to present appeals against the provisions of the Militia Bill. Not only were there complaints that it had been passed without proper consultation, but the cry of 'Down with the recruiting houses' was also raised. Although the crowds dispersed peacefully, the two currents of discontent over the recruiting issue had clearly flowed into each other. Handbills were circulating which said that men were being kidnapped and sent to Canada and elsewhere. On Tuesday there were riots at Shoe Lane, Holborn. Although troops were sent, a general attack had begun on recruiting houses and suspected crimps in the capital. The Lord Mayor, Paul Le Mesurier, reported to the Home Secretary that the intention of the rioters was 'to pull down every house which had been opened as a House of Rendezvous'. Houses were attacked at several different places in Moorfields, Holborn, Westminster and the City. Meanwhile crowds had been parading Fleet Street during the afternoon and early evening to cries of 'No War – No Soldiers', 'Liberty and no Crimps'. At least three recruiting houses were 'pulled down' on the night of 20–21 August, the peak of the riots. Thereafter the authorities gradually reassumed control. Initially harassed by the rapidity with which mobs moved from one part of the capital to the other and melted away after making an attack, the armed associations were called out, large numbers of special constables sworn in, and detachments of troops posted at various strategic points in the capital. On the 21st and 22nd attempts to attack other recruiting houses were defeated and crowds which continued to assemble in the City were dispersed. By Saturday morning the crisis had passed and the authorities began to take stock of the situation.

The crimp riots had been the most serious disturbances in the capital since the Gordon riots. Compared with 1780, however, the amount of damage was trivial. Four houses were damaged sufficiently to be classed as 'pulled down', although this in fact meant a degree of damage far short of complete destruction. Similarly the death toll was small: the rioters, for all their threats, killed no one, although there were reports of people being beaten up for their alleged involvement in crimping. Of the twenty-three people committed for trial for their part in the disturbances, four were eventually executed.

The riots were clearly a response to the twin threats of 'crimping' and being balloted for the militia. Elaborate rumours of kidnappings signified a state of acute anxiety during a period of intense recruitment to the armed forces. As such, the crimp riots were a largely spontaneous outburst of hostility to the agencies which recruited the armed forces. That the City Militia issue should have come to a head at the same time was largely fortuitous, but served to broaden the base of discontent to include many elements of 'respectable' opinion in the City. But the authorities were suspicious that the riots might have been fomented by the radical societies. Patrick Colquhoun, one of the magistrates most active in dealing with the disturbances, reported to the Home Secretary that he had 'strong grounds to believe that these riots have been excited by the leaders of the seditious societies whose views extend very far beyond the recruiting houses'. The next day he elaborated on his suspicions, writing that 'I have strong grounds to believe that the riots are the result of a deliberate system originating with the corresponding societies for the purpose of overthrowing the government'. A number of newspapers echoed this view that there was a 'hidden hand' behind the riots. The strongest evidence for this is provided by printed handbills which circulated during the riots. The most common was one which ran:

> Beware Britons of the hordes of crimps and kidnappers that infest the metropolis and its environs, who rot and imprison its peaceful inhabitants. Oh! think of the number of parents that are made wretched, in having their blooming sons torn from them by these monsters – Would such atrocious acts have been suffered in the days of Alfred? If you bring the Demons before the magistrates you cannot get redress, they will screen them in defiance of the law. Is this the land so famed for liberty? Did Sidney and Russell bleed for this? – Oh my poor country!

This handbill was circulated with others which denounced the London Militia Bill on the grounds that it infringed the traditional liberties of the citizens of London. There appeared to be an attempt to encourage disturbances on the crimp and militia issues. Although they breathed the traditional spirit of 'liberty' with their appeal to the memory of the Whig 'martyrs' and the Norman Yoke, the handbills were clearly inflammatory, but their source is obscure; at the time of the riots, the leaders of the LCS were in prison awaiting trial for high treason, whilst the society's official line was firmly against violent proceedings of any kind. The Society would hardly be likely to endanger its leaders at such a time by being involved in these riots.[9] That the handbills were produced at all, illustrated that in the context of the early 1790s, there were people who would seek to take advantage of the Government's unpopularity and fan the flames of discontent. But there is little evidence to suggest that the riots were preplanned. The handbills, whoever lay behind them, were only fuel to a fire that was already raging.

The riots were suppressed without the crimping system being abolished. Two owners of crimp houses were brought before the magistrates, including Mrs Hannah, the owner of the house outside which Howe's body was found, but were dismissed without facing any charges. Opposition to the Militia Act was more successful, and in December 1794 the City of London authorities decided to raise the necessary men by levying a general rate on the wards which would be used to purchase recruits, thus stilling discontent with the militia issue for the rest of the decade.

The LCS and opposition to the war

The latter months of 1794 also witnessed a striking degree of popular support for the radical leaders being tried for high treason. Thomas Hardy, leader and founder of the London Corresponding

Society, was brought up for trial at the Old Bailey on 28 October on a charge of high treason. After an epic trial of nine days and a three-hour recess by the jury, Hardy was acquitted. Although he attempted to make a discreet escape from the court to his brother-in-law's house in the Strand, his coach was spotted by an enthusiastic crowd in Snow Hill and forced to turn into Fleet Street, where the horses were unhitched and the crowd drew Hardy in triumph through the Strand, Pall Mall, St James's Street, Piccadilly, Haymarket and eventually back to the Strand. According to his own account, 'the people frequently stopped, and shouted at different places, such as Charing Cross, Carlton House and St James's Palace. At No. 9, Piccadilly, his (Hardy's) former comfortable habitation, they stopped a few minutes in *solemn silence*'. This triumphant reception was repeated when Horne Tooke and John Thelwall also received verdicts of not guilty.[10]

Following this defeat there began a critical time for the Government, for 1795 marked in many ways the culmination of discontent with the war against revolutionary France. The disappointments of the war, the dislocation of trade, and the continued burden of recruiting stimulated considerable anti-war sentiment. To this was added the threat of famine, for one of the severest winters in English history was followed by a very poor harvest. As early as January 1795 a correspondent warned Henry Dundas, that 'want and war will accord very ill with each other'. In parliament, even some Government supporters began to agitate for peace, while a crowded meeting of the Common Hall of the City of London held on 23 January passed a resolution for a 'speedy peace' by 4,000 votes to 100. News of the defeat and defection of one after another of Britain's allies in the war and higher taxes increased the popularity of the radical societies and enhanced the hopes of the Foxite opposition.

The recruiting service continued to occasion sporadic disorders. On 9 January a mob attacked a recruiting in Southwark, releasing eighteen men. One of the prostitutes who worked from the house was ducked by the crowd and the door of the house chalked with the words 'the empty Bastille'. Discontent with the activities of recruiting parties simmered through the spring and early summer. In April over a thousand people were reported to have rushed into Charles Street, Westminster, with a man they said had attempted to kidnap a boy of fifteen; he had been doused under a pump and one of his ears slit to make him reveal the location of the crimp house from which he was operating. The youth's story sounded all too typical of the activities of the crimps. He claimed to have been given a shilling by the man to buy some food, but was then seized on the grounds he had taken the 'King's Shilling'. During June a very 'hot press' was conducted in the riverside districts with the usual affrays between press-gangs and populace. One gang which boarded a Liverpool trader was fiercely resisted; some of the gang were thrown overboard and the lieutenant killed by a shot fired from the vessel.[11]

In this atmosphere and with widespread food riots taking place in the country, the anti-war platform of the LCS was bound to prove attractive. On 29 June, two days after parliament had gone into recess, the Society held an open-air meeting in St George's Fields, Southwark, attended by several thousand people. The meeting approved an address to the nation which reaffirmed the Society's determination to pursue the cause of universal suffrage and annual parliaments. An address to the King demanded 'free and equal representation', a purge of 'guilty ministers', and an immediate end 'to the ravages of a cruel and destructive war'. It was reported that while the meeting was in progress, biscuits were distributed among the crowd stamped with the words 'unanimity, firmness, and spirit' and others with 'freedom and plenty, or slavery and want'. In spite of the fiery nature of the addresses, the meeting passed off peacefully. The authorities held troops in readiness at several strategic points in the capital and the magistrates from Union Hall public office were ordered to attend the meeting, but to maintain 'a prudent, discreet, and firm, but temperate conduct in every exigency which may occur'. Although at three in the afternoon the magistrates were ordered by the Home Office to read the Riot Act and disperse the meeting 'as a riotous, unlawful, and tumultuous assembly', the meeting had already broken up without any violence occurring.[12]

The capital remained unaffected by serious rioting until July, when disturbances broke out which reflected antagonism to the war, discontent over the price of food, and opposition to the crimp houses. On 7 July a crowd attacked a suspected crimp house at Newington and destroyed its furniture; in the evening another house in Soho was attacked. On the following morning, something approaching a 'food panic' seized parts of the capital; it was reported that 'such was the outcry for bread on Thursday morning that great numbers of people crowded the doors of the bakers in different parts of the town, fearful they would not be served'. A large crowd in Bow Street grew tumultuous when a distribution of bread from the public office there ran out, leaving many of them unsatisfied. To cries of 'Give us bread', the crowd became so threatening that the Riot Act had to be read. In the evening crowds gathered outside a baker's shop in Seven Dials and had to be dispersed by the Horse Guards; even so, they returned the next day and smashed the shop's windows before they were driven away by local constables.[13]

For two days the capital was quiet, but on Sunday the 12th there was a renewal of trouble at the King's Arms, Charing Cross, one of the recruiting houses attacked in the riots of the previous August. Two soldiers who had been drinking in the house incited a crowd to search the house for imprisoned recruits. This they did, finding no one, but wrecking the interior and throwing the furniture into the street. By now the authorities were thoroughly alarmed. Some believed the renewed attack on the crimp houses to be a premeditated attempt to stir up the populace; one magistrate claimed that the riots were carried out 'by a set of persons not very numerous either hired or lovers of riot, who escape the instant they have done mischief'. Sir James Bland Burges, who had already warned his wife that it was unsafe for her to return from the country to London, believed that the reformers were behind the riots, writing that he had heard 'several well-dressed men haranguing the populace in a true Parisian style by addressing them as citizens and exhorting them to assert their rights'. Fears that the riots had a wider purpose seemed confirmed on the next day, when a mob assembled at Charing Cross and marched down Whitehall, breaking Pitt's window in Downing Street on the way and forcing passers-by to remove their hats. Passing over Westminster Bridge to Southwark the crowd attacked two recruiting houses, making a bonfire of the contents of one of them in the street. A troop of cavalry was sent to disperse the crowd and a cannon was placed in the street to overawe them. The riots continued on the next day when early on the morning of the 14th some prisoners were rescued from custody in the Watch-House in St George's Fields. In the evening another recruiting house was attacked and a detachment of the crowd went down Parliament Street, shouting 'No war, No Pitt', before being dispersed. Bland Burges feared the worse on the 15th: 'What has passed has, I am convinced, merely served to do mischief by encouraging the mob, and by exposing the soldiers to ridicule. The most violent and inflammatory papers are circulated and stuck up everywhere with impunity and everything denotes a still more violent explosion.'[14]

In fact, the riots died out almost as quickly as they had begun. Although the radicals were widely blamed for causing them and there was evidence of handbills circulating during the disturbances, popular concern about prices and recruiting appears to be sufficient explanation. Reports of food riots in the country must have reached London by July and the recruiting issue was fresh in people's minds as men continued to be sought for all branches of the armed forces. So inflammatory was the recruiting issue that vicious little affrays over crimping continued after the worst of the anti-war rioting had died down. On 22 July a sergeant and corporal of 12th Light Dragoons who had just seized a deserter were attacked by a crowd who raised the cry of crimping; while the deserter was rescued, the corporal was hit in the face with a hammer, and according to another report the crowd 'knocked him down, and beat [him] very severely and the populace had proceeded so far as to have laid one of them down in the street that a cart might run over his neck'.[15]

In the midst of a worsening crisis, the Ministry announced an early summons to Parliament and drew up a speech from the throne which held out the possibility of peace negotiations. The LCS decided to hold another mass meeting on 26 October, three days before the opening of parliament, at Copenhagen Fields, Islington. The authorities were thoroughly alarmed by this plan; one of the Under-Secretaries at the Home Office informed the commander of a volunteer corps in the capital that it was a step 'exactly resembling that which fifteen years before had nearly led to the destruction of the metropolis'. Notwithstanding, the meeting was allowed to proceed, but a careful watch was kept upon it; the authorities posted men in the crowd to watch and report on the proceedings, with troops and constables standing by to intervene if necessary. The newspapers reported figures up to 150,000 for the attendance and, although the true figure will never be known with complete accuracy, the number was certainly both large and impressive. Three rostra had to be used so that the crowd could hear the proceedings. An 'Address to the Nation and Remonstrance to the King' was approved, once again demanding reform of parliament, dismissal of ministers and a 'speedy PEACE'.[16]

Although this meeting passed off without incident it was followed three days later, by one of the most famous incidents of the decade. On 29 October, a large crowd assembled for the state opening of parliament. Estimates of the crowds varied, but most put the figure in the region of 150,000 to 200,000. As the King in the State Coach passed through St James's Park on his way to Parliament, the crowd hissed and groaned at him, calling for 'No Pitt', 'No war', 'Bread, bread', 'Peace, peace', 'Give us bread', and 'No famine'. Outside the Houses of Parliament, in St Margaret's Street, a stone, at first thought to be a bullet, struck the window of the King's carriage. When he returned from the Lords to St James's Palace he was again hissed and hooted by the crowd. The King changed from the State Coach to his private coach at St James's Palace and left via Stable Yard for the Queen's Palace (Buckingham House). On his way, he was pursued by a portion of the crowd and 'one miscreant in a green coat' was reported to have attempted to open the door and pull the King out before the Horse Guards arrived to rescue him. Meanwhile the empty State Coach which was being driven back to the Royal Mews was attacked and its windows broken. The *Gentleman's Magazine* reported that 'a stout fellow, with a bludgeon, completed the demolition of the only glass, of which a single part remained and was proceeding to destroy the carved work, etc., when one of the King's footmen interposed'. A crowd continued to press around Westminster Hall and when Storey's Gate was locked against them, sledgehammers were brought and an attempt made to force an entry. A 'gentleman' who remonstrated with the crowd was set upon and had to be rescued by the troops.[17]

The Lords immediately undertook an enquiry into the events. On the 31st both Houses presented loyal addresses to the King. A Royal Proclamation was issued against seditious meetings, clearly implying that the LCS meeting of the 26th had been responsible for the attack on the King, and offered a £1,000 reward for the arrest of the authors of the attack. As loyal addresses flowed in from the country, almost 600 in all, the Government turned the attack on the King into an opportunity to check the radical movement by bringing before parliament two Bills on Treasonable and Seditious Practices and Seditious Meetings. The preamble to the former referred to

the daring outrages offered to your Majesty's most sacred person, in your passage to and from your Parliament at the opening of the present session, and also the continued attempts of wicked and evil disposed persons to disturb the tranquillity of this your Majesty's Kingdom, particularly by the multitude of seditious pamphlets and speeches daily printed, published, and dispersed.

The effect of the Bill was to extend the law of treason to 'compassing' the use of force to change the King's councils or intimidating Parliament and to make spoken and written words, even when followed by no overt act, treasonable. The Seditious Meetings Act restricted the calling and holding of public meetings, and was aimed directly at the mass meetings called by the LCS.[18]

Although the radicals were blamed for the attack on the King, there is little evidence of their direct involvement. Four people were examined in connection with the affair; all were charged with throwing stones at the King's carriage on the way back, but only one, Kyd Wake, a journeyman printer who was seen throwing stones at the carriage, was committed for trial. Although heavily punished, he was never at any time accused of being a radical. Important clues to the affair are provided by the evidence of two members of the LCS, Francis Place and John Binns. Place claimed that the man in a green coat against whom the Proclamation was issued was John Ridley, a bootmaker of York Street, Covent Garden and member of one of the London Corresponding Society's divisions. Place claimed that Ridley had only touched the door of the King's coach to save himself after he had nearly slipped under its wheels. But the evening of the attack John Binns met an LCS member in Moorfields who told him that he was the one who had tried to pull the King from his coach.[19]

But while it is quite possible that individual members of the LCS had a part in the demonstration, the connection of the Society's meeting of 26 October and the attack on the King was indirect. Undoubtedly their anti-war campaign had contributed to bitterness of feeling among the populace and in that sense, the Government's argument for the 'Two Acts' was not entirely specious. What is clear is that the official line of the LCS was to disavow violence of any kind; Hardy claimed that he 'abhorred the very idea of having recourse to violence of any sort'. This policy was expressed in a pamphlet *Reformers No Rioters*, published in 1794, which said: 'One of the fundamental principles of this society and a lesson we have industriously inculcated is, that riot, tumult and violence are not the fit means of obtaining redress of grievances.' The official policy of the Society's leaders in 1794 and 1795 was to eschew violence and concentrate upon 'constitutional' methods of attaining reform.[20] They argued that the lesson of 1780 was that 'public commotions may occasion disorders, far more prejudicial than the evils they are intended to remove'.

Indeed the LCS continued its programme of mass meetings, using them as a basis to oppose the Two Acts. An emergency demonstration on 12 November at Copenhagen Fields attracted a crowd estimated at up to 300,000.

Petitions were sent to both Houses of Parliament, condemning the administration, while another called on the King to exert his authority and prevent the passage of the Bills. At a further meeting on 7 December at Marylebone Fields 'an immense concourse' passed more resolutions, but apart from an abortive attempt to hold a meeting in May 1797, this was the last of the mass meetings held by the Society, as it was forced to comply with the provisions of the Seditious Meetings Act.

Place believed that the attack on the King's Coach was deliberately exaggerated to destroy the prospects of the radical societies and to facilitate repressive measures. He claimed that it 'had long been the custom for the spectators to show their dislike of the proceedings of the court by hissing and groaning as the King went to the Parliament, and the practice still continues'. 'Everybody expected that the King would be assailed by the clamours of the ill fed discontented people, and ministers might if they had wished have prevented it.'[21] In fact there is no clear evidence from the Government side that the attack was expected, nor is it likely that the Government would willingly risk the life of the King.

Place was nearer the mark in suggesting that it was not unusual for members of the Royal Family or the Ministry to be attacked or jeered as they passed through the streets of the capital. On 17 December as Pitt was riding back from the Commons through St James's Park, he was attacked by a group of men who pelted him with mud, one of whom tried to seize his horse's bridle. At a time when Pitt was being bitterly attacked as the author of the nation's misfortunes and some of the rhetorical taunts of the radical societies included references to 'King William Pitt' such attacks were to be expected. John Gales Jones was reported to have stated that he wanted him to be the first victim sacrificed to the 'just resentment of an injured and insulted nation' and in an ironic reference to Pitt's usual guard of soldiers, hoped that the next time he had such a guard it would be to accompany him to the scaffold. Nor were they the only occasions upon which Pitt or members of the Royal Family were attacked during the 1790s. In February 1796 the Queen's coach was stoned, and the Queen and a servant were slightly injured. In June 1796 Pitt's house was attacked by a crowd which had to be dispersed by soldiers, and again in December 1797 he was hissed and pelted as he went to St Paul's for a thanksgiving service for the victory at Camperdown and had to be escorted home by the troops.[22]

A reduction of food prices, the failure of peace overtures, and the repressive measures of the Government blunted the edge of radical activity and popular discontent in the period after 1797. The threat of invasion, discontent in Ireland, and a severe financial crisis tended, if anything, to rally support for the administration. Although Pitt was still the occasional object of radical attacks and popular indignation, there was evidence that the immediate crisis for the administration had passed. In July 1797 the LCS attempted to defy the Acts by holding a mass meeting in St Pancras. Magistrates from the public offices were mobilised with a large force of constables and several thousand troops were placed on standby. The meeting was allowed to begin, but then the magistrates stepped in and arrested six of the Society's leaders. The crowd was dispersed and the military galloped about the ground for an hour to prevent it reconvening.[23]

Moreover the autumn witnessed renewed 'Church and King' demonstrations in the capital. The news of Duncan's hard-fought victory over the Dutch at Camperdown reached London on 13 October. An impromptu illumination was enforced by crowds going about the streets crying 'Lights', 'Duncan for ever', 'No Jacobins'. Some minor fracas took place between the 'loyalists' and anti-war demonstrators, but three days later the loyalists took their revenge during a 'General Illumination' by attacking Hardy's house in Fleet Street. According to Hardy, he was interrogated by a crowd which asked him whether he was going to illuminate his house or not; when he shut the door on the crowd there were rival cries of 'Duncan for ever' and 'Hardy for ever' and he was eventually forced to send for help from the London Militia as a full-scale assault on his house was threatened. After the incident a letter to the *True Briton* alleged that Hardy's house had been filled 'with a set of Ruffians, armed with cutlasses, sword-sticks, bludgeons, &c.' who 'sallied out, and indiscriminately assaulted every person who had not the good fortune to escape'. Although Hardy denied that the house was filled with defendants, he admitted that 'a number of my friends' assembled to defend it. Writing at a safe distance, some years later, and with a somewhat hazy memory of the date, John Binns recollected that

> about 100 men, chiefly members of the society, many of them Irish, armed with good shillelahs, took post early in the evening in front of and close to the front of Hardy's home. As night approached, an immense crowd gathered in the street; many and violent were the attacks and efforts made to get possession of the house, and many were the wounds inflicted by fists and sticks.

Eventually a troop of mounted guards from the London Militia were called out to disperse the crowds.[24]

Bread or blood!

The situation in the capital remained relatively quiet until 1800 when London became affected by the general harvest crisis discussed in an earlier chapter. Fear of disturbances had already led the authorities to introduce relief operations, advocate the consumption of coarser bread, and initiate proceedings against middlemen for monopolistic offences. The most significant of these actions in the London context was the trial and conviction in July 1800 of John Rusby, a London corn dealer, for regrating at the Mark Lane market. This trial was accompanied by less well known proceedings against dealers involved in the sale of vegetables, meat, and fruit. Ill-feeling against the dealers in foodstuffs and considerable anxiety about the prospects in the coming harvest created a tense situation in the summer months. Wheat and bread prices fell during August, temporarily defusing the situation, but by the beginning of September the authorities were alarmed to find that the capital was threatened not so much with high prices, but an 'absolute scarcity of bread' because the bakers complained that they could not afford to purchase wheat at the going rate and still make a profit under the Assize. As a result the authorities raised the Assize price of the quartern loaf by $1\frac{1}{2}d$ on 2 September and by $1\frac{3}{4}d$ a week later; these were the sharpest price increases to have occurred throughout the whole crisis. The magistrates were ordered to attend at their public offices throughout the week from 6 September. The Home Secretary, the Duke of Portland, remained confident, however, that in spite of the riots in the rest of the country 'nothing of a similar nature is likely to take place in the capital'.[25]

He was to be proved wrong. On the night of Saturday 13 September 1800, placards were put up in the Mark Lane Corn market and on the Monument, calling on the people to rise and attend the corn market on Monday. One of these proclaimed: 'Bread at 6d. if people assemble at corn market on Monday. Ye are the Sovereignty.' Another contained a fuller exhortation to the populace:

> Fellow Countrymen, how long will you quietly and cowardly suffer yourselves to be thus imposed upon and half-starved by a set of mercenary slaves and government hirelings? Can you still suffer them to proceed in their extensive monopolies and your families are crying for food? No! Let them exist not a day longer. Ye are the sovereignty. Rouse then from your lethargy and meet at the Corn Market on Monday.

Although the authors of these notices were never discovered, they had an effect. On Monday morning a crowd of about a thousand assembled in the corn market. As the mealmen and cornfactors arrived at about ten o'clock they were hissed and pelted by the crowd who singled out a Quaker and rolled him in the mud. The Mayor, Harvey Combe, arrived shortly after and urged the crowd to disperse. Though interrupting him with cries of 'bread, bread, give us bread, and don't starve us!', the crowd remained noisy rather than particularly threatening, and the Mayor eventually returned to the Mansion House. As the crowd remained assembled during the afternoon, the Riot Act was read and the Mayor once again retreated to the Mansion House to write a report for the Duke of Portland; volunteers and militia were brought up to clear the streets, leaving the area quiet by midnight, and at 1.00 a.m. the troops were withdrawn.

Unknown to the Mayor, a crowd had gone out from the City into Surrey and attacked Rusby's shop in Blackfriars Road; his family were allowed to escape before the house was gutted and the furniture destroyed. On the next day, the Mayor gave an account of his actions to the Court of Aldermen and received their thanks. He reported to the Home Secretary at 5.00 p.m. that the City was quiet, but three hours later the calm was disrupted by reports that a mob was attacking a wholesale cheesemonger's shop in Bishopsgate; bacon and cheese shops were also attacked in Chiswell Street and Fore Street before it could be dispersed by troops. Wednesday was quiet, but on Thursday 17 September new posters appeared in the City. One on Bow Church in Cheapside ran:

> Liberty or Death! Citizens to Arms! Cold Bath Fields on
> Sunday night, 10,000 men will meet you there! Remember the
> Bastile! Be firm, courageous and Bold your enemies tremble!
> Strike! Citizens – the soldiers of despotism must be murdered!

For a few hours nothing occurred. Then in the early evening a crowd assembled in Finsbury Square and marched down Bishopsgate towards Smithfield, where they broke the windows of a few shops; more windows were broken as the crowd marched out through Saffron Hill to Holborn, then on to Snow Hill, and eventually back to Fleet Market. They then set off up Ludgate Hill, smashing shop windows and street lamps as they passed, before dispersing on the City limits. Disturbances continued until the 20th. Notices were circulated urging the crowd to attack particular food-sellers, whilst the slogan 'Bread or Blood' was found chalked on many walls. Notices continued to be found which indicated wider aims than regulating the price of food. Posters put up in Spitalfields and Shoreditch demanded, 'Britons. Who will live free or Die? Meet with firmness on Monday. The soldiers are your friends. Cowards stay in your hovels and starve.' Even so the riots were virtually over by the weekend. The last incident occurred on 24 September when a baker's windows were broken by a group of people who were being driven from Fleet Market. The following day, the authorities began dismissing the constables and volunteer corps who had assembled to help them.[26]

The food riots of September 1800 were significant in that London had usually escaped food rioting in the past and there were clear signs that there existed in the capital some groups who would take advantage of economic discontent. The handbills and posters played a vital part in focusing discontent at a time when food riots were taking place in many other parts of the country, and as close to the capital as Rochester and Chatham. Such disturbances could easily have taken place without the posters to encourage them, but these did give a focus in time and place for genuine grievances. Equally significant, however, the attempt to broaden the issue into an insurrectionary attempt failed. Attacks on the prisons, Cold Bath Fields in particular, were urged but not carried out, at least on this occasion. A longhand notice found on the 17th in Bankside, on the Surrey side of the river, formed another unanswered call to arms:

> Starved Fellow Creatures. Assemble on Thursday next at 10.00
> at night with proper weapons in St George's Field, where you

will meet friends to defend your rights. Never mind the blood thirsty soldiers. We shall put them to flight, our schemes are sure to be attended with success. The cause is honourable and ought to be prosecuted as such. Rouse to Glory ye slumbering Britons.

The most likely authors of the crude posters found in September 1800 were members of the group of more determined radicals who had persisted in their activities during the late 1790s. These years saw significant changes in the nature of London radicalism and in the nature of the threat faced by the government. Growing disillusionment with France, the patriotic fervour aroused by the war and especially the threat of invasion, and government repression had brought to an end the expansive public phase of the LCS. Already isolated by 1795, the Society had lost much of its more moderate leadership by 1796-7 and was attracting recruits like Colonel Edward Marcus Despard, Dr Watson, and John Binns; although reduced in size and effectiveness, it attempted to maintain a legal existence, but some at least of its members were also involved in the shadowy conspiracies of the United Irishmen, United Scotsmen, and United Englishmen.[27]

The full extent and nature of conspiratorial activity in the capital in the late 1790s, as in the country at large, is still not clear. Nonetheless the Government was seriously concerned that the remaining radicals posed a real threat to public order. In April 1798 the leading members of the LCS and the various United Societies were arrested and Habeas Corpus was once again suspended. During these arrests, troops were mobilised in case of a sympathetic or pre-emptive rising. Nor were these fears mere scaremongering: the Government's informants had become aware of the conspiratorial activities of the United Irishmen and following the trial of James O'Coigley, an Irish priest, for attempting to pass over to France, they acted to outlaw the LCS and the radical United Societies. In March 1799 the Secret Committee of the House of Commons reported that it had 'the clearest proof of a systematic design ... to overturn the laws, constitution, the Government'. When defence arrangements to counter the threat of a French invasion were drawn up in 1799, the Government reasoned that invasion would pose a less immediate threat to the capital than action by French sympathisers. It urged that 'internal conspiracy and insurrection cannot be too soon met and crushed', recommending 'immediate Military Execution' for any incendiaries or looters found in the act. The early detection 'of known leaders of sedition and Mischief' and the 'immediate punishment of persons detected in the active promotion of Riot' were regarded as vital to the security of the capital.[28]

Despard and the insurrectionary tradition

Certainly among Despard and some of his associates the idea of a *coup d'état* had taken root. Seizure of the principal symbols of authority of the capital, the Bank and the Tower, was to provide the signal for a general rising. Recent work has suggested that the London part of the activities, later known as the 'Despard conspiracy', was part of a wider plan in which risings in London, the industrial areas, and Ireland would be abetted by the French. Released from prison in 1800, Despard had undoubtedly been involved in conspiratorial activity in which he toured the taverns of London's poorer districts to win over followers, especially from among members of the London garrison. The exact details of the conspiracy are in some dispute; it is not clear whether Despard was in fact the main instigator of the 'plot' or whether he was made the scapegoat. Although neither its ramifications among London guardsmen and workmen nor the full extent of the provincial and foreign links have been fully explored, a conspiracy there certainly was. The interesting point about the plan was the belief that there would be a spontaneous response to the coup, both in London and in the provinces. This was not dissimilar from earlier plots, indeed as Thompson has noted, Despard's activities appear to owe as much to the tradition of Elizabethan and Jacobean conspiracy as to the revolutionary movements of the nineteenth century, a seizure of the principal buildings of the capital followed by foreign assistance, in this case from France.[29]

Despard was seized in November along with thirty-five other people, five of them soldiers. Although it has been suggested that there was little enthusiasm for a rising in November 1802, except among some of the London guardsmen, the Government may well have acted to nip the conspiracy in the bud and also to furnish itself with more detailed evidence of the activities of the conspirators. Whether the conspiracy was primarily Despard's and whether a rising was planned for 23 November, when parliament was to be opened, must remain a matter of contention. Certainly much of the evidence brought forward at Despard's trial in February 1803 must be treated with caution. Even so, the 'Despard conspiracy', for which he and five others were executed, suggested an insurrectionary potential among *some* London radicals; nor did the idea die on the scaffold with Despard, for it was to be taken up by the followers of Thomas Spence in the post-war period. In the Spa Fields Riots of December 1816 and again in the Cato Street conspiracy, men like Arthur Thistlewood and, perhaps also the Watsons, inherited the idea 'that London must perform the role of Paris in an English revolution either by means of riots culminating in general insurrection directed at the Tower, the prisons, and the Houses of Parliament, or by means of the *coup d'état*.'[30]

9 London and the kingdom

The capital remained the focus for many of the major political agitations in the early decades of the nineteenth century. The decline of the principal radical societies by the end of the 1790s and the execution of Despard and his fellow conspirators marked the end of one era of activity but did not extinguish some of the advances in political organisation and extra-parliamentary activity which had taken place. Although the industrial areas and provincial towns and cities were coming increasingly to the fore, the capital was still the most important urban community in the country, the security of which dominated the mind of the government. To reformers and radicals alike, it retained an enormous potential for generating support and orchestrating opposition. By 1802 a new popular champion had emerged in the person of Sir Francis Burdett, whose election for Westminster in 1807 and conflicts with the Government in 1810 were to mark important episodes. With the end of the Napoleonic Wars London was the scene of several popular agitations, including those in opposition to the passing of the Corn Laws, the reform campaign of 1816–17, and the support for Queen Caroline. The period also witnessed two insurrectionary attempts, at Spa Fields and Cato Street, which, though total failures, had important repercussions on the conduct of Regency politics and the development of popular radicalism.

Burdett and liberty

Sir Francis Burdett emerged as a popular champion at the time of the imprisonment of the radical leaders in Cold Bath Fields prison. A wealthy baronet, and protégé of John Horne Tooke, Burdett took up the cudgels in defence of the prisoners, coining the description of the prison as the 'English Bastille'. His securing of an enquiry into conditions at the prison ensured that his name became well known in London. Cold Bath Fields prison achieved further notoriety on 16 August 1800 when a large crowd gathered around it as cries of 'Murder' and 'Starving alive' came from within; cries of 'To arms' and 'Pull down the Bastille' were heard among the crowd. Although the crowd was dispersed and the

London *c.* 1815

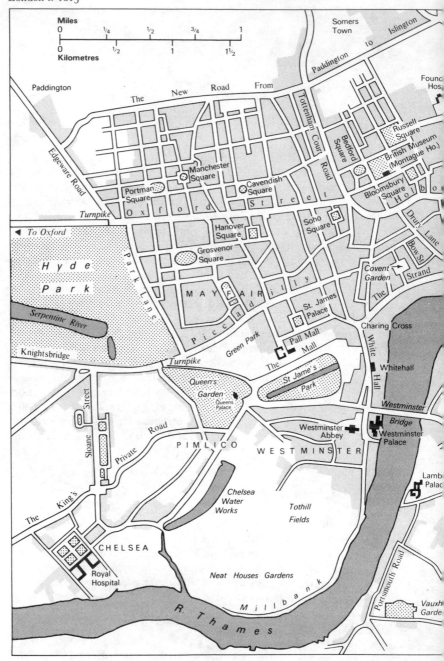

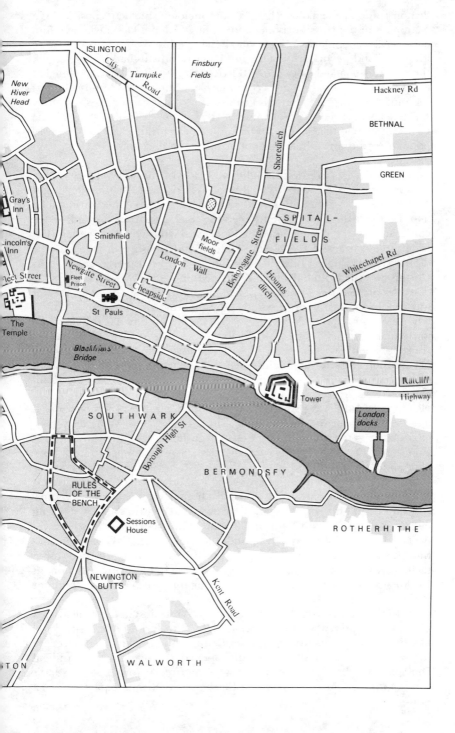

ISLINGTON

New
River
Head

City

Turnpike
Road

Finsbury
Fields

Hackney Rd

BETHNAL

GREEN

Shoreditch

Gray's
Inn

Lincoln's
Inn

Smithfield

SPITAL-

FIELDS

Moor
fields

Bishopsgate Street

Whitechapel Rd

Fleet Street

Newgate Street

London Wall

Hounds
ditch

Fleet
Prison

Cheapside

St Pauls

The
Temple

Blackfriars
Bridge

Ratcliff

Tower

Highway

SOUTHWARK

London
docks

Borough High St

BERMONDSEY

RULES
OF THE
BENCH

Sessions
House

ROTHERHITHE

NEWINGTON
BUTTS

Kent Road

TON

WALWORTH

demonstration passed off without serious incident, Burdett's position as a champion of oppressed prisoners, including Colonel Despard, gave him considerable popularity. Even when the conditions in the prison were improved and the majority of the imprisoned radicals had been released, the cry and chalked slogans of 'Burdett and No Bastille' and 'Burdett and Liberty' were to become a commonplace after 1798. Because some of the mutineers of 1797 were also the victims of Governor Aris's regime, Burdett also earned the nickname of the 'sailors' friend'. It was on the basis of this popularity that he brought to electoral politics a degree of popular enthusiasm which had not been seen in the capital since the days of Wilkes.[1]

From 1802 Burdett fought a series of tumultuous elections, culminating in 1807 with his victory at Westminster. In 1802 he fought Middlesex against the ministerial candidate William Mainwaring. The 'No Bastille' slogan was reinforced by his supporters providing an elaborate pageant of emaciated prisoners and whip-wielding gaolers. His programme attacked the waste of blood and treasure in the war, the destruction of English liberties symbolised by the suspension of Habeas Corpus and the Cold Bath Fields issue. Mainwaring was attacked as the defender of 'that new system of police, of secret imprisonment and secret torture': in contrast Burdett posed as the champion of 'Bread and Plenty'. The election campaign was rowdy and tumultuous rather than particularly violent; Cobbett described how 'The road from Piccadilly (Burdett's house was in Piccadilly) to the hustings at Brentford is a scene of confusion and sedition, such as never was beheld, except in the environs of Paris, during the most dreadful times of the revolution.' His successful election was greeted by an enthusiastic illumination. In 1804 a by-election at Middlesex provided another opportunity to test his support. Taking as his slogan 'Independence' he attacked both Whig and Tory candidates, to the applause of the crowds gathered around the hustings at Brentford. For several days pro-Burdett crowds terrorised the Tory candidate, George Mainwaring (William Mainwaring's son): whenever he appeared on the hustings he was shouted down; his committee rooms in Carey Street were attacked, as was his house, and the house of his sons. Constables and magistrates had to be posted to control the crowds going out to Brentford from central London. On 15 August Burdett was declared elected by a majority of one vote. A triumphant cavalcade bore him back to London, only to have his election overturned on a technicality the following morning. He failed to secure election at Middlesex in 1806, although once again greeted with popular enthusiasm.[2]

In that year, 1806, the scene shifted to Westminster: the radicals, led by Francis Place and now supported by the formidable writings of Cobbett, put up a candidate, James Paull. Although he failed to secure the seat, he polled respectably and opened the seat up for a radical challenge in the following year. A committee to organise Burdett's candidature was formed, in which Place played a leading part. Out of a committee of twenty, no less than six were former LCS members. The aim of the committee was to elect Burdett and a last minute choice, Lord Cochrane, without recourse to bribery, treating or violence, all of which were denounced by Cobbett and Place as vestiges of a corrupt electoral system. Instead they sought to pin their faith on the honesty and independence of the electors, demonstrating the virtues of 'independence'. Although Burdett kept the committeee at arm's length, refusing to assist in any way, the result was a triumph for the radicals with both Burdett and Cochrane elected.[3]

Burdett's attitude to the Westminster candidature in 1807 would have put off less determined men than Place and the Westminster Committee. He had almost brought the campaign to disaster by fighting a duel with the first choice of running-mate, James Paull; only the tireless efforts of the Committee in organising the vote for Cochrane and Burdett rescued the situation. Moreover Burdett's commitment to reform fell short of that of some supporters, his position owed more to the traditions of Wyvill and the Yorkshire Association than to the new urban radicalism which was pushing to the fore. His stand was that of the classic 'independent', in which reform was regarded as a means of checking the influence of the Ministry and reviving the power of the country gentry. But whatever Burdett's shortcomings, he was to prove the figurehead for the metropolitan radicals during the next few years. Although representing Westminster, he had the support of City radicals, such as Matthew Wood and Robert Waithman, ensuring him the backing of the City's political machinery and considerable popular influence. As the 'sailors' friend' and the candidate of 'Bread and plenty' he offered a focus for the feelings and aspirations of much of the populace of the capital. It was this influence with the City radicals and the London crowd which was to make the Burdett affair of 1810 a particularly dangerous one for the administration.

By 1810 the Government was under considerable pressure. Already in some disarray over the war issue, the scandal of the Duke of York's mistress had aroused sufficient public indignation to permit the passing of Curwen's Act against the open purchase of seats. But the refusal of the country gentlemen to trust the Whigs, and the persistent divisions between Whigs and radicals, vitiated attempts at more extensive reform. Nonetheless, the radicals were determined to seize any opportunity to embarrass the Government, expose its deficiencies, and thereby further the cause of reform. The parliamentary session opened with petitions for reform from Middlesex and Westminster, as well as considerable criticism of the conduct of the war. Then in February John Gale Jones was summoned before the House of Commons for a libel on the House at the British Forum. Place sought Jones out and urged him to resist the warrant, question its authority, and force the House to arrest him, thereby exposing its arbitrary and corrupt nature. Alternatively cajoling and bullying Jones, Place pointed out to him that 'he would be better accommodated in Newgate than he was at home', and would be there 'visited and cheered by many opulent and influential persons, and that he now had an opportunity of pushing himself forward advantageously in the world'. A subscription of between £300 and £1,000 was promised should he agree to play the martyr of liberty; but should he refuse 'he would be neglected in prison and abandoned by everybody'. Having promised to play the part, Jones decided to surrender himself to the House's mercy and was committed to Newgate for the duration of the sitting.[4]

But the situation was rescued when Burdett published a letter in Cobbett's *Political Register* for 24 March, attacking the House's action in imprisoning Jones. On 5 April the Government ordered Burdett to be committed to the Tower: the London radicals had been given a tremendous opportunity to pit his popularity against the unreformed House. Burdett declared the warrant illegal and defied the Government to arrest him from his house in Piccadilly; he also appealed to the Sheriffs of London and Middlesex to protect him, thus placing the jurisdiction of the City of London between himself and the Government. The Ministry acted as if Burdett's defiance might lead to popular insurrection; several thousand regular troops and artillery were drafted into the capital and posted to protect all important buildings and the West End squares. Almost 10,000 Volunteers were placed on standby at the public offices and three of the most experienced stipendiary magistrates formed into a coordinating committee at the Gloucester Coffee House. Although the Lord Mayor of London was relatively neutral, as was one of the sheriffs, the other sheriff, Matthew Wood, was radically inclined and a stickler for City 'liberties'. The scene had been set for a classic confrontation between the radical champion and the administration, in which the side issues of City 'liberties', 'freedom of expression', and the use of the army against the populace were also involved.[5]

In addition to the backing of other metropolitan radicals, Burdett could count on widespread popular support. Crowds gathered outside his house in Piccadilly and had to be dispersed by the troops. Papers were pushed under doors which ran, 'Britons, if you do not now resist the Right Honourable thieves by force of arms you will be still further trampled on,' while the walls around Piccadilly were festooned with inscriptions of 'Burdett for Ever', 'Liberty or Death', and 'Magna Carta and the Bill of Rights'. Crowds of people, many of them festooned with blue ribbons and cockades, the colours of Sir Francis, forced passers-by to remove their hats in respect and pelted them if they refused to comply. Attempts by the soldiers to clear the crowds were complicated by the sheriffs' objection that it was their responsibility not that of the troops. After the Riot Act had been read on the afternoon of the 8th and the troops had cleared the streets, Sheriff Wood protested and said that he would indict the soldiers should anyone be killed. Later in the evening crowds gathered and events took an uglier turn; two soldiers were wounded by shots fired from an alley off Piccadilly and when the troops tried to clear the area the crowd made a make-shift barrier with a ladder and some bricks from a building site. Meanwhile, a section of the crowd moved off to the West End where they called for a general illumination and a few windows were broken in the fashionable squares.[6]

As it became clear that the Ministry would soon have to arrest Burdett rather than allow the farce of his defiance to continue, both Government and radicals prepared their ground. The Home Office was confident it now had control of the situation with almost 20,000 troops on duty; meanwhile the Tower was prepared to receive Burdett: the ditches were filled with water, cannon placed in the gateway and primed with grapeshot, and the Tower Hamlets Militia called out. The Government's plan was for the Serjeant-at-Arms to arrest Burdett early on the morning of 9 April and take him with an escort of troops on a long circuitous route north of London to avoid any obstruction by the City authorities.

The radicals had been granted an impressive publicity success during the siege of his house, but there were some among Burdett's associates whose ideas stretched to even higher flights of fancy. Place recalled some years later that he had been called to a meeting with Burdett at 11.00 p.m. on Sunday evening; under the influence of Arthur O'Connor, Burdett was toying with the idea of actively defending the house and Place was asked if he had twenty men who would defend it. In reply he posed the decisive problem: 'It would be easy enough to clear the hall of constables and soldiers, to drive them into the street or to destroy them, but are you prepared to take the next step and go on?' According to Place this was sufficient to induce everyone present to rely on the more pacific measure of calling out the *posse comitatus* under Sheriff Wood to protect Burdett, thus causing an embarrassing confrontation between the authority of the sheriffs and the House of Commons. Place hoped that the sheriffs would arrest any army officer who refused to leave the scene, thereby vindicating the constitutional proprieties and forcing the Government to escalate the situation at the risk of offering still more opportunities to the radical press. He therefore advised Burdett to 'go to bed and sleep soundly'. In a remarkable passage, he articulated his rationale for not resisting more actively.

> I did not then, I do not now [1827], disapprove of Sir Francis Burdett's notions. Had circumstances been such as to promise effectual resistance, not only at the house of Sir Francis but anywhere else, had there been anything like a sufficient body organised to have assured the soldiers that power enough existed to protect them ... there would have been a fair chance in the then disposition of men, and no small portion of the army, that a successful effort at the outset would have given them confidence, and that many and perhaps nearly all the troops in London would have revolted. But there was no organisation and no arms, and to have resisted under such circumstances would have been madness.[7]

Having rejected 'physical force', primarily on pragmatic grounds –

a useful draught of realism in the heated atmosphere of Burdett's house – a *posse comitatus* was prepared for Monday morning, but he was arrested too early for the plan to be put into operation. Climbing into the house, the Serjeant-at-Arms arrested Burdett who he found engaged in instructing his family from Magna Carta. He was conveyed to the Tower under military escort without mishap, but the news of his arrest spread like wildfire through central London so that by midday the Tower was surrounded by an 'immense concourse'. As the soldiers returned to their quarters, they were pelted with mud, stones and other missiles. One group of cavalry opened fire killing two people and wounding about a dozen more, while others beat their way through the crowds with the flat of their swords. Nonetheless Sir Francis was securely imprisoned and after the mêlée with the troops, the crowds dispersed.[8]

Burdett could only be kept in the Tower for the duration of the parliamentary sitting and his impending release led to an interesting sequel. His arrest was made much of by the radicals, allowing them to attack even more bitterly the corruption of a House of Commons which permitted such 'tyranny'. Petitions demanding his release flowed into parliament, whilst in London a series of banquets and resolutions attacked the abuse of privilege by parliament. Accordingly, the Burdettites planned a triumphal procession to escort their leader from the Tower. Place was reluctant at first to organise the demonstration, but, urged on by Major Cartwright, an elaborate and peaceful display of reformist strength was arranged. Once involved, Place was concerned that the procession should be orderly and well-conducted, for 'had there not been the greatest order, the whole would have got into confusion, terminating in a riot, and the people would have been slaughtered'. Marshals were appointed and printed notices prepared detailing the arrangements.

The Government feared that Burdett's release might lead to serious rioting or even a rising and they prepared an elaborate plan to garrison the capital with regular troops, artillery, militia, and volunteers. Liaison with the civil authorities was arranged and a headquarters set up in the Gloucester Coffee House opposite Burdett's house in Piccadilly where the procession was to end; all important streets and buildings were given guards of a magistrate and some troops; squadrons of cavalry were allotted to the command of the public offices, platoons of infantry were appointed to guard the houses of prominent individuals, and vestry clerks were told to assemble the 'respectable' inhabitants in order to be ready to swear them in as special constables. Finally, a semaphor system was arranged so that news of the dissolution of parliament could be passed instantly to the Tower.[9]

The episode ended not in a repetition of 1780, as many feared, but a fiasco. Large crowds assembled on 21 June, thousands of blue-cockaded figures standing on wagons or scaffolding erected specially for the occasion. A procession of Westminster electors proceeded to the Tower at 2.00 in the afternoon where they awaited news of their hero. But at

3 o'clock they were told that Burdett had left secretly by water and returned to his country home at Wimbledon. He had informed no one, not even Place, with whom he had earlier agreed to take part in the procession. Place was so disgusted that he broke off contact with Burdett for several years. What then of Burdett? He clearly feared being the centre of an event which might lead to widespread bloodshed. No one in his position could ignore the events of thirty years before and that Lord George Gordon had found himself charged with High Treason as a result. His rumoured fear that Place was a government spy, trying to implicate the leader of popular radicalism in a potentially disastrous disturbance, while untrue, nevertheless showed the way in which his mind was working. As he recorded: 'Our enemies . . . have been base enough to charge him with the blood that had been shed, and had he by gratifying his personal vanity been the cause of a single accident, or the death of any person, he should have reflected upon it with pain the rest of his life.'[10]

The Burdett affair illustrated many of the dilemmas that were to dog the radicals in their attempt to direct and stimulate extra-parliamentary agitation. Place's overriding concern was to expose the arbitrary actions of the Commons and promote the case for reform. In this the affair was moderately successful. It produced meetings, resolutions, and petitions which not only condemned the arrest of Burdett and Gale Jones but also demanded various degrees of reform. In that sense it marked a revival of the Wilkes situation in the 1760s, especially in so far as popular enthusiasm was focused on a particular individual. But Burdett was no Wilkes. Aristocratic, humane, and diffident, he was not prepared to risk the consequences of popularity with the London crowd; indeed such incidents as had occurred had served to frighten off elements of 'respectable' opinion from support for reform, including many of the Whigs. Three weeks after Burdett's release from the Tower, Grey denounced the radicals' attempt to obtain reform by 'popular clamour', and stressed that 'the path they are treading is dangerous in the extreme, and demands the most vigilent caution to prevent it from leading to a fatal termination'.[11]

Moreover the dilemma for popular leaders like Burdett, and later men like Cobbett, Hunt, and the Chartist leaders, was that they were operating in a grey area between 'moral' and 'physical' force; they all knew advocates of more violent action against the unreformed system and Place himself had clearly looked the question straight in the face in April 1810. Burdett, Hunt, Place, Cobbett, and Cartwright had personal knowledge of people with more extreme views such as Arthur O'Connor, Arthur Thistlewood, and the Watsons. Their problem was to make the most of popular support, while avoiding giving the Government an opportunity for repression and alienating 'respectable' opinion. Only an understanding of this ambivalent position explains the sometimes contradictory attitudes of radical reformers in the post-war years to popular disturbances and agitations.[12]

The passing of the Corn Laws

The passing of the Corn Laws of 1815 have received less attention than their repeal thirty-one years later, yet in both the capital and the country it produced a petitioning movement of unprecedented scale and in London created scenes which once again evoked memories of the Gordon Riots. The proposal to prohibit all imports of foreign wheat until the domestic price reached 80s a quarter aroused opposition as early as 1814. Designed to protect the living of landowners who had invested heavily in improvement and increased acreage during the war years, it aroused the opposition of manufacturers, poor law overseers, humanitarians and other representatives of urban interests. As a select committee of the House deliberated on the issues, an intense pamphlet war was being waged which involved many of the important economic and political writers of the day. In spite of the opposition the Bill received its first reading on 1 March 1815. Metropolitan feeling towards the measure was expressed by the *London Chronicle*:

> This question is now brought to an issue between the owners and occupiers of land on the one hand and on the other between all the rest of the community who do not derive their income from land . . . the landed interest want to have a law for raising the price of corn to double the amount of what it was before the war began. . . . the landed interest who constitute so comparatively small a majority tell the rest of the people that they must not obtain corn from abroad, except at such price as they shall fix upon it.

At parish meetings in many parts of the capital, similar sentiments were expressed, in the poor East End parish of Bethnal Green it was resolved 'that the evils resulting from such a measure will be the increase of poverty and paupers, and consequently an alarming advance of poor rates'.[13]

Popular opposition to the Bill emerged during the chairing of the newly elected member for Southwark, Charles Barclay, on 28 February 1815. Barclay was surrounded by a large crowd who pelted him with stones, hurting him quite severely. Taking refuge in the Horns Tavern at Kennington, he was besieged by the crowd who had to be dispersed by troops. The origins of his rough reception was that he was rumoured to be in favour of the Corn Bill. During the incident, the cry of 'Burdett for ever' was heard again and a number of able people seen parading the streets bearing loaves covered in black crèpe on the end of poles,[14] though in fact, Burdett was somewhat equivocal on the measure, fundamentally favouring protection. The Westminster constituents and the City of London prepared petitions against the Bill and made ready to oppose it tooth and nail through its various stages; A second reading passed on 3 March without serious incident, but during the debate on the third reading on the 6th, the scene outside Parliament began to resemble what it had been at the height of the excise crisis or the early stages of the

Gordon Riots. By the afternoon several thousand people had assembled outside the Commons where they interrogated members going into the House; carriage doors were opened and members were grabbed by the collar and asked on which side they intended to vote. Late in the evening, soldiers were called in to disperse a crowd estimated at between 10,000 and 20,000 strong, but a section moved off to attack the houses of known supporters of the Bill. The windows of Lord Eldon, Lord Ellenborough, Charles Yorke, and Frederick Robinson – the mover of the Bill – were among those to suffer. Lord Eldon sallied from his house and seized two of the crowd, recalling: 'I brought into the house by their collars two of the mob, and told them that they would be hanged. One of them bid me look to myself, and told me that the people were much more likely to hang me than I was to procure any of them to be hanged.'[15]

On the next day inscriptions of 'Bread or Blood' appeared on the walls of Spital Square, as well as the ominous 'We want a Bellingham', referring to the assassin of Perceval. Hanging from a tree in Islington was found an effigy with a white apron, designated as Frederick Robinson, with a placard announcing 'this is the post of honour for those who support the corn laws'. Crowds who assembled in Palace Yard were addressed by two men who demanded: 'Do none of you remember Hampden, Russell, Sydney. And do you not remember Oliver Cromwell who so gloriously dissolved the Parliament? We had patriots in those times, why should we not have them now? Patriots where are ye all? . . . they have taken off the property tax, only to lay on one that will scourge the poor man still worse. Rise!'

Once again dispersed by soldiers, the crowd moved off to attack houses in Westminster: windows were smashed and minor damage done at about a dozen houses; at Frederick Robinson's house, the crowd who assembled were fired on by the butler and guard of three soldiers, killing a sailor and a woman. The attacks were not blind outrages, but directed against known or suspected supporters of the Corn Bill. Some other scores were settled at the same time; Meux's brewhouse was attacked on 7 March, and his private house the previous night, allegedly because he had laid off a number of his workmen. A rationale for the attack on the West End was also offered by the *Morning Post* who claimed that the crowds which assembled complained that the West End parishes had not called vestry meetings to oppose the Bill.[16]

The Government had now begun to assemble its forces. Five regiments of cavalry, a regiment of infantry, and a militia regiment were drafted into the metropolitan area. Notwithstanding a crowd assembled on Wednesday morning and smashed the windows of the *Morning Herald*, a supporter of the Bill, then went off to huzza an opponent, the *Morning Post*. More houses were attacked and those of George Ponsonby and Sir Joseph Bankes were ransacked; several effigies were found and one of Vansittart was burned at Lewisham; posters and scrawled inscriptions were found threatening death to the Prince Regent if he gave his assent to the Bill; one placard put up on the Pantheon on Thursday simply read

'Depraved Prince – Corrupt Ministers, Ruined Country'. Rumours of attacks on the prisons flew around but the only disturbance was described as an 'uproar march' through Oxford Street in the evening which was broken up by cavalry. On Friday 10 March in spite of a petition from Westminster signed by 42,473 people, the Bill received its third reading. Although petitions to the Lords and to the Prince Regent were to continue until the bill received the royal assent on 23 March, the 10th witnessed the last of the anti-Corn Law disturbances when some windows were broken in Fitzroy Square. Apart from a spate of threatening letters to lawyers who had been involved in drawing up the Bill, some of whose houses and offices had been attacked during the last nights of the riots, the disturbances were over.[17]

The opposition to the passing of the Corn Laws was significant in several ways. The disturbances owed much to the eighteenth-century traditions of the London 'mob', acting in collusion with its leaders in City of London, in an agitation which was one of the last to stir the City's grassroots political institutions, the wards and parishes. The crowds which assembled outside parliament and the mobs which went out to attack the premises of those associated with the Bill appear to have derived little impetus from the agencies of popular radicalism. Indeed the most prominent radical leader in London, Burdett, was in favour of the Bill, and the actions of the London populace were derived primarily from the traditions of crowd action seen on many occasions in the past. Although slogans and posters were found which clearly emanated from a more radical tradition, the rioters in March 1815 showed the same discrimination and moderation in their attacks that had been seen many times before. No known radicals were arrested for taking part in the riots and the Government found no suspicious background to those it seized, even at a time when it was inclined to do so. Instead, they dealt with the riots for what they were – a traditional display of opposition – in which protest ranged from the 'respectable' elements in the House of Commons to the streets. While in the rest of the country the opposition to the Corn Laws marked an important stage in the development of 'public opinion', along with opposition to the Orders in Council, in the capital it served to show the survival of the traditional methods of metropolitan pressure upon the government.[18]

As so often happened, popular disturbances again proved a double-edged weapon, and severely compromised the Bill's opponents. In presenting the Westminster petition Burdett was forced to disavow such methods of agitation and newspapers which had initially taken a neutral line on the issue were alienated by the riots. On 2 March the *London Chronicle* urged the Blackstonian doctrine that the 'legislature should never submit to popular clamour' and in the midst of the disturbances, a week later, was simply stressing the need to suppress them without further debate of the pros and cons of the measure. The *Morning Post*, which had consistently opposed the Corn Law, claimed later that but for the riots the Bill would not have passed. Once again the lesson seemed to be that the popular radicals either had to organise popular pressure skilfully and avoid the embarrassment of disturbance, or risk seeing the alienation of 'respectable' opinion and a fresh opportunity given for government repression.[19]

The insurrectionary tradition: from Spa Fields to Cato Street

London was heavily affected by the distress which followed peace with France: the loss of war contracts brought unemployment to the London trades and to the port and its associated industries; the release of men from the armed services brought crowds of often destitute men on to the streets so that the parochial and philanthropic resources of the metropolis were stretched almost to breaking point. With increasing prices due to a poor harvest, London shared in the reform agitation taking place in the country at large, with the Common Hall of the City of London demanding parliamentary reform in August and November. While the Government made preparations for what the Home Office described as a 'very awkward winter', the main focus for their attention was the small group of Spenceans, led by Dr Watson and Arthur Thistlewood.[20] This group could be considered as the extreme left wing of a large number of radicals and reformers who partook of the London political scene. Whereas the prevalence of distress united all reformers in the desire for reform there was considerable disagreement about tactics. The veteran radical Major Cartwright and Sir Francis Burdett concentrated on public meetings, petitions, and what a later generation would describe as 'moral' force. Place was also by this time convinced that the only effective way forward was by constitutional methods and utilitarian improvement. Of the radical leaders, the two most prominent in the post-war period, Henry Hunt and William Cobbett, came nearest to taking a more active stance. Whereas the latter eventually came out openly against violent proceedings in *A Letter to the Luddites*, Henry Hunt often seemed to come near to approving violence in his rhetoric and became for much of the post-war period the man to whom many poor and distressed working men looked for leadership.[21]

Hence when Dr Watson and his colleagues planned a programme of mass meetings to petition against distress and for reform in the autumn of 1816 it was to Hunt above all, and to a lesser extent Burdett and Cobbett, that they looked to provide charismatic leadership. At what point in this plan the Spenceans adopted the insurrectionary idea is not clear; much of the evidence brought against them at their trial in 1817 was elicited from paid informants and the crown witness John Castle, who had been involved in the conspiracy. Hunt's own evidence is also somewhat suspect as it was produced when he was languishing in prison for his part in the Peterloo affair and trying to do his best to exonerate himself from any part in violent proceedings. None the less, it is clear that the Spenceans planned a meeting at Spa Fields on 15 November to which they invited Hunt, Burdett, Cobbett and Cartwright. Only Hunt accepted, and he was seriously alarmed when he heard that they planned to march on Carlton House to present a petition to the Prince Regent in person; he dissuaded them from this course and, although a few posters calling on the people to arm themselves and rise were circulated, the meeting was well attended and largely peaceful. Only after the crowd of several thousands had been urged by Hunt to disperse peacefully and put their faith in petitioning did a breakaway group cause any trouble; a body of boys and 'poor-looking men' gathered near St Clement's Church and paraded through part of Westminster breaking the windows of food shops; by 9.00 p.m. the incident had ended, but it was a symptom of the popular discontent over prices and conditions which was present among many of the capital's poorer inhabitants.[22]

According to later evidence, the Watsons were so encouraged by the large number – up to 20,000 – attracted to the meeting that they planned a rising in which the Bank, the Tower, and the prisons would be attacked. Although, as in the Despard conspiracy, the Crown may well have filled out the details of the conspiracy in more detail than ever existed in reality – and lurid detail at that, including combustibles to burn down the barracks, 'infernal devices' to disable cavalry, and a list of radical notables to provide a 'Committee of Public Safety' – some preparations were made by the Spenceans for what could only be an attempted rising. Arms were secured and loaded into a wagon, tricoloured flags and banners calling on the soldiers to join them were prepared, and some of the Spenceans were reported distributing bread and cheese among the poor of the East End parishes so that they would attend the meeting. By the end of November the Home Office was receiving information about possible disorder at the meeting scheduled for Spa Fields on 2 December. An informant told them on 30 November of a plan to 'Burn and destroy all the Jails in the Metropolis and let out the prisoners'; another reported a plan to seize the arms deposited in the Artillery Ground belonging to the Honourable Artillery Regiment. As a result the Home Office took a number of precautions: the City constables were placed to police the meeting at Spa Fields and the Lord Mayor stationed in the Mansion House to report half-hourly to the Home Office; the stipendiary magistrates were alerted and asked to report every two hours on the state of their districts, and small detachments of troops were placed at important buildings. Even so, the scale of preparations was moderate compared with many other occasions in the period, and Lord Sidmouth confided to Lord Liverpool on 31 November that he did not expect any serious disturbances from the Spenceans.[23]

Hunt had disassociated himself from the Spenceans by leaving London and arranging to turn up at the meeting at one o'clock. Since the first Spa Fields meeting he had had an interview with Lord Sidmouth, who congratulated him for counselling against the proposed march on

Carlton House, which Sidmouth assured him would have been dispersed by troops. Whether this had served as a warning to him or not, the issue was taken out of his hands. On the day of the meeting the Spenceans arrived early at Spa Fields, about midday, with a wagon bearing flags, banners, and possibly some arms. One of the banners bore the inscription 'The brave soldiers are our Brothers treat them kindly'. A considerable portion of the 2,000 or so people assembled in the fields clustered round the wagon, where they were first addressed by the elder Watson and then by his son. Where the father had denounced the evils suffered by the nation, the younger Watson went further, declaiming: '"If they will not give us what we want shall we not take it? (answers of yes, yes). Are you willing to take it? (Yes, yes). If I jump among you will you follow me?" At that he jumped from the wagon, seized the largest of the flags and set off towards the City followed by a crowd of about two hundred; by far the greater part of the assembled throng remained to hear Hunt who had not yet arrived.'[24]

The mob marched unopposed past Cold Bath Fields prison – the Mayor's constables having been caught taking lunch – entered the City at West Smithfield and marched towards the Royal Exchange, plundering a gunshop on the way. At the Royal Exchange they were met by the Lord Mayor and a group of hastily assembled constables who overpowered several of the crowd. Many fled, throwing away their weapons, but a party moved on towards the Tower arming themselves from a shop in the Minories; one group left the area by going towards the East End along the Whitechapel Road where they were now somewhat belatedly pursued by Dragoons. Part of the crowd approached the Tower, where two men, 'one with a drawn sword and the other with two pistols', harangued the garrison. A soldier later testified that they were offered a hundred guineas to open the gates, but were called from the ramparts before anything could happen. At the approach of cavalry the two men disappeared into the crowd. This occurred just before 2.00 p.m. Within the next couple of hours the authorities dispersed the remaining crowds and seized several of the rioters and most of the weapons. The elder Watson, Thomas Preston, and John Hooper of the leading group had been arrested and within three days a reward of £500 was on the head of the younger Watson.[25]

Many contemporaries regarded the incident as being more of a riot than a serious insurrectionary attempt. None the less, the Spenceans had caught the authorities napping, if not entirely unprepared. The gang were given free rein for several hours in an area which contained large stocks of arms in the various warehouses and gunshops near the Tower, more than 50,000 in all according to the authorities. As it was, the rioters had seized over 200 muskets and pistols, as well as swords, pikes, a three-pounder carronade, and two small field pieces; but many of the crowd in the Minories had no idea how to use the weapons and several of them loaded the muskets with stones, buckles, and buttons, injuring themselves in consequence when the weapons burst. The whole affair could have gone badly wrong for the authorities had they been faced with a more determined and capable group of conspirators; indeed, had the Spenceans but known it, the Tower lay at their mercy as on 5 December the commander admitted that throughout the afternoon of the 2nd he had been without ammunition, which had been sent to the Hyde Park magazine, and fresh supplies did not arrive until late in the evening.[26]

Meanwhile, Hunt encountered groups of rioters as he proceeded to Spa Fields, claiming in his *Memoirs* that he was told by the Crown witness Castle that the Tower was taken and was urged to join the rising. Ignoring this information he went on to Spa Fields where he addressed the large crowd as planned. In his own account he stressed that he counselled the people against violence and warned them to disperse peacefully. This they did, apart from a small group who tore up some railing in the West End and broke the windows of some shops before dispersing at the sight of some cavalry. Hunt's account of his actions was substantially corroborated by the newspaper accounts and by witnesses at the later trial of the Spenceans in June 1817. After the event, Hunt – like most other prominent radicals – condemned the Spenceans for their 'disgraceful and contemptible riot'.[27] But suspicion remains that the full story was never told. A mysterious man on a white horse was seen directing the crowd in the Minories at much the same time as Hunt had left the Spa Fields meeting on horseback, but it seems improbable that the Government would have allowed Hunt to escape from prosecution had the slightest opportunity presented itself to produce a case against him. However, after his acquittal, Thistlewood was reported as saying that the Spa Fields plan failed because 'Sir Francis Burdett was not to be depended on' and that if he or Hunt had stood forward 'the people would have followed and the Business would have been done'; he alleged that all that was required was a leader, because the Watsons were not well enough known to the general populace. Whether the incident was a semi-spontaneous insurrection or a well laid plan which failed because of Hunt's caution will perhaps never be known for certain, but certainly Sidmouth was given to understand from his informants that radicals in the provinces were expecting the non-appearance of the mail coaches to signal a successful rising. An additional hint that the Spa Fields incident had not been fully explained occurred during a bitter dispute in the press between Hunt and Dr Watson in 1819, where the former suggested that the full truth about the riots had not been revealed at the trials of 1817.[28]

Even more significant was the impact of the riots. Even before they started Lord Sidmouth had intimated his desire to bring in fresh repressive legislation; the events of 2 December gave him an unanswerable case. Committees of Secrecy appointed in January concluded that: 'a traitorous conspiracy has been formed in the metropolis for the purpose of overthrowing, by means of a general insurrection, the established Government, laws, and Constitution of this kingdom, and of effecting a general plunder and division of property'.

Plans for repressive legislation were set in train as a result of the Spa Fields riots and the widespread disturbances in the country; although the

Government exaggerated the threat it faced, there was an element of genuine alarm. The case for legislation was strengthened by a small-scale repetition of the events of October 1795: at the opening of parliament on 28 January the Prince Regent's coach was booed and hissed, and some stones or gravel broke the windows. Bills were brought before parliament to suspend Habeas Corpus, make permanent parts of the Treason Acts of 1795, make subverting the armed forces a capital offence, and prevent seditious meetings. To the protests of Whig and radical MPs, Lord Castlereagh pointed to the events of 2 December as proof of the existence of a conspiracy to subvert the country. When Samuel Romilly protested that Habeas Corpus was not suspended in 1780, the Solicitor-General rounded on him with the comment that 'in the year of 1780 there was no plan to disorganise the state; that no clubs for revolutionary reforms were on foot; no plans for the subversion of Church and State were ramified'. By March, the repressive measures had been passed.[29]

At least one of the participants in the Spa Fields disturbances, Arthur Thistlewood, retained faith in the idea of a dramatic blow which would spark off a spontaneous rising. Only three months after the acquittal of the Spa Fields conspirators the Government had information from one of its spies that a rising was due to take place at the end of Bartholomew Fair in September 1817. Thistlewood and Thomas Preston were said to be confident of raising 2,000 men from the crowds attending the fair who would then attack the Tower armoury. The Home Office took the plot seriously enough to post troops at key points, mobilise magistrates and constables, and alert the Lord Mayor, but no appearance of a rising took place; later it was claimed that the conspirators had been frightened off by the sight of soldiers and constables. Nothing daunted, Thistlewood continued to crop up in the reports of government informers. In October 1817 he was reported to have suggested for the first time a plan to murder the Prince Regent and the Privy Council while they were at dinner, but it was not until December 1819 that his plot began to take shape. In the meantime he had been imprisoned without trial from February 1818 to the summer of 1819 for challenging Lord Sidmouth to a duel, he also participated for a time in the autumn in a London 'Committee of Two Hundred', but grew increasingly distrustful of the cautious policies of many of his fellow radicals and especially of the hero of 'Peterloo', Henry Hunt. Urged on by the government spy George Edwards, Thistlewood and a group of fellow conspirators planned to assassinate the cabinet when attending a dinner at Lord Harrowby's house in Grosvenor Square on 22 February. Fully informed of these plans by Edwards, the Government pounced on the conspirators as they assembled in Cato Street. Thistlewood and four of his fellows were convicted of High Treason and executed on 1 May 1820. Five others were transported.[30]

Although often dismissed as a rather pathetic gamble by desperate men, the Cato Street conspiracy was not quite the isolated gesture it appeared. Like Despard, Thistlewood believed in the prospect of a spontaneous reaction to his coup. There is evidence that the Scottish 'rising' and some of the events in Yorkshire later in the Spring may have been part of a concerted plan for a nationwide rising. Certainly Lord Sidmouth thought so, writing on 4 March that 'an expectation prevailed amongst the disaffected in the northern parts of the Kingdom that an important blow would be struck in London, previous to the expiration of the month of February'. Rumours of a widespread rising were abroad in the manufacturing districts and Sidmouth believed the weaving centres of Leeds, Manchester, Carlisle, and Glasgow to be implicated. While the true extent of this activity in the provinces remains obscure. Thistlewood was not quite as alienated from radical opinion in the capital as is sometimes suggested by a crude dichotomy between 'physical' and 'moral' force; although they disagreed with his methods, many radicals regarded him with sympathy as a man driven to desperation by adversity and fatally trapped by a particularly dangerous and odious *agent provocateur*. Thus even men who would have had no part in Thistlewood's kind of plotting, lamented his execution and hounded Edwards the spy out of the country.[31]

While Thistlewood was led towards the scaffold, other reformers were learning to live with repression. While the radical journalists hammered away at the Government, people such as Place, Dr Watson, and Thistlewood himself, concentrated on organising meetings and demonstrations after the expiry of the Seditious Meeting Act. In doing so they re-established the right of peaceful assembly to influence opinion at a time when government was habituated to see in almost every such occasion the threat of insurrection. They organised a huge reception for Hunt when he entered the capital after the Peterloo 'massacre'. At the end of the parade, Hunt made his now customary admonition to the populace; in the course of which 'he then advised them as they valued the cause for which they were contending to disperse quietly, and not by any ebullition [*sic*] of feeling to give their enemies any advantage over them'.[32] Similarly at the mayoral elections in London in the following month, he was able to use his popularity to support the radical candidates. A newspaper grudgingly noted his command over the crowds: 'We must give the devil his due. . . . He had at his back a dirtier rabble than the day before, and he directed their manoeuvres with admiral precision. . . . This monarch of the Mobility had his commands obeyed with a submissive deference, which few people now-a-days think of showing to the judges and great men of the land.'[33]

This development of peaceful protest, participated in for a time even by Thistlewood, was to be of far greater significance in the long term than the Cato Street conspiracy. The revival of forms of extra-parliamentary pressure which fell short of anything the Government could call treasonable was to play a vital part in the political struggles of the rest of the century.

The Queen Caroline Affair

These developments found their most remarkable expression in London, not in response to Peterloo, but in the unlikely cause of Queen Caroline. The struggle of George IV to divorce his estranged wife, Caroline of Brunswick, after he became King on 29 January 1820, provided a spectacular opportunity for opponents of the Government to orchestrate the most sustained and widespread agitation in the capital since the days of Wilkes. For almost a year the Queen's affair dominated politics. Taken up by many as a means of opposing the existing administration, the campaign for 'Caroline and Liberty' soon developed a powerful momentum of its own, in which the attempt to deprive Caroline of her royal title for alleged, and almost certainly actual, misconduct became a symbol of the assault upon English liberties.

For several months the Queen's cause not only provided a focus for radical groups but also threatened to fashion an alliance between the Whig opposition in the House of Commons and the extra-parliamentary agitation in the streets. The Queen not only provided a common focus of discontent, she provided a seemingly legitimate one too, acting in the tradition of the 'reversionary interest' of the eighteenth century. The veteran radical Major Cartwright ominously compared her return to England on 5 June 1820 to the landing of William III; certainly her arrival threw the Liverpool administration into disarray. Having failed to obtain from her the compromise settlement they expected, namely a pension in return for her staying out of the country, they now found themselves with little choice but to try to pass a Bill of 'Pains and Penalties'. The Queen was to be 'tried' before the House of Lords and the evidence of her misconduct abroad since 1814 used against her. In doing so, however, the Government gave her supporters an opportunity to mount an intensive campaign on her behalf, whilst the radical press had a field day in exposing the irony of the situation in which a notoriously immoral monarch was attempting to divorce his wife for misconduct.[34]

From her arrival in London on 6 June, after a triumphal journey from Dover, the Queen's campaign was effectively managed by Alderman Wood; this gave her access to the formidable resources of popular agitation possessed by the City of London. With William Cobbett acting as speechwriter, courtier, and adviser, Caroline was assisted by the most brilliant publicist of his day; in addition, she was supported by almost every important radical in the capital, including not a few who found her personally vulgar and her cause somewhat dubious. With Brougham and Denman as her principal Whig advisers, the Queen was certainly in a position to embarrass the Government and some believed that she would be the occasion of its overthrow. For some days in June, there was a peculiar atmosphere of expectancy: no one knew what was to happen, only that the Queen's arrival had been met by spontaneous demonstrations of support and that the King and his Ministers were at odds. At one point it even appeared that the troops might mutiny in her support; some soldiers in the London garrison refused to stand to duty, following persistent rumours that they sympathised with the Queen's cause. In fact, the men were primarily complaining about the onerous round of duties imposed by the crisis and the absence of extra pay for it and the affected troops were quickly marched out of the capital; thus the incident was closed, but significantly Lord Sidmouth was later to record it as the most serious crisis in the whole of the post-war period. But apart from this incident and some window-smashing, the feature which most impressed contemporaries were the series of parades and processions organised by the Queen's supporters. One recorded that:

> Often riding to Windsor have I been detained by an army of working men, with bands, and banners, and placards, headed by deputations of their several committees with wands of office – all terribly in earnest – all perfectly convinced of the Queen's immaculate purity – all resolved that oppression should not triumph – a peaceful multitude, but one that in any other country would have seemed the herald, if not the manifestation of, Revolution.

In similar vein, Creevey wrote that:

> Every Wednesday the scene which caused such alarm at Manchester is reported under the very nose of Parliament and all constituted authorities and in a tenfold degree more alarming. A certain number of the efficient population of the town march on each of these days in a regular lock-step, four or five abreast, banners flying, music playing. I should like anyone to tell me what is to come next if this organised army loses its temper.[35]

During the summer and autumn London tradesmen, representatives of parishes, wards, and other groups of opinion within the capital presented scores of addresses and resolutions to the Queen; similar displays of support flowed in from the country at large. While the more sober-minded radicals lamented on the diversion of the people's attention from more fundamental issues, Alderman Wood continued to keep the Queen at the head of a seemingly inexhaustible wave of popular support. But one or two of the shrewder politicians in the capital were already beginning to wonder precisely what the torrent of extra-parliamentary agitation was going to achieve; in a conversation with the Queen on 2 October, J. C. Hobhouse warned her not to rely upon 'the people', because 'they had been so often opposed to government and always failed'.[36]

The abandonment of the Bill of Pains and Penalties in November was greeted by tremendous rejoicing in the capital. Anne Cobbett wrote that within half an hour of the decision being known 'guns were firing in all directions, bells ringing, and illuminations in every street and suburb'.

She described the spectacle as

> fine beyond anything you can imagine. All the ships in the river
> lighted to the mastheads, processions marching with bands of
> music carrying busts of the Queen with the crown on her head
> covered with laurel, playing God Save the Queen and bearing
> torches.

Creevey described the river as

> the most beautiful sight in the world; every vessel is covered
> with colours, and at the head of the tallest mast in the river is
> the effigy of a Bishop, 20 or 30 feet in length, with his heels
> uppermost, hanging from the masthead.

Not only the main streets, but also 'the most obscure and most quiet
streets' were illuminated.[37] On 29 November the Queen attended a
thanksgiving ceremony at St Paul's. Although she was given no formal
marks of respect by the Government, she was accompanied by the
Common Council of the City of London and a guard of honour composed
of 1,000 gentlemen on horseback, organised by Wood. Sir Robert Wilson
described it as 'a most imposing exhibition and the enthusiasm as high
and general as can be imagined', calculating there were almost half a
million people on the streets. Anne Cobbett described it as an 'immense
mob' and *The Times* as the largest crowd in the history of the capital. But,
although the Government had placed the police and soldiers on the alert,
there were no disturbances during the procession.[38]

But Caroline's victory soon proved hollow. Once the Ministry
decided not to resign, the agitation began to falter. Divisions grew
between the radicals and, after the Whigs' attempt to defeat the Ministry
in the Commons in the New Year had failed, it was difficult to see where
Caroline's campaign could go. Although addresses continued from the
representatives of trade groups and others in the capital, the desertion of
the Whigs left the extra-parliamentary movement bereft of direction or
effectiveness. When the Queen accepted a pension of £50,000 in the New
Year, her cause was all but lost. She had a last chance to bring her
followers on to the streets at the King's coronation. As early as April
Caroline was informed that she would not be allowed a place in the Abbey,
still less any official marks of honour, nevertheless she was determined
to attend; in this she was mainly encouraged by Alderman Wood. The
Queen set out for Westminster Abbey accompanied by a 'thin and shabby
mob'; at the entrance to the Abbey she was refused admittance and was
forced to make her retreat in a rather embarrassing anti-climax.
Although her partisans claimed that the venture had been a success, that
the crowds supporting her had been large, and that the soldiers had once
again shown their favour, her opponents noted the rather surprising
warmth shown towards the King and the rather ludicrous spectacle of
Caroline going from door to door in Westminster Abbey and being
refused admittance. Croker summed up his feelings: 'We had rumours all

day of mobs and riots. I went myself to see what had happened; it turned out that half a dozen windows were broken in half a dozen places, and that was all. There was no more crowd opposite the Queen's door than served to fill the pavements.'[39]

The Queen's health proved incapable of withstanding the physical and emotional shock of the episode: she was taken unwell on the evening of the Coronation and in spite of a brief recovery died on 6 August. The Government wanted to dispose of her remains as quickly and discreetly as possible, and seized on her deathbed wish to be buried in Brunswick as providing an opportunity to avoid further embarrassment. It was planned to move the body to Harwich by the route least likely to lead to demonstrations. At first it was thought that the route by water from Hammersmith could be used, but a nervous Lord Liverpool decided it would facilitate obstruction from the City of London and it was finally decided to send the Queen's cortège by road on a circuitous route north of the City of London. An escort of Horse Guards was provided and other soldiers, police, and magistrates were put on the alert for the funeral procession.[40]

Early on 14 August the Queen's funeral procession set off. Almost immediately, the Government's plans were thrown out by the very large numbers of people on the streets; carts were found to be blocking the intended route with masses of people behind them. After consultation with Lord Liverpool, the procession was rerouted through Hyde Park by the magistrate in charge, Sir Robert Baker. The Life Guards were called out and the crowd began to pelt the troops with dirt and stones, crying 'Through the City, through the City'; Baker became alarmed as the crowd seemed to increase and all routes except that through the City seemed blocked and barricaded by carts or wagons. In the meantime a detachment of Life Guards became involved in a fracas with the crowd at Cumberland Gate. The troops attempted to keep the gate clear and were forced to draw their swords, but the mob, twice succeeded in shutting the gate and the troops were heavily pelted with stones and mud, injuring many and unhorsing two. The troops charged the crowd and when this proved of no avail they opened fire; two men were shot, Richard Honey, a cabinet maker of Compton Street Soho, and George Francis a bricklayer. Sir Robert Wilson, who was riding in the funeral procession, remonstrated with the troops, saying that 'the people will have her go through the city'. Sir Robert Baker still hoped to find a route avoiding the City, but as the embattled procession made its way forward, 'an immense concourse of people' and new barricades 'of coaches and carts which seemed chained together and loaded with people' blocked alternative routes and inexorably turned it towards Temple Bar. At Fleet Street the procession was met by the City Marshal who informed Baker that the Lord Mayor was on his way to act as escort through the City; the troops were dismissed and Sir Robert Baker retired defeated to the Home Office in Whitehall. The Lord Mayor then escorted the procession through the streets of the City on to the Romford Road for Harwich.[41]

The disturbances at the Queen's funeral, although not particularly serious in themselves, were regarded as a major defeat by the Government. Henry Hobhouse, Under-Secretary at the Home Office, complained to Lord Sidmouth that 'immense assiduity has been used by the radicals' to disrupt the procession and continued: 'I dread the moral effect of this day. The mob glory in having carried their object by force, in having beaten the military. . . . it strikes me that it is highly important to postpone all military reductions until the effect of this day is seen.' The Tory press fulminated against Sir Robert Baker's failure to ensure that the cortège adhered to the prescribed route; John Bull referred to a 'head of police, who evidently had no head of his own' and warned that 'a magistrate incompetent in times of difficulty, either from moral or physical inbecility to enforce laws and ordinances of the government is the most dangerous character in the country'. But although Baker was ultimately removed from his post as Chief Magistrate at Bow Street, it was difficult to see what more he could have done without risking greater bloodshed – indeed this was precisely his principal excuse. The Government also blamed the radicals for orchestrating the obstruction to the route and suspicion focused especially on Sir Robert Wilson, MP for Southwark, who had remonstrated with the troops; as a result he lost his army commission, although this only provided the radicals with further opportunities to protest about another exercise of 'arbitrary power'. Some collusion had taken place, because the City authorities clearly expected the procession be rerouted; there were reports of City constables recruiting men to build the barricades and of well-dressed men organising the crowd at different points on the route. The Queen's supporters in the capital had used their influence with the crowds to defeat the Government's plans, just as it had been feared that they might.[42]

The deaths of Honey and Francis gave the radicals an opportunity to recreate in a minor key the furore caused by Peterloo. The radical press made as much of the deaths as possible, the *Black Dwarf* headlining them for three weeks. Led by Dr Watson, John Gale Jones, and the trade union leader, John Gast, the London trades were again mobilised, this time to honour the dead men with a public funeral. Moreover with the sympathetic Whig, Robert Waithman as Sheriff of London and Middlesex, the radicals extracted the maximum political capital from the event through the inquest proceedings. These made it clear that the troops had opened fire without orders and without the Riot Act being read. But although some of the Life Guards were forced to parade before the coroner's jury, no specific charges could be made. The public funeral of Honey and Francis on 26 August provided the last 'spin-off' from the Queen's affair. An estimated 70,000 or 80,000 people took part in a procession meticulously organised by Gast and the Watsons. Representatives of the trades were to attend with emblems of their craft; a rendezvous was made at Smithfield at noon and the route took the procession past the Knightsbridge barracks used by the Life Guards.

Although only angry words were exchanged between the soldiers and the procession on the way to the graveyard, on the return in the early evening fighting broke out between members of the procession and off-duty soldiers, and a full-scale brawl took place during which the Riot Act had to be read. Although Sheriff Waithman had intervened to break up the fighting, he was blamed by the Government for not controlling the members of the procession more successfully: this reopened old quarrels between the City and the Home Office about the respective jurisdiction of the civil and military powers. After an acrimonious correspondence between the City authorities and Lord Bathurst, the affair subsided, but not before the Common Council of the City had set up an enquiry and the opposition press vented their displeasure at 'praetorian licentiousness', 'military dominion', and the descent of the army into a 'lawless mob'.[43]

Even by the end of the Napoleonic Wars, however, London's pre-eminent role in providing extra-parliamentary support for political agitations was beginning to be eclipsed by the rise of the manufacturing districts and the growth of the major provincial cities. The Queen Caroline affair marked the last of the great agitations in the traditions of Wilkes in which a largely metropolitan-based movement dominated the political scene. The focus of attention, especially in the reform movement, was shifting towards the provinces and it was they who were to play the most important role in the years after 1815. While London's place as the seat of government, the centre of commerce, and the most important source of journalistic activity ensured its continuing place in almost any political cause, it was increasingly more as a 'stage' for demonstrations which derived most, if not all, their support from outside; as a result, it is necessary to treat the capital from the 1820s as a part of the larger movements which provoked or threatened to provoke major upheaval.

10 The reform struggle

Waterloo to Peterloo

Not for the first nor the last time, the transition from war to peace produced serious economic difficulties. War-torn Europe was unable to buy British goods in the quantities expected and extensive commercial competition had to be faced from countries which had previously been swept from the seas by the British navy or restricted by the Napoleonic system of blockade. As a result Britain's overseas trade in 1816 was only two-thirds what it had been in 1814. More seriously, those industries which had expanded to meet wartime needs were plunged into depression by the ending of government contracts. The iron industry was particularly badly hit. In Shropshire, 7,000 ironworkers were thrown out of work and the depression spread through the collieries and metalware industries of the Midlands. A similar story was repeated in the ironworks of South Wales, the shipyards of the Thames and the South Coast, as well as among many other trades. In addition, the coming of peace released 300,000 soldiers and sailors, who flooded the labour market, depressing wage levels when they found work and adding to the pool of unemployed when they did not. As a result poor rates rose alarmingly in both industrial and rural communities. To make matters worse, exports of grain and a poor harvest in 1816 pushed up the price of wheat from 77s. 4d. a quarter in August to over a 100s. in December.[1]

Economic distress was accompanied by renewed agitation for reform. By the end of the war there was growing evidence of interest in reform not only from manufacturers and gentry, but also from the better educated workmen. The first Hampden Club had been founded in 1812 and during the next three years Major Cartwright made a series of tours of the manufacturing districts to carry his message to all who would listen. By 1816 Hampden Clubs and Union Clubs were springing up, many of them formed entirely by working men, often subscribing a small sum to purchase pamphlets and newspapers, and meeting in chapels, cottages, and alehouses. In November 1816 Cobbett wrote his *Address to the Journeymen and Labourers*, published as the sole contents of the first cheap edition of the *Weekly Register*, priced at twopence. Cobbett's linking of 'our present miseries' to the need for parliamentary reform had an immense effect, with an estimated 200,000 copies of the *Register* sold in two months. Samuel Bamford wrote:

> ... the writings of William Cobbett suddenly became of great authority; they were read on nearly cottage hearth in the manufacturing districts of South Lancashire, in those of Leicester, Derby and Nottingham; also in many of the Scottish manufacturing towns. Their influence was speedily visible; he directed his readers to the true cause of their sufferings – misgovernment; and to its proper corrective – parliamentary reform. Riots soon became scarce, and from that time they have never obtained their ancient vogue with the labourers of this country.[2]

In spite of the element of *post hoc* reasoning, Bamford's comments illustrated the growing political awareness of the labourers and artisans in these years. Cobbett, like Cartwright, sought to turn the labourers away from disturbances, seeing in riots and machine-breaking only an opportunity for further government repression. Cobbett also warned his readers that: 'I know of no enemy to reform and of the happiness of the country, so great as that man who would persuade you that we possess *nothing good* and that all must be torn to pieces. . . . We want great alteration, modification to suit the times and circumstances; but the great principles ought to be, and must be, the same, or else confusion will follow.' Cartwright too opposed 'any attempt to excite the poor to invade the property of the rich'.[3] On the whole, the leading radicals and publicists of the post-war era took up an essentially constitutional stance, believing that the political education of the people and the exertion of pressure upon the Government through the press, petitions, and public meetings would eventually prevail. The Government, on their side, saw in the progress of political ideas and the attempts of radicals to turn economic grievances into a political crusade the threat of revolution. To conservatives like Sidmouth, distress was regrettable, but inevitable, therefore radicals attempts to capitalise upon it were both mischievous and dangerous, destroying 'all respect for established authority and ancient institutions'. As a result the Government after 1815 was often to act with great harshness, making little distinction between reform agitation and 'sedition'. At the local level too, magistrates often tended to view all manifestations of lower class organisation as dangerous and reacted accordingly.[4]

In fact the majority of disturbances in 1816 were entirely apolitical. During the spring there were increasing signs of discontent in East Anglia, with rick burnings and threatening letters. The opening of French ports to imports resulted in prices for wheat going up in May by over 16*s.* in Cambridge and Norfolk. On 24 May riots were reported from the Isle of Ely, where crowds of agricultural labourers had marched into the market towns of Littleport and Downham, headed by banners inscribed 'Bread or Blood', and to the accompaniment of horns, fife and drum. In the towns they mobbed the magistrates and demanded higher wages and lower prices but did little other damage. The Government reacted sternly to these fairly minor disturbances. Troops were despatched to quell the riots and on 18 July a Special Commission was set up to try the offenders; twenty-four were condemned to death, five of whom were ultimately executed, the remainder being transported or imprisoned. These relatively savage sentences presaged growing alarm, and a cold, wet summer meant the certainty of high prices and discontent in the coming winter, one which Lord Eldon anticipated with 'fear and trembling'.[5]

During July gangs of unemployed colliers from the Midlands dragged carts piled with coal around the countryside to draw attention to their distress. When a party reached the outskirts of London they were firmly turned back, but given money and food for the return journey. Food riots had already occurred at Bridport and Frome in the South-West in spring and more disturbances were reported during the summer at Stockport, Bolton, Coventry, Hinckley, and Birmingham. Frame-breaking had flared up again in February at Huddersfield, whilst in May began a renewed period of frame-breaking by the Midlands stockingers, mainly directed at the lace-frames in Leicestershire, but also affecting Nottinghamshire by the autumn. Reviewing a bulging pile of letters detailing disturbances in South Wales, the North-East, Lancashire, and the Midlands, Lord Sidmouth could be forgiven for his comments to Lord Sheffield on 1 November that 'We must expect a trying winter, and it will be fortunate if the Military establishment which was pronounced to be too large for the constitution of the country shall be sufficient to preserve its internal tranquillity'.[6]

By this time the Government was alarmed at the mass meetings being organised in the capital by Henry Hunt, with the backing of a group of followers of Thomas Spence. The 'Spenceans', including Dr Watson, his son, and Arthur Thistlewood, were being watched carefully and the Government was also concerned about the meetings being held in provincial towns to organise petitions for reform – a campaign inaugurated by Major Cartwright and Sir Francis Burdett in September 1816. The petitioning movement involved sending delegates into neighbouring towns and villages from the provincial Hampden Clubs, to culminate in a meeting of delegates in London on 23 January 1817. In the interim the Spa Fields meetings in London erupted into an insurrectionary attempt led by Thistlewood and the Watsons. It met with little response in the country at large, where the Hampden Clubs maintained as discreet a profile as possible, subject as they were to magisterial harassment and urged by Cartwright and Cobbett to give no opportunity for repression. An exception was Sheffield where a meeting was held in the marketplace on 3 December to consider the results of the Spa Fields meeting the day before. When the organisers moved to adjourn for two days, John Blackwell led a group of several hundred on a parade through the town behind a blood-stained loaf carried on a pole. After smashing the windows of a flour dealer the group agreed to meet two days later, but by this time the soldiers and constables had been called out, the Riot Act read, and Blackwell arrested. A meeting was held secretly the next day addressed by an unknown 'Orator' who referred to other meetings being held in Birmingham, Nottingham and Manchester; on the following day the soldiers dispersed the reconvened main meeting. The usually level-headed Earl Fitzwilliam believed the meeting to be the counterpart to those in London. It was not he believed 'the consequence of distress', but 'the offspring of a revolutionary spirit'.[7]

The Spa Fields riots, reports of discontent in the country, and the attack on the Prince Regent's coach at the state opening of Parliament on 28 January strengthened the Ministry's hand in calling for new repressive measures. As in 1795, Committees of Secrecy were formed to collect information on the state of the country. Although there was certainly some evidence of plotting by groups in Yorkshire, Lancashire, the Midlands and London, the *Report* submitted to parliament in mid-February was a lurid exaggeration both of the extent and organisation of subversive activity. All discontents in the country were seen as part of a gigantic plot to promote a revolution. Echoing the sentiments of Lord Sidmouth, the petitioning campaign of the Hampden Clubs was claimed to be simply a mask for revolutionary preparations. As a result parliament sanctioned the suspension of Habeas Corpus and passed a Seditious Meetings Act which required any meeting of fifty or more to obtain prior permission from a magistrate, and gave magistrates permission to disperse any meeting they thought seditious. The Government's fear of 'tumultuous assemblies', such as those at Spa Fields and at Sheffield, was well illustrated in the debate on this Seditious Meetings Bill. To Erskine's protests at the infringement of traditional liberties and argument that everything that was free must on occasion prove irregular, Lord Eldon replied that he remembered the Gordon Riots of 1780, 'and if he were asked what was the most orderly public meeting he ever saw in his life, he should answer, that which assembled to meet Lord George Gordon. Nothing could have been more regular and orderly than that meeting was in the morning; and yet its consequences were, in the evening, to set London in flames.'[8]

Even before the Seditious Meetings Act was in force, the Government had acted firmly against the attempt by Lancashire weavers to march to London to petition the Prince Regent. Although ostensibly peaceful, the Middleton radical, Samuel Bamford, was sufficiently alarmed to take no part in the 'March of the Blanketeers' and warned his followers against it. He recorded that the Lancashire organisers, William Benbow and Joseph Mitchell, had come under the influence of the Spenceans while in London, and that where previously their maxim had been Major Cartwright's 'Hold fast by the laws', 'doctrines varying from this now began to be broached, and measures hinted, which, if not in direct contravention of the law, were but ill-disguised subterfuges for evading its intentions'. The Government obviously agreed. When the 4,000 or 5,000 weavers assembled on 10 March in St Peter's Fields with their blankets rolled up as knapsacks on their backs or under their arms, the magistrates read the Riot Act and called in the cavalry and special constables to disperse them. Only 300 struggled out towards Stockport where they were turned back by yeomanry who had taken possession of the bridge; a party who crossed the river into Cheshire were pursued and dispersed, one man being killed and several others sabred; a few reached as far as Leek.[9]

In spite of this tragic fiasco, reformers like Bamford continued to persevere with meetings in secret and some at least also dabbled in conspiracy. These months were the time when Oliver the spy was involved in gathering information for the Government. Oliver, whose real name was W. J. Richards, offered his services in March 1817 and undertook to gain the confidence of the leading radicals and feed the information back to the Home Office. Touring the country in the company of the Liverpool radical, Joseph Mitchell, he encountered a number of groups and plans for insurrection. The extent of this activity and the degree to which Oliver himself fomented and exaggerated it is debatable. Not every secret meeting was evidence of conspiracy, because even moderate reformers had been driven underground by the Seditious Meetings Act. Nor is it possible to estimate precisely the extent of the support for these groups through the veil of 'tainted' evidence. The Government was informed of four main centres of activity run by secret committees in the East Midlands, Birmingham and district, Lancashire and Yorkshire. At the end of March, the leading Lancashire radicals had been arrested for an alleged plot to 'make a Moscow' of Manchester. In places like Sheffield and Barnsley it has been argued that Oliver merely discovered already existing groups of insurrectionists, some of whom traced their pedigree back to the 1790s and who acted as a 'physical force' party within the Yorkshire reformers. Oliver reported talk of a 'simultaneous rising' at a conference at Wakefield on 5 May attended by 'delegates' from Northern and Midland towns. On 29 May the Sheffield magistrates raided a secret meeting in Sheffield which an informer claimed was planning an insurrection for 10 June, the day after the actual rising at Pentrich.[10]

Talk of insurrection was undoubtedly in the air in spring 1817, but even Oliver confessed the schemes were 'weak and impractical'. Nonetheless, Sidmouth was informed on 23 May that an insurrection would take place on 9 June and Oliver was despatched to encourage it with promises of support in London. The arrest of the Sheffield men on 29 May threw that promising centre of unrest into confusion and on 6 June a meeting of delegates at Thornhill Lees near Dewsbury was betrayed by Oliver, and the men were seized by troops. Moving on to Nottingham on the 7th, he assured his contacts there that all was ready for a rising on 8 June and that lavish promises of support from Birmingham and London had been made. In fact the men of Pentrich were to rise alone, apart from a group of weavers from Holmfirth who set out for Huddersfield on the evening of the 8th; after exchanging a few shots with the military the men dispersed into the night; although two men were arrested and eventually tried, they were acquitted by the jury.[11]

The principal activist in the Nottingham and Pentrich area was the veteran radical Thomas Bacon. A framework-knitter and ex-ironworker he provided Oliver's main contact. He was also a travelling delegate between the Midlands, Lancashire, Yorkshire and London. He had attended the meeting of Hampden Club delegates in London in January and had been at the Wakefield meeting reported by Oliver. It was he who suggested Pentrich as the base, allegedly because of its proximity to the Butterley ironworks which it was hoped to use for the manufacture of pikes and cannon during the coming insurrection. But Bacon took no part in the rising. Its actual leader was Jeremiah Brandreth, a twenty-seven-year-old man who had worked in a number of trades, and had only recently moved into the area. Taking charge a few days before the 8th, he organised support from the area around Pentrich. On the evening of the 8th between 50 and 300 stockingers, iron-workers, and labourers from the villages of Ripley, Pentrich, Alfreton, and South Wingfield gathered and set out to march the fourteen miles to Nottingham, collecting more men and arms on the way. Brandreth assured his followers that Nottingham would already be secured, that 100,000 men from other towns would meet them, and that London would be the next objective. Roast beef, rum and a hundred guineas a man were promised to the reluctant. The prospect of ending the National Debt and all taxes (an echo of Cobbett) and releasing some 'great men' from the Tower were also offered. Arriving at Nottingham and finding no support – apart from a group of about a hundred who gathered briefly in Nottingham Forest with pikes and poles and dispersed without of their own accord – the Pentrich band fled at the first contact with soldiers and were rounded up during the next few days.[12]

The Pentrich 'rising' had involved only a few hundred men at most, many of those virtually coerced into taking part during the night march to Nottingham. Armed with a few guns, home-made pikes, scythes, and pitchforks they had killed only one man during the whole episode. The Government, however, decided to make an example and forty-five were tried for High Treason by Special Commission at Derby in July. Three were hanged, including Brandreth, and thirty sentenced to transportation, including Bacon. The Government's reaction could be interpreted as one of genuine alarm, and in a sense the attempts by historians to prove that there was genuine conspiracy in spring 1817 have provided justification. But the sentences were widely interpreted as excessive; even more serious for the Government the exposure of Oliver's role gave the Whigs and the radical press another stick with which to beat the administration. Not only could the Government be accused of restricting traditional liberties, but it appeared to be enveigling 'the nameless and the friendless' – to use Prentice's phrase, into fatal conspiracy. Prentice claimed that he and fellow middle-class reformers in Manchester warned their lower-class contacts in future to 'Beware of Spies' and only this warning kept the Lancashire radicals from following Brandreth's example.[13] Undoubtedly the revelation of the role of spies helped to turn the tide of opinion against the Government, or at least limit its excesses. Thus the Government failed to secure the conviction of the Spa Fields conspirators in July 1817 and was also to fail in its attempts to convict the radical printers Wooler and Hone. The growing isolation of government, although still secure in its majority in parliament, was to become an increasingly important factor in the political climate after 1817.

If the Pentrich affair was the outcome of the insurrectionary conspiracies which had been fermenting for several years in the North and Midlands, the most significant development of these years, was the growing articulation of extra-parliamentary pressure through legitimate channels. The post-war years witnessed the growth of the radical and independent press, exemplified by Cobbett's *Register*, the *Black Dwarf*, the increasingly influential *Times*, and provincial papers such as the *Leeds Mercury*. The rise of a free press through the various vicissitudes of prosecution is not one to describe here, but it was an important part of the process by which legitimate pressure could be brought to bear upon parliament. Increasingly the press defined the political context in which the Government and its opponents conducted their affairs. The exposure of Oliver's role in the *Leeds Mercury* and the reaction to Peterloo were part of this process; another was the development of mass meetings, taking up the developments of the 1790s: peaceful meetings to pass resolutions, promote addresses, and organise petitions became increasingly common after 1815. Although prevented by the Seditious Meetings Act, its lifting in mid-1818 made this method of orchestrating opinion increasingly important. Unlike the county meetings of the past, many of these were now organised by working men.[14] An equally important development lay in the organisation of petitioning. The reform campaign of 1817 saw more than 700 petitions presented from over 350 towns, many of them from unrepresented manufacturing towns. Again in 1818 there were over 1,500 petitions for reform, many of them with only a few signatures, but an impressive number nonetheless.[15] Although these campaigns were vitiated by divisions between Whigs and radicals, between the radicals themselves, and by the hostility of middle-class opinion to demagogues such as Hunt, they also witnessed the emergence of 'public opinion', the organisation and manipulation of which was to become crucial during the reform crisis of 1830-2.[16]

Peterloo and after

Following the lead given by the Hampden Clubs, other political societies were founded after 1818 among artisans and workmen, such as the Union Clubs, reading clubs, and penny-a-week clubs. The radical press continued to flourish in spite of Government persecution, to the extent that it became a major preoccupation of Lord Sidmouth and his law officers to check the progress of 'sedition' and 'blasphemy'. In 1818 a magistrate from Lancashire reported to the Home Office that while he thought reform had not yet 'taken root in the mind of the mass of the population', yet he believed 'that this idea gains ground, and that in consequence the working classes have become not only more pertinacious but more insolent in their demands and demeanor'. By the following year it was being reported from the North-East that the *Black Dwarf* and the *Black Book* 'are to be found in the *Hat Crown* of almost every pitman you meet'.[17] In 1819 plans for a campaign of mass meetings to promote reform were set in train and widely publicised in the radical press.

On 15 January 1819 Henry Hunt presided over a meeting 8,000 strong at St Peter's Fields. Setting a more aggressive tone than in the past, he advised people to leave off petitioning parliament and instead to draw up a 'Remonstrance' to the Prince Regent demanding universal suffrage and annual parliaments. Another meeting was held at Stockport on 15 February and another 'Remonstrance' passed; after the meeting there were disturbances in the town and the Riot Act was read three times.[18] In summer more meetings were organised in Lancashire and Yorkshire and a meeting was held on 7 June at Oldham with delegates from twenty-eight towns, in which it was proposed to support a national meeting of radical delegates in London. On the 15th an anxious Manchester magistrate warned the Home Office that 'a very short period of two *Months* at the longest is spoken of as the great Day of Trial'. On the 28th there was a large meeting at Stockport attended by organised groups of workmen from the surrounding towns, some bearing caps of Liberty, others carrying banners with radical slogans. At the meeting Sir Charles Wolseley declared he had been present at the storming of the Bastille and 'was not idle on that glorious day' and that he would 'not be inactive in endeavouring to annihilate those dungeons of despotism in his own'. The Rev. Harrison asserted that the people had a right to approach the Crown with petitions, but were being prevented, and that 'this was a barrier of corruption and the people must blow it up or blow it down'. At the beginning of July Hunt accepted an invitation to speak at Manchester by the Patriotic Union Society; the temper of the situation was illustrated when the writer inviting him claimed, 'I believe nothing but the greatest exertions can prevent an insurrection. Oh, that you in London were prepared for it!'

A dramatic chain of events had begun in which the radicals appeared to be moving closer and closer to insurrection. A series of tumultous mock elections were held to elect 'legislatorial attorneys' for the unrepresented towns. On 12 July Wolseley was elected at a meeting in Birmingham, and on the 19th a meeting at Leeds agreed to hold a similar election. At a mass meeting on 21 July in Smithfield in London it was resolved that as parliament was not properly constituted, its Acts would have no binding force after 1 January 1820. Poll books were prepared on the basis of universal suffrage and Lord Sidmouth was declared to have committed high treason. The Manchester meeting planned for 9 August was to provide the Lancashire component of the movement to coerce parliament; for their part, the Lancashire magistracy were thoroughly alarmed, believing that the meeting would be used to launch an insurrection and, backed by a royal proclamation of 30 July against seditious assemblies, seditious libels, and drilling, they banned the proposed meeting on 9 August. The organisers therefore took legal advice and announced a new date, the 16th.[19]

The purpose of the meeting was somewhat ambiguous. The organisers of the meeting for the 9th had been advised that holding a meeting to elect a 'legislatorial attorney' was illegal, and therefore requested the meeting on the 16th only 'To consider the propriety of adopting the most LEGAL and EFFECTUAL means of obtaining a REFORM in the Commons House of Parliament'. In his memoirs, Samual Bamford stressed that the organisers wanted the meeting to be as 'morally effective as possible' through a 'display of cleanliness, sobriety, and decorum, such as we never before had exhibited'. The organising committee's first injunctions, he recorded, were 'CLEANLINESS', 'SOBRIETY', 'ORDER', to which Hunt added 'PEACE'. To secure order, the contingents to the meeting were to march in disciplined formation to St Peter's Fields, equipped only with banners, flags and musical instruments. According to Bamford this was the sole purpose of the drilling which took place before the meeting, but which appeared to the magistrates far more sinister.[20] The meeting was clearly intended as a show of force, a display of the organised power of the unrepresented; the question was, how much further did it go? The tone of the radical press was frankly intimidatory during the summer, the *Medusa* producing a song on 5 June:

Britons, rise, the time is come,
To strike the opposition dumb,
For though we arc oppress'd by some,
Our wish is to be free:
Rise, unite, demand Reform,
Let no tyrant you alarm,
And if refus'd, then let us arm,
And fight for liberty.[21]

Bamford himself reported hearing William Benbow urge a crowd near Middleton in 1819 to 'present their petitions at the point of sword and pike'. On the other hand the leading actor in the proposed meeting, Orator Hunt, was well versed in keeping just the right side of the law. Although Whigs often denounced his reliance on public meetings with the dangers, as they saw it, of prejudicing reform by the outbreak of disturbances, Hunt and his supporters clearly believed in their ability to influence Parliament by the pressure of organised 'public opinion'.[22]

The Manchester magistrates were in a high state of alarm. They were forced by the law to permit the meeting to assemble, but retained the option of arresting Hunt and dispersing the crowds at their own discretion. Lord Sidmouth had in fact advised them on 4 August to 'abstain from any endeavour to disperse the mob' and left the magistrates to manage the affair themselves. No evidence of a ministerial or Home Office plot to initiate the events of the 16th has been established, and the tragic events of 'Peterloo' probably owed far more to the incompetence of the magistrates and the Manchester and Salford Yeomanry than to premeditated action. Having decided to dispense with the help of the experienced General Byng, the magistrates had made their own preparations to deal with the disturbances they were almost certain would ensue. According to the *Manchester Mercury* on 3 August, they had 'come to a determination to act with decision and to suppress all Seditious Meetings immediately as they assemble'. Hunt meanwhile had urged his supporters to be peaceful and orderly, his instructions were for them to come on Monday the 16th, 'armed with no other weapon but that of a self-approving conscience: determined not to suffer yourselves to be irritated or excited, by any means whatsoever, to commit any breach of the public peace'. He also offered to surrender himself to the magistrates in advance of the 16th in order to leave them no pretext for breaking up the meeting. The magistrates declined his offer, and instead concentrated on organising a mixed force of Yeomanry, Hussars, infantry, artillery, and special constables to police central Manchester.

The crowds began to assemble in St Peter's Fields from nine in the morning of 16 August 1819. Orderly contingents came in from the surrounding towns to swell a crowd of at least 60,000 by late morning. The crowd included many women and children and the atmosphere was entirely peaceful, even cheerful. Many had banners with inscriptions such as 'Unity and Strength', 'Libery and Fraternity', and 'Parliament's Annual'. A platform had been erected from which Hunt was to speak on which representatives of the press also sat. When Hunt arrived at about one o'clock the magistrates immediately decided 'that the whole bore the appearance of insurrection', though no disturbance of any kind had occurred. Nadin, the Deputy Constable of Manchester and an inveterate enemy of the radicals, was told to execute a hastily signed warrant for Hunt's arrest. Forty yeoman cavalry broke into the tightly packed crowd, some of them striking out with their sabres. Hunt was arrested and bustled away, but the yeomanry were now hemmed in and Hussars were called in. The huge crowd began to flee in panic, many being trampled and others beaten down with the flat of swords or sabred and slashed by the troops. Within ten or fifteen minutes 11 people had been killed and 400 injured.[23]

Although the Government was later to claim that the troops had been assailed by brickbats and shots fired before they dispersed the meeting, the evidence was only that some had resisted the soldiers with makeshift weapons. Whatever the excuses, an unarmed crowd of men women and children had been savagely dispersed; even if many of the dead and injured had suffocated or been trampled on, there were also 140 suffering from sabre cuts. Whether the magistrates had intended all along to disperse the meeting once Hunt arrived cannot be proved with certainty; at the very least they had acted with spectacular incompetence for which eleven innocent people had paid with their lives.

Peterloo was significant on several levels. Although the Government saw itself as having no option but to stand by the magistracy – the Prince Regent conveying his thanks to the authorities for their 'prompt, decisive, and efficient measures for the preservation of public peace' – the action had exposed the Ministry to violent recrimination from Whigs and radicals. In private Lord Liverpool confided that the magistrates action had been 'injudicious' and even an ultra-Tory such as Lord Eldon admitted that though the magistrates had to be supported they were 'generally blamed'. Meetings condemning the Peterloo 'massacre' were held in London, presided over by Sir Francis Burdett, and also at Birmingham, Leeds, Sheffield, Newcastle upon Tyne, and Huddersfield. At a Yorkshire County Meeting summoned by Lord Fitzwilliam, resolutions were passed condemning unlawful interference with the right of public assembly and demanding an inquiry into the events at Manchester. For drafting these resolutions Fitzwilliam was dismissed from the lord lieutenancy. More than any other single event, Peterloo gave the Whigs an opportunity to broaden their basis of support and helped to convert many sections of middle-class opinion to the view that some reform was necessary.[24]

Moreover, compared to the Luddite outbreaks, Peterloo received enormous publicity. The hustings had contained reporters from several major papers, including John Tyas of The Times, John Smith of the Liverpool Mercury, and Edward Baines of the Leeds Mercury, the first time special reporters had been sent to a provincial meeting of this kind. The presence of the press meant that the Government had not only blundered, but it had blundered in the full gaze of the increasingly powerful provincial and metropolitan press. For example The Times published an influential account on 19 August which was very critical of the Manchester Yeomanry and exonerated the crowd from blame. The radical press, however, reached a crescendo of fury, the Cap of Liberty denouncing the Government for 'High Treason against the People' and openly calling on the people to arm in self-defence. The Briton called on 'Fellow countrymen' to 'learn the use of arms and practise a soldier's discipline'. The very name 'Peter-loo' was a creation of the press, an ironic echo of the famous victory of 1815, and this was emphasised by a flood of caricatures showing fat, drunken soldiery hacking down a defenceless throng of women and children; this fierce condemnation was to make Peterloo an emotive symbol well into the nineteenth century.[25]

In the immediate aftermath of the 'massacre' Manchester had to be patrolled by troops, and for a time it appeared that an insurrection was imminent. Bamford spoke of arms being prepared, but the only disturbances were some clashes with troops at New Cross in Manchester and the killing of a special constable.[26] However, news of Peterloo sparked off riots in Macclesfield on 17 August when a crowd of 700 men and boys attacked the office of the pro-ministerial *Courier* newspaper, as well as the houses of forty people who were yeomanry or special constables.[27] Other disturbances occurred at Stockport. By October there was considerable alarm. The *London Chronicle* described the district around Manchester as being in a 'truly frightful state. . . . There the war between the poor and the rich is almost openly proclaimed'. When a friend tried to assure Lord Sidmouth that the country was mostly peaceful and 'anti-radical', Sidmouth pointed to the volumes of papers on his desk in which he said the pictures were 'frightful'. Briskly practical as ever, Wellington opined that as the radicals were clearly out to dispossess the gentry, it was vital to prevent them acquiring the arms 'which we know they have not'.[28]

When parliament reassembled on 23 November, the Ministry went on the counter-offensive, laying before the House alarming evidence from lord lieutenants and county magistrates to support a new battery of repressive measures, the 'Six Acts'. In spite of the opposition's advances over Peterloo, the threat of violent upheaval was still one of the strongest cards the government had to play. Whigs like Lord Erskine were caught in a dilemma, he wrote on 23 November: '. . . as to the mob, he had stood within the Temple gates in 1780 with a field piece, and a match in his hand, resolved to blow the mob to the devil, and would again if necessary; but was against all changes giving power to Government.'[29] Nonetheless, radical indignation and liberal sympathies could avail little against the Tory majority in both houses. By the end of the year legislation had been passed restricting meetings and the press, empowering the seizure of arms in disturbed districts, preventing delays in trials for misdemeanour, and preventing military training.[30] The political fruits of Peterloo were not very great in the short term. Parliament rejected an inquiry and in March 1820 Hunt and his associates were tried for 'conspiring to disturb the peace, exciting discontent and disaffection, arousing hatred and contempt of the government and constitution, and unlawful assembly'. Hunt was sentenced to two and a half years' imprisonment.[31]

With returning prosperity and stronger powers, the Government was able to deal with such incidents as occurred. Rumours of a rising began to circulate again late in 1819, with reported journeys by Arthur Thistlewood to the North. The discovery of the Cato Street conspiracy in February was followed by a number of small 'risings'. In Scotland on 5-6 April, small groups of weavers rose following a shortlived 'general strike' of Glasgow workers. Defeated by the troops at the 'Battle of Bonnymuir' three men were later executed; no links with the metropolitan radicals could be proved but there was a suggestion that there had been contacts with Lancashire and other weaving strongholds in northern England. On the night of 31 March groups of weavers mustered on the moors outside Huddersfield with the alleged aim of seizing the town and taking arms from the soldiers. When no other groups joined them they melted away. Again on the night of 11-12 April a party of 300 to 500 men marched to Grange Moor outside Barnsley with flags, drums, and weapons. They also carried banners inscribed with slogans such as 'Hunt, the intrepid champion of the Rights and Liberties of the People' and 'May the Tree of Liberty spread its hands throughout the earth'. Arriving at the Moor and finding no contingents awaiting them from other towns, the men fled when some yeomanry appeared; twenty were eventually put on trial for High Treason and condemned to death, the sentences being later commuted to transportation for periods of fourteen years or life. Sheffield too was involved in these schemes. On the evening of 11 April John Blackwell led a party of 200 men in an attack on the Attercliffe barracks to cries of 'Hunt and Liberty' and 'the Revolution'; their resolution failing at the last minute, the attack was postponed. Blackwell was arrested the next day and sentenced to thirty months' imprisonment.[32]

These events showed that Peterloo and the Six Acts had revived in some the hopes of a nationwide rising similar to the projects of 1817 or 1801–2. As in those events it is difficult to determine their real strength or degree of support, but on the face of it the plan for a 'rising' had failed because of the familiar problems of lack of coordination and the unwillingness of large numbers to throw in their lot with schemes of this kind. As in 1817, groups of determined insurrectionists found themselves waiting for support which never arrived in the quantities required to make a successful revolutionary attempt.

By the summer of 1820 attention among reformers was increasingly focused on Queen Caroline's return to England. Although primarily a metropolitan affair in the traditions of the Wilkite agitation, the press which had made Peterloo a *cause célèbre* brought news of the progress of her case to all parts of the country. The enthusiasm which her cause generated in many different communities illustrated a curious mixture of popular loyalism and anti-Government feeling. News of the dropping of the Bill of Pains and Penalties in November was received in Shropshire by the ringing of bells, bonfires, and public barbecues; several Cornish boroughs witnessed illuminations and at Oxford the Riot Act had to be read when the celebrations led to fighting between town and gown. In Lincoln, the Queen's affair brought out the latent spirit of opposition between the Tory and Cathedral establishment and the Whig-backed lower classes. During the Queen's trial the latter paraded with torches, tar barrels, and 'transparencies', and smashed the windows of local clergy. Liverpool too gave remarkable support to the Queen, celebrating her birthday on 17 May with bell-ringing and flags on churches and ships in the river. The dropping of the Bill of Pains and Penalties was celebrated with an illumination and a monster procession of an estimated 35,000 people, including members of the trade societies with their insignia and bands. The Coronation celebrations for George IV also led to some minor disturbances by the Queen's supporters at places such as Lincoln and Manchester.[33]

Both Peterloo and the Queen Caroline affair helped to discredit the Government as an increasingly self-conscious middle-class began to demand greater representation. It was in May 1820 that Peel wrote his famous letter to Croker:

Do you not think that the tone of England – of that great compound of folly, weakness, prejudice, wrong feeling, right feeling, obstinacy, and newspaper paragraphs, which is called public opinion – is more liberal – to use an odious but intelligible phrase – than the policy of the Government? Do not you think that there is a feeling, becoming daily more general and more confirmed – that is, independent of the pressure of taxation or any immediate cause – in favour of some undefined change in the mode of governing the country?[34]

The reform crisis

The events of 1830–2 were the result of long-term developments, some of which we have noted earlier. This is not the place to discuss in detail the origins of the reform movement or the break-up of the Tory dominance which had existed with only short breaks since 1784. But, as many other historians have recognised, the years of Peterloo and the Queen Caroline affair had played an important part in strengthening reform sentiment. Elie Halévy identified the 1820s as the crucial decade for the 'conversion' of the 'squires' to reform, with issues such as 'Cash, Corn, and Catholics' provoking discontent even among the already enfranchised and leading them to support reform as a means of obtaining more effective representation than 'Old Corruption'. To these demands from within the political nation were increasingly being added those of the unrepresented manufacturing towns and the emergent voices of middle and working class opinion.[35]

From the latter half of the eighteenth century reformers had developed a battery of devices for bringing extra-parliamentary pressure to bear upon government. But faced with administrations hostile to reform, who refused to acknowledge or concede to this pressure, reformers had been forced to recognise the limitations of extra-parliamentary agitation and the need to refine their tactics if it were to have decisive effects. Thus James Mill argued that 'where the people have not the power legally and peaceably of removing their governors they can only obtain any considerable ameliorations of their governments by resistance, by applying physical force to their rulers, or at least by threats so likely to be followed by performance, as may frighten their rulers into compliance'. The answer to an obdurate parliament then, was 'the language of menace', backed up by impressive displays of support, so that the people 'should appear to be ready and impatient to break out into outrage, *without actually breaking out*'.[36] Middle-class reformers such as Mill, Francis Place, and Joseph Parkes had no wish to see a revolution unless there was no possible alternative. They hoped an impression of overwhelming and irresistible force would be sufficient without the risks of defeat or chaos which a genuine rising could bring. This meant that popular demonstrations had to be orderly and well-conducted, for men who remembered the 1790s and the 'Six Acts' knew only too well that intemperate displays of popular violence could rebound on the reform movement by providing the Government with an opportunity to rally support among propertied opinion, frighten off the moderates, and justify repressive legislation.

It was in this frame of mind that many radicals viewed the accession of Grey's administration in November 1830. In an atmosphere already excited by the July Revolution in France and the mounting wave of industrial and agricultural reactions to distress, the radicals intended to spur the Whigs to implement their pledge to reform, prevent any backsliding, and block any attempt by opposition, Lords, or monarch to halt the progress to reform. The main agencies of extra-parliamentary pressure were the political unions which sprang up in many towns and cities, usually under middle-class leadership, and, as in the case of the Birmingham Political Union, sometimes uniting middle-class and working-class reformers in a common front. Others were in the hands of artisan or working-class radicals, especially in the North, whilst others were primarily dominated by the middle classes, with few if any working-class participants.[37]

The autumn of 1830 witnessed reform meetings in many areas. A meeting at Blackburn witnessed events similar to the heyday of post-war radicalism, with tricolour flags and banners inscribed with 'Unity is Strength' and 'Liberty and Fraternity'. At the height of the labourers' disturbances, there were reform meetings and lectures at Horsham, Maidstone, and Battle. The elections which followed the resignation of the Wellington government saw riots at Bristol, Northampton, Norwich, Preston, and Banbury. At Preston Henry Hunt was elected MP and tricolour flags and banners inscribed with 'Bread or Blood' and 'Liberty or Death' were paraded through the streets.

During the winter of 1830–1 the first reform bill was drafted with the support of around 3,000 petitions sent in from the country, some of those from the larger cities bearing tens of thousands of signatures. In the country itself, there were meetings, processions, and bonfires in support of the Bill, with Joseph Parkes of the Birmingham Political Union setting the tone by saying 'if the Whigs intend to realise their promises, they cannot object to strong demonstrations: if they mean to break their vows, it is wholesome to remind them of them'. In April 1831 the Bill passed its second reading by only one vote, forcing the Whigs to go to the country and broaden their base of support in the lower House. On 27 April there was a great illumination in the capital in which the windows of opponents of the Bill were smashed, including those of the Duke of Wellington and the Bishop of London. During the election, in which the Tories lost heavily, there were disturbances in several Scottish towns where anti-reform voters were kidnapped or pelted and the Lord Provost of Edinburgh nearly thrown over the North Bridge. In England there were disturbances at Malmesbury, Boston, Banbury, Rye, Horsham, and

Whitehaven. At Wigan the son of one of the patrons of the seat, an anti-reformer, was fatally injured. In spite of this incident, few regarded the disturbances as particularly threatening or the amount of disturbance as unusual for an election of the period.[38]

The rejection of Grey's second Bill by the House of Lords on 8 October 1831 led to serious rioting. In Birmingham the bells tolled all night and a protest meeting was attended by an estimated 100,000 people. On 12 October a procession was organised in the capital by two London radicals, Bowyer and Powell, helped by Francis Place, to present an address to the King. The number taking part was variously estimated at between 6,000 and 300,000 and the windows of several houses were smashed, including those of the Duke of Wellington at Apsley House; another group gathered in St James's Square, to the alarm of the King, before being dispersed by the police. There was some evidence that the disturbances came from a group who followed the main procession which was reported to be 'perfectly peaceable' and consisting of 'shopkeepers and superior artisans'. Bowyer frankly admitted that the purpose of the event was 'to create, if possible, an impression that popular violence would be provoked if the Reform Bill were any longer obstructed' and reported to Place that 'scarcely a single cheer, or, when we felt it necessary, a groan was given, except by word of command. Little things of this sort keep the public mind up to concert pitch'.[39] These relatively minor incidents in the capital represented more an attempt by the radicals to keep up the pressure for reform than evidence of a massive underlying discontent ready to break to the surface.

On the face of it the country appeared riper for an outbreak of insurrectionary fervour. Riots broke at Derby on the evening the Bill was rejected, the houses of anti-reformers were attacked and three men taken into custody. The next day a crowd demanded their release and when this was refused marched on the City gaol, where although fired on from the prison, and a bystander killed, they smashed the gate in and released twenty-three prisoners before moving on to the county gaol. There the crowd was repulsed after three men had been wounded and one killed by the defenders. More windows were smashed in the evening and an attack made on a house at Little Chester. On the 10th a group of stalls set up for signing petitions against the Lords' rejection were destroyed, the crowd having called for a public protest meeting; the Riot Act was read and the troops opened fire, killing one man. With troops brought to the town and the yeomanry mobilised, the disturbances died down; their most significant feature is that they could probably have been avoided if the mayor had given in to the request to release the prisoners and hold the public meeting.[40]

Disturbances also broke out at Nottingham on 9 October when some windows were smashed. On the next day, following a Reform meeting in the Market Square, a mob went out to Colwick Hall where they wrecked the interior before returning to Nottingham and attacking and burning down the unoccupied (and undefended) Nottingham Castle.

The 11th witnessed an attack on a factory at Beeston and attacks on houses in neighbouring towns, as well as an assault on Woollaton Park where no serious damage was reported. The main targets were the property of known anti-reformers, including Nottingham Castle, seat of the Duke of Newcastle, who had evicted pro-reform tenants. Although troops had been available, they were insufficient to stop the disturbances in widely scattered parts of the town and its neighbourhood; when reinforcements arrived on 12 October, the riots quickly came to an end.[41]

There were minor episodes at Leicester, Tiverton, Yeovil, Blandford, Sherborne, Exeter, and Worcester; but the biggest disturbances took place in Bristol almost three weeks after the Lords' rejection of the Bill, when meetings had already been held in the town to protest against the failure of the Bill. The Bristol Political Union had already shown its opposition to anti-reformers. On the 24th the Bishop of Bath and Wells came to consecrate a new church and because he had voted against reform had to be protected from a hostile crowd. The main riots, however, were occasioned by the visit of the Recorder, Sir Charles Wetherall, a vehement anti-reformer, who was due to open the Assizes on 29 October. Opposition was widely expected and ninety-three dragoons were despatched to the city under the command of Lieutenant-Colonel Brereton, a semi-retired officer who lived in the area. Assembling on the 29th, crowds stoned any buildings thought to be occupied by Wetherall, including the Guildhall and the Mansion House. The Riot Act was read and the troops called out when threats were made to fire the Mansion House. Sir Charles having hastily left Bristol for Newport, it was widely believed the riots would subside; the authorities tried to get a notice printed that Wetherall had left, but it being weekend, a printer was hard to find. Although troops had cleared the streets on Saturday evening (29th), Brereton ordered the soldiers to return to quarters while he waited for reinforcements from Gloucester, presumably hoping that the absence of the troops would help to calm the situation. He was proved disastrously wrong, for there were now attacks on the Bridewell, the New Gaol, toll houses, the Gloucester County Prison, the Bishop's Palace, the Mansion House, the dock gates, the excise house, and several private houses around Queen's Square. Having looted several houses the rioters held an impromptu feast in the middle of Queen's Square with plundered food and drink, the statue of William III in the midst being surmounted with a cap of liberty. On Monday the authorities rallied themselves and began to clear the streets with an ease which suggested that they could have done so at any point with very little difficulty. The official casualties were later put at 12 killed and 94 wounded; of 102 prisoners taken, 31 were capitally convicted of whom 4 were eventually executed.

The Bristol riots were by far the most destructive of the reform disturbances, estimates of the damage done ranging up to £300,000. The riots were partly the result of genuine hostility to the anti-reformers, but the real cause of their magnitude lay in Brereton's handling of his forces. Later court-martialled for his conduct, he claimed to have been unwilling to take the lives of rioters without the backing of the civil magistrates, a frequent point of confusion which had led to the paralysis of military forces on more than one occasion in the past. This confusion, together with a humane dislike of taking the lives of men from a neighbourhood in which he lived, left the city open to the rioters on the Sunday. The riots had also been aggravated by a dispute between the Bristol Political Union and the municipal authorities. The magistrates had approached the Union before Wetherall's arrival to seek some means of ensuring the peace, but the Union declined to cooperate, merely stepping up their demand that the Corporation resign and allow an election to take place among all the inhabitants for a new Corporation. None of the Union members, however, could be directly implicated in instigating the riots, rather they had withdrawn any possibility of an effective restraint of the crowds and helped to undermine the authority of the civil officers.

Although it was widely alleged that the rioters were drawn from criminals and paupers and included 'a set of reprobates' driven from London by the professional police, the trials revealed that almost all the rioters arrested had no previous convictions and most were employed. They included some small property-owners, as well as a miscellany of semi-skilled and unskilled workers; most were natives of the city, although drawn from the poorer districts. Far from being a symptom of impending revolution, the Bristol riot was a reprise on an old theme, the extremely thin line which lay between 'order' and 'disorder' in the era before the introduction of professional policing. The paralysis of the military commander and the failure of the magistrates to take a more active lead, provided the context in which disturbances could pass beyond the normal level. As in the case of Birmingham in 1791 or London in 1780, the failure of the authorities had provided the opportunity for disorder of an exceptional scale.[42]

The disturbances which followed the Lords' rejection were the most serious to occur during the whole reform crisis. They did not in themselves betoken a 'revolutionary' crisis because the disturbances were largely unconnected and had no organisation to direct and control them as part of a larger and more politically effective movement. Although the riots, especially those at Bristol, alarmed the Government, the reaction to the Lords' rejection was significant less for its size than for the ease with which it was suppressed. Far from being evidence that reform would have to be passed at any cost, the lesson could be drawn that even the most flagrant obstruction to the wishes of the 'people' would only cause a reaction well within the capacities of the Government to cope with it.

Moreover, although some radicals welcomed the disturbances as a useful reminder to Whigs and Tories alike that attempts to frustrate reform might lead to insurrection, most moderate reformers were fearful that undirected popular violence of this kind might precipitate a conservative reaction and therefore dissociated themselves from it. Attwood blamed the violence at Bristol on the absence of well-organised political unions, drawing the conclusion that reformers must organise if they were to make their agitation effective. The question of tactics remained paramount: how was extra-parliamentary pressure to be brought to bear on the still unreformed House of Commons?

It was here that the growth of the political unions was most important. Organised by essentially moderate leaders such as Place, Attwood, and Parkes, they had already begun to develop the 'language of menace' in order to influence the reform struggle. When a deputation of Westminster reformers prepared to visit Lord Grey on 12 October, Roebuck recalled a speech – probably by Place – in which he declared; 'We must frighten them. . . . No reality we can create will be sufficient for our purpose. We must work on Lord Grey's imagination. We must pretend to be frightened ourselves.' Place and Parkes also fed Lord Melbourne's private secretary, Tom Young, with stories of the 'explosive' temper of the people. Further evidence of a potentially threatening situation came when the middle-class reformers began to speak of forming a 'National Guard', ostensibly to protect householders from rioters, but with the clear threat that they might provide the basis for armed resistance should the Reform Bill be further obstructed or delayed. There were, however, limits to such tactics, for they so genuinely alarmed Grey and Melbourne that they threatened to lead to suppression of the unions. Even before the Bristol riots Grey warned the Westminster deputation on 12 October that any disturbances would be firmly put down; and he agreed with the King that the formation of the unions was 'far more mischievous and dangerous than any proceedings of a more avowed and violent character, palpably illegal and treasonable'. To Tories they appeared no less menacing, Lord Eldon recording on 2 November: 'I have seen a great deal of mischief going forward in the country, but till those institutions were becoming general, and till the Government by connivance and apathy, can be said rather to encourage than discourage them, I had hopes that matters might get right. The crisis is formidable, because of those unions.' Among some Tories there was talk of forming 'counter-associations'; Peel even began to stockpile arms to defend his property, but Croker warned him that such manoeuvres could lead to civil war and opposition should be confined to parliament.[43]

In fact, the Whigs had already begun to react to the threat posed both by popular disorder and by the unions. Greville reported that Lord Melbourne had been 'frightened to death' by the Bristol riots and had given the authorities *carte blanche* to deal with any disturbances in the capital. Thus when the London National Union of the Working Classes announced a mass meeting in White Conduit Fields for 7 November, in coordination with other meetings in the country, to which each man was invited to attend with a twenty-inch stave, Melbourne told its leaders that they would be prosecuted for treason if they went ahead. Although its leaders agreed to postpone it, massive preparations were put in hand in case the meeting still took place; it was recorded that the Government 'scraped together every disposable *Sword and Bayonet* within 50 miles of London'! 629 marines and 400 Greenwich pensioners were called up,

7,490 special constables enrolled, 2,000 police mobilised, and communications set up to coordinate arrangements between the civil and military forces. As a final precaution warrants were filed to stop letters addressed to the letters of the NUWC in Manchester and London. It was Greville who recorded that these preparations 'paralysed the malcontents' and, although a few hundred men and boys did assemble, they were easily dispersed.[44] When the Birmingham Political Union then proposed to arm and adopt a paramilitary structure, the Government issued a proclamation on 22 November declaring such actions illegal and unconstitutional. The leaders of the BPU accepted this edict, abandoning their plans even before the proclamation was issued.

Although there were continued reports of arming both in the capital and in the provinces and the political unions continued to grow apace, the influence of extra-parliamentary pressure on the complex sequence of events which followed the introduction of a new Reform Bill in December 1831 is difficult to gauge. The essential manoeuvres were taking place within the context of 'high politics', but it was a context which was influenced to some extent by extra-parliamentary agitation. Place was later to claim that the mobilisation of public opinion through the political unions was decisive and that but for their pressure the Whigs would have abandoned reform. Yet there were moments early in 1832 when the political temperature appeared to have fallen far below the heady excitement of autumn 1831. On 17 January Croker wrote to Lord Hertford that he believed 'the danger *narrowed*. . . . I really believe that if the king were tomorrow to send for the Duke of Wellington and make him first Minister, we should not have even as much of riot or disturbance as we had on the rejection of the Bill by the Lords. The *Bill* has no friends out of office.'[45] But as the reform crisis came to a climax in May 1832, the extra-parliamentary movement was ready to support the Whigs and threaten any obstruction by the Tories with 'general rebellion'. Following Grey's resignation on 9 May and the King's unsuccessful attempts to find a Tory administration willing to serve, the reformers would claim that it was their pressure which had ultimately decided the issue. Certainly in the May crisis the extra-parliamentary agitation reached almost fever pitch in which the political unions almost outdid each other in their minatory language. Place concerted plans with Birmingham for an armed rising, while Attwood reminded his followers of their constitutional right to bear arms. Fiery language was used at meetings both in the capital and in the country and there were reports of men moving from the manufacturing districts to London 'to carry the Bill'. Petitions flowed into parliament in favour of reform and meetings in several cities threatened to refuse to pay their taxes unless the reform bill was passed. There was also an attempt to promote a run on the banks with the famous slogan 'To Stop the Duke Go for Gold' which was placarded in London and the provinces from 13 May. Although the effect of these economic pressures is disputed they certainly added to an atmosphere of crisis.[46]

A number of historians have doubted the efficacy of the activities of the reformers in this crisis.[47] The immediate initiative after 9 May had passed to the Tory leaders and the King and it is extremely difficult to assess the extent to which they were influenced by the threats of popular insurrection. Attempts to form a stable Tory administration were compromised by the King's insistance on a comprehensive Reform Bill as a condition of office. This effectively excluded Peel and deprived Wellington of the support of his party when he attempted to float an administration in the days following the Whig resignation. After 15 May, when the King was forced to make renewed overtures to Grey because of the absence of an alternative administration, the plans of Place and others for resistance had, according to M. Brock, 'become politically irrelevant'.[48] Nonetheless they remained influential through their contacts and were able to exert some influence over the Whigs in their negotiations with the King. These came to a successful conclusion on 18 May when the King assured Grey that he would, if necessary, create enough peers to carry the Bill should it encounter further obstacles in the Lords.

The extent to which reformers would have been able to mount effective resistance to a determined and repressive Tory government is difficult to assess. It is quite certain that significant quantities of arms had been prepared in various parts of the country, but the organisation and leadership for a rising were rather suspect. The plan was for the delegates who gathered in London following Grey's resignation to return home should Wellington's appointment be announced; demonstrations were to be organised in London by a committee of deputies in order to tie down 7,000 of the 11,000 troops the government had available. Once this was accomplished, Birmingham was to lead the rising, to be followed by other towns and cities if the Government had still not conceded. Place confidently asserted that he was in communication with leaders in the provinces, that the soldiers would soon join them and all would be over within a few days. The suspicious point about this plan is that it was meant for the consumption of the Whig Minister of War and may well have contained a large element of exaggeration; it does seem, for example, that experienced military commanders were lacking. Although it was claimed that Colonel William Napier was sympathetic, he always denied that he sought to take up arms 'with a Birmingham attorney and a London tailor against the Duke of Wellington'; other potential commanders were claimed to be 'general Johnstone', probably the ex-MP for Boston, William Johnson, a half-pay colonel, and a Polish emigré, 'Count Chopski', Count Joseph Napoleon Czapski. In spite of an air of unreality, it is quite feasible that the radicals would have staged some sort of rising had a Tory administration been formed; Place and Parkes were both adamant that they would have tried 'whatever the cost'. Even if their revolution had failed, at least they might have faced the Government with the task of dispersing a series of organised and armed movements in the country, a task from which the consequences might have been a climb-down by the Government or a spiral of violence and repression with unknown outcome. In fact the overwhelming impression given by Place and Parkes was that revolution was a tactical ploy rather than the main objective. Place summed it up when he claimed that the NUWC wanted reform to promote revolution, whereas his followers wanted it to prevent one. Throughout the crisis he represented to the Whigs that the moderate radicals did not want to be forced to extremities for:

> The defeat of the duke when in power might be an instant destruction of the government in Church and State, and the formation of a purely representative government, for which the people were by no means well fitted as they ought to be, and it is most of all desirable they should be, before any such change were made. This revolution was therefore undesirable, not only on account of the present mischief . . . but of the future trouble and peril a premature revolution could not fail to produce.'

Even with these views, however, Place could still write privately at the end of the crisis, 'We were within a moment of general rebellion, and had it been possible for the Duke of Wellington to have formed an administration, the king and the people would have been at issue.'[49]

A further question must remain over the readiness of 'the people' to rise at the behest of Place and Parkes. Place argued that if a revolution had occurred it 'would have been the act of the whole people to a greater extent than any which had ever before been accomplished'. But he was not completely in control, indeed not in control at all, of many of the 'low unions' which had been formed during the crisis, and even in the capital, his National Political Union was rivalled by the more radical National Union of the Working Classes at which gathered men such as James Watson, John Gast, William Lovett, and William Benbow. Though smaller than Place's union the NUWC had better links with the 104 provincial 'low unions' and maintained a programme of weekly debates at the Rotunda and discussion through the pages of the weekly *Poor Man's Guardian.* Elsewhere in the country, the Birmingham Political Union was something of an exception for its close harmony between middle-class and working-class elements and remained more amenable to Thomas Attwood's leadership. In other towns middle-class influences were less strong; several places had seen splits between moderate and radical reformers during the autumn and winter of 1831–2 or the formation of more radical unions. Whether these men would have been prepared to rise for a Bill which they saw as hopelessly inadequate is doubtful, though some at least saw it as a 'wedge' to start the process of radical reform. There were certainly some who, as in 1816–17 or 1819–20, would have been ready for an opportunity to mount an insurrection, but because the situation never arose, we can never know how widespread the response would have been.[50]

It is, however, important to recognise, as Professor Hamburger has shown, that there was very little open violence in 1832 compared with 1831. Although there were some disturbances arising out of wage disputes in Manchester and the North-East, there was a marked absence of political disturbances during the critical spring months. A meeting called by the NUWC in Finsbury Square was dispersed by police in March and a number of police injured, two seriously; there was also a disturbance at Carlisle where an effigy was burnt by 500 people. But in the May days the only serious disturbances occurred at York where the Bishop's Palace was attacked and his effigy burned, and at Worcester, where an effigy of the Duke of Wellington was burned; in neither case was there a serious clash with the authorities. Elsewhere, such meetings as convened passed off peacefully. Crucially, London itself was largely peaceful during the May crisis. Some crowds assembled outside the Houses of Parliament but confined themselves to hissing a few of the more unpopular peers. On 12 May Lord Ellenborough wrote 'In London all is quiet. The meetings have been rather failures. In the country all is quiet.' Greville was more anxious, noting 'There is so much of wonder, and curiosity, and expectation abroad that there is less of abuse and exasperation than might have been expected, but it will all burst forth. The town is fearfully quiet.'[51]

Indeed it was the *absence* of disturbances which seemed most ominous. 'All seemed reserved', wrote Sir Robert Heron, 'for a tremendous explosion.' The calm seemed evidence of the discipline and organisation of the reformers, but many feared either that an unsuccessful outcome would precipitate an insurrection or that prolonged uncertainty would take matters out of the hands of the more moderate leaders. Place himself did nothing to disturb this impression by risking a public meeting of metropolitan reformers which might have revealed less support than many supposed. Nor were the NUWC any more desirous of an open confrontation with the authorities during the May days. Although the *Poor Man's Guardian* had published extracts from Colonel Marcerone's manual in street fighting, *Defensive Instructions for the People*, in April and some, at least, of its members were taking lessons in sword exercises in March, the NUWC officially rejected plans for drilling in May and also rejected Benbow's call for a National Congress in the capital.[52] Thus even the body that Wellington regarded as the real danger in the capital maintained a low profile during the May days.

Preoccupation with the 'May days' and events leading up to the passing of the Reform Bill has sometimes led to a failure to appreciate that there was another period of tension once its provisions became clear. To some extent there was more danger of serious disturbances in the immediate aftermath of the crisis than there was before and during it. For many of the more militant radicals the first Reform Act was only the beginning of the attempt to widen the franchise further and to implement a radical reform similar to that adopted by the Chartists. Spring 1833 witnessed a revival of reform activity with a mass meeting at Birmingham attended by an estimated 180,000 people at which the 'treachery' of the

Whigs was denounced. During the winter of 1832–3, the NUWC in London came under the influence of more militant members and plans were made for a mass meeting at Cold Bath Fields on 13 May to discuss preparations for a National Convention. The London police and the Home Secretary were seriously alarmed, fully expecting an attempt at an armed demonstration: it was reported to them that before the meeting a group of forty men assembled at a public house in Lambeth were told: 'Tomorrow will be your day of glory. Let every man resist the oppressors to the death. Every one of you must go armed. Rally to the flag – Liberty or Death – you and your families have endured starvation and poverty long enough. Arm, arm against the foe.'[53] By 2.30 p.m. on the 13th between 500 and 1,000 people had assembled, while more contingents arrived bearing banners with inscriptions such as 'Holy Alliance of the Working Classes' and 'Equal Rights and Equal Justice'. One body carried a black flag with a skull and crossbones and the motto 'Liberty or Death', others American flags and caps of liberty. The meeting was broken up by a group of seventy police who baton-charged the crowd, injuring many men, women and children; portions of the crowd fought back with stones, railings, and staves during which a policeman was stabbed and killed.

The killing of Constable Culley in what became known as the 'Clerkenwell Riot' developed into a political controversy about the conduct of the police. The London inquest demonstrated its independence by returning a verdict of justifiable homicide; it also led to a Select Committee to investigate the activities of the New Police.[54] This was the last serious disturbance to arise from the reform movement of the early 1830s. From the events of 1831–3, the radical reformers had to try to regroup their forces in the face of their exclusion from the franchise and the increasing cohesion of the new middle-class voters and the landed interest. As the Chartist movement developed the central problem remained of how to force change upon a still only partially reformed parliament.

11 Unions and labourers: industrial and agricultural protest

The years between the end of the Napoleonic Wars and the 1840s witnessed important developments in the forms of economic protest. Even before the repeal of the Combination Laws there was an increasing tendency to replace some of the features of 'collective bargaining by riot' by stronger union organisation. Although many of the early unions foundered and ambitious attempts to form general unions were defeated, the period saw an increasing sophistication of tactics and growing emphasis upon 'respectability', and although violence was still often associated with trade union activity, especially among the less well-organised trades, its use was already being condemned by a generation of trade union leaders who sought to operate within the existing legal and political framework. These years also marked the most dramatic movement by the agricultural labourers to protect their position in the face of both long- and short-term changes in their economic and social position.

The rise of the unions

The post-war period was marked not only by increasing political interest by many groups of workmen but also by the increased growth of trade union activity, not only in the traditional craft trades, but also in such diverse groups as cotton operatives, colliers, ironworkers, and lead miners. Although often using clandestine or *ad hoc* organisation, many of these groups were beginning to use strikes rather than riots to obtain improvements in living standards or halt their erosion. For example in 1819 the colliers of the St Helen's area struck for the first time; their case came to light because they had mobbed an inn to free a collier who had been arrested, but the sophistication of their strike tactics took the local magistracy by surprise. The miners used the technique of 'strike in detail', a succession of strikes in different pits, so that the working miners could support those who were on strike.[1]

Equally significant was the strike of the Manchester cotton spinners in 1818. A group of over 2,000 factory operatives conducted a well-organised strike in 1810 and in July 1818 struck again for higher wages; by the end of the month, 20,000 workers were idle in the Manchester area as strikes spread to carpenters, joiners, glassworkers, dyers, and colliers. The spinners' strike was organised by two delegates from each mill with a committee of twelve to manage the funds which came in from sympathetic trade groups in other parts of the country. Addresses stating the men's case were printed and a system of intimidation developed in which groups of several hundred would form up early in the morning and march to any mills still working 'and so carry off by force or intimidation though without any violent breach of the peace the hands who might be disposed to go to work'. The local army commander, General Byng, commented that 'the peaceable demeanour of so many thousand unemployed men is not natural'. But still more evidence of the growing sophistication of peaceful tactics was seen in the twice daily parades organised through Piccadilly; the government informer, Bent, described how they took '23½ minets in going Bye', one man from each shop organising his own ranks of marchers. During August there were some violent incidents as the men's strike fund ran low and factories began to reopen, but the spinners also reacted by lending their support to the idea of a 'General Union of the Trades' and delegates were sent out to seek support in other industrial areas.

The gradual collapse of the strike overtook these developments. The arrest of five of the spinners' committee on 29 August led to a mass meeting at Stockport on 1 September, addressed by some of the radical orators from the area; on the next day the most violent incident occurred when the spinners attacked Gray's mill in Stockport where a quarter of the workforce was continuing to work at the old rate and where there was ill-feeling against the superintendent, John Frost, an ex-union man. When the crowd attacked at midday they were resisted with musket fire, one man being killed and several others wounded and at the inquest the dead spinner was declared to have been 'justifiably and of necessity shot and killed'. The attack was a last desperate attempt to enforce the strike and with its failure the men were forced to return to work by the end of the first week of September.[2]

The authorities had been greatly alarmed by the discipline and organisation of the strikers. A local witness reported to the Home Office that 'the System of delegates is in every point of view so pregnant with danger and mischief that so long as it is unchecked by the *strong* arm of the Law the system of general turn outs will be kept alive and may by such means become more formidable and extensive than they have hitherto been'. This was vindicated when the Lancashire weavers struck at the end of August. The strike was set in motion by a meeting of weavers' delegates at Bury on 27 July who issued a handbill addressed to the cotton manufacturers of Lancashire, Yorkshire, Cheshire, and Derbyshire, asking for a wage increase of 7s. in the pound. Further meetings of delegates made the final decision to strike, with a refusal to weave for less than the requested wage. In early September there were parades of striking workers, marching about their own towns and going to others to swell the ranks there; at Stockport 1,222 men and 355 women paraded on 3 September with flags and banners – a favourite device being a shuttle draped in black crêpe. As in 1808 the weavers impounded shuttles to prevent work taking place and in some places adopted the tactic of billeting workless weavers out among those still in work with masters who had paid the wage advance. Although a small advance in wages was gained for a time, the arrest of some of their leaders and a declaration of the magistrates that they would use the Combination Acts to prevent the collection of subscriptions brought the strike to an end. By the end of September the weavers in the Manchester area had begun to drift back to work.

Although it was the orderliness of the weavers' strike which impressed and frightened some contemporary observers, there were a number of disturbances around Burnley and Blackburn. The weavers at Burnley sent the town bellman round to give notice of a meeting to enforce their wage demands, and when the authorities seized the bellman and threw him in the town lock-up, the weavers broke it open and released him before being themselves overpowered by a troop of yeomanry cavalry. Following a series of nocturnal meetings attended by several thousand men, the Blackburn weavers paraded the streets in files four abreast. On 17 September Dr T. D. Whitaker, a local magistrate, wrote to Lord Sidmouth that the hundred of Blackburn

> is in a state approaching to that of a general insurrection in consequence of a dispute betwixt the weavers and their employers on the subject of wages. . . . We have in consequence been compelled hitherto to use conciliation, which has only had the effect of emboldening the mob and encouraging them to acts of greater outrage. The ringleaders which had been apprehended have been liberated by violence . . . The houses of the weavers who are willing to work are visited, their looms and work marked, and themselves inhibited from proceeding, by threats of fire or other mischief.

At Padiham a troop of soldiers leading prisoners away after disturbances in Burnley were stoned. By the 22nd the disturbances were over. A year later two weavers were tried at Lancaster for conspiring to raise wages. One could not be found having been released from custody by an attack on the constables, but the other, James Watson, was given a year's imprisonment for using the words 'Stand firm; live on air; burn your looms; bear any extremity rather than work'.[3]

These disturbances showed that in spite of growing organisation both skilled and unskilled workers still frequently had to resort to violence to enforce a stoppage. During a keelmen's strike on Tyneside in September–November 1819, the men stopped all movement on the river and a keelman was killed when a crowd stoned a party of marines and constables who escorted some laden keels to South Shields.[4] The iron-workers and colliers of Shropshire enforced a strike against wage reductions in January 1821 by moving round the collieries and ironworks, forcing the working miners to come to the surface and stopping boilers and blast furnaces. A group of 3,000 gathered on the 'cinderhills' near Old Park ironworks, refused to disperse when the Riot Act was read and attacked a party of yeomanry who tried to carry away two arrested men. In the ensuing mêlée two colliers were killed and several cavalrymen wounded by lumps of slag.[5] During a series of disputes among the Liverpool ropemakers and sawyers in 1823-4, in which Scottish workers were brought in to take the place of striking hands, there were several attacks on the 'blacklegs', two of whom were murdered, and several cases of arson.[6]

Although many textile workers had become involved in reform agitation and in demands for repeal of the Combination Laws, and were increasingly sophisticated in their bargaining techniques, machine-breaking remained a common tactic. In the South-Western woollen industry there were disturbances at Frome over the use of fly shuttles in 1822, and an attack on a worsted power loom at Shipley in 1822.[7] The biggest and one of the last outbreaks of machine-breaking occurred not primarily as an extension of wage-bargaining, but as a protest by the handloom weavers of north Lancashire against distress and unemploy-ment. The years 1821-5 had seen the widespread adoption of power looms in the cotton industry and the steady deterioration of the handloom weavers' position. In the winter of 1825-6 a sharp depression in the cotton trade led to several commercial failures and widespread unemployment; at Blackburn it was reported that 14,000 people were being kept from starvation by poor rates and public subscription. As late as 5 April the Blackburn weavers were being praised for having shown 'no symptoms of discontent, disaffection, or sedition', but already coaches carrying manufacturers between Manchester and Blackburn had been stoned on coming into the town and some windows on a mill were broken at Accrington in mid-April. By the 20th it was reported that the weavers were planning to destroy all power looms and all yarn which was awaiting export to be woven abroad. After the disturbances had started the Home Office was informed that 'emissaries have been travelling about the country urging the people to rise and destroy the power looms before any military could arrive, and that for several weeks past numbers of pikes have been preparing in the neighbourhood of Blackburn and Burnley'.

On Monday 24 April a crowd attacked and destroyed power looms in the factory at Accrington whose windows had been broken earlier. Evading the military sent from Blackburn, the mob attacked the undefended town and by the evening had reportedly destroyed every power loom within six miles of Blackburn. During the next two days mobs attacked mills in the Irwell valley from Bacup to Bury, and looms were broken at Darwen, Rossendale, Wigan, Bolton, Clitheroe, Rawtenstall Long Holme, Edenfield, Chadderton, and Summerseat. More than twenty-one mills were attacked in east Lancashire and over a 1,000 looms smashed. On the whole the loom-breakers displayed remarkably successful tactics in evading the military, but at Chadderton the troops killed seven rioters and wounded several others, and two or three men were killed in other clashes. The mobs had a few pikes, but were mainly armed with bludgeons. Even so, Major Ekersley remarked that 'the obstinacy and determination of the rioters was most extraordinary, and such as I could not have credited had I not witnessed it myself'.[8] The attitude of the machine-breakers was shown by a participant who later recalled a brush with the military:

> That morning we set off to the loom-breaking. When we had got on the road we saw horse soldiers coming towards us. There was a stop then. The soldiers came forward, their drawn swords glittering in the air. The people opened out to let the soldiers get through. Some threw their pikes over the dyke and some did not. When the soldiers had come into the midst of the people, the officers called out, 'Halt!' All expected that the soldiers were going to charge, but the officers made a speech to the mob and told them what the consequences would be if they persisted in what they were going to do. Some of the old fellows from the mob spoke. They said, 'What are we to do? We're starving. Are we to starve to death?' The soldiers were fully equipped with haversacks and they emptied their sandwiches amongst the crowd. Then the soldiers left and there was another meeting. Were the power-looms to be broken or not? Yes, it was decided. They must be broken at all costs.[9]

The disturbances spread to Manchester on 27 April when a body of men marched through the streets calling others to join in a meeting of unemployed in St George's Square. Assembling at six in the evening a crowd of 5,000–6,000 people were urged by one or two speakers to destroy the power looms and assured that 'no military force could withstand them, if they would only assert their rights like men'. Archibald Prentice tried to dissuade them from violence, reminding them of the relief subscriptions that had been collected and that 20,000 lb of bacon and 100,000 lb of meal were ready for distribution on the following day. Although part of the crowd accepted this advice, another group moved off and burnt down a mill in Jersey Street and broke into some bread shops.[10] The disturbances spread to Skipton, where a mill at Gargrave was attacked and twenty looms destroyed, and to Bradford on 3 May where a group of worsted workers attacked Horsfall's mill, one of the first to introduce power looms in the district. The mill had been garrisoned by soldiers and two youths were shot as the crowd unsuccessfully tried to gain entry; the reading of the Riot Act and two troops of dragoons eventually dispersed them.[11]

Alarm continued into the summer but there were no more attacks, in spite of several threatening letters passed on by informers and magistrates to the Home Office. Eventually sixty-six rioters were tried at Lancaster and ten sentenced to death, but all were later reprieved and transported, another thirty-three receiving short terms of imprisonment. The disturbances were primarily a protest against distress and except for the incident in Manchester there is no evidence of radical involvement. In a sense, the machine-breaking of 1826 was almost a gesture of despair, a last ditch attempt in a period of severe hardship to destroy the machines which the weavers believed to be responsible for their distress. With no strong organisation behind them, attempts to form a weavers' union having failed, machine-breaking appeared the only alternative available. As a form of direct action to remove the source of their distress, the riots were not just the blind 'vandalism' they have sometimes been painted. Nonetheless, they were ineffective; manufacturers soon bought new looms, many from money received in compensation by actions brought against the county for damages.

Renewed trade depression led to further disturbances in 1829. There were widespread strikes against wage cuts and some attacks on factories and provision shops. In April during a strike of silk-workers in Macclesfield the windows of a factory were smashed and on the next two days the workers paraded the streets, bearing banners saying 'We only wish to live by our labour'. It was reported that 'Men, dressed as mourners, carried black flags as emblems of their position. A weaver and his loom were borne on a cart with a red herring suspended just beyond reaching distance of his hungry mouth.' At Rochdale weavers once again impounded shuttles to enforce a strike, but also destroyed some factory machinery; when sixteen men were placed in the town lock-up, a crowd attempted to release them, pelting the soldiers on guard with stones until they opened fire and several were killed.[12] In May four weaving shops in Manchester were attacked and over 150 power looms smashed, finished work destroyed, and one factory set on fire. On the next two days provision shops were sacked and contributions of food and money levied on the neighbouring houses. At Bolton, Wigan and Preston strikes were organised against milk and butter dealers and at Bolton some shop windows were smashed.[13]

Machine-breaking and intimidation died only slowly, being a necessary complement to weak or non-existent union organisation. Even as organisation developed, as it undoubtedly did in the 1820s and especially after the repeal of the Combination Laws, violence continued. Attacks on new ribbon-making machinery took place at Coventry in 1831 and at Preston in the same year. It was around 1830 that the word 'rattening' came into common usage in Sheffield for the practice of damaging the grinding-wheels of unpopular grinders.[14] Even among the spinners, perhaps the best organised of the textile groups, vitriol attacks on individuals were recorded in 1824-5.[15]

But the trend was clear. The first generation of notable trade union leaders, men like John Gast, John Doherty, and Thomas Hepburn were, at least in public, opposed to violence, putting their trust in firm union organisation. During the spinners' strike in Manchester of 1830 the men at first paraded the streets with pistols and bludgeons, breaking windows and compelling non-union workers to come out, but Doherty, recognising that the patience of the authorities was wearing thin, ordered an end to all processions and turned instead to a call for a general strike. This failed, but a local magistrate, commented shrewdly that its failure 'lessens the security we had for their peaceable conduct whilst they were strong and united and under the control of leaders with sufficient sense to know, that nothing was so likely to defeat their object as the attempt to attain it by open and violent disturbances of the peace'. Notwithstanding, Doherty remained wedded to peaceful methods of organisation and political education in the years that followed.[16] Similarly in the great miners' strikes in the North-East in 1831–2, Thomas Hepburn adopted as his watchwords moderation and abstention from violence, on the grounds that these offered the greatest hopes of winning public sympathy. On the whole this policy was maintained, although pit machinery was destroyed at Blyth, Bedlington and Jesmond Dene. As the Hammonds remarked 'considering that 17,000 men were idle, and for the most part hungry, the absence of serious outrage was remarkable'. When attacks were made on men brought in to break the strike, Hepburn urged his members not to prevent others from working, though to little avail, nor could he prevent crowds from resisting the wholesale evictions from tied cottages by the coalowners. But Hepburn's fears that any disorder would rebound on the union received clear vindication when a magistrate, Nicholas Fairles, was murdered on 11 June by two pitmen. At the trial of Jobling, the only man arrested, Mr Justice Parks blamed the murder on the union and sentenced Jobling to be executed, tarred and exhibited in chains throughout the neighbouring villages so that 'others may take warning from your fate'. Lord Melbourne too regarded all disturbances in the region as a natural consequence of strike activity and urged the magistrates to enforce the law against illegal meetings and 'unlawful combinations'.[17]

This strike illustrated features which were to dominate the relationship of trade unionists to violence in the years after 1832. Violence could still be used to enforce a strike, whether in the initial stages or to resist the introduction of strike-breaking labour, but trade unionists were conscious of their ambivalent legal status and wished to avoid provoking the authorities into acting against them; secondly at the same time, the more sophisticated trade unionists, like popular politicians, were coming to terms with the 'rise of public opinion', conscious that public sympathy at a local level was a valuable asset and could also affect the attitude taken by the authorities in London. As studies of several disputes in the North-East during the period 1815–70 have shown, the employers were 'often outwitted by the strike leadership, which frequently managed to obtain public support and the sympathy of impartial observers'.[18]

The early 1830s were marked by a series of attempts to form general unions and national unions of groups such as the potters and builders.

John Doherty's National Association for the Protection of Labour, founded in 1831, and the Grand National Consolidated Trades Union of 1833 were the most sophisticated attempts to achieve through organisation the realisation of the Owenite millennium.[19] Although Owen stressed the peaceful nature of the struggle that would ensue, there was often a tinge of revolutionary violence behind the movement as conducted in the localities. The Society for Promoting National Regeneration, founded in 1833 by Robert Owen and John Fielden, aimed to establish an eight-hour day by a general refusal to work for more than eight hours on a specified day in spring 1834. Faced by the hostility and alarm of employers and magistrates, there were disturbances in places such as Oldham when trade union leaders were arrested and freed by local crowds. Calls by Doherty and other leaders for a general strike in April 1834 received some ragged support in Lancashire, Yorkshire and the Midlands, but were eventually defeated; troops were sent into the most strike-prone areas and arrests and prosecutions under a variety of existing laws were instigated. The most famous of these arrests were of the six Dorsetshire labourers from Tolpuddle for administering illegal oaths in connection with an Agricultural Labourers' Friendly Society.[20]

In the midst of the defeats of the strike movement of 1833-4, the agitation in support of the Tolpuddle 'martyrs' was a significant display of organised trade union pressure. Protest meetings were held in many parts of the country, including a march of at least 25,000 in London.[21] Though the sentence of seven years' transportation was not rescinded as a result of these demonstrations, they confirmed the growing ability of trade unionists and radical sympathisers to orchestrate a campaign against unpopular and discriminatory actions by the authorities. Subscriptions for the Glasgow cotton spinners convicted of intimidation and arson in 1837 further illustrated the ability of trade unionists to organise in defence of their own kind. At the local level too, Dr Foster has shown how in towns such as Oldham trade unionists were already beginning to manipulate the machinery of local government to their own advantage, harassing the police for entering union premises and exerting pressure to prevent the building of a barracks in the town.[22]

Thus, if by the mid-1830s some of the high hopes of men like Doherty had been dashed amidst the wreckage of schemes for a general union, they had also seen important developments in the organisation of trade union activity and an increasing tendency towards the institutionalisation of working-class protest. The process was by no means complete in the 1830s, but it was to gather momentum in the Victorian period.

Captain Swing

While industrial workers were slowly showing signs of dispensing with 'collective bargaining by riot', one of the largest and most widespread outbreaks of disturbances occurred in the rural areas from 1830 to 1832. Known as the 'Captain Swing' disturbances from the signature placed on threatening letters, this 'last labourers' revolt', as the Hammonds called it, consisted of more than a thousand separate incidents of machine-breaking, arson, and other disturbances. Although almost all English counties were affected, the disturbances were heavily concentrated in the agricultural areas of southern and eastern England, where the origins of the Captain Swing outbreaks lay in the growing poverty and unemployment during the first decades of the nineteenth century, and especially after 1815. Population growth in areas which did not experience industrial development and often saw the decay of cottage industry produced a situation of chronic rural poverty and unemployment, eloquently described by Cobbett in his *Rural Rides*. Although historians have disputed about the role played by enclosure and other changes in agriculture, growing dependence on wage labour left the rural worker competing in an overcrowded labour market and vulnerable to agricultural depression, technical improvement, and high prices.[23] Evidence of rural distress can be found in the growing expenditure on poor rates which rose rapidly from the 1790s and reached a peak in the years 1815 to 1820. It has been estimated that by 1830 over ten per cent of the total population of the southern and eastern counties was in receipt of poor relief and the largest poor rates were being paid not in the manufacturing districts but in rural counties such as Berkshire, Wiltshire, and Sussex. During the 1820s poor law authorities made almost desperate efforts to reduce the amounts spent on poor relief, often making conditions of relief harsher, encouraging emigration, or hiring out unemployed labourers at 'knock-down' wages.[24]

In their authoritative study of the Captain Swing disturbances, Hobsbawm and Rudé have identified some tendency for crime and cases of arson to increase during the 'bad' years after 1800, such as 1812, 1816–17, 1822, and 1829–30; poaching also was increasing after 1815, especially in East Anglia. With due caution, the authors have suggested that these features might indicate increased social tension in the countryside prior to 1830, but they have also recognised the other important feature of the situation, which was that the agricultural labourers had not figured very prominently in English disturbances in the past, and they comment that 'on the whole the observer of the southern English countryside would hardly have predicted a general outbreak of active discontent, because there was virtually nothing to announce it'.[25] An exception was East Anglia, the scene of the first major protest by agricultural labourers in 1816. Here agricultural change had gone furthest, farms were larger, and the system of wage-labour was most common. A. J. Peacock has expressed the opinion that 'no year in the first half of the nineteenth century was a quiet year in the East. Every year was violent, and the amount of violence that took place was very great indeed.'[26] But even here it was only in the peak years of distress, such as 1816 and 1822, that large-scale collective action occurred, much of the other protest taking the form of clandestine cattle maimings, arson attacks, and destruction of farm property which left little trace. But if East Anglia seemed ripe for revolt at almost any time, this picture was not typical of the agricultural districts as a whole where the passive 'Hodge' of popular caricature appeared to offer little resistance to deteriorating circumstances. In seeking an explanation for the outbreak of the disturbances in 1830 rather than any other time, Hobsbawm and Rudé have isolated the effects of a poor harvest in 1830 which promised the prospect of a hard winter of poverty and unemployment, combined with a sense of 'vaguely stirred expectation' caused by the revolutions on the continent and the beginnings of the reform crisis within England. They have summed up the situation:

> The conditions of the southern labourer was such that he required only some special stimulus – admittedly it would probably have to be exceptionally powerful to overcome his demoralised passivity – to produce a very widespread movement. The economic conditions of 1828–30 produced a situation which made his already bad situation worse, and almost certainly increased both rural unemployment, the attempts to diminish in some way or another the financial burden of poor relief on the rate payers, and the discontent of farmers and all those who depended on agriculture. The combined effect of continental revolution and British political crisis produced an atmosphere of expectation, of tension, of hope and potential action. They did not provide the actual spark. In North and East Kent it may have been Irish labourers and threshing machines, in the Weald the cut in poor relief, elsewhere in the country other local factors may have revived action here and there in those occasional villages where, for one reason or another, a tradition of resistance and action survived.[27]

The introduction of cheap Irish Labour and threshing machines have been identified as primary precipitants of the disturbances which began in Kent during the summer of 1830; the first threshing machine was broken in the village of Lower Hardres, near Canterbury on 28 August and within a few weeks more than a hundred were broken in the area. As well as machine-breaking there were cases of arson and a flurry of threatening letters, many of them signed by the mythical 'Captain Swing'. During the autumn, disturbances quickly spread into the Medway valley, Surrey, Sussex, Hampshire, Wiltshire, Berkshire, Oxfordshire, Buckinghamshire, Bedfordshire and East Anglia. Although 'Swing' letters were found as far west as Herefordshire and rick-burnings occurred as far north as Carlisle, the disturbances were heavily concentrated in the counties below a line drawn between the River Severn and the Wash. Taking all incidents, including threatening letters, arson, demonstrations of various kinds, cases of robbery and assault, as well as of machine-breaking, the most disturbed counties were (in order): Hampshire and Wiltshire, Berkshire, Kent, Sussex, and Norfolk. Reaching a peak in November 1830 the main wave of disturbances was over by early 1831, though there was a revival of activity in Kent and Norfolk later in the year and sporadic cases of arson and other disturbances continued in some areas into the mid-1830s.[28]

Although machine-breaking accounted for the largest single category of incidents, the disturbances had many different forms and targets. Demands for higher wages were particularly prevalent in Essex and Suffolk. Tithes were a particular grievance in parts of East Anglia and Sussex, and led to attacks on parsons and demonstrations for a reduction in tithes. In East Sussex, workhouses were a principal target of the disturbances. Wiltshire, Kent and Berkshire witnessed the largest number of machine-breaking incidents, but in the last there were also attacks on paper-making machinery by unemployed paper workers. In East Anglia, there were attacks on Irish labourers. In Lincolnshire, arson attacks were the principal symptoms of 'Swing' with virtually no other disturbances. In one or two areas, discontent took the form of strikes.[29] Elsewhere, the 'Swing' disturbances flowed into already existing quarrels. The resistance of the small farmers and other inhabitants of Otmoor in Oxfordshire to new drainage schemes had led to attacks on embankments before 1830, but the acquittal of some farmers for breaking down banks and hedges led to a wholesale attack on enclosures on Otmoor during July and August 1830 and the despatch of troops to the area. When prisoners were brought back in wagons to Oxford on 6 September they were released by a crowd drawn from those attending the annual St Giles's Fair. The main connection with the 'Swing' disturbances lay in the hostility to enclosure shown in several disturbances on the Oxfordshire/Berkshire border.[30] The Forest of Dean was another area affected by enclosure disturbances: although long enclosed, in 1831 a general feeling appears to have arisen that now the trees in enclosed areas were mature, the plantations should be thrown open to grazing. A local man, Warren James was reported to have been 'for some time urging others to join him in the recovery of their rights, which they considered to be usurped by foreigners, in whose hands the principal coal works of the Forest are, by purchase or lease from free miners'. On 3 June 1831 he had a handbill printed calling on 'all persons' to meet and clear the forest on the 8th, when in spite of the presence of constables and woodmen, 200 miners equipped with axes cut down trees and loosed animals on the enclosures. The military were called in and ultimately James was transported for life.[31]

This 'contagious' aspect of the disturbances was one which frightened the authorities most. The movement spread extremely rapidly, taking less than a week to move from Sussex to Wiltshire. Disturbances radiated out from particular villages as bands of men, usually not more than fifty strong, went out to neighbouring settlements and farms; news of them passing rapidly from village to village through gossip and rumour, sometimes carried by itinerant workmen, canalmen or gypsies. Organisation was almost entirely local, as in the case of the Luddites, with leaders or 'captains' drawn from the community. A fairly typical sequence of events occurred around Thatcham in Berkshire during November 1830. It was reported that the labourers assembled to induce their employers to raise wages on the 15th. 'A sufficient number of them being gathered together, they marched off (preceded by one of their company blowing a horn) to visit each of the farms, for the purpose of compelling the labourers to unite with them.' Assembling in the churchyard, they asked the select vestry to provide them with work and higher wages; when work was offered, but no guarantee of higher wages, the men reassembled and over the course of the next three days destroyed sixty-three machines and levied contributions from farmers, in many cases forcing them to pay a fee for the work of breaking the machines.[32]

Although labourers were often forced to join the ranks and there were several instances of people being roughly handled, the dominant feature was the orderliness and ceremony with which these disturbances were carried out. Few, if any, arms were carried and although the language of the protesters was often bloodcurdling, they killed no one, and discipline was also shown in the ritual elements of being preceded by a flag or horn, while a party at Ashampstead in Berkshire was described as having 'the rear kept up by whippers-in as at a hunt'. Often parties had a 'treasurer' to keep the money collected from farmers at least until the evening when it was frequently spent in the local alehouse. In large part this organisation simply reflected local groupings; labourers accustomed to working together could easily provide the nucleus of a gang and this could be swollen by friends, relations, and other members of the village community who were not working directly in agriculture. Among those involved were a high number of village craftsmen, such as carpenters, wheelwrights, blacksmiths, and cobblers; often these provided the 'treasurer' or 'captain', probably because they were likely to be slightly better educated than the common run of labourers. The use of 'treasurer' also suggests the influence of club life upon the organisation of the Captain Swing bands. Societies such as the Oddfellows, Druids, Foresters, and various forms of benefit society had penetrated many villages since the Friendly Societies Act of 1793 and given some other experience of organisation to add to existing patterns of village ritual and cooperative labour. Dissent too seems to have played a part in providing some villages with a focus of organisation which helped them to mobilise.[33]

'Swing' was not a universal phenomenon. It was primarily a movement of the most depressed sections of the agricultural workforce in the low wage areas of the South and East. Even there, disturbances did not take place in every village. Accepting that only the broadest generalisation is possible, Hobsbawm and Rudé have nevertheless concluded that the villages which saw outbreaks tended to be of above average size, were more totally dependent on agriculture than others, and had a higher than average ratio of labourers to farmers; they were also villages with a large number of artisans and often also a propensity to religious dissent. 'Open' villages were more likely to be disturbed than 'closed' ones and places on communications networks or with a history of past activity were more likely to be disturbed. That being said, the spirit of unrest could be carried from centres of unrest, such as Thatcham in Berkshire, to places which might otherwise have remained unaffected. It is important not to categorise too far in an episode which had so many aspects and local variations, nonetheless the propensity of the larger villages, as in 1816, to show signs of unrest, and also those having contact with a wider culture of news and opinion, do not seem unreasonable propositions in explaining why some villages should be more disposed to disturbance than others. Moreover, the rural character of the disturbances requires emphasis for it left the county towns virtually unaffected, as well as the suburban fringe of London, where wages were traditionally higher and employment opportunities greater.[34]

The authorities reacted rather slowly to 'Swing', for Wellington's administration was more preoccupied with disturbances in the manufacturing districts in the first part of 1830; as a result, although some troops were despatched to the rural counties, the Government urged rural magistrates to deal with the disturbances themselves. Grey's administration took office as the riots were reaching a climax in November 1830 and the new Home Secretary, Lord Melbourne, issued a proclamation offering a reward of £500 for bringing rioters and incendiaries to justice. In the absence of a professional police in the rural areas and with relatively small numbers of troops available, the authorities were forced to depend on various expedients to deal with the problem: yeomanry were mobilised, special constables sworn in, and *ad hoc* forces of tenants and servants organised by local landowners. Although Melbourne adopted a more systematic policy, appointing military commanders to supervise small detachments of troops in the most disturbed areas, the bulk of the troops remained stationed near the bigger towns and manufacturing centres. In practice these measures were adequate because many of the disturbances lasted no more than a few days, the labourers and artisans involved being unable to stay away from work for much longer; merely providing a guard or nightly watch was often sufficient to deter further outbreaks. It soon became a relatively easy task for the authorities to round up suspected rioters with little opposition, and by December 1,976 men and women were awaiting trial. By then judicial proceedings had already started in Kent, but they were so lenient that the Government reacted by appointing special commissions to try nearly 1,000 offenders in Winchester, Salisbury, Reading, Dorchester, and Aylesbury; about the same number were tried in 85 other courts. Of these prisoners, 252 were sentenced to death, 19 of whom were eventually executed, the rest being sentenced to transportation or terms of imprisonment. Nearly 500 were transported and over 600 imprisoned. While the number of executions was smaller than for the Luddites, the number of people transported was exceptional.[35] This in part reflected the smaller number of capital offences on the statute book since Peel's reforms of the criminal code and had 'Swing' occurred before 1822 the toll of executions might have been higher, but even so, the repression was undoubtedly severe, especially in Hampshire and Wiltshire. At the local level, the transportation of two or three villagers, perhaps for life, left a lasting impression, a farmer of Great Holland in Essex recorded that following the transportation of three men from the village 'the prompt measures taken to suppress the disturbance frightened the labourers alarmingly'.[36]

Analysis of the people tried has revealed that the majority were drawn from the broad category of 'labourers', a term which included a wide range of more specialised jobs and men who had more than one occupation. Generally, they appear to have earned above average wages and were not in any sense the poorest elements in the village community; although there were paupers among them, there were also some who were considered among the best paid. There was also a sizeable minority of village craftsmen who appear to have played a highly significant part in leading and organising the disturbances. What surprised contemporaries was that it was not a 'paupers revolt', but one in which the most 'respectable' elements in the working population had played a dominant part. This was borne out by the fact that while many of those convicted were in their middle or late twenties, more than half were married. These were not the rootless young, or the desperate poor, still less outside agitators, but a representative sample of the village community. One group who were under-represented were women: far fewer were involved than in many other disturbances and only two were transported; this probably reflects the small number of food riots (usually dominated by women) during the disturbances, and that the 'mobs' who went about the farms were based on male-dominated labour gangs.[37]

While the disturbances were in part generated by political excitement, the labourers showed few political aims. Their horizons were largely bounded by the world of the parish, or at most the county; references to parliament show little real awareness of the political struggles going on in the country. 'Agitators' were widely blamed for stirring up the labourers and Cobbett was tried and acquitted for allegedly fomenting the movement, but there was little evidence that they played a crucial part. Cobbett had toured the South-East to lecture in various towns during October 1830, but the disturbances began before he arrived. Equally, while there was considerable sympathy with the labourers' plight from radical groups in some of the small towns of southern England, places like Maidstone and Horsham where small groups of radicals existed and who certainly made some attempts to agitate both labourers and small farmers, they rarely did more than contribute to a movement which was derived from the hardships and grievances of the agricultural labourers. The striking feature of the men's demands was that they were almost entirely economic and backward-looking. They sought a restitution of lost rights, of customary wages and levels of poor relief, and felt themselves to be resisting innovations such as the use of machinery. In that sense the motivation of the labourers was deeply conservative. They posed no revolutionary threat to the Government or to the local authorities, having neither the organisation or the ideology to do so. It was no less an authority than Cobbett who claimed that 'I never heard amongst common tradesmen, little farmers, artisans or labourers, anything indicating a wish to see the nobility pulled down ... the change that they wanted was a change from bad living to good living: a single thought about the change of the constituent parts of the state, never, even by accident, came athwart their minds'.[38] Hence there was no *jacquerie*, no wholesale plunder of the rich, no burning of churches, and no massacres such as have occurred in other rural revolts, rather individually shortlived manifestations of protest which were, on the whole, more remarkable for their restraint than for their venom. In this way the 'Swing' disturbances bore close resemblances to some of the Luddite attacks of 1811–12 and 1826: they were a protest against distress in which machinery was a principal but not the only target. Moreover, although in the short term these protests were functional in that machines were destroyed and some concessions wrung from local farmers and authorities, the 'Swing' bands were operating in a much more localised and *ad hoc* way than many contemporary urban workmen. Fragmentary evidence exists to suggest that unions of agricultural labourers were emerging in some areas, as the Tolpuddle incident was later to show, and some strikes and 'turn outs' occurred during the 'Swing' months, but the development of large-scale effective unionism lay almost half a century away. The rural labourer, hindered by illiteracy and less frequent exposure to the world of pamphlets and newspapers, lagged almost a generation or more behind their urban counterparts in the forms of their protest. This is not to say their methods were primitive, but they were different from those taken by groups like the cotton spinners of Lancashire or the skilled trades of the capital. It is interesting too, that in some sense, 'Swing' was a retrospective protest against the changes in agriculture which had been affecting the English rural labourer for a century or more. It was only in the circumstances of acute distress in 1829–30 that the labourers of south-eastern England reacted against the gradual erosion of their living standards caused by the exogenous pressures of population growth and agricultural change.[39]

Rural protest did not come to an end with the suppression of 'Swing'; poaching, cattle-stealing, and animal maiming continued into the 1830s and 1840s, as did a miscellany of disturbances over tithes, enclosures, and wages. As shown later, poor relief remained a frequent source of irritation and the introduction of the New Poor Law after 1834 met widespread resistance in many country areas. But perhaps the most typical crime after 1832 was arson, running consistently at higher levels than before 1830 and in some years reaching new peaks; in 1843–5 there was an epidemic of arson in Norfolk and Suffolk which attracted considerable public attention. Although not all fires were arson, and not all arson attempts malicious, some at least being started by farmers to obtain the insurance, a significant number of them have to be considered as genuine symptoms of unrest. Moreover, detailed work on the East Anglian outbreak has shown that arson was often pre-planned and preceded by a threatening letter. Far from being always a spasmodic and solitary crime, some attacks were pre-planned by groups of villagers and often preceded by a threatening letter to the victim. Once fires were started, it was not uncommon for the villagers to turn out and hamper the firemen, loot the premises, or even stoke up the blaze. 'Dumb insolence' from locals when questioned about the instigators or men casually lighting their pipes from a smouldering hayrick or barn spoke volumes for the way in which arson had become a part of social protest.[40]

Thus in some areas, 'Swing' was only the largest of a series of waves of rural protest which had begun in 1816. In others, however, it appears more of a once and for all affair, an exceptional reaction to distress from a group of workers who were not to be seen again as a threat to order until the days of Joseph Arch and the National Agricultural Labourers' Union.

12 The Chartist era

The 1830s and 1840s witnessed a number of waves of disturbances beyond those already discussed. Attacks on cholera hospitals, protests against the New Poor Law, and resistance to the new police form a superficially diverse group of incidents, most of them minor in themselves, but with a common theme in that they were often reactions to administrative change in a period which has sometimes been characterised as witnessing a revolution in government. Moreover, some of these issues flowed directly into the Chartist agitation, the movement which above all others appeared to offer a threat of major upheaval. At times in the period 1839–48 Britain seemed to some observers to be as near to revolution as at any time in the nineteenth century. In fact, Chartism was a many-sided phenomenon which displayed several different aspects of the role and place of popular violence in British society.

The impact of cholera

Although the early 1830s were dominated by the reform agitation and the disturbances in agricultural and industrial areas, another cause of popular unrest was the arrival of Asiatic cholera in England in the autumn of 1831. It was less fear of cholera itself which led to disturbances, than the resentments caused by the hastily organised public health campaign mounted by the authorities. This triggered off deep-lying anxieties about hospitals, dissection and body-snatching. The background to the disturbances lay in the problems faced by medical men in obtaining bodies for dissection; the only bodies which could legally be used were those of executed felons, but as demand exceeded supply others were obtained from a semi-criminal fraternity of 'body snatchers'. As a result there was a history of attacks on medical premises, usually because they were suspected of using bodies stolen by grave-robbers or even murdered to sell for dissection. In 1832 the Anatomy Act permitted medical schools to take the unclaimed bodies of those who died in workhouses, prisons and hospitals. In spite of being widely regarded as a just compromise between the needs of medical education and the concern of relatives and friends to prevent the deceased from ending up on the dissecting table, the Act did not end suspicions concerning both hospitals and doctors. Hence when in reaction to the arrival of cholera in England, the Government recommended that cholera victims should be put into isolation hospitals and interred in special burial grounds, they aroused widespread alarm. The overhasty dissection of cholera victims in the initial stages of the epidemic as doctors sought to investigate the disease only fuelled popular anxieties about the regulations. Moreover, the regulations governing the interment of cholera victims frequently disrupted traditional customs: burials were often carried out without allowing time for a 'wake' and what was thought of as a 'proper' funeral. The use of tar and quicklime to dress the bodies, a practice associated with the treatment of felons, further upset relatives and friends. The use of unconsecrated ground for the burial of suicides had caused disturbances in the past and did so again during the first cholera outbreak as local boards of health tried to comply with the regulations for the isolated burial of the victims.

The main wave of resistance to these administrative measures occurred during the spring of 1832. In London a mob of Irish people prevented the authorities from burying a woman and child who had died of cholera in a special burial ground; instead a large crowd escorted them to the Bayswater Cemetery. Crowds also attacked the cholera hospital at St George's in the East, but were stopped when shown that the patients were being well-treated; at St Marylebone hospital a man was carried away naked by a crowd who believed he was going to be 'burked'.[1]

There were also extensive riots in Scotland, especially at Edinburgh, Glasgow, and Paisley, accompanied by rumours of murders by the medical practitioners to provide corpses for dissection and troops had to be called in to deal with the situation. The most serious riots in England occurred in Manchester in September when a crowd carried the body of a partly dissected boy through the streets; they attacked the Swan Street cholera hospital, 'liberated' the patients and began to wreck the interior. When the police were called in the crowd attacked the local lock-up and only stopped when the troops were called out and the Riot Act read. The discovery of the boy's body had come as the climax to a long process of accusations against the cholera hospital amongst the poor Irish who lived nearby and a series of incidents which had focused suspicion on the hospital.

The riots in both England and Scotland showed some common features: they occurred near medical schools or cholera hospitals where there had been rumours or actual instances of body-snatching. There was also a strong Irish element in most the crowds; they had already formed tightly-knit communities in several cities and were the group who attached most importance to their 'rites de passage'. Normally, the amount of violence was limited, a striking illustration that even when deep popular feelings were touched, the result was still fairly restrained; Moreover, the authorities reacted sensibly by making some concessions on the quarantine arrangements.[2]

Anti-poor law disturbances

Resistance to alterations in the provision of poor relief were not uncommon in early nineteenth-century England and grievances about the operation of the poor laws had formed a significant feature in the disturbances in the southern counties in 1830-2. By that time the poverty and unemployment which had given rise to the 'Swing' disturbances forced many labourers to rely on 'outdoor relief' for at least part of the year and on the Speenhamland system to provide them with a supplement to their wages in times of high prices or unemployment. Whatever its demoralising character, the Old Poor Law at least provided for flexible arrangements to deal with poverty and had clearly come to be regarded by many labourers as their right in times of hardship. Hence attempts by individual parishes or unions to economise on poor relief or alter the conditions on which it was given were always likely to cause opposition and there had been several instances of this happening in the years before 1834.[3]

But it was the introduction, or more precisely the implementation, of the Poor Law Amendment Act of 1834 which provoked the most widespread hostility and opposition. The Act was the result of the Royal Commission on the Poor Laws of 1832-4 and its intentions were to ease the burden of rising poor rates and the demoralisation of the poor by making unlawful any relief to able-bodied persons outside the workhouse; this was now to be a well-regulated and spartan institution designed to discourage all but the genuinely needy. The Act grouped hitherto independent parishes into unions to be governed by elected boards of guardians. Three centrally appointed Poor Law Commissioners with the aid of salaried assistants were to supervise the implementation of this plan and, once set up, to guide the unions in the gradual withdrawal of outdoor relief and the conduct of the new workhouse regime.[4]

As such the Act was intended to solve the problem of rising poor rates and the maladministration of existing workhouses by an application of *laissez faire* principles. As a result the Act had a relatively easy passage through parliament, but it aroused the opposition of traditionalists such as Cobbett, who in his pamphlet *The Legacy to Labourers*, saw it as an attack on the 'right' to relief and an assault upon the traditional 'social compact' between the propertied and the poor. Others were more concerned with the centralising tendency of the measure. In an age when most government was still local government, the extensive powers given to the Poor Law Commissioners created unease as a radical departure from existing practice. To popular radicals, the new Act appeared part of an attack upon the livelihood of the poor by a penny-pinching Government. The *Sheffield Iris* referred to the Commissioners as 'the travelling legalised Shylocks with their weigh scales and sharp knives'.[5]

The first reaction to the implementation of the Act came in the agricultural areas; Dr Edsall has shown that the attempt to enforce the Act from 1835 was followed by numerous disturbances in East Anglia and the southern counties.[6] The situation was aggravated by a hard winter which forced many unemployed labourers to apply for poor relief, so that they quickly encountered the harsher conditions of the new regime. Announcements of the implementation of the Act were also greeted with hostility. In Wiltshire it was reported that the farm-workers marched out of church when it was announced and assembled in the churchyard. At Christian Malford the labourers occupied the church, while other bodies marched on the Devizes Petty Sessions to protest against the overseers. Elsewhere there were attacks on guardians and attempts to prevent paupers being moved to a central workhouse; other disturbances were caused when applicants for relief were offered tickets for provisions instead of cash. In May 1835 a crowd assembled at Ampthill in Bedfordshire, demanding 'Blood or bread', 'All money' and 'No bread', and were only dispersed when the Riot Act was read. In other places labourers occupied the workhouse, demanding that customary relief should be granted. Attempts to separate male and female paupers under the new regulations gave rise to rumours that this was part of a Malthusian plot to stop the poor from breeding; an elaboration of this rumour was that workhouse food was being adultered with an anti-fertility substance or even poisoned.

The disturbances in Suffolk were the most serious. There, the assistant commissioners met with severe criticism in several parishes when they went to implement their enquiries. Anglican churchmen in the area were openly opposed to the new law and strong local feeling was more evident than in many other parts of the country. In December 1835 the Ipswich board of guardians began to impose the workhouse test on able-bodied paupers and to alter the workhouse buildings for the separation of the sexes and classification of different categories of pauper. A crowd assembled on the 16th and partly demolished the St Clement's workhouse, and were only prevented from completely destroying it by the arrival of troops. In many of the smaller villages poor law officials were insulted or attacked and workhouses were threatened at Stradbroke and Cosford. All the attacks took place within a week of the riot at Ipswich and eventually troops and London police had to be called on to deal with the situation. In February 1836 disturbances also spread to Devon and to the north-east corner of Cornwall at Camelford and Stratton early in 1837, forcing delay in the replacing of the old workhouses.

The disturbances in southern England against the implementation of the poor law illustrated the sensitivity of the population to changes in the customary administration of poor relief. Rumours of being poisoned or maltreated in the new 'Bastilles' achieved wide circulation in the atmosphere of anxious expectancy which preceded the arrival of commissioners and the alteration of workhouses and their regimes. Resistance, however, was sporadic: hundreds of parishes were grouped into Unions without any show of open opposition and such disturbances as took place were largely uncoordinated; except around Eastbourne where an Agricultural Labourers' Benefit Society was established and organised meetings and protest marches against the board of guardians, they were local and spontaneous reactions similar to the 'Swing' disturbances. There was little serious violence, other than some property being damaged and a few people roughed up. Even in Suffolk, the disturbances were quickly over with only one instance of large-scale damage – that at Ipswich.

Although there was often considerable sympathy with the rioters and many gentry and parsons petitioned against the Act or protested locally against its implementation, the disturbances did virtually nothing to disturb the implementation of the New Poor Law. In some places, such as Suffolk and Cornwall, there was some delay, but within a few months the new system was operating. Even in the unions which had shown the most resistance the system was operating with full rigour within less than a year of the disturbances. With no permanent organisation to facilitate resistance and with the growing confidence of the new poor law authorities, the anti-poor law movement never gained the support and partial success it was to achieve when the system was applied to the North.[7]

Opposition to the Poor Law Amendment Act was far more organised north of the Trent. Initially the Act was received favourably by the powerful provincial press in the North, largely because it was felt that it was irrelevant to the industrial areas where poor rates were much lower and parochial relief had often already been reorganised. But when the New Poor Law began to be implemented in the North from the end of 1836 it aroused serious and sometimes violent opposition, much of it organised by Tory radicals such as Michael Sadler and Richard Oastler, who had already been campaigning for factory reform under the banner of the Ten Hours movement and now turned their attention to the New Poor Law. These middle-class reformers provided an organisation against the new Act which the resistance in the South had not had. Local committees in the textile towns of Lancashire and Yorkshire prepared to resist the poor law commissioners by petitions, public meetings, demonstrations and a well-organised press and pamphlet campaign. The campaign orchestrated by the anti-poor law movement stressed the Christian duty of the rich to assist the poor and accepted Cobbett's argument that the Act was intended as a denial of basic rights. In vindication of this view, the abuses of the New Poor Law were stressed and the fearful reputation of the 'poor law Bastilles' played up. Moreover, the assistant commissioners arrived to form the new unions just at the time that trade depression was beginning to affect many of the textile districts, adding greatly to the fears of the manufacturing population, especially the increasingly vulnerable handworkers.

In the face of this movement it was hardly surprising that the arrival of the commissioners should lead to violence. Assistant Commissioner Alfred Power was greeted by hostile crowds and his meetings with local poor law officials interrupted by noisy demonstrations, some of the most serious occurring at Keighley, Bury, and Bradford. On the whole the leaders of the movement preferred to maintain control over their followers and direct the campaign in a peaceful direction without causing outright violence. Boycotts of the new unions were organised by local opponents and the protest campaign came to a climax in mid-May with a giant meeting organised by the Yorkshire anti-poor law movement on Hartshead Moor, attended by an estimated 100,000 to 250,000 people.

At Huddersfield on 5 June 1837 the meeting of the board of guardians was surrounded by crowds of several thousand people, part of whom wrecked the workhouse and prevented the election of officials. The crowd had been called together for a rally addressed by Oastler, who urged the crowds to resist, led them to the workhouse, but also counselled them against causing any disturbance. This show of force played an important part in forcing the poor law commissioners to put off the implementation of the New Poor Law until the next year. During the following summer and autumn, meetings of boards of guardians were attended by threatening crowds and the burning of effigies. When Oastler stood for Huddersfield during the general election of July 1837 there was a full-scale attack on his Whig opponents which was only quelled by the troops; another election riot took place at Wakefield at the end of July when he marched 30,000 of his supporters to the town. Although these disturbances arose mainly from confrontation between Whig and Tory supporters, Oastler was prominent at the head of the anti-Whig faction. At Dewsbury in July and August 1838 there were disturbances at the first meeting of the guardians under the new Act. Anti-poor law guardians moved wrecking amendments, but were overruled by the chairman. At a mass meeting on 1 August the crowds were urged to support the opposition guardians and at a second meeting the guardians were stoned by the crowd and only rescued by troops. When in October, some overseers at Todmorden were convicted for obstructing the Act and on refusing to pay their fines had their property seized and auctioned, a crowd repossessed the goods and drove the auctioneer out of town. A further attempt to seize the goods of another opponent on 16 November led to a crowd attacking the constables, one of whom was stripped naked and beaten up. A week later a mob reassembled and attacked the houses of guardians, relieving officers, and supporters of the new Act; windows were smashed and furniture destroyed in about a dozen houses. But by the end of 1838 the violent phase of resistance had died down as the unions were gradually established and the poor law commissioners made concessions which allowed boards of guardians to give relief in Lancashire and Yorkshire on the traditional basis of the Old Poor Law if the situation required it. By 1839 the anti-poor law campaign began to disintegrate as working-class resentment was appeased by the continued use of 'outdoor relief' and rivalries between the middle-class and working-class elements began to come to the fore. Increasingly the more radically inclined were attracted to the Chartist movement with its wider political objectives, which promised repeal of the New Poor Law as one of the results of the granting of universal suffrage. Indeed out of the anti-poor law agitation emerged one of the most prominent Chartist leaders, Fergus O'Connor, whose *Northern Star* campaigned actively against the New Poor Law, but increasingly after 1838 gave its support to the struggle for the Charter. Middle-class members of the movement were increasingly alienated by the growing Chartist influence and concentrated their efforts on mitigating the law's operation through the local boards of guardians.[8]

Thus the anti-poor law movement in the North represented a temporary alliance between working class and middle class against what was widely regarded as an injust and intrusive measure; in a sense it was also a local reaction against centralization which cut across class lines. Eventually the differences in emphasis and ideology between Tory radicals such as Oastler and the emerging Chartist leaders ruptured this alliance. In tactics too, the movement was transitional. The disturbances were only a minor part of a well-orchestrated campaign in which the threat of popular violence was far more important than its reality; as such the Tory radicals were using the 'language of menace' in much the same way as the parliamentary reformers in the reform crisis. Their major effort, however, building on the experience of the ten hours movement, was directed to exerting pressure through press, pamphlets, and meetings. These peaceful methods were to be increasingly influential in the political campaigns of the early and mid-Victorian period, notably in the campaigns of the Anti-Corn Law League. The sophisticated campaign in the North directed by the middle classes stood in contrast to the more traditional, less organised and less effective reactions in the agricultural areas.

The new police

Another administrative innovation which provoked sometimes violent resistance was the introduction of professional policing. The creation of municipal forces under the provisions of the Municipal Corporations Act of 1835 and county forces under the County Police Act of 1839 gave rise to a series of disturbances, some of which at least can be seen as anti-police riots. Although the establishment of professional policing was regarded as desirable by social reformers and 'improvers' of many types, its introduction often led to intense hostility. Many radicals regarded the police as agents of a repressive government and union organisers often feared that the police would prove a strike-breaking force. Even those unaffected by these concerns resented the introduction of a body which would enforce the law in hitherto unregulated areas of everyday life. It was this regulatory and intrusive character of the police which probably led to more hostility than almost anything else, at a time when the authorities saw it as part of the police function to control an increasingly wide range of everyday activities.

Some of the most serious disturbances occurred in Colne during the spring and early summer of 1840. The creation of a police force for the town in April led to somewhat officious attempts to keep the streets clear for 'respectable' inhabitants by 'moving-on' the crowds of onlookers who were accustomed to congregate in the town centre. The situation was complicated by the fact that the constables were almost all strangers to the area, many being Scots, and that Colne was a strongly pro-Chartist community at a time when the Chartists had already bitterly attacked the new police through the pages of the *Northern Star*. Attacks on the Colne police began on the evening of 24 April when a large crowd put out the street lamps and 'in a disciplined manner' began to stone the constables. Eventually the disturbances were quelled by the arrival of troops. More riots occurred in August and in a fierce battle on the 10th in the main streets of the town a force of special constables and police encountered a large body of the inhabitants marching 'in military array, four abreast', armed with bludgeons and iron railings. During the clashes a special constable was killed. Eventually the Colne police had to be backed up by a military garrison to prevent further trouble.[9]

Similar resentment of a police presence was shown at the Lancaster races in July 1840 when a force of Lancashire county police were attacked without, it seems, having made themselves offensive in any other way than by being there. More typical, perhaps, were the incidents at Leeds in June 1844, when a party of Leeds corporation police arrested some soldiers accused of beating a man up. Their compatriots rallied in their defence attacking the police with belt buckles and bludgeons. Issuing from the pub where the original incident had taken place, the soldiers raised the cry of 'Down with the police' and encouraged a general attack on local policemen which lasted for several days.[10] Major risings against the police were largely concentrated in the period 1839–44, when forces were being introduced in several towns for the first time; attacks on police offices also occurred during the so-called 'Plug-plot' riots of July–August 1842. Although these attacks and some of the earlier ones coincided with periods of Chartist activity, their most important element seems to have been the attempt by local communities to resist the intrusion of professional police who were seen as an imposition from 'outside'.[11] Indeed, the anti-police character of these disturbances has been confirmed by similar incidents in West Yorkshire in 1856–7, when the Chartist agitation had long subsided; characteristically, however, they occurred near, or at, the point where the police were first introduced and came into conflict with some local activity. Individual or collective resistance to the police undoubtedly continued well into the mid- and late Victorian period, but it was at the point when they were first established that the heaviest concentration of anti-police riots occurred.

The early Chartists: 'physical' and 'moral' force

Chartist agitation grew out of several different strands of activity in the 1830s. Finding common focus in the campaign for the People's Charter, with its promise of radical parliamentary reform, it derived partly from a growing sense of disillusionment with the limited nature of the 1832 Reform Act and the exclusion from the franchise of all except the propertied middle and upper classes. By the middle of the 1830s the introduction of the New Poor Law, the creation of new municipal authorities on a propertied franchise, and the prosecution of trade unionists at Tolpuddle in 1834 and Glasgow in 1837 seemed to many radicals to indicate a consolidation of the middle and upper classes against the unenfranchised. But Chartism also grew out of distress: it revealed the strains of increasing urbanisation and industrialisation and the years when it came nearest to becoming a mass movement coincided with the troughs of the trade cycle. The peak years of Chartist activity were also the years of unemployment, when the demands of an articulate artisan intelligentsia were combined with protests of the factory operatives and the declining handicraft workers.

For many radicals, the reform struggle had only started with the Reform Act of 1832. Groups of activists, heavily concentrated among the artisan elite of the capital and the major manufacturing centres, recommenced their activities once it became apparent that the Whigs were unlikely, indeed were actively opposed to, any further measure of parliamentary reform. The formation of the London Working Men's Association (LWMA) in 1836 provided one such focus of activity and it was this body which provided the programme for a revival of agitation with the publication of the People's Charter in May 1838. This document, drawn up with the help of Francis Place and a number of radical MPs, formulated the famous six points of universal manhood suffrage, annual parliaments, votes by ballot, the abolition of property qualifications for MPs, equal electoral districts, and payment of members. The Charter was accepted as the common basis for agitation by several provincial groups in the months which followed. Thus in August 1838 the powerful Birmingham Political Union adopted universal suffrage as its major programme in place of its traditional policy of currency reform. By the autumn, the Chartist agitation was in full swing with the formation of political unions in Newcastle upon Tyne and Leeds and a series of large, but peaceful, mass meetings in London and provincial centres to accept the Charter and elect delegates for a national convention to be held early in 1839.

Marking as it did the revival of political activity in many areas where the reform struggle had left off and the emergence of many thousands of working men into political agitation for the first time, Chartism ought not to be solely, or even primarily, seen as a violent movement. Its fascination to historians lies in the almost bewildering complexity of its local character and personalities, which reveal so much about the conditions, attitudes and aspirations of its participants. Yet, as Dorothy Thompson has reminded us, the issue of violence lies somewhere near the heart of the Chartist 'movement', at least as a national force.[12] At several points, the struggle for the Charter appeared to threaten upheaval on a revolutionary scale. It forced the government to take measures which had not been used since the days of the Luddites, including the use of several thousand troops to garrison the manufacturing districts, and a major effort by the Home Office, under successive Secretaries of State, to prevent or suppress the threat of a Chartist uprising. As late as 1848 the Chartist movement was to give rise to the famous *cause célèbre* of the Kennington Common meeting of 10 April, a date remembered by some Victorians at least as the turning point between the threat of revolution and the 'order' of mid-Victorian prosperity.[13]

However fanciful these fears and however distorted a picture they give of the Chartist movement, the Chartist era did see a large number of popular disturbances, some at least of which took the form of insurrectionary attempts. Although only an imperfect record of the 'true' level of activity, reflecting as they do the offences known to the authorities and the vagaries of enforcement, the number of committals and convictions for riotous offences (Table 12.1) gives an indication of the increasing scale of activity in the early Chartist years.

Table 12.1 Committals and convictions for indictable offences of riot and rescue, 1835–45[14]

	Committed	Convicted
1835	1,905	1,717
1836	2,013	1,687
1837	1,693	1,280
1838	2,168	1,589
1839	4,730	2,181
1840	4,758	1,951
1841	4,353	1,633
1842	4,394	1,960
1843	5,673	2,099
1844	4,962	1,750
1845	3,693	1,339

In his important study of public order in the Chartist period Dr Mather has identified four main 'clusters' of disturbance. These were: (a) spring 1837–January 1840; (b) the summer months of 1842; (c) November 1842–October 1843; (d) February–August 1848.[15] Although (c) was almost entirely confined to Wales, the dozen years from 1837 witnessed a series of waves of disturbances of different types and in different areas. Although by no means all Chartist-inspired or even directly related to the Chartist agitation, they provide one of the most disturbed periods of the nineteenth century and in which the role of the Chartists was considered central by both government and many of the propertied classes alike.

Chartism inherited from the reform struggle and from the anti-poor law movement a tradition of militant extra-parliamentary agitation.

With only a handful of radical MPs in parliament likely to be sympathetic, the Chartists saw themselves as attempting to repeat the process which they believed had operated in 1831–2. By building up a head of agitation, they aimed to create an impression of irresistible force which would intimidate a reluctant parliament to accept their demands. A group of early Chartists meeting in London in February 1837 argued that 'in 1832 the working classes by their moral and physical organisation beat the Tories for the sake of the Whigs – by the same means they can in 1837 beat both Whigs and Tories for the sake of themselves'.[16]

The assessment of the Chartist movement is therefore heavily coloured, as is that of the reform movement, by the 'language of menace'. Chartism embraced a wide variety of opinions on the question of 'physical' or 'moral' force. These ranged from the intimidatory language of O'Connor and veterans of the anti-poor law movement to the more genuine insurrectionary plans of some of the Sheffield and Bradford Chartists. In fact, the dichotomy between physical and moral force was never quite so clear as some of the Chartists or later historians have made it out to be. Almost every leader of early Chartism had recourse to what has been called 'the rhetoric of violence'. Many of the northern Chartist leaders who had emerged during the anti-poor law movement had urged direct defiance of the law and colluded in mass demonstrations which sometimes spilled over into violent acts. A typical aspect of this 'verbal bellicosity' was that the people had a right to arm in their own defence and that the ability to resist oppression was the only means to ensure a successful outcome. The position of many Chartists in 1838–9 was summed up by Harney in his famous election speech in Derby in January 1839:

> What is it that we want? Not to destroy property and take life, but to preserve our own lives, and to protect our own property – viz, our labour. We are for Peace, Law, Order; but if our oppressors shall break the peace – if our tyrants shall violate the law – if our despots shall trample upon order – then we will fall back upon the Constitution, and defend the few remaining of the blood bought rights left us by our fathers. The Whigs shall never violate the constitution of this country as they have done in Canada. They charge us with being Physical Force men; I fling the charge back in the teeth of these canting liberals. Let them call to mind their own words and deeds during the humbug reform agitation. ... Again I say, we are for peace, but we must have justice – we must have our rights speedily: peaceable if we can, *forcibly if we must*. ... Time was when every Englishman had a musket in his cottage, and along with it hung a flitch of bacon; now there is no flitch of bacon for there is no musket; let the musket be restored and the flitch of bacon will soon follow. ... You will get nothing from your tyrants but what you can take, and you can take nothing unless you are

properly prepared to do so. In the words of a good man [Oastler], then, I say, 'Arm for peace, arm for liberty, arm for justice, arm for the rights of all and the tyrants will no longer laugh at your petitions.' . . .[17]

O'Connor embraced a similar position:

He counselled them against all rioting, all civil war, but still, in the hearing of the House of Commons, he would say, that rather than see the constitution violated, while the people were in daily want, if no other man would do so, if the constitution was violated, he would himself lead the people to death or glory. . . . His desire was to try moral force as long as possible, even to the fullest extent, but he would always have them bear in mind, that it is better to die freemen than to live slaves.[18]

The threat that 'moral' would give way to 'physical' force was the most powerful argument the Chartists could use against the government. It seemed the answer to the question posed by the Heckmondwike Chartists in 1839: 'How are the people to obtain the Charter, there being a majority of the Commons against it?' While some continued to believe that 'we have sufficient moral power to gain all we ask', O'Connor continually hinted at a barely controlled force ready to break loose should 'oppression' last too long. At the Kersal Moor meeting in September 1838, attended by between 50,000 and 300,000 people, O'Connor proclaimed: 'Here is moral power with a vengeance, which will be turned ere long, in spite of me, or of the most wise counsellors of the age, into physical force, because the people know that they have borne oppression too long and too tamely.'[19]

The main purpose of this meeting, however, as of the others held in the summer and autumn of 1838, was to elect representatives to a Chartist convention in order to prepare a petition to Parliament. The Convention met on 4 February 1839 in the British Coffee House at Charing Cross, the day before parliament met. It was attended by fifty-four representatives representing a wide spectrum of opinion. Although the decision to petition parliament provided common ground, there was considerable disagreement about further aims and objectives. A moderate group wished to restrict the purpose of the gathering solely to preparing the petition; some to turn the Convention into a true rival to parliament by styling themselves MCs and enacting 'legislation'; others to develop more extensive plans to intimidate Parliament by organising a run on the banks, a general strike, or resort to 'physical force'. Several of the moderate delegates, including J. P. Cobbett, son of the famous publicist, left the Convention in alarm at the more violent tones of men like Dr Fletcher, the Bury delegate, and Harney with his demands for 'universal suffrage or death'. On 13 May the remaining members of the Convention decided to move to Birmingham, retaining as its motto 'peace, law and order', but only 'so long as our oppressors shall act in the same spirit'.

Up to the move of the Convention to Birmingham, the most serious disturbances occurred when the Convention sent out missionaries to drum up support for the petition. The West Country cloth towns had provided early and enthusiastic support for the Charter, but the arrival of Henry Vincent at the end of March to hold a public meeting in Devizes sparked off an attack by a crowd of 'drunken farmers, lawyers, clerks [and] parsons' led by the under-sheriff. When the meeting was adjourned to an inn, the magistrates and constables only with difficulty prevented the crowd from breaking in. When a second meeting was held on 1 April the local Chartists rallied their forces from Trowbridge, Bradford, Chippenham, and Bromham; when the meeting assembled in the Market Place a hostile crowd attacked with stones and bludgeons: Henry Vincent was knocked senseless and the Chartist banners captured. Although the attack ended Chartist meetings in Devizes, the West Country remained disturbed with reports of arming and small meetings organised by Chartist speakers. At Trowbridge church windows were smashed at the end of April and on 5 June there was a small-scale attack on the barracks in the town. By this time, however, the borough and county magistrates had convened to take measures to preserve public order, assembling 130 police, 600 special constables, a troop of Hussars, and six troops of Yeomanry, as well as special constables and Chelsea pensioners from Bath.[20]

Throughout the winter and spring of 1838–9 the Home Office received reports of arming, drilling, arson, and various revolutionary plots. But although there was considerable excitement among the Chartists as the campaign to organise the petition to parliament got under way and frank alarm from many local authorities, the Government reacted cautiously. It banned torchlight processions and rallies in December 1838 and arrested the Rev. J. R. Stephens, probably the most violent Chartist orator, for a speech he had made at Hyde. The correspondence of some Chartists was opened in the post and troops were moved from Ireland to England; Major-General Sir Charles Napier was appointed commander of the Northern District with 5,000 troops under his control to cover the area north of Nottingham. Drilling was forbidden by a royal proclamation, but the Home Office urged local authorities to call on local resources of special constables, yeomanry, and armed associations, rather than use large numbers of troops. On the whole, the Home Office urged restraint upon the local authorities, as the Home Secretary, Lord John Russell, was determined to avoid any action which would precipitate a series of 'Peterloos' and provide a pretext for armed insurrection. However, in May the arrests of local Chartist leaders began in Wales, Lancashire, and the West Country. At Llanidloes, the arrival of three London policemen with some unpopular special constables from Newtown and Welshpool provoked rioting; the arrest of three local men led to an attack on the inn in which the men were rescued and some of the constables manhandled, one of them being stabbed. The local Chartists did their best to calm the situation, rescuing the policemen and patrolling the town to prevent further disturbances until the military arrived; eventually thirty-two people were arrested, several of whom were imprisoned and four transported; the Government also acted to arrest the local Chartist leaders, Charles Jones and Thomas Powell. The riot, which seems to have been as much the product of anti-police feeling than anything else, was blamed on Powell's oratory and he was imprisoned for twelve months. This incident showed how easily the Chartists would be blamed for any disorder which arose in the atmosphere of 1838-9.[21]

In spite of an excited atmosphere the Devizes and Llanidloes disturbances were the only major disturbances to occur before the reconvening of the Convention at Birmingham on 1 July; even before that date, the Birmingham Bull Ring had become the regular meeting place for the more ardent local Chartists. Although in the past regarded as an exemplar of class harmony, Birmingham Chartists had become radicalised during the winter of 1838-9, increasingly throwing their support behind O'Connor rather than the more moderate Attwood. During early May there were complaints about the almost constant crowds congregating in the Bull Ring to hear addresses from radical speakers and on 10 May the Magistrates prohibited all public meetings. Some of the Chartist orators, notably John Fussell, were ready to make this a test case of their determination to assert the right of free speech. At an open-air meeting on the outskirts of Birmingham at Holloway Head, Fussell affirmed the right to meet where they liked; if he were arrested, he claimed Birmingham would be made a 'hell on earth'. In fact, he was arrested without serious trouble by a magistracy now backed up by 2,300 special constables and two companies of riflemen. But even after his arrest, meetings continued in the Bull Ring, in spite of petty prosecutions for obstructing the traffic. The adjournment of the Chartist Convention to Birmingham left the Mayor, William Scholefield in a dilemma. Having failed to cow the local Chartists by 45s. fines, he was faced with the prospect of nightly gatherings of an excited local population with the added stimulus of some of the most famous popular leaders of the day to encourage them; the mayor therefore sent for reinforcements of sixty policemen from London, who arrived on the evening of 4 July. Proceeding virtually straight to the Bull Ring, where a meeting was taking place, the Mayor called on the crowd to disperse. On their failing to do so the police baton-charged the crowd, who armed themselves with pieces of wood and iron railings and defended themselves until troops were called in to add their weight to the police. During the next two days further clashes took place as police and soldiers attempted to clear the streets. The Bull Ring meetings were suppressed and the magistrates arrested two of the Chartist leaders, William Lovett and John Collins, who were imprisoned in Warwick Gaol. A week later a further disturbance took place in the Bull Ring when a mob of boys followed a Chartist procession protesting about the arrest of Lovett and Collins and burned two houses and looted shops.[22]

By the time this disturbance had occurred, the first Chartist petition had been refused a hearing in the House of Commons by 235 votes to 46.

The remaining members of the Convention were now faced with the awkward dilemma of how next to proceed. Rejecting the idea of another petition, the delegates first voted for a 'Sacred Month' (a general strike to start on 12 August), then abandoned it when it became obvious they had insufficient support. Moreover the growing toll of arrests did much to deter the delegates from taking any step which might precipitate wholesale repression. A series of clashes between Chartist supporters and strikers in the North-East culminated in the 'Battle of the Forth' on 30 July when police and soldiers broke up a Chartist meeting, an incident remembered by R. G. Gammage as the 'Peterloo of Newcastle', but which led to no serious casualties. Although further disturbances occurred during the summer at Bolton, Ashton, and Loughborough, and some districts of Lancashire and the North-East struck work in support of the 'Sacred Month', the arrest of Chartist leaders, the extensive preparations of the authorities, and the disintegration of support left the Convention increasingly isolated. After further days of discussion at the end of August and early September, it voted to dissolve itself on 6 September.[23]

In fact the dissolution of the Convention preceded the major outbreak of disorder in the year. Although September was described by Napier as a month of 'unvarying quietude', some of the remaining leaders, notably Peter Bussy, William Cardo, Julian Harney, and Dr Taylor began to make plans for a rising in which the Welsh were to take a leading part. The full nature of these plans is not clear and they present the same difficulties of interpretation as earlier episodes of conspiracy, mainly because many of the Chartist leaders who did know something of the plans for an insurrectionary attempt in the winter of 1839–40 tended later to play down their role. The story of the Newport Rising on the night of 3–4 November has been told in full elsewhere by Professor David Williams.[24] The crucial incident had occurred before the dissolution of the Convention with the arrest of Henry Vincent on 7 May: an immensely popular figure with the industrial workers of Monmouthshire, his arrest seemed to herald a declaration of war on the Chartists and encouraged the 'physical force' party. The Convention delegate from the area, John Frost, who was later to be charged with treason for his part in the Newport 'rising' in fact warned William Lovett as early as May that Vincent's arrest would lead either to a complete collapse of Chartism in the area or to an insurrectionary outbreak. Frost, an ex-magistrate dismissed from the bench for his Chartist activities, was himself by autumn under the threat of prosecution for using 'violent and inflammatory language' at a demonstration earlier in the year, and appears to have oscillated between moderation and active conspiracy, pushed on in the latter by the militant temper of the Monmouthshire workers and two of his local aides, William Jones and Zephaniah Williams. As late as 3 October Frost urged the staging of a peaceful mass demonstration to secure the release of Vincent, but was opposed by Williams and Jones. In spite of Frost's seeming reluctance to take part in any conspiracy, the Northern leaders by 29

October knew of a rising to take place in South Wales on 3 November; according to one account, O'Connor was to lead it once they were under way, but he left for Ireland on 4 October and did not return until 6 November. To this day the full extent of the plan remains obscure, but, at the very least, large numbers of Monmouthshire Chartists were prepared to make an armed demonstration against Newport to secure Vincent's release.

On the evening of Sunday 3 November contingents of Chartists from Blackwood, Nantyglo, and Pontypool, led by Frost, Williams, and Jones respectively, marched through a wet and stormy night towards Newport. Jones returned to Pontypool, ostensibly to seek reinforcements, and when by Monday morning he had not returned Frost and Williams pressed on without him. The authorities had by this time received warning of the attack and placed twenty-eight soldiers in the upper rooms of the Westport Hotel. When the Chartists converged on the building they fired a few shots, but were taken almost completely by surprise when a volley came in reply from the troops causing them to break and run, leaving fifteen dead and the authorities with a relatively simple job of rounding up prisoners. Frost, Williams, and Jones were eventually tried for high treason and condemned to death in January 1840, a sentence ultimately commuted to transportation for life. Throughout his examination and trial, Frost alleged that he had simply wanted to mount a demonstration, and Professor Williams has argued that this appears the most likely explanation for what occurred, even if some of the contingent may have thought otherwise. Frost's dilemma was that he had either to join the demonstration with whatever consequences might fall on him if it got out of hand or was misconstrued by the authorities, or of deserting the cause and being branded a traitor. It was an unenviable predicament and Frost nearly paid with his life.

Although the evidence for a wider conspiracy in the autumn of 1839 remains inconclusive, it is almost certain that parts of Yorkshire, especially Bradford and Halifax, were involved in plans for a rising; there is evidence too, that in the North-East Ainge Devyr awaited a signal. Frost's failure ruined any immediate chance of success, but by the end of the year widespread rumours of plots to rescue him or precipitate an insurrection were in common circulation, leading Napier to warn his local commanders to take necessary precautions. The centre of the conspiracy was a secret committee at Dewsbury, where representatives met from several parts of the North and settled on 12 January as the date for the rising. By the end of December men such as Samuel Holberry from Sheffield were touring South Yorkshire and the Midlands in order to raise support. For a time it appeared that O'Connor would be ready to act as leader once the rising was under way, but like other radical leaders before him he was reluctant to become involved in a conspiracy until it was seen to be successful; fearing its failure, he withdrew his support and counselled his followers against joining it.

Nonetheless, preparations went ahead in Yorkshire with plans for

12 January. The Dewsbury Chartists were to rise independently, as were those at Sheffield, with other joining when the signal reached them through the stopping of the mail coaches. On the 12th, 100 men armed with bludgeons and guns marched through Dewsbury, fired some shots in the Market Place, but then dispersed. At Sheffield, Holberry, an ex-soldier, planned to create diversions by firing isolated houses and barracks, and then marching 400 armed men into the centre of Sheffield during the early hours of the 12th to seize and barricade the Town Hall and Tontine Inn. In fact, the Sheffield plans were betrayed and Holberry was arrested at midnight before he could begin his 'diversions'; the bulk of his followers dispersed; only about fifty 'rose' at 2.00 a.m., and they either fled or were arrested after skirmishes with the authorities in which some watchmen were wounded.[25]

There is some evidence that had the Dewsbury and Sheffield risings been successful, other places might have joined in. On the 11th it was reported that coaches from Sheffield were being stopped in neighbouring towns by workmen who wanted to know if Sheffield was up in arms; an anonymous informer told the head of the Metropolitan police that two armed meetings, held in Bethnal Green on 14 and 16 January were part of the same scheme.[26] Newcastle, too, was once again said to be awaiting the signal, and on the 26th there was an attempt to take Bradford, led by a Scottish radical, Robert Peddie, but this plan was betrayed and the whole effort ended in complete failure.[27]

Thus as on several occasions in the past, a few activists had led their followers in an insurrectionary attempt which lacked the coordinated and widespread support necessary for any chance of success. The plan for simultaneous risings was not intrinsically a bad one, but the problems of maintaining secrecy and at the same time ensuring a wide basis of support presented an almost insuperable task. Whether, if these technical difficulties had been overcome, the rising would have received wide support is a question which it is probably futile to attempt to answer. Nevertheless, these failed attempts are clear evidence that some Chartists had retained a belief, however misplaced, in the possibilities of a successful insurrection.

By the spring of 1840 Chartism was in retreat. The failures of the previous year and a growing toll of arrests and prosecutions deprived the agitation of most of its momentum. Many moderate supporters were frightened off by the Newport episode and the attempts of January, while even some of the more determined were forced to proceed more cautiously in the face of a wave of arrests which totalled over 500 by the early summer. Faced with a government which was prepared to pick off local leaders at the first sign of illegal activity, many Chartists had to learn to live with a policy of 'gradualism' whether they liked it or not. The upshot was the formation of the National Charter Association in July 1840, a legal, nationwide body which would provide a federal structure for local wards and councils. By 1842 the National Charter Association had 48,000 members and provided the basis on which the Chartists reorganised for the presentation of a second petition to parliament in May 1842. Once again, however, the Charter was refused a hearing by a large majority in the Commons.

The 'Plug-plot' riots and the general strike of 1842

The failure of the second national petition left the Chartists with the familiar problem of what to do when constitutional methods failed. Once again there was talk of violence and angry meetings were held in some of the centres of Chartist support, but the national leaders seemed unprepared to take any steps which might again initiate a cycle of arrest and prosecution. However, the year of 1842 provided a different kind of opportunity, for serious trade depression and high prices produced one of the most disturbed years of the century. Probably at no point in the 1840s did the 'Condition of England' question seem more acute, and in March the Home Secretary reported that a tenth of the total population was on poor relief. As depression, unemployment, and wage cuts spread in the spring and summer, one of the factory inspectors reported that the operatives had either to choose 'employment on any terms, or starvation'. As the price of wheat and bread rose to new heights in July, one of the traditional months for food riots in the past, a series of strikes began which were eventually to embroil fifteen counties in a movement which was regarded by the Home Secretary, Sir John Graham, as being more serious than the events of 1839. By the time of its peak in August 1842 the attempt to turn the stoppages into a 'general strike' for the Charter added another dimension to what was initially a purely economic movement.

The strikes began in the North Staffordshire coalfield in early July, against wage cuts and truck payments. A prominent feature was the drawing of plugs from the boilers of pit engines to enforce a stoppage; colliers also marched around the district forcing other pits to stop work, some reaching as far north as Stockport. At the end of the month strikes broke out in the Ashton cotton mills against a 25 per cent wage cut; and by early August there were extensive strikes in the Lanarkshire coalfield and further stoppages in East Lancashire, especially around Stalybridge and Ashton. Touring groups of striking workers carried the stoppage to new areas, bringing 130 mills to a standstill in Manchester, and drawing plugs from factory boilers in many parts of Lancashire, Cheshire, and Staffordshire. Strikes also spread to West Yorkshire, the East Midlands, the North-East and South Wales.[28]

The objectives of the crowds of 'turn-outs' who moved around Lancashire and Cheshire were primarily to enforce the stoppage for better wages, shorter hours, lower rents, and an end to truck payments. Usually the crowds were intimidating rather than violent, but some more serious clashes took place, especially when the strikers were opposed: a girl was killed by missiles thrown from a roof at a factory in Stalybridge at the end of July, and on 6 August a police station at Newton was demolished and two constables fatally injured; at Stockport the workhouse was attacked and troops wounded seven people at Salford; at Preston there was a serious riot on the 13th when a crowd attacked soldiers with stones and refused to give their ground when the Riot Act was read and the soldiers opened fire, killing five people. Not untypical, if less bloody, were the events at Macclesfield where a crowd, augmented it was said by 'a mob from Stockport and Bollington', attacked Brocklehurst's factory. One of its defenders recorded:

> The leaders thundered on the door. 'Where are the masters?' they inquired. 'In the counting house,' we replied. 'Show us the way in,' they said. We took them in as we had been instructed to do. From the masters they inquired, 'Will you turn all the workpeople out of the mill?' 'Yes,' was the reply. 'Will you let us see the engine fires put out?' 'Yes, if you do no injury,' was the reply. So out went the fires and out went the workpeople into the streets.[29]

From the second week of August, however, the strike took on a new aspect when a meeting of trade delegates in Manchester attempted to turn it into a strike for the Charter. Some meetings early in the month has already embraced the Charter as one of the strike's objectives, a meeting on Mottram Moor near Stalybridge on 7 August declared for 'a fair day's wage for a fair day's work', but also that 'all labour shall cease until the People's Charter becomes the law of the land'. Moreover, some of the local strike leaders were men who had been engaged in Chartist activity and now saw the stoppage as a means of resurrecting the idea of the 'Sacred Month' – the almost millenarian 'Grand National Holiday' which in William Benbow's words would 'disorganise the whole fabric of the old world, and transfer, by a sudden spring, the whole political government of the country from the master to the servant'.[30] Delegates were sent out into the areas where strikes were going on to convert the industrial stoppages into a strike for the Charter. One of these missionary endeavours led to some of the most severe rioting when the Leicester Chartist Thomas Cooper addressed a meeting of striking miners at Hanley in the Potteries on Sunday 14 August. A further meeting was held early the next day attended by several thousand people, but after voting in favour of the resolution 'that all labour cease until the People's Charter becomes the law of the land' the crowd marched away and began a two day riot during which the house of Lord Granville's mine agent was burnt down, the police office demolished, the debtor's court invaded and its records destroyed, and pits and potteries stopped from working. Arriving in Stoke the crowd destroyed another police station, then broke into bread shops, and attacked and plundered the houses of some clergymen. The houses of a lawyer and a stipendiary magistrate were also destroyed. On the morning of the 16th, crowds of miners assembled with large sticks and marched on Burslem, where they attacked an inn and fought with soldiers and special constables. When the commander of the troops, Major Powys, rode out of the town to intercept a party from Leek, Congleton and Macclesfield and asked them what they wanted, they replied 'Our rights and liberties, the Charter, and more to eat'. Having failed to persuade them to disperse and coming under volleys of stones, the troops opened fire, killing one man and wounding several others. Gradually troops brought the situation under control, but the extent of the disturbances can be gauged by the scale of arrests, 800 in all. Further disturbances occurred towards the end of the month, when the strike began to break down and the Riot Act was read at Kingswinford and Dudley. In October a Special Commission tried 276 men from the Potteries and the Black Country, five of whom were transported for life.[31]

There were also serious disturbances as the strike movement spread to Yorkshire. Frank Peel recorded how as a child he has seen a 'compact mass of 25,000 men' march from Todmorden and Bradford to close the mills at Halifax.

> The sight was just one of those which it is impossible to forget. They came pouring down the wide road in thousands, taking up its whole breadth – a gaunt, famished-looking desperate multitude, armed with huge bludgeons, flails, pitch-forks and pikes, many without coats and hats and hundred upon hundreds with their clothes in rags and tatters. Many of the older men looked sore and weary, but the great bulk were men in the prime of life, full of wild excitement. As they marched they thundered out to a grand old tune a stirring melody, of which this was the opening stanza:
> 'Men of England, ye are slaves
> Though ye rule the roaring waves,
> Though ye shout, From sea to sea
> Britons everywhere are free.'[32]

Events in Halifax took a still more violent turn the next day when a troop of cavalry returning from escorting prisoners to Elland railway station was ambushed at Salterhebble by crowds of people who had gathered on hearing news of the removal of the prisoners. Showering the troops with stones from the rooftops and the neighbouring hillside, they knocked two soldiers from their horses, one of whom subsequently died, and wrecked the carriage used to carry the prisoners; the soldiers then brought up reinforcements who fired on the crowds, killing two people and wounding several others. An eye-witness, Benjamin Wilson, commented that 'those who attacked the soldiers at Salthebble were neither Lancashire people or people from a distance, but principally young men from the surrounding districts; the mills had been stopped about two days. The struggle was short, but fierce'.[33]

Meanwhile in Manchester a national conference of the National Charter Association and conferences of the trade delegates continued to meet attended by large crowds. These trade delegates' meetings were originally distinct from the NCA meeting, but by 12 August had accepted a general strike until the Charter was accepted. On the 16th, however, the magistrates broke up the meeting and began to arrest its members. Although a minority of delegates began at this point to talk in terms of militant action, most continued to urge their followers to maintain 'peace, law and order' and rely on the strike to carry the day. But by the end of August, support for the strike was crumbling. The trades had insufficient resources to maintain their members during a season of high food prices and unemployment; attempts to mobilise the support of shopkeepers in order to extend credit failed and a drift back to work began accompanied by widespread arrests of the strike leaders.

The general strike of 1842 was testimony to the well-tried strike tactics of some of the Northern trades by the 1840s. Delegate conferences and coordinated strike action had been a feature of earlier disputes, but the acceptance by trade delegates of the political objectives of the Charter was new: for a time at least, an alliance between the trades and the Charter had been forged. It was not universal, nor was it to last. Several groups of strikers maintained more interest in their immediate economic objectives; moreover many of trade delegates represented the skilled 'labour aristocracy' or the declining handicraft trades rather than the staple industries. The cotton operatives, miners, and potters were less well represented and their adherence to the Charter was often only temporary;[34] some groups of workers, notably the potters, actively resented the intrusion of Chartist orators as 'outsiders' and retreated after 1842 into an acrimonious relationship.[35]

Although the 'Plug-plot' riots were the most serious of the 1840s, one of the most remarkable features of the episode was the emphasis placed by the trades delegates and Chartist leaders on orderliness. Time and again the strike organisers sought to prevent any outbreak of disorder which might provoke repression. In fact, this was an almost hopeless task given their only partial control over the strike wave and the severe distress of many of the workers, nonetheless it reflected the continuing emphasis of many Chartists and early trade unionists on moral rather than physical force. For trade union organisers, as we have seen, it was already a dominant theme in the conduct of strikes. It was hardly surprising that they carried this over in the infinitely more dangerous situation of a political strike. Given the warning of the treason charge used against Frost and the already high number of arrests and trials prior to 1842, it was little wonder that the 'moral force' party of the Chartists and the trade delegates should have attempted to avoid any opportunity for repression; even so, by October over 1,000 arrests had been made and 749 people imprisoned for various offences.[36]

Although the acceptance of the Charter by many of the strikers in the summer of 1842 marked it out as a significant development from what had occurred in the past, the disturbances revealed many traditional features. While the Chartists and Anti-Corn Law League were widely blamed for the 'Plug-plot', the strike movement had begun and was conducted in a similar way to earlier movements. Itinerant bands, enforcing a stoppage by damaging pit machinery, quenching engine boilers, and intimidating non-strikers had been seen many times in the past. Chartist and trade union leaders might counsel non-violence, but the plunder of provision shops and houses as occurred at Stockport and the Pottery towns were clearly a throwback to other incidents in the early nineteenth century; they were not traditional food riots, but nor were they the considered and pacific actions increasing sought by the more moderate working class leaders. In this, as in so many other ways, the disturbances of the summer of 1842 were transitional: they combined the most sophisticated tactic of all – a general strike organised and led by trade delegates – with less directed incidents of violence and looting.

The disturbances of 1848 and the National Petition

A poor harvest and trade depression in 1847 contributed to a revival of Chartist agitation. The average price of wheat in 1847 was higher than any previous year since 1819, with the one expection of 1839, and the average price of bread was higher than in any year since 1812. Food riots broke out in some of the remoter parts of the British Isles, mainly in Scotland and the West Country, while spring 1848 witnessed disturbances in several large cities. At Glasgow on 6 March several thousand unemployed and poor who had assembled to receive meal provided by a relief committee marched on the City Hall to see the treasurer and secretary of the fund because of a complaint about the quality of the food. Ordered to leave the building, the crowd divided into two groups who ransacked gunsmiths, jewellers, and breadshops. Marching past the Exchange, some fired the guns in the air before being restrained by troops. It was reported that the majority were Irish, and 'chiefly lads in bonnets and fustian jackets'. The following day there was an attempt to seize the gasworks and stop mills, but the workmen manned the walls and 'bade the rioters defiance'. A small group of 'pensioners' (veteran soldiers) were trapped by a crowd who pelted them heavily with stones until they eventually opened fire, killing two outright and fatally wounding three others. Far from being cowed the mob carried the dead body of one of their number back into central Glasgow, to cries of 'Blood for blood' and marched right up to the muzzles of a line of soldiers drawn up to stop them: for a moment it appeared that a bloody confrontation would ensue, but the agitators were eventually persuaded to move away without further violence.[37]

Two days later disturbances broke out in Manchester when groups of youths began barracking paupers entering the temporary Tib Street workhouse and insulting those who maintained the 'Bastilles'. Over the next two or three days slogans calling on the unemployed to meet together were chalked on the walls, and people entering the workhouse were jostled or, in the case of girls, stripped of their clothes. Parading round the town, the youths tried to persuade mills to close, but in almost every case they were resisted by those at work; on one occasion the hands issued from the factory to beat up the youths assembled at the gate, and elsewhere armed themselves to protect the factories in which they worked. In one of the last incidents a group of men and boys marched down Chester Street following a boy with a loaf stuck on the end of a pole before they were broken up by the police. These disturbances owed little or nothing to Chartist activity. The *Manchester Guardian* commented somewhat haughtily that 'mobs more insignificant, in point of moral or physical force or number, it has never been our lot to witness; and it is scarcely necessary to say that they were wholly without any political object whatsoever, but that of creating a sensation and doing mischief to the extent of their ability'. The local Chartist leaders agreed, blaming the disturbances on 'mischievous imps and lads' and offering to help to preserve the peace. In fact, the disturbances were really a protest about the imposition of the 'labour test' of picking oakum for several hours a day in order to qualify for relief; meetings to protest about oakum-picking were a regular feature in Manchester during the spring, groups of up to several thousand unemployed meeting in Stevenson Square. The action of the youths appears to have been an attempt to take some direct action against the labour test, but one which broke down when faced with the refusal of other unemployed or workmen to join in.[38]

The distress of which these disturbances were symptoms had encouraged Chartist hopes for another large-scale agitation in order to petition parliament. As early as 1845 the idea of a petition with five million signatures was being mooted and this project was already under way by the winter of 1847–8. As well as renewed disturbances in the country, the Chartist revival also received stimulus from the revolutions occurring on the continent. The February Revolution in France was celebrated by meetings in several Chartist strongholds in the North and comparisons between England and France became the common fare of Chartist orators; the *Northern Star* openly rejoiced at the flight of the French monarch and declared that 'as France has secured for herself her Republic, so Ireland must have her Parliament restored and England her idolised Charter'. Ominously, the rioters in Glasgow were reported to have shouted 'Bread or revolution' and '*Vive la République*'.[39] The fall of European monarchies led some Chartists to see themselves as part of a wider struggle and to encourage the more militant into hoping that the meeting of a new Convention in April would be only the preliminary to more forceful measures. When the Convention met on 3 April in London, some at least of the delegates talked of 'ulterior measures' to be adopted should the petition, now allegedly totalling almost six million signatures, be rejected. Some advocated the calling of a large assembly to consider what these measures might be, while the London journalist G. M. Reynolds moved that if the petition were refused the Convention should declare itself in permanent session and proclaim the Charter as the law of the land. In the event the Executive, dominated by O'Connor, won the day; the petition was to remain the focus of attention and the Chartists were to rely once again on the ambiguities of 'moral force' to carry the day against a reluctant parliament and Government. Should the petition fail, the Convention was to prepare a National Memorial to the Queen to dissolve the present parliament and 'call to her council such ministers only as will make the People's a cabinet measure'. A National Assembly would meet to prepare the Memorial, to continue in permanent session until the Charter were accepted. Friday, 21 April was set for meetings in support of the Memorial and the election of delegates to the National Assembly which would meet on 24 April.

The Chartist strategy was not the ignorant folly it was sometimes later to be dubbed. Clearly many Chartists expected the petition to be refused and prepared their plans accordingly; arming and drilling were again under way among the more militant in Lancashire and Yorkshire, while even those who believed that only 'moral force' could work might hope that the published plans for an Assembly might serve to persuade the Government that this time the Charter was irresistible. In part at least, the plans for the rejection of the petition were a strategy of bluff, to give it some chance of acceptance. The Charter was to be carried in procession to the House of Commons on Monday 10 April, following a mass demonstration on Kennington Common on the south bank of the Thames, only a mile from Westminster as the crow flies. Mass meetings were also to be held in the provinces to demonstrate the overwhelming support for the Charter. These preparations were conducted openly and the Chartists publicly announced their determination to meet and make an 'unarmed moral demonstration' for the Charter.

If the plan was by no means as naïve as has sometimes been represented, it nonetheless contained a number of weaknesses. The most obvious was that the Government might choose to call the Chartist's bluff. While some of the militants assumed that the 'real work' would start after the 10th, a great deal of emotional capital had been invested in the petition and its reception was bound to have an important effect on morale. Moreover, while a mass demonstration in the capital might have considerable symbolic advantages for intimidating parliament, it also increased the risks of a confrontation with the authorities in which the Chartists would either have to fight or back down. Traditionally, the government had always been wary of large meetings in the capital and it was hardly likely to allow the Chartists a free hand to dictate terms to the country. As recently as 6 March, the Whig Government had banned a meeting in Trafalgar Square to protest against a rise in income tax; when the meeting took place under the auspices of the journalist G. W. Reynolds the police broke it up, resulting in fighting in the Square and surrounding streets for the next two or three evenings.[40]

The attitude of the Government was clearly critical to Chartist plans. But if they hoped that it was to be panicked or overawed they were very much mistaken. Dr Mather has argued that although the preparations made to deal with the demonstration on the 10th were extensive, they were less evidence of panic than of the Government's desire to strengthen its domestic and external position by making a firm stand and prevent the Chartists approaching parliament.[41] This was the critical decision, for it stood in marked contrast to the behaviour of the Peel administration in May 1842. This had allowed the Chartists to carry their petition to parliament in a huge two-mile long procession which had started out from Lincoln's Inn Fields. Instead, in 1848, a somewhat reluctant administration was prevailed upon by the 'hawkish' sections of opinion, led by the Duke of Wellington, and the influential sections of middle-class opinion in the capital, represented by *The Times*, to leave nothing to chance. Dr Large has concluded that 'it was a combination of pressure from the hysterically excited and consciousness of how this might be exploited to the government's political advantage that led to the massive overkill of 10 April'.[42] It was an 'overkill' which left all the advantages with the government. Although Wellington was brought in to advise the Cabinet on preparations for the defence of the capital and had been busy drawing up elaborate schemes for the purpose, the principal planning was carried out by the Metropolitan Police.[43]

Having decided to make a show of force, the Government acted carefully and methodically. Arrangements were made to police the provincial meetings and communications ensured through the takeover of the Telegraph Company. Shorthand reports by the police as well as the public statements of the Convention provided the government with a reasonably reliable account of how the demonstration was likely to proceed. Perhaps most crucial of all, especially in the light of Peterloo, Chartists were banned from presenting their petition *en masse*, as being contrary to an Act of Charles II against 'tumultuous petitioning', the meeting itself was not banned and a small number of Chartists were to be allowed to present their petition. As a result, the authorities were not in any way committed to breaking up the Chartist meeting, but if any disorder occurred, it would quite clearly be blamed on the Chartists.

In this almost symbolic confrontation between the forces of 'order' and the Chratists, the press played a crucial role. In an important respect, the Chartists had been losing the initiative in the war of propaganda which had been waged by the radical press for almost half a century. Where once the middle-class press had been an ally of reform, it was almost universally hostile to the Chartists. For a time, the spectacularly successful *Northern Star* looked as though it could provide an outlet for Chartist ideas which would rival the London dailies and the provincial press, but though it had a meteoric rise, reaching a circulation of over 50,000 a week in 1839, by 1844 it had fallen to a mere 7,000. *The Times* alone sold 30,000 copies a day by February 1848, reflecting the major proportion of an aggregate sale for London dailies of 60,000; Sunday newspapers sold still more, over a quarter of a million, while the provincial press dwarfed even these figures.[44] Although radical news-papers still existed, a few of which supported the Chartists, the overwhelming coverage of their activities lay in the hands of a press which, while becoming more 'political' in a party sense, was also becoming profoundly conservative.[45] Thus in 1848 one of the most pertinent features was a growing press campaign which depicted the Chartists as the likely authors of outrage and violence. Events both on the continent and in the country provided a theme of social chaos for the newspapers; for example, *The Times* had no hesitation in blaming the disturbances on 6 March in London on 'the Chartist rabble' and speculation about social revolution spreading to England from the continent grew apace.[46]

Faced by a determined Government and a largely hostile press, another difficulty was whether London Chartism could provide the numbers necessary for an intimidating and impressive show of support. The relative strength of London Chartism is still a matter of debate, but it had certainly proved disappointing on the occasion of the first petition in 1839. It had sufficiently strengthened by 1842 to provide 200,000 signatures for the petition of that year and to host thirty-eight Chartist meeting places. Although the capital probably reached support approaching the same level in 1847-8, the familiar problems of mobilising metropolitan opinion remained. While London had its share of the declining craft industries which provided so much support for the Charter elsewhere in the country, the very variety of its manufacturing and service industries tended to lessen the impact of trade depression because not all trades were likely to be depressed at the same time. The worst areas of poverty in the notorious 'rookeries' of St Giles or Saffron Hill were not noted for their political activism. The most fertile sources of Chartist support lay in the numerous trades of the East End, but even here the Spitalfields' weavers remained less responsive than some of the handworkers in the provinces. Perhaps most important of all, the impact of Chartist support, however significant in absolute terms, was always likely to be diffused in a vast metropolis of two and a half million people.[47]

The mood of the authorities was shown on 13 March when a meeting called on Kennington Common to celebrate the French Revolution was treated almost as a dress rehearsal for 10 April: the troops were called out to guard the bridges across the river and important public buildings, 20,000 special constables were mobilised and 2,000 metropolitan policemen put on duty. Although there were only some minor scuffles after the meeting, the mounting hysteria of the London press ensured that the Chartist convention and the presentation of the petition would be attended with considerable public alarm. So it proved. The preparations made to guard the capital were among the most extensive ever seen; 8,148 regular troops and 1,231 'pensioners' composed the military force to deal with any serious disorder, backed up by thirty pieces of artillery in the Tower ready to be carried by hired river steamer wherever they were needed. The troops were placed in detachments to support the civil forces and to garrison the major public buildings, the most important, such as the Bank of England, being barricaded with sandbags and provided with loopholes. Virtually the whole force of the metropolitan police, over 4,000 men, was to provide the first line of defence, supported by large numbers of special constables. By 6 April the Duke of Wellington was able to inform the Prime Minister that an attempt by the Chartists to march on parliament could be stopped at any point the Government chose; on the same day, it was officially announced in parliament that the procession to present the petition would be prohibited, and notices to this effect were posted throughout the capital. Attempts by Chartist leaders to assure the Home Secretary of their peaceful intentions were of no avail and the procession remained prohibited, while the Convention delegates had unanimously declared that it must proceed.

As the 10th approached, one of the most significant features was the response of the metropolitan middle classes to the 'patriotic' call to join up as special constables. The response was remarkable. In the absence of a definitive return of all the constables sworn in, we have to rely on press estimates which varied between 120,000 and 200,000 on duty by the day of the Kennington Common meeting. Something approaching a popular 'fad' for volunteering affected the capital, reminiscent of the invasion scares of the Napoleonic period and perhaps not paralleled again until the outbreak of the First World War. The Chartist 'threat' seemed to tap deep reserves of support for the established order which embraced people as diverse as William Gladstone, Prince Louis Napoleon, and even some of the London trades; indeed, one group of recruits to the special constabulary were the London coalheavers, who, having come to a favourable settlement with their employers in 1843, now proceeded in a body to the Mansion House to be sworn in as specials and protect the capital against the Chartists.[48] The workmen of some of the larger industrial concerns were also sworn in *en bloc*, though under how much duress is unknown. Nevertheless, there was no mistaking that a great rallying of the propertied classes was taking place and that the newly sworn in special constables were to be given, with the police, the major task of policing the capital, with the troops acting as a reserve and only to be used if necessary.

When the Convention reassembled on the morning of the 10th, Fergus O'Connor was faced with a dilemma which had dogged extra-parliamentary agitation for years. Faced with a Government ban, could the Chartists risk the consequences of trying to force their way to the House of Commons? In words which might have been uttered by Henry Hunt thirty years earlier, O'Connor made a last appeal to the Convention to abandon the plan of the procession in case it should 'throw their cause into the hands of pickpockets and scoundrels, and give the Government an opportunity of attacking them'. Unimpressed, the delegates joined the organised bands of Chartists making their way from various venues toward Kennington Common. True to their earlier professions, the Chartists were unarmed and organised by their own marshals. The usual caps of liberty, tricolours, and cockades were in evidence, as well as bands and banners with slogans such as 'Voice of the People' and 'Universal Suffrage'. The petition was loaded onto a great cart drawn by horses from the Land Company estate at Snig's End. Although O'Connor had urged the Chartists to leave him to present the petition alone should Kennington Common prove to be occupied by police or troops, the meeting was allowed to assemble according to plan. The number which gathered was variously estimated at between '400,000 and 500,000' (O'Connor) and *The Standard's* 9,000–10,000. The police estimated somewhere between 12,000 and 20,000 and these were the figures reported by Russell to the Queen and by *The Times*. Dr Large has calculated that the Common itself could not have held more than 54,560 people packed tightly into its 13,640 square yards.[49] At 11.30 a.m. Police Commissioner Mayne and Superintendent Malalieu arrived and summoned O'Connor to a conference where he was told that the procession would be opposed and that he would be held responsible for any consequences should it take place. These were ominous in the light of the fate of Frost and other Chartist leaders, not to mention the fate of Lord George Gordon seventy years earlier. O'Connor, tired, ill and looking 'pale and frightened', readily agreed to the ban on the procession and to allow the petition to be taken by cab to the Commons; he then returned to the meeting to report his account of the interview and urge his followers to disperse peacefully. By 2.00 p.m. the crowd had dwindled to about 5,000 and was reported to be dispersing quietly.

While the Charter was being conveyed peacefully by cab to the House of Commons and the authorities breathed a collective sigh of relief, the provincial meetings also passed off without disturbance. During the weekend of 7–10 April Manchester presented a similar scene, if in miniature; 11,000 specials were mobilised, cannons were placed in the streets, and cavalry with drawn swords paraded the town. The Manchester Chartists held their main meeting on Sunday, the 9th, at Smithfield market, attended by between 8,000 and 20,000 people, believed by the *Manchester Guardian* one of the largest ever held in the city. Smaller meetings were held in other towns in the cotton districts, some on the 9th, others on the 10th; none of them provoked any disturbances, although there were reports of parties of armed men moving towards Manchester who were disuaded by the show of force put up by the local authorities. In Sheffield a meeting of an estimated 10,000 people on Monday afternoon, also passed off quietly.[50]

Chartism was not killed by the events of 10 April. To some Chartists the petition was always likely to be rejected and they had planned accordingly. But it was certainly a defeat for those who retained any faith in the 'language of menace' to make the Charter the law of the land. Militants almost vied with each other to find a sufficiently damning description of the uselessness of moral force in the circumstances of 1848 – the Manchester delegate to the Convention declaring that one might as well 'whistle a jig to a millstone' as present petitions to the House of

Commons. But although Chartists might declare after the event that the Kennington Common meeting was unimportant, it had taken two sides to make a confrontation. If the Government had overreacted, the Chartists had done little to avoid the trap laid for them. They had allowed themselves to be outmanoeuvred in such a way that the 10th could be celebrated by Government and the bulk of the press as a triumph of 'order' over the forces of chaos and anarchy; moreover, the campaign was to be even further discredited by the exposure of some of the signatures on the petition as forgeries or nonsense names; even dedicated Chartist leaders in the provinces could not escape the sense of having been outwitted, one at least laying the blame on 'the lying statements of a corrupt press'.[51]

But plans for simultaneous meetings on Good Friday, 21 April, went ahead. Large meetings were held outside Halifax and Bradford, and smaller ones in Lancashire and the Midlands.[52] While 'physical force' and arming was strongly advocated at some of these, it was plain that serious divisions about tactics remained. Some moderate Chartists took the view that the best chance of gaining their objectives lay in broadening their basis of support with middle-class allies, even at the expense of compromising their programmes, others turned again to conspiracy and insurrectionary plotting. The situation was in some ways analogous to what it had been in the winter of 1839–40, with the important difference that some Chartists now saw their struggle in an international perspective. The Irish influence had become quite pronounced and the Government was seriously concerned about the links between the Chartists and the insurrectionary plans of the 'Young Ireland' movement which were also coming to fruition in the spring and early summer of 1848.[53] As in 1839–40, the full story remains uncharted. One centre of activity was London, where there were reports of meetings on Clerkenwell Green during May, followed by parades of armed Chartist supporters through the streets on the edge of the City of London. The Government was sufficiently alarmed to initiate another spate of arrests and to ban all further meetings, but there were clashes with the police in the East End on 4 June when groups of Chartists persisted in their efforts to meet. Although these disturbances were more serious than anything that had happened in the capital earlier in the year, they offered little real threat in the face of the mobilisation of police and soldiers to deal with them.

Reports that the 12 June had been set as the date for an insurrection led to another confrontation between the authorities and the London Chartists. Large numbers of police and soldiers were posted to prevent a meeting at Bonner's Fields in Bethnal Green; faced with a choice between a pitched battle with the authorities and abandoning the meeting, the principal speaker, Peter McDougal, advised those who had assembled to disperse rather than risk inevitable defeat. After a few minor scuffles with the police, the meeting broke up.[54]

Reports linked the activities of the London Chartists with renewed conspiracies in the North. Drilling and purchase of arms was undoubtedly taking place in some areas and at Bradford pikes were reported to be openly on sale; in Manchester supporters of repeal of the Union and local Chartists made common cause to hold meetings at the end of May. Rumours of plans to stop the mills and that armed bands from the neighbouring towns would descend on Manchester led the local authorities to ban the meetings. Widespread arrests of known leaders took place in several northern towns at the end of May. One of the biggest operations took place at Bradford, where 3,000 were reported to have drilled openly. The arrest of two men by the police, backed by 200 infantry, two troops of dragoons and 1,000 special constables, led to serious fighting in which the prisoners were rescued and the magistrates' clerk attacked by a crowd who threatened to drop him from a bridge into the Aire. When the authorities tried to take a reputed pike-maker, they were resisted by a large crowd who blocked the street and assailed the police with stones and bludgeons; eventually, the dragoons fought their way through the police and cleared the area.[55]

Concern about insurrectionary plots continued and further arrests took place in London in which quantities of powder and shot were seized. Subsequent trials specified the night of 14–15 August as the planned occasion for a rising. In the North, a number of disturbances occurred on that night. The plan appears to have followed the pattern familiar from 1817, 1820 and 1839–40: groups of armed men from Stalybridge, Ashton, Oldham and Dukinfield were to assemble and attack the police before marching on Manchester. At Ashton a group of armed men did in fact parade through the streets and shot a special constable; at Hyde a group of 80–100 men armed with hammers, pikes and guns attempted to stop mills. But as in the past, the small groups who assembled or made their way to the chosen rendezvous found they lacked the numbers to mount a successful effort. The arrests of leaders earlier in the year, infiltration by informers, and only half-hearted support from the local population, denied the activists any real chance of mounting an effective challenge to the authorities. By the autumn the leaders of these abortive risings has also been committed to prison or transported.[56]

13 The transition to order

By the 1870s a Victorian historian of crime in England could write that 'it may well with little fear of contradiction be asserted that there never was, in any nation of which we have a history, a time in which life and property were so secure as they are at present in England'; while admitting that there remained areas where assault and robbery occurred frequently, he averred that

> any man of average stature and strength may wander about on foot and alone, at any hour of the day or night, through the greatest of all cities and its suburbs, along the high roads, and through unfrequented country lanes, and never have so much as the thought of danger thrust upon him, unless he goes out of his way to court it.[1]

Accordingly, historians of the 'Age of Equipoise' have done little more than reflect the overwhelming impression conveyed by contemporaries that they lived in an 'orderly' society. Professor Best has remarked that this sense of 'safety after storms' emerged remarkably quickly after 1848, so that the Great Exhibition of 1851 could be celebrated as a great national festival, not least because the thousands who thronged to the Crystal Palace did so 'not only without disorder, but almost without crime'.[2]

Within a relatively short space of time, the 1840s were being regarded as a kind of dark night before the dawn of mid-Victorian peace and prosperity, when industrial expansion and rising living standards underpinned a strong mood of national progress and self-confidence. Compared with the seeming imminent social conflicts of the 1840s and the uncertainties of the 'Great Depression', the mid-Victorian years appeared a time of relative stability. But however plausible the concept of a transition to order in mid-Victorian England, Asa Briggs has reminded us of the 'instinct for violence and interest in violence' which remained.[3] England did not suddenly change overnight from the disorders of the Hungry Forties into a perfectly peaceful and orderly land. Popular disturbances continued on a number of issues, notably over religious and ethnic conflicts, at election times, in labour disputes, and during political demonstrations in the capital, especially those surrounding the agitation for the Second Reform Act. It is important therefore to examine these major areas of disturbance, many of which continued to promote violence in the late Victorian era and beyond, and also to assess to what extent the mid-Victorian era marked a significant turning-point in the overall level and nature of popular disturbances in nineteenth-century England.

Anti-Catholic and anti-Irish disturbances

One of the most striking features of the period between the Gordon Riots and the passage of Catholic Emancipation in 1829 was the apparent decline of anti-Catholic rioting. Where once the Catholics had been the targets of abuse or attack in times of national crisis, this attitude appeared to be softening in a more tolerant atmosphere. Although anti-Catholicism or 'No-Popery' continued to provide one of the themes of Englishmen's 'liberties', the Gordon Riots had no obvious sequel in the capital or in the provinces before the Victorian era. Even during the Napoleonic Wars when the threat of invasion, Irish rebellion, and bellicose patriotism might have provided the raw material for renewed attacks on Catholics, they did not do so. Rather, the scapegoats for 'gut' patriotism were radicals or dissenters, though it was perhaps significant that some at least of the rioters who sacked the homes of Birmingham dissenters in 1791 did so to the cry of 'No-Popery'.

Anti-Irish sentiment was more diffuse than anti-Catholicism, for the immigrant Irish roused animosities other than those of religion. One of the most important was the threat of cheap labour undercutting the livelihood of English workmen. Riots against Irish harvest labour were common in the eighteenth century and the employment of Irish labourers in London had provoked serious rioting in 1736. Periodic clashes between English and Irish workers were common when the latter were used as strike-breakers; here the conflicts were not necessarily anti-Catholic or anti-Irish. Strike-breakers could just as easily be other Englishmen, Welsh, or Scots, and tended to provoke hostility as much as the Irish. Although eighteenth-century reformers tended to view the Irish as a 'problem' class, there was some evidence towards the end of the century that the most violent anti-Irish feeling had subsided as they became integrated into the lower strata of manual employments. London, with one of the largest Irish communities, was already familiar with them as construction workers, dock labourers, coalheavers, porters and chairmen.

The issue of Catholic emancipation brought new tensions into the relationship between Irish and English. Orange Lodges originated among the Ulster peasantry as a reaction to increasing pressures from Catholic political and economic movements. Their organisation acquired legitimacy not only from the support of the Protestant gentry in Ireland, but also from ultra-Tory opinion in England. The first British lodges were set up in Lancashire around 1800 as clubs for ex-soldiers and can be regarded as the Protestant reply to the United Irishmen, with the important difference that they revised their rules successfully to escape the provisions of the Act of 1799, which forbade secret oath-taking. Dr Senior has calculated that by 1822 Orange lodges were established in most industrial areas in England and included civilians as well as veteran soldiers, with a membership of 6,000 organised in about 300 lodges.[4]

The activities of the Orange Lodges were eventually to lead to their suppression in England by a temporary Act in 1825 and a definitive statute in 1836. In the interim, however, Orange clubs had provided an indication of anti-Catholic and anti-Irish feeling in those parts of the country most affected by Irish immigration. Lancashire in particular was heavily involved in the Orange movement, providing a quarter of the total number of lodges in 1835 (eighty-five in all), with 3,000 members. The organisation of processions to celebrate the Battle of the Boyne caused disturbances in England as early as 1819 when an Orange procession in Liverpool, organised with the usual insignia of 'the lamb, the ark, the Bible, men dressed in ermine, pontificial robes, leopard skins, Etc.', was attacked by Irishmen armed with brickbats and stones, who tore down the banners and injured several of the participants. There were more riots in Liverpool in July 1835 when gangs of Catholic Irish, some of them armed, gathered to prevent an Orange procession from taking place; when one of the leaders was arrested, the crowds turned on the police, breaking open the lock-up in Vauxhall Road; reassembling next day, the crowds demanded that no Orange procession should be allowed to take place and remained on the streets to prevent it.[5]

But although Liverpool witnessed these disturbances, the potent fusion of Irish and English politics failed to create widespread unrest before the 1850s. An important factor was the investigation carried out by the Whig Government of 1835 into the Orange Movement in England and Ireland after the exposure of the 'Fairman plot' in which Lt-Col. W. C. Fairman, the Grand Secretary of the Orange Movement in Britain, was alleged to have planned to place the English Grand Master, the Duke of Cumberland, on the throne in place of the then Princess Victoria. Although the strength of the Orange order in the army and in the country was probably exaggerated by radicals and Irish nationalists, the pressure on the Government to suppress the order led the Duke of Cumberland to accept the inevitable and dissolve the British lodges. In doing so, one focus of local conflict was removed. Protestant and 'Orange' opinion could surface in many other ways, but the public processions and parades which might have provoked more serious sectarian violence were avoided.[6]

In fact, the most numerous disturbances involving the Irish in the 1830s and 1840s arose from the itinerant 'navvy' gangs building the railways. Although there was no doubt a good deal of exaggeration in the image of the railway navvies, there were almost endemic brawls between these different groups, and between navvies and the local population. In 1837 a group of Irish navvies marched on Preston to support the radical and pro-Irish candidates in the election; after some serious fighting anti-

Irish mobs raced through the Irish quarters smashing windows and attacking houses. In the following year there were more disturbances between Irishmen building the North Union Railway and English spinners, during which some people were killed and the military had to be called in. Battles between Irish and English were frequent, but reached a culmination in the mid-1840s when lines were being pushed into Scotland. Attacks by Scottish and English workers on the Irish occurred on several occasions in the border country and in Scotland itself. One of the most serious riots occurred at Penrith in February 1846 when after a quarrel between an Irish navvy and an English ganger, the English drove the Irish from their camp, burning their huts, and turning their wives and children out into the cold; the next day, 500 Irish returned for revenge, but the English fled to recruit more forces. Overnight the word was spread to camps up to ten miles away, so that by the following morning 2,000 English navvies had assembled in Penrith. Prudently, the Irish fled or hid themselves in the town, but the English navvies ransacked the town, dragging out any Irish they found and beating them unmercifully with bludgeons and pickshafts. The Westmorland Yeomanry imposed some temporary order, but over the next fortnight were twice faced by gangs of Irish bent on revenge who had to be dispersed by force. At Kendal, the Irish appealed to the mayor for protection and were accompanied back to work by mayor, magistrates and police. The riots also spread into Scotland with serious outbreaks at Gorebridge, south of Edinburgh. Disturbances also occurred at Doncaster in August when English workmen set on the Irish.[7]

While disturbances between navvy gangs formed one major group of incidents in which the Irish were involved, another was the so-called 'Murphy' riots, after the anti-Catholic lecturer, William Murphy. The resurgence of popular Protestantism in the mid-Victorian period derived from many sources. As Professor Best has shown, it traded on the traditional 'No popery' of the past and the strong strain of antisaceradotalism which pervaded English culture.[8] To some extent at least, anti-Catholicism continued to fulfil its traditional role of defining English nationalism for, as a *Times* editorial declared in 1853, 'We very much doubt whether in England, or indeed in any free Protestant country, a true Papist can be a good subject.'[9] At a time when some sections of the press, were already beginning to pander to what would later be described as 'jingoism', anti-Catholicism provided a powerful and emotive force which could channel a complex mixture of religious and political prejudices.

The themes of 'No popery' could be found, for example, in the 'Surplice riots' of the 1840s the late 1850s. The fears of a neo-Catholic movement in the Church of England, brought into sharp focus by the tractarian controversy, led to a series of disturbances in Anglican churches against 'ritualism'. Anti-ritualism surfaced in many areas during the 1840s and 1850s, occasionally taking violent forms. In the South-West in November 1844 parochial meetings, placards, and anonymous letters greeted a pastoral letter of the bishop, Henry Phillpotts, advising that clergy should hold a weekly collection and preach in a surplice. When the curate of St Sidwell's parish in Exeter preached in a surplice on Sunday 12 January 1845, two-thirds of the congregation walked out, and a mob of 200 booed him as he left the church in the evening; the next Sunday, 700 people assembled, rising to 2,000 by the afternoon, forcing the curate to seek police protection to and from the church. Later disturbances at Exeter in 1848 illustrated a continuing distrust of the Anglican laity in some areas for what they saw as 'Romish practices'. [10] Sporadic incidents of this kind occurred in many parishes during the 1840s and 1850s. In London, Bishop Blomfield's definition of the rubric to be followed by Anglican clergy led to serious disagreements among a clergy and laity used to a wide diversity of practice. During the 'Papal aggression' scare of 1850 crowds of protesters gathered on successive Sundays outside 'Ritualistic' churches and were not condemned by the bishop. Controversy and ill-feeling flared up in a number of churches and parishes during the 1850s but the most notorious incidents centred around the mission church of St George's-in-the-East where, in spring and early summer 1859, members of the congregation howled down the curates conducting the service. For a time the church had to be closed and was only reopened with the protection of 300 policemen. [11]

A foretaste of the explosive combination of Irish immigration and anti-Catholicism was shown in the disturbances in Stockport in 1852. The town, like many others in the North-West, already had its 'Little Ireland' of settlement, but had seen a rapid increase in recent immigration, some of which, it was alleged, had replaced English labour in the cotton factories. A large and well-furnished chapel already served the Catholic community and a mission chapel had been opened in a disused theatre as recently as 1851. Ill-feeling between Catholic and Protestant appears to have been inflamed by Lord John Russell's proclamation against religious processions on 15 June 1851. This was defied by the Catholics who held a children's procession on the 27th. A day later, a quarrel in a public house between an Irishman and an Englishman flared up into a full-scale neighbourhood brawl which had to be broken up by police. The next night the Irish assembled and attacked the house of a prominent protestant Alderman and a protestant school in St Peter's Square; a general fight broke out in the Square, some of the Irish harvest workers present being armed with sickles and scythes. An attack was now made on the Irish quarter and the chapel of SS Philip and James. This was broken into and the interior wrecked, pews, statues, crosses, organ, and pictures being broken to pieces. Fearing the worst, the priest hid in the tower behind a locked door, having cut the bell-rope in case anyone tried to climb in. His presbytery was ransacked and his library of 400 books burnt; attempts to fire both house and chapel failed and the crowds were driven away by the reading of the Riot Act. Instead they proceeded to the Mission Chapel and wrecked the contents before being stopped by the intervention of troops. In a short but fairly destructive riot, two chapels had been severely damaged, a hundred people injured and one killed. Out of sixty-two people arrested, ten English and ten Irish were later tried. Most received minor terms of imprisonment, but one was transported for fifteen years.[12]

The Stockport riots were by far the most destructive of the 1850s, but there were some other symptoms of religious and ethnic rivalries in London, when there were a series of minor disturbances between the Irish Catholics of Clerkenwell and some recent Italian refugees, many of whom were fiercely anti-clerical. The Irish rallied in defence of their priests, who were being insulted by the Italians, and several hundred police had to be brought in to control the situation. Renewed disturbances came in 1858 with the lecture tour of the Catholic 'apostate', the Baron de Camin. At Wolverhampton in June 1858 he gave a series of lectures attacking the Pope and the Catholic church, the first of which was broken up by a crowd of Irish labourers. At the second lecture, a crowd assailed the hall with stones, so that the Riot Act had to be read and the police sent in to disperse the protesters, which they only accomplished after a brisk fight.[13] A proposed lecture at Wigan in the following year led to a wholesale attack by the English upon Roman Catholic churches, pubs, and houses; De Camin's lectures also provoked attacks on Catholic chapels in Wakefield, Bradford, and Leeds during the summer and autumn of 1862.

In late September there was fighting in Hyde Park between English working men who supported Garibaldi's struggles in Italy and pro-Papal Irishmen; off-duty soldiers from the nearby Guards' barracks joined in on the side of the English, wielding walking sticks and belt buckles. The conflict was renewed in the Park a week later, several thousand people gathered and there was a prolonged struggle for possession of the Redan, a mound in the park used for addressing meetings. The mound changed hands several times as Irish, Italians, and Englishmen charged and countercharged each other. Eventually after two or three hours fighting, rain and a squad of 500 soldiers gained control; although bludgeons, belts, and park rails were freely used, only one man was seriously injured. During the next few weeks further brawls occurred in the rookeries and slums of West and Central London, in which Irishmen fought with soldiers or Italians, or anyone who was deemed an opponent of the Pope or the Irish. Some sections of the press saw in these disturbances the hand of a 'Catholic conspiracy' which hired mobs; even a pastoral letter by Cardinal Wiseman condemning the riots was denounced for coming out only after the police had taken steps to ban 'the public discussion of popular and exciting topics' in the parks. However, the police action, combined with levelling the mound used by speakers and the mustering of a strong force of 1,100 police to patrol the park confined the fighting to a few scuffles on subsequent Sundays.[14]

There were also disturbances in Birkenhead in October 1862 when an Irish Protestant clergyman whose church lay in the midst of an area heavily populated by Catholic Irish dock labourers decked out his church with Orange slogans and announced a meeting to debate a motion of 'Sympathy with Garibaldi'. The hall and church were attacked by an Irish mob; police forays into the surrounding streets were met by hails of bricks and stones from the houses, and the inhabitants fired their chimneys to provide clouds of soot and smoke to confuse them. The next day groups of Irish paraded the streets and Orange shops and taverns were sacked. Although there were rumours of the impending rescue of the eleven rioters taken, the situation was calmed by the priests urging their people to remain off the streets. Protected by 1,000 Orange constables from Liverpool and local police, the lectures went ahead unmolested.[15]

A new edge to Anglo-Irish hostility was given by the rise of the Fenian movement during the 1860s. Fenian 'outrages', including a bomb attack on Clerkenwell prison which killed twelve people and injured 120 more, the shooting of the Duke of Edinburgh in Australia, and a plot to capture Chester Castle, provided a focus for Protestant hysteria.[16] In September 1867, the rescue of two Fenians from a coach taking them to the New Bailey prison in Salford, when an unarmed police sergeant was killed, provided a prelude to the tours of William Murphy, the most notorious of the anti-Catholic lecturers. An Irish ex-Catholic, Murphy was sponsored by the Protestant Evangelical Mission and Electoral Union on a series of lecture tours which provoked the most serious wave of disturbances in the mid-Victorian period. His talent for virulent anti-Catholicism brought him to the attention of the Home Office in February 1867, when a series of lectures in Wolverhampton led to fighting inside and outside the hall. County police and cavalry had to be brought in to control mobs of several thousand Irishmen who gathered outside for his final lectures. Further lectures in the Midlands caused apprehension rather than disturbance, but in June 1867 Murphy's lectures in Birmingham produced the most serious rioting in the city since 1791. Refused a hall, Murphy and his supporters set up a 'tabernacle' for 3,000 people on an empty space in central Birmingham. His first lecture on Sunday, 16 June was broken up by a mob of men, women, and children. The next day, crowds estimated at between 50,000 and 100,000 thronged the streets, one group of Irishmen parading the streets with a great wooden cross bedecked in green ribbons while others assailed the tabernacle. Shops were broken into and the mayor was forced to read the Riot Act, swear in 600 specials and use 400 soldiers to supplement the regular police force of 580 men. During the evening some of Murphy's supporters moved into the Irish district breaking into Catholic houses and a chapel. Nearly 100 people were arrested and dozens injured, but in spite of rumours of attacks on the Catholic cathedral and local armouries, Murphy's lectures were allowed to proceed under heavy protection.

During Murphy's tour of Lancashire in 1868 the most serious riots occurred at Ashton and Stalybridge. An attack on some men who had been attending one such lecture in May led to an attack on a Catholic chapel in Stalybridge which was defended by the Irish and their priest, and at Bacup there were scuffles between rival groups of Murphy's supporters and opponents, but the most violent incidents occurred in Ashton-under-Lyne. A group of Irish attacked a gathering of 'Murphyites and Orangemen', and a retaliatory attack by the English swept in to Ashton's 'Little Ireland', wrecking twenty houses and a Catholic chapel; one Irishman died as a result of the fighting. In September Murphy's visit to Manchester led to further disturbances when he announced himself as the 'Protestant candidate' in the forthcoming election and held a series of 'election' meetings which provided a focus for the anti-Murphyite Irish to attack his supporters. In fact, Murphy did not present himself for election; by next spring he was touring the North-East, where a lecture at Tynemouth Oddfellows Hall was broken up by a column of Irish armed with sticks and hammers. Further lectures in April 1870 at Woolwich also led to scuffles and attacks on the halls being used. Considerable disquiet at this riotous progress was growing, especially after the Liberal triumph at the polls in 1868, but Murphy's career was cut short before the dilemma of reconciling freedom of speech with concern for public order was resolved: starting a lecture series at Whitehaven in Cumberland in April 1871, he was seized by a group of Irish miners who savagely kicked him senseless before he was rescued by police; almost a year later he died of his injuries. [17]

Clashes between Catholic and Protestant continued sporadically for many years after Murphy's death, especially in areas of high Irish immigration. Liverpool, in particular, was marked by frequent disturbances between 'Orange' and 'Green', and religious animosities gave Lancashire politics a peculiarly intense flavour which was remarked upon by contemporaries in the late Victorian era. [18] But there was no comparable wave of sectarian rioting in England after the 1860s to that which had been seen in the mid-Victorian period. Gradually the Irish were integrated into the institutions and social life of the areas in which they lived, a pattern of development which had been interrupted by suddenly increased immigration and the revival of anti-Catholic feeling. Significantly, the next major occasions for attacks upon religious groups, came not against Catholics, but in the attacks made on the evangelizing missions of the Salvation Army in the late 1870s and 1880s. [19]

Respectability and 'outrage': Victorian labour disturbances

The years from the 1840s have been characterised as a period of growing organisation among industrial workers. The mid-Victorian era was to become the heyday of 'new model' unionism with its emphasis on 'respectability' and self-improvement. By the end of the 1860s, the Trades Union Council had been formed, many of the skilled artisans had obtained the vote, and trade unions were a recognised force in both national and local politics. But during this period and after, labour disputes provided a persistent undercurrent of violence. As in the past, it was strikes which usually occasioned the disturbances, with intimidation of strike-breakers and conflicts over picketing providing the principal occasions for disorder. Trade unions still had no legal status, employees could be threatened with breach of contract under the Master and Servant Act if they went on strike, and the laws of picketing remained obscure. Thus, although 'organisation' is often counterposed to the presence of violence in industrial conflicts, the crucial determinant was what might be termed 'effective' organisation. Even unions which were relatively well organised might have to resort to violence in order to maintain solidarity, or to strike and resist the use of strike-breaking labour. Some smaller trade groups, however well organised internally, might find themselves in such a weak bargaining position that they were forced to use violence in an effort to bargain effectively.

Nonetheless, one of the most striking characteristics of industrial bargaining from the 1840s was the increasing emphasis placed by union leaders on 'respectability' and non-violence. To take one example, the formation of county unions in the coal-mining industry led in 1842 to the creation of the Miners Association of Great Britain and Ireland, which within two years could claim 70,000 members. Largely eschewing the Chartist movement, the Miners' Association began a campaign for better wages and working conditions which in 1844 produced a bitter four-month conflict in the North-East and other coalfields. From the outset, the strikers determined to keep the peace as much as possible and even newspapers hostile to their cause commented on the self-discipline and restraint. Although there were attacks on blacklegs, the union leaders tried to deal with the problem at source by sending representatives to other areas in order to discourage them from providing strike-breaking labour, publishing notices in newspapers to inform people that the strike was taking place and explaining the issues involved. A principal fear of the union leaders was that violent proceedings would be turned against them in the courts and press. Numerous resolutions were passed to keep the peace, with warnings that anyone who did not do so would be deemed a traitor to the cause.[20]

As in earlier disputes, it was difficult to prevent unrest at the spate of mass evictions ordered by some of the coalowners. Faced with the eviction notices, one of the leaders urged the strikers: 'Stay in the house, your families around, lock the door (as against an ordinary housebreaker), sit down or go to bed, firmly and quietly state that you have read in a book that "an Englishman's home is his castle". Beyond that, offer no resistance whatever. Let them *carry* you out.'[21] Although this advice was not always followed, the *Newcastle Courant* admitted that it would be 'unjust to the great body of men not to state that distinctly their general demeanour is remarkable peaceful.' Elsewhere the introduction of strike-breakers did provoke disturbances. The use of Derbyshire miners to break the strike in the Sheffield pits, led to an attack upon their temporary 'barracks' in the pityard at the Soap House pit; scaling the walls, a crowd entered the buildings and attacked the strike-breakers, for which three men eventually received sentences of fifteen years transportation. On 25 August, strikers blew up the boiler of the Deep pit near Sheffield to prevent it working, killing one man when the powder went off accidentally. By this time, however, the strike was beginning to crumble and men were drifting back to work, exactly the point at which counsels of non-violence were least likely to be heeded by men who had been on strike for several weeks.[22]

The general determination of union leaders to preserve an officially 'moderate' tone was partly conditioned by the vague legal status of trade unions, and it was the Miners' Association solicitor, W. P. Roberts, 'the Pitmen's Attorney- General', who had done much to shape this policy in 1844. Similar determination to win a strike without resort to violence was shown by the Amalgamated Association of Operative Cotton Spinners who struck work in 1853-4. A successful strike in Stockport supported by funds from other districts was followed by a protracted dispute in Preston. Almost equally matched in funds and determination, the masters and men were locked in a dispute from October 1853 to May 1854. But it was not until strike-breaking labour was brought in from Ireland in February that any disturbances occurred. Almost as soon as they did, the local magistrates began to arrest the strike leaders on charges of 'molesting and obstructing' the imported labour. Even so, Dickens, who visited the town in February 1854 was deeply impressed by the peaceful atmosphere and the good order of the strike meetings.[23]

By the 1860s there was a revival of mining trade unionism in Northumberland. Although there were evictions and conflicts with bailiffs during a fifteen-week strike at Cramlington in 1865, this dispute has been described as 'the last strike in the mould of 1832 and 1844'. Increasingly, union leaders such as Thomas Burt sought to organise 'model unions' based on high subscriptions and dependable members, their aim being to avoid strikes and secure union recognition.[24] One of the most notable examples of a disciplined and publicity-conscious strike occurred during the campaign of the engineers on Tyneside to reduce working hours in 1871. The 'Nine Hours' League' was sufficiently strong to prevent its men returning to work on compromise terms during a protracted dispute and went to considerable lengths to avoid disturbances in the face of the introduction of blackleg labour and the prosecution of union members for breach of contract. Some disturbances occurred, but the strike leaders vigorously and publicly declared their opposition to such incidents; and although they knew full well that their words would have little effect on their more militant members and sympathisers, they maintained a strenuous defence of moderation and non-violence in order to appeal to public sympathy. The historians of this dispute have written: 'It would be ingenuous indeed to accept at face value all assurances given by Leaguers that their activities were invariably peaceful. The combination of a skilful and conspicuously non-violent leadership equipped with a large supply of emollient phrases, together with a good deal of successful intimidation in practice, was a singularly effective one.'[25]

Similarly in his study of public order in the Black Country, Dr Philips has emphasised the difference between the colliery strikes in the early 1840s and those of the late 1850s. Although colliers still marched about the district attacking provision shops and intimidating blacklegs, there were fewer large-scale riots. Dr Philips has stressed here the importance of the use of the police as a more flexible instrument for dealing with the situation, troops and yeomanry being called out but kept in reserve. What was also important was the restraint show by the strikers themselves, in spite of considerable provocation; during meetings held in the midst of a nine-week strike in 1858, speakers urged their hearers to refrain from violence. The Lord-Lieutenant of Staffordshire acknowledged that the longest strike he could remember had 'been unattended with a single instance of violence'. Dr Philips has also made the interesting observation that this characteristic of greater restraint was more prevalent in the expanding industries, such as mining and the iron industry; on the other hand, groups such as the Black Country nailmakers, who were increasingly threatened by machinery, fought a series of strikes which if anything became more rather than less violent: during strikes in the late 1850s, the nailers cut the bellows of blacklegs and non-union members, as well as attacking the shops of nailmasters;[26] similiar cases of intimidation occurred during the strike of the Northampton boot and shoe-makers in 1857–8, a strike caused by the introduction of sewing machines for closing the uppers on shoes.[27]

That respectability had another face was shown by increasing concern about trade union 'outrages', the most famous of which occurred in Sheffield in 1866. The Sheffield incidents arose out of a series of attacks on non-union members of the cutlery trades. A long series of instances of 'rattening' and intimidation had preceded what was to become a *cause célèbre* of trade union history, the blowing up of a workman's house by gunpowder in October 1866. Bitterly attacked in the newspapers, the trade unions found themselves being subjected to a Royal Commission of enquiry which investigated many aspects of trade union practice; the evidence collected provided many examples of restrictive practices and minor forms of 'outrage', especially in the building trades. In their evidence before the Commission, however, trade unionists concentrated on the beneficial functions of the unions and their peaceful intentions; they also used the inquiry as a platform from which to air their grievances about their legal disabilities. As a result, the Majority Report of the Commission came out in favour of legalising trade unions, a proposal which was enshrined in the Trade Union Act of 1871.[28]

The protection which the 1871 Act gave to trade union funds and the legalisation of peaceful picketing in 1875 under the Conspiracy and Protection of Property Act provided the framework which initiated the era of 'new unionism' and the creation of general unions. While the great majority of strikes passed off peacefully, however, there were some bitter conflicts in the late Victorian era which led to violence. One of the most serious occurred during a nine-week weavers' strike in North-East Lancashire in 1878, when the house of the employers' association leader in Blackburn was looted and burnt down. Disturbances also occurred in Preston, far more so than in earlier conflicts of the mid-Victorian period. Similarly in 1893 the strike of the Yorkshire colliers led to clashes between pickets and strike-breakers. When the troops were called in at the Ackton Hall Colliery, near Featherstone, in September 1893 they were greeted with vollies of stones and the troops opened fire, killing two people.[29] Again in the Edwardian period, especially during the period of rapid trade union growth between 1906 and 1913, some clashes between troops, police and strikers achieved national notoriety. Picket-line disturbances, especially where strike-breakers were being used, were to become probably the most frequent source of violence during strikes in the twentieth century. But the number of disturbances was small compared with the total volume of strike activity. The fact that incidents such as those at Featherstone or Tonypandy achieved wide coverage illustrated that they were regarded as exceptions rather than the rule. Thus although strikes were often to appear a major cause of popular disturbances after 1870, they in fact reflected a characteristic which was becoming clear during the first half of the nineteenth century, the increasing emphasis on order and restraint in the conduct of industrial disputes.[30]

Election disturbances

Elections continued to be one of the most persistent sources of popular disorder in nineteenth-century England. Although the first generation of reformers had pledged themselves to maintaining a policy of 'no treating' and disavowed electoral violence, there was little evidence either immediately before or after 1832 that the more tumultuous traditions of the eighteenth century had been left behind. Early nineteenth-century elections, such as those of 1802 or 1820 continued to occasion disturbances little different in kind to those to be found a hundred years earlier. Even the radical triumph of winning Westminster in 1807 with a policy of 'no treating', had turned sour by the post-war years, when the Westminster elections of 1818 and 1819 were once again scenes of uproar and fighting between rival factions. Cobbett, who had declared himself for the borough of Honiton in 1806 and was shocked by the venality of the voters who remonstrated with him for his endeavours to deprive them of the profit of their vote, could still at Coventry in 1820 find himself at the mercy of the same pressures and the most blatent forms of intimidation. He vividly described the scene as his opponents' hired men set upon his supporters at the hustings:

> The Ruffians came, not less than five hundred in number, in regular order, about eight or ten deep, with drums and banners at their head. They made their approach by the higher part of

the ground, (and) began the attack on my voters. All attempts to resist were in vain. And, in five minutes, three hundred of my voters were as completely driven as if an army had made an attack upon them. After this, not a man dared to show his face to vote for me.[31]

As Professor Gash has shown, the First Reform Act made little difference to the traditional tactics of electoral intimidation and violence. As well as redistributing seats and rationalising the franchise on the basis of property qualifications, the Act also raised the level of constituency organisation by enforcing the registration of voters, thus stimulating the formation of political clubs and associations. These clubs continued to develop during the Victorian era, providing focal centres for the loyalties of enfranchised and unenfranchised alike during elections. Partisanship and various forms of political influence and pressure remained a major feature of the electoral system. As in the past, physical intimidation or violence was often only the tip of an iceberg of more subtle, if often just as forceful, influences brought to bear on electors, and practices such as 'cooping' - the sometimes forcible removal of pledged or wavering voters from the scene until it was time to vote - continued to be used; gangs of hired thugs such as the semi-regular Lewes 'bullies' and Nottingham 'lambs' were still used to intimidate rival sets of supporters and voters, while elections continued to provide a source of free drink and entertainment at which a certain amount of rowdy behaviour was expected and sometimes actively encouraged.[32]

The election disturbances which achieved some public notoriety only stand out from a generally tumultuous atmosphere at contested elections in the Victorian period. Those at Wolverhampton in May 1835 were considered among the most violent of the 1830s because the Riot Act had to be read and troops were ordered to fire on a crowd which was attempting to attack the successful Tory candidate and his organisers; more typical, perhaps, were the scenes at Coventry in 1832 where one sailor hired to stop rival voters reaching the hustings recorded how 'we cut them down and kicked them about like a football'. Nor did the situation alter markedly during the mid-Victorian period: it was still possible for Lady Guest to watch a battle between rival groups of supporters for possession of some flags and banners at Poole in Dorset in 1850, or for fighting to break out at the nomination meetings in the Coleshill division of North Warwickshire in 1852, in which several people were injured. The paucity of contests in 1857 and 1859 contributed to what some saw as a slow improvement in public behaviour at elections; but those of the 1860s and the decades that followed showed that the tradition of electoral disorder was far from dead. The large number of contests in 1865, double the number of the previous election, led to widespread disturbances in some of the Midland constituencies. At Nuneaton 'about ten minutes before the poll commenced, fifty or sixty men, well primed with beer, marched down and placed themselves in front of each booth, ready to do battle in the Conservative interest'.[33]

Fighting also broke out at Leamington and Atherstone in 1865, while at Warwick one of the Tory candidates was plastered with mud by a Liberal mob and in a general mêlée between the rival factions one man was seriously injured; at Nottingham a mob of several thousand surged through the market place and sacked the Liberal Party offices. The 1868 election saw a renewal of disturbances in which the Murphyite lectures added to the temperature of the Lancashire contests. At Blackburn, rival mobs destroyed the headquarters of the candidates and fought in the streets with police. The *Annual Register* recorded: 'All along the pavement streams of blood were flowing, and the sickening sight of men with blood flowing from their heads and faces met one at every turn.' At Bristol it was alleged that the Liberals had employed 'flying columns' of several hundred men armed with bludgeons to beat away Conservative voters; at the end of the election a solicitor on a white horse paraded the streets followed by Liberal supporters who broke the windows of their opponents.[34]

Although many election addresses in 1868 mentioned the secret ballot as a means of ending the most blatant forms of influence, including violence at the hustings, its introduction did not end the electoral disorder of the period; Dr Richter has estimated that there were at least seventy-one separate incidents of serious electoral disorder between 1865 and 1885, many of which occurred after 1872.[35] The abolition of public nomination, the increased number of polling places, and the secret ballot did not prevent a short campaign of three weeks in February 1874 from frequently erupting into violence; although only two petitions were presented alleging riot and intimidation (Dudley and North Durham), there were disturbances at Willenhall (near Wolverhampton), Stour-bridge, Barnsley, Newcastle, Nottingham, Sheffield, the Forest of Dean and Wolverhampton itself. The scene at Willenhall where local colliers and locksmiths armed themselves with staves to defeat an invading party of Tory 'roughs' was reported in *The Times* on 5 February:

> Blood flowed freely and they (the 'roughs') were terribly kicked, one so shockingly about the head and face that his life is in much jeopardy. . . . The victorious mob then paraded the streets, smashing the windows of three public houses where the landlords are Tories, and similarly attacked the residence and factory of the chairman of the Conservative Committee.[36]

As both Dr Richter and Dr Bailey have shown, election disturbances continued into the late Victorian and Edwardian period, surviving the 1883 Corrupt Practices Act just as they had the Ballot Act.[37] There was some evidence however that the pattern of election disorders was altering. Most disturbances now took place during the campaign, rather than at the polls, an obvious comment on the open hustings and centralised voting as a cause for disorder prior to 1872. In London it was said that the Ballot Act alone had transformed the situation so that 'the places that used to be the worst are now the best'. Disturbances also still took place after the result was declared, a factor little altered by the ballot; even the presence of a strong local police force was not necessarily a deterrent because the populace of some towns was likely to attack the police on sight, especially during the excitement and 'licence' of an election: this happened on more than one occasion in 1874. Attempts to improve the electoral machinery and local policing still left elections as one of the most common sources of popular disturbance in late Victorian England.[38]

London's public spaces and the Second Reform Act

Victorian London continued to provide an important stage for movements of national importance. The capital had been the focus of the Chartist petitions and the Kennington Common meeting of April 1848 had illustrated the almost symbolic context in which confrontations between governments and demonstrators could take place. During the mid-Victorian period and later, the right to demonstrate in the public spaces of the capital, notably Hyde Park and Trafalgar Square, became a frequent source of acrimony and occasionally of disorder. An issue which in a provincial city or town would have been of little national significance developed in the capital during this period into a series of confrontations which reached a climax in the 'Hyde Park railings' incident in July 1866, which has been accorded an important place in the passage of the Second Reform Act.

Many of the traditional meeting grounds in the capital had been built up by the mid-Victorian period. Places such as Spa Fields and St George's Fields had already been covered in buildings by the 1840s and the spaces which were left were private property. Legally, there was no unrestricted right of public assembly in the two major open spaces in central London, Hyde Park and Trafalgar Square; the former was crown property, as were several of the other major parks; the latter had also been vested in the Queen's possession by an Act of 1844 and came under the control of the Commissioner of Works. Other places in the capital came under the direct control of the Home Office through the Metropolitan Police. Between them, the Crown and the Home Office had the power to restrict access to almost all the available public meeting places in the capital; in addition, the Seditious Meetings Act of 1817 had placed restrictions on meetings of fifty or more people within a mile of Westminster while parliament was in session. But the way in which these powers were used lay almost entirely within the discretion of the Home Office and the Metropolitan Police. Meetings might be given tacit approval or subjected to bans, such as those used against Chartist meetings in the East End in 1848, enforced by the police or even troops. After 1848, however, attention increasingly shifted to the issue of the right to demonstrate in Hyde Park, which therefore became the scene of several clashes between police and demonstrators in mid-Victorian London.[39]

The use of Hyde Park for meetings occasioned some violent clashes in July 1855. With some reluctance, the authorities had permitted a meeting to be held there to protest against the Sunday Trading Bill which was coming before parliament; the Bill was unpopular with many of the workmen and traders of the capital, who used Sunday as a principal shopping day. When the meeting was held on 24 June 1855 there was some disorder; the police later alleged that wealthy passers-by had been hooted and jeered, and that gangs of 'thieves, pickpockets and other reckless and disorderly persons' had used the meeting as a cover for criminal activities. News of a further meeting to be held on the following Sunday, 1 July, led Police Commissioner Mayne to issue a notice on 29 June declaring the use of Hyde Park for popular demonstrations illegal. This was widely regarded as being of dubious legality and ignored, so that further demonstrations became an assertion of the right to assemble in the London parks. This confrontation led to a particularly bitter clash on 1 July, when an estimated 150,000 people assembled in the Park in defiance of Mayne's notices and began to heckle wealthy passers-by; the police on duty endured a certain amount of provocation, but eventually they baton-charged the crowd and took seventy-two prisoners. Though there were further demonstrations, none provoked as fierce a reaction by the police. The press took up the issue of police brutality and the Government was forced to appoint a commission of inquiry.[40]

After considerable delay the inquiry began, and a number of serious allegations were made about the administration and conduct of the police at the 1 July demonstration. The number of police assembled to deal with the demonstration seemed excessive and the absence of the police commissioner on the spot was criticised; when questioned upon this Sir Richard Mayne admitted that he remained at Whitehall throughout the demonstration and would not expand on his reasons for this conduct. The officer on the spot, Superintendent Hughes, was accused of undue excitement and improper language, and of ordering his men to use their staves too early. The report admitted that some policemen had acted badly, but on the whole asserted its confidence in the force.[41]

In an article on the riots Dr Harrison has thrown a great deal of light on the incident and the commission which followed; in particular he has found an explanation for the fierce reaction of the police to the demonstration and for Sir Richard's conduct on the day in question. Before the demonstration of 1 July the Government had received intelligence from the French police, through the British ambassador in Paris, that it might be used by a group of Chartist agitators and French refugees to initiate an insurrection. It was this intelligence which determined the disposition and action of the forces on the day. A large force was assembled in anticipation of a serious threat to the security of the capital; Sir Richard Mayne had remained in his headquarters because he could direct operations more easily from Whitehall than from the Park itself. The severity of the police response was also explained by this information. At the commission Sir Richard Mayne had been unable to reveal anything of this and the Government had delayed the commission so as not to compromise itself or the police. In essence the report was an embarrassment to the Government and they took little action on it.[42]

Although the police came out badly, the commission's report still declared that Hyde Park was not an appropriate 'arena for the discussion of popular and exciting topics'. This did not prevent meetings and lectures from being held and, as shown elsewhere, further disturbances took place in Hyde Park in 1862 over meetings in support of Garibaldi. At first the police had permitted meetings to take place, recognising that many radical groups were ready to pounce on what might be interpreted as a denial of free speech and rights of public assembly. Eventually, however, the fighting that ensued had forced the police once again to prevent meetings in the Park. That the right to assemble in other places in the capital was not established was shown in the incidents at Primrose Hill in April 1864. During Garibaldi's visit to England earlier in the year he was greeted by large and enthusaistic crowds. Fearing disorder at other meetings in the country, the Government had asked him to leave the country. This provoked a meeting on Primrose Hill, organised by the London Workingmen's Reception Committee and a middle-class Garibaldi committee led by Edmund Beales. The ostensible purpose of the meeting was to celebrate Shakespeare's tercentenary, but in reality it was to protest at Garibaldi's expulsion. As the meeting was to take place in a public park, the police mustered over 200 constables who violently dispersed the assembled crowds. This action again brought the issue of the right to public assembly to the fore and led in the following year to the formation of the Reform League which sought to ensure the right of peaceful meetings in public parks.[43]

The issue of the right to meet in the public parks of the capital flowed directly into the agitation surrounding the Second Reform Act. The minority Tory Government which came to power in June 1866 announced that it would not pledge itself to deal with the issue of parliamentary reform during the next session, and as a result the Reform League announced its intention to hold a meeting in Hyde Park on 23 July. The Home Office concurred with the Commissioner's decision to prohibit the meeting, but the organisers decided to defy the ban. The Home Secretary had the gates of the Park locked and arranged for a large force of police to guard the entrances. The League's organisers had no wish to precipitate a riot which might prejudice their cause and arranged to march to Hyde Park, but to adjourn to Trafalgar Square if prevented from entering. Notices were distributed to supporters informing them of· this plan. A large, peaceful march of demonstrators arrived at Marble Arch to find the gates closed and police assembled to oppose them; Beales led one part of the procession off to Trafalgar Square, but other sections pressed forward against the railings, breaking them down along Park Lane and the Bayswater Road. Fighting between police and demonstrators continued until darkness fell, but although troops were brought up, it was thought inadvisable to order them to fire.

The significance of this celebrated episode has aroused controversy between historians who apportion differing weight to the role of extra-parliamentary agitation in the passing of the Second Reform Act.[44] At the very least, it can be argued that the 'Hyde Park railings' incident helped to stimulate pressure for reform and make it more certain that a Reform Bill would be passed. The Government, however, did not appear unduly alarmed, parliament being prorogued from August 1866 until early February 1867. Although John Stuart Mill recorded that he had to persuade some radical reformers against pursuing confrontation with the authorities, there was little evidence of a 'revolutionary' temper in the meetings held in London and in the country. A meeting of 25,000 reform supporters, mainly trade unionists, had to be held at Beaufort House, Kensington, on 3 December because the Government refused permission to use Hyde Park and this prohibition was accepted; the trade societies' own marshals kept order at the meeting. However, when discussion of the Reform Bill reopened in February 1867 the Reform League demanded to meet in the Park. The Home Secretary issued a proclamation that the 'meeting is not permitted' and urged people not to attend; large numbers of police and special constables were mobilised, but the Park gates were permitted to remain open. On the evening of 6 May the Reform League marched to the Park and filled it with a large crowd of 200,000 people who listened to speeches from ten different platforms. The meeting ended with cheers for the Queen and dispersed peacefully. The confrontation was recognised by the Government as something of a humiliation, and the Home Secretary resigned.[45]

As suggested above, the significance of these events in the reform struggle has been disputed. Some have regarded the events of July 1866 and May 1867 as helping to propel a government towards reform for fear of revolutionary violence emerging. In this interpretation, the events of 6 May could be regarded as a kind of revenge for April 1848, only this time with the government's bluff being called. Historians who have emphasised the 'high politics' of the reform crisis have argued that this picture is overdrawn: the violence in July 1866 was minimal and the Government had lost some face in May 1867 but little more. In the event, the theory of a 'revolutionary' crisis in 1866–7 cannot be tested, any more than that of 1831–2. Whether widespread violence would have followed the failure of a reform measure to pass in 1867 is impossible to say with certainty, though it appears that many middle-class supporters of reform would have been alienated by widespread disorder; as it was, the Second Reform Act had received the Royal assent by August and the issue was never put to the test. The crucial difference in 1867 compared to 1848 was that reform had a substantial body of support inside the House of Commons; unlike the Chartists, the Reform League were not battering their heads against an intransigent parliament. The government was ready to grant a measure of reform, the only issues to be settled being the exact terms of the measure and who would gain the credit for its passing. In this context the extra-parliamentary pressure for Reform was important, but it is still not clear that it had a decisive impact on the political manoeuvring taking place at Westminster.[46]

In the more limited context of the demand for the right of free assembly in the parks and squares of the capital, the events of 1866–7 represented a partial triumph. The Government's climb-down in May 1867 effectively led to Hyde Park becoming recognised as a forum for public meetings and demonstrations. Its position was defined in the Royal Parks and Gardens Act of 1872 which, while it rejected the existence of any common law right of public meeting, left the public free to assemble under the restrictions of the rules of the Park. During the 1870s and 1880s Hyde Park was to be the scene of many large demonstrations and meetings.[47] The situation in regard to Trafalgar Square was less clear; meetings had taken place there in 1866 over parliamentary reform and in 1870 and 1871 over the Franco–Prussian War, but it took a series of clashes between the authorities and demonstrators, particularly 'Black Monday' (8 February 1886) and 'Bloody Sunday' (13 November 1887), before a position of 'cautious tolerance' became the norm.[48]

The transition to order

Popular disturbances also occurred on other issues and occasions in mid-Victorian England. Although the traditional food riot had largely died out by the 1840s there were still occasional disturbances in periods of unemployment or distress; food shops were plundered in Liverpool in 1855, in London in the winter of 1860–1, and again in 1866–7.[49] Although Victorians were later to praise the fortitude displayed by the Lancashire cotton operatives during the 'cotton famine' of the American Civil War, troops had to be called in and the Riot Act read at Stalybridge in March 1863 when the local relief committee suddenly reduced their grant to the unemployed and tightened up on provisions. The windows of the police station and of the houses of members of the relief committee were smashed and the committee's store plundered of £800 of goods.

Over the next few days, disturbances spread to Ashton, Hyde and Dukinfield, where the unemployed 'turned out' from the compulsory sewing and reading schools they had to attend in order to receive relief. Concern that further disturbances might break out among the unemployed led to urgent consideration of more effective relief measures, leading to a Public Works Act in July 1863 which offered cheap loans to local authorities to carry out works of public utility. Dr Rose has commented that its passage 'reveals the extent to which the growing discontent of the Lancashire unemployed, dramatically illustrated by the Stalybridge riots, had persuaded public opinion that poor relief and private philanthropy had failed, and that some new policy was imperative if Lancashire was not to be pauperised'.[50]

Given the persistence of different kinds of popular disturbance in this period, we can go some way towards assessing mid-Victorian perceptions of the orderliness of their society by examining the criminal and judicial statistics, which provide annual summaries of those committed to trial for indictable offences. Available from as early as 1805, it is only from 1835 that they permit the total number of committals for riotous offences to be abstracted from the returns; these returns allow an appraisal both of the general level of committals for riotous offences in relation to committals for all offences and some appreciation of their movement over time; from 1857 another category of information is available in the form of indictable offences 'known to the police'. As several historians of nineteenth-century crime have noted, these statistics must be approached with caution; as a record of committals for trial on the more serious offences they are not a record of 'actual' crime – an unknown number of offences always occurred without the intervention of the police or other authorities. Nor can it be assumed that this was a constant figure during the period which saw the establishment of both borough and county police forces. The introduction of a professional force could often lead to an increase in the number of committals, not only distorting the general sequence of figures, but also altering the relationship between actual crime and the recorded incidence; in addition, the number of committals for any particular offence was subject to fortuitous factors such as changes in police strength and policy. However, approached with these reservations in mind, the criminal and judicial statistics provide a valuable indication, if no more, of some of the long-term movements in public order offences and their distribution.[51]

Table 13.1 shows the number of committals for indictable offences of riot in England and Wales from 1836 to 1870, as well as the total of all committals for England and Wales and the percentage of all committals made up by public order offences; from 1857 it also shows the number of riotous offences known to the police. One of the most striking features of this table is the relatively small number of committals for riotous offences, running only once above 5 per cent in 1842. In most other years, the level of committals for riotous offences was much smaller, dropping below 1 per cent of all committals in eleven of the thirty-five years. We are dealing then with a very small proportion of total crime as reflected in the numbers of people committed for trial on indictable charges. However dramatic or politically significant popular disturbances might be, they show up nationally as one of the smaller areas of criminal activity. More detailed analysis of the figures for each county presents serious difficulties because of the small numbers of committals; a not untypical county such as Berkshire has only 104 indictments for serious riotous offences for the whole period 1836–70. One or two large disturbances or the movement of a body of rioters across a county boundary, not to mention the alterations in policing arrangements or policy, could easily affect figures of this magnitude.

Table 13.1 Committals for indictable riotous offences* 1836–1870 (England and Wales)

	Committals for all indictable riotous offences	Indictable riots known to police (from 1857)	Committals for all indictable offences	Committals for riotous offences as % of all committals
1836	524	–	20,984	2.497
1837	523	–	23,612	2.215
1838	421	–	23,094	1.822
1839	792	–	24,443	3.240
1840	630	–	27,187	2.317
1841	565	–	27,760	2.078
1842	1628	–	31,309	5.199
1843	663	–	29,591	2.240
1844	571	–	26,542	2.151
1845	363	–	24,303	1.493
1846	307	–	25,107	1.222
1847	386	–	28,833	1.338
1848	644	–	30,349	2.121
1849	279	–	27,816	1.003
1850	318	–	26,813	1.186
1851	220	–	27,960	0.786
1852	370	–	27,510	1.345
1853	217	–	27,057	0.802
1854	230	–	29,359	0.783
1855	132	–	25,972	0.508
1856	155	–	19,437	0.797
1857	138	302	20,269	0.680
1858	173	160	17,855	0.968
1859	136	187	16,674	0.815
1860	54	50	15,999	0.337
1861	162	53	18,326	0.883
1862	169	79	20,001	0.845
1863	209	81	16,461	1.269
1864	173	89	15,308	1.130
1865	203	133	15,411	1.317
1866	200	46		
1867	196	78	15,208	1.288
1868	249	161	16,197	1.537
1869	257	102	15,722	1.634
1870	126	53	14,010	0.899

*Includes offences of riotously and feloniously demolishing buildings, machinery, etc.; riot, breach of the peace, and pound breach, and (from 1839) riot and sedition. Indictments for High Treason (14 in 1840; 12 in 1848) have been excluded and offences of rescue and refusal to help the police.

(Source: *British Parliamentary Papers*, 1835–1870).

However, taking some of the counties with larger populations, such as Lancashire and Yorkshire, which also contained a substantial manufacturing population, it is clear that the pattern did not significantly alter from the national one. Calculating the proportion of committals for riotous offences as a proportion of all committals in these counties, the figures work out at just over 2 per cent in each case, slightly higher than the national average but not dramatically so. Public order offences in

Lancashire and Yorkshire, even including the peak years of the Chartist movement, were still a very small proportion of the offences for which people were committed for trial. Counties are a somewhat indiscriminate category from which to analyse variations between different types of area as boundaries often cut though important manufacturing districts such as those on the Lancashire-Cheshire border, or include rural and urban districts, often with widely different occupations and conditions. However, in his important study of the 'Black Country', Dr Philips has attempted to analyse crime in a primarily manufacturing district which covers several counties; his analysis suggests that riotous offences for the period 1835-60 accounted for 2.7 per cent of all committals, far outweighed by the larger categories of larceny, offences against property with violence, and assaults.[52] Nor is the pattern substantially altered if we use such statistics as are available for the larger cities. The parliamentary papers contain a useful analysis of the police returns for all offences, indictable and summary, for the year 1848 in London, Manchester and Liverpool. This was by no means the 'quietest' year in the period we are considering, yet the number of public order offences was again very small: out of a total of 64,480 people taken into custody in the Metropolitan Police area in 1848, only 239 were taken for riot, rescue offences or sedition (30,200, and 9 respectively), 0.37 per cent of the total; in Manchester the figures were 70 out of 6,277 (25 for riot, 22 for rescues, 33 for sedition), 1.12 per cent of the total; in Liverpool there were only 150 rescue offences from over 21,000 people taken into custody and discharged, committed, or summarily punished.[53] While it is possible that a large number of riotous offences were disguised as summary convictions for assault, disorderly conduct, vagrancy and other offences, not to forget the unknown 'dark number' of unrecorded offences, it remains the case that public order offences represented only a small proportion of all recorded crime.

The major exceptions to this pattern were in some of the manufacturing counties during the peak years of Chartist and industrial unrest. These can best be shown in Table 13.2

Table 13.2 Riotous offences (including riot and sedition) as a percentage of all committals in each county, selected years

	1839	1840	1842	1848	Average 1839-48
Lancashire	5.72	4.19	12.14	3.46	7.5
Cheshire	4.25	4.22	7.27	5.51	8.2
Staffordshire	4.08	3.14	19.46	0.89	10.2
Yorkshire	3.76	3.32	9.39	6.77	4.1

The number of committals for riotous offences in Staffordshire in 1842 stands out as the highest percentage experienced by any county in the whole period 1835 to 1870, clearly reflecting the extensive strike movement and rioting of that year. With the one exception of Staffordshire in 1848, all these counties experienced a number of committals for riotous offences which far exceeded the national average.

In examining the distribution of committals for riotous offences over the whole period, it is clear that the years 1836–48 were the most 'disturbed'. Nationally, however, there was a reduction in the years which followed, as shown in Table 13.3

Table 13.3 Committals for riotous offences by decade (England and Wales)

	Riotous offences per year (including riot and sedition)	Riotous offences per year (excluding riot and sedition)
1839–48	654.9	486.4
1849–58	223.2	221.7
1859–68	175.1	175.1

Table 13.3 makes clear the sharp fall in the number of riotous offences in the decades after 1848. This holds true even if the category of offences which came under the heading 'riot and sedition' (introduced in 1839) is excluded; riotous offences still stand considerably higher in the decade 1839–48 than in subsequent ones.

This pattern of fewer committals for riotous offences in the mid-Victorian period holds good for individual counties, although the small number of committals makes it extremely treacherous to undertake elaborate statistical investigation. In every instance the late 1830s and 1840s marked the peak; all experienced a diminution of activity during the 1850s and 1860s, in some cases to the point where committals for riotous offences almost ceased altogether: for example between 1856 and 1870 only three people were committed for riotous offences in Bedfordshire; only four in Buckinghamshire, and only nine in Hereford-shire, all primarily agricultural counties. But the situation was little different in the urban and industrial counties, the number of committals also falling sharply as shown in Table 13.4.

Table 13.4 Riotous offences per 10,000 population, selected counties

	1839–48	1849–58	1859–68
Lancashire	7.5	1.9	0.6
Yorkshire	4.1	0.9	1.1
Staffordshire	10.2	1.8	1.0
Cheshire	8.2	1.6	2.3
Warwickshire	3.3	0.8	2.1

This picture has also been confirmed by Dr Philips's study of the Black Country, where 'a definite trend away from violence and public disorder' has been identified for the period 1835–60.[54]

On the basis of the criminal statistics we can see that Victorians were correct in claiming that they lived in a more orderly society. We need not, of course, rely on statistics alone to illustrate the decline of Chartism and the receding threat of social and political upheaval, nonetheless the statistics do suggest that there was a decline in the incidence of popular disturbances, at least as measured by the number of committals for serious riotous offences. Few things, perhaps, better illustrate the differences between the 1840s and the years which followed than the number of people committed for offences under the heading 'riot and sedition'. The ten years 1839–48 saw 1,725 committed for trial on these charges, as well as another 26 on charges of High Treason; in the two decades which followed the numbers fell dramatically, with only 15 people being committed for riot and sedition, and none for High Treason. Nor was the tendency confined to these 'political' offences, but was represented across the board as a decline in committals for all indictable riots in the years after 1848, a decline which was reflected in rural as well as urban areas, in industrial as well as agricultural communities. Mid-Victorian society may not have been entirely free of popular disturbances, but it was certainly less prone to them than the early Victorian period.

There was more to Victorian perceptions of the orderliness of their society than can be expressed in criminal statistics. In part, at least, one is dealing with attitudes and beliefs which represented a particular moment in social and political development. One crucial perspective for Victorians was that whatever the dangers and difficulties of the past, Britain had escaped the revolutionary upheavals which had affected other nations; 1848 had been particularly important in confirming a sense of the efficacy of English institutions and way of life, no doubt all the more fervent because it came after a decade or more of genuine concern about the 'condition of England' question and the threat of social upheaval. For example, within ten days of the 'defeat' of the Kennington Common meeting, the *Sheffield Iris* of 20 April 1848 boasted:

> In no other country in the world could what occurred last Monday and the preceding days take place. . . . There is full liberty to play the braggart, full liberty to play the fool, full liberty to run the head against the wall, the full resolution to maintain the barriers of order and stand by them manfully. . . .
> Often and often as the example of England has served the world, never did it render a greater more signal service, than last Monday . . . while Europe is swept by the hurricane, England alone is hardly stirred. . . . But to what is this security owing? – to knowledge which every intelligent man has, that upon the maintenance of order depends his all; that his condition must be impaired by any calamity: the commotion must cost him dear: that revolution would be followed by ruin and beggary. Every part of our social system is sympathetic, a wound anywhere is felt everywhere, the nerves have their ramifications throughout. Consequently each, in acting for the good of all, does his best himself. The policy of every man is to spare no exertion, no petty sacrifice for the maintenance of peace and order.

The decline of riot and disorder was seen by many Victorians as one among many signs of social improvement. Some reformers, like Francis Place, were claiming as early as the 1820s that there had been a decisive change in the manners and habits of the population. Such claims, however, seemed premature in the light of the upheavals of the Chartist period. For several years, the country appeared to be locked into a vicious cycle of trade depression and social unrest, in which a full awakening to the consequences of industrialisation created real dismay and seemed to pose problems of an entirely new order. Nevertheless, within a generation, there were those who recognised that even the worst years of unrest had offered a glimmer of hope. It was the Manchester historian J. Reilly, writing in 1865, who noted that 'A turn-out like that of August, 1842, occurring twenty years previously, would have occasioned a civil war.'[55] Similarly, L. O. Pike, in his *History of Crime in England* (1873-6) regarded the 1840s as a watershed, arguing that increased education and changes in the law had produced a more orderly and law-abiding society. Education had taught working men respect for the law, whilst the end of cruel and degrading punishments both reflected and encouraged more humane and civilised attitudes.[56]

By the 1860s Victorian social reformers were far more concerned with the general problems of crime than the specific question of disorder. Even when a particular incident did achieve public notoriety, such as the Sunday Trading riots in Hyde Park, there was a tendency to blame violence on a well-defined 'criminal' or 'dangerous class'.[57]

The large cities, especially London, were believed to retain a potential for violence of this kind and increasingly attracted the attention of social reformers who sought to eliminate what they saw as the breeding grounds of both physical and social disorders. In his famous study, *The Rookeries of London*, published in 1852, the Rev. Thomas Beames described St Giles, Westminster, as

> inhabited by the various classes of thieves common to large
> cities – the housebreaker, who did not profess to have any other
> means of livelihood; the tramp and vagrant, whose assumed
> occupation was a cloak for rogery; the labourer who came to
> London to look for work; the hordes of Irish who annually seem
> to come in and go out with the flies and the fruit.

These were the areas, he alleged, which had provided the French revolution of 1789 with its recruits, drawn from 'St Antoine, the St Giles of Paris'.

> We say, not that these divisions of the body social originate
> popular disturbances, but they are the fuel on which agitation
> feeds, ready to take fire the moment the flame is kindled by
> great party feuds. . . . England's domestic difficulties, her foreign
> embroilments, a crisis in her councils, a split in her parties, will
> alike evoke ready instruments to do by violence what should

have been done by a paternal Government . . . when rebellion recruits her forces she is fed by the denizens of these retreats. It is on record that during the combats in Paris in 1848, and on the famous 10th of April here, multitudes of strange figures issued from these lurking places distinguished by their appearance from the rest even of the poor population. They bide their time; the agitator calls, and 'they will come when he doth call'.[58]

These fears, amplified in the writing of other social investigators in the mid-Victorian period could assign the persistence of disorder to a clearly defined 'dangerous class', seen at its most threatening in the capital's 'rookeries'. Thus when disturbances appeared in the capital in the 1860s, the dangerous class provided an explanation for disorder which did not contradict the main tenets of 'improvement'. Violence was the product of a residuum which remained to be brought under the ameliorative influences of Victorian philanthropy. In the country at large, the persistence of violence was also blamed primarily on specific groups, such as the 'roughs' or the Irish, who remained an exception to the general progress of society.

Victorians were not indulging in self-deception when they claimed to be living in a more stable and orderly society. They were acutely conscious of having escaped the revolutionary upheavals which had swept the continent and of having left behind the divisive conflicts of the early Victorian era. Increasingly, popular disturbances were regarded less as a threat to the political structure of the country than as a social 'problem' to be dealt with like many others. Indeed, the concept of a 'dangerous class' permitted Victorians to accept a degree of minor disorder while maintaining that their society was generally improving. One result was a slightly complacent attitude towards popular disorder which led to a degree of shock when serious incidents occurred, as in the 1880s and in the years before the First World War. Essentially, the Victorians had reached a position which was to be maintained for much of the twentieth century, that of only intermittent concern with the problem of public order, usually in the wake of some exceptionally violent or embarrassing incident.

14 Conclusion

It is extremely hazardous to attempt to draw general conclusions about the many diverse disturbances examined in the previous pages. They cover a wide range of issues, illustrate complex motives, and occurred in many different environments. Many, particularly in the eighteenth century, remain tantalisingly obscure, although considerable progress has been made in examining particular areas and forms of activity. First-hand accounts of disturbances are not so common that we can always be definite about the motivation and objectives of the participants. These have often to be inferred from the actions of the people concerned, a particularly treacherous procedure which can lead to misrepresentation of an event in the search for neat categories and clear patterns. Moreover, popular disturbances were, and still are, a highly complex phenomenon. One has only to observe the enormous output of analysis and interpretation about the disturbances in American cities and universities in the 1960s to be aware that there are no simple answers to why they occurred or about their role in larger social and political processes. Many commentators find current examples of collective violence, such as that which occurs in football crowds, difficult to explain, even though we are in a far better position to collect data, interview participants, and observe the events at first hand than we are in the case of a disturbance in a small village in the early eighteenth century. What follows here therefore is not an attempt to provide a grand general theory of the causes and role of popular disturbances, rather the intention is to suggest some of the main lines of thinking and to comment on them in the light of current research and the material discussed in these pages.

The causes

There is no simple answer to why disturbances occurred at one time rather another or in some places rather than others. Earlier writers, such as Rudé, have done much to dispel the customary association of riots with the criminal, the unemployed, and the marginal. Many of the most persistent or extensive waves of unrest, including food riots, machine-breaking, and the 'Captain Swing' disturbances have been recognised as involving fairly typical cross-sections of the local population. If then, many of these involved relatively ordinary people, are there any factors which can be isolated as generating popular disturbances?

Probably the most persistent attempts have been made to relate popular disturbances to economic factors. One of the most influential of these was W. W. Rostow who produced a 'social tension' chart constructed from the movement of wheat prices and the fluctuations of the trade cycle between 1790 and 1850.[1] Similarly, T. S. Ashton highlighted the coincidence of popular disturbances and harvest failure in the course of the eighteenth century. E. J. Hobsbawm also attempted to correlate economic fluctuations in the nineteenth century with a wide range of social movements, including not only such things as food riots, but the growth of trade unionism and political militancy.[2] Some historians, notably E. P. Thompson, have condemned the 'gross economic reductionism' of these explanations, arguing that the disturbances which did occur resulted from a more complex and sophisticated response of the populace to events.[3]

There is no doubt that the relationship between economic hardship and protest is extremely complex. Initially it can be said that many food riots occurred in times of high prices, taking broad averages year by year; with the growth of industrialisation there also appears a rough correlation between periods of trade depression, distress, and unemployment with the incidence of protest and political agitation. Cobbett's dictum that 'I defy you to agitate a man on a full stomach' is almost a cliché and must be respected in the sense that it reflects the experience of many early reformers that periods of distress provided the most fertile soil for the development of mass agitation. Whatever the frustration felt with Rostow's 'social tension' chart, its peaks in 1795, 1800, 1812, 1819, 1830-1, 1839, 1842, and 1848 do mark significant years of social unrest, political agitation, and popular disturbances; in the light of the evidence presented in the preceding pages, however, it must also be seen as insufficient in itself. One of the most interesting features of any period of unrest was the way in which disturbances were confined to particular places and times within these years of 'social tension'. There are too, many types of disturbance, such as those associated with the Sacheverell trial, the Gordon Riots, the Militia Act, and the religious upheavals of the nineteenth century, which owe little or nothing to economic circumstances. Often one can find a contributory economic motive in some attacks on minority groups, such as the Quakers or the Irish, but these too have usually to be placed in a wider context in which the economic factor was one among many.

The most detailed accounts of events such as Luddism or the 'Captain Swing' episodes also illustrate complexity of motive. What was often most important was less the absolute level of deprivation than popular perceptions of status, living standards, or accepted practice; the state or 'relative deprivation' rather than absolute deterioration was crucial in many instances. Carlyle wrote: 'It is not what a man outwardly has or wants that constitutes the happiness or misery of him. Nakedness, hunger, distress of all kinds, death itself have been cheerfully suffered, when the heart was right. It is the feeling of injustice that is insupportable to all men. . . . No man can bear it or ought to bear it.'[4] This element of perceived injustice mobilising discontent operated in many disturbances: food riots tended to occur where malpractice was suspected, militia riots against innovatory balloting procedures, attacks on press gangs for straying outside the customary categories of men to be taken, and machine-breaking attacks against 'unfair' machines or work practices. As a psychological factor it is extremely difficult to be precise about the extent of such feelings or the way in which individuals perceived their situation. Some have criticised the idea of 'relative deprivation' for its vagueness, but it provides a useful if not entirely determinable perspective from which to judge why some places were disturbed and others were not, why conditions accepted in some years were rebelled against in others. It also provides an explanation for the occurrence of protest not at moments of maximum hardship, but often when a situation was improving.

The concept of 'relative deprivation' is thus close to the view of de Tocqueville that discontent within societies usually arises when conditions are actually improving or reforms being undertaken, situations in which new expectations and aspirations are aroused.[5] One of the favourite models for explaining the cause of revolution and social unrest is a statistical updating of de Tocqueville which sees a 'J-curve' in which expectations rise only to be frustrated by a short-term crisis: the crisis point occurs at the down-turn, when discontent is at its maximum and disturbances or even revolution can occur.[6] A rather similar idea can be applied to many aspects of popular disturbances. Clearly there have been periods of economic deprivation when groups have suffered with little or no overt response, but have reacted when there was some mitigation or prospect of mitigation of their condition; the case of the farm labourers in 1830 would appear an instance of this, a group who had not been conspicuously turbulent in times of hardship became so during a period of political crises at home and abroad with the possibility of some change in their conditions. Rising aspirations also fits the case of the early artisan reformers, men whose slight but often decisive advantages of living standards and education enabled them to make the first attempts at political organisation among the working population; similarly too, it was the 'labour aristocracy' of skilled trades, already active in the eighteenth century who were the most active in strikes, 'collective bargaining by riot', and in the formation of more permanent trade union organisation.

Moreover, in studying any particular disturbance it is often possible to pinpoint a moment when things might have turned out differently. There were many occasions when crowds assembled or milled about, rumours circulated, and a kind of 'pre-riot' situation developed. At this stage a great deal depended on relatively fortuitous factors: time and again disturbances were averted by the intervention of magistrates addressing angry crowds or by a judicious show of force, and leaders of agitations themselves often took decisive action to urge their followers to disperse when it appeared events might pass beyond their control. But inevitably in many of these situations, an inexperienced troop commander, an over-zealous policeman, a particularly determined section of a crowd, or some other event could tip the balance one way or another. Often it was the reaction of the authorities which ultimately decided what occurred. Charles Tilly has written:

> As odd as it may seem, the authorities have far greater control over the short-run extent and timing of collective violence, especially damage to persons rather than property, than their challengers do. This is true for several reasons. The authorities usually have the technological and organisational advantage in the effective use of force, which gives them a fairly great choice among tactics of prevention, containment and retaliation. . . . The authorities also have some choice of whether, and with how much muscle, to answer political challenges and illegal actions that are not intrinsically violent: banned assemblies, threats of vengeance, wildcat strikes. A large proportion of European disturbances turned violent at exactly the moment when the authorities intervened to stop an illegal but non-violent action. This is typical of violent strikes and demonstrations.[7]

One needs only to think of Peterloo, the Clerkenwell riot, and the Sunday trading disturbances to see the importance of this discretionary power in the English context.

Thus the origins of outbreaks are extremely complex. The relationship between deprivation and the incidence of disturbances is by no means simple and the reactions of the authorities play a considerable part in determining the nature and scale of what occurs. One of the most detailed examinations of these elements was conducted by the National Advisory Commission on Civil Disorder in the United States to investigate the causes of the wave of riots in American cities in the 1960s. This suggested that timing and location was often dictated by 'precipitating' factors of a largely fortuitous nature, little related to the underlying social economic grievances of the Negro ghettoes. Such discontents were a necessary precondition of the riots, but were not in themselves the decisive factors: it was the 'trigger' incidents which determined whether a disturbance took place at all and there were many instances of what were perceived as 'near riots' without any violence actually occurring.[8] The same can be said for England in this period: innumerable instances of crowds assembling but dispersing peacefully either under their own volition or through the effective management of the authorities.

Frequency and distribution

Although many of the major waves and spectacular episodes of popular disorder have generated a considerable literature, we still know relatively little about the 'normal level' of disturbances in English society. A great deal of work remains to be done on court records, local newspapers and other sources before we can be more certain of how common they were. This is especially true of the period before the expansion of the provincial newspaper press and the growth of judicial statistics in the nineteenth century. As a result it is difficult at present to assess how frequently particular communities experienced some form of tumultuous activity. It is deceptively easy to assume that because a large number of different types of disturbance can be found in the eighteenth century, that they were an everyday occurrence; in fact, such evidence as we have suggests that this was far from being the case. J. M. Beattie's study of crime in Sussex and Surrey provides one attempt to examine the number and nature of riotous offences as reflected in indictments for the period 1660 to 1800: he notes that in the rural areas the number of indictments for these offences are 'too few in most years' to make an examination of trends very meaningful; the urban parishes of Surrey, however, including the Borough of Southwark, show an average of five indictments for riotous offences in the 1670s and 1680s; during the early part of the eighteenth century, the numbers rose to an average of fifteen per year in 1722–3, with a peak of twenty-three in 1723; by the 1730s the number had fallen to an average of five per year and apart from a small 'bump' in the figures during the 1760s, the number continued to fall to a yearly average of one or two indictments by the late eighteenth century.[9]

As Beattie is at pains to point out, the number of indictments for riotous offences is a blunt tool with which to estimate the level of 'violence' in a community, but his figures do suggest that even in an area as populous as the Southwark parishes of London only a relatively small number of riots are reflected in the criminal indictments. Although the number rose between the 1670s and the 1720s, so too did the average number of indictments, from about 160 to about 200 per year. Moreover, the rise in the number for riotous offences could be the result of the insecurity of the early Hanoverian government acting to repress any signs of discontent, a view which has received corroboration from other sources. As a result, it is difficult to assess accurately whether the number of disturbances had increased or merely the sensitivity of the authorities. Turning to other parts of eighteenth-century England, the problem is more acute because of the lack of analysis of long runs of court records for particular communities and the poorer quality of newspaper sources. Historians still have to rely upon relatively impressionistic evidence in assessing how often some of the large provincial towns were 'disturbed'. J. D. Chambers, for example, recorded his opinion that in the years between 1700 and 1760, Nottingham experienced serious riots 'very infrequently'.[10] This appears a valid generalisation for almost any major town in the eighteenth century: occasional major riots involving significant damage, serious injury, or large numbers, against a background of more frequent minor disturbances. On the whole, local historians have tended to note only the most significant or notorious episodes whereas the extent of smaller-scale disorder remains obscure.

For the latter part of the eighteenth and for the early part of the nineteenth centuries more studies are available. Dr Bohstedt has carried out an examination of riots in England between 1790 and 1810 and found a total of 740 'full-scale' riots, 26 of which involved loss of life. He has broken down the total into the categories shown in Table 14.1:

Table 14.1   Riots in England, 1790–1810[11]

Food riots	335.5
Riots against impressment, militia, and crimps	148.0
Political riots	58.5
Labour riots	43.5
Brawls	38.0
Rescues and resistance to authorities	16.0
Collective assaults on individuals	13.0
Enclosure riots	10.0
Theatre riots	8.0
Smuggling and excise riots	6.0

Here the importance of food riots and recruiting disturbances is clearly shown, although it must be borne in mind that this period was peculiar in witnessing two periods of severe harvest failure and was also one of almost continuous warfare. It would therefore be dangerous to regard it as in any way a 'typical' twenty-year period from which it is possible to extrapolate evidence about the period before or after.

This breakdown can be compared with one for disturbances in London between 1790 and 1821. Taking all disturbances in which there was some damage to persons or property and three or more people involved, the number is shown in Table 14.2.

Table 14.2   Disturbances in London, 1790–1821

1790	5	1801	9	1812	5
1791	3	1802	5	1813	3
1792	9	1803	5	1814	4
1793	1	1804	9	1815	12
1794	12	1805	3	1816	5
1795	13	1806	3	1817	4
1796	9	1807	5	1818	12
1797	7	1808	6	1819	12
1798	5	1809	4	1820	10
1799	4	1810	15	1821	11
1800	12	1811	2		

While Table 14.2 may not be a complete record of all disturbances in the London area, because of the inevitable limits of newspaper reporting, indictments and other sources, it does reach down to a fairly low level of incident and cover all the parishes within the metropolitan bills of mortality. It includes many incidents which can be described simply as aggravated brawls, but no doubt omits many incidents which newspapers thought too trivial to be beyond their interest. However, the suggestion of these figures is that in a city of around a million people, we are dealing with a situation in which some disturbances occurred every year with peaks in years such as 1794-5, 1800-1, 1810, and 1820-1. These peaks clearly reflect the major episodes of disorder described earlier, but what is more important here is the general level, running at an average of seven per year in 1790-1800, six in 1801-11, and eight in 1812-21. It would be impossible to select a 'typical' year – none was – but outside the years marked by major disturbances, which in London tended to be linked with some great political campaign or issue, we are left with a relatively small total of incidents each year. Numbers, of course, mean little in themselves, but it can be added that the great majority of disturbances in the capital during these years were fairly minor in the sense that they were over quickly (46 per cent within an hour), involved at most minor damage to property or assaults on persons (88 per cent), and were highly localised, affecting one or two streets (over 70 per cent). The percentages in which the troops were called out, the Riot Act read, or in which capital proceedings followed were also small, running at 12, 10, and 7 per cent respectively.

The distribution of disturbances by type is also interesting, reflecting a different pattern to that found for the country as a whole by Bohstedt, although there is also some difference in categorisation (Table 14.3).

Table 14.3 Types of riots in London, 1790–1821

Political	60	Prison	10
Brawls	40	Community	
Recruiting	36	Justice	10
Resistance to		Labour	7
Authorities	25	Religion	3
Price	20	Others	12

Compared to England as a whole, the importance of political disturbances in London is well marked; recruiting played a large part as a source of disorder, as it did in the country as a whole; brawls, a high percentage of which occurred between groups of sailors in the riverside district, were also a more significant feature of the disturbances in the capital than in the country. Equally striking are the small number of religious disturbances in London, a category which would almost certainly have been higher in any similar examination a hundred years earlier.[12]

A critical question is to what extent the level and pattern of disturbances altered with urbanisation and industrialisation in the first half of the nineteenth century. Historians of crime have recognised an increase in the number of committals for indictable offences between the first decade of the nineteenth century and the middle of the century (Table 14.4).

Table 14.4 Total committals for trial, England and Wales

1805	4,605
1810	5,146
1815	7,818
1820	13,710
1825	14,437
1830	18,107
1835	20,731
1840	27,187
1845	24,303
1850	26,813

The number of indictments increased at a much faster rate than that of the population as a whole, rising nearly six times between 1805 and 1850, while the population less than doubled. Within this period, there were also periods when the number of indictments rose particularly sharply: between 1815 and 1819 the number of committals rose from 7,818 to 24,254; between 1835 and 1842 from 20,731 to 31,309; between 1845 and 1848 from 24,303 to 30,349.[13]

The relationship between the level of indictments and 'actual' crime has been raised earlier, but is particularly relevant to assessing the changing levels of disturbances because the numbers involved are often small and fluctuate wildly. For the period up to 1835, the level of indictments for riotous and allied offences clearly reflects major riots or waves of disturbances discussed in the text: 202 people indicted for Luddite offences in 1812-13; 148 in 1815-17; 62 in 1826; 282 in 1831; other years, such as 1806, 1811, 1822-5, and 1829-30 yield no indictments at all for riotous offences. Moreover, as many disturbances were no doubt classed as assaults or other crimes, the number of indictments, even in the most disturbed years, bears little relation to their significance.

The judicial statistics appear a more sensitive barometer when the years of Chartist activity are examined. Here the number of committals for riotous offences and the offence of resisting the police rose above earlier levels. In 1839 the London Statistical Society estimated that the total number of committals in England and Wales had averaged 22,174 per year over the period 1834-9; of these, the offences of riot and breach of the peace averaged 607 per year and resisting peace officers 579 per year.[14] These were much higher numbers than anything seen earlier, reflecting to some extent the presence of professional police forces and an increased sensitivity to crime of all types. In an industrial community such as the Black Country, Philips has shown that the number of indictments for riotous offences averaged over forty-one per year in 1835-42, a number which would have been regarded as high for the whole country in some of the quieter years of the early nineteenth century.[15]

Taking the country as a whole, the number of public order offences averaged 411 per year between 1834 and 1892. Within that figure, as seen in the last chapter, there was a peak in the 1830s and 1840s followed by a decline in the mid-Victorian period. In this respect, public order offences followed a similar pattern to other serious crime, showing an increase in numbers during the 1830s and 1840s and falling off later in the century. Within that broad pattern, as might be expected, periods of particular unrest could leave their mark as a 'bump' in the statistics. In a real sense, however, the 'increase' in riotous offences after 1835 must be considered as more apparent than real, a reflection as much of a more intense level of policing than of an 'actual' increase in offences. Many of the offences being recorded in the 1830s and 1840s were results of attempts by the police to regulate previously unregulated activities, ranging from prizefights, wakes and fairs to the conduct of public houses and everyday behaviour. The stage at which this took place varied from area to area. In London, it began in the eighteenth century and was evident in some of the reactions to the 'peelers' in the early 1830s. In many industrial districts, however, the years between 1835 and 1860 marked the decisive stages in the introduction of the professional police forces and it was no accident that 'recorded' crime increased during those years, as the police effort produced hostility and resistance. In the years after the 1850s, a more stable relationship was achieved between the police and their communities, one which was assisted by the development of more orderly and less violent means of protest.[16] The combination of these elements was complex, but it was showing itself in the incidence of public order offences by the 1850s.

Motives and beliefs

The most striking feature of many English popular disturbances was their essentially defensive character. Whether brought about by high prices, recruiting, new machinery, turnpikes, enclosures, Methodist itinerants, or a myriad of other causes, they occurred most frequently as attempts to resist interference of innovation of some kind. In doing so, the participants were acting in ways which were not unique to the eighteenth or nineteenth century; many which conform to similar patterns could be found before 1700. Examples of price-fixing riots, collective bargaining by riot, resistance to enclosure, community justice, and many other types discussed here can be found in early modern England. Although there is a tendency to think of the 'mob' as a peculiarly eighteenth-century phenomenon, we may be doing no more than recording the greater availability of source material and the sensitivity of social reformers and evangelicals from the latter part of the century to social evils, of which crime and disorder was one. Popular direct action to preserve threatened values, community norms, or customary living standards certainly has its roots far earlier. It is not too fanciful to see some of the major episodes of the early modern period, especially the anti-enclosure revolts of the 1620s or the 'Clubman's' revolt of the Civil War years, as bearing many of the characteristics of some of the events discussed here.[17] These characteristics might be said to be a sense of the legitimacy of the protest being made, a 'backward-looking' or conservative ideology, and a degree of restraint and propriety in the means of protest, often expressed in ritual or ceremonial elements. These have been illustrated often enough not to require reiterating here. What is important to recognise is that they were present at least as much in the seventeenth century and earlier and continued into the industrial era: although sometimes regarded as 'pre-industrial' forms of protest or communal expression, they can be found in Luddism, 'Captain Swing', anti-Poor Law disturbances, reactions to cholera hospitals, to the professional police, and to the immigrant Irish. Even in late Victorian and Edwardian England examples of popular resistance to innovation which are recognisable in these terms can be found, as in the reactions to compulsory vaccination during the 1870s, attacks on the Salvation Army in the 1880s, and the actions of 'jingo' crowds during the Boer and Great Wars.[18]

Probably the most ambitious interpretation of the eighteenth century 'crowd' has been Thompson's conception of the 'moral economy' which underpinned popular direct action:

> It is possible to detect in almost every eighteenth-century crowd action some legitimising notion. By the notion of legitimation I mean that the men and women in the crowd were informed by the belief that they were defending traditional rights and customs; and, in general, that they were supported by the wider consensus of the community. On occasion this popular consensus was endorsed by some measure of licence afforded by the authorities.

Taking his evidence primarily from food disturbances, he has argued that the various forms of action designated as food riots not only represented reaction to soaring prices and the malpractice of dealers, but also expressed 'a popular consensus as to what were legitimate and what were illegitimate practices in marketing, milling, baking, etc.'. These views were grounded on 'a consistent traditional view of social norms and obligations, of the proper economic functions of the several parties within which, taken together, can be said to constitute the moral economy of the poor'. Thompson has argued that this 'moral economy' might be seen at work in other aspects of popular resistance to change and used in the context of other infringements of popular rights over such matters as enclosures, game laws, work practices, popular recreations, and rights of access.[19]

In many respects this is a highly plausible perspective. As we have seen, many episodes were either direct interventions to preserve some threatened 'right' or a call upon the authorities to do so; participants in food disturbances commonly made appeal to the concept of a 'fair' or 'just' price for foodstuffs and the same appeal to custom can be seen in many labour disputes, with resistance to changed work practices, new machinery, or the dilution of skilled labour which might result in a threat to living standards. The principal danger lies in applying a too rigid notion of 'moral economy' to the many complex situations out of which disturbances could occur. Many of the changes in marketing and pricing to which Thompson refers in his work on food riots had occurred before the main waves of disturbances took place.[20] As in the case of the 'Captain Swing' disturbances, we seem often to be seeing a retrospective protest against earlier changes, the full import of which was only brought home at a time of particular crisis. Hence the incidence of protest did not necessarily correspond to actual changes in food marketing or other customary arrangements. Indeed there is a further difficulty here, in that there is a danger of taking too static a view of popular attitudes and assumptions. There is, for example, some evidence that even in asserting a 'fair' price for foodstuffs, the population did not 'fix' prices at a constant level, but one which took some account of the long-term changes in prices.[21] Price-fixing was a gesture of displeasure at exploitation and malpractice rather than a rejection of the market mechanism as a whole. Similarly, machine-breaking was not a reaction against machinery as such, but against the adoption of machines of a type or used in such a way that they presented an exceptional threat to living standards. If a 'moral economy' existed, it was remarkably flexible and resilient to change, for the most significant feature of eighteenth-century society was less the frequency of protest at innovation or deprivation than the ways in which such changes were accepted more often than not without causing protest.

Nonetheless when protest did occur it was most frequently justified in terms of accepted practice: this has often been characterised as 'backward looking'. Past experience and traditional arrangements provided the most obvious sanctions for resisting change, and much early protest sought its legitimacy in lost 'rights', even when these rights had been discarded many years earlier. They also tended to be couched in terms of loyalty to the existing political system, so that a breach of 'order' was prefaced by expressions of loyalty to the King or a readiness to accept the intervention of authority, provided specific grievances were met. Protest movements often existed in an ambivalent situation to authority, obviously inflicting a short-term rebuff on normal social hierarchies, while at the same time asserting their loyalty and law-abiding nature. This ambivalence is well-expressed by a handbill circulated in Gateshead during disturbances against the Militia Act in 1761:

> This is to give notice to all in general, that it is far from the hearts of any of us that is here met to-day, to be Rebellious against his Royal Majesty; but far from it, only what common men desire, is men of estates to hire men for the Militia as they were formerly; being very fit that they who have lands should

hire men to maintain them; for it is a thing that none of us will submit to, to be ballotted after this manner, as it is in vain to enlist or draw any belonging to this country; for we are resolved not to go out amongst us after this manner. – God save his Majesty King George the Third.[22]

Although it would be dangerous to see in this one document the 'typical' motives and beliefs of protestors in eighteenth-century England, it carries the authentic flavour of many of the episodes discussed in these pages: an affirmation of 'loyalism', a protest against a measure perceived as innovatory or burdensome, a hint of antagonism to the rich and powerful for not fulfilling their traditional obligations, and a strong sense of the legitimacy of the cause. These elements combined to provide many popular movements with their most striking characteristics, their discrimination, restraint, and ceremony.

Discrimination and restraint were usually shown in attacks on persons and property. Where either were attacked it was most commonly because they were seen as the legitimate targets of popular displeasure. Rioters often moved considerable distances to seek out the houses or property of their victims, totally ignoring the opportunities for assault and looting which their numbers and the powerlessness of the authorities gave them. In London, it was frequently remarked that the characteristic bouts of window-smashing were carried on by bands who moved about the streets with almost military precision, posting look-outs, and even sometimes ringing the doorbell to find if their intended victim was at home. Small notices or papers manufactured in the heat of the moment might direct rioters to targets often at considerable distance from their point of first assembly. Another frequent tactic was the 'uproar march' of a band of people through the streets, stopping off to break windows, huzza friends, or groan and hiss opponents and enemies. In country disturbances too, the movement of bands of people from one village to another or a series of forays from a town to neighbouring villages, farms or mills permitted protesters to visit 'justice' on widely separated targets. Rarely would violence or damage occur in a random way, but was characteristically directed at those who had made themselves 'obnoxious' or refused to cooperate. There could, however, come a point when such discipline as existed broke down. There were several occasions where a protracted disturbance could pass from a stage of relatively restrained activity to more general looting and violence. The Gordon Riots provide an example of the development over several days of more random and criminal acts by the participants. A similar transition has been noted in the later stages of Luddism, where the original machine-breaking attacks gave way to raids by semi-professional gangs in which common robbery was the main motive.

A similar qualification ought to be made in the case of the violence in popular disturbances; some were undoubtedly violent, disputes between mobs and press gangs and excise officers particularly so; even election crowds could prove intimidating enough and lead on occasion to serious casualties. Nonetheless, some of the larger disturbances in this period and some of the most frequent occasions of disorder led to very few fatal casualties. Although the death toll in the Gordon Riots was eventually over 300, they were accounted for by accidental deaths, people killed by the soldiers, or those subsequently executed. Similarly the shooting of William Horsfall during the Luddite outbreaks stands in marked contrast to a movement otherwise distinguished by the absence of serious casualties inflicted by the machine breakers. Perhaps most striking of all, the extensive 'Captain Swing' disturbances claimed no lives other than those executed by the authorities. As far as the evidence suggests, other major categories of disturbances, such as food riots, led to few fatal casualties being inflicted by the participants, although there was a steady trickle of people killed or executed for taking part in them. But this is not to turn every disturbance into a tea-party, for there were ample occasions on which people resorted to arms, men were killed, and those involved registered real fear. At least a dozen people were killed in disturbances in London between 1790 and 1821, most commonly in riverside brawls between sailors and in clashes between press gangs and local inhabitants, when as in the case of the more organised smuggling gangs, little quarter was given and serious casualties resulted.

While there is no doubt that vicious and bitter violence could occur, it remains the case that the balance of fatalities was heavily weighted against the participants. The casualties inflicted in suppressing the Gordon Riots alone probably outweighed the total number of people killed by rioters between 1700 and 1870. This does not imply that England was populated by a breed of noble savages, but reflects that many disturbances sought to inflict humiliation or exert pressure rather than indulge in indiscriminate bloodshed for its own sake. The attitude to property was similar. It has to be considered that for much of this period any large crowd that assembled was in a position to do as it pleased for several hours before the authorities could hope to have a chance of suppression by force. What remains striking is less how often crowds turned to indiscriminate damage, than how often they refrained from doing so. Attacks on persons and property tended to be more remarkable for the control exercised than for its absence.

The description of disturbances as 'ritualised' conveys the ceremonial and structured quality which many displayed. By no means all did, but it was sufficiently frequent for historians to have come to regard it as the hallmark of early protest movements. It was not necessarily restricted to protest, for much of the 'theatre' used in disturbances derived from popular festivals, trade rituals, and other communal occasions; its use provided both a sense of communal solidarity and marked out the specialness of the occasion.[23] Ceremony and ritual asserted a sense of self-importance which it was often hoped would be recognised by those in authority. Ritual elements survived in many industrial conflicts, strikers were called out by the local bellman, communal punishment visited on strike-breakers, and parades and demonstrations organised with some of the ceremony found in non-industrial environments. Bands of protesters marching before a loaf stuck on the end of a pole could be found in the Manchester of 1848 and some of these elements survived in the opposition to anti-Catholic lecturers in the middle of the century. In so far as ritual expressed communal feeling, it continued to exist in the new environment of the industrial district or the factory village.

Politically, it can be argued that much eighteenth-century protest was ultimately deferential. Apart from those elements in the early part of the century which were explicitly Jacobite, participants in disturbances either expressed no political feelings at all or affirmed their loyalty while protesting against specific grievances. Mobs who acted against dissenters, Catholics, and other minorities often claimed to be doing so on behalf of 'Church and King'. Handbills and anonymous letters often ended with a 'loyalist' slogan and there was even an occasions when food rioters, having concluded the unloading of a barge, gave a rendition of 'God Save the King'. This form of deference to higher authority has frequently been regarded as characteristic of popular movements among people who have no rationale for protest beyond that provided by existing frameworks of authority. As Hobsbawm and others have shown it can be found in many parts of the world in what is often designated as 'primitive' rebellion. The 'lost' and 'Pretender' Tsar movements of nineteenth-century Russia or the powerful myths of the 'just' Prince provide interesting parallels to the frequently expressed 'loyalism' of eighteenth-century crowds. Even the adoption of Jacobitism as an 'oppositionist' creed in some parts of Britain during the first half of the eighteenth century can be seen as the attempt to find a source of legitimacy for expressing grievances about wartime hardships, antagonism to dissent, or other grievances against the ministry of the day. Although only partly explored, Jacobitism fulfilled this role for many different groups at various points in the first half of the eighteenth century. Increasingly, however, the consolidation of the Hanoverian dynasty and Walpole's firm repression (and exploitation) of the 'Jacobite' menace reduced its importance as an alternative focus of loyalty and legitimation.

Even in the years of Whig oligarchy there were limits to the deference showed by English 'mobs'. Rudé has noted the 'levelling' instinct which showed itself in so many disturbances, in which crowds forced the wealthy to join in their shouts, acknowledge their champions, or bear a degree of abuse which would not normally be tolerated. In local fairs and wakes, numbers and the licence of the occasion allowed wealthy passers-by to be taunted or pelted. Many local festivals were built around a burlesque of local authority, as in 'Mock-Mayor' ceremonies, and on 'Mischief Nights' the well-to-do were favoured targets of pranks. More seriously, these instincts were revealed in the major disturbances, such as the Gordon Riots, when it was the houses of wealthy Catholics rather than poor ones who were attacked by the London populace. Antagonism to wealthy farmers, expressed in folk-songs, anonymous letters, as well as the writings of Cobbett, also played an important part in the 'Captain Swing' disturbances. Similarly, many of the major disturbances which moved beyond immediate objectives saw attacks on the symbols of, authority: the Newcastle Guildhall in 1740; Newgate prison in London in 1780, the town gaol and debtor's prison in Birmingham in 1791, the Bishop's Palace at Bristol and Nottingham Castle in 1831.

During the eighteenth century the London 'mob' displayed the most frequent political awareness, in part at least derived from its tradition of opposition to government, the collusion of City politicians, and the presence of a relatively wealthy artisan, tradesman and shopkeeper class who had their own sources of information in trade clubs, tavern societies and chapels. Rudé has shown that London crowds in the eighteenth century frequently asserted the 'rights' and 'liberties' of Englishmen and that these concepts enshrined an interrelated network of ideas, including popular chauvinism, no-popery, and a belief in the distinctive rights of Englishmen. The beliefs that Englishmen were not 'slaves', did not wear 'wooden shoes', and were possessed of a 'birthright' were frequently articulated in slogans, handbills, and popular rhymes, and appear often to have been derived from the religious and constitutional struggles of the seventeenth century. Appeals were commonly made to the 'Norman Yoke' and the 'Golden Age' of Alfred and Saxon Democracy, to the memory of Cromwell and the dismissal of the Rump, and the Whig martyrs, Sidney and Russell. During the anti-crimp house riots in 1794 a handbill was circulated which ran:

> Beware Britons of the hordes of crimps and kidnappers that infest the Metropolis and its environs, who rot and imprison its peaceful inhabitants. . . . Would such atrocious acts have been suffered in the Days of Alfred? . . . Is this the land so famed for Liberty? Did Sidney and Russell bleed for this? – Oh my Poor Country![24]

In 1815 the crowds who gathered outside the House of Commons during the passage of the Corn Laws were harangued with words: 'Do none of you remember Hampden, Russell, Sidney? And do you not remember Oliver Cromwell who so gloriously dissolved the Parliament? We had patriots in those times, why should we not have them now? Patriots, where are ye all?'[25] Sometimes slogans and notices conflated older struggles with more recent ones as when 'No 45, Liberty or Death. A Second Oliver Cromwell' was found chalked up in Banbury marketplace in September 1801. Libertarian rhetoric can be found well into the nineteenth century when the names of early radical leaders such as Burdett and Hunt were linked to the word 'liberty'.

The other great theme of handbills and slogans was patriotism. Handbills were addressed to 'Britons', 'Fellowcountrymen', 'Sons of Albion' and 'Patriots'. Even a conspicuously radical group such as the Spenceans used the patriotic slogan of 'England expects every man to do his duty' to summon people to the Spa Fields Meeting in December 1816, while another called for 'Our King and a free country'. Nor were these elements entirely lost in the Chartist period. The Bradford Chartists who assembled to initiate a rising in January 1840 were also addressed with the 'Englands expects . . .' theme. Clearly popular chauvinism was a theme which survived to be used by men who went much further in their demands than the characteristic eighteenth-century protester. The rhetoric of patriotism, like that of other 'backward-looking' elements could be turned to account to mobilise or attempt to mobilise opposition to the Government even if that opposition was of a more radical nature.

From the French Revolution, however, much of the ephemeral literature produced breathes a different spirit. It also raises greater difficulties. During the years between the 1790s and the 1840s there were undoubtedly groups such as the United Irishmen, the Spenceans, and the more militant Chartists whose aims were insurrection and agitation. Many of the handbills and notices sent into the Home Office by magistrates appealed to the example of France and expressed a more radical ideology than had been seen in the past; their presence in itself was significant, illustrating the growth of a radical ideology which although it sometimes used the libertarian rhetoric of the eighteenth century now made more open challenges to government. During the food riots of 1800–1 and in the disturbances of the Regency period, the Home Office received many examples of handbills, both printed and handwritten, anonymous letters, and other agitational literature which had been posted up, pushed under doors, handed about at meetings, or simply dropped in the street. As already suggested, the crucial problem is how far this material can be seen as representing those who took part in disturbances. Agitational literature was collected where no riots or disturbances took place, whilst many disturbances occurred without any obvious agitation. There is no denying that from the 1790s there were groups of men in England who had embraced a revolutionary ideology and sought to mobilise support. The critical question remains to what extent these men ever obtained a mass following for their ideas and how far a revolutionary ideology penetrated into the consciousness of significant numbers of the population as a whole. It is clearly established that there were several insurrectionary attempts in the years between the French Revolution and the Great Exhibition; it is also clear that many food riots, strikes, machine-breakings and other disturbances continued to follow earlier patterns without embracing a radical ideology.

The changing face of protest

The great change which appears to lie in the period under discussion is the growth of organised and pacific means of articulating demands. In fact, the contrast between 'riot' and more organised action is one that historians have done much to modify. Once many 'riots' are recognised as a more restrained and rational procedure, the gap between them and more permanent and institutionalised forms of action is substantially narrowed. Charles Tilly has argued that there are five reasons for seeing so-called 'primitive' protest in a more rational light: (1) it was frequently successful as a tactic, (2) it was effective in establishing or maintaining the solidarity of the groups involved, (3) it obeyed certain constraints, (4) it recruited its participants from ordinary people, and (5) it tended to evolve in cadence with peaceful action.[26] Examples of all these factors have been seen in many of the disturbances discussed in the preceding pages. Nonetheless, there is clear evidence of the development of more organised and permanent means of articulating grievances and presenting demands. We have seen how the rise of the reform movement depended on the development of middle- and lower-class organisations and the methods of effective agitation, notably the press, petitioning, and peaceful meetings and demonstrations. The growth of trade unionism, though by no means a straightforward process, also illustrates the increasing emphasis on more effective and more permanent forms of organisation.

This process was by no means simple, but there was a growing reliance by both middle- and lower-class groups on peaceful and orderly methods of protest. The first generation of artisan radicals emphasised their constitutional approach and disavowal of violent methods. Although some undoubtedly turned to conspiracy and insurrectionary plotting at points between the French Revolution and the mid-Victorian era, the absence of a major breakdown of government meant that protests had to be channelled within the existing political situation. Popular radicals, such as Place, Hunt, Cobbett and O'Connor, were often aware that whatever the frustrations and difficulties of gradualism, they had more to lose from violence and its subsequent repression than from broadening the basis of support and relying on the education of opinion. Operating within a pre-existing framework, the reform movement concentrated on orchestrating extra-parliamentary agitation in ways which would avoid repressive action by government. The apparent success of these tactics for middle- and upper-class pressure groups over the Orders in Council and the income tax turned the mainstream of reformers towards these methods. Men like Place seem to have taken an entirely pragmatic attitude; they may have wanted a more wholesale change, but having to work in the face of an undefeated and potentially repressive government the only option to fruitless rebellion was organisation. It was this attitude which often left the more passionate radical spokesmen out on a limb, forced to indulge in the 'language of menace' in order to wring concession from the government and build up mass support, yet forced to back down when faced with a challenge which would almost certainly lead to defeat. One result was that reformers were forced to concentrate on developing impeccably peaceful methods, ones which it was hoped would mobilise 'independent' members in the

Commons, influence Ministers, and impress voters.

As Chartism showed, there were limits to the 'language of menace', particularly for movements of men largely without the vote and faced with a hostile press and almost entirely hostile parliament. The growth of the electorate and the press did have important influences: the battle for opinion was less sharply focused on the House of Commons, and more sophisticated pressure-group tactics could be used. Charles Tilly has argued that Britain was the first country to develop 'modern' protest in which 'specialised associations with relatively well-defined objectives' make demands upon the political system. He has suggested that such modern disturbances as occur tend to 'develop from collective actions that offer a show of force but are not intrinsically violent'.[27] The demonstration that got out of control was the more likely source of political violence in late nineteenth- and twentieth-century Britain than the threat of violent insurrection.

The case of trade unionism is also complex. 'Collective bargaining by riot' existed where it was necessary as a substitute or complement to other methods of bargaining. Increasingly trade unions sought to obtain effective organisation in order to avoid resort to such means, fearing that they might lead to prosecution and bad publicity; early unions, hindered by legal ambiguities, weak organisation and disunity, were often forced to resort to violence on the frontier of effective organisation. Violence was characteristically employed against strike-breakers or those who threatened living standards, whether employers or other workmen. As a result violence occurred among weak trades such as the nailmakers of the Black Country well into the nineteenth century because it was the only means by which they could impose some form of discipline within a declining craft industry. A striking example of the way in which a short-term deterioration of bargaining position could lead to violence was that of the Sheffield trades in the 1860s, when a normally well-organised and effective groups of workers found themselves faced with a vulnerable situation and reacted with a series of attacks on those they believed were undercutting their livelihood.

Harold Perkin has argued that the years between 1780 and 1880 witnessed the emergence of a 'viable class society' in which conflicts between social groups evolved into a process of mutual bargaining. Threats of violence, demonstrations of strength, even the prospect of revolutionary upheaval were utilised first to wring concessions from the old order and then to bargain with it.

> The crucial factor in the rise of a viable class society was in fact the institutionalisation of class, the creation, recognition and acceptance of the political, social and industrial institutions through which the classes could express themselves, safeguard or ameliorate their standards and conditions of life, and channel their conflicts out of the paths of violence into those of negotiation and compromise.

The most likely period of violent upheaval was therefore when demands for a share in political and industrial power were met by repression and resort to the threat of violence appeared the only means of exacting recognition. For some at least the threat was not merely tactical, for there were those who adopted a revolutionary ideology which committed them to the overthrow of the existing order. These, however, always appear to have been a minority and by the mid-Victorian period relations between the classes in Britain could be characterised as 'a familiar kind of marriage in which the partners cannot live together without bickering but are perfectly aware than apart they cannot live at all'.[28] It was significant that some of the most celebrated disturbances in mid- and late nineteenth-century England occurred to safeguard the means of peaceful bargaining: the right to free assembly and of effective strike action.

The situation had been reached by mid-century where there were forms of organisation, methods of expressing grievances, and sufficient effective influence for the major interest groups to contain conflicts within the existing political framework. The broad cultural and economic forces which brought this situation about lie outside the scope of this study, but we can see the changing nature of protest as one of the symptoms. Alongside the story of the decline of certain forms of disturbances and their substitution by more organised and permanent institutional procedures, must also be placed those of economic growth, political and social reform, and the distinctive cultural influences which shaped English society.[29]

Revolution and order

It is important to recognise that there are two very different questions involved in discussing the growing 'orderliness' of British society, one which involves the threat of revolution and one which refers to a diminishing degree of more general disturbance. The question of how near England came near to revolution during this period is bedevilled by problems of terminology – what precisely is meant by revolution? Definitions vary between those who regard only major upheavals in which there is a major restructuring of political, economic and social forces as true 'revolutions' and those who are prepared to admit any sudden, violent change of regime into the category.[30] Each kind of definition can have its own validity, but it raises the difficult problem for British historians who have no recent model of revolution to draw upon of deciding when, if ever, Britain came close to a revolutionary crisis. What exactly does a 'revolutionary situation' look like? – the spring and summer of 1780?, the summer of 1795?, spring 1812?, May 1832?, April 1848?, or July 1867? The conventional wisdom usually assumes that any period of protracted unrest marks some kind of crisis in that it can undermine the authority of the regime. Violence other than that controlled by the state and its agents is therefore a potentially destabilising element to be contained or suppressed.[31] But clearly there are many kinds of violence which do not threaten the stability of the state and the relationship between popular disturbances and 'revolutionary situations' is by no means clear. Revolutions are not always heralded by a swelling volume of violent protest and it has been plausibly argued and documented by Charles Tilly and others that more violence and bloodshed customarily take place after a revolution than before.[32] It is also the case that many regimes have proved themselves able to exist with extensive and protracted violence. As Adam Smith remarked, 'there is a deal of ruin in a nation' and it is important not to see in what appear to be symptoms of a crisis, the crisis itself.

That being said, there are a number of factors which might be considered as the requirements for an upheaval which extends beyond a *coup d'état* in a narrow elite. Economic deterioration, particularly after a period of improvement, is usually necessary to provide significant mass support. There needs to be a group equipped with the kind of ideology to make them want to seize power when the opportunity arises. Lastly, there has to be some division or crisis in the ruling order which prevents it from suppressing opposition and operating the normal instruments of government. One can see that one or more of these factors were present on occasions in the period in question, but never together in such a way as to turn possibility into reality. Popular disturbances provide evidence of discontents which might have been mobilised by a revolutionary group; they could too, if serious or extensive enough, precipitate political crises within governments. But in themselves, popular disturbances were never sufficient to bring about a revolution without the coincidence of some of the other factors mentioned above.

Two other factors are also important in the English context. The pre-eminent role of London and its fascination for would-be in-surrectionists masked the fact that England was one of the most decentralised polities in eighteenth- and nineteenth-century Europe. Insurrection at the centre would have left local government intact and functioning at least for some time. Conspirators from the seventeenth century through to the early nineteenth thought in terms of capturing the prominent public buildings in London – the Bank and the Tower figure prominently in 1722, 1802, 1816, and 1820. The difficulty was always what to do next for, as Despard glumly admitted, a hundred determined men could seize prominent buildings in London, but it required many times that number to hold on to them. Moreover, with the growth of the industrial districts of the North and Midlands, the potential recruits for a rising were at a considerable distance from the capital. Although London had extensive working-class districts, the peculiarities of the metropolitan environment were such as to make them less of a threat than the population of contemporary Paris.[33] Simultaneous insurrection in the provinces was certainly a dangerous threat to the government particularly before the railway and telegraph added immeasurably to the efficiency of central government, but contact between different groups in the provinces was difficult to both carry out and keep secret. It was precisely when attempts were made to coordinate a nationwide conspiracy that it became most vulnerable to penetration by spies and informers. As a result, the kind of coordinated rising that might have been a real threat to the government during the most troubled years of this period was never realised.

Earlier historians have always included in the catalogue of factors which contributed to the security of English governments the simple fact of geography: that the insularity of mainland Britain provided one of the principal guarantees of domestic tranquillity. This is perhaps truer of the nineteenth century than the eighteenth; in the years after 1815 the United Kingdom had nothing to fear from foreign invasion in spite of a number of shortlived invasion scares. The point can be exaggerated for the period before 1815: both Jacobite and Jacobin conspirators looked to foreign aid to assist them and it was Walpole who claimed in the 1730s that what had been true in the fifteenth century remained so in the eighteenth:

Five or six thousand men may be embarked in such a small number of ships, and so speedily, that it is impossible to guard against it by means of our fleet. Such a number may be landed in some part of the island, before we can hear of their embarkation: and if such a number were landed, with the Pretender at their head, there is no question that they would meet with many, especially the meaner sort, to join them. In such a case, we could not march our whole army against those invaders and their assistants; because, if we should draw all our regular forces away from the other parts of the Kingdom, the disaffected would rise in every county so left destitute of regular troops; and the rebels being thus in possession of many parts of our sea coasts, would be continually receiving supplies, by single ships, from those who had at first invaded us.[34]

The Jacobite rebellion of 1745 illustrated the vulnerability of English regimes to invasion of this kind, even if ultimately unsuccessful. As it was, the security of English governments remained dependent on the ability of the fleet to intercept such threats and to prevent the kind of problems that might have been caused by successful invasion from the continent. The ability to prevent such incursions remained an important prerequisite of political stability.

It has not been the primary concern of this volume to examine in detail the growth and administration of the police, the role of the armed forces in dealing with popular disturbances, or the wider aspects of preventing civil disorder. At one time, the introduction of a professional police force was regarded as the social equivalent to the steam engine in the process of industrialisation: the 'heroic' invention which transformed the situation from one of persistent disorder to one of relative tranquillity. Just as the steam engine has been put within its appropriate context as a factor in the industrialising process, so the police have increasingly been seen to be as much a symptom as a cause of changes in social conditions. Although improvements in policing arrangements can be found as early as the mid-eighteenth century, particularly in the capital, the major developments of professional policing came after the most serious period of concern. London received a small group of professional constables and stipendiary magistrates in 1792, who proved extremely useful in policing demonstrations and regulating everyday life, but it was not until 1829, almost fifty years after the Gordon Riots, that a full-scale Metropolitan Police Force was established.[35] Boroughs and counties were only gradually brought within the orbit of professional policing in the years between 1835 and 1856 and even in the late Victorian period many towns had pathetically small forces of professional constables.[36]

Those who have been puzzled by the failure to establish a fully fledged police force earlier than this have perhaps tended to exaggerate the weaknesses of the authorities in the years before 1829. *Ad hoc* arrangements proved themselves adequate even during the Regency period and acceptable to a parliament which was at least as much concerned with reducing the burden of taxation as with combatting crime and disorder. The small force of professional police in London were used to deal with some of the most delicate problems of policing, providing a more sophisticated instrument than the troops for crowd control. In many towns, including the burgeoning industrial areas, reliance was placed on the local magistracy and constables, backed up if necessary by yeomanry and troops. In non-industrial areas, it was not until the 1830s and 1840s that it was felt necessary to supplement the traditional apparatus of public order and the time-honoured processes of social control. The expedients to deal with disorder ranged far beyond those of brute force, including the mobilisation of charity, conciliation where possible, and the exercise of selective terror where repression did become necessary; for example, the harsh treatment of the 'Captain Swing' disturbances illustrates the sensitivity of the governing classes to a threat from a group who had not previously been a serious problem. Increasingly, however, it became recognised that the police provided not just a more flexible instrument of control, but also one which could assist in the regulation of popular amusements and other areas of activity. The role of the police in mid-Victorian England was at least as important in this area as it was in the business of direct crowd control.[37]

Moreover, such evidence as we have suggests that the police were not in themselves the decisive instrument in producing a more orderly society. If the statistics for assaults on the police are anything to go by, late Victorian England was far from quiescent.[38] Nonetheless there had been a decline in popular disorder. This, however, was at least as much a result of cultural changes within English society as it was of the purely technical solution of the use of professional police forces. In perhaps the most detailed studies we have of this process, it has been recognised that the authorities were only able to operate with relative economy of force within a cultural context which permitted them to do so.[39] Hence from one perspective, the most significant feature of English development is not that disturbances occurred but that they did not occur more often: even in the largest waves for every village or town to witness some incident or other there were countless places where nothing happened. Equally it is striking to compare the statistics for public order offences in Ireland to those of England for a troubled decade such as the 1840s, a comparison which reveals that the level of disorder in the former was on a completely different scale as measured by the number of committals to trial.[40] The presence of some insurrectionary activity and a degree of ambivalence on the part of others should not obscure the readiness with which the majority of English reformers and trade union leaders were absorbed into conventional politics at both national and local levels. Their followers too, were not in the main prepared to risk life and limb in the face of intermittent distress when opportunities for piecemeal reform and gradual improvement were being offered to them. Here again, broad cultural factors conditioned the development of a more 'orderly' society in which protests were transmitted through organisations and a relatively harmonious relationship achieved between different groups without the need for a vast repressive apparatus. In that sense, the English 'mob' tamed itself, at least as much as it was tamed by government or its agents.

Writing in the early years of the Second World War, George Orwell considered that 'gentleness' and respect for the law were two of the essential qualities of English society. In doing so, he was doing no more than expressing one of our most enduring myths of ourselves.[41] Neither quality has always been present in English society or present to anything like the same degree in different localities. Nonetheless, like most myths, it has a core of reality. England did not experience revolutionary upheaval or counter-revolutionary violence to the degree experienced by many other societies in this period, in spite of the stresses imposed by urbanisation, industrialisation, and the transition from oligarchic government to the beginnings of mass democracy. The evolutionary perspective remains valid in dealing with English society, but clearly the issue was never quite so simple and straightforward as it has sometimes appeared. Nor, I would contend, is it sensible to regard those cohesive elements which operated in the English context with such force, most notably the faith in constitutionalism and patriotism, as having the same validity in other parts of the British Isles. If we have come to regard a relatively peaceful evolution as a cultural attribute of English society, we should always remember that the picture would look very different if viewed from the Highlands of Scotland or the Irish countryside. But, as an English working man once told Mr Gladstone, 'Damn all foreign countries, what has old England to do with foreign countries'![42]

References

Abbreviations used in references

BM British Museum
HMSO Her Majesty's Stationery Office
HO Home Office Papers, Public Record Office
PC Privy Council Papers, Public Record Office
PP [British] Parliamentary Papers
UP University Press
WO War Office Papers, Public Record Office

Chapter 1 Introduction

1. **R. Cobb,** *The Police and the People: French popular protest, 1789-1820,* Oxford UP, 1970, p. 3.
2. See **R. J. White,** *Waterloo to Peterloo,* Heinemann, 1957; for a recent study in this genre see **M. I. Thomis** and **P. Holt,** *Threats of Revolution in Britain, 1789-1848,* Macmillan, 1977.
3. **J. L. Hammond** and **B. Hammond,** *The Village Labourer,* Longmans Green, 1911, 5th edn 1966; *The Town Labourer, 1760-1832: the new civilisation,* Longmans Green, 1917; 4th edn 1966; *The Skilled Labourer, 1760-1832,* Longmans Green, 1919.
4. A not untypical reflection on this theme can be found in **G. M. Trevelyan,** *English Social History,* Longmans Green, 1944, pp. 347-9.
5. **R. F. Wearmouth,** *Methodism and the Common People of the Eighteenth Century,* Epworth, 1945.
6. **G. Lefebvre,** 'Foules révolutionnaires', *Annales historiques de la Revolution française,* **11** (1934), pp. 1-26.
7. **E. J. Hobsbawm,** *Primitive Rebels: studies in archaic forms of social movement in the 19th and 20th Centuries,* Manchester UP, 1959; **G. Rudé,** *The Crowd in the French Revolution,* Oxford UP, 1959 and *Wilkes and Liberty,* Oxford UP, 1962.
8. **G. Rudé,** *Paris and London in the Eighteenth Century,* Collins, 1970, p. 319.
9. See **E. J. Hobsbawm,** 'The machine breakers' in *Labouring Men,* 2nd edn, Weidenfeld and Nicolson, 1968, pp. 5-22.
10. Rudé, *Paris and London,* pp. 310-17.
11. See **E. P. Thompson,** *The Making of the English Working Class,* 2nd edn, Penguin, 1968, pp. 66-83; 'The moral economy of the English crowd in the eighteenth century', *Past and Present,* **50** (1971), pp. 76-136; and 'Eighteenth-century

English society: class struggle without class?', *Social History*, May (1978), pp. 133-65.

12. **J. B. Owen,** *The Eighteenth Century, 1714-1815*, Nelson, 1974, p. 74.

13. The repercussions of the change are noted in **W. A. Speck,** *Stability and Strife, England 1714-1760*, Arnold, 1977, pp. 255-6; for a contemporary account of the effects, see *The True Briton*, **4** (20 Sept. 1752), 117.

14. See **I. Taylor,** 'Football mad' in **E. Dunning** ed., *The Sociology of Sport*, Cass, 1970 and 'Soccer consciousness and soccer hooliganism' in **S. Cohen** ed., *Images of Deviance*, Penguin, 1971. The most ambitious attempt to analyse football 'hooliganism' has been **P. Marsh, E. Rosser,** and **R. Harré,** *The Rules of Disorder*, Routledge and Kegan Paul, 1978.

15. There is a useful discussion of some of the issues involved in **G. R. Elton's** introduction to *Crime in England, 1550-1800*, ed. **J. S. Cockburn,** Methuen, 1977, pp. 1-14.

16. This approach derives largely from the work in phenomenology, enthomethodology, and the 'new' criminology: see for example **P. L. Berger** and **T. Luckmann,** *The Social Construction of Reality*, Penguin, 1966. Some of the implications of this approach are covered in the introduction to S. Cohen ed., *op. cit.* There is also the more traditional Marxist view of 'bourgeois' order as represented by the law and social institutions. For a discussion of this view see **E. P. Thompson,** *Whigs and Hunters: The origin of the Black Act*, Allen Lane, 1975, pp. 258-69.

17. See the introduction to **A. P. Donajgrodski** ed., *Social Control in Nineteenth Century Britain*, Croom Helm, 1977, pp. 9-26; also G. Stedman Jones, 'Class expression versus social control? A critique of recent trends in the social history of "leisure"', *History Workshop*, **4** (1977), 162-70.

18. See **V. Bailey,** 'The Dangerous classes in late Victorian England. Some reflections on the social foundations of disturbance and order with special reference to London in the 1880s', Warwick University Ph.D. thesis, 1975; **D. Hay,** 'Property, authority and the criminal law' in D. Hay, P. Linebaugh, J. G. Rule, E. P. Thompson, and C. Winslow, *Albion's Fatal Tree: crime and society in eighteenth-century England*, Allen Lane, 1975, pp. 17-63; and **R. S. Storch,** 'The policeman as domestic missionary: urban discipline and popular culture in northern England, 1850-1880', *Journal of Social History*, **9,** 4 (1976), 481-509.

19. **D. Williams,** *Keeping the Peace: the police and public order*, Hutchinson, 1967, pp. 236-48; **W. S. Holdsworth,** *A History of English Law*, Methuen, 1938, VIII, 301-33; **I. Brownlie,** *The Law relating to Public Order*, Butterworths, 1968.

20. See Thompson, **Whigs and Hunters**, pp. 21-3.

21. The Treasonable and Seditious Practices Act, 36 Geo. III, c. 7; see Holdsworth, pp. 302-22.

22. **W. Firth,** *Commentary on the Late Treason Trials*, London, 1817, p. 48.

23. **E. R. A. Seligman** ed., *The Encyclopedia of the Social Sciences*, New York, 1948, XIII, 386.

24. **G. Le Bon,** *Psychologie des Foules*, Paris, 1895 (London, 1896). Le Bon can be regarded as the father of crowd psychology, but see also **G. Tarde,** *L'opinion et la foule*, Paris, 1901 and **R. E. Park,** *Masse und Publikum (The Crowd and the Public)*, Bern, 1904.

25. For a discussion of Park's contribution to the field of 'crowd' studies, see H. Elsner's introduction to **R. E. Park,** *The Crowd and the Public and Other Essays*, Chicago UP, 1972, pp. vii-xxxii.

26. **N. J. Smelser,** *Theory of Collective Behaviour*, Routledge and Kegan Paul, 1962, pp. 73-5.

27. **E. L. Faris** ed., *Handbook of Modern Sociology*, Rand McNally, 1966, p. 386.

28. **R. H. Turner** and **L. M. Killian,** *Collective Behaviour*, Prentice-Hall, 1957, p. 103.

29. Rudé, *The Crowd in History*, p. 244.

30. Turner and Killian, pp. 103-19; Smelser, pp. 255-6. For some recent contributions on crowd behaviour during riots see **E. L. Quarantelli** and **J. R. Hudley,** jr.

'A test of some propositions about crowd formation and behaviour' in R. R. Evans ed., *Readings in Collective Behaviour*, Rand McNally, 1969, pp. 538-54, also **J. R. Hundley,** jr. 'The dynamics of recent ghetto riots', *loc. cit.*, pp. 485-9. A similar variety of activities in football crowds has been observed, see Marsh, *et al.*, pp. 58-82.

31. See **H. Mannheim,** *Comparative Criminology*, Routledge and Kegan Paul, 1965, ii, 644. Looting in American city riots of the 1960s was carried out both by 'typical' riot participants and some existing 'delinquent gangs'. See **E. L. Quarantelli** and **R. Dynes,** 'Looting in civil disorders', in L. H. Masotti and D. R. Bowen, *Riots and Rebellion: civil violence in the urban community*, Sage, 1968, pp. 131-41.

32. The line is inevitably an arbitrary one. There is a useful discussion by **A. Arblaster,** 'What is violence?' in *The Socialist Register*, 1975, pp. 224-49.

33. See **W. Hawkins,** *A Treatise of the Pleas of the Crown*, 8th edn, London, pp. 513-16.

34. *London Chronicle*, 27 Oct. 1810.

35. See Rudé, *The Crowd in History*, pp. 3-16, 195-269.

36. Thompson, *The Making of the English Working Class*, pp. 67-83 and 'The moral economy of the English crowd in the eighteenth century', pp. 76-9.

37. See above, n. 30 and **R. J. Holton,** 'The crowd in history: some problems of theory and method', *Social History*, May 1978, pp. 219-33.

38. For the functions of the Home Office and the workings of central government at different points in this period see **M. Beloff,** *Public Order and Popular Disturbances, 1660-1714*, Oxford UP, 1938, pp. 129-51; **D. G. Isaac,** 'A study of popular disturbances in Britain, 1714-54', Edinburgh University Ph.D thesis, 1953, Pt II, Ch. vii; **R. R. Nelson,** *The Home Office, 1782-1801*, Durham, N.C., 1969; **F. O. Darvall,** *Popular Disturbances and Public Order in Regency England*, Oxford UP, pp. 218-49; and **F. C. Mather,** *Public Order in the Age of the Chartists*, Manchester UP, 1959, pp. 29-47.

39. Cobb, pp. 5-7. For other discussions of the role of informants see Darvall, pp. 274-303; Mather, pp. 182-225; and Thompson, *The Making of the English Working Class*, pp. 529-42.

40. Walpole's operations against Jacobite conspiracy are discussed in **P. S. Fritz,** *The English Ministers and Jacobitism between the Rebellions of 1715 and 1745*, Toronto UP, 1975, esp. pp. 99-101. An important reassessment of the nature of the informers used in the period after the French Revolution is available in **J. Ann Hone,** 'The ways and means of London radicalism, 1796-1821', Oxford University, D.Phil thesis, 1975, Ch. ii.

41. See **D. Vincent's** introduction to *Testaments of Radicalism: memoirs of working-class politicians, 1790-1885*, Europa, 1977, pp. 1-23 and **M. Thale,** *The autobiography of Francis Place*, Cambridge UP, 1972, pp. ix-xxxvii, especially pp. xix-xxvii.

42. See **G. Rudé,** *The Crowd in History, 1730-1848*, Wiley, 1964, pp. 10-14, 195-213.

43. See **V. A. C. Gatrell** and **T. B. Hadden,** 'Criminal statistics and their interpretation' in **E. A. Wrigley** ed., *Nineteenth-Century Society: essays in the use of quantitative methods for the study of social data*, Cambridge UP, 1972, pp. 336-96.

44. For the growth of the press, see **G. A. Cranfield,** *The Press and Society: from Caxton to Northcliffe*, Longman, 1978.

45. For Tilly's quantitative approach, see **C. Tilly,** 'Methods for the study of collective violence' in R. W. Conant and M. A. Levin eds., *Problems in Research on Community Violence*, Praeger, New York, 1969; 'How protest modernised in France' in W. Aydelotte, A. Bogue, and R. Fogel eds., *The Dimensions of Quantitative Research in History*, Princeton UP, 1972; and **C. Tilly, L. Tilly,** and **R. Tilly,** *The Rebellious Century, 1830-1930*, Dent, 1975, pp. 15-16.

46. **R. A. E. Wells,** 'Dearth and distress in Yorkshire, 1793-1802', *Borthwick Paper*, no. 52, 1977, p. 30.

Chapter 2 The age of riots

1. **Roger North,** *Examen: or an enquiry into the credit and veracity of a pretended complete history*, London, 1740. The *Shorter Oxford English Dictionary* dates the first use of the noun 'mob' to 1688.
2. See **W. L. Saches,** 'The mob and the revolution of 1688', *Journal of British Studies*. **4** (1964), 23-41 and Beloff, *Public Order and Popular Disturbances*, pp. 34-55.
3. *The Life and Times of Anthony A Wood*, Oxford UP (World's Classics), 1961, pp. 351-2.
4. See **D. Hirst,** *The Representative of the People?*, Cambridge UP, 1975, pp. 1-25, 42-3, 187-8.
5. **G. Holmes,** *British Politics in the Age of Anne*, Macmillan, 1967, p. 218.
6. J. Cannon, *Parliamentary Reform, 1640-1832*, pp. 36-7.
7. Beloff, pp. 49-50.
8. Beloff, pp. 54-5; **G. Holmes,** 'The Sacheverell riots', *Past and Present*, **72** (1976), pp. 55-7.
9. The fullest account of these disturbances is in **D. G. D. Isaac,** 'A study of popular disturbances in Britain, 1714-54' Edinburgh University Ph.D. thesis, 1953, Ch. viii.
10. *Ibid;* also **W. H. Thomson,** *History of Manchester* to 1852, Altrincham, 1967, pp. 144, 153; **J. A. Picton,** *Memorials of Liverpool*, Longman, 1873, I, 187.
11. **C. W. Boase,** *Oxford*, Longmans, 1890, pp. 182-3; **J. R. Green,** *Oxford Studies*, Macmillan, 1901, pp. 141-9; **J. C. Jeaffeson,** *Annals of Oxford*, Hurst and Blackett, 1871, ii, 231-8; **W. R. Ward,** *Georgian Oxford*, Oxford UP, 1958, pp. 55-6.
12. **F. D. Willmore,** *A History of Walsall*, 2nd edn, Walsall, 1972, pp. 352-3.
13. **S. Glover,** *The History of the County of Derby*, Derby, 1829, II, 608; Ward, pp. 62-3.
14. See **P. S. Fritz,** *The English Ministers and Jacobitism between the Rebellions of 1714 and 1745*, University of Toronto Press, 1975, pp. 20-9; Ward, pp. 64-5; **R. Sedgwick,** *The House of Commons, 1715-1754*, HMSO, 1970, p. 319; **R. W. Greaves,** *The Corporation of Leicester, 1689-1836*, Oxford UP, 1939, pp. 92-4.
15. Sedgwick, pp. 203-4.
16. See **L. B. Namier,** *The Structure of Politics at the Accession of George III*, Macmillan, 1929, I, 242.
17. **P. Langford,** *The Excise Crisis*, Oxford UP, 1975, pp. 120-3.
18. Namier, I, 101, 302-3.
19. Thomson, p. 185.
20. **R. F. Wearmouth,** *Methodism and the Common People of the Eighteenth Century*, Epworth, 1945, pp. 22-3; Picton, I, 208. A Catholic chapel was also attacked at Durham and a priest's house sacked, see **E. Hughes,** *North Country Life in the Eighteenth Century: the North-East, 1700-1750*, Oxford UP, 1952, pp. 24-5.
21. Ward, pp. 170-1; Sedgwick, p. 319, see also **J. M. Fewster,** 'The keelmen of Tyneside in the eighteenth century', **19** Pt II, *Durham University Journal*, **19** (1957-8), 73-4.
22. Quoted in Willmore, p. 368; *Gentleman's Magazine* (1750), p. 331.
23. Cannon, pp. 36, 41.
24. **R. J. Robson,** *The Oxfordshire Election of 1754*, Oxford UP, 1949, p. 128; Boase, pp. 184-5.
25. Greaves, pp. 101-2.
26. **J. Brooke,** *The House of Commons, 1754-1790*, 2nd edn, Oxford UP, 1968, pp. 13, 47, 115.
27. See **J. Brewer,** *Party Ideology and Popular Politics at the Accession of George III*, Cambridge UP, 1976, pp. 176-80.
28. **R. W. Davis,** *Political Change and Continuity, 1760-1885*, David and Charles, 1972, p. 29.
29. See **D. R. McAdams,** 'Electioneering techniques in populous constituencies, 1784-96', *Studies in Burke and His Time*, **14** (1972), 43-4.

30. **C. B. Jewson,** *The Jacobin City*, Blackie, 1975, pp. 22–3, 72.
31. Wearmouth, p. 41.
32. Brooke, p. 20.
33. See **W. Cobbett,** *Rural Rides*, Penguin edn, 1967, pp. 108–9.
34. See **I. Grub,** *Quakerism and Industry before 1800*, London, 1930, pp. 124–7. See Ch. 5, pp. 108–9.
35. See **J. Walsh,** 'Methodism and the mob in the eighteenth century', in G. J. Cuming and D. Barker, *Popular Belief and Practice*, Studies in Church History, VIII, Cambridge UP, 1972, pp. 213–27.
36. See **F. E. Halliday,** *A History of Cornwall*, Duckworth, 1963, pp. 266–7; and for his reception in the Sandgate district of Newcastle see Wesley's *Journals Deut* (Everyman edn), I, 374–5.
37. See **J. Ede,** *A History of Wednesbury*, Wednesbury, 1962, pp. 206–13.
38. Halliday, pp. 266–70.
39. *Ibid.*; also Walsh, pp. 226–7 and Wearmouth, pp. 249–52. Wearmouth records that two London newspapers, the *London Evening Post*, 16–18 February 1744 and the *London Daily Post and General Advertiser*, 17 February 1744, alleged that the Methodists had caused an insurrection and arson in the county of Staffordshire.
40. Walsh, pp. 222–5.
41. See **T. Shaw,** *A History of Cornish Methodism*, Barton, 1967, pp. 28–31; Wearmouth, pp. 258–9.
42. Shaw, p. 31.
43. *Ibid.*
44. Wearmouth, pp. 252–6.
45. Shaw, p. 29.
46. Wearmouth, p. 257.
47. An extract from the conference minutes was printed in a letter in the *Gentleman's Magazine* for December 1792. See also the *Arminian Magazine*, (1792), p. 493.
48. See the account in Wearmouth, pp. 260–2.

Chapter 3 Manifold disorders

1. **J. R. Western,** *The English Militia in the Eighteenth Century*, Routledge, 1965, esp. Ch. vi. For general background to the history of the militia the chapter draws extensively on pp. 128–9, 247–8.
2. *Ibid.*, pp. 245–64.
3. *Ibid.*, pp. 299–300.
4. *Gentleman's Magazine* (1757), p. 431.
5. See Western, pp. 290 ff.
6. *Ibid.*
7. *Ibid.*, p. 298; *London Chronicle*, 5, 14 Mar. 1761; *Gentleman's Magazine*, (1761), p. 138; **R. B. Turton,** *The History of the North York Militia*, Patrick and Shotton, 1973, pp. 44–6.
8. Western, p. 426.
9. *Ibid.*; **J. Prebble,** *Mutiny*, Secker and Warburg, 1975, p. 439.
10. **M. Howard,** *Studies in War and Peace*, Oxford UP, 1970, p. 51.
11. See **C. Lloyd,** *The British Seaman*, 2nd edn, Paladin, 1970, p. 116.
12. See Isaac, 'A study of popular disturbances' (thesis), Ch. ix.
13. See Lloyd, Ch. vii; **D. A. Baugh,** *British Naval Administration in the Age of Walpole*, Princeton, New Jersey, 1965, Ch. iv.
14. **R. B. Rose,** 'A Liverpool sailors' strike in the eighteenth century', *Transactions of the Lancashire and Cheshire Antiquarian Society*, **68** (1958), 85–6.
15. Quoted in Lloyd, p. 131; **H. R. Hikins** ed., *Building the Union*, Liverpool, 1973, p. 21.

16. *London Chronicle*, 3 August 1790.
17. C. Lloyd, pp. 132-3; *St James's Chronicle*, 28 Feb.-1 Mar. 1972.
18. Hammond and Hammond, *The Village Labourer*, p. 73.
19. **W. E. Tate**, 'Opposition to parliamentary enclosure in the eighteenth century', *Agricultural History*, **19** (1945), 137.
20. See **G. Slater**, *The English Peasantry and the Enclosure of Common Fields*, Constable, 1907, p. 112.
21. See J. D. Chambers and G. E. Mingay, *The Agricultural Revolution, 1750-1880*, Ch. iv. See also the discussion by **J. D. Chambers**, 'Enclosure and labour supply in the Industrial Revolution', *Economic History Review*, 2nd ser. **5** (1952-3), 325-7.
22. See the anonymous letters referred to by **E. P. Thompson** in 'The crime of anonymity' in D. Hay, P. Linebaugh, J. G. Rule, E. P. Thompson, and C. Winslow, *Albion's Fatal Tree*, Allen Lane, 1975, pp. 275-6. See also **A. J. Peacock**, 'Village radicalism in East Anglia, 1800-1850' in **J. P. D. Dunbabin**, *Rural Discontent in Nineteenth Century Britain*, Faber, 1974, p. 27.
23. Beloff, pp. 76-80; Slater; **H. C. Darby**, *The Draining of the Fens*, Cambridge UP, 1940, pp. 46-76; **F. Hill**, *Georgian Lincoln*, Cambridge UP, 1966, pp. 106-7.
24. See **H. G. Nicholls**, *Nicholls's Forest of Dean and Iron Making in the Forest of Dean*, David and Charles, 1966, pp. 37, 54-5; **C. E. Hart**, *Royal Forest*, Clarendon Press, 1966, pp. 91, 107, 125, 149, 171, 184, 189, 192, and 195. For the 'Black Act' see above pp. 46-7.
25. *Gentleman's Magazine* (1758), p. 286; *London Chronicle*, 28 Mar. 1761; Hammond and Hammond, *The Village Labourer*, p. 73.
26. **F. K. Donnelly** and **J. L. Baxter**, 'Sheffield and the English revolutionary tradition, 1791-1820', *International Review of Social History*, **20** (1974).
27. *Gentleman's Magazine* (1799), pp. 801-2.
28. The fullest account of these disturbances is in Isaac, Ch. v. See also *Gentleman's Magazine* (1749), pp. 376-7 and (1753), p. 343.
29. Figures from **W. Albert**, *The Turnpike Road System of England, 1663-1844*, Cambridge UP, 1972.
30. See Isaac, Ch. xi. There were further disturbances in the Bristol area in September 1793 when a group of people forced the toll gates on a turnpike near the centre of the city. Troops who were called up were attacked with stones and oysters! Eventually the troops opened fire, killing and wounding several; see *Gentleman's Magazine* (1793), p. 951.
31. See **C. Winslow**, 'Sussex smugglers' in Hay *et al.*, *Albion's Fatal Tree*, pp. 119-66. Also **D. Phillipson**, *Smuggling: a history 1700-1970*, David and Charles, 1973, pp. 77-85; **E. E. Hoon**, *The Organisation of the English Customs System, 1696-1786*, Appleton-Century, 1938, pp. 231-2 gives an account of the 'punishment' of customs officers in 1721 and 1764.
32. In 1783 it was estimated that there were at least 120 large armed vessels and 200 smaller ones involved in the smuggling trade. The most notorious of the professional gangs was that based on Hawkhurst on the Sussex-Kent border. They were responsible for the murder of a revenue officer and an informer in 1748, see Phillipson, pp. 79-85. Smuggling gangs in Suffolk were blamed for a series of armed robberies in 1749-50, see *Gentleman's Magazine* (1751), pp. 232-3 and *The London Gazette*, 7-11 and 11-14 May 1751.
33. See Halliday, *History of Cornwall*, pp. 263-4. Smuggling boats tended to be owned by individuals who both carried out the voyage and distributed the goods in contrast to Sussex and Kent where distribution was often carried out by known middlemen. Nonetheless some of the craft engaged in the Cornish trade were large and well-armed; a return of 1785 mentions one of 250 tons with 26 guns (12 and 9-pounders) and a crew of 60. See Phillipson, pp. 85-9.
34. **J. G. Rule**, 'Wrecking and coastal plunder' in D. Hay, *et al.*, pp. 167-88 and Picton, *Memorials of Liverpool*, I, 242-3.
35. See Thompson, *Whigs and Hunters*.

36. **D. Hay,** 'Poaching and the game laws on Cannock Chase', in D. Hay, *et al.*, pp. 189-253. There were attacks on rabbit warrens in Sussex in 1714, see **J. M. Beattie,** 'The pattern of crime in England, 1660-1800', *Past and Present,* **62** (1974), 64.

37. **F. Hill,** *Georgian Lincoln,* Cambridge UP, 1966, pp. 39-41. Bishop Reynolds claimed the disturbances were a result of the success of earlier riots in the Fens.

38. *Lloyd's Evening Post,* 20 Sept. 1765.

39. See **R. W. Malcolmson,** *Popular Recreations in English Society, 1700-1850,* Cambridge UP, 1973, pp. 126-35.

40. **A. F. J. Brown** ed., *Essex People, 1750-1900,* Essex County Council, 1972, pp. 36-7.

41. **G. Herbert,** *Shoemaker's Window: recollections of Banbury before the railway age,* ed., B. S. Trinder, 2nd edn, Chichester, 1971, pp. 73-4.

42. For 'skimmington' see **E. P. Thompson,** 'Rough music: le charivari anglais', *Annales: Economies, Societies, Civilisations,* **27,** 2 (1972), pp. 285-312.

43. **A. J. Peacock,** 'Village radicalism in East Anglia, 1800-50' in Dunbabin, *Rural Discontent,* pp. 47-8.

44. **W. L. Burn,** *The Age of Equipoise: a study of the mid-Victorian generation,* George Allen and Unwin, 1964, p. 238. Other 'legitimising' views were that the 'stang riders' could not be touched if it was carried out in three parishes or if the ride marched around the parish church three times, see Storch, 'The policeman as domestic missionary . . .', pp. 489-90. For another late survival of a 'rough music' see **F. Thompson,** *Lark Rise to Candleford,* Penguin, 1977, p. 140. F. Hill mentions that at Lincoln the effigy burnt on Guy Fawkes night could sometimes be of a man with a wanton wife, see his *Georgian Lincoln,* p. 286. In Wales a wooden horse or 'Ceffyl Pren' was carried to the door of those who offended against local standards.

45. Versions of 'skimmington' were used against strike-breakers in the North-East, in the East Midlands, and against those who informed against sailors for the press gangs. See Storch, p. 490. The activities of the Hawkhurst gang probably lie outside the orbit of any attempt at 'community justice' but see the punishments inflicted on the officer of a naval cutter in 1764 in Hoon, p. 232.

46. **K. Thomas,** *Religion and the Decline of Magic: studies in popular beliefs in sixteenth- and seventeenth-century England,* Penguin, 1973, pp. 538-40.

47. *The True Briton,* 1 May 1751, p. 426.

48. *London Chronicle,* 21 July 1790.

49. See the *London Chronicle,* 19 Oct. 1810 for an account of a man found indecently exposing himself being ducked, stripped and pelted by a group of 'mechanics' in St Marylebone Fields; *London Chronicle,* 7 July 1817 for an attack on a butler said to resemble Oliver the spy. The attack happened on the 6th; Oliver's part in the Pentrich affair was revealed in the second edition of the *Leeds Mercury* on 14 June. See pp. 210-11.

50. See the *London Chronicle,* 10-12 Oct., 31 Oct.-2 Nov., 3-5 Dec. 1799.

51. *London Chronicle,* 10-11 July, 23 Sept., 6 Nov. 1810.

52. **L. O. Pike,** *A History of Crime in England,* 2nd edn, Patterson Smith, 1968, p. 378.

53. *London Chronicle,* 23 Sept. 1810; BM Place Papers, Addit. MSS 27826 ff. 172-3.

54. See Cobbett's comment quoted in Thompson, *The Making of the English Working Class,* p. 662: 'An immense crowd of people cheered him during the whole hour: some held out biscuits, as if to present him with: others held him out glasses of wine, and others little flags of triumph and bunches of flowers. While the executioner and officers of justice were hooted! *This it was that was the* real cause of putting an end to the punishment of the pillory!' For the debate see Cobbett's *Parliamentary Debates,* XXXII, 803-5; the Act was 56 Geo. III, c. 138, leaving the pillory for perjury and subordination of perjury.

55. See Malcolmson, pp. 15-33, 75-8, esp. pp. 83-4.

56. Halliday, p. 261; **B. Trinder,** *The Industrial Revolution in Shropshire,* David and Charles, 1970, p. 360.

57. Malcolmson, pp. 83-4; **G. L. Gomme,** *The Village Community*, Walter Scott, 1890, pp. 240-2.

Chapter 4 Eighteenth-century London

1. **L. S. Sutherland,** 'The City of London in eighteenth-century politics', in *Essays presented to Sir Lewis Namier* ed. R. Pares and A. J. P. Taylor, Oxford UP, 1956, p. 59; for London's role in the seventeenth century see **V. Pearl,** *London and the Outbreak of the Puritan Revolution*, Oxford UP, 1961 and **B. Manning,** *The English People and the English Revolution*, Heinemann, 1976.
2. The average price of bread was higher in the two previous years, at 7.0*d.* for the 4lb loaf in 1708, 8.7*d.* in 1709 and 6.2*d.* in 1710.
3. See **G. Holmes,** 'The Sacheverell Riots', *Past and Present*, **72** (1976), 55-85.
4. **R. R. Sharpe,** *London and the Kingdom*, Longmans Green, 1894, II, 628-35. For the best study of the trial see **G. Holmes,** *The Trial of Doctor Sacheverell*, Eyre Methuen, 1973.
5. **G. Rudé,** *Hanoverian London, 1714-1808*, Secker and Warburg, 1971, pp. 206-7; Sharpe, III, 5.
6. **N. Rogers,** 'Popular protest in early Hanoverian London', *Past and Present*, **79** (1978), 70-100; See also **J. L. Fitts,** 'Newcastle's mob', *Albion*, **5** (1973) and Rudé, pp. 207-8.
7. Sharpe, III, 12-30.
8. Sharpe, III, 35-8; Rudé, pp. 149-51, **P. Langford,** *The Excise Crisis*, Clarendon Press, 1975.
9. Rudé, p. 151; Sharpe, III, 38.
10. See **G. Rudé,** 'Mother Gin and the London riots of 1736', in *Paris and London in the Eighteenth Century*, Fontana, 1970, pp. 201-21.
11. *Ibid.*; also Rudé, *Hanoverian London . . .*, pp. 187-90.
12. See **N. Rogers,** 'Popular disaffection in London during the forty-five', The London Journal, **1** (1975), 22; Sharpe, III, pp. 41-8.
13. *Ibid*, Rogers, pp. 22-3; see also **N. Rogers,** 'Resistance to oligarchy: the City opposition to Walpole and his successors, 1725-47' in **J. Stevenson** ed. *London in the Age of Reform*, Blackwell, 1977, pp. 6-13.
14. Rogers, 'Popular disaffection . . .', pp. 29-5; for City reactions to the Jacobite rising, see also Sharpe, III, pp. 50-6.
15. For the 1761 estimate, see **Namier,** *The Structure of Politics at the Accession of George III*, I, 100. For some analysis of its social composition see Rudé, *Hanoverian London*, pp. 127-32.
16. **N. Rogers,** 'Aristocratic clientage, trade and independency: popular politics in pre-radical Westminster', *Past and Present*, **61** (1973), 70-2.
17. *Ibid.*, pp. 74-7.
18. *Ibid.*, pp. 98-9; **P. Pringle,** *Hue and Cry*, Museum Press, 1955, pp. 83-5.
19. Pringle, pp. 85-6 quotes Fielding as saying that he could only remember two prosecutions under the riot act in thirty-four years.
20. Rogers, 'Aristocratic clientage . . .' pp. 98-100.
21. *Ibid.*, Pringle, pp. 86-7.
22. Rogers, pp. 100-1.
23. Sharpe, III, p. 69.
24. Rudé, *Hanoverian London . . .*, pp. 162-74.
25. For further discussions of the development of politics in the 1760s, see Rudé, *Wilkes and Liberty*, and **L. S. Sutherland,** *The City of London and the Opposition to Government, 1768-74*, Athlone, 1959.
26. See Rudé, *Hanoverian London . . .*, pp. 191-2; **W. J. Shelton,** *English Hunger and*

Industrial Disorders, Macmillan, 1973, pp. 155–63.
27. For the London trades, see the rather sketchy account of developments in **S. Webb** and **B. Webb,** *The History of Trade Unionism* 2nd edn, Longmans Green, 1920, Ch. 1. **M. D. George,** *London Life in the Eighteenth Century*, 2nd edn, Penguin, Ch. 4 has some useful background. There is no systematic study of the London trades organisations in the eighteenth century.
28. Shelton, pp. 199–202.
29. See Rudé, *Wilkes and Liberty*, pp. 17–36; Sharpe, pp. 73–7.
30. Hammond and Hammond, *The Skilled Labourer*, pp. 205–6.
31. The quartern loaf weighed 4lb 5½oz. (2 Kg).

**Average price of bread in London, 1766–70
(old pence per 4lb. [1.8 Kg])**

1766	6.0
1767	7.3
1768	7.1
1769	5.7
1770	5.8

---

32. For the importance of parish settlement see George, *London Life* . . ., pp. 220–1; for trade conditions, see Shelton, *op. cit.*, pp. 156, 161.
33. Rudé, *Wilkes and Liberty*, pp. 39–45; Sharpe, III, 80–1; Pringle, pp. 174–5.
34. Rudé, *Wilkes and Liberty*, pp. 46–8; Sharpe, III, pp. 81–2.
35. Rudé, *Wilkes and Liberty*, pp. 49–51.
36. For conditions among the coalheavers see W. J. Shelton, pp. 165–72 and **M. D. George,** 'The London coal-heavers', *Economic History*, **1** (1929).
37. Rudé, *Hanoverian London* . . ., pp. 196–7.
38. Shelton, pp. 172–4.
39. *Ibid.*, pp. 174–5; Pringle, p. 176.
40. Pringle, p. 177; Shelton, pp. 175–7; Rudé, *Hanoverian London* . . ., p. 197.
41. Shelton, pp. 192–4.
42. Rudé, *Hanoverian London* . . ., p. 198.
43. *Ibid.*, Shelton, pp. 194–5; see also **G. Henson,** *The History of the Framework-Knitters*, 2nd edn, David and Charles, 1970, pp. 373–80.
44. Shelton, pp. 198–9; Rudé, *Hanoverian London* . . ., pp. 198–9; *Annual Register* (1768), p. 57.
45. Henson, pp. 380–1.
46. *Annual Register* (1769), pp. 81, 124, 136, 138.
47. The Spitalfields Act only applied to London, Westminster, and the County of Middlesex; for comment on the Act see Hammond and Hammond, *The Skilled Labourer*, pp. 208–9; George, *London Life* . . ., pp. 186–7; Shelton, pp. 198–9. George comments (p. 186); 'The Act brought peace to Spitalfields but not prosperity.' Although individual weavers undoubtedly played a part in political movements after 1773, this was the last time they acted as a trade group in defence of their economic interests.
48. Shelton, pp. 184–9; Rudé, *Hanoverian London* . . ., p. 193.
49. Shelton, pp. 189–92.
50. Rudé, Hanoverian London, p. 201.
51. Rudé and Shelton concur on the point and there is no evidence for a different opinion, see Shelton, pp. 160–1 and Rudé, Wilkes and Liberty, pp. 103–4.
52. Rudé, *Wilkes and Liberty*, pp. 59–60.
53. *Ibid.*, pp. 57–73.
54. Sharpe, III, 106–16.
55. Rudé, *Paris and London in the Eighteenth Century*, p. 263; for analysis of the rioters see his *Wilkes and Liberty, App. III.*

56. Rudé, *Wilkes and Liberty*, p. 46; see also **J. Brewer,** *Party Ideology and Popular Politics at the accession of George III*, Cambridge UP, 1976, Ch. 9.
57. Rudé, *Paris and London in the Eighteenth Century*, p. 307.
58. *Ibid.*, pp. 316-18; Thompson, *The Making of the English Working Class*, pp. 75-6.
59. Brewer, pp. 199-200.
60. Thompson, p. 76.
61. For the early history of the Protestant Association see **J. P. de Castro,** *The Gordon Riots*, Oxford UP, 1926, pp. 1-19 (quotation from p. 17); for the disturbances in Scotland, see **T. C. Smout,** *A History of the Scottish People, 1560-1830*, 2nd edn, Fontana, 1972, pp. 210-11.
62. De Castro, p. 16; Sharpe, III, 178-9.
63. For these and later developments in The Gordon Riots see de Castro, *passim* (quotation from p. 25); additional sources as noted.
64. Rudé, *Paris and London in the Eighteenth Century*, p. 270.
65. Sharpe, III, pp. 180-2.
66. *Ibid.*
67. *Ibid.*, pp. 183-5.
68. R. R. Sharpe, *op. cit.*, pp. 184-5.
69. De Castro, p. 142.
70. Sharpe, pp. 186-90.
71. Rudé, *Paris and London in the Eighteenth Century*, pp. 275-6, 280-91.
72. **P. Toynbee** ed., *The Letters of Horace Walpole*, Clarendon Press, 1904, vol. XI, p. 223.
73. For the table see **B. R. Mitchell** and **P. Deane,** *Abstract of British Historical Statistics*, Cambridge UP, p. 498; for the monthly returns of bread prices see the *Gentlemans Magazine*, 1780.
74. De Castro, pp. 210-15.
75. *Ibid.*, p. 194.
76. *Ibid.*, pp. 211, 230 (Romilly quoted).
77. J. P. de Castro believed that the aim of the City was the fall of the administration and its replacement with one which would terminate the war with America. For the attitude of the City of London towards the American crisis see P. Langford, 'London and the American Revolution', in Stevenson ed., *London in the Age of Reform*.
78. When challenged on this point in parliament on 19 July by, of all people, Wilkes, Bull admitted that his men had worn cockades, but that he had made four remove them (Sharpe, III, p. 190).
79. **W. Belsham,** *Memoirs of the Reign of George III*, London, 1795, III, p. 22.
80. For Mansfield's judgement, see *Parliamentary History*, XXI, 694.
81. **H. Butterfield,** *George III, Lord North, and the People, 1779-80*, Bell, pp. 379-80.
82. *Ibid.*, p. 380; P. Brown, *The Chathamites*, Macmillan, 1967.
83. **I. R. Christie,** *The End of North's Ministry, 1780-1782*, Macmillan, 1958, pp. 24-5; see also **J. Norris,** *Shelburne and Reform*, Macmillan, 1963, pp. 132-5.
84. **Sutherland,** 'The City in eighteenth-century politics', p. 73.
85. Christie, p. 24.
86. Brown, p. 87.

Chapter 5 Food riots in England

1. See Rudé, *The Crowd in History*, pp. 33-8; **C. Tilly,** 'Collective violence in European perspective' in **H. D. Graham** and **T. R. Gurr** eds, *Violence in America*, Bantam, 1969, pp. 16-19.
2. See **J. Walter** and **K. Wrightson,** 'Dearth and the social order in early modern

England', *Past and Present*, **71** (1976), 22–42; **P. Clark,** 'Popular protest and disturbance in Kent, 1558–1640', *The Economic History Review*, second ser. **29** (1976), 365–81; **M. Beloff,** *Public Order and Popular Disturbances, 1660–1714*, Oxford UP, 1938, pp. 56–75; **R. B. Rose,** 'Eighteenth-century price riots and public policy in England', *International Review of Social History*, 6 (1961), 277–92; and **J. Stevenson,** 'Food riots in England, 1792–1818' in **J. Stevenson** and **R. Quinault** eds, *Popular Protest and Public Order*, George Allen and Unwin, 1974, pp. 33–74. I am grateful to Dr C. S. L. Davies, Dr J. Maddicott, Mr J. Cambell, and Dr A. S. Saul for their advice on the early modern and medieval periods.

3. See, for example, the budgets printed by Eden in **F. M. Eden,** *The State of the Poor*, Cass reprint edn, 1966, II, 586, III, 796. See also **W. Ashley,** *The Bread of our Forefathers*, Oxford UP, 1928, pp. 22–5; **J. Middleton,** *View of the Agriculture of Middlesex*, London, 1798, p. 389; Rudé, *Wilkes and Liberty*, p. 8; and **W. Cobbett,** *Rural Rides*, Penguin edn, ed. A. Briggs, 1967, pp. 305–6.

4. **C. Smith,** *Three Tracts on the Corn Laws*, 2nd edn, London, 1766, pp. 140, 182–5; see also Ashley, pp. 1–26.

5. See **H. C. Darby,** *A New Historical Geography of England after 1600*, Cambridge UP, 1976, pp. 104–12; Eden, I, 496–517; Ashley, pp. 6–20. For potatoes, see **R. N. Salaman,** *The History and Social Influence of the Potato*, Cambridge UP, 1947, p. 493, and Eden, *op. cit.*, I, pp. 501–6.

6. See **A. H. John,** 'The course of agricultural change, 1660–1760', in L. S. Pressnell, *Studies in the Industrial Revolution*, London, 1969; **T. S. Ashton,** *An Economic History of England: the eighteenth century*, Oxford UP, 1955, p. 86; **N. S. B. Gras,** *The Evolution of the English Corn Market*, Cambridge, Mass., 1915, pp. 109–24. On the corn trade to London see O. A. K. Spate, 'The growth of London, A.D. 1660–1800' in **H. C. Darby,** *An Historical Geography of England before A.D. 1800*, Cambridge UP, 1936, pp. 541–2 and **F. J. Fisher,** 'London as an "Engine of economic growth"', in **J. S. Bromley** and **E. H. Kossman,** eds, *Britain and the Netherlands: IV*, The Hague, 1971, pp. 3–16.

7. See **A. Everitt,** 'The marketing of agricultural produce' in **J. Thirsk** ed., *The Agrarian History of England and Wales*, IV, Cambridge UP, 1967; **E. P. Thompson,** 'The moral economy of the English crowd in the eighteenth century', *Past and Present*, **50** (1971), 79–94. See also **J. Burnett,** 'The baking industry in the nineteenth century', *Business History*, **5,** 2 (1963).

8. Gras, 1915, pp. 109 n. 1, 124, 127–8.

9. M. Beloff, p. 73. Young's comment is quoted in Ashton, p. 86.

10. PC 4/6: Sockett to Dundas, 26 Oct. 1795.

11. **W. J. Shelton,** *English Hunger and Industrial Disorders*, Macmillan, 1973, pp. 42, 44.

12. *Lloyd's Evening Post*, 10 Oct. 1766.

13. See the reports in HO 43/7 and HO 42/35.

14. For the Midlands see HO 42/35: Fowks to Portland, 24 June 1795; and for the North, HO 42/34: reports to Home Office, April 1795; see also **D. J. V. Jones,** *Before Rebecca: popular protests in Wales, 1793–1835*, Allen Lane, 1973, pp. 20–1; and HO 42/35: Mayor, Carlisle, to Home Office, April 1795.

15. *London Chronicle*, 10 May 1816; **A. J. Peacock,** *Bread or Blood*, Gollancz, 1965.

16. See **T. S. Ashton,** 'The coal-miners of the eighteenth century', *Economic Journal*, **1,** 1929, pp. 316–17; *London Chronicle* 4 March 1817, 3 Nov. 1818.

17. **A. K. Hamilton Jenkin,** *The Cornish Miner*, David and Charles reprint, 1972, p. 150.

18. HO 42/34: report to Home Office, 30 March 1795.

19. HO 42/51: report from Witney, 22 Sept. 1800; Hughes to Portland, 15 Sept. 1800.

20. For Banbury see HO 42/51; Hughes to Portland, 15 Sept. 1800; for East Anglia, HO 42/35: Clayton to Portland, 11 Aug. 1795, and reports from Wisbech, 25 July and 1 Aug. 1795; for the Thames Valley, Thompson, 'The moral economy of the English crowd' p. 119; and for Stony Stratford, HO 42/50: Buckingham to Portland, 6 May 1800.

21. PC 1/27, A.54: Mayor of Weymouth to Privy Council, 7 July 1795. PC 1/27, A.54: Mayor of King's Lynn to Privy Council, 7 July 1795.
22. HO 42/34: Elford to Home Office, 6 April 1795.
23. See **J. W. Rowe,** *Cornwall in the Age of the Industrial Revolution*, Liverpool UP, 1953, pp. 160-1; **W. Borlase,** *The Natural History of Cornwall*, 2nd edn, London, 1970, pp. 89-90; **E. S. Maxwell,** 'Cornish farming, *c.* 1800', *Report of the Royal Cornwall Polytechnic Society*, new ser., **10** (1942), 30-1.
24. **W. Marshall,** *The Rural Economy of the South-West*, London, 1796, pp. 36-7. Marshall commented on the backwardness of agriculture inland from the coast which he blamed upon the poverty of communications. He proposed the construction of a canal across the peninsula from Exeter to the north coast.
25. Shelton, pp. 37-8.
26. Rudé, *Paris and London in the Eighteenth Century*, pp. 310-11, and 56-7.
27. *Ibid.*, p. 55; **L. A. Clarkson,** *The Pre-Industrial Economy in England, 1500-1750*, Batsford, 1974, pp. 176-7.
28. See P. Colquhoun's report on prices in the capital, PC 1/27, A.54: Colquhoun to Portland, 9 July 1795. Colquhoun was involved in the development of soup kitchens in the capital during the 1790s, see HO 42/66: An Account of the public services of Patrick Colquhoun, (undated) 1804. On the Assize, see **S. J. Webb,** and **B. Webb,** 'The Assize of Bread', *Economic Journal*, **14** (1904) 211-16.
29. See J. Stevenson, 'Food riots', pp. 43-6; **Wells,** 'Dearth and Distress in Yorkshire, 1793-1802', **A. Booth,** 'Food riots in North-West England, 1790-1801', *Past and Present*, **77** (1977); Booth has added considerably to the number of disturbances in the North-West in 1795-6 and 1800-1; although many of these took place in small towns, such as Northwich, Delph, Nantwich, others took place in the larger manufacturing towns and major cities. More detailed work requires doing on the other areas before a clearer picture of the distribution of disturbances in 1795-6 and 1800-1 is obtained, particularly whether the manufacturing areas were more disturbed than southern England and East Anglia, see Booth, p. 90.
30. Stevenson, pp. 45-6.
31. Rudé, *The Crowd in History*, p. 45.
32. Thompson, 'The moral economy . . .' p. 119.
33. See PC 1/26, A.51: Willoughby to Carter, 28 June 1795; PC 1/27, A.54: Mayor of Weymouth to Privy Council, 7 July 1795. A similar situation pertained in corn riots in Wales and Scotland, see Jones, pp. 31-2 and **S. G. E. Lythe,** 'The Tayside meal mobs 1772-3', *Scottish History Review*, **46** (1967), 35.
34. See Peacock, chs 1-3.
35. **E. J. Hobsbawm** and **G. Rudé,** *Captain Swing*, Penguin, 1973, Appendix I.
36. **O. Hufton,** 'Women in revolution, 1789-96', in *French Society and the Revolution*, ed. D. Johnson, Cambridge UP, 1976, pp. 161-2.
37. For Dover, see *Ipswich Journal*, 31 May 1740; for the Taunton incident, *Gentleman's Magazine*, 1753, p. 390; and for Blandford Forum, HO 42/51: Mayor of Blandford to Portland, 9 Sept. 1800.
38. *The Star*, 20 Sept. 1800.
39. Darvall, p. 98.
40. *Gentleman's Magazine*, 1766, pp. 386, 388.
41. HO 42/51: report from Chesterfield, 8 Sept. 1800; *London Chronicle*, 16-18 Nov. 1816.
42. See Olwen Hufton's comments in 'Women in revolution, 1789-1796', p. 153 and n. 18 on the distinction between *Pauvreté honnête* and *indigence* in France.
43. See especially Rudé, *The Crowd in History*, chs 1-2, 13-16; Thompson, 'The Moral economy . . .', **R. B. Rose,** 'Eighteenth-century price riots and public policy in England', *International Review of Social History*, 6, 1961.
44. **R. F. Wearmouth,** *Methodism and the Common People of the Eighteenth Century*, Epworth, 1945, pp. 20, 24-5.
45. 36 Geo. III c. 9. The Act received its third reading on 18 Dec. 1795.

46. HO 42/51: Willoughby to Portland, 5 Aug. 1800.
47. Darvall, p. 95; *Annual Register*, 1816, Chronicle, p. 68.
48. Hammond and Hammond, *The Village Labourer*, 5th edn, p. 117.
49. HO 42/51: Hughes to Portland, 7 Sept. 1800.
50. **A. Prentice,** *Historical Sketches and Personal Recollections of Manchester*, 3rd edn, Cass, 1970, p. 52.
51. Darvall, pp. 96-9; *Annual Register*, 1812, Chronicle, p. 104.
52. See **O. A. Westworth,** 'The Albion steam flour mill', *Economic History* (1932), pp. 380-95.
53. See *Gentleman's Magazine*, 1766, pp. 386, 388.
54. HO 42/35: report from Dudley to Home Office, 23 June 1795; *Annual Register*, 1816, Chronicle, p. 174.
55. The Banbury incident was reported in HO 42/51: Hughes to Portland, 15 Sept. 1800; for this London series see *Gentleman's Magazine*, **70** (1800), 894-5. See also Rudé, *The Crowd in History*, pp. 252-7 for the restraint with which many of these incidents were conducted.
56. See Woodforde, pp. 427-8, entries for 28 Nov. and 8 Dec. 1792.
57. HO 42/34: report from Gloucester, 11 May 1795; HO 42/51: Walford to Portland, 11 Sept. 1800.
58. Darvall, pp. 96-7; *Annual Register*, 1816, Chronicle, pp. 70-1.
59. Thompson, 'Moral Economy . . .', pp. 110-11; *Gentleman's Magazine*, 1866, p. 437.
60. HO 42/51: Willoughby to Portland, 21 Sept. 1800; see also the actions of the mob who marched out from Exeter and made farmers sign a contract to sell at reduced prices, **W. G. Hoskins,** *Industry Trade and People in Exeter 1688-1800*, Manchester UP, 1935, p. 148.
61. *Annual Register*, 1812, Chronicle, p. 52.
62. Ashton, 'The coal-miners of the eighteenth century', p. 327.
63. The Newcastle incident is reported in HO 42/50: Turner to Portland, 29 April 1800; Peacock, pp. 79, 60-1, records the East Anglian crowds.
64. See, for example, the incident at Nottingham in 1812 quoted by Thompson, *The Making of the English Working Class*, p. 70. For the London demonstrations see *Gentleman's Magazine* (1795), pp. 965-6; *Morning Chronicle*, 16, 22 Nov. 1816.
65. Thompson, 'The moral economy. . .', pp. 94-107 discussed the 'popular justice' aspect.
66. *Ibid.*, pp. 107-15.
67. At least thirty people, on the most conservative estimate, were killed or executed for their part in eighteenth century food riots.
68. Hamilton Jenkin, p. 152.
69. **A. Rowe,** 'The food riots of the forties in Cornwall', *Report of Royal Cornwall Polytechnic Society*, **10** (1942), 51-67.
70. For the seasonality of riots see E. J. Hobsbawm in *Labouring Men*, p. 131; Stevenson, pp. 52-3; this view has been confirmed in Booth's study of the North-West between 1790 and 1801, Booth, p. 90.
    Pre-harvest shortage could lead to ill-feeling even in years of average prices, see for example the account of disturbances in May 1737 near Burford. Corn believed to be for export was stopped by about sixty people 'who knocked down the fore horse, brake the wagon in pieces, cut the sacks, and strewed about the corn', **E. L. Jones,** *Seasons and Prices*, Allen and Unwin, 1964, p. 138. See also Hobsbawm.
71. Rudé, *The Crowd in History*, p. 39.
72. See Darvall, pp. 96-7; Prentice, p. 53.
73. Average prices of wheat per quarter from the *Gentleman's Magazine*, *1816*.

1816	Cambridge	Norfolk
February	52*s* 11*d*	54*s* 8*d*
March	50*s* 3*d*	52*s* 9*d*
April	62*s* 11*d*	61*s* 1*d*
May	77*s* 1*d*	77*s* 5*d*

74. There were also riots in Cornwall in 1737 when prices were entirely normal, possibly caused by rumours of exports.
75. HO 42/51: Bracebridge to Home Office, 19 Sept. 1800.
76. Shelton, pp. 95 ff.
77. *Ibid.*; see also Stevenson, pp. 53-5.
78. See **D. G. Barnes,** *A History of the English Corn Laws,* Routledge, 1930, pp. 81-2. For hostility to the Quakers, see **I. Grub,** *Quakerism and Industry before 1800,* London, 1930, pp. 124-7; Chapman, pp. 186-7.
79. Hamilton Jenkin, p. 151.
80. HO 42/51: Hughes to Portland, 15 Sept. 1800.
81. For Liverpool, see Rose, p. 289; for Nottingham, Chapman, pp. 180-1; and for Norwich **C. B. Jewson,** *The Jacobin City: a portrait of Norwich, 1788-1802,* Blackie, 1975, pp. 98-103.
82. Wearmouth, p. 21.
83. **A. P. Wadsworth** and **J. De Lacy Mann,** *The Cotton Trade and Industrial Lancashire, 1600-1780,* Manchester Up, 1931, pp. 359-60.
84. *Ibid.*, p. 360.
85. For a general perspective see **P. Laslett,** *The World we have lost,* 2nd edn, Methuen, 1971, pp. 113-34 and **A. B. Appleby,** 'Disease or famine? Mortality in Cumberland and Westmorland, 1580-1640', *Economic History Review,* 2nd ser., **26** (1973), 403-41.
86. **R. S. Schofield,** 'Crisis mortality', *Local Population Studies,* **9** (1972).
87. See **D. E. Williams,** 'Were "hunger" rioters really hungry? Some demographic evidence', *Past and Present,* **71** (1976), 70-5; **A. Gooder,** 'The population crisis of 1727-30 in Warwickshire', *Midland History,* **4** (1971-2), 10-22; **M. F. Pickles,** 'Mid-Wharfedale, 1721-1812', *Local Population Studies,* **16** (1976), 35. On the continuing debate about the relative role of disease and famine see **J. D. Post,** 'Famine, mortality and epidemic disease in the process of modernisation', *Economic History Review,* 2nd ser., **29** (1976), 14-37 and **A. B. Appleby,** 'Famine, mortality and epidemic disease: a comment', *Economic History Review,* 2nd ser., **30** (1977), 508-12 in which Appleby questions the causal relationship between famine and disease.
88. See **Wells,** 'Dearth and distress in Yorkshire, 1793-1802', pp. 22-4. Appleby has concluded that the London Bills of Mortality fail to show a significant correlation between bread prices and the incidence of epidemic disease for the period 1650-1750, see **A. B. Appleby,** 'Nutrition and disease: the case of London, 1550-1750', *Journal of Interdisciplinary History,* **6** (1975-6), 1-22. A recent study has also cast doubt upon the relationship between prices and mortality in the East End in the late eighteenth and early nineteenth century, see **L. D. Schwartz,** 'Conditions of life and work in London, *c.* 1770-1820, with special reference to East London', Oxford University D Phil. thesis, 1976, pp. 157ff.
89. The term 'famine' is applied somewhat loosely by Wells, (p. 25). 'Famine conditions were responsible for the wave of intense rioting which swept across West Yorkshire during the summer of 1795'. Booth relies upon more impressionistic evidence, but nonetheless concludes that 'in the winter of 1800 and the early months of 1801 the poor were literally starving'. No demographic evidence is provided. For more particular usage see Laslett, and Appleby, 'Disease or famine . . .'.
90. See, for example, **M. D. George,** *London Life in the Eighteenth Century,* 2nd edn, Penguin, 1965, pp. 173-4, for evidence of starvation in the capital, usually among women.

Chapter 6 Labour disputes before the Combination Laws

1. See Hobsbawm, *Labouring Men*, pp. 5-10.
2. Beloff, *Public Order and Popular Disturbances*, pp. 81-2; Hoskins, *Industry, Trade and People in Exeter, 1688-1800*, pp. 58-61.
3. J. de L. **Mann**, *The Cloth Industry in the West of England from 1640 to 1880*, Oxford UP, 1971, pp. 108-12; Hammond and Hammond, *The Skilled Labourer*, p. 157. See also G. **Henson**, *History of the Framework-Knitters*, 2nd edn, David and Charles, 1970, pp. 125-6 and Webb and Webb, *The History of Trade Unionism*, pp. 34-5; also *House of Commons Journals*, **20**, 598-9.
4. Mann, p. 109.
5. Henson, pp. 245-6; *Gentleman's Magazine* (1738), p. 658.
6. Mann, 109-11. The weavers' actions in 1738-40 were similar to those in 1726 when they had asked the justices how to proceed with their grievance.
7. See Hammond and Hammond, *The Skilled Labourer*, pp. 157-8; Mann, p. 112.
8. Hammond and Hammond, *ibid.*, pp. 145-6, 159-61; Mann, pp. 123, 125-6.
9. Mann, pp. 115, 142-6.
10. Beloff, p. 81.
11. Hammond and Hammond, pp. 140-3.
12. *Ibid.*, pp. 192-6; Beloff, p. 87.
13. H. **Heaton**, *The Yorkshire Woollen and Worsted Industries*, 2nd edn, Oxford UP, 1965, pp. 316-19; *London Evening Post*, 15-17 June, 1775.
14. Hammond and Hammond, pp. 53-4; R. S. **Fitton** and A. P. **Wadsworth**, *The Strutts and the Arkwrights, 1758-1830*, reprinted edn, Manchester UP, 1973, pp. 79-80; Wadsworth and Mann, *The Cotton Trade and Industrial Lancashire, 1600-1780*, reprint edn, Manchester UP, pp. 380, 497-9.
15. Hammond and Hammond, pp. 54-6.
16. D. **Bythell**, *The Handloom Weavers*, Cambridge UP, 1969, p. 198. On the peaceful introduction of machinery see the example at Stroud given in the Hammonds, p. 160.
17. Hammond and Hammond, pp. 221-3.
18. *Ibid.*, pp. 223-5; see also Fitton and Wadsworth, p. 54 and G. Henson, *op. cit.*, pp. 401-9.
19. *Public Advertiser*, 5, 7 July 1783.
20. *Gentleman's Magazine* (1790), p. 1045.
21. Henson, pp. 95-6.
22. Beloff, pp. 82-7.
23. Rudé, *Hanoverian London*, pp. 185-7.
24. See J. M. **Fewster**, 'The keelmen of Tyneside in the eighteenth century', *Durham University Journal*, new ser., **19** (1957-8), 24-33.
25. *Ibid.*, pp. 33, 112-16.
26. *Ibid.*, pp. 33, 116-19.
27. *Ibid.*, pp. 66-8, 119.
28. *Ibid.*, pp. 68-75.
29. *Ibid.*, p. 123; R. F. **Wearmouth**, *Methodism and the Common People of the Eighteenth Century*, Epworth, 1945, p. 43.
30. D. J. **Rowe**, 'The strikes of the Tyneside keelmen in 1809 and 1819', *International Review of Social History*, **13** (1968), pp. 58-9.
31. See R. B. **Rose**, 'A Liverpool sailors' strike in the eighteenth century', *Transactions of the Lancashire and Cheshire Antiquarian Society*, **68** (1958), 86; *Gentleman's Magazine* (1762), p. 596. According to R. B. Rose the crowd who released the sailors were attending a fair at Magull.
32. W. J. **Shelton**, *English Hunger and Industrial Disorders*, Macmillan, 1973, pp. 187-9.
33. See Rose, pp. 87-92; also J. A. **Picton**, *Memorials of Liverpool*, Longmans, 1873, I, pp. 696-7.

34. **T. S. Ashton** and **J. Sykes,** *The Coal Industry of the Eighteenth Century*, 2nd edn, Manchester UP, 1929, p. 118; **E. Welbourne,** *The Miners' Unions of Northumberland and Durham*, Cambridge UP, 1923, p. 21.
35. Hammond and Hammond, pp. 12-15; also Ashton and Sykes, pp. 89-91 and Welbourne, pp. 21-2.
36. Hammond and Hammond, pp. 15-17.
37. Ashton and Sykes, p. 127.
38. For early disturbances in the Royal yards see **J. Ehrman,** *The Navy in the Wars of William III, 1689-1697*, Cambridge UP, 1953, pp. 91, 328, 475, 489. The disputes of the 1740s are considered in **D. A. Baugh,** *British Naval Administration in the Age of Walpole*, Princeton, New Jersey, 1965, pp. 287-8, 323-32. For Portsmouth see **A. Geddes,** 'Portsmouth during the great French wars, 1770-1800', *The Portsmouth Papers*, **9** (1970), pp. 18-19 and **D. Wilson,** 'Government dock-yard workers in Portsmouth, 1793-1815', Warwick Univ., Ph.D. thesis, 1975, pp. 309-53.
39. **H. R. Hikins** ed., *Building The Union*, Liverpool, 1973, pp. 11-23; HO 42/22: R. Burdon to H. Dundas, 3 Nov. 1793; see also **N. McCord** and **D. E. Brewster,** 'Some labour troubles of the 1790s in North-East England', *International Review of Social History*, **12** (1968), pp. 366-78; Wearmouth, pp. 44-5; **C. G. Down** and **A. J. Warrington,** *The History of the Somerset Coalfield*, David and Charles, 1972, p. 32. Some of the documents relating to these disturbances are reprinted in **A. Aspinall,** *The Early English Trade Unions*, Batchworth, 1949, pp. 2-14.
40. Aspinall, p. 19; McCord and Brewster, p. 376.
41. For Tyneside see McCord and Brewster, pp. 375-80; for the shipwrights, *Kentish Register* (1795), p. 115; and the weavers Hammond and Hammond, pp. 58-61, see also Aspinall, pp. 25ff, and **C. J. Hunt,** *The Lead Miners of the Northern Pennines*, Manchester UP, 1970, p. 122.
42. **Thale** ed., *The Autobiography of Francis Place*, p. 112.
43. British Museum, Addit. MSS (Place Papers), 27, 834, f.108 (1834).
44. These instances are recorded in the Middlesex sessions papers or the *London Chronicle*.
45. Webb and Webb, pp. 28-9.
46. The list of combinations or strikes has been compiled from the London newspapers, Home Office and Middlesex sessions papers. For the survival of trade union activity in the capital see the Place papers, recording successful strikes by the breeches makers in 1795, 1802, 1810, and 1813. Place commented that the London trade clubs in 'spite of the Combination Laws, did from time to time raise their wages by means of strikes'. See also **A. E. Musson,** *British Trade Unionism, 1800-1875*, Macmillan, 1972, p. 24 and **M. D. George,** 'The Combination Laws', *Economic History Review*, **6** (1936).
47. *Gentleman's Magazine* (1792), p. 109.
48. Hobsbawm, p. 7.
49. James Hargreaves left Blackburn after the disturbances of 1768-9 and moved to Nottingham. The attacks on the elder Peel's premises at Altham in October 1779 led him to move to Burton-on-Trent and set up business there, see Hammond and Hammond, pp. 53-4.
50. The 'habit of solidarity' is the phrase he uses, see Hobsbawm, pp. 9-10.
51. Quoted in Webb and Webb, pp. 36-7 from *A Short Essay upon Trade in General* (1741) by 'A Lover of His Country'.
52. See Wadsworth and Mann, pp. 497-9 and E. J. Hobsbawm, pp. 10-12.
53. This reluctance has been seen in other disturbances, see E. P. Thompson, 'The moral economy of the English crowd in the eighteenth century', *Past and Present*, **50** (1971), 121.
54. See McCord and Brewster, pp. 370-2.
55. The author of the *Essay on Riots* was Thomas Andrews of Seend in Wiltshire, described by Mann as 'a stern moralist'.
56. Hammond and Hammond, p. 17.

57. McCord and Brewster, p. 372.
58. *General Evening Post*, 11–14 July 1795.
59. Rose, p. 91; Fitton and Wadsworth, pp. 79–80; Hammond and Hammond, p. 225.
60. *Ipswich Journal*, 6 Sept. 1740.
61. See Shelton, pp. 199–202.
62. The point is made Ashton and Sykes, pp. 125–6. See **T. Tooke,** *A History of Prices and of the State of the Circulation from 1793 to 1847*, London, 1938.
63. Webb and Webb, p. 46.
64. See, for example, the evidence quoted by Wearmouth, pp. 71–2.
65. See the evidence from the Place Papers cited above. For the larger issue, see Musson, pp. 22–8.
66. Webb and Webb, p. 69.
67. See Aspinall, p. xii.
68. See the discussion in Musson, pp. 23–4.
69. J. Stevenson, 'Food Riots', pp. 62–4 and D. Bythell, *The Handloom Weavers*, pp. 180–1.

Chapter 7 The age of revolution

1. Hammond and Hammond, *The Town Labourer*, 4th edn, p. 101.
2. See **P. A. Brown,** *The French Revolution in English History*, Crosby Lockwood, 1918, pp. 29–31.
3. **A. Prentice,** *Historical Sketches and Personal Recollections of Manchester*, 3rd edn, Cass, 1970, pp. 1–11; **G. S. Veitch,** *The Genesis of Parliamentary Reform*, 2nd edn, Constable, 1965, pp. 103–7.
4. **R. B. Rose,** 'The Priestley riots of 1791', *Past and Present*, **18** (1960), pp. 68–88. See also the important study by **J. Money,** *Experience and Identity: Birmingham and the West Midlands, 1760–1800*, Manchester UP, 1977, pp. 219–25. Money places the riots within the larger context of the development of Birmingham as a more sophisticated political community in the late eighteenth century. He emphasises the importance of depression in the buckle and button trades upon local politics during 1790–1, but also suggests that the riots had a less decisive impact than has sometimes been claimed.
5. **M. I. Thomis,** *Politics and Society in Nottingham, 1785–1835*, Blackwell, 1969, pp. 160–2, 170–2.
6. Prentice, pp. 6–7.
7. *Ibid.*, pp. 5–14.
8. Quoted in Veitch, pp. 235–6. For a list of other Paine burnings see **M. D. Conway,** *The Life of Thomas Paine*, Putnam, 1892, I 369–71. Priestley was burnt in Hertfordshire, though it was alleged that some of the crowd thought the clerical effigy was a bishop. See **A. O. Aldridge,** *Man of Reason: the life of Thomas Paine*, Cresset, 1959, pp. 182–3.
9. Thomis, pp. 173–7.
10. Quoted in Prentice, p. 9.
11. See Veitch, pp. 194–5.
12. **J. Woodforde,** *The Diary of a Country Parson, 1758–1802*, ed. J. Beresford, Oxford UP, 1949, p. 427.
13. *Sheffield Register*, 30 Nov. 1792.
14. PC1/29, A.64: G. Pane to Privy Council, 7 Aug. 1795.
15. See **G. A. Williams'** somewhat enthusiastic account in *Artisans and Sans-Culottes*, Arnold, 1968, pp. 58–61. Significantly P. A. Brown also regarded the case for Sheffield as a centre of physical force 'Well-authenticated', see Brown, pp. 145–7. For the incident in 1795 see Wells, 'Dearth and distress in Yorkshire

...' pp. 25-7 and more generally **F. K. Donnelly** and **J. L. Baxter,** 'Sheffield and the English revolutionary tradition, 1790-1820' in **S. Pollard** and **C. Holmes** ed., *Essays in the Economic and Social History of South Yorkshire,* South Yorkshire County Council, 1976, pp. 93-6 and W. A. L. Seaman, 'Reform politics at Sheffield, 1791-1797', *Trans. Hunter Archaeological Society,* **6** (1957), 215-28.

16. Wells, *op. cit.,* p. 35 (for a reference to the SCCI meeting); see also **J. R. Dinwiddy,** 'Christopher Wyvill and reform, 1790-1820', *Borthwick Paper,* 39, 1971, pp. 8-10.

17. See Thale ed., *The Autobiography of Francis Place,* pp. 141-8.

18. Picton, *Memorials of Liverpool,* pp. 271-3. **C. B. Jewson,** *Jacobin City: a portrait of Norwich in its reaction to the French Revolution, 1788-1802,* Blackie, 1975, pp. 66-7. Prentice, pp. 17-25.

19. Lloyd, *The British Seaman,* pp. 177-83; Picton, pp. 273-4.

20. Western, pp. 294-302.

21. J. Prebble, *Mutiny,* Constable, 1975, p. 439.

22. *Annual Register* (1795), Chronicle, pp. 39-40.

23. Stevenson, 'Food riots in England, 1792-1818', pp. 47-8; Western, pp. 418ff.

24. See **A. Geddes,** 'Portsmouth during the great French wars, 1770-1800', *The Portsmouth Papers,* **9,** 1970, pp. 3-6. I am grateful to J. Langston Field for drawing my attention to this article.

25. For the mutiny see **C. Gill,** *The Naval Mutinies of 1797,* Manchester UP, 1913; **B. Dobrée** and **G. E. Manwaring,** *The Floating Republic,* London, 1935; **J. Dugan,** *The Great Mutiny,* Deutsch, 1966.

26. Thompson, *The Making of the English Working Class,* pp. 183-5.

27. See the reports in the *London Chronicle,* 13-16, 25-27, May 1797; **F. Duncan,** *History of the Royal Regiment of Artillery,* London, 1873, pp. 71-2; **J. Holland Rose,** *William Pitt and the Great War,* Bell, 1911, pp. 318-20. The Act granting a pay rise was 37 Geo. III, c. 41. The Incitement to Mutiny Act and Unlawful Oaths Act can both be seen as reactions to the naval mutinies.

28. E. P. Thompson puts the case for the bifurcation of activity and the beginning of a 'revolutionary underground' in *The Making of the English Working Class,* pp. 182-203. For the Lancashire evidence in 1800-01, see Booth, 'Food riots . . .', pp. 99-107.

29. Dinwiddy, pp. 10-12; Wells, p. 40.

30. Booth, p. 103 and Wells, pp. 34-46.

31. Thompson, pp. 515-28; Donnelly and Baxter, pp. 99-101. For the debate on the 'Black Lamp' evidence, see **J. R. Dinwiddy,** 'The "Black Lamp" in Yorkshire, 1801-1802' and **J. L. Baxter** and **F. K. Donnelly,** 'The Revolutionary "Underground" in the West Riding: Myth or Reality?', both *Past and Present,* **64** (1974), pp. 113-35.

32. See especially **M. D. George,** 'The Combination Laws', *Economic History Review,* **6** (1936) and 'The Combination Laws reconsidered', *Economic History* (supplement to the *Economic Journal*), **2** (1927). For a general perspective, see **A. E. Musson,** *British Trade Unionism, 1800-1875,* Macmillan, 1972, pp. 22-8.

33. Webb and Webb, *The History of Trade Unionism,* p. 83.

34. The first major dispute occurred in spring 1801 with a joint petition from the Royal Yards to the Navy Board for an increase in wages, see **D. Wilson,** 'Government dock-yard workers in Portsmouth, 1793-1815', Warwick University Ph.D. thesis, 1975, pp. 341-5 and **J. S. Tucker,** *Memoirs of Admiral Earl St Vincent,* London, 1844, p. 133. For the dispute in the Thames Yards in 1802 see HO 42/66: August 1802 and the *London Chronicle* for August and September. The strike of caulkers and shipwrights lasted over sixteen weeks and there were disturbances when men from the Royal Yards were brought in to break the strike in the private yards. John Gast, the shipwrights' leader, published a pamphlet stating the men's grievances and defending them from the charge of initiating the riots, see **J. Gast,** *Calumny Defeated or a Compleat Vindication of the conduct of the working Shipwrights during the late disputes with their employers,* London, 1802.

35. **D. J. Rowe,** 'The strikes of the Tyneside keelmen in 1809 and 1819', *The International Review of Social History*, **13** (1968), pp. 58–66.
36. See Hammond and Hammond, *The Skilled Labourer*, pp. 167–90.
37. *Ibid.*, p. 176.
38. *Ibid.*, p. 178. The Hammonds prefaced this letter of January 1803 with the comment that it was written 'as if there was no such law as the Combination Act'.
39. *Ibid.*, pp. 72–81. See also Bythell, *The Handloom Weavers*, pp. 189–91.
40. Hammond and Hammond, *The Skilled Labourer*, Chs 4, 6, 8, 9, and 10 contain a detailed account of the industrial background and the main regional aspects of Luddism. Darvall, *Popular Disturbances and Public Order in Regency England*, provides an excellent account of Luddism as seen from the centre but less sensitive to the local context than either Thompson, *The Making of the English Working Class*, pp. 569–659 or **M. I. Thomis,** *The Luddites*, David and Charles, 1970. For the quotations see Thompson, pp. 594, 604 and Thomis and Holt, *Threats of Revolution in Britain*, p. 33.
41. Thompson, p. 616.
42. Donnelly and Baxter, *op cit.*, pp. 102–4.
43. Fitzwilliam MSS, Fitzwilliam to Sidmouth, 25 July 1812.
44. For the role of Bent see Thompson, pp. 538–9, 644–55, and Thomis, *The Luddites*, pp. 90–2.
45. For the debate on Henson's role see **R. A. Church** and **S. D. Chapman,** 'Gravenor Henson and the Making of the English Working Class' in **E. L. Jones** and **G. E. Mingay** eds, *Land, Labour and Population in the Industrial Revolution*, London, 1967 and Thompson's defence of his position, pp. 924–34.
46. Darvall, *Popular Disturbances . . . in Regency England*, pp. 194–5.
47. Prentice, p. 46.
48. See Darvall, pp. 310–13. For a discussion of the wider political situation, see **A. D. Harvey,** *Britain in the Early Nineteenth Century*, Batsford, 1978, pp. 285–99.
49. For Wyvill see Dinwiddy, pp. 24–6; for Cartwright's activities see **F. D. Cartwright,** *Life and Correspondence of Major Cartwright*, London, 1826, II, 17–55.
50. Darvall, pp. 325–7.
51. See Thompson, pp. 614–15 and Thomis, pp. 103–19.
52. See Rudé, *The Crowd in History*, pp. 226–7.
53. Webb and Webb, *The History of Trade Unionism*, pp. 58–9.

Chapter 8 London in the age of revolution

1. *The Memoirs of Francois René, Vicomte de Chateaubriand*, London, 1902, IV, 92.
2. See **J. Brooke,** *The House of Commons, 1754–1790*, Oxford UP, 1964, pp. 126–41; **L. G. Mitchell,** *Charles James Fox and the Disintegration of the Whig Party, 1782–1794*, Oxford UP, 1971, pp. 92–8.
3. **C. Hobhouse,** *Fox*, John Murray, 2nd edn, 1964, pp. 162–4; **J. Holland Rose,** *William Pitt and the National Revival*, Bell, 1911, pp. 167–8.
4. Hobhouse, p. 163.
5. See **D. R. McAdams,** 'Electioneering techniques in populous constituencies, 1784–96', *Studies in Burke and His Time*, **14**, (1972), pp. 43, 45–6.
6. The Letters of Horace Walpole, ed. P. Toynbee, Clarendon Press, 1905, XV, 21.
7. **G. S. Veitch,** *The Genesis of Parliamentary Reform*, 2nd edn, Constable, 1965, pp. 269–71.
8. See *Memoir of Thomas Hardy*, London, 1832, pp. 36–8.
9. For a fuller discussion of the disturbances, see **J. Stevenson,** 'The London "crimp" riots of 1794', *International Review of Social History*, **16** (1971), pp. 40–58.

10. *Memoir of Thomas Hardy*, pp. 38-43.
11. *Morning Chronicle*, 10 Jan. 1795; *London Chronicle*, 16-18 April 1795.
12. *Gentleman's Magazine*, **2** (1795), 609-10; *Morning Chronicle*, 30 June 1795; HO 65/1: J. King to Union Hall, 29 June 1795.
13. *British Chronicle*, 8-10 July 1795; *Morning Chronicle*, 11 July 1795.
14. Morning Chronicle, 13, 14, 15 July 1795; *Letters and Correspondence of Sir James Bland Burges*, ed. J. Hutton, London, 1885, p. 186.
15. HO 42/35: J. Floud to Home Office, 22 July 1795; *London Evening Post*, 22-24 July 1795.
16. See *Account of the Proceeding of a Meeting of the London Corresponding Society*, London, 1795; HO 65/1: King to Herries, 24 October 1795.
17. *Gentleman's Magazine*, **2** (1795), 965-6; *Annual Register*, 1795, Chronicle, pp. 37-9.
18. Treasonable and Seditious Practices Act, 36 Geo. III, ch. 7; Seditious Meetings Act, 36 Geo. III, ch. 8.
19. BM Place Papers, Addit. MSS 27808, ff.41-9; **J. Binns**, *Recollections of the Life of John Binns*, Philadelphia, 1854, p. 55.
20. *Reformers No Rioters*, London, 1794.
21. Thale, ed. *The Autobiography of Francis Place*, p. 145.
22. *London Chronicle*, 17 Dec. 1795; 2-4 Feb. 1796; 14-16 June 1796; 19-21 Dec. 1797.
23. *New Annual Register*, 1797, pp. 120-1.
24. London Chronicle, 17-19 October 1797; *Memoir of Thomas Hardy*, pp. 79-87; Binns, *Recollections*, pp. 42-3.
25. HO 65/1: J. King to Public Offices, 6 Sept. 1800.
26. This account is complied from the Home Office file 42/51, *London Chronicle*, and *Gentleman's Magazine*. See also Corporation of London Record Office, Repertory 204, ff. 414-34.
27. For this phase see Thompson, *The Making of the English Working Class*, pp. 161-203 and **G. A. Williams**, *Artisans and Sans-Culottes*, Arnold, 1968, pp. 101-11.
28. HO 42/47: Proposed General Arrangement for the Defence of the Capital, April 1799.
29. See Thompson, pp. 521-8 and **M. Elliott**, 'The "Despard conspiracy" reconsidered', *Past and Present*, **75** (1977).
30. Thompson, pp. 674, 692-6.

Chapter 9 London and the kingdom

1. For Burdett's emergence see **M. W. Patterson**, *Sir Francis Burdett and his Times*, London, 1931, I, Ch. iv and J. Ann Hone 'Radicalism in London, 1796-1802' in J. Stevenson, *London in the Age of Reform*, Blackwell, 1977, pp. 90-5. For the disturbances see HO 42/50: Baker to Portland, 15 Aug. 1800.
2. Hone, pp. 93-5; Thompson, *The Making of the English Working Class*, pp. 493-4; Patterson, Chs. iv-vii.
3. Thompson, *The Making of the English Working Class*, pp. 500-10; **J. M. Main**, 'Radical Westminster, 1807-1820', *Historical Studies (Australia and New Zealand)*, (1966), pp. 186-204.
4. BM Place Papers, Addit. MSS 27850, ff.158-61.
5. For the political context of the affair, see **M. Roberts**, *The Whig Party, 1807-1812*, 2nd edn, Cass, 1965, pp. 265-7; **S. Maccoby**, *English Radicalism, 1786-1832*, Allen and Unwin, 1955, pp. 258-62.
6. See *London Chronicle*, 7-8 April 1810; PC 1/3912: report of Baker, 22 April 1810.
7. BM Place Papers, ff.194-202.
8. *Anon, Memoirs of the Life of Sir Francis Burdett*, London, 1810, pp. 101-9. For the

fighting outside the Tower see Corporation of London Record Office, MSS 95/3: Report of Committee on the deaths of 9 April 1810.

9. BM Place Papers, ff.229-35; HO 42/109 for June 1810 is mainly concerned with the arrangements for Burdett's release.
10. BM Place Papers, ff.238-9.
11. Quoted in Roberts, pp. 271-2.
12. See E. P. Thompson, pp. 683-6.
13. *London Chronicle*, 28 Feb.-1 March 1815; *Morning Chronicle*, 3 March 1815.
14. *Morning Chronicle*, 1 March 1815.
15. **H. Twiss,** *Life of Lord Chancellor Eldon*, London, 1844, II, 260-5. For the disturbances outside the Palace of Westminster see *Annual Register*, 1815, Chronicle, pp. 20-1.
16. See HO 42/143 for reports on the disturbances. The principal man involved in the speech outside parliament was an unemployed harness-maker, Charles Farrer. There is no record of prosecution in the Westminster sessions papers.
17. HO 42/143. For the presentation of the Westminster petition see *Hansard*, 1815, 97-102.
18. See **A. Briggs,** 'Middle-class consciousness in English politics', *Past and Present*, **9** (1956).
19. *London Chronicie*, 2, 9 March 1815; *Morning Post*, 9 March 1815.
20. For the Spenceans see **T. M. Parsinnen,** 'The revolutionary party in London', *Bulletin of the Institute of Historical Research*, **45** (1972) and O. D. Rudkin, *Thomas Spence and His Connections*, London, 1927.
21. There is no satisfactory life of Hunt, but see the short description in Thompson, pp. 681-3.
22. *London Chronicle*, 16-18 November 1816.
23. For the preparations see HO 42/156.
24. HO 40/3, ff. 895-9: evidence of Vincent Dowling, (undated) 1817. See also **J. Fairburn,** *Whole Proceedings on the Trial of James Watson, Snr, for High Treason*, London, 1817.
25. *London Chronicle*, 3-4 Dec. 1816; HO 40/3, ff. 881-3: evidence of Matthew Wood, 3 Dec. 1816. Accounts of how many men approached the Tower differ, some saying one, others two. See HO 42/156: evidence of privates Edmonds and Darlington, 13 Dec. 1816. Thomas Preston later claimed to be the man who addressed the soldiers, see **S. Bamford,** *Passages in the Life of a Radical*, MacGibbon and Kee, 1967, p. 26.
26. HO 42/156: Maj. Elsington to H. Torrens, 5 Dec. 1816.
27. **H. Hunt,** *Memoirs of Henry Hunt*, London, 1822, pp. 334-73. Place called them 'a contemptible set of fools and miscreants'.
28. HO 40/7, ff. 32-33: anonymous information to Home Office, 2 October 1817; *London Chronicle*, 26 Oct., 2 Nov. 1819.
29. Reports of the debates in *London Chronicle*, 25, 26, 27, 28 Feb. 1817. See also **J. E. Cookson,** *Lord Liverpool's Administration: the crucial years 1815-1822*, Scottish Academic Press, 1975, pp. 107-12 and Thompson, pp. 699-701.
30. For the fullest account, see **D. Johnson,** *Regency Revolution: the case of Arthur Thistlewood*, Compton Russell, 1974; also Thompson, pp. 769-80.
31. Devon Record Office, Sidmouth MSS, Lord Sidmouth to B. Bloomfield, 3 and 4 March 1820. Matthew Wood, the ex-Lord Mayor of London led the attack on Edwards see *Annual Register*, 1820, History, pp. 34, 36; *Hansard*, new series, 1820, I, 54-7; 242-6.
32. *Gentleman's Magazine*, 1819, p. 269.
33. *London Chronicle*, 1 Oct. 1819. An attendance of 50,000 was estimated at a meeting called by Place after Peterloo on 3 Sept.
34. For the ministerial side of the affair, the best treatment is Cookson, pp. 200-300; see also Stevenson, 'The Queen Caroline affair' in *London in the Age of Reform*.
35. **H. Maxwell** ed., *The Creevey Papers*, London, 1905, p. 332.
36. BM (Broughton Papers), Add. MSS. 56541, diary entry for 25 October 1820.

37. Nuffield College Library, Cobbett Papers, A. Cobbett to J. P. Cobbett, 15 November 1820; Maxwell, p. 341.
38. BM, Addit. MSS (Wilson Papers), 30123, ff. 213-16, 30 November 1820; Cobbett Papers, A. Cobbett to J. P. Cobbett, 6 December 1820; *The Times*, 30 Nov. 1820.
39. **L. J. Jennings** ed., *The Croker Papers*, London, 1884, I, 361-2.
40. For the funeral arrangements see HO 44/9: Memorandum on moving the Queen's body by water, 14 Aug. 1821 and Memorandum on military arrangements for the Queen's funeral, Aug. 1821.
41. See **J. Stevenson,** 'Disturbances and public order in London, 1790-1821', unpublished D Phil. thesis, Oxford University, 1973, pp. 153-60.
42. For a fuller discussion of the evidence of 'collusion', see Stevenson, 'The Queen Caroline affair', pp. 138-9.
43. *Ibid.*, pp. 139-40.

Chapter 10 The reform struggle

1. For conditions in 1816 see **J. E. Cookson,** *Lord Liverpool's Administration: The Crucial Years, 1815-1822*, Scottish Academic Press, 1975, pp. 90-116.
2. **S. Bamford,** *Passages in the Life of a Radical*, Fitzroy edn, MacGibbon and Kee, 1967, p. 13ff.
3. *Political Register*, 11 Feb. 1816, cols. 454-5; F. D. Cartwright, *The Life and Correspondence of Major Cartwright*, London, 1826, vol. 1, pp. 292-3, Cartwright to Thomas Hardy, 5 Jan. 1801.
4. For the views of other radical leaders see *ibid.*, pp. 665-90 and *Waterloo to Peterloo*, pp. 131-47. For the attitude of the administration, see Cookson, pp. 102-16 and **A. Temple Patterson,** 'Luddism, Hampden Clubs, and trade unions in Leicestershire, 1816 17', *English Historical Review*, **63** (1948).
5. For the disturbances in East Anglia see **A. J. Peacock,** *Bread or Blood*, Gollancz, 1965.
6. *Annual Register* (1816), Chronicle, pp. 95-100; Darvall, *Popular Disturbances in Regency England*, pp. 152-5. Sidmouth was referring to the heavy reduction of the armed forces in Britain, especially the cavalry arm, about which there was considerable debate between the military men (backed by Sidmouth) and other politicians in the Government. Sidmouth and the military feared that excessive reductions would make it difficult to suppress domestic disturbances, see Cookson, pp. 116-21.
7. See Donnelly and Baxter, 'Sheffield and the English revolutionary Tradition', Pollard and Holmes, pp. 105-6.
8. Twiss, *Lord Chancellor Eldon*, 3rd edn, 1846, I, p. 550.
9. Bamford, pp. 29-32. Prentice says that twenty reached Derby and that both Cartwright and Cobbett had approved the plan at the Crown and Anchor meeting on 7 Feb., see Prentice, *Historical Sketch of Manchester*, pp. 92-4.
10. The 'Ardwick Plot' was dismissed by Prentice, (pp. 94-100) as a concoction of the magistracy, but Bamford indicates that some more radical voices were obtaining a hearing (see MS, pp. 34-7, 40, 62-9). Bamford was one of the dozen men taken. See also Thompson, pp. 702-22, and Donnelly and Baxter, pp. 106-8.
11. Darvall (p. 164) makes the interesting point that the Huddersfield 'rising' has every right to be considered as comparable with that of Pentrich in terms of numbers, object and outcome, but has always attracted less attention because the Yorkshire event had no leader as picturesque as Brandreth, no convictions, and less publicity than that stirred up by Brandreth's advocate Denman. News of Oliver's involvement and the political purposes to which it could be put ensured

further publicity, see **A. Mitchell,** *The Whigs in Opposition, 1815-1830,* Oxford UP, 1967, pp. 108-9.

12. There are several accounts of the Pentrich 'rising'. See especially Thompson, pp. 723-34 and White, pp. 170-83. The crucial distinction between Thompson's account and earlier ones is his belief that it was 'one of the first attempts in history to mount a wholly proletarian insurrection, without any middle class support' and was an expression of a growing consciousness, not merely a creation of Oliver. For a review of the evidence see Thomis and Holt, *Threats of a Revolution in Britain,* pp. 44-61.

13. Prentice, pp. 108-9.

14. For the rise of the press in these years see Cranfield, *The Press and Society,* pp. 88-119.

15. See **P. Fraser,** 'Public petitioning and parliament before 1832', *History,* **46** (1961), 195-211 and **C. Leys,** 'Petitioning in the 19th and 20th centuries', *Political Studies,* **3** (1955), pp. 45-64, esp. pp. 45-8.

16. See esp. **A. Briggs,** 'Middle-class consciousness in English politics, 1780-1846', *Past and Present,* **9** (1956) and Fraser, 'Public petitioning'.

17. Quoted in Hammond and Hammond, *The Skilled Labourer,* pp. 26 and 101.

18. **D. Read,** *Peterloo: the 'Massacre' and its background,* reprint edn, Manchester UP, 1973, p. 108.

19. *Ibid.,* pp. 108-22. Read's remains the most authoritative account of the affair. Recent attempts to exonerate the magistracy in **R. Walmsley's,** *Peterloo: the case re-opened,* Manchester UP, 1969, are criticised by **D. Read** in *History* (1970), pp. 138-40. Thompson's views are stated in *The Making of the English Working Class,* pp. 734-60, and criticised in **J. D. Chambers** *History,* **51** (1966), 183-8. Thompson claims that the magistracy intended to employ force to arrest Hunt and disperse the meeting *and* that Sidmouth knew this even though he was unprepared for the violence which took place. Read exonerates Sidmouth from responsibility for the actions of the magistrates and this view is supported in **P. Ziegler,** *Addington,* Collins, 1965, pp. 374-5. It is often not recognised that the meeting exposed a particularly difficult legal problem, see Eldon's comment to William Scott, 'An unlawful assembly, *as such merely,* I apprehend can't be dispersed; and what constitutes *riot* enough to justify dispersion is no easy matter to determine, where there is not actual violence begun on the part of those assembled' in Twiss, I, 583.

20. Bamford, pp. 131-41.

21. *Medusa,* 5 June 1819.

22. This is precisely Bamford's position (pp. 131-2); his account of the meeting retains its power and ought to be read in conjunction with any secondary account; see also Prentice, pp. 159-71.

23. Read, *Peterloo . . . and its background,* pp. 126-37.

24. *Ibid.,* pp. 137-54 for the immediate consequences. For the Whigs and broader aspects, see Cannon, *Parliamentary Reform . . .,* pp. 180-5 and Mitchell, pp. 125-37. Fitzwilliam's reaction is discussed in **E. A. Smith,** *Whig Principles and party politics: Earl Fitzwilliam and the Whig party, 1748-1833,* Manchester UP, 1975, pp. 346-53.

25. See Cranfield, *The Press and Society,* pp. 100-2 and **M. D. George,** *English Political Caricature, 1793-1832,* Oxford UP, 1959, pp. 181-3. See also Read, *Peterloo . . . and its background,* pp. 206-9.

26. Bamford, pp. 158-61. Bamford speaks of men grinding 'scythes, others old hatchets, others screw-drivers, rusty swords, pikels, and mop-nails: anything which could be made to cut or stab was pronounced fit for service'. But continues 'no plan was defined, - nothing was arranged, - and the arms were afterwards reserved for any event that might occur'. The disturbance at New Cross arose when a crowd attacked the shop of a man believed to have been a special constable at Peterloo, see Read, *Peterloo . . . and its background,* p. 140. Thompson argues that there was a more widespread movement towards arming and plans for

347

insurrection than Bamford suggests, see Thompson, pp. 755-61. For evidence of drilling in Yorkshire, see **F. J. Kaijage,** 'Working-class radicalism in Barnsley, 1816-1820' in **Pollard** and **Holmes,** *Essays in the Economics and Social History of S. Yorkshire,* pp. 120-2. For reactions in the North-East see **N. McCord,** 'Tyneside Discontents and Peterloo', *Northern History,* **2** (1967), 91-111.

27. See **K. W. W. Aitkin,** 'Notes on popular unrest in Macclesfield, 1812-32', History Resources Group, Macclesfield, 1975. I am grateful to Mr M. Greengrass for drawing my attention to this collection of documents.

28. *London Chronicle,* 4 Oct. 1819. For Sidmouth's advocacy of strong measures after Peterloo, see Cookson, pp. 178-99, and his letters to Eldon in Twiss, pp. 587, 589; see also *Memoirs of the Political and Literary Life of Robert Plumer Ward,* ed. **E. Phipps,** London, 1850, II, 16-23.

29. *Ibid.,* pp. 32-3. I am grateful to Dr A. Macintyre for these references.

30. For the passage of the 'Six Acts' see Cookson, pp. 180-99. The Acts were (i) the Training Prevention Act (60 Geo. III, c. 1), which made any person attending a gathering for the purpose of training or drilling liable to transportation for up to seven years or imprisonment for a maximum of two years (ii) the Seizure of Arms Act (60 Geo. III, c. 2) gave magistrates in 'certain disturbed counties' the power to search for and seize arms from any persons or property on the oath of one witness (iii) the Misdemeanours Act (60 Geo. III, c. 4) prevented defendants postponing their pleas (iv) Seditious Meetings Prevention Act (60 Geo. III, c. 6) prohibiting the holding of public meetings of more than fifty people without the consent of a sheriff or magistrate; six days notice to be given in writing by seven resident householders of the parish; prohibitions placed on carrying banners, flags, weapons or emblems. Meetings must disperse within fifteen minutes if commanded to do so or become liable to transportation for up to seven years. Justices and others indemnified in case of death or injury caused while dispersing such unlawful assemblies (v) Blasphemous and Seditious Libels Act (60 Geo. III, c. 8) which increased the penalties against such publications to include seizure of the documents and banishment for the authors on the second offence (vi) Newspaper and Stamp Duties Act (60 Geo. III, c. 9) which made 'certain publications' (pamphlets and printed papers) liable to Stamp Duty.

31. Indicted with Hunt were John Knight, Joseph Johnson, John Thacker Saxton, Joseph Healey, James Moorhouse, Robert Jones, George Swift and Robert Wild. Johnson, Knight, Healey and Bamford were found guilty, Johnson, Bamford and Healey receiving a year's imprisonment and Knight two years in prison for attending a meeting at Burnley in November. In addition, Sir Francis Burdett was fined £2,000 and sentenced to three months' imprisonment for his pronouncements after Peterloo and Sir Charles Wolseley and the Reverend Harrison received eighteen months in prison for the Stockport meeting. Harrison also received two years' on another charge. James Wroe of the *Manchester Observer* received twelve months' imprisonment, plus a fine of £100 for seditious publication. Wooler of the *Black Dwarf* and Major Cartwright received fifteen months imprisonment and £100 fine respectively for taking part in the Birmingham meeting before Peterloo.

32. There is a rather partisan account of the Scottish episode in **P. B. Ellis** and **S. Mac A'ghobainn,** *The Scottish Insurrections of 1820,* Gollancz, 1970; see also Thompson, pp. 775-6 and Thomis and Holt, pp. 71-84. There is an account of the Barnsley events in Kaijage, pp. 122-3. For a fuller discussion see **F. K. Donnelly,** 'The general rising of 1820: a study of social conflict in the Industrial Revolution', Sheffield University Ph.D. thesis, 1975. For Sheffield, see Donnelly and Baxter, pp. 108-10.

33. Trinder, *The Industrial Revolution in Shropshire,* p. 383; **W. R. Ward,** *Victorian Oxford,* Oxford UP, 1965, p. 42; Hill, *Georgian Lincoln,* pp. 228-9; Picton, *Memorial of Liverpool,* pp. 427-31.

34. Jennings ed., *The Croker Papers,* I, 170.

348

35. See Fraser, pp. 204-6; **E. Halévy,** *The Liberal Awakening,* 2nd English edn, Benn, 1949, pp. 146-50; Dinwiddy, 'Christopher Wyvill . . .' pp. 29-31; and Cannon, pp. 183-5.
36. See **H. Perkin,** *The Origin of Modern English Society, 1780-1880,* Routledge, 1969, pp. 340-7, 365-9.
37. See **A. Briggs,** 'The background of the parliamentary reform movement in three English cities, 1830-32', *Cambridge Historical Journal,* **10** (1950-2).
38. **J. Hamburger,** *James Mill and the Art of Revolution,* Yale UP, 1963, pp. 139-47.
39. *Ibid.,* pp. 147-54.
40. *Ibid.,* pp. 158-61.
41. *Ibid.,* pp. 154-8; Thomis, *Politics and Society in Nottingham,* pp. 225-7.
42. Hamburger, pp. 161-81; **S. Thomas,** *The Bristol Riots,* Bristol Historical Association, 1974.
43. Twiss, II, 283-4, letter of Lord Eldon to Lord Stowell; Jennings, *Croker,* II, pp. 136-9.
44. **P. Whitwell Wilson** ed., *The Greville Diary,* Doubleday, 1927, I, 370. See also Hamburger, pp. 240-2.
45. Jennings (Croker), II, p. 148.
46. See especially **M. Brock'**s discussion of the role of the extra-parliamentary movement, in *The Great Reform Act,* Hutchinson, 1973, pp. 268-310.
47. *Ibid.,* esp. pp. 307-9; see also Cannon, pp. 238-40.
48. Brock, p. 305.
49. *Ibid.,* pp. 307-9. See also Thomis and Holt, pp. 87-99.
50. For the situation in the capital, see **D. J. Rowe,** 'London Radicalism in the era of the great Reform Bill' in Stevenson, *London in the Age of Reform,* pp. 149-76. For some of the divisions among reformers see Briggs, and Thompson, pp. 888-908. There is evidence that the May 'crisis' brought middle- and working-class reformers together, but whether this cooperation would have lasted through an insurrectionary phase is questionable.
51. Hamburger, pp. 195-9.
52. Rowe, especially pp. 166-70 and n. 68.
53. **P. Hollis,** *The Pauper Press: a study in working-class radicalism of the 1830s,* Oxford UP, 1970, pp. 45-6.
54. *Ibid.,* see also **G. Thurston,** *The Clerkenwell Riot: the killing of Constable Culley,* Allen and Unwin, 1967.

Chapter 11 Unions and labourers: industrial and agricultural protest

1. **T. C. Barker** and **J. R. Harris,** *A Merseyside town in the Industrial Revolution, St Helens, 1750-1900,* Liverpool UP, 1954, pp. 159-63.
2. Bythell, *The Handloom Weaver,* pp. 193-6; Hammond and Hammond, *The Skilled Labourer,* pp. 96-121.
3. **E. Hopwood,** *A History of the Lancashire Cotton Industry and the Amalgamated Weavers' Association,* Amalgamated Weavers' Association, 1969. pp. 23-4, 27-8.
4. Rowe, 'The strikes of the Tyneside keelmen in 1809 and 1819', pp. 66-73.
5. Trinder, *The Industrial Revolution in Shropshire,* pp. 384-5.
6. Webb and Webb, *History of Trade Unionism,* p. 91; Picton, *Memorials of Liverpool,* pp. 446-7.
7. Mann, *The Cloth Industry in The West of England . . .,* p. 161.
8. See Hammond and Hammond, pp. 126-8; Bythell, pp. 198-204.
9. **C. Aspin,** *Lancashire, the First Industrial Society,* Helmshore, 1969, pp. 45-9.
10. Prentice, *Historical Sketch of Manchester,* pp. 274-80.

11. Hammond and Hammond, pp. 194–5.
12. **C. Stella Davies,** *A History of Macclesfield,* E. J. Morten, 1976, p. 192.
13. Bythell, pp. 180–1.
14. **M. Walton,** *Sheffield: its story and its achievements,* Sheffield, 1948, p. 151.
15. Another method used was the 'black-cat', a brick tied to a string and thrown over the warp. When pulled it broke the threads of the work. See Hopwood, p. 30.
16. For Doherty's evolution see **R. G. Kirby** and **A. E. Musson,** *The Voice of the People: John Doherty, 1798–1854,* Manchester UP, 1975, especially pp. 31–2.
17. The best account of the colliers' disputes remains Hammond and Hammond, pp. 31–46, but see also **E. Allen, J. F. Clarke, N. McCord,** and **D. J. Rowe,** *The North-East Engineers' Strikes of 1871,* Frank Graham, 1971, pp. 70–4.
18. *Ibid.,* pp. 142–3, 182–6.
19. See Hammond and Hammond, pp. 128–35 and Musson, *British Trade Unions, 1800–1875,* pp. 29–35; see also **G. D. H. Cole,** *Attempts at General Union, 1818–1834,* London, 1953.
20. Webb and Webb, pp. 115–68. For the reactions in Oldham, see **J. Foster,** *Class Struggle and the Industrial Revolution,* 2nd edn, Methuen, 1977, pp. 107–14. Musson is more cautious about the significance of this phase than either Cole or Foster, see Musson, pp. 31–4. Even if Foster's account somewhat exaggerates the degree of 'class conflict' present in the detriment of sectional conflicts between rival groups of workmen, he nonetheless captures something of the flavour of near-millenarian expectation aroused amongst some workmen by Owenite schemes. On the General Strike, see **W. H. Crook,** *The General Strike,* Chapel Hill, 1931 and **William Benbow,** *Grand National Holiday and Congress of the Productive Classes,* London, 1832. Benbow's career is discussed in **I. J. Prothero,** 'William Benbow and the Concept of the "General Strike"', *Past and Present,* **63** (1974), 132–71.
21. Webb and Webb, pp. 147–8. Greville's estimate was 25,000 see Wilson ed., *Greville Diary,* p. 423. *The Times* put the figure at 30,000 as did Alexander Somerville. Somerville's account is interesting for his claim that a rising was planned at the demonstration. He claimed to have been invited to join in the plotting, but declined close involvement. His warnings to Government and other unionists helped to ensure that the preparations made to safeguard the capital were the most extensive prior to 1848, with several additional regiments of troops brought into the capital, with extra artillery, and five thousand 'specials' sworn in. These preparations forestalled any attempt by the plotters and without a lead from London, the provincial conspirators refused to act. Somerville mentioned Leeds, Oldham, Birmingham, Manchester, Nottingham and Derby as 'ready to rise'. See **A. Somerville,** *Somerville's Diligent Life,* Montreal, 1860, pp. 177–93.
22. Foster, pp. 56–61.
23. The highly coloured account of the Hammonds in *The Village Labourer,* has been substantially modified by further research. Few doubt the reality of rural immiseration, the question remains of its principal causes and the role of changes such as enclosure, see Chambers and Mingay, *The Agricultural Revolution, 1750–1880,* Ch. 4 and Hobsbawm and Rudé, *Captain Swing,* Ch. 2.
24. *Ibid.,* pp. 53–4. For a glimpse of the chronic problem of rural unemployment in a particular parish, see **H. Colvin,** *A History of Deddington,* SPCK, 1963, pp. 74–7. In a parish of about 2,000 inhabitants, sixty men regularly reported to the parish overseers for work or payment each morning.
25. Hobsbawm and Rudé, pp. 54–61.
26. **A. J. Peacock,** 'Village radicalism in East Anglia, 1800–50', in Dunbabin, *Rural Discontent,* p. 39.
27. Hobsbawm and Rudé, *op. cit.,* p. 68.
28. *Ibid.,* pp. 71–160.
29. *Ibid.,* pp. 163–87.
30. **B. Reaney,** *The Class Struggle in 19th Century Oxfordshire,* History Workshop, 1970, esp. pp. 29–45.

31. **H. G. Nicholl**, *Nicholl's Forest of Dean and Iron Making in the Olden Times*, David and Charles, 1966, pp. 110-12; C. E. Hart, *Royal Forest*, Clarendon Press, 1966, p. 214.

32. *Reading Mercury*, 22 Nov. 1830. I am grateful to Brother Geoffrey Scott for this reference.

33. Hobsbawn and Rudé, Ch. 12 and pp. 254-6.

34. *Ibid.*, pp. 140-60; see also **E. P. Thompson**, 'A very English rising', *The Times Literary Supplement*, 11 Sept. 1969, pp. 989-92.

35. Hobsbawm and Rudé, pp. 215-240. More people were executed and exiled than in the near contemporary Decembrist revolt, while it is necessary to go back to the Jacobite rising of 1745 for a larger toll, for the figures see **G. H. Jones**, *The Main Stream of Jacobitism*, Harvard UP, 1954, p. 239.

36. A. J. Brown ed., *Essex People, 1750-1900*, p. 75.

37. Hobsbawm and Rudé, pp. 201-11. For the role of women in food riots, see pp. 101-2.

38. **W. Reitzel** ed., *The Autobiography of William Cobbett*, 2nd edn, Faber, 1967, pp. 212-13.

39. See Dunbabin, *Rural Discontent . . .*, pp. 11-20.

40. See **D. Jones**, 'Thomas Campbell Foster and the rural labourer: incendiarism in East Anglia in the 1840s', *Social History*, **1** (1976), 5-43 and Peacock, 'Village radicalism in East Anglia, 1800-50', pp. 27-55. Hobsbawm and Rudé, pp. 241-59, discuss the legacy of rural crime and protest. They also raise the interesting question of the role of religion as a 'passive' response to defeat. A less passive response was the curious affair of the following obtained by J. N. Tom who styled himself as 'Sir William Courtenay' in the area between Canterbury and Faversham in 1838. Raising several labourers to join him with his mixture of millenarian prophecy and the promise of fifty acres a man, Courtenay killed a constable sent to arrest him and retired to Blean Wood with fifty men. Armed only with bludgeons, the labourers resisted the military sent to arrest 'Lord Courtenay'. Courtenay, eleven or twelve of his followers, and an officer were killed in the ensuing fight. See Thompson, *The Making of the English Working Class*, pp. 880-2 and **P. G. Rogers**, *Battle in Bossenden Wood*, Oxford UP, 1962.

Chapter 12 The Chartist era

1. **R. J. Morris**, *Cholera 1832*, Croom Helm, 1976, pp. 101-2, 108-17. The term 'burking' was derived from the Burke and Hare murders in Edinburgh. For eighteenth-century disturbances over dissection, see **P. Linebaugh**, 'The Tyburn riot against the surgeons', in Hay, *et al.*, *Albion's Fatal Tree*, pp. 65-117. There had been attacks on a London dissecting house in 1801; attacks on doctors in Glasgow in 1803, 1813-14 and 1823. The Aberdeen Anatomy Theatre was 'pulled down' in 1831.

2. Morris, pp. 113-4.

3. See Hobsbawm and Rudé, *Captain Swing*, pp. 18-33 and Peacock, 'Village radicalism . . .', pp. 36-7.

4. See **N. C. Edsall**, *The Anti-Poor-Law movement, 1834-44*, Manchester UP, 1971, pp. 2-16.

5. *Ibid.*, pp. 16-24; *Sheffield Iris*, 31 May 1836.

6. See Edsall, pp. 25-44.

7. *Ibid.*, Peacock, pp. 37-9; Hobsbawm and Rudé, pp. 243-4.

8. Edsall, Chs iii-vii; see also **M. E. Rose**, 'The Anti-Poor Law movement in the North of England', *Northern History*, **1** (1966), 70-91.

9. See **R. D. Storch**, 'The plague of blue locusts', *International Review of Social History*, **20** (1975), 61-90.

10. *Ibid.*, pp. 72-9. Soldiers often felt a keen sense of rivalry with the new police.
11. Plans to murder the police featured in some of the Chartist insurrectionary plots of 1839-40, see Storch, p. 71.
12. **D. Thompson,** *The Early Chartists*, Macmillan, 1971, pp. 16-27.
13. **W. E. Houghton,** *The Victorian Frame of Mind, 1830-70*, Yale UP, 1957, pp. 54-8.
14. Figures from **G. R. Porter,** *The Progress of the Nation*, John Murray, 1847, p. 675.
15. **F. C. Mather,** *Public Order in the Age of the Chartists*, Manchester UP, 1959, p. 305.
16. Quoted in **A. Briggs,** *The Age of Improvement, 1783-1867*, Longmans, 1959, p. 305.
17. *The Operative*, 10 Feb. 1839.
18. On 'physical' and 'moral' force, see also **F. C. Mather,** *Chartism*, Historical Association, 1965, pp. 15-18.
19. Quoted in **J. T. Ward,** *Chartism*, Batsford, 1973, p. 105.
20. See **R. B. Pugh,** 'Chartism in Somerset and Wiltshire' in **A. Briggs** ed., *Chartist Studies*, Macmillan, 1959, pp. 174-94.
21. **D. Williams,** 'Chartism in Wales', in Briggs, *Chartist Studies*, pp. 228-32.
22. **T. R. Tholfsen,** 'The Chartist crisis in Birmingham', *International Review of Social History*, **3** (1958), 461-80.
23. See **W. H. Maehl,** 'Chartist disturbances in north-eastern England in 1839', *International Review of Social History*, **8** (1963), 389-414 and **D. J. Rowe,** 'Chartism on Tyneside', *International Review of Social History*, **16** (1971), 17-36.
24. **D. Williams,** *John Frost: a study in Chartism*, Evelyn, Adams and Mackay, 1969. Most of what follows is taken from William's account. See also Ward, pp. 133-6.
25. See **J. L. Baxter,** 'Early Chartism and labour class struggle: South Yorkshire 1837-1840' in Pollard and Holmes, *Essays in the Economic and Social History of South Yorkshire*, pp. 146-50.
26. Mather, *Public Order in the Age of the Chartists*, pp. 23-4.
27. See **A. J. Peacock,** 'Bradford Chartism, 1838-40', *Borthwick Paper*, **36** (1969).
28. See **F. C. Mather,** 'The General Strike of 1842: a study in Leadership, organisation and the threat of revolution during the Plug Plot disturbances' in Stevenson and Quinault, *Popular Protest and Public Order*, pp. 115-35. See also **G. Rudé,** *The Crowd in History*, Wiley, 1964, pp. 183-91.
29. Quoted in **C. Stella Davies,** *A History of Macclesfield*, E. J. Morten, 1961, p. 293.
30. See Mather, 'The General Strike . . .', pp. 122-9 and p. 136 n. 9. Mather believes the early strikes were conceived primarily for economic objectives. See also on this point D. Philips, 'Riots in the Black Country, 1835-1860' in Stevenson and Quinault, pp. 151-6. For the origins of the General Strike as a concept in early radical thought see **N. Carpenter,** 'William Benbow and the Origin of the general strike', *The Quarterly Journal of Economics*, **35** (1921), 491-9; **A. Plummer,** 'The general strike during one hundred years', *Economic Journal*, Supplement (1927).
31. See Philips, pp. 156-7; **W. H. Warburton,** *The History of Trade Unionism in the Potteries*, London, 1931, pp. 119-22; see also **T. Cooper,** *The Life of Thomas Cooper*, London, 1873, pp. 187-95; **Old Potter,** *When I was a Child*, Stoke, 1903, pp. 158-66.
32. **F. Peel,** *The Risings of the Luddites, Chartists and Plug-Drawers*, 3rd edn, Heckmondwike, 1895, pp. 338-9.
33. See **B. Wilson,** *The Struggles of an Old Chartist*, reprinted in D. Vincent ed., *Testaments of Radicalism*, Europa Press, 1977, pp. 199-201; Mather, *Public Order* . . ., pp. 174-5.
34. See Mather 'The general strike of 1842 . . .', pp. 130-5.
35. For the conflict between the Potters' Union and the Chartists, see Warburton, pp. 118-36.
36. See **R. Challinor** and **B. Ripley,** *The Miners' Association: a trade union in the age of the Chartists*, Lawrence and Wishart, 1968, pp. 18-19, 34-6.
37. *Manchester Guardian*, 8, 11, March 1848.
38. *Ibid.*, 11 March 1848; HO 45/2410 Part I (Manchester) and Part IV (Military correspondence of Lt-Gen. Sir T. Arbutnott, C-in-C Northern and Midland Districts).

39. *Northern Star*, 11 March 1848. The judgement on the riots is that they were more a reaction to distress than Chartist inspired, see **A. Wilson,** *The Chartist Movement in Scotland,* Manchester UP, 1970, pp. 218-21.
40. See **D. Large,** 'London in the year of revolutions, 1848', in Stevenson ed., *London in the Age of Reform,* p. 183.
41. **F. C. Mather,** 'The Government and the Chartists', in Briggs, ed., *Chartist Studies,* pp. 395-6.
42. Large, p. 188.
43. Mather, 'The Government and the Chartists', p. 396.
44. See G. A. Cranfield, *The Press and Society,* pp. 160, 194-203.
45. See Twiss's comments contrasting the role of the press in the late eighteenth century with the position it had achieved by 1846, '. . . according to all present appearance, the newspapers, conducted as with few exceptions they are, and adapting themselves, as for the chief part they do, to the general sentiments of the most respectable classes of society, appear likely, instead of abetting an inroad upon property, to be among its most effective protectors'. Twiss, *Life of Lord Chancellor Eldon, 1846 edn,* I, pp. 80-1. See also Cranfield, pp. 188-98.
46. Large, pp. 182-3.
47. On London Chartism see **D. J. Rowe,** 'The failure of London Chartism', *The Historical Journal,* **11** (1968), pp. 472-87; **I. Prothero,** 'Chartism in London', *Past and Present,* **44** (1969), pp. 76-101; also **F. Sheppard,** *London 1808-1870: The Infernal Wen,* Secker and Warburg, 1971, pp. 322-30.
48. **M. D. George,** 'The London coal-heavers', *Economic History,* **1** (1929), 24-8.
49. Large, p. 192.
50. *Manchester Guardian,* 8, 12 April 1848. Among the 11,000 specials were 400 volunteers from the clerks and porters of the Manchester warehouses. *Sheffield Iris,* 13 April 1848.
51. See the report of the Meetings at the People's Institute, Heyrod Street, Manchester attended by 300-400 people on 14 April, *Manchester Guardian,* 15 April 1848; see also the reports of meetings in Stevenson Square and at Smithfield, *ibid.,* 12 April 1848.
52. *Ibid.,* 22 April 1848.
53. See **F. C. Mather,** *Chartism,* Historical Association, 1965, pp. 23-6; **R. O'Higgins,** 'The Irish Influence in the Chartist Movement', *Past and Present,* **20** (1961), 83-96.
54. Large, pp. 193-201.
55. *Manchester Guardian,* 31 May 1848.
56. *Ibid.,* 16, 19 Aug. 1848. The total commitals for the period 1839-48 was given in *British Parliamentary Papers,* **54** (1850), pp. 134-5 as follows:

Year	Riotously and feloniously demolishing building and machinery	High treason	Riot and sedition	Riot, breach of peace, and pound breach
1838	9	–	231	592
1840	–	14	212	413
1841	7	–	5	553
1842	71	1	962	595
1843	60	–	60	543
1844	2	–	2	567
1845	–	–	–	363
1846	5	–	–	302
1847	13	–	–	373
1848	4	12	253	387

Commitals for seditions offences in 1848

Murder of policeman by armed rioters	1
Feloniously compassing to levy war	12
Unlawfully drilling and training	35
Conspiracy to send arms to Ireland	8
Seditiously conspiring to make an insurrection	60
Seditious and unlawful conspiracy, assassination, and riot	96
Riot, assault on peace officers and rescue in connection with seditious association	54
Total	**266**

(*Ibid.* 44 (1849) 56)

Chapter 13 The transition to order

1. **L. O. Pike,** *A History of Crime in England,* 2nd edn, Patterson Smith, 1968, II, 480.
2. **G. Best,** *Mid-Victorian Britain, 1851-75,* Weidenfeld and Nicolson, 1971, p. 229.
3. **A. Briggs,** *Victorian People: a reassessment of persons and themes,* 1851-67, Penguin, 1965, p. 13.
4. **H. Senior,** *Orangeism in Ireland and Britain, 1795-1836,* Routledge, 1966, for the history and activities of early nineteenth-century Orange Lodges in Britain.
5. Picton, *Memorials of Liverpool,* I, 408-9, 544-6.
6. See Senior, pp. 271-84 and *Report from the Select Committee on Orange Institutions in Great Britain and the Colonies with Minutes of Evidence,* PP **17** (1835) (605).
7. **T. Coleman,** *The Railway Navvies,* 2nd edn Penguin, 1968, pp. 63-5, 93-114; *Manchester Guardian,* 16 Aug. 1848.
8. **G. F. A. Best,** 'Popular Protestantism in Victorian Britain' in **R. Robson** ed., *Ideas and Institutions of Victorian Britain,* Bell, 1967, pp. 115-42.
9. *Ibid.*; see also **E. R. Norman,** *Anti-Catholicism in Victorian England,* Allen and Unwin, 1968, pp. 13-79.
10. *Ibid.,* pp. 61-5, 105-21; **O. Chadwick,** *The Victorian Church,* A. and C. Black, 1966, I, 219-21, 289.
11. F. Sheppard, *London ... The Infernal Wen,* pp. 241-3.
12. **W. Astle,** *History of Stockport,* 2nd edn, S. R. Publications, 1971, pp. 51-2. For the background in 1851-2, see Norman, pp. 52-79.
13. See **S. Gilley,** 'The Garibaldi riots of 1862', *The Historical Journal,* **16** (1973), 697-732. Philips, 'Riots and public order in the Black Country, 1835-1860', p. 164.
14. Gilley.
15. *Ibid.*
16. **F. S. L. Lyons,** *Ireland Since the Famine,* 2nd edn, Fontana, 1973, pp. 122-38.
17. The best account of these disturbances is **W. L. Arnstein,** 'The Murphy riots: a Victorian dilemma', *Victorian Studies,* **19** (1975). See also **H. J. Hanham,** *Elections and Party Management: politics in the time of Disraeli and Gladstone,* Longmans, 1959, pp. 304-9.
18. See, for example, **P. F. Clarke,** *Lancashire and the New Liberalism,* Cambridge UP, 1971, pp. 51, 139-41.
19. See **V. Bailey,** 'Salvation Army riots, the "Skeleton Army" and legal authority in the Provincial Town', in Donajgrodzki, *Social Contrast in Nineteenth-century Britain,* pp. 231-53.
20. Allen, *et al.,* *The North-East Engineers' Strikes of 1871,* pp. 76-83.
21. **R. Challinor** and **B. Ripley,** *The Miners' Association: a trade union in the age of the Chartists,* Lawrence and Wishart, 1968, p. 135.
22. *Ibid.,* pp. 164-5.

354

23. **A. Hewitson,** *History of Preston,* 2nd edn, S. R. Publishers, 1969, p. 178; **R. E. Frow** and **M. Katanka,** *Strikes: a documentary history,* Charles Knight, 1971, pp. 60–76.
24. Allen *et al.,* pp. 83–4.
25. *Ibid.,* p. 143.
26. Philips, pp. 158–63.
27. Frow and Katanka, pp. 78–9.
28. See **S. Pollard,** 'The ethics of the Sheffield outrages', *Transactions of the Hunter Archeological Society,* **17** (1953–4), 118–39 and *A History of Labour in Sheffield,* Liverpool UP, 1959, pp. 152–8. On the building trades, see **R. N. Price,** 'The other face of respectability: violence in the Manchester brick-making trade, 1859–1870', *Past and Present,* **66** (1975), 110–32.
29. Hewitson, p. 180; Hopwood, *A History of the Lancashire Cotton Industry,* p. 37. For the Featherstone incident, see *Report of the Committee to inquire into the Circumstances connected with the disturbances at Featherstone on 7th September 1893,* House of Commons, 1893–4 (Cmd 7234).
30. For a general perspective, see **H. Pelling,** *A History of British Trade Unionism,* Penguin, 1963, pp. 59–148 and for the complexities of the relationship between 'organisation' and violence, see Price, pp. 130–2.
31. Reitzel, ed., *Autobiography of William Cobbett,* p. 174.
32. **N. Gash,** *Politics in the Age of Peel,* Longmans, 1953, pp. 137–53; **C. O'Leary,** *The Elimination of Corrupt Practices in British Elections, 1868–1911.* Clarendon Press, 1962, pp. 1–26.
33. See **R. Quinault,** 'The Warwickshire County magistracy and public order, *c.* 1830–1870', in Stevenson and Quinault eds, pp. 198–201.
34. **D. Richter,** 'The role of the mob riot in Victorian Elections, 1865–85', *Victorian Studies,* **15** (1971–2), 19–22.
35. *Ibid.,* p. 23.
36. *Ibid.,* p. 22.
37. *Ibid.,* pp. 19–28. Also Bailey, 'The dangerous classes in late Victorian England . . .'.
38. Richter, pp. 21–8.
39. On the legal issues surrounding the use of Hyde Park and Trafalgar Square, see Williams, *Keeping the Peace,* pp. 70–86.
40. Sheppard, p. 333; **B. Harrison,** 'The Sunday trading riots of 1855', *The Historical Journal,* **8** (1965).
41. PP, *Report from the Royal Commission on the alleged disturbances in Hyde Park and on the Conduct of the Police,* (1856), (2016), **23** pp. 239–40, 459–75.
42. Harrison, pp. 234–5.
43. PP, *Primrose Hill Meeting: reports from the Superintendent and Inspector in charge with police institutions,* 348 (1864) (252) **48.**
44. For the debate on the Second Reform Act, see **G. Himmelfarb,** 'The politics of democracy: the English Reform Act of 1867', *Journal of British Studies,* **6** (1966), 97–138.
45. *Ibid.,* pp. 97–138. For another view laying more emphasis on the extra-parliamentary movement, see **R. Harrison,** *Before the Socialists,* Routledge, 1965, 'The tenth April of Spencer Walpole: the Problem of Revolution in Relation to Reform, 1865–67'.
46. Perhaps the most cautious of the assessments of the extra-parliamentary influence can be found in **M. Cowling,** *1867: Disraeli, Gladstone and Revolution. The passing of the second Reform Bill,* Cambridge UP, 1967.
47. See, for example, those cited by **H. Cunningham** in 'Jingoism in 1877–8', *Victorian Studies,* **14** (1971), 429–53 and Williams, p. 74.
48. *Ibid.,* pp. 74–86 and **R. Mace,** *Trafalgar Square: emblem of Empire,* Lawrence and Wishart, 1976, pp. 137–203. See also Bailey, 'The Dangerous classes in Late Victorian England . . .'.
49. Picton, pp. 608–9; **G. Stedman Jones,** *Outcast London: a study in the relationship between classes in Victorian society.* 2nd edn, Penguin, 1971, pp. 43–7.

50. **M. E. Rose,** 'Rochdale man and the Stalybridge riot. The relief and control of the unemployed during the Lancashire cotton famine', in A. Donajgrodzki, pp. 185-206.
51. See Gatrell and Hadden, 'Criminal Statistics . . .' pp. 336-96 and **D. Philips,** *Crime and Authority in Victorian England: the Black Country, 1835-1860,* Croom Helm, 1978, pp. 13-24, 41-52.
52. *Ibid.*, p. 142.
53. *PP* **54** (1850), 153, 167.
54. Philips, p. 274.
55. **J. Reilly,** *The History of Manchester,* London, 1865, p. 395.
56. Pike, II, 450-80.
57. For the idea of a 'dangerous class', see **V. Bailey,** 'The dangerous classes in late Victorian England . . .'; G. Stedman Jones, pp. 10-16, pp. 281-314.
58. **T. Beames,** *The Rookeries of London,* 2nd edn, Cass, 1970, pp. 26, 65-7.

Chapter 14 Conclusion

1. **W. W. Rostow,** *British Economy in the Nineteenth Century,* Oxford UP, 1948, pp. 122-5.
2. **T. S. Ashton,** *Economic Fluctuations in England, 1700-1800,* Oxford UP, 1959; E. J. Hobsbawm, 'Economic fluctuations and some social movements since 1800' in *Labouring Men,* pp. 126-57.
3. Thompson, 'The moral economy of the English crowd in the eighteenth century', esp. pp. 76-9.
4. **T. Carlyle,** *Chartism,* Chapman and Hall, 1892, p. 23.
5. See **W. G. Runciman,** *Relative Deprivation and Social Justice,* Cambridge UP, 1966.
6. See **J. C. Davies,** 'The J-curve of rising and declining satisfactions as a cause of some great revolutions and a contained rebellion' in Graham and Gurr eds, *The History of Violence in America,* pp. 690-730.
7. **C. Tilly,** 'Collective violence in European perspective', in Graham and Gurr eds, p. 41.
8. *Report of the National Advisory Commission on Civil Disorders,* Bantam, 1968, pp. 116-20.
9. Beattie, 'The pattern of crime in England, 1660-1800', pp. 66-7.
10. *Ibid.,* pp. 58-60, 66-73; **J. D. Chambers,** *Nottinghamshire in the Eighteenth Century,* 2nd edn, Cass, 1966, pp. 49-50.
11. **J. H. Bohstedt,** 'Riots in England 1790-1810, with special reference to Devonshire', Harvard Ph.D. thesis, 1972; table quoted in Harvey, *Britain in the early nineteenth century,* pp. 59-60.
12. **J. Stevenson,** 'Disturbances and public order in London, 1790-1821', Oxford University D.Phil. thesis, 1973, pp. 231-53.
13. Porter, *The Progress of the Nation,* p. 642 and *PP* (1835-50).
14. *Journal of the Statistical Society of London,* **2** (1839), 325.
15. Philips, *Crime and Authority in Victorian England,* p. 275.
16. Pike (*A History of Crime in England,* p. 479) noted the relationship between improvements in policing and crime figures as early as the 1870s. A more stable relationship did not necessarily mean an end to disturbances or assaults upon the police, see Storch, 'The policeman as domestic missionary . . .', pp. 481-509. Storch's figures (pp. 502-9) show that assaults on the police *increased* in some areas during the 1860s and 1870s, only falling after 1880. Storch makes the point that while the more spectacular attempts to drive the police from their district by 'riotous resistance' declined, other forms of resistance continued or even grew.
17. We still await a definitive study of popular movements in early modern England, but there is little doubt that many of the features regarded as 'typical' of the eighteenth century can be found in England before 1700.

18. See Bailey, 'The Salvation Army Riots . . .', Cunningham, 'Jingoism in 1877-8', **R. Price,** *An Imperial War and the British Working Class: Working Class Attitudes and Reactions to the Boer War 1899-1902,* Routledge, 1972, Ch. 4.
19. Thompson, 'The moral economy of the English crowd in the eighteenth century'.
20. **E. Fox Genovese,** 'The many faces of moral economy', *Past and Present,* **58** (1973), 161-8.
21. See Stevenson, 'Food Riots in England, 1792-1818', pp. 64-5.
22. Quoted in Turton, *The History of the North York Militia,* p. 44.
23. For the role of ritual in early protest movements, see Hobsbawm, *Primitive Rebels,* pp. 150-74.
24. *Old Baily Sessions Papers,* 1794, pp. 1326-1332.
25. *Morning Chronicle,* 9 March 1815.
26. See **C. Tilly,** 'The chaos of the living city', in **H. Hirsch** and **D. C. Perry** eds, *Violence as Politics,* Harper and Row, 1973, p. 103.
27. Tilly, 'Collective violence in European perspective', pp. 28-45.
28. Perkin, *The Origin of Modern English Society,* pp. 340-7.
29. *Ibid.,* esp. Ch. 9; see also **A. Briggs,** *The Age of Improvement, 1783-1867,* Longman, 1959, Ch. 8.
30. See **L. Stone,** 'Theories of revolution', *World Politics,* **18** (1966) and **P. Amann,** 'Revolution: a redefinition', *Political Science Quarterly,* **77** (1962).
31. This has been called the 'natural history' theory of revolutions, see, for example, **C. Brinton,** *The Anatomy of Revolution,* rev. edn, Vintage, 1965.
32. **J. Rule** and **C. Tilly,** '1830 and the unnatural history of revolution', *Journal of Social Issues,* 1971. Tilly's views form part of an attempt to place collective violence within the context of larger political processes, see **Tilly, Tilly,** and **Tilly,** *The Rebellious Century,* pp. 271-300.
33. See Rudé, *Paris and London in the Eighteenth Century,* pp. 35-60 and Stevenson ed., *London in the Age of Reform,* pp. xiii-xxvi.
34. Quoted in Fritz, *The English Ministers and Jacobitism . . .,* p. 137. The role of the invasion 'scare' in British politics is one which still requires analysis, spanning both the eighteenth and nineteenth century and providing continued evidence of the powerful role of xenophobic sentiment whether real or manipulated.
35. See Stevenson, 'Social control and the prevention of riots in England, 1789-1829', in Donajgrodzko ed., *Social Control . . .,* pp. 27-50.
36. See Bailey, 'The dangerous classes in Late Victorian England . . .'.
37. See especially Storch, 'The policeman as domestic missionary . . .', and the essays by Donajgrodzki, Storch, and Cunningham in A. P. Donajgrodzki ed., *op. cit.* Also on the control of leisure see **R. W. Malcolmson,** *Popular Recreations in English Society, 1700-1850,* Cambridge UP, 1973, pp. 89-157, and Philips, *Crime and Authority . . .,* pp. 84-7.
38. Storch, 'The policeman as domestic missionary . . .', pp. 502-9.
39. See **T. R. Gurr,** *Rogues, Rebels, and Reformers: a political history of urban crime and conflict,* Sage, 1976, esp. pp. 163-84.
40. *Committals for indictable riotous offences, 1842-8.*

	England and Wales		Ireland	
	Riot	Rescue	Riot	Rescue
1842	595	12	2,890	1,594
1843	543	18	3,343	2,330
1844	567	13	3,018	1,944
1845	363	14	2,574	1,119
1846	302	11	3,471	983
1847	373	2	2,437	2,251
1848	387	9	3,222	4,131

Source: PP **44** (1849), 226-7 and **54** (1850), 134-5.

41. **G. Orwell,** *Inside the Whale and Other Essays,* Penguin, 1957, pp. 68–72.
42. **J. Morley,** *Life of Gladstone,* London, 1908, I, p. 54; quoted in Thompson, *The Making of the English Working Class,* p. 899.

Select Bibliography

Chapter 1 Introduction

Cobb, R., *The Police and the People: French popular protest, 1789-1820*, Oxford UP, 1970.
Cockburn, J. S., ed. *Crime in England, 1550-1800*, Methuen, 1977.
Hobsbawm, E. J., *Primitive Rebels: studies in archaic forms of social movement in the 19th and 20th centuries*, Manchester UP, 1959.
Rudé, G., *The Crowd in History*, Wiley, 1964.
Smelser, N. J., *Theory of Collective Behaviour*, Routledge, 1962.
Stevenson, J., and **Quinault R.,** eds. *Popular Protest and Public Order: six studies in British history, 1790-1920*, Allen and Unwin, 1974.
Tilly, C., 'Collective violence in European perspective', in H. D. Graham and T. R. Gurr eds., *Violence in America*, Bantam, 1969.
Thompson, E. P., 'The moral economy of the English crowd in the eighteenth century', *Past and Present*, **50** (1971).
Williams, D., *Keeping the Peace: the police and public order*, Hutchinson, 1967.

Chapter 2 The age of riots

Beloff, M., *Public Order and Popular Disturbances, 1660-1714*, Oxford UP.
Brooke, J., *The House of Commons, 1754-1790*, 2nd edn, Oxford UP, 1968.
Holmes, G. *Party Politics in the Age of Anne*, Macmillan, 1967.
Isaac, D. G. D., 'A study of popular disturbances in Britain, 1714-54', Edinburgh University Ph.D. thesis, 1953.
Jones, G. H., *The Main Stream of Jacobitism*, Harvard UP, 1954.
Sedgwick, R., *The House of Commons, 1715-1754*, HMSO, 1970.
Walsh, J. 'Methodism and the mob in the eighteenth century', in G. J. Cuming and D. Barker, *Popular Belief and Practice: studies in Church history*, vol. 8, Cambridge UP, 1972.
Wearmouth, R. F., *Methodism and the Common People of the Eighteenth Century*, Epworth, 1945.

Chapter 3 Manifold disorders

Beattie, J. M., 'The pattern of crime in England, 1660-1800', *Past and Present*, **62** (1974).

Hay, D., Linebaugh, P., Rule J. G., Thompson, E. P., and Winslow, C., *Albion's Fatal Tree*, Allen Lane, 1975.
Lloyd, C., *The British Seaman*, 2nd edn, Paladin, 1970.
Malcolmson, R. W., *Popular Recreations in English Society, 1700-1850*, Cambridge UP, 1973.
Thompson, E. P., *Whigs and Hunters*, Allen Lane, 1975.
Western, J. R. *The English Militia in the Eighteenth Century*, Routledge, 1965.

Chapter 4 Eighteenth-century London

Brewer, J., *Party Ideology and Popular Politics at the Accession of George III*, Cambridge UP, 1976.
Castro, J. P. de., *The Gordon Riots*, Oxford UP, 1926.
Holmes, G., 'The Sacheverell riots', *Past and Present*, **72** (1976).
Rogers, N., 'Aristocratic clientage, trade and independency: popular politics in pre-radical Westminster, *Past and Present*, **61** (1973).
Rogers, N., 'Popular disaffection in London during the Forty-five', *The London Journal*, **1** (1975).
Rogers, N., 'Popular protest in early Hanoverian London', *Past and Present*, **79** (1978).
Rudé, G., *Hanoverian London, 1714-1808*, Secker and Warburg, 1971.
Rudé, G., *Paris and London in the Eighteenth Century*, Fontana, 1970.
Rudé, G., *Wilkes and Liberty*, Oxford UP, 1962.
Stevenson, J., *London in the Age of Reform*, Blackwell, 1977.
Sutherland, L. S., 'The City of London in eighteenth-century politics', in R. Pares and A. J. P. Taylor eds, *Essays presented to Sir Lewis Namier*, Oxford UP, 1956.

Chapter 5 Food riots in England

Barnes, D. G., *A History of the English Corn Laws*, Routledge, 1930.
Beloff, M., *Public Order and Popular Disturbances, 1660-1714*, Oxford UP, 1938.
Jones, E. L., *Seasons and Prices*, Allen and Unwin, 1964.
Rose, R. B., 'Eighteenth century price riots and public policy in England', *International Review of Social History*, **6** (1961).
Shelton, W. J., *English Hunger and Industrial Disorders*, Macmillan, 1973.
Thompson, E. P., 'The moral economy of the English crowd in the eighteenth century', *Past and Present*, **50** (1971).
Webb, S. and Webb, B., 'The Assize of Bread', *Economic Journal*, **14** (1904).

Chapter 6 Labour disputes before the Combination Laws

Ashton, T. S. and Sykes, J., *The Coal Industry of the Eighteenth Century*, 2nd edn, Manchester UP, 1929.
Aspinall, A., *The Early English Trade Unions*, Batchworth, 1949.
Beloff, M., *Public Order and Popular Disturbances, 1660-1714*, Oxford UP, 1938.
George, M. D., *London Life in the Eighteenth Century*, 2nd edn, Penguin, 1965.

Hammond, J. L. and Hammond, B., *The Skilled Labourer, 1760-1832*, Longmans, 1919.
Hobsbawm, E. J., 'The machine breakers' in *Labouring Men*, 2nd edn, Weidenfeld and Nicolson, 1968.
Mann, J. de L., *The Cloth Industry in the West of England from 1640 to 1880*, Oxford UP, 1971.
Shelton, W. J., *English Hunger and Industrial Disorders*, Macmillan, 1973.
Webb, S. and Webb, B., *The History of Trade Unionism*, 2nd edn, Longmans, 1920.

Chapter 7 The age of revolution

Brown, P. A., *The French Revolution in English History*, Crosby Lockwood, 1918.
Darvall, F. O., *Popular Disturbances and Public Order in Regency England*, 2nd edn, Oxford UP, 1969.
Harvey, A. D., *Britain in the Early Nineteenth Century*, Batsford, 1978
Hammond, J. L. and Hammond, B., *The Skilled Labourer, 1760-1832*, Longmans, 1919.
Prentice, A., *Historical Sketches and Personal Recollections of Manchester*, 3rd edn, Cass, 1970.
Rose, R. B., 'The Priestley riots of 1791', *Past and Present*, **18** (1960).
Thale, M. ed. *The Autobiography of Francis Place*, Cambridge UP, 1972.
Thomis, M. I., *The Luddites*, David and Charles, 1970.
Thomis, M. I. and Holt, P., *Threats of Revolution in Britain, 1789-1848*, Macmillan, 1977.
Thompson, E. P., *The Making of the English Working Class*, 2nd edn, Penguin, 1968.
Veitch, G. S., *The Genesis of Parliamentary Reform*, 2nd edn, Constable, 1965.
Williams, G. A. *Artisans and Sans Culottes*, Arnold, 1968.

Chapter 8 London in the age of revolution

Brown, P. A., *The French Revolution in English History*, Crosby Lockwood, 1918.
Elliott, M., 'The "Despard conspiracy" reconsidered', *Past and Present*, **75** (1977).
Stevenson, J. ed. *London in the Age of Reform*, Blackwell, 1977.
Thomis, M. I. and Holt, P., *Threats of Revolution in Britain, 1789-1848*, Macmillan, 1977.
Thompson, E. P., *The Making of the English Working Class*, 2nd edn, Penguin, 1968.
Veitch, G. S., *The Genesis of Parliamentary Reform*, 2nd edn, Constable, 1965.

Chapter 9 London and the kingdom

Cookson, J. E., *Lord Liverpool's Administration: the crucial years 1815-1822*, Scottish Academic Press, 1975.
Main, J. M., 'Radical Westminster, 1807-1820', *Historical Studies* (Australia and New Zealand), (1966).
Parsinnen, T. M., 'The revolutionary party in London', *Bulletin of the Institute of Historical Research*, **45** (1972).
Patterson, M. W., *Sir Francis Burdett and his Times*, Oxford UP, 1931.

Stevenson, J., *London in the Age of Reform*, Blackwell, 1977.
Thompson, E. P., *The Making of the English Working Class*, 2nd edn, Penguin, 1968.

Chapter 10 The reform struggle

Bamford, S., *Passages in the Life of a Radical*, MacGibbon and Kee, 1967.
Briggs, A., 'Middle-class consciousness in English politics, 1780–1846', *Past and Present*, **9** (1956).
Briggs, A., 'The background of the parliamentary reform movement in three English cities, 1830–32', *Cambridge Historical Journal*, **10** (1950–2).
Brock, M., *The Great Reform Act*, Hutchinson, 1973.
Cannon, J., *Parliamentary Reform, 1640–1832*, Cambridge UP, 1973.
Fraser, P., 'Public petitioning and parliament before 1832', *History*, **46** (1961).
Hamburger, J., *James Mill and the Art of Revolution*, Yale UP, 1963.
Read, D., *Peterloo: The 'massacre' and its background*, reprint edn, Manchester UP, 1973.
Rudé, G., 'English rural and urban disturbances, 1830–1', *Past and Present*, **37** (1967).
Thompson, E. P., *The Making of the English Working Class*, 2nd edn, Penguin, 1968.

Chapter 11 Unions and labourers: industrial and agricultural protest

Aspinall, A., *The Early English Trade Unions*, Batchworth, 1949.
Bythell, D., *The Handloom Weavers*, Cambridge UP, 1969.
Cole, G. D. H. and Filson, A. W., *British Working Class Movements: Select Documents, 1789–1875*, Macmillan, 1965.
Dunbabin, J. P. D., *Rural Discontent in Nineteenth Century Britain*, Faber, 1974.
Hammond, J. L. and Hammond, B., *The Skilled Labourer, 1760–1832*, Longmans, 1919.
Hobsbawm, E. J. and Rudé, G., *Captain Swing*, Penguin, 1973.
Musson, A. E., *British Trade Unions, 1800–1875*, Macmillan, 1972.
Pelling, H. M., *A History of British Trade Unionism*, Penguin, 1963.
Webb, S. and Webb, B., *The History of Trade Unionism*, 2nd edn, Longmans, 1920.

Chapter 12 The Chartist era

Briggs, A., ed. *Chartist Studies*, Macmillan, 1959.
Edsall, N. C., *The Anti-Poor Law Movement, 1834–44*, Manchester UP, 1971.
Jones, D., *Chartism and the Chartists*, Allen Lane, 1975.
Mather, F. C., *Public Order in the Age of the Chartists*, Manchester UP, 1959.
Mather, F. C., *Chartism*, Historical Association, 1965.
Morris, R. J., *Cholera 1832*, Croom Helm, 1976.
Rose, R. E., 'The anti-poor law movement in the North of England', *Northern History*, **1** (1966).
Stevenson, J. and Quinault, R., *Popular Protest and Public Order: six studies in British history, 1790–1920*, Allen and Unwin, 1974.
Storch, R. D., 'The plague of blue locusts', *International Review of Social History*, **20** (1975).

362

Thompson, D., *The Early Chartists*, Macmillan, 1971.
Ward, J. T., *Chartism*, Batsford, 1973.

Chapter 13 The transition to order

Arnstein, W. L., 'The Murphy riots: a Victorian dilemma', *Victorian Studies* **19** (1975).
Best, G. F. A., 'Popular protestantism in Victorian Britain' in R. Robson ed., *Ideas and Institutions of Victorian Britain*, Bell, 1967.
Donajgrodzki, A. P., *Social Control in Nineteenth Century Britain*, Croom Helm, 1977.
Gilley, S., 'The Garibaldi riots of 1862', *The Historical Journal* **16** (1973).
Harrison, B., 'The Sunday trading riots of 1855', *The Historical Journal,* **8** (1965).
Harrison, R., *Before the Socialists*, Routledge, 1965.
Pelling, H., *A History of British Trade Unionism*, Penguin, 1963.
Philips, D., *Crime and Authority in Victorian England*, Croom Helm, 1978.
Richter, D., 'The role of the mob riot in Victorian Elections, 1865–85', *Victorian Studies*, **15** (1971–2).

ndex

Admiralty, 127
affray, 5–7 *passim*, 9–10, 11
age of riots, Ch. 2
agricultural labourers, 229
    'Captain Swing' disturbances, 237–44
    and food riots, 100–1
    unions of, 243
Agricultural Labourers' Benefit Society, 248
Agricultural Labourers' Friendly Society, 236
Allen, William, 67, 73
Althorpe, Colonel, 144
Amalgamated Association of Operative Cotton Spinners, 284
American Civil War, 293
American Non-Intercourse Act 1811, 156
American War, 39–40, 46, 124, 127
Amherst, Lord, 80
Anatomy Act 1832, 245
Ancaster, Duke of, 146
Anne, Queen, 39, 57, 58
Annual Register, 15, 167, 288
anti-Catholicism, anti-Catholic riots, 25, 28, 29, 79, 81–2, 84–6, 276–81; *see also* Gordon Riots; Murphy; Sacheverell riots; religious riots
Anti-Corn Law League, 251, 265
anti-crimp-house riots, 166–9, 315
anti-enclosure riots, 42–3, 143, 239, 310
anti-Irish disturbances, 61, 85, 276–8, 310
    'Murphy' riots, 278, 281–2
anti-Jacobin feeling, 165
anti-police riots, 251–2, 257–8, 290, 310, 322
anti-poor law disturbances, 247–51, 254–5, 310
anti-ritualism, 278–9
anti-war feeling, 144–6 *passim*, 150, 165–6, 170–1
prenticeship laws, 129
ouse of, 115–16, 120, 123, 128, 152

Arch, Joseph, 244
Aris, Governor, 184
Arkwright, Richard, 117–19, 132
Armistead, Mrs, 164
army, 38–9, 144
    mutinies in, 149–50
    recruitment for, 38–9, 146, 166–8, 170–
Ashburnham, Lord, 78
Ashton, T. S., 302
Aspinall, A., 134
Assize of bread, 85, 100, 108, 177
Atholl, Duke of, 38
Attwood, Thomas, 222–3, 224, 226, 258
Aylesford, Earl of, 138

Bacon, Thomas, 210
Bailey, V., 4, 288
Baines, Edward, 215
Baker, Sir Robert, 202–3
bakers, 94, 171
Ballot Act, 288
Bamford, Samuel, 206, 208–9, 213, 215
Bank of England, 57, 81–3 *passim*, 86, 2
Banks, Sir Joseph, 191
Barclay, Charles, 190
Barnard, Sir John, 60
Bath and Wells, Bishop of, 221
Bathurst, Lord, 78, 83, 204
Battle of the Boyne, 277
Beales, Edmund, 291
Beames, Rev. Thomas, 299
Beattie, J. M., 305
Beckford, William, 65, 68–9
Bedford, Duke of, 38, 66
Bellingham, John, 160, 191
Beloff, M., 19, 42
Benbow, William, 208, 213, 226, 227, 2
Bent (informer), 230
Best, G., 275, 278
Billiers, Sir William, 60
Bill of Pains and Penalties, 199, 200, 2